A History of
the Middle East

A History of the Middle East

Saul S. Friedman

McFarland & Company, Inc., Publishers
Jefferson, North Carolina, and London

"There is really no limit to historians' lies."
— Livy, *The War with Hannibal*

LIBRARY OF CONGRESS CATALOGUING-IN-PUBLICATION DATA

Friedman, Saul S., 1937–
A history of the Middle East / Saul S. Friedman.
p.   cm.
Includes bibliographical references and index.

ISBN 0-7864-2356-0 (softcover : 50# alkaline paper) ∞

1. Middle East — History.   I. Title.
DS62.F79 2006   956 — dc22   2006000209

British Library cataloguing data are available

Cover photograph ©2006 Flat Earth Photos

Manufactured in the United States of America

*McFarland & Company, Inc., Publishers
Box 611, Jefferson, North Carolina 28640
www.mcfarlandpub.com*

For Rebekah and Maya and
all the children of the Middle East.

May you play together in peace.

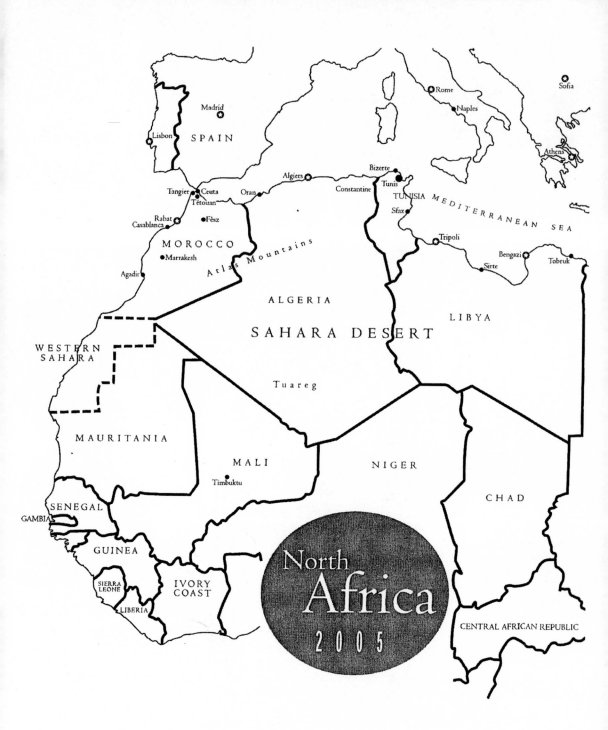

Map by Youngstown State University Graphic Services

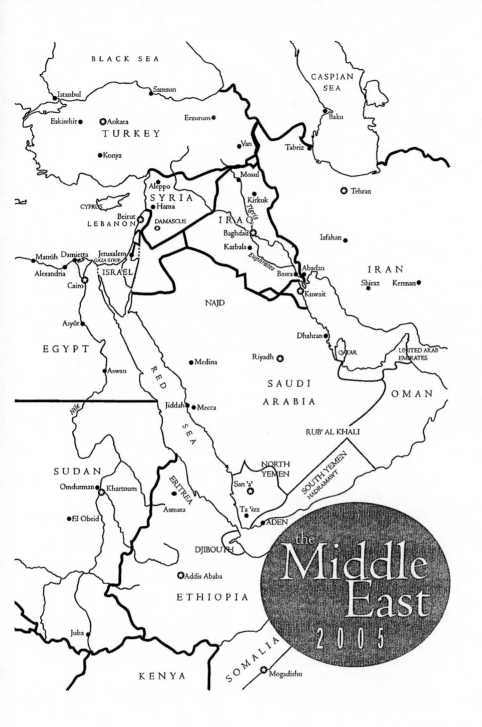

Map by Youngstown State University Graphic Services

A Note on the Transcription

Those who labor in foreign script know there will be difficulties in transcription. One author may offer *Kheyder* or *Hanukkah* for *cheder* or *Chanukah*. Responding to nationalist sensitivities, *Peking* becomes *Beijing*. The problem is especially acute within Arabic where there is no E or O and yet some writers continue to refer to "Mohammed" or Mohammedanism." For purposes of this volume, I have tried to adhere to the system favored by *The Oxford History of Islam*, ed. John Esposito (Oxford University Press, 1999). Personal idiosyncrasies exist. Proper reference is sometimes eschewed for the familiar (e.g. Yasser over Yasir Arafat, Suleiman the Magnificent instead of Suleyman, Hejira over hajrah, kibla instead of qibla, jahiliya instead of jahilya, and the omission of diacritical marks representing glottal stops.) I trust, however that this will not present insurmountable impediments for the reader.

Contents

Preface

More than 2000 years ago, the Greek Polybius offered instruction to those who dedicated themselves to retelling the story of mankind. For Polybius, there were three essential tasks before the historian: first, to familiarize himself with sources; next to travel to the actual sites where great events had occurred (what Polybius termed *autopsy*); and finally to compose a text that would offer utility to contemporary society. Unfortunately, much of what historians from Livy and Polybius to Macaulay and Graetz had to say was marred by nationalist impulse. It was not until the end of the nineteenth century that the German historian Leopold von Ranke reminded his colleagues that their primary commitment should be to objectivity, scientific methodology and a sense of balance. Many scholars have conceded difficulty in this pursuit as the phraseology employed by an historian, let alone his or her selection of sources, identified a text with some ideological wing in the profession. By its very nature, history becomes subjective, its worth based on the prestige or numbers of supporters. Objectivity, as Jacques Barzun and Henry Graff have written, "is a delusion."[1]

Nowhere is the dilemma more acutely noted than in the field of Middle East studies.[2] Until recently the region was regarded as arcane, its principal raconteurs religious pilgrims, agents for oil companies or government functionaries who had retired from imperial postings. Much of what they wrote was tainted with the traditional European bias (what Edward Said denounced as "Orientalism").[3] As the world came to appreciate the strategic importance of the region, university chairs were endowed and the quality of both those teaching and those studying Middle Eastern civilization increased. Not without certain preconditions, however. Criticism of cultural flaws (e.g. the oppressed status of women, the nature of slavery, restrictions on *dhimmi*, existence of anti–Semitism and other forms of ethnic harassment) had to be muted if friendly relations between East and West were to be maintained. Unlike other fields of history, which have permitted the debate of ideas, a catechism has been created about the Middle East leaving even public school teachers to wonder what they may say in classrooms. As Anatole France despaired: "An original historian is the object of distrust, contempt, and loathing from everybody."[4]

I do not claim parity with France's historian hero, but I do understand what it means to write something that challenges orthodoxy. I may not have visited as many places as Polybius but I have seen the sun rise over Agamemnon's Mycenae and Hatshepsut's Luxor. I have observed the religious protocols that operate in St. Peter's and the Mosque of Umar.

I have spent more than fifty years of my life with scholars like William McDonald, Sydey Fisher, Moshe Zeltzer, Marie Syrkin, Howard Sachar, Daniel Pipes and Ben Halpern, studying and teaching about the Middle East, always with the vain hope that some day it will all be better.

My thanks to the many individuals who assisted with this project: secretary-typists Mary Bellotto, Bonnie Harris and Jason Lehman; research assistants Jim Guy, Dirk Hermance, Carol Salmon, Mary Ann O'Toole, Aziz Alhadi, and Sam DiRocca, and, as ever, my wife Nancy.

1

An Introduction
to the Middle East

What Is the Middle East?

In April 1986, my son Jonathan and I journeyed to Egypt with a tour group from Israel. Colleagues back home warned us against making the trip because American aircraft had just attacked Libya and tensions in the region were high. Still, it was an opportunity to see the land of Tutankhamen, and the irony of entering Egypt at Passover did not escape us.

After three hours at the border checkpoint of Rafiah, our Egged bus continued into the Gaza Strip. Our tour skirted the squalor of refugee camps within Gaza City. What we saw were neatly cultivated orange groves separated by clusters of cacti and palms. As we moved forward, a small boy, no more than five or six years of age, came running up behind our vehicle. I thought he was going to wave. Instead, he reached down, grabbed a rock, and with all the fury in his little body, flung it against the bus. We did not know it at the time, but that stone was a harbinger of a greater torrent of missiles that were to fly in December 1987, with the outbreak of the Palestinian Intifada.

Time and hatred, like the crescent moon, move with their own relentless grace in this part of the world. This is the Middle East, a stretch of land predominantly (not exclusively) Arab in population and Islamic in culture. British colonialists coined the term "Middle East" at the end of the nineteenth century. Then, it encompassed everything east of the Suez Canal to the borders of China, including the subcontinent of India. Today, it is understood to include Iran, Mesopotamia, Anatolia, the Holy Land (Syria, Lebanon, Jordan and Israel), and the Arabian Peninsula, but also the states bordering the Sahara Desert from Egypt to Morocco.

Why Study Middle East History?

1. **Confronted with daily crises in the Middle East, responsible citizens should form conclusions based on reason, not intuition.** No longer has any world citizen the luxury of ignoring famine in Africa or sectarian violence in Ireland. In recent years, Americans have become all too familiar with strange-sounding sites and personalities that have intruded

1

onto the front pages of hometown newspapers. They have learned that the war waged against Iraq in 1991 is only a slice in the whole loaf of crisis and tragedy that is Middle Eastern history. Since July 1974, two NATO allies (Greece and Turkey) have threatened war against one another on the island of Cyprus. The state of Israel has been under siege since its creation in 1948, six wars ago. Between 1980 and 1989, Iraq and Iran embarked on mutual crusades that bled more than 500,000 youths of their lives. When that war ended, Saddam Hussein turned against Kuwait. Only then did the rest of the world react to the threat of poison gas, which had already been used against royalists in Yemen, Kurds in Iraq, and rebellious Sunni Muslims in Syria.

The Middle East is a region that breeds terror. Assassins struck down Emir Faisal of Saudi Arabia in 1975 and Egypt's Anwar Sadat in 1981. Terrorism has left Lebanon a gutted battleground for roving armed gangs. Massacres and retaliatory raids like those at Munich and Lod Airport in 1972, Kiryat Shmona and Maalot in 1974 and 1975, Damour in 1976, Sabra-Shatilla in 1982, Hebron and Jerusalem are grim reminders of the Palestinian refugee problem that has festered for four decades. Other minorities (Kurds, Armenians, Druze, Copts, and Baha'is) have failed to achieve self-determination. And despite a number of well-meaning proposals (the Eisenhower, Nixon and Carter doctrines, the Rogers Plan, the Jarring Mission, Camp David, Kissinger and Baker Shuttle Diplomacy), the United States has felt the sting of Middle East partisans. The murders of Robert Kennedy, Leon Klinghoffer, Robert Stethem, and Rabbi Meir Kahane; the destruction of marine barracks in Beirut, of Pan-Am 103 over Lockerbie, Scotland, and of New York's World Trade Center; and attacks against U.S. embassies in East Africa were executed because Middle East factions viewed American policy with disfavor.

2. The Middle East was the birthplace of Western Civilization. Modern archaeology and science have shown that the Middle East was the seedbed of ancient civilization. In this region occurred, the origins of the Neolithic Revolution, domestication of animals, organized agriculture, urbanization, metallurgy, pottery, the wheel, the natural sciences, astrology and astronomy, writing, literature and mythology, political and legal institutions, philosophy, and religion.

3. The Middle East was the cradle of three principal religions. Fifteen million Jews regard *Eretz Yisrael* as a land given to them by divine covenant. Two billion Christians trace their heritage not to some crag in Eire or Poland but to the Church of the Nativity in Bethlehem or the Church of the Annunciation in Nazareth. A billion Muslims revere the prophets of Judaism and the apostles of Christianity but stress the special mission of Muhammad, whose warriors conquered much of the civilized world in the seventh century. Over the past 2,000 years, adherents of these three related faiths have waged countless wars for control of territory deemed holy by all.

4. The Middle East is a region of great cities, confronting problems common to urban society. A tourist in the Old City of Jerusalem can walk from the Church of the Holy Sepulchre (the site of Golgotha) to the *Kotel ha-Ma'aravi* (the Western Wall, said to be the last vestige of Herod's temple), then to the Mosque of Umar (from which Muhammad made his miraculous ascent to heaven) within a few moments. Through the ages, Canaanites, Israelites, Assyrians, Babylonians, Egyptians, Romans, Byzantines, Persians, Macedonians, Arabs, Turks, Crusaders, Britons, Jordanians and Israelis have all liberated David's city of peace. Yet Jerusalem, with its population of 600,000, is more than a symbol of religious or national passion. It also represents the urban revolution that has transformed the Middle East. Today Algiers, Casablanca, Alexandria, Teheran, Baghdad, Tel Aviv, Beirut, Istanbul, Ankara, and Damascus count between one and four million residents. Cairo, with eight million (and another two million clustered on its outskirts), is among the 10 largest cities in the world.

Sewage lines and storm drains are virtually unknown in many large cities. Decent drinking water is available in bottles; the World Health Organization cautions against the presence of salmonella and enteric viruses that cause meningitis, respiratory disease, hepatitis, conjunctivitis, rash, vomiting or diarrhea.[1] Half the drinking water pumped in Istanbul comes from an ancient pipeline poisoned with industrial chemicals and human waste.[2]

Cairo, whose modern hotels, parks, museums, and subway hold a fascination for tourists, has another, seamier side. From the Mokattam hills in the city's east to the Nile, there are endless rows of mud-wattle huts without heat, light or sanitation. An earthquake in the fall of 1992 left many of these primitive homes in shambles. A similar situation prevails in Istanbul, where hundreds of thousands of impoverished newcomers cling to hovels in the more than 200 shantytowns that circle the city.[3]

5. In the Middle East, population increase constantly outstrips food supply. Cairo is one of the most densely populated centers in the world. The ratio per square mile is 69,000, twice the density of Tokyo or Bombay. Most Egyptians are also inadequately fed. In many nations (Libya, Egypt, Jordan, Iran, Saudi Arabia, Iraq) less than one-tenth of the land area is cultivable. Food production rises at the rate of 3.1 percent annually. Despite food shortages and epidemics, population increases at 3.5 percent per year, doubling every 35 years. Between 1961 and 1981, Egypt's population rose from 26 million to 42 million, that of Turkey from 29 million to 44 million, Syria from 5 million to 8 million. In July 1994, the United Nations projected that by the year 2025 Egypt and Turkey would count 98 million and that Iran's population would be 152 million.

Efforts to combat food shortages have not succeeded. The 364-foot high Aswan Dam was supposed to increase arable land in Egypt by 40 percent. But the nation's population increased 50 percent between 1956 and 1975. Even then, defective Russian engineering resulted in cracks of the dam's masonry. To create the Lake Nasser reservoir above the dam, more than 100,000 Nubians were displaced from their homes. Irrigation taps resulted in a diminution of water flushing from the Nile into the Mediterranean. By late 1970, the *New York Times* could report that fish had all but disappeared from coastal waters, that harmful salt deposits have developed, and that the Delta, noted for 5000 years as the most fertile regions of the world, was now a breeding ground for malarial mosquitoes and other parasites.[4]

6. The Middle East has been and continues to be a breeding ground of disease. Malaria, yellow fever, leishmaniasis (a parasitic disease causing facial deformities), filariasis (a disease of the blood and lymphatic channels), trypanosomiasis (sleeping sickness) leprosy, anthrax, dysentery, typhus, and hemorrhagic fever are all endemic to the region and no British or American passport is an effective talisman. History records numerous instances of plagues carried by merchants from the Middle East to European ports (including the Black Death, which took 30 million lives between 1348 and 1350). Though the world prides itself on having controlled diseases such as smallpox and diphtheria, the possibility of contamination from regions of primitive hygiene remains.

Consider these findings by the World Health Organization in the past two decades:

(a) the tuberculosis rate in the Middle East is seven times that of Western Europe; (b) a majority of Saudis suffer from some ophthalmic disorder (glaucoma, trachoma) and several million Egyptians and Tunisians have been afflicted with cataracts and blindness; (c) at one time spirochete bejel or related venereal diseases afflicted 25 percent of the Saudis and Egyptians; (d) large numbers of Egypt's *fellaheen* (peasants) suffer from ancylostomiasis (hookworm) or bilharziasis (snail fever); (e) in September 1977, more than 2600 persons in Jordan, Lebanon, Syria and Saudi Arabia fell victim to cholera, which flared up again in Egypt in the summer of 1983; (f) there were outbreaks of paralytic polio affecting 966 children in Jordan in 1983, bubonic plague (226 victims) in Sudan in March 1979, and Rift Valley Fever (600 deaths) in Egypt in 1977. Assessing data from Egypt, Algeria and Iran, which revealed that as many as 20 children in 1000 suffered from rheumatic heart disease, the World Health Organization concluded that high mortality rates in these countries were due, in part, to the prevalence of acute respiratory infections (flus, bronchitis, pneumonia, and related diseases). Nations that spend as much as 40 percent of their income on weapons (cf. Iraq and Syria) average 1500 persons per doctor, 500 persons per hospital bed. Little wonder that the infant mortality rate in Egypt in 1994 was 68 per 100, in Iran 64 per 1000 — seven times that of Israel. Only half the populations in Morocco, Oman, Yemen or Sudan can read or write. And yet every nation in the Middle East claimed that they had managed to increase life expectancy from 48 to 66 years in a single generation.[5]

7. The Middle East is a storehouse of natural resources. People have mined for copper, zinc, lead, nickel, magnesium. Algeria, rich in uranium, supplies the bulk of liquefied natural gas to France and Italy. The Jordan Valley produces some of the richest phosphates in the world. Morocco produces more cobalt and manganese than the United States. Apart from oil, Iran also exports manganese and tobacco. Turkey, the world's sixth largest grower of tobacco, is fourth in production of chromium. The Sudan is the chief supplier of gum arabic, a source of mucilage and pharmaceutical excipients. Asbestos, once a prized commodity, comes from Cyprus.[6] Most important, the Middle East sits atop 60 percent of the world's known petroleum deposits.

8. The Middle East is of great strategic importance to world powers. Long before Lord Montgomery and Erwin Rommel clashed here, other empire builders understood the strategic value of the region. Thutmose III and the Prince of Kadesh, Alexander the Great and Darius, Antiochus and Ptolemy, Romans and Parthians, Richard the Lionheart and Saladin, Napoleon and Palmerston, Allenby and the Ottomans all squared off in this vital land bridge connecting southeast Asia, Europe and Africa.

For the past half century Jews and Arabs have faced one another as willing or unwilling surrogates in a greater global conflict. Despite momentary optimism generated by the Camp David Accords in 1979, the Israel-Lebanon treaty of 1982, the Gulf War of 1991, the preliminary accords reached by the PLO and Israel in 1993, events in Lebanon, Syria, Iran and Iraq have demonstrated that lasting peace in the Middle East is a phantasm.

A fable from 1975 may illustrate the point. It is said that Premier Leonid Brezhnev of the Soviet Union, President Gerald Ford of the United States and Prime Minister Yitzhak Rabin of Israel were summoned before the throne of God and told they could ask one question of the Almighty. Brezhnev inquired, "When will my Russian people be able to feed themselves?" God thought a moment, then replied, "In another generation." Brezhnev broke down and wept, saying, "I'll not live to see it in my lifetime." Then Gerald Ford stumbled before the throne of God and asked, "When will there be an end to lawlessness on the streets of America?" Again, God mused and responded, "In another fifty years." Whereupon, Ford broke down and wept, saying, "I'll not live to see it in my lifetime." Finally, Israel's Prime Minister Rabin came before the throne and asked, "When will there be peace in the Middle East again?" Again, God pondered. Then *God* broke down and wept, saying, "I'll not live to see it in my lifetime."

No government has ever been able to control the dialectic of war. Once a conflict starts, it obtains a life of its own. The dangers are especially acute in the Middle East where, until recently, civilian centers had rarely been targets of military assaults. Given the intemperate nature of Middle East politicians and the availability of long-range missiles and chemical, bacteriological and nuclear weapons, the future can only be termed grim.

2

The Dry Land

Earthquakes and Deserts

More than 2000 years ago, the historian Polybius stressed that climate and geography influenced the development of civilizations. This was especially true in the Middle East where the lack of water makes for a rigorous existence. In this vast expanse, only two great river systems — the Tigris-Euphrates and the Nile — may be found. The region was not always so arid. Fifteen thousand years ago, during the last glaciation, moisture-bearing westerly winds shifted and in their place came desiccating breezes.

Mountain ranges that gird the coasts of most Middle Eastern lands present an obstacle to precipitation. In northern Turkey, the 8000-foot high Pontic Mountains loom less than five miles from the Black Sea. To the west, the Taurus/anti-Taurus chains serve as barriers before the more imposing Caucasus and the 17,000-foot high Mt. Ararat, legendary resting place of Noah's Ark. Further east, along the Caspian Sea, Mt. Demavend, an 18,934-foot volcanic peak, is the highest point west of the Hindu Kush. Shielding Iran's southern coast for more than 1000 miles are the 10,000-foot high Zagros Mountains. Across the Persian Gulf in Arabia, the mountains of the Hadhramaut and Hejaz average 9000 feet, while those in Yemen reach 14,000 feet.[1]

These jagged peaks lie astride one of the world's most active earthquake belts. Some 200 destructive shocks were recorded in Turkey before 1900. Quakes with a ferocity comparable to the San Francisco disaster of 1906 have altered the course of rivers and resulted in numerous human casualties. In Turkey, 24,000 persons died as a result of a tremor that occurred during a winter blizzard in 1939. Hundreds perished in Turkish resort towns in the fall of 1999. In Iran, 25,000 lost their lives in September 1978, another 50,000 in June 1990, when quakes rocked that country.

Where the mountains do not inspire fear, they block rain-bearing clouds. The Lebanon/anti–Lebanon mountains rise pleasantly from the seacoast to a pinnacle of 11,000 feet, along the snowy ridges of Mt. Hermon. On the coast at Beirut, the annual rainfall is 35 to 38 inches. Damascus, less than 60 miles away beyond the mountains, receives 10 inches per year. Baghdad, 500 miles inland, receives only five inches of precipitation each year. Further to the south, Aden, with an annual rainfall of three inches, has been described as "Hell with the sun beaming down on it."

In the Middle East, the rainy season may last from three to six months. Normally the season runs less than 50 days and is the product of the *sirocco*, or southeast winds. At other times, winds may not bring any kind of relief. From the west come locusts in the *dibba*, or hopper stage, blown out of Africa on their way to Iran, Iraq and Pakistan. The locusts strike across a five-mile front, devastating bushes and grass, leaving sheep and goats to starve for want of forage.

During the summer months, wells dry up and temperatures on the desert floor may reach 150 degrees as the *shamal*, or north wind, brings its withering heat across Mesopotamia into Arabia. The north wind is also the source of the dreaded *khamsin* or *idyah*, the sandstorm that strikes with hurricane-like velocity in some locations as often as a dozen times each year. The sight of a two-mile wide billowing wall of sand moving across the plain and blackening out the sky to an elevation of 5000 feet is harrowing. On rare occasions, the storms may be accompanied by lightning discharges that add a terrifying, primal element to the atmosphere. When sandstorms hit, shutting down visibility to less than a few yards, the proper action is to take shelter and wait them out.

The caprice of winds and mountain outcroppings have worked to create vast deserts. The region is a continuation of wastelands that stretch from the Sahara in Mauritania through the Gobi of Mongolia. The barren Libyan Desert sprawls over 50 percent of the land surface of that nation and Egypt. The 500-mile-long Syrian desert spills into Jordan and Iraq. More than one million square miles, 30 percent of Saudi Arabia, is sand dune. In the Rub' al-Khali, the Empty Quarter in the peninsula's east, sand mountains rise 600 to 700 feet, sand ridges extend for 30 to 40 miles. The Rub' al-Khali is an immense wasteland covering more territory than all of Western Europe. There are few permanent habitations, fewer wells and roads in the 300,000 square miles of the Empty Quarter, where midday temperatures hover above 130 degrees and devilish jinn create fanciful images for lost travellers.[2]

Sand eroded from soil, quartz, granite and sandstone makes up the most common form of desert, known as *erg*. The Dashti-Lut (Desert of Salt or Death) is a gravel plateau or *sammada* that covers 1000 miles south of Teheran. There are no cities, no airports in this rocky desert, which Alexander the Great chose to avoid. Mountainous deserts may also be found in eastern Egypt and Sudan, along the North African coast, in southern Jordan and throughout Turkey. A third type of desert is that of the Negev in Israel. Much like the Mohave in California, this flat, dusty land of scrubgrass needs only irrigation to bloom.[3]

The Camel

Fortunately for the inhabitants of this region, nature has provided a beast that eases their existence. The Arabian camel, or dromedary, is a good example of natural selection at work. Easily distinguished from his Bactrian cousin, which is stubbier, shaggy of hair and in possession of twin humps, the Arabian variety has longer eyelashes, spongy hoofs that splay out over the sand, and a single hump. Because of fatty tissue and its three-section stomach, the camel is capable of going two weeks without being fed or watered.

Domesticated between 1800 and 1200 B.C., the camel fulfilled most of the needs of the bedouin. Not particularly swift, it was primarily a means of transport. The camel could carry 1000 pounds of merchandise 25 miles— in some instances as much as 100 miles— in a day. During long treks through the desert, it served as companion. More than a beast of burden, the camel supplied tents, rugs and clothes from its hair, water containers and sandals from its hide. Camel flesh had the taste of tough beef. Camel urine was mixed with unguents to make *bahl*, a medicinal salve nomads found effective in the treatment of eye diseases. Camel droppings were dried on the rooftops and walls of primitive hamlets, then used as fuel.

An entire system of jurisprudence was based upon precedents involving camels that strayed onto others' property, were stolen, or were the object of communal lotteries. Status in tribal councils, the marriage price of a bride, compensation for criminal or civil wrongs were reckoned in terms of this animal. The temperamental beast has made such an impact upon the Middle East that the bedouin sometimes have been called *Ahl-al-Bayir* (people of the camel).[4]

Flooding and Salination

Not even the camel, however, could protect the bedouin from the capricious flow of water in the region. In some areas, a complete year's rainfall may come down on a single day. When this happens, dried-up wadis and mountain passes become raging streams that destroy everything in their path. Exactly such a disaster occurred in southern Jordan in the spring of 1966. Pilgrims to the ancient rock city of Petra were devastated by mountain floods.[5]

Even where flooding is anticipated, annual surges of water may be destructive. The 1700-mile-long Tigris and 1200-mile Euphrates rivers are credited with the development of civilization in Mesopotamia. Between April and June, the two streams deposit huge amounts of black alluvium, excellent for growing cereals. The Tigris alone removes 3,000,000 tons of eroded material in a single day; some estimate as much as 8000 cubic feet annually. Maps show the Sumerian towns of Eridu and Ur, originally seaports, now 65 to 100 miles away from the Persian Gulf, testifying to the amount of soil dredged up by the two rivers in historical times.

In Egypt, with few exceptions, the Nile flows placidly through 500 miles of deep limestone channels. In contrast, the Tigris and Euphrates are subject to many variables. The amount of winter snow or mountain rain, landslides, seacoast gales all affect the rivers, which plunge from elevations of 8000 to 10,000 feet into flat plains below. Not without reason was the Tigris nicknamed the *Idiglat* (swift as an arrow). In 1831, it shifted its course and destroyed 7000 houses in Baghdad in a single night. Even the slower, more manageable Euphrates has been known to burst its banks, most notably during the reign of Alexander the Great in 323 when the river shifted 11 miles to the east. Modern governments in Iraq have tried to implement flood-control programs (no less than four major dams and reservoirs were constructed between 1956 and 1961 to protect Baghdad) and to convert land in the Shatt al-Arab into farms, without much success.

The rivers also carry with them the bane of Middle East existence: salt. Archives from Lagash around 2400 B.C. complain of salt ruining agriculture. A 13th-century boundary stone from the region offers a curse: "May Adad, the supreme director of irrigation in heaven and earth, bring forth most salt to destroy his fields and dry up the barley, nor let the green herbs grow." More than 40 years ago, Thorkild Jacobsen and Robert Adams of the University of Chicago analyzed records of the Diyala region from 2600 B.C. to A.D. 1400 and attributed a northward shift of power here to progressive salination that left the soil uncultivated in the south. Wheat disappeared, barley shrivelled in a 500-year span.[6] Floodwaters were leaching calcium, sodium and magnesium carbonates from rocks, then spreading the insolubles throughout the floodplain, where evaporation did the rest. Whitish crusts of salt turned into "hardpan," crumbless soil in which seeds could not germinate and plants could not extend their roots or breathe.

Politics and Water

Logic dictates that people faced with common problems of food and water shortages should share resources. Lamentably, this has not been so in the Middle East. Egypt and Sudan offer one example.

In ancient times the pharaohs sought to control the land they called Cush. More recently, the two states were jointly administered by British imperialists. When the first Aswan Dam was opened at the Elephantine rapids in 1902, it was supposed to benefit both countries. When Egypt and the Sudan finally cast off British control between 1954 and 1956, Muslim Arabs dominated both societies. Sudan followed Egypt's lead in foreign affairs, hosting the Arab summit at Khartoum in August 1967. For a time after 1979, Sudan was one of the few Middle East states that supported the Camp David Accords.

Thus it was remarkable that Sudan contested Egypt's second Aswan Dam project when it was begun in 1957. Eighty-five billion cubic meters of water flow through the Nile annually. Under old arrangements, Sudan tapped into the river for four billion cubic meters, Egypt for 48, and 33 billion went to the Mediterranean or evaporation. Somehow, the Sudanese worried that the new dam with gigantic Lake Nasser would impair agriculture upstream. After tense negotiations, arrangements were made to increase the flow of water to Sudan to 18.5 billion cubic meters, Egypt would receive 55 billion, and the Mediterranean would get 11.5. While this may have placated politicians in both countries, environmentalists have been disturbed by increased erosion in the Nile waterway and along the shores of the Delta, destruction of sardine fisheries and increased pestilence in the same area, unstable levels of Lake Nasser and loss of agricultural nutrients, increased soil salinity and waterlogging.

Egypt and Sudan were able to work out their differences. Not so Turkey, Syria and Iraq, who share the waters of the Euphrates. Since 1966, the three nations have been constructing their own massive dams and barrage systems designed to increase arable land and hydroelectric power from the Euphrates. The 670-foot rock-filled dam at Keban, Turkey, was programmed to produce six billion kilowatt hours of energy for north-central Turkey, one of the Middle East's most underdeveloped areas. Syria countered with a series of projects that dot the Euphrates as it flows 300 miles through its territory. The greatest of these was the 300-foot high Tabqa dam. Stretching 8,200 feet across, it was built with Soviet assistance and designed to spearhead the irrigation of nearly three million acres of land when it opened in 1973. Within two years, Iraqi officials complained that the brackish, polluted flow coming from Syria was unfit for human consumption. The Iraqis also claimed that Syrian discharges were killing children, sheep and cows, and had deprived three million farmers of their irrigation. Though both governments were controlled by anti–Israel Baathists (Arab socialists), and were populated mainly with Sunni Muslims, their dispute over water periodically erupted in artillery duels along the border. A significant fallout of the Euphrates water squabble was Syrian support for non-Arab, non–Baathist, Shiite Iran in its war with Iraq and its participation in the anti–Iraq coalition in 1990.

The most notable case where failure to agree on sharing a stable water supply generated political controversy has been the Jordan River system. This famed river falls from 9000 feet at the Golan Heights to 1300 feet below sea level at the Dead Sea in just 110 miles. The figures are deceiving, for the river is not some raging torrent, but rather a serpentine stream with a generally placid flow. Nevertheless the Jordan does have a sudden gravitational fall in spots (200 feet in the ten miles between the Huleh Basin and the Sea of Galilee, a 60-foot waterfall at the Bareighit River at Tannur) and is the principal artery for parched sections of Lebanon, Syria, Jordan and Israel. Common sense suggests that regional cooperation would be the first step toward peace in the area. Just such a scheme was proposed by the Eisenhower Administration in 1953. Known as the Johnston Plan (after special representative Eric D. Johnston), this proposal would have reclaimed nearly 400,000 acres and supplied enough hydroelectric power to secure employment for nearly all of the then one million Palestinian refugees. The U.S. promised to fund the project, which would have supplied 200,000 new homes to the Palestinians. Sixty percent of the water flow would have been reserved for Arab states. Unwilling to work with Israel, the Arabs rejected this and several other plans offered by the U.N. General Assembly.[7]

The result was a race on the part of four nations to tap into available water supplies before their neighbors. Using $80 million of U.S. assistance, Jordan constructed its East Ghor Canal in 1958, ostensibly to reclaim 125,000 acres of land. Shortly after, Syria began work on a diversion canal from the Wazzani and Baniyas Rivers to the Yarmuk, in the hope of thinning the flow of water southward. Lebanon, too, invested $100 million for the construction of dams and tunnels on the Litani and Hasbani Rivers, to irrigate nearly 200,000 acres in the Bekaa Valley and the coastal hills between Sidon and Tyre.

For its part, Israel pushed ahead with a pipeline from the Sea of Galilee, circumventing the Jordanian-occupied West Bank to the Negev. The 10-inch concrete pipe ran 160 miles and took nearly 10 years to complete. When it was opened in January 1964, the National Water Carrier had an annual capacity of a million cubic meters and was designed to accommodate immigrants and development towns in Israel's southern desert.

The pipeline also had an undesired side effect. Representatives of Arab nations convened in Cairo to plot a response. In a rare moment of accord, Syria and Iraq urged warfare. But Egypt's Nasser, noting that his country was unprepared for a third round of hostilities with Israel, advised the Summit to pursue a different course instead. A united Arab command, subsequently dubbed the Palestine Liberation Army, the fighting organization of the Palestinian refugees, was placed under the direction of Egyptian General Abdel Hakim Amer. Members of the Arab League were expected to tithe better than a million dollars each year in support of a new Palestinian political apparatus headed by onetime Saudi diplomat Ahmed Shukeiry. In Cairo and again in Jerusalem in May 1964, delegates of Palestinian councils vowed to carry on the fight for the liberation of their homeland. They were encouraged by Nasser, who told them on May Day: "We will not liberate Palestine today, but time is on our side. We shall liberate Palestine by building up our strength and our armies. We shall enter Israel not on a red carpet, but on fields of blood."[8]

It is instructive to note that the maps that festooned the halls in Cairo and East Jerusalem in 1964 showed the Palestinian homeland to be not Gaza (which Egypt controlled since 1948), Jerusalem or the West Bank (annexed by Jordan in 1952), but the Galilee, Haifa, Tel Aviv, Lod, Beersheba, and the Negev. Had the Arab states seriously been interested in creating a Palestinian state, they could have done so at any time between 1948 and 1967. However legitimate the aspirations of Arab refugees may be, the Palestine Liberation Organization came into existence in 1964, an artificial creation of the Arab League.

3

The Blessings of Oil

From Titusville to Dhahran

If lack of water is the curse of the Middle East, the glut of petroleum has been a mixed blessing. The Industrial Revolution of the 19th century brought with it a demand for more and better lubricants. In America, petroleum was known to the Indians who used globules of pitch as a medicine or cast it into ceremonial objects—beads, bowls, amulets. Even after Colonel Edwin Drake tapped into deposits along Oil Creek in Venango County Pennsylvania in 1859, the black substance still was not regarded as an energy panacea.[1]

As late as 1850, 90 percent of the fuel burned in the United States was wood. Coal, which passed wood for the first time in 1885, supplied 65 percent of the nation's energy needs by the turn of the century. Coal was generating power for homes, streetlights, blast furnaces, and naval vessels. At the same time, a number of factors combined to displace coal as the favored energy source. Ships propelled by coal were dependent upon supplies cached about the world in remote colonies. An energy revolution was signaled in 1904 when Admiral Edwin Fisher, Lord of the British Admiralty, championed conversion of the fleet to what seemed the cleaner, more efficient fuel—petroleum. About the same time, Henry Ford and others were demonstrating the practicality of the gasoline-powered automobile.

All of this still might have proved insufficient without the marketing genius and ruthlessness of John D. Rockefeller. Though the Russians claimed they were the first to appreciate the potential of oil, it was Rockefeller, operating out of Cleveland, Ohio, who secured a virtual monopoly on American, European and Chinese markets. His Standard Oil company accounted for 90 percent of oil produced, refined, and distributed in the United States and helped bring about the Sherman anti-trust law of 1890.[2]

Rockefeller's competition came from Royal Dutch Shell, the Rothschilds, Alfred Nobel, and some Armenian and German bankers, all of whom were searching for cheap concessions throughout the world. The Middle East appealed for several reasons. For a token, medieval shaykhs were willing to grant long-term leases. Second, labor was cheap and the task of oil recovery required little skill. Most important, there was little need to explore, for in several places oil seeped through springs of sulphur water and could be ladled off the surface. Herodotus offered directions to such spots along the Euphrates and near Susa. In certain sections of Palestine, surface limestone was so saturated, it emitted an oily odor when struck a light blow. In one form or another, petroleum had been used to caulk the vessels of ancient sailors, and as brick and mortar for the ziggurats of Ur and Babylon. Natural gas leaks served as the basis of sacred fires of Persia. When the first British gusher came in at Abadan, Persia, in May 1908, it confirmed what everyone had known. Oil was there, in great abundance, just for the taking.

Fear of the Rockefellers produced an unofficial cartel that shut the Americans out of Middle Eastern oil on the eve of World War I. British Petroleum already owned the Persian concession. In June 1914, British and Dutch interests combined with Germany's Deutsche Bank to create the Turkish Petroleum Company, which monopolized resources in Mesopotamia. Blocked from the rich fields of Mosul-Kirkuk and Abadan, the various branches of Standard Oil plumbed the soil of Palestine and the more remote regions of the Persian Gulf. By 1928, Socony-Vacuum and Standard of California were making hydrographic soundings and surveying boundaries in the wastes of the Rub'al-Khali.

The principal beneficiary of this interest was the Emir Abdul Aziz ibn Saud. An irascible fundamentalist who considered the world flat, ibn Saud had spent 10 years of his youth in exile at the court of Kuwait. This legendary ruler first gained prominence when, at the age of 22 in January 1902, he directed the reconquest of the Najd in northern Arabia. Accompanied by 40 armed tribesmen, ibn Saud seized control of the provincial capital Riyadh and restored his family's rule. He remained relatively obscure over the next two decades, until Hussein ibn Ali, the heavily subsidized protégé of the British, proclaimed himself king of the Hejaz in 1919 and caliph in 1924. Outraged, ibn Saud, who belonged to the puritanical Wahhabi Muslim sect, attacked with bands of holy warriors and forced Hussein into exile. In January 1926, ibn Saud was proclaimed king in Mecca. Six years later, the combined territories of the Hejaz and Nejd were renamed Saudi Arabia. Literally the father of his country, ibn Saud left a royal family that numbers 3000 princes and has produced all of the nation's monarchs.

Initially, Saudi Arabia was a bankrupt kingdom, unable to meet its international bills, even with revenue generated by pilgrim traffic to the sacred city of Mecca. Then, in 1933, it signed a 66-year agreement with Standard Oil of California providing the government a royalty of four shillings on every ton of oil extracted. In January 1944, this California-Arabian Oil company joined with Texaco, Standard of New Jersey (Exxon) and Socony-Vacuum (Mobil) to become the Arab-American Oil Company, Aramco, a giant conglomerate that by 1967 had more than $2 billion in capital investments in the area.[3]

The Americans had to wait five years before the field at Dhahran yielded oil in September 1938. Once again, a world war intervened to frustrate American exploitation of Middle Eastern oil. In the next six years, however, oil companies and the U.S. government ingratiated themselves with ibn Saud. President Franklin Roosevelt made a special side trip from Yalta in February 1945 to consult with the Arab monarch about the future of Palestine. Even though Saudi Arabia declined to enter the war against the Axis until the last week of February 1945 (when the outcome was predictable), it was granted charter membership in the postwar United Nations. Most important, through the conflict Saudi Arabia was paid $50 million in "Lend-Lease," from a program designed to bolster Allied belligerents. The monies were to secure the goodwill of this oil-rich nation.

The Threat of OPEC

The practice of paying subsidies to rulers of states in strategic locations was common in the British Empire. With regard to Saudi Arabia it seemed to make little sense. In 1950, the continental U.S. produced two-thirds of the world's petroleum. As recently as 1960, this nation imported a mere 3 percent of its oil from the Middle East. Americans, who constituted 6 percent of the world's population, were consuming one-third of all its energy. Some experts projected that at such a rate by the year 2000 we would require 100 percent of the world's energy.

While Japan and Western Europe became increasingly dependent upon Middle Eastern oil, Americans were bemused. Few expressed concern over the nationalization of oil companies or the formation of OPEC (the Organization of Petroleum Exporting Countries, comprised mainly of Middle Eastern states, but including also Nigeria, Venezuela, Ecuador, and Indonesia), a true cartel. So long as rival service stations in the United States waged price wars, there was no cause for alarm. Economists in the Eisenhower Administration predicted that the energy binder would have to end by the 1970s, but politicians and the public ignored such warnings. Despite large reservoirs of high-grade petroleum in shale deposits of the American West, the Nixon Administration cut the budget of the Bureau of Mines by one half. Despite the existence of a 10-year supply of oil in Alaska, environmentalists succeeded in delaying construction on the North Slope–Prudhoe Bay project. Despite bituminous coal reserves sufficient to power the nation for 200 years, no efforts were mounted by lessees of America's 15 major coalfields to spearhead research that would purge the coal of its sulfur content. Small wonder, since five of those leases were held in perpetuity by the Continental, Shell, Sun, Gulf, and Atlantic-Richfield oil companies.

Americans did not worry because the Arab states had engaged in a brief and ineffective boycott during the Six-Day War of 1967. The winter of 1973 and 1774 changed everything. Early in 1973, Arab members of OPEC began to threaten the U.S. if it did not abandon a pro–Israel stance. On May 14, Libya's Qaddafi and Egypt's Sadat called for use of oil as a "self-defense" weapon. A day later, Libya, Iraq, Kuwait, and Algeria halted oil flow as a symbolic protest against the anniversary of the independence of the state of Israel. Two months later, Saddam Hussein suggested that American interests might be better served by tilting toward a pro–Arab policy. Following the lead of Libya, the Iraqi leader nationalized his nation's oil reserves early in October and called for a halt to all shipments of oil to the West. With the outbreak of the Yom Kippur War, Middle Eastern states announced a 17 percent increase in the price of oil. As Arkansas Senator J. William Fulbright fretted that some major power might invade Middle East oil fields, Saudi Arabia threatened to cut back shipments of oil if the U.S. resupplied Israel, then threw its lot in with Abu Dhabi (October 19), Libya (October 20), Algeria (October 21), Kuwait, Bahrain, Qatar and Dubai by instituting a total embargo against the U.S. and Holland (October 22).[4]

America was now importing more than 25 percent of its oil from the Middle East and the pinch was felt everywhere. Overnight, the price of gasoline, tires, roofing asphalt, tar, plastic garbage bags—anything with an oil derivative—doubled. Lines formed at gas stations on Fridays because few stations were open on weekends, and there was talk of rationing. Students and government employees shivered in public buildings where thermostats were set at 68 degrees. Workers were treated to the glory of the rising sun as Daylight Savings Time was proclaimed during the winter months. For the first time in America's history, the inflation rate passed 10 percent. Economists quarreled about whether domestic oil companies were profiteering, but there was no disputing the three to five points in inflation, the result of increased costs of oil. Auto, steel, and rubber plants shut down because of a drop in consumer confidence, and Secretary of State Henry Kissinger reported 500,000 jobs lost in the process. Subsequently, the Brookings Institution, a Washington-based think tank, would link the loss of two million jobs in 1976, and three million in 1977, to a trade deficit caused by manipulation of oil supplies and prices.

In the spring of 1973, King Faisal of Saudi Arabia (Saud's second successor) and the Shah of Iran, two figures generally regarded as friends of the West, joined with Libya's Qaddafi in raising the cost of a barrel of crude oil (approximately 42 gallons) from $2.75 to $13.00. Journalists and political cartoonists likened Europe and America to helpless drug addicts, willing to pay outrageous sums—$40 per barrel by 1980. America's dependency grew to the point where it was importing nearly 50 percent of its oil by the time President Carter finally capped the import limit during the Iranian hostage crisis of 1979 and 1980. The pinch was felt not merely at the pump, where prices soon crossed the magic barrier of $1 per barrel. The increases also affected America's balance of payments—$42 billion in 1974, $60 billion in the Gross National Product of 1976, $80 billion in 1977.[5]

During that first year of withdrawal-dependency, some pundits envisioned the collapse of Western economies. It was argued that the drain of cash reserves and gold would destroy the U.S. and Europe. The catastrophe did not materialize for several reasons: first, because the OPEC nations spent much of the money in the West for luxuries, economic development projects, and military hardware; second, because the nations invested much of their newfound wealth in enterprises located in the West; third, because the most secure place for whatever cash surpluses existed was in Western banks; fourth, because of concerted conservation programs and plans to develop alternate sources of energy; and fifth, because of political differences that prompted competition among OPEC's members and dropped the price of crude oil back to $18 by 1987.

The Middle East, possessing a disproportionate share of the world's known petroleum reserves, acquired new political and economic power. Libya's Qaddafi could not be dismissed as an upstart who had expelled the U.S. from Wheelus Air Force Base. He commanded the seventh largest oil-producing nation in the world, one whose four billion tons of petroleum would make Libya a major exporter for the next 50 years. Iran's 5.8 million barrels per day gave this country 10 percent of the world's market by 1976. Since 1980, its temperamental leaders have sometimes menaced, sometimes disrupted, the flow of oil through the Straits of Hormuz — eight million barrels per day, which is 25 to 70 percent of the supplies needed by Japan, France, West Germany and the United States.

Along the Persian Gulf a host of kingdoms have been shaken from the doldrums of feudalism. Previously, rulers of Bahrein, Qatar, and Abu Dhabi preferred to hold court in their tents or hawk after bustard. Now, with millions of dollars pouring in weekly, they reacted as most instant millionaires. Shaykh Rashid of Dubai, Zaid of Abu Dhabi, Isa of Bahrein, and Khalifa bin Hama at-Thani of Qatar spent freely and conspicuously. Their prestige baubles included Dubai's $10 million airport, an $8-million mosque in Abu Dhabi, Bahrein's gleaming Secretariat Building, an olympic-sized stadium for the United Arab Emirates, passenger planes for newly formed national airlines, the Dorchester Hotel, Mereworth Castle, Fort Belvedere, and St. Martin's Property Corporation in England. Wary of the colossi of Saudi Arabia, Iran, Iraq, the U.S. or Soviets, the erstwhile feudal states coveted helicopters, howitzers, anti-tank guns, armored personnel carriers, corvettes, frigates, minesweepers, fighter bombers and interceptors.[6]

The Miracle of Saudi Arabia

In Saudi Arabia, the power of oil enabled ibn Saud's son, Faisal, and his half brothers to hobnob with American presidential aspirants, and demand that the dream of pilgrimage to Jerusalem be fulfilled. Saudi Arabia possesses one of the largest pools of oil in the world, perhaps 530 billion barrels. For the past decade, it has been the region's leading producer of oil, averaging between six and nine million barrels per day. The impact upon its economy has been phenomenal. Back in 1939, state revenues totaled $3.2 million. By 1973, the figure was $4.34 billion. The next year, after OPEC quadrupled crude prices, Saudi Arabia received $22,573,500,000. By 1987, the figure was $130 billion, with substantial sums stashed in reserves and more than $60 billion invested in Western banks.

With such windfalls, the Saudis purchased real estate on the Champs Elysees, Fifth Avenue, the Strip in Las Vegas, as well as in Georgia, Kentucky, and Southern California. They also invested in Nippon T and T, the Krupp Steel Works in Germany, Delta Airlines, and securities offered by the Federal National Mortgage Association. Much of the new-found wealth was applied to internal improvements. Successive five-year plans called for the construction of modern jetports at Dhahran, Jidda, Riyadh, and Damman. Saudi Arabia developed archaeological and religious projects, phosphate mining, cement factories, and a new steel industry. Its ports were modernized. Foreign experts were invited in to assist with land reclamation, desalination, and the construction of the Wadil Jizan dam that irrigated 70,000 acres. In the reign of Saud ibn Saud (1953–64) 600,000 trees were planted in the Northern Provinces. Health and education were also priorities. One decade after the death of Ibn Saud, the number of teachers had increased five times, the number of students four times. Seven hundred dispensaries were opened about the country and several world-class hospitals were established.

Though reckoned as a friend and ally, Saudi Arabia frustrated or disappointed its Western patrons. During the Six-Day War, King Faisal (1964–75) called for an economic boycott of the West. Later, he endorsed the three negatives of Khartoum (no negotiations, no recognition, no peace with Israel.) King Khalid (1975–82) opposed the Camp David Accords and in January 1981 asserted that the liberation of Jerusalem "from the claws of Zionism is a must." His successor, King Fahd, called for a jihad against Israel, opposed the use of Western troops in Israel in 1982 and the U.S. bombing of Libya in 1986, yet was silent when an attack on U.S. marines in Beirut left 260 dead in 1983. At a time when the United Nations was attempting to impose economic sanctions against South Africa, Saudi Arabia was supplying the apartheid regime with 50 percent of its petroleum needs. Yet in 1982 Saudi Arabia supported the United States in one of four votes in the United Nations General Assembly, a figure surpassed by former Soviet satellites Poland and Albania. Without Western intervention, it is questionable whether the Saud dynasty would have survived invasion from Iraq in 1990 and 1991.

Saudi Arabia's oil wealth also created internal tensions for this staunchly conservative society. Writing in the *New York Times* in November 1976, Edward Sheehan likened the port city of Jidda to "Calcutta with diamonds." It was, said Sheehan, "wrappings and junk all over." On the docks lay tons of merchandise — tape recorders, bulldozers, television sets, automobiles. In the harbor, 100 newly acquired fiberglass patrol boats sat idle because there was no one trained to operate them. City streets were being ripped up to accommodate repairs on inadequate water, sewage, telephone, and electricity lines.[7] Three years later, Sheehan described the same roads in disrepair, a proliferation of X-rated cinemas, a rising crime rate, and an extraordinary inflation where a two-bedroom apartment was renting for $20,000 per year.[8]

In the passing years, Westerners posted to Saudi Arabia noted how gracious and scrupulously kind their hosts have been. The compounds outside Dhahran seem like subdivisions in the Arizona desert. Within the Western community, however, mixed swimming is frowned upon. Outside, hours of access to grocery stores and other shops are limited. In

Saudi Arabia, women are discouraged from driving. They enter busses from a separate door and those who dress immodestly (without hair covering or ankle-length gowns) may be chastised by cane-wielding *mutawwas* (religious police). Australian reporter John Laffin told how in 1977 a German woman, the victim of rape, was "righteously punished" (i.e., flogged) as an "accomplice to immorality" because she was wearing a Western dress.[9]

There are all sorts of dangers for the millions of foreigners who have come hoping to participate in the economic miracle of Saudi Arabia. The worst menial jobs are taken by poor, uneducated Yemenites and Bengladeshis. Thieves share subterranean cells with 15 others for an indefinite period. A number of Philippine nurses have been victims of rape or vanished into captivity. Three employees of the Bucheir Corporation of Youngstown, Ohio, were denied exit from the country in the summer of 1984 because of contractual disputes. Personal safety became more than an abstract for most Americans when in 1995 terrorists bombed the Khobar Towers complex outside Dhahran, killing five American servicemen.

Despite promises to the contrary in 1958 and 1984, Saudi Arabia has no constitution, no political parties, no elections, no trade unions. Adultery, murder, idolatry, conversion to another faith, even the presence of a non-Muslim in the holy city of Mecca are all capital crimes. Punishment is meted out publicly and can take the form of stoning, beheading (four murderers in 1997), "drawing and quartering" or "crucifixion" (sanctioned by, but never implemented by, Muslim teachers against 170 extremists who seized the Great Mosque in Mecca in November and December 1979). At the start of the 21st century, Saudi Arabia is one of the world's great paradoxes. Here is an important nation whose boundaries have never been completely defined and which has never taken an accurate census. It has access to one of the most precious commodities of the industrial world and yet is a hidebound society. The princes nurture a military that mutinied on at least three occasions. The economic gap between the royal family and its subjects continues to widen. There are also problems concerning the perceived religious morality of the Saudis. Yet some experts argue the regime is stable.

Kuwait

The most startling material transformation in the Arab world due to the oil revolution occurred in Kuwait. After 1756, this ill-defined confederacy located in the corner of the Persian Gulf was run by 70 shaykhs, chief among whom were the Sabah clan from Arabia. As late as 1939, Kuwait had no formal government. Most of its 350,000 people were illiterate bedouin, shepherds, goat herders, caravan merchants or pearl fishers, with an income averaging $35 per year. Few diplomats from Great Britain, the nation that assumed protector status over Kuwait, relished being posted to a stark desert where there were no roads, no hospitals, and only a handful of doctors.[10]

When World War II ended, geologists from British Petroleum discovered that the flat, porous soil of Kuwait was literally saturated with oil. No large derricks were required to extract the precious liquid, which spurted from pumpers. After 1952, more than 100 consecutive digs yielded the world's least costly bonanza. Once among the poorest countries in the world, Kuwait was suddenly reckoned among the richest. Its gross national income, only $300,000 in 1939, exploded to $8 billion in 1974. While not every 500th Kuwait was a millionaire (as some statisticians reckoned) the per capita income in 1985 ($18,000) was the highest in the world.

Over the past three decades, Kuwait's population quadrupled as engineers, technicians, and their families from other Middle Eastern lands flocked to Hawalli and Kuwait City seeking jobs in the petroleum industry. The capital, Kuwait City, once a dusty, provincial town, sprouted pink, purple and chartreuse stuccoed office buildings ("Detroit Modern," some critics said). Six-lane highways, lined with fluorescent lights and 200,000 trees (the latter costing $125 each) disappeared into the city's desert outskirts. Such roads were necessary for Kuwait's motor vehicles, numbered more than those in Lebanon, Syria and Jordan combined.

Some shaykhs squandered much of their revenue. One purchased a carpet woven of solid gold thread. Another imported a menagerie of lions, antelopes, and monkeys. Another constructed palaces for each of his four wives and instructed them to keep lunch ready in case he came by for an afternoon siesta. Another built 50 pink-marble air-conditioned palaces. The biggest spender of all was Shaykh Abdullah Mubarak. Once unable to afford third-class passage to Europe, he squandered more than $800,000 during a trip to Paris in the early 1960s, lavishing $500 tips on cigarette girls in restaurants and, on the spur of the moment, purchasing three Rolls-Royce automobiles. The possessor of a Cadillac with an 18-carat gold grillework, Shaykh Abdullah summoned more than 80 vehicles to greet King Saud on a state visit in 1961.

In recent years, Kuwait's leaders evinced a more responsible attitude toward spending. With $400 million, Kuwait purchased 14 percent (controlling interest) in Daimler-Benz (Mercedes). Another $320 million went to five oil tankers, enabling the Arab state to get into the "downstream" (distribution) aspect of the petroleum industry. Kuwaitis own shipping and mining works in Africa and a cement firm in Canada. Kuwaiti fishing trawlers, manned by Scandinavians, sail the New England Banks off the coast of the U.S. Kuwait owns a $100-million hotel-office complex in downtown Atlanta, and another $17-million resort (Kiawah Island) near Hilton Head, South Carolina.

Internally, the Sabahs tried to forge a modern welfare state while retaining traditional power in their own hands. They almost succeeded. Before Iraq's armies stormed across Kuwait's borders on August 2, 1990, the only taxes paid in Kuwait were for customs. In a land where cigarettes cost less than 50 cents per pack, the government supplied free medical attention. Prewar statistics on hospital care and life expectancy compared favorably with that of Israel. Free education, compulsory through eighth grade, virtually wiped out illiteracy. The student-teacher ratio was less than 15:1 in modern schools equipped with libraries, Olympic-sized swimming pools and apartments for boarders. A few years ago, the government opened a $20-million technical school to service nine students. The government paid cash bonuses to students who received top grades. The state also provided clean, inexpensive public housing to the poor and immigrants, as well as subsidies for gasoline and the telephone.

Granted complete independence from Britain in 1963, Kuwait had many serious problems. Though CBS' news program *60 Minutes* would extol Kuwait as a model constitutional monarchy, the Parliament outlined in Kuwait's constitution had little power (many of the 66 seats were appointed and the king could veto measures he disliked) and rarely met (Parliament was prorogued between 1976 and 1981). Despite postwar rhetoric from Shaykh Jarullah, women still have no political rights in Kuwait. Neither have the immigrants from Palestine, India, and Pakistan who came to Kuwait to share in its prosperity. This wave of newcomers, more than a million in all, created the spectre of native Kuwaitis becoming a minority in their own land. To prevent this, the government imposed a series of increasingly harsh naturalization laws designed to raise the years required for citizenship to 10, 15, then finally no limit. To become a Kuwaiti, an individual must demonstrate that such action is vital to the nation's welfare.

Among those especially hurt by such legislation were 400,000 Palestinians who resided in Kuwait. Unable to serve in the military or government, Palestinians suffered discrimination through quotas for jobs, admission to schools, and technical institutes. In prewar Kuwait, the joke was told that when a Palestinian took his examination for a driver's license, he was asked, "To whom do you yield at an intersection?" Reflecting the melancholy existence of his countrymen in this wonderland, the Palestinian responded, "To any Kuwaiti."

That sentiment may explain why some Palestinian residents welcomed Saddam Hussein's invasion of Kuwait. The ruling Kuwaiti caste was as oblivious to their resentment as they were to grievances presented by Saddam Hussein. The latter complained that his armies had bled for nearly a decade fighting the Iranians not merely to protect the interests of Iraq but of all the Gulf shaykhdoms as well. And what was his reward? Iraq, which had possessed $30 billion in cash reserves in 1980, was more than $70 billion in debt to the very nations of Arabia for whom it had sacrificed so much. Worse, Kuwait was allegedly stealing oil from Iraqi fields by slant-drilling near Rumaila. And whether that charge was true or not, there was no question that the freewheeling pumping policies of Kuwait and Saudi Arabi were combining to keep oil at $14 a barrel, far below any figure that would enable Iraq to recover from the hardships of its war with Iran.

When Iraq overran Kuwait in a matter of hours, some academics, using the benefit of hindsight, alleged that the invasion was inevitable, considering the Kuwaitis' alleged "arrogance." The explanation given was that for years the parvenu Kuwaitis had flaunted their wealth before their poor Arab brothers. Moreover, the matter was merely a family dispute, to be settled among the Arabs, without interference from the outside world. Finally, from an historical standpoint Kuwait was nothing more than a part of Iraq.

The facts are otherwise. There never was a nation called Iraq until Winston Churchill and the British Colonial Office insisted upon creating another state as compensation for the Emir Faisal from the old Ottoman provinces of Mosul, Baghdad and Basra at Cairo in 1921. Another band of British colonialists acknowledged the suzerainty of the Sabah clan 170 years earlier in a little hut that gave the name to the oil-rich principality south of Mesopotamia. Few would dispute the show of superiority displayed by Kuwaitis in the past twenty years. Kuwait's success was envied by its poorer neighbors and those who did not share its prosperity, much the way Lebanon in the 1960s was reviled.

None of this warranted, however, the aggression of Saddam Hussein. Throughout July 1990, Kuwait was negotiating with Iraq. The day before the invasion, August 1, Kuwait offered to absolve Iraq of major indebtedness, extend use of an island depot in the Persian Gulf, and submit the question of slant-drilling to third-party arbitration. Despite these proposals, the Iraqis proceeded with their invasion.

Prompted by the United States and other industrial nations that are dependent upon oil, the United Nations reacted swiftly, demanding an Iraqi withdrawal. Four months later, on January 16, 1991, political and economic sanctions proving useless, the multinational force that had been assembled in the Gulf attacked. Land operations for "Operation Desert Storm" lasted less than one week. When the Allies reentered Kuwait, they found cities that had been plundered of everything from personal belongings to plumbing. Highways leading to the north were blocked with the burning hulks of stolen automobiles and school busses. Virtually all of Kuwait's booby-trapped oil wells were ablaze, evoking warnings of an atmospheric disaster from scholars like Carl Sagan. There were atrocity tales, some true, some never substantiated: newborn infants dumped from confiscated incubators, women raped, men shot at trenches. And there was the lingering impact of poison gas, which affected 100,000 veterans of the Gulf War.

After the initial exuberance of flag-waving and posing for pictures, undisciplined Kuwaiti units attacked "collaborators." The objects of their rage were once more the Palestinians. Troops of the multinational forces stood by as Kuwaitis tortured Palestinians, as Saddam Hussein's Republican Guard massacred Shiites in Kerbala, as a million Kurds fled for their lives to Turkey and Iran. The Shaykh of Kuwait waited more than a month to make his return to his capital — until an air-conditioned palace with proper chandeliers and bathroom fixtures could be made ready. Meanwhile, the common people waited for drinking water, electricity, and food.

The allies had succeeded in restoring the ruling faction to Kuwait. The U.S. had never been in a more favorable position vis-à-vis its trading partners in the Middle East. Yet after the Gulf War no real demands were imposed, no tribute sought. By 1999, it was business as usual with OPEC forcing prices at the pump to $2.25 a gallon. As economists explained that the price ("adjusted for inflation") really wasn't that bad and domestic oil companies attributing wide fluctuations cost to supply and demand, the U.S. was importing 60 percent of its energy needs. Since then, promises of reform have evaporated. In late January 2006, Exxon-Mobil reported annual profits of $36 billion.

4

The Cradle of Civilization

Destiny's Catalysts

It seems incongruous that the genesis of civilized man would take place in a region scant of water and other conveniences essential to comfortable existence. More remarkable that it would take place among marsh dwellers who tattooed their bodies, pierced their ears, and lived in wattle huts. Several factors worked to make the Middle East the navel of civilization:

1. **Favorable climate.** In some Middle Eastern myths, the sun is regarded as an agent of death and destruction. More often, as with Shamash, who bestowed the Babylonian law code upon Hammurabi, or Aton, the Egyptian solar disc through which all life force descended to men in the time of Ikhnaton, the sun was an agent of help. The warm rays of a constant sun enabled people to remain in one location year-round, rather than flee extremes of temperature. The tepid climate made possible, moreover, two growing seasons in a single year. The reaping of grain was so important that people celebrated the New Year with sacrifice in the spring month of Nisan (April). Six months later came a second festival of fruits. The impact of such rituals was not confined to the Middle East. When the Pilgrims offered thanksgiving after one year in the Plymouth colony in 1621, they modeled their holiday after the ancient fall harvest.

2. **Occurrence of emmer wheat and barley in a free state.** The transformation from haphazard food gathering to meticulous agriculture is generally credited to women. While males were off hunting or fishing, their mates tended the young, kept protective fires burning, and did the cooking. Women picked fruits, nuts, roots. When garbage was pitched from a campsite, they noticed how pits or seeds germinated over a period of time. Their quest for food was made simpler by the presence of emmer wheat and barley. Emmer, a small-kernelled wheat with a thick hull and spiky beard, is the prototype of domestic wheats and grows wild only in the Middle East. Carbonized evidence of barley, a sturdier grain, has been dated back 8000 years. Apparently in the Paleolithic period (before 10,000 B.C.), women observed these flowering cereals and cut away the hulls with stone knives. The kernels were softened by pounding with stones, the first milling instrument. The rough flour could then be made into mush or bread.

3. The fertile soil. In some spots of Mesopotamia, floodwaters may have deposited as much as 36 feet of topsoil in historic times. Territory acquired a new significance as orchards and fields of cereals were cultivated and towns evolved. The resulting assured supply of wheat, barley, fish and wild fowl from the lagoons stimulated population growth and other changes in life — the division of labor, development of arts and crafts, public works, music, government.

4. Need for trade. No single location in the Middle East was capable of autarky, total self-sufficiency. The deltas may have possessed grain and dates, naptha and bitumen, but they lacked wood and metals. Conversely, the uplands were rich in gold, silver, jasper, iron, cooper and flint. Consequently, trade grew up along the rivers with people exchanging food for weapons, articles of adornment and eating utensils. One conduit of raw materials from Asia Minor was the Euphrates, whose Sumerian name was the *Urudu* or "copper" river. The absence of geographical barriers in the plains was an invitation to migrating traders or bands of warriors who periodically descended from the mountains for booty. Between 4000 and 3000 B.C., a series of peoples penetrated Mesopotamia — from Tell Halaf in Turkey, highlanders from Iran, more primitive al-Ubaid people from the south, Anatolians responsible for the culture of Uruk, and finally Iranians who founded Jemdet Nasr. The result, according to some historians, was the fusion of peoples known as Sumerians.[1]

5. The genius of the Sumerians. There are times when destiny, or providence, seems to bless a particular people. The Greeks in the fifth century B.C., Rome for 700 years, Arabs in the medieval period, England after the 17th century, and modern America achieved some degree of hegemony. Between 4000 and 2000 B.C., Sumerian civilization flowered in southern Mesopotamia. In their walled city-states, the *Ki-En-Gi* (as Sumerians called themselves) constructed ziggurats, stepped pyramids, to their gods. They developed religious hymns, heroic tales, and legal codes. Their sophisticated artwork was a byproduct of commerce that ranged from Anatolia to India. According to Berossos, a Babylonian priest of the third century, the Sumerians were a race of monsters, half man, half fish who came out of the sea. Under their leader, Oannes, they settled in the coastal towns and introduced the arts of writing, agriculture, and working in metal. "In a word," said Berossos, "all the things that make for the amelioration of life were bequeathed to men by Oannes and since that time no further inventions have been made."[2]

To this day, the origins of the Sumerians remain obscure. They differed in appearance from the predominantly Semitic population of Mesopotamia. Inscriptions and amulets show Sumerians to be clean-shaven, bald, with prominent eyes and noses, and favoring unusual skirts called kaunakes. What evidence there is of the Sumerian language preserved in bilingual dictionaries of Assyrian libraries indicates the tongue was not Semitic. The monosyllabic roots and grammar are reminiscent of Chinese, Zulu or Oceanian. Because of such confusion, numerous theories of their origins have been propounded, from Seton Lloyd and Georges Roux, who believe them to be an amalgam of previous civilizations, to the more preposterous suggestion of Erich von Daniken that the wall-eyed Sumerians came from the cosmic sea to control earth.[3]

Sumerian legends stress that the ancestral homeland lay somewhere in the East, in a mountainous region filled with river streams and lush vegetation that became their image of paradise. Their skill with stone temples and sculpture implies familiarity with mountain terrain. The substance most favored for seals, vases, and statues was a black stone called steatite. A popular motif etched in steatite was that of a bull with a hump.

The likeliest spot east of Mesopotamia where one finds rich valleys, mountains, use of steatite, veneration of cows, and a surplus population is India. Between 2700 and 2200 B.C., the Indus Valley achieved a high level of civilization. The principal cities, Mohenjo-Daro and Harappa, resembled those of Sumeria, with streets laid out according to a specific grid, busy harbors unloading goods imported from far-off lands, multi-tiered houses, a social system stratified along specific economic and racial lines. Philologists have noted, moreover, a resemblance between the Sumerian language and that of the ancient Dravidians.[4] The one flaw in the link, however, is that the Indus civilizations flourished more than 1000 years after the arrival of the Sumerians in Mesopotamia. It is possible, of course, that a pre-Aryan Indian civilization may have been devastated by disease, war, famine or natural catastrophe. Mediterranean history abounds with examples of peoples forced to migrate for these very reasons. Archaeology of the Indian sub-continent may one day reveal sites pointing to the common source of both Mohenjo-Daro and Sumeria.

A Legacy of Firsts

The Middle East does not possess the world's oldest fossilized bones of man. Africa and India contest that distinction. Neither does the Middle East any longer lay claim to the invention of every life-improving device. The Middle East does, however, supply the most continuous record of man's social evolution. Along the way, the region could cite numerous firsts which transformed crude hominids into civilized men. Among these:

1. **The oldest traces of man-made fire.** Just south of Haifa, Israel, one mile off the coastal highway, lies a series of caves. Three hundred feet up, one camel-shaped opening contains traces of the oldest man-made fire anywhere in the world. The ashes date back 150,000 years to a Neanderthal creature known as Mt. Carmel Man. Fire was not discovered in the Middle East. Peking Man, *Sinanthropus Erectus*, is generally credited with this remarkable breakthrough between 500,000 and 300,000 years ago. That discovery expanded man's diet and served as a weapon against wild beasts. Fire was a tool, as vital as the first club or chopper, but more important because primitive man could not rely on chance to supply a new blaze. Somehow, men and women had to communicate through grunts and gestures the means of keeping a flame going. With fire, culture and tradition were born, for man the firemaker was also man the wordmaker. Fire was a life-preserving gift that was to be venerated.[5] The Romans dedicated temples to this eternal substance. To this day the hearth and fireplace remain the center of icons and photographs of loved ones.

2. **The first domestication of animals.** In a region as arid as the Middle East, it was natural that animals would congregate at watering holes. Quite soon, man learned there were certain beasts that were to be avoided. Not so the scavengers hovering near campsites waiting for scraps. The first domesticated animal was the dog, a gregarious descendant of wolves. Long before 10,000 B.C., canines were accompanying men on hunting expeditions. By way of contrast, the cat, an austere creature regarded by the Egyptians as a god, may never have been domesticated.

The next group of animals to be domesticated were those that served as a supply of food. Decoys were employed to lure herds of sheep, goats and cattle into captivity. After 7000 B.C., all of these animals were bred, along with fowl, originally trained for game-fighting. Several thousand years would pass before the final group of animals—beasts of burden — would be tamed. These included elephants used for the hunt, the wild ass and horse fit for chariots and carts, and the last cantankerous draft animal, the camel.

3. The beginnings of the Neolithic Revolution. The Neolithic Revolution is defined as that time when men first settled down in fixed communities and began raising their own food. We have already seen how chance induced men or women to grow their own wheat and barley about 8000 B.C. Shortly after, rye and oats, beginning as weeds in other fields, were planted and harvested. Neither rice nor corn grew free in the Middle East, but flax and cotton both were spun or woven into fabric, and hemp, the basis of rope, was also used as a narcotic 6000 years ago. About the same time the produce of vineyards was being fermented into wine, people in the Middle East realized that untended grain turned to beer. By the year 3000 B.C., nearly 1000 years before mainland Europe discovered the mixed joys of tippling, 40 percent of the cereal crop in Mesopotamia was being diverted to brewing.

4. The first division of labor. Food surpluses mandated the first division of labor. People fortunate enough to harvest more than they could consume needed storage vessels for the surplus. Others, holding lands that were not as fertile, or proving less adept at farming, turned to handicrafts. Baskets of tree bark or reeds were exchanged for supplies of grain. By 5000 B.C. at Hassuna, a site 25 miles south of Mosul, clay was being modeled by hand into monochrome pots of uneven shape. In the next 1000 years, pottery acquired a slip (liquid second glaze), with decorations ranging from simple whorls or chevrons to abstract representations of animals cavorting about a water hole, swastikas, and the Maltese Cross. These designs and the color of pottery — apricot for Tel Halaf (4500–4000), green at Ubaid (4000–3500), plum or brick red in Uruk (3300–3100) — offered the most reliable means of distinguishing various stages of ancient civilization in Mesopotamia.[6] The shape of pottery also changed during this period. Handles, spouts, beveled rims, and bell-shaped Glockentöpfe were designed to meet specific needs. What made possible stylistic changes in pottery was another Sumerian invention — the potter's wheel. A simple horizontal revolving disc that guaranteed a smooth clay surface, the potter's wheel carried with it a more substantial benefit to mankind.

5. The first practical application of the wheel. From the potter's wheel, the Sumerians drew inspiration for crude wagons, carriages and chariots. In the fourth millennium, they fostered a revolution in transport, as carts drawn by draft animals bore loads greater and farther than any mule or onager. Warfare was altered forever, as two-man chariots, their tripartite wooden wheels hinged with wooden pegs, offered a terrifying, if cumbersome, dimension to clashes between armies.[7]

The circle shape had been known since the dawn of man. Circles were drawn on tents or etched in stone, some of which were naturally round. To appreciate what the Sumerians did with this geometric form, one need only look at civilizations that were late in adopting the wheel or those which never did. Egypt apparently lacked the potter's wheel until the beginning of the Bronze Age. Thereafter, the wheel in its many variations became a vital ingredient — in pulleys that made possible the raising of colossi, in pottery that was unrivalled in the Middle East, on delicate spoked chariots that pivoted with an agility that facilitated Egyptian domination of the eastern Mediterranean. Without a proper application of the wheel and its experimental offspring, some societies remained backward and vulnerable.

6. The development of fine and plastic arts. Invention of the potter's wheel only whetted man's creative instincts. Those first instructional grunts about tending fires or signals on the hunt became whistles, notes, music. Man experimented with drums, gongs, blown instruments and much later the first stringed instruments. By 20,000 B.C., he was scrawling images of game or supernatural creatures on the walls of his caves. Such images eventually turned into bas-reliefs, which bedecked the walls of great palaces. Chimera, serpopards, griffin, genii and other mythical beasts embellished the halls of Sargon, Thutmose and Rameses, along with glazed tiles, scenes of victorious hunts and banquets.

Obese idols (Venuses) of the paleolithic period gave way to sculpture like the Warka Head, a 12-inch marble image of a woman whose delicate features predate the famed bust of Nefertiti by 1600 years. Pre-literate peoples wore all kinds of ornaments, necklaces, bracelets, of stone, amber, chalcedony and ivory.[8] Smelting, which began about 7000 years ago, changed the forms of gold and silver. The Egyptians began working with faience and glass about 4000 B.C. In Mesopotamia, copper was hammered into mirrors, swords, shields and studs for military capes. The Sumerians designed filagreed headdresses of electrum, 14-karat gold drinking vessels, daggers whose hilts were dotted with precious stones. Tin was alloyed with copper to make bronze before the Hittites introduced iron, the metal that afforded them military supremacy about 1500 B.C. People skilled in such crafts were anxious to trade their goods— grain for copper, leather for wine. Thus the city came into being.

7. The first identifiable cities. The most ancient cities in the world were found in the Middle East. Damascus is the oldest continuously inhabited city, dating back more than 4000 years. The beehive settlements of Khirokitia in Crete and Byblos in Lebanon date to 6000 B.C. Archaeologists date Jarmo in Iran to 6500 B.C. Čatal Hüyük in the Anatolian highlands, replete with plastered homes built into the walled perimeter of the town, ventilator shafts or chimneys, storehouses, and shrines devoted to a vulture deity, is dated to 7000 B.C.[9] And the oldest city of all, Jericho, offers a tower that may date beyond 8000 B.C.[10]

Some of these towns developed by accident, others according to specific plan. Wandering clans may have decided to occupy a specific locale because it was where they had won a great victory or had captured a herd of life-sustaining animals. More likely, the settlers were drawn to a body of fresh water (preferably upstream from another group on the same river). Nearby fields guaranteed an adequate food supply. Natural heights provided a refuge to which the people could retreat in times of peril.

A primitive shrine would be erected and sacrifice made to the gods. From this hut would grow the impressive temples of Egypt and Mesopotamia with their rambling compounds. Such shrines served as the nexus of cities. People craved a location where exchange of goods could be made safely without fear of deceit or robbery. What better spot than in the shadow of the gods' house, itself enveloped in a taboo zone where sin of any kind was forbidden. Thus, the first markets grew up as adjuncts of the temples. Some merchants made their permanent homes in these precincts. Paths became streets. Landings grew into docks. Campsites became cities.[11]

8. The first major architectural innovations. Natural fortifications proved inadequate against determined besiegers, so earthen ramparts were raised to protect the town. These evolved into the batter-fortress walls of cyclopean rock (16 to 20 feet high, 40 feet thick) that earned their architects the status of demi-gods. Simple gateways could not serve these great walls. Instead, arcades extending 30 yards or more spilled into the city, their openings arched or vaulted like Gothic cathedrals. The residences of rulers were transformed from single-celled hovels to multi-tiered palaces like that of Nebuchadnezzar, regarded as one of the wonders of the world, or that of the rulers of ancient Mari, which sprawled over eight and one-half acres. Within the city temenos rose homes of the heavenly pantheon — the U-shaped cluster in Tepe Gawra, the quixotic Eye Temple of Tel Brak, the 40-foot high White Temple of Anu in Uruk, the greater ziggurat of Nannar in Ur, and the 480-foot high pyramid of Khufu.

Such buildings were not merely static or square-cut. Archaeology has disclosed rounded columns recessed in palace walls at Uruk (3300–3100) and Sakkara (c. 2800). About 1100 years before the Greeks allegedly invented the pillar temple, Egypt's Queen Hatshepsut embellished the desert necropolis near Thebes with her pillared temple of Deir el-Bahri. Much earlier, the Sumerians hauled palm logs, seven feet in diameter, to the second platform of a temple in Uruk. The columns were smeared with bitumen into which pieces of shell and mother-of-pearl were laid. Set in double rows, the pillars served as a portico for the greatest limestone temple of the city 2500 years before the age of Pericles.

9. The first empires. The existence of shrines and palaces suggests that power which had rested with tribal elders was being transferred to a more central authority. In Mesopotamia, warlords emerged and arrogated to themselves titles like *lugal* (great man), *patesi* (duke) or *ensi* (priest-count). Lacking large, well-trained armies, at the mercy of flood waters, and controlling, for the most part, regions adjacent to their city walls, Sumeria's feuding city-states resembled ancient Greece more than a unified empire. Not until 2400 B.C., when Sargon of Agade subjugated the Amorites in the west, Assyrians in the north, Elamites in the East and Sumerians in the south, could anyone truly lay claim to the title of king. Thereafter, Mesopotamian history is the saga of the ebb and flow of empires— Akkadian, Sumerian revival, Babylonian, Kassite, Hittite, Assyrian, Lydian, Median, Persian, and Greek.

Along the Nile, tradition has it that the 34 nomes or counties were united by Menes about 3100 B.C. A convenient invention of the ancient Egyptians, on the order of King Arthur, Menes probably was a fusion of several lords— Narmer, "Scorpion," Antjab Merpeba, all of whom labored to conquer the land between 3400 and 3100 B.C.[12] Afterward, Egypt reckoned its history in dynasties (royal families) of pharaohs, living gods whose title derived from the term "great house." At a time when Sumeria looked to the first dynasty of Ur for cultural leadership about 2700 B.C., the Old Kingdom of Egypt (fourth-sixth dynasties) was directing massive public works projects that involved thousands of peasants. When Isin, Larsa, Ur and Babylon contested for hegemony in the Fertile Crescent, the 12th dynasty of Egypt was undergoing a renaissance. Finally, between 1500 and 1100 B.C. the 18th and 19th dynasties (New Kingdom) provided some of the most celebrated monarchs in history— the valiant warrior Thutmose III, the religious reformer Ikhnaton, his successor, the boy-king Tutankhamen, and Rameses of the oppression.

10. The first organized religions. Religion is one of the universals in human society. Belief in gods stems from primitive man's wish fulfillment.[13] Unable to control the elements that bless or confound him, man projects personality into the forces of nature. If dependent upon a particular animal (such as the buffalo) for sustenance, he venerates totemic or animist forms. At the mercy of storms, floods, winds or the beating sun, he may invent celestial deities. To placate these gods, he engages in repetitive chants and sacrifices that may have been performed at the end of a past hurricane, pestilence or drought.

Whatever form his rituals or gods take, fertility will be a major factor in his religion.

Without the bounty of the land ripened by precious water, there would be no survival. Ancients equated the process with human sexual activity, the male fertilizing the female with sacred juices. It was no accident that the Egyptians perceived the land in female form — the goddess Isis— that was periodically impregnated by the male Nile — the resurrected Osiris. In Mesopotamia, a bull, the most potent male animal, served as the consort of Ishtar, goddess of love and war.

Not coincidentally the king-priests combined the responsibilities of fertility and war. Before leading their people in combat, the kings were required to perform ablutions that would guarantee victory. During the flood season, they were required to perform the annual rites of renewal, whether they took the form of the *akhitu* festival in Babylon or saw the pharaoh draped in a wolf's tail for the *Sed* ceremony along the Nile. The king's potency in the bedchamber, as well as the battlefield, was necessary to guarantee prosperity, and if this ever faltered, the good of the people required that he be deposed.[14]

11. The first science. Judaism, Christianity, Zoroastrianism, and Islam have traveled far from simple fertility cults. Shanties designated as sacrosanct by a flag or totem became temples. Those in the service of the gods included, diviners, augurs, exorcists, ritual slaughterers, prostitutes ("virgins" who were not to bear children), scribes and nascent scientists. The latter were especially important, for if the priestly hierarchy was to retain its position in a community, it was essential that some of their prayers be effective. Some warning against the flood season was needed and the only way this could be achieved was by an accurate calculation of the year. To protect their own interests, priests turned to the skies for their most convenient clock. By noting the movements of specific bodies in the heavens, they were able to work out a lunar calendar that operates (awkwardly) to this day. The Babylonians discovered the wonders of the sexagisemal system (based on the figure 60, which was divisible by 30, 20, 15, 10, 6, 5, 4, 3, and 2) and so was born the concept of 60 seconds in a minute, 60 minutes in an hour, 360 degrees in a circle. From the ancient Egyptians came a rough, but proximate, solar calendar. The fanciful garble that was astrology gave way to astronomy.[15]

As an extra hedge for the accuracy of their predictions, priests in Egypt established observation posts at the first cataract, 700 miles from the Delta. There, niches were cut into the limestone rock jutting from the river bed. The height of the water at these so-called Nilometers could foretell a good or bad harvest. If the river stood at 25 feet, it meant a good growing season. A drop of 30 inches meant a pinch, 60 famine. Information garnered here would be relayed to the Delta several days before the arrival of the floodwaters and in time for the priests to make their predictions.

To keep order in the land, especially during the flood season when boundaries might be destroyed, the king, assisted by priests, delimited specific landholds. To do so, they employed the basic tenets of mathematics and geography, roping off and measuring plots, devising miniature maps of the region. When viewed from the air today, irrigation channels in Egypt and Mesopotamia resemble geometric grids. Tools devised for agriculture were used to perfection with pyramids, ziggurats and other monumental structures.

On occasion, the priests enhanced their reputations by "raising the dead." They accomplished this by administering herbs, leeches, secret draughts, or bleeding the sick. The ringing of iron gongs, placement of raw meat on a wound, and the examination of animal entrails also were said to have a salutary effect. In the 17th century B.C., the Edwin Smith Surgical Papyrus in Egypt offered a clinical description of and treatment for broken bones and a fractured skull and dismissed the notion that some demon was responsible for fever.

An earlier manuscript from the fifth dynasty, the Ebers Medical Papyrus states that the heart "speaks" in various parts of the body and that a physician may "measure for the heart" (pulse) in this fashion.[16] While such documents may be rarities, they, along with manuscripts offering pharmacological formulas, advice about rest, diet and cleanliness, laid the basis for more sophisticated medicine.

12. The first writing. By the middle of the fourth millennium, priests recognized the need for an improved system of non-oral communication that could record the movement of the stars and the height of nilometers, distinguish the nature and size of sacrifices (so appropriate prayers might be said for donors), and preserve sacred hymns that otherwise might be lost if left solely to an oral tradition. Monarchs required some kind of mnemonic devices to assist with resolving boundary disputes and the dissemination of imperial edicts. Farmers and merchants required a medium of commercial honesty that could be guaranteed by an objective third party.

With the invention of pottery, people applied their talents to decorating vases and bowls with geometric patterns or stick figures. It was, after all, not such a great leap from painting a cow's head on a pot to drawing the same head in clay to convey the idea of one cow. The first glyphs, then, were pictographs, simple attempts to represent an object in a recognizable form. The oldest example of such writing — a man's head and foot etched in stone at Kish about 3500 B.C. — probably was an attempt at graffiti.

Subsequently, written communication became more complex. Depiction of a foot could represent running, kicking, to stand or go, carry off, a leg injury. A star could be interpreted to mean heaven, sky, high. An arrow also symbolized life. A picture of the *mons veneris* meant not only female, but also slave girl, for Sumerians abducted slaves from the mountains. Such ideographs often were found amid pictographs, in which case their meaning was determined by context. Adding to the confusion was the development of syllabic or rebus-writing, where signs carried specific sounds that when joined with other sign-sounds resulted in a totally new concept. By the time the ancient Phoenicians devised the alphabet about 1200 B.C., the process of writing was unfathomable to all but the most skilled professionals.

Those scribes early on discovered that adherence to detail was dolorous. Just like potters, they employed abstractions, which proved as acceptable as life-like replicas of objects. To a certain extent, the form these abstractions took was determined by the nature of available writing materials. In Egypt, where fibers of the aquatic plant papyrus could be pressed into layers and rolls resembling heavy paper, scribes used pen and ink. It was possible to portray animals in delicate form or to develop a cursive style of writing. In Mesopotamia, where neither stone nor papyrus could be found, clay proved the likeliest medium. Shaped into rectangular tablets, the clay would be incised with a wedge-like stylus, baked hard, then placed into a second "sleeve" of clay for protection against the elements for more than 3000 years. The peculiar, but identifiable, chicken scratches of cuneiform were preferable to smears and blurs that otherwise would have resulted from attempts to write on a wet, clay surface.[17]

If ancient man found it difficult to read or write, recent decipherment has been even more complicated because of obstacles inadvertently thrown up by scribes. Generally, but not always, Middle Eastern scripts are written from right to left. Some ancient inscriptions were to be read in the direction their pictographs faced. In Egypt, this could be either right or left, or in the case of obelisks, up and down. In Persia, some royal inscriptions ran alongside the frames and lintel of doorways. The Hittites mastered bustrophedon (ox-plowing) script where the reader followed one line from right to left, then the next from left to right, alternating direction for each line of the manuscript. Some symbols were polyphones (one sign with many sounds), others homophones (one sound with many signs or meanings). Various Semitic words derived from the same basic root, which, lacking diacritical marks, confounded the novice. Some languages, like Sumerian, were so old, much of their vocabulary was forgotten. And frequently there were misspellings, which made translation virtually impossible.

In spite of these many problems, an incredibly dynamic written culture did develop in the ancient Near East, one that has enriched Western civilization with its message of law, philosophy, creation, mythology, folk tales, and science.

5

Foundations of the Bible

Reputable theologians agree that the Bible is a composite of history, geography, mythology, law, ethics, and revelation. Materials from the Cairo *geniza* (a ninth-century repository of religious documents), the Dead Sea Scrolls, and other discoveries in Israel demonstrate a surprising amount of agreement between the Bible as we know it and ancient texts. Scholars have detected no less than four distinct sources of the Pentateuch — the Jahwist component dating from the ninth century B.C.; the Elohist, which followed by a century and is probably Canaanite in origin; the Deuteronomist of the seventh century; and a priestly code influenced by the Persians stemming from the fifth century. The notion that the Pentateuch is a syncretism rather than the work of a single man, Moses, is consistent with the saga offered by the Hebrews themselves. A primitive people, they migrated from southern Mesopotamia to Syria to Palestine and Egypt, and in so doing were influenced by traditions which operated in each of these areas.

Mesopotamian Influences upon the Bible

The Bible states that the first Hebrew was Abraham (originally called Abram) from Ur of the Chaldees (Gen. 11:28). Such a claim is problematic for several reasons: (a) if there was an actual Abraham, cultural evidence would date him to the 19th century B.C.; (b) Ur, a Sumerian city, was by this time in a state of decline; (c) the Chaldaean empire did not rise in Mesopotamia until the seventh century, 1200 years after Ur had crumbled. Ancient sources may have confused the Babylonian dynasty of Nebuchadnezzar with that of Hammurabi. Allowing that Abraham came from Sumeria, it is possible that he elected to flee his home city during a period of strife. He might have followed trading routes up river to Syria, then crossed the Orontes into Canaan and Egypt. A second possibility, suggested by discoveries from Tell Mardikh (Ebla), is that there was a second Ur somewhere in Syria. Whatever the origin of the patriarchs, the book of Genesis owes much to beliefs and folk tales from the Fertile Crescent:

The Creation of the Universe. The Sumerians devised several cosmological theories. Common to each was the belief that the universe was ordered by the gods from chaos. After the gods created male and female principles, life sprang into being upon a cosmic mountain. The gods were limited by a set of absolutes called *me's* (including weariness, fear, wisdom, peace, power, art). Best elaborated in the *Enuma Elish*, a lengthy prayer that accords special prominence to Marduk, patron deity of Babylon, the Mesopotamian creation epic parallels the opening chapter of Genesis. In both, an immense primeval body of water contains the component parts of the earth. In both, the creation of the firmament is accompanied by a separation of the waters. The sequence of ordering the universe—creation of light, the firmament, dry land, luminaries, man—is the same. The abyss of Genesis is the *apsu* of the Enuma Elish. The Hebrew word for "deep" is *tehom* and in the Enuma Elish, Marduk combats a leviathan-dragon whose name is Tiamat. From the corrupt innards of the beast (a sea serpent or crocodile in Isa. 27:1, Ps. 104:235, and Ps. 74:12–17), Marduk fashions man as the capstone of his labors, then rests. [1]

Creation of Mankind. Marduk is not alone in claiming responsibility for the creation of mankind from base materials. Other Babylonian documents credit the air deity Ea who "nipped off clay in the Apsu" and Ninhursag (goddess of vegetation and birth) who mixed clay with the blood of a slain god. The theme of the gods sacrificing their own to fashion servants appears also in a ninth-century tablet from Ashur, where the great gods in assembly decide to slay two of their own craftsmen gods, from whose blood men would be created. Another Assyrian document credits Ninigiku (Ea in another incarnation), while a cuneiform text from Nippur awards the honor to a divine team — Anu, Enlil, Enki and Ninhursag — working in tandem.

Creation of Woman. When Jehovah in the Bible decided that it was not good for Adam to be without a helpmate, he cast a sleep over him, then from a rib made Eve (*Chave* in Hebrew, from "she who gives life"). Another Sumerian hymn, "Enki and Ninhursag," offers a striking parallel. According to this legend, Ninhursag cultivated eight new plants, then left them unattended. Along came the water deity Enki, who had impregnated Ninhursag, her daughter and her grand-daughter. He spied the rare flowers and ate them. Furious, Ninhursag cursed whoever had profaned her garden, and Enki became ill in eight separate parts of his body. As he lay moaning, Ninhursag, moved to pity by his aches, forgave him. Repeatedly she asked, "My brother, what hurts you?" For each lament (jaw, arm, tooth) she created a goddess of healing. When Enki said, "My rib hurts me," Ninhursag responded, "To the goddess Ninti, I have given birth for you. In Sumerian, the name Nin-Ti, "Lady of the Rib," also meant "lady who makes live."[2]

Eden-Paradise. The ode of Ninhursag that is the inspiration for Eve offers a glimpse of Sumerian paradise. Located in the region of the rising sun, Dilmun is a land "pure, clean and bright," where waters never cease to flow and every conceivable fruit and animal may be found. It also foreshadows the messianic hope of Isaiah, for in Dilmun "the lion kills not, the wolf snatches not the lamb." The Garden of Eden is a duplicate of Dilmun, watered by the four world rivers, rich in gold, bdellium and onyx and filled with all kinds of trees "fair to behold and pleasant to eat." The name Eden itself may be derived from a fertile pastoral strip, the Gu-edinna, which was the subject of a territorial dispute between the Sumerian city-states of Umma and Lagash between 2600 and 2500 B.C.E.[3]

The Underworld. In Mesopotamia, paradise was reserved for the gods. Mortals faced an eternity in the Land of No Return, the House of Dust, "wherein the entrants are bereft of light, where dust is their fare and clay their food, where they see no light, residing in darkness, where they are clothed like birds with wings for garments and where over door and bolt is spread dust." The same bleak idea is expressed in Job 10:18–22 as "the land of darkness and blackness; a land of darkness and without order." The Hebrew word for this murky concept is *Sheol*, at times defined "the shades" (Deut. 32:22, Ps. 49:16, Ps. 139:8, Amos 9:2) or "the grave" (Josh. 7:26; 8:29; 2. Sam. 18:17, Isa. 14:18–20).

Loss of Immortality. Just as Adam and Eve, the heroes of Mesopotamian legend, squandered the gift of eternal life, in the tale of Adapa, a Sumerian fisherman from Eridu breaks the wing of the south wind, which was tormenting him. Summoned before the sky god Anu, Adapa is warned by Ea (Enki) not to accept any food or water, for it might be poisoned. Thus "when the bread of life they brought him, he did not eat, when the water of life they brought him he did not drink."[4] In the epic of Gilgamesh, also the hero twice is offered a talisman to stave off death. Instructed to stay awake for one week, Gilgamesh instantly passes out and sleeps for seven days. Given a plant that will rejuvenate him (appropriately named "The Old Man becomes Young Again") Gilgamesh pauses to bathe before re-entering his city of Uruk. As he swims, a snake comes forward to deprive man of his last opportunity for immortality.

Cain and Abel. Expelled from Paradise, Adam must earn his bread by the sweat of his brow. Chapter 4 in Genesis proceeds with the tale of Abel's death at the hand of his brother Cain. A Sumerian document labeled "The Wooing of Inanna" may have been the model for this fratricide. In the Sumerian tale, two gods, Dumuzi (farming) and Enkimdu (a shepherd deity) vie for the affection of Inanna, goddess of love and war. The two offer a number of gifts, promise to bedeck her with exquisite garments and jewels if the great goddess favors one of them. Unlike the biblical tale, in the Sumerian legend the shepherd prevails. More significantly, there is no murder. Rather, the poem ends with the two singing praise to Inanna.[5]

Tower of Babel. The story of the Tower of Babel (Gen. 11:1–9) where men vainly tried to reach the heavens and had their speech confounded may be derived from a Sumerian text from the 20th century. "Enmerkar and the Lord of Aratta" first recites how there were no ferocious animals, no fear or terror. The inscription then tells how the people of Shubur, Hamazi, Sumer, Ur, and Martu, "the whole universe, the people in unison to Enlil in one tongue gave praise."[6] Whether such a golden age ever existed, Mesopotamian ziggurats may have seemed like skyscrapers to the nomadic descendants of Abraham.

The Epic of Gilgamesh. Among some 30,000 clay tablets recovered from the library of seventh-century Assyrian monarch Ashurbanipal, 12 tablets told the saga of a demigod king of Uruk. Amazingly, the Gilgamesh epic was deciphered by a self-taught cuneiformist named George Smith. An engraver at the Bank of England, Smith labored several years on his own time at the British Museum. When he finally presented his findings before the Royal Society of Biblical Archaeology in 1872, what he said literally jarred the foundations of Western theology.

Gilgamesh was a Sumerian hero whose name appears on the royal list of Uruk dating back to 3300 B.C. As the first tablet of the epic explains, it was Gilgamesh who raised the walls of the city and dedicated sanctuaries to its gods. Having recounted these deeds, the purpose of the epic is revealed. For Gilgamesh, who is two-thirds divine, a giant 11 cubits high (18 feet tall) and nine spans across the chest, knows that he will eventually die and end up in the House of Dust. With such a melancholy future and no real challenges in this life, the hero acts with arrogance, raping wives, daughters and brides. In dismay, the people of Uruk pray to the gods asking for the creation of an adversary for Gilgamesh.[7]

True to form, the goddess Aruru "pinched off clay" and creates Enkidu, a virtual double for Gilgamesh, though his entire body was shaggy with hair. Some scholars liken Enkidu, a wild man who roamed with creatures of the plain, to the uncivilized Semites who lived on the periphery of the cultured Sumerians. When Enkidu repeatedly opens traps set by an unnamed hunter, the latter hires a temple prostitute to "treat him to a woman's task." Seduced by this woman for no less than six days and seven nights, Enkidu is rejected by the beasts. As he sits mournfully at the feet of the harlot, she counsels him to accompany her to Uruk where Gilgamesh "yearns for a friend."[8]

Dutifully, Enkidu follows her back to Uruk where the two heroes clashed before the gate to Gilgamesh's home. The epic's second tablet tells of a ferocious battle, but does not reveal the winner. Instead, the two become great friends and Gilgamesh confides his fear of dying, of being forgotten. To make an everlasting name, he proposes an expedition to chop down one of the trees in the sacred Cedar Forest. Though the elders of Uruk try to dissuade them, the two heroes assemble their weapons (axes weighing 180 pounds, swords 120 pounds) and set off for the one spot in the Middle East where the cedars grow—Lebanon.[9]

Gilgamesh and Enkidu need their fabulous weapons, for the forest is guarded by a terrible monster, Humbaba. With the assistance of every conceivable type of wind, they trap and kill Humbaba even after he pleads for his life.[10]

Their mission accomplished, a cedar cut down, Gilgamesh and Enkidu return to Uruk. Before entering the city, however, the civilized Gilgamesh must wash away the grime of the journey. As he does, the goddess Ishtar attempts to seduce him with a chariot of lapis and gold, goats that cast triplets, racing horses, sweet smells, and the deference of kings. Gilgamesh icily rejects these offerings, comparing Ishtar to a charcoal brazier that goes out in the cold, a back door that gives no shelter from the wind, pitch that soils its bearers, or a waterskin that soaks through its bearer, a shoe that pinches the foot of its owner. Then tauntingly, he recites a list of Ishtar's previous, short-term lovers: Tammuz, her consort in youth, who must die each year; the dappled shepherd bird that sits in the grove with a broken wing chirping sadly about its broken wing; the lion, confined to pits; the stallion, spurred, whipped, and forced to drink muddy water; the herdkeeper who was turned into a wolf; the gardener Ishullanu who brought her dates and was turned into a mole. "If thou shouldst love me," sneered Gilgamesh, "thou wouldst treat me like them."[11]

What follows is one of the more amusing exchanges in literature, as Ishtar proceeds to the throne of Anu, her father, screeching about how Gilgamesh insulted her by reciting her past indiscretions. To which Anu responds, "But surely thou didst invite ... and so Gilgamesh has recounted thy stinking deeds, thy stench, and thy foulness."

Enraged, Ishtar threatens to smash the door of the underworld so that the dead would outnumber the living and famine sweep the land, unless Anu releases a terrible Bull of Heaven upon the earth. Concerned about the loss of sacrifice, Anu caves in and the Bull kills 300 men with its first two snorts. As Ishtar watches from celestial ramparts, however, Gilgamesh and Enkidu stab the animal in the head and fling its right thigh back in her face. Once again the two heroes celebrate their victory and bathe. Back in heaven, Ishtar demands compensation: the death of either Gilgamesh or Enkidu. The gods agreed that the stripping of the cedar mountains constitutes a profanation and decree death—for poor Enkidu.

Depending upon which version of the Gilgamesh epic one reads, there follows a lengthy interpolation of Enkidu descending into the House of Dust or merely falling ill. After bitterly cursing the hunter, the harlot and everyone else responsible for making him leave the blissful steppes, he becomes comatose. Meanwhile, Gilgamesh sits by his side, regaling his friend with glorious images of his impending funeral. The tiger, hart, leopard, lion, oxen, deer, kings, princes, nobles, all of Uruk's people will weep for Enkidu. After 12 days of this, Gilgamesh touches his friend's heart and it is still. The Sumerian demigod tears his clothes and hair and mourns seven days and seven nights "until a worm fell out of [Enkidu's] nose."[12]

Weeping bitterly, Gilgamesh sets out in a quest of the one man who had eluded death — Utnapishtim the Faraway. Before he can reach the land of eternal life, he must pass through the district of Mashu where the Scorpion people (an historic tribe located in the Elamite Mountains) reside. Seven, eight, nine "double hours" he trekked through darkness before coming to an alehouse at the edge of the Waters of Death, the separation between Dilmun and the mortal world. Denied entry by a maid, Sidduri, Gilgamesh threatens to tear the building apart unless he is given sustenance. Once inside, he pours out his grief about the loss of his friend, his own fear of death. In words evocative of Ecclesiastes, Sidduri tells him:

> Gilgamesh, whither rovest thou?
> The life thou pursuest thou shalt not find.
> When the gods created mankind,
> Death for mankind they set aside,
> Life in their own hands retaining
> Thou, Gilgamesh, let full be thy belly,
> Make thou merry by day and by night.
> Of each day make thou a feast of rejoicing,
> Day and night dance thou and play!
> Let thy garments be sparkling fresh,
> Thy head be washed; bathe thou in water.
> Pay heed to the little one that holds on to thy hand,
> Let thy spouse delight in thy bosom!
> For this is the task of mankind![13]

Similar words would be uttered by Utnapishtim when Gilgamesh forces a boatman (Urshunabi) to ferry him across the Waters of Death and confronts the one mortal who cheated death. Gilgamesh, however, refuses to be put off by such counsel. Since Utnapishtim is no different in appearance from himself, how was he permitted to join the assembly of the gods? Utnapishtim told Gilgamesh how he once lived in the city of Shuruppak along the Euphrates River. Upset with the noise made by men, the great gods decided to wipe them all out by the disaster common to Mesopotamia — a flood. Because Utnapishtim was a righteous man, however, the water deity Enki spoke to him through the wall of his reed-hut, saying, "Man of Shuruppak, son of Ubar-Tutu, tear down this house, build a ship."

As instructed, Utnapishtim fashioned a mammoth wooden ship, 120 cubits high, caulked with bitumen. Aboard her six decks he brought "the seed of all living things," grain, wine, gold, silver, the beasts of the field, all manner of craftsmen, and his family. At a signal from Shamash, he battened up the entrance and waited.

The ensuing storm was so frightening that even the gods cowered like dogs behind the throne of Anu. For six days and six nights the wind raged, then "the sea grew quiet, the tempest was still, the flood ceased." Utnapishtim opened a hatch and light fell upon his face. His ark had come to rest on a rocky peak (Mt. Nisir), but there was no other visible land. After seven more days, he sent out a series of birds— a dove, a swallow, a raven — to find a landing place. The first two returned without success, but the last cawed and flew off for good. Utnapishtim and his family could now descend from the ark and offer thanks to the gods:

> Then I let out all to the four winds
> And offered a sacrifice
> I poured out a libation on the top of the mountain.
> Seven and seven cult-vessels I set up,
> Upon their pot-stands I heaped cane, cedarwood, and myrtle.
> The gods smelled the savor,
> The gods smelled the sweet savor,
> The gods crowded like flies about the sacrificer.
> When at length as the great goddess arrived,
> She lifted up the great jewels which Anu had fashioned to her liking
> "Ye gods here, as surely as this lapis
> Upon my neck I shall not forget,
> I shall be mindful of these days, forgetting them never.[14]

The epic contains additional episodes where Utnapishtim offers Gilgamesh two chances to retain life or youth. But it is this tale of a destructive flood that so closely approximates the story in Genesis 6–9, which has commanded the greatest attention. More than 50 years ago, Sir Leonard Woolley excavated sites in southern Mesopotamia seeking to verify a universal deluge. Woolley claimed to have located a specific stratum that bore out the tale.[15] Subsequent charlatans inspired by the Bible and Gilgamesh have scoured the Middle East in quest of Noah's ark.

Apart from the common themes of an angry god or gods (Gen. 6: 5–7), a warning to a just man (Gen. 6:13), construction of an ark (Gen. 6:14–16), rescue of various species of animal life (Gen. 6:19) and supplies (Gen. 6:20), a protracted storm and flood (Gen. 7:19), the grounding of the vessel atop a mountain (Gen. 8:4), the dispatch of birds (Gen. 8:6–12), sacrifice (Gen. 8:20), and a covenant sealed with a heavenly necklace or rainbow (Gen. 9:13–15), there are other indications of a borrowing from the Gilgamesh tale.

In true Mesopotamian fashion, the biblical ark is of gopher wood, made water-tight with pitch (Gen. 6:14). A Babylonian version of the flood epic credits the king Xisuthros with having preserved life. According to Berossus (a third-century priest responsible for Babylonian chronology), Xisuthros was the 10th king of his dynasty, just as Noah was 10 generations removed from Adam. In other legends, the hero is called Atrahasis ("exceeding wise") or Ziusudra ("he who laid hold on life"). Most compelling, however, is a Hurrian tale of the deluge dating from the 17th century where the hero is called Na-ah-um-iel ("a servant who brings comfort to god"). This document predates Moses, the Pentateuch, and Hebrew reference to Noah by 400 years.[16]

The Patriarchal Age Confirmed

The Bible's treatment of a more historical period, the Patriarchal Age, redounds with personal names, places, and customs identical to those in documents retrieved from Egypt and other Middle Eastern sites. One that may eventually prove invaluable is the archive of ancient Ebla, 40 miles southwest of Aleppo. Italian archaeologists first scratched the surface of Tell Mardikh in 1964. Since then more than 18,000 tablets detailing religious observance, commerce, diplomatic correspondence, and military dispatches covering Hittite, Egyptian, and Aramaean kingdoms in the years between 2900 and 2250 have been recovered. Some scholars have detected references to biblical figures (Eber, Abraham, Ishmael, Esau) and the destruction of Sodom and Gomorrah (Gen. 14) in the Ebla tablets. Others, currying favor with the Syrian government, have denounced alleged linguistic links. Meanwhile, translation proceeds so slowly some scholars doubt the Ebla tablets will be completely published in the next 300 years.[17]

From Tell Hariri on the right bank of the Euphrates, seven miles from the border of Syria, French scholars in the 1930s extracted 20,000 clay tablets containing royal correspondence and records of the Mari people who controlled this region about 1750 B.C. Further east at Nuzu, 12 miles south of Kirkuk, archaeologists uncovered thousands of Indo-European Hurrian (Horites in the Bible) tables dating from 1500 to 1370 B.C.

If a people whose antiquity is clouded by mystery or mythology (e.g., the Hebrews of the Bible) shares common patronymic and toponymic names with another that can be scientifically dated, the historicity of the former may also be assumed. Such is the case with the genealogy of Abraham, eight generations removed from Shem, the son of Noah. Among his forebears were Peleg, Serug, Nahor, and Terah, all of whose names appear as towns in the Mari and Nuzi letters. Reference is also made to Haran, Abraham's brother (designated as an important Hurrian town 60 miles west of Tell Halaf), Jacob, his uncle Laban (the chief moon god of Haran), the Dawidum (David), the Bini-Yamina (the tribe of Benjamin, regarded at Mari as a predatory tribe), and Abamram or Abi-rama himself.

Babylonian, Mari, Kassite, and Assyrian records dating from 2000 to 1700 B.C. allude to troops hired from the ranks of a primitive wandering folk variously called the Sa-Gaz, Harbi-Shihu, Habireans, or Habiru, from which the term *Hebrew*, first used in Genesis 14:13, could easily be derived. In Genesis 14, Abraham appears as a warlord allied to several Canaanite princes, leading 318 men against four kings of Mesopotamia — Chedorlaomer, king of Elam (whose name appears as Kurdur Lagamar, servant of a god, in Elamite sources); Arioch of Ellasar (possibly Arriwuk or Arriukki of Nuzi letters); Tidal, king of the Goim (perhaps the Hittite monarch Tudhaliyas, but more likely a reference to the wild Guti people who ravaged Sumeria about 2000 B.C.); and Amraphel of Shinar (often identified with Hammurabi of Babylon).[18] This tale of Lot and Abraham battling in the Vale of Slime to preserve the feeble monarchs of Canaan jibes with archaeological research showing Palestine in the Middle Bronze period to be relatively underdeveloped and politically divided.

The correspondence of Zimri-Lin, lord of Mari, with neighboring kings, including Hammurabi before he razed Mari in 1700, and the Nuzi archives contain the following Biblical parallels:[19]

Wife-Sistership. On the order of Abraham's ruse when he took Sarah to Egypt, the Nuzi letters confirm this institution designed to guarantee inheritance for a wife Beltakkadummi.

Adoption of an Heir. In Genesis 15:2, an 86-year-old Abraham, fearing that he would die without a son, adopts the slave Eliezer of Damascus. The practice is permitted at Nuzi, with the provision that should the lord subsequently have a natural son, the adopted son will share less in the final disposition of property.

Concubinage. The Nuzi documents tell how a slave woman from the land of Lulu is given in concubinage, much the same as Sarah's gift to her husband noted in Genesis 16:3.

Expulsion of Concubine. Following the birth of Isaac, Sarah orders the expulsion of the concubine Hagar along with her child Ishmael. The Code of Hammurabi provides for punishment of a presumptuous woman, who is to be "counted" back among the ranks of slaves, but does not sanction expulsion.

Betrothal Gifts. The correspondence of Zimri-Lin tells of gold rings and bracelets borne by intermediaries like Eliezer who negotiated the marriage of Isaac and Rebecca (Gen. 24:22).

Fratriarchy. In the Bible, permission for Rebecca's marriage (Gen. 24:50) must be secured from her brother Laban. The same practice is noted in a Nuzi letter ("With my consent my brother Akkulenni gave me as wife to Hurazzi").

Negotiable Birth Rights. Famished from his labors in the field, Isaac's elder brother Esau sells his inheritance to Jacob for a mass of potage (Gen. 25:31). Documents from Nuzi bear out this practice.

Deathbed Blessing. The second of the fables involving Esau and Jacob (Gen. 25:18–41) is supported by a Hurrian letter that speaks of a father's deathbed gift of a wife to a younger son.

Marriage of Eldest Daughters First. Jacob labors seven years in the mistaken notion he will earn the hand of Rachel (Gen. 29:21–29), then has to work another seven because it was the custom (noted at Nuzi) for the eldest daughter (in this case Leah) to be married off first.

Teraphim. Rachel absconds with the household deities of Laban (Gen. 31:19–34), figurines that were venerated as far back as the golden age of Sumeria. The Nuzi letters provide for an equitable sharing of the idols among a person's heirs.

Prostration. Upon returning to Canaan to meet with Esau, Jacob prostrates himself seven times (Gen. 33:3). The phrase "at the feet of my lord, seven times and seven times I fall" appears frequently in ancient inscriptions.

Compensation for Rape. After "defiling" Jacob's daughter Dinah, the prince of Shechem offers "double the marriage portion" for her shame (Gen. 34:12). The Mari letters speak of similar offers.

Levirate. If a husband has died without having a son, Deuteronomy 25:5–10 instructs his surviving brother to marry the widow. The eldest son of such union will be considered the son of his deceased brother. The same practice is mentioned in the Nuzi letters.

The Pentateuch is indebted to the Fertile Crescent for other precedents. When Abraham offered up Isaac to God as a sacrifice in Genesis 22, he was following a ritual long practiced in his native land. His substitution of animal sacrifice for human is regarded as one of the more significant steps for civilized man, but his substitution of a ram is no accident. Votive statuettes from the first dynasty of Ur, 1000 years earlier, portray goats trapped in a ceremonial thicket of gold leaf. When Abraham purchased the Cave of Machpelah as a tomb for Sarah and his family from Ephron of the sons of Heth, he was required to secure possession of the surrounding lands as well (Gen. 23:17–20), according to practices outlined in 17th century Hittite contracts. When the names of Abraham, Sarah, Jacob and Joseph were changed (Gen. 17:5, 17:15, 32:31, 41:45) it was in keeping with the practice of both Egypt and Mesopotamia where name changes reflected the blessing of the gods. From Canaanites came the custom of making covenants to guarantee safety and honesty, the veneration of high places, even the circumcision ritual (Gen. 17:11). From the Akkadians there even came the following, familiar tale:

> Sargon, the mighty king, king of Agade, am I
> My mother was a changeling (temple prostitute),
> My father I knew not.
> The brothers of my father loved the hills.
> My city is Azupiranu, which is situated on the banks of the Euphrates.
> My changeling mother conceived me, in secret she bore me.
> She set me in a basket of rushes, with bitument she sealed my lid.
> She cast me into the river which rose not over me.[20]

Sargon did not perish in the stream. As in all such legends, he was rescued, rose to prominence in the service of a lord, and eventually established his own dynasty in Mesopotamia. The tale of Sargon is important not only because it offers a glimpse of the common roots of the first great emperor of the ancient world, but also because it provides us with a convenient bridge to that other region that imprinted the thoughts and mores of the Hebrews—Egypt.

Egypt: The Hyksos Interlude

Ancient Egyptian history is based upon the reconstruction of Manetho, a priest from Heliopolis who lived in the third century B.C. Manetho's reckoning of 26 dynasties is interrupted only twice by confused eras referred to as the First Intermediate Period (2200–2050) and the Second Intermediate Period (1800–1570). The latter is especially interesting, for it was a time when "men of lowly birth from the eastern regions" subdued Egypt by weight of numbers. Known as the Hequa-Khasut or *Hyksos*, these so-called Shepherd Kings gained supremacy through the use of a composite bow, the quiver, new swords, axes, and chariots.[21] They caused so much chaos and disruption by some accounts that 118 rulers (four dynasties) vied with one another in little more than a century. In the process, they introduced new gods to the Egyptian pantheon, improved fortifications, and founded several camp cities, one of which was called Tell el-Yahudiyah.

The ancient Jewish historian Flavius Josephus identified the Hyksos with the Tribes of Israel who began their 400-year sojourn in Egypt as overlords. There is evidence that some Semites entered Egypt peacefully during the Patriarchal Age. Wall paintings in the tombs of Beni-Hasan in Middle Egypt portray followers of a nomadic chief named Abisha bringing stibium pigment into the land. Dating from the 19th century B.C., these dark-bearded figures wear striped tunics of several colors, are shown to be tinkers bearing bellows, and also carry musical instruments like the harp and cymbal. Their means of transport was the donkey. As such, they bear a remarkable resemblance to the family of Lamech (Gen. 4:21–22), donkey caravaners who played the lyre and pipe and "forged all implements of copper and iron." Other Egyptian documents of that era tell of dozens of slaves imported from Palestine as domestics, brewers, and cooks. Military penetration almost certainly accompanied commerce. A stele from the reign of Sesostris III (c. 1850) tells of a defensive campaign against Sekmen (Shechem). Further evidence of military pressure from the East is supplied by a series of Middle Kingdom execration texts (broken bowls inscribed with the names of enemies) where Zebulon, Ashkelon, Jerusalem, and Byblos all are cursed.[22]

Josephus' equation of the Hyksos with the ancient Israelites is no longer accepted. The modern interpretation is that the sons of Jacob entered Egypt along with other Semitic tribes and shared power for a time. When native rule was restored by Kamose and Ahmose, the Hebrews were enslaved, along with other aliens. Documents from the reign of Rameses II in the 19th dynasty refer to the fierce "Khabiri" or "Apiru" who were forced to drag stones for the construction of granaries in Pithom, Per-Rameses and Tanis-Zoan. Involuntary corvée was also demanded by Rameses III (pressing grapes, work on a temple at Heliopolis) and Rameses IV (quarrying at Wadi Hammamat). While the Children of Israel clearly did not build the pyramids (raised nearly 1000 years earlier), the Hyksos interregnum approximates that period described by the Book of Exodus when a pharaoh arose who knew not Joseph.

Joseph and his brothers in Egypt. The tale of Joseph and his brethren contains many elements that are of Egyptian origin. The Dothan road where Joseph was first abandoned then sold into slavery (Gen. 37:17) was the most prominent caravan route from Gilead east of the Jordan through the Jezreel Valley and Philistia into Egypt. In times of want, it was advisable to purchase "corn" from Egyptian granaries (Gen. 42:1–4). Egypt in the Middle Kingdom had already developed vast bureaucracies with various departments headed by lords who arrogated to themselves grand-sounding titles like governor of Upper or Lower Egypt, royal prince, supreme judge, prophet of Maat, superintendent of the works of kings, the six great houses. They also included the chief butler (scribe of the sideboard) and chief baker (superintendent of the bakehouse). Both of these figure prominently in Genesis 40–41 where Joseph, having fallen into disfavor with the captain Potiphar, is placed in a house of detention. The term employed for "prison" (*bet sohar*, Gen. 39:20), is of Egyptian origin. So, too, the reed grass (*achu*, Gen. 41:2) and river (*yeor*, Gen. 41:1) in pharaoh's dream of lean and fat cows. One way to regain status in this superstitious land was through dream divination (Gen. 41:17–36), precisely what Joseph does at the expense of native magicians (*chartumin*, Gen. 41:8), another word borrowed from Egypt. The Pharaoh then invests Joseph with fine linen (*biqday shaysh*, Gen. 41:42) and compels his courtiers to kneel (*abrech*, Gen. 41:43) before him. In keeping with Middle East custom, Joseph is granted a new name (*Zaphenath-paneah*, food man of life, Gen. 41:45). Ultimately reunited with his family, he presides over a 40-day mummification period for his father Jacob (Gen. 50:3).

Joseph and the Tale of Two Brothers. The temporary power the Hyksos-Hebrews-Amorites enjoyed was not without its drawbacks. Genesis 39:6–20 tells how Joseph, raised to the position of steward in the house of his benefactor, Potiphar, is sent to prison for allegedly attempting to seduce Potiphar's wife. The same tale of lust and jealousy is found in an Egyptian manuscript from the 13th century B.C. The D'Orbiney Papyrus relates the story of two brothers, Anubis and Bata.[23] Orphaned as youths, the elder brother, Anubis, eventually married and took his sibling into his own house. Later, when the two were plowing in the fields, Bata, now 18 and in full manhood, was sent back to obtain seed.

Upon reaching the house, he found his sister-in-law doing her hair and unwilling to help. "Go and open the bin and take what you want!" she snapped. Bata loaded up five sacks of emmer and barley on his shoulders and was about to return to work when the woman caught sight of him and changed her tone. "There is great strength in you!" she exclaimed. "Now I see your energies every day!" And, the tale continues, "She wanted to know him as one knows a man." She seized him and said, "Come, let's spend an hour sleeping together! This will do you good, because I shall make fine clothes for you." At this suggestion, the younger brother became "like a leopard," rejecting her: "See here — you are like a mother to me, because being older than I, he was the one who brought me up. What is this great crime which you have said to me? Don't say it to me again! And I won't tell it to a single person."

After Bata tramped off to the fields, the sister-in-law became frightened about the possible consequences. She ate fat and grease and lay disheveled, vomiting, when Anubis returned that evening. Aghast, the older brother asked what had happened. His wife responded weakly that his brother attempted to rape her. When this failed, he beat her, leaving her this way in the dark. Now it was the turn of the elder brother to become like "a leopard." Sharpening the point of his lance, he waited near the barn door for Bata. As the latter approached, cows spoke and warned, "Here's your elder brother waiting for you, carrying his lance to kill you! Run away from him!"

When Bata saw the feet of Anubis protruding from under the barn door, he ran away. Pursued by his elder brother, Bata called on Ra of the Horizons to protect him. The god caused a stream filled with crocodiles to spring up between the two brothers. All night, Anubis roared his anger while Bata pleaded his innocence. Finally, in the morning, the younger man swore, "As for your killing me falsely, you carried your lance on the word of a filthy whore." Then he took his knife, emasculated himself, and died. The tale has a "happy" ending, though, for Anubis returned home, threw his wife to the dogs, and mourned for his brother.

The Historical Moses. The presence of so many Egyptian words and themes in Genesis 37–50 cannot be ascribed to coincidence. The question has been raised whether Moses was an Egyptian whose life was embellished with local legend. That very hypothesis was advanced by Sigmund Freud, who suggested that Moses was a devotee of the Aton cult that preached the divinity of the physical sun disc.[24] Introduced into Egypt by Ikhnaton (Amenhotep IV), about 1380 B.C., Aton worship was henotheistic or monolatrous (venerating one god while recognizing the existence of others). It was regarded as a serious heresy by the dominant Amon-Ra cult, which succeeded in persecuting its adherents following the death of Ikhnaton. Not all of the Aton devotees were eliminated, however. When Egypt underwent a series of inexplicable plagues in the 14th century, one of the surviving Aton priests may have led a rabble out into the desert to cleanse the land. Hence, the tale of the Exodus.

Most scholars have rejected Freud's notion, and certainly the renowned psychiatrist was out of his element playing historian. But what really is known of Moses? The motif of miraculous rescue at birth is common enough in the ancient world, but generally the hero's claim of divine ancestry has been dismissed as puffery. In Moses' case, the assertion of lowly roots has been seen as an attempt on the part of a noble to identify with the masses. A papyrus from the Middle Kingdom tells of one courtier who made such a transition. Following the death of Amenemhet I, one of his family, Sinuhe by name, fearing civil war and purge, fled Egypt. In the rugged hills of Upper Retenu (Palestine) he married the daughter of a chieftain, championed his adopted people against a giant, prospered, and eventually returned to Egypt where he was welcomed by relatives.[25] The similarities with Moses' adventures in the land of Midian where he married Zipporah (Exodus 2:15–22) are striking.

James Henry Breasted, the great American Egyptologist, offered another twist to the study of the historical Moses. Toward the end of his reign, Seti I felt obligated to nominate a successor. The honor went to his first-born son, whose name is unknown. Ceremonial steles were prepared and the figure of this prince was chiseled onto the walls of Karnak in battle scenes with the Libyan enemies of Seti. Subsequently, another of the Pharaoh's sons, Rameses II, usurped power from his elder brother and desecrated his memory, replacing the unnamed prince's figure at Karnak with his own.[26]

While Breasted never specifically named Moses as the elder prince, the intimation is clear. Rameses was, after all, the Pharaoh of the oppression. Though Moses brought down on Egypt the wrath of Adonai, Rameses was strangely reluctant to have him executed. The Exodus may be dated toward the end of his reign (middle of the 13th century) since a stele of Merneptah, his successor, refers to a people Isireil in Palestine. It is possible that some royal diehard may have persisted with the Aton worship.[27] Linguistically, there seems to be a connection between the Adonai of the Bible (a euphemism for the ineffable name of God) and the Aton of Egypt. There is also a link between the commandment "Thou shalt have no other gods before me" (Ex. 20:3) and the monolatry of Aton. An absolute monotheistic creed would have said bluntly: "Thou shalt have no other gods."

Finally, as Professor Breasted and John Wilson have pointed out, there exists an extraordinary set of parallels between the Hymn of Aton and an ancient Psalm (104) ascribed to David. In virtually identical order, both sacred chants tell of (a) a deity whose daily disappearance creates darkness; (b) beasts that creep forth from the forests; (c) young lions that "roar after their prey"; (d) men who wake and go to work when the sun returns; (e) an earth whose riches have all been made according to the deity's wisdom; (f) a primordial sea that was tamed by the deity; (g) streams of precious water that have come from the skies and mountains. The hymns also invoke their respective deities with a unique phrase: "How manifold are thy works!" Such parallels cannot be written off to coincidence.[28]

Miracles and the Exodus. Study of Egypt and its environs may help unravel some of the puzzles that surround the tale of the Exodus. No miracle was required of Moses to change the Nile to blood (Ex. 7:20). The annual sweep of floodwaters from the Atbara and Blue Nile may cause the color of the main channel of the Nile to appear ruddy. During this season, all manner of vermin, frogs (Ex. 8:2), gnats (Ex. 8:12) and flies (Ex. 8:17) are displaced from their normal habitats in the delta or swamps. Locusts (Ex. 10:4) are a frequent summertime pest in the Middle East. The death of first-born children (Ex. 11:5) may be attributed to a combination of circumstances: diseases that were endemic to the region, exaggerations that glossed over or ignored the deaths of other offspring in the same family, or even a variant on the archaic Egyptian practice of offering the first-born as a sacrifice to Osiris.

Other biblical plagues (death of cattle, Ex. 9:7; boils, Ex 9:10; hail, 9:18; darkness, Ex. 10:21) may be more difficult, but not impossible, to explain. The scholars Galanopolous and Marinatos have theorized that eruptions on the volcanic isle of Thera-Santorin, 500 miles north of the delta, may have had impact upon Egypt.[29] The Aegean isle, which some have identified with Atlantis, became particularly active between 1550 and 1200 B.C. Its rain of burning ash not only forced natives of the island to migrate, but evidence exists that substantial amounts of volcanic ash were also deposited upon the island of Crete more than 100 miles south. Seismologists reckon that the size of the crater born of these upheavals indicates one or more eruptions that dwarf that of Krakatoa in 1883. (Clouds of smoke and ash from that fabled eruption were noted in New York State, 7000 miles from their origin.)

Galanopolous and Marinatos suggest that the biblical pillar of smoke and pillar of fire (Ex. 13:21) that guided the Israelites out of Egypt were nothing more than the smoke and flame generated in the heavens from Santorin-Thera. When the mixed multitude was led by Moses through a parted sea, it was not the Red Sea (Ex. 14:22) but rather the shallows of the Reed Sea near the Bay of Pelusium. The marshy waters here supposedly receded because of a quake at Thera-Santorin. When the Pharaoh's army tried to follow, they may have been wiped out (Ex. 14:28) by the gushing waters of a tsunami.

Natural phenomena may also account for miracles that rescued the Israelites during their Sinai wanderings. The quail that materialized suddenly in their camp in response to appeals for food (Ex. 16:13) were migratory birds common to the region that fly with prevailing winds. The honey-sweet white manna of Exodus 16:31 may well have been the sap of some plant affected by parasites. The blossoms of the wild acacia plant, a bright bush that grows in the desert, may have provided Moses with his epiphany of God in a burning bush (Ex. 3:2). When the Israelites complained about their thirst (Ex. 17:6), Moses smote the rock in Horeb, probably a limestone spring, and brought forth water.

No one can establish absolutely that the Hebrews borrowed from the writings of their contemporaries or developed their own mythology-religion in a vacuum. The greater likelihood is, however, that this primitive folk did accept, consciously or otherwise, what appealed to them and rejected the rest.

6

The Origins of Law and War

The Evolution of Law

Historians often credit the Romans with the foundations of European law. The first system was supposedly engraved by a commission upon the Twelve Tables circa 449 B.C. Over the next 10 centuries, the Roman Senate and various plebeian assemblies elaborated thousands of additional decrees that affected commerce, citizenship, diplomacy, the family. To preserve this rich tradition from extinction in the Dark Ages, Byzantine emperors Theodosius (346–395) and Justinian (518–610) had their greatest scholars compile digests of legal decisions and statutes. From these developed the later codes of the Holy Roman Empire, the Bourbon and Hapsburg monarchies, Frederick the Great, and Napoleon.

In law, as elsewhere, Roman civilization owed much to Hellenic elders in the east. In 508 and 507, the Athenian Cleisthenes altered the political and social structure of his city, democratizing some of its institutions and expanding its citizenship. A century before (594) the single archon Solon enacted so many reforms (including tax relief to poor farmers) that his name became synonymous with that of "lawmaker." Another descriptive legalism — draconian punishment — derived from the Code of Draco (620), where death was meted out for the least offense. Athens was not unique in its quest for order. Every Greek city, including Sparta — which traced its rigid, authoritarian form of government to Lycurgus about 675 B.C. — possessed its own patron deity and system of law.

Urukagina: The First Code. Schoolchildren are aware of a much earlier set of laws from the Near East — the Code of Hammurabi. Recovered from the dusty wastes of Persia, the ancient Babylonian code dates from the 18th century B.C.e. The Code of Hammurabi may be the most complete set of laws from the ancient period, but it is not the oldest. From Urukagina, patesi of Lagash (2415–2400 B.C.), comes a text that tells how this ruler established *amargi* (freedom, social justice). After paying homage to his gods at the beginning of the inscription, Urukagina described the miserable conditions that existed in former times. His government engaged in massive public works, digging several canals that brought "clear water to Nanshe." He (Urukagina) intervened to stamp out corruption that was rampant among wealthy boatmen, at the fisheries, and in storehouses. Not only were debt farmers amnestied, but Urukagina made it impossible for anyone to be victimized by excessive taxes by abolishing the tax collector "from the borders of Ningirsu to the sea." Peasants who had been robbed when they attempted to bring offerings to the cemetery were now protected. So, too, orphans, widows, and the blind, who previously had been deprived of their meager possessions. No one, not indigent artisans nor "gala" priests, need beg any longer as Urukagina's government provided bread and beer, a guaranteed dole, for all.

Two additional reforms sound as if they were instituted by a modern government. If a seller had a change of heart and did not wish to complete a transaction, he could not be coerced by buyer or government. More important, Urukagina commanded the introduction of a "fair" price, a progressive idea that Europe would not embrace until the late Middle Ages.[1]

Ur-Nammu: The Introduction of Fines. In many ways, Urukagina's text is closer to the standard boasts of eastern monarchs than a legal hornbook. The writings of one of his successors in Lagash — Gudea, who ruled about 2200 B.C. — exhibited the same debt to the gods (Gudea was inspired by Ningirsu in a dream), similar reforms (he erected a great temple and chased witches from the city), and the same absence of humility (Gudea literally strewed the region with statuettes proclaiming his glory). In nearby Ur, Shulgi (also called Dungi) brought prosperity (new ziggurats, military expeditions to Kurdistan) and the rule of law (a new calendar, reforms in weights and measures). Sumerian documents of the era also speak of the laws of Nisaba and Hani.

Puffery aside, none of these works provides an organized list of legal precedents. We are left with partial codes that fill the gap between Urukagina and Hammurabi. One of these was left by Shulgi's father, Ur-Nammu, who ruled Ur about 2100 B.C. Inscribed on both sides of a table, eight inches by four, the Code of Ur-Nammu opens with familiar references to the gods and the monarch's military exploits. Ur-Nammu claims to have eliminated corruption from his society, promoted justice, protected the orphan and widow, and revived business and agriculture. Where his code differs is on the obverse side of the cuneiform tablet. Here there is space for 45 ruled entries, only five of which have been partly deciphered. Each entry is an actual rule of law, dealing with such diverse subjects as trial by water ordeal or the return of a fugitive slave. Especially enlightening are three items that mandate fines for personal assaults. As restored by Professor Samuel N. Kramer of the University of Pennsylvania, they read:

> If a man to a man with a [...?] instrument
> his [...] the foot has cut off,
> 10 silver shekels he shall pay.
> If a man to a man with a weapon
> his bones of [...] severed
> 1 silver mina he shall pay.
> If a man to a man,
> with a geshpu-instrument, the nose has cut off,
> two-thirds of a silver mina he shall pay.[2]

What is remarkable about these entries is not just that ancient man finally developed a sense of legal organization, but the Sumerians recognized that society had a vested interest in controlling disorder. The primitive *lex talionis*, "law of retaliation," must be constrained, lest feuds continue endlessly. Hence the imposition of a fine.

Unfortunately, this sophisticated concept of jurisprudence was soon abandoned. The law codes of Bilalama (King of Eshnunna about 1900 B.C.) and Lipit-Ishtar (fifth king of Isin, c. 1868) continued the practice of fining wrongdoers: "If a man bites the nose of another man and severs it, he shall pay one mina of silver.... If a man severs another's finger he shall pay two-thirds of a mina of silver." The two codes also provide insight into such diverse matters as the price of commodities, labor disputes, marriage and divorce, inheritance, property rights and slavery, negligence, and the ubiquitous ox that has run amok.[3]

The Code of Hammurabi: Lex Talionis. Such law codes could not prevent a reversion to the more brutal *lex talionis*, which is the hallmark of the Code of Hammurabi. Of 282 precedents incised on this monumental stele, at least two dozen condone personal retaliation. While fines are imposed for some violations, most offenses are punished by mutilation or death sentences. The code opens with four separate rules warning that the penalty for bearing false witness is death. Anyone who steals property of the church or state or receives stolen property "shall be put to death" (#6). Robbery is punishable by death (#22) as is looting ("if fire broke out in a freeman's house and a freeman who went to extinguish it cast his eye on the goods of the owner of the house and has appropriated the goods of the owner of the house, that freeman shall be thrown into that fire," #25). Cheating in the sale of real estate is a capital crime (#10). So, too, child stealing (#14), the killing of a husband by his wife (#153) and sexual relations between mother and her son (#157).

Several picaresque entries carried with them grim consequences. Thus, an individual who tried to avoid military service by hiring a surrogate in his place would not only lose his property, but also his life (#26). Death was also meted out to a priestess who set foot in a grog shop (#110), a wife who shamed her husband (#143), a builder whose structure collapsed upon a free man (#229). A physician whose operation caused the blindness or death of a patient was only to lose a hand (#218).

The Code of Hammurabi was a dour, merciless document, central to which was brute force. If, for example, an adopted son publicly denounced his foster parents, authorities were to cut out his tongue (#192). If he tried to return to the home of his paternal family, his eye was to be plucked out (#193). If a child in the care of a wet nurse died, the woman was to be punished by having a breast cut off (#194). If a son struck his father, "They shall cut off his hand" (#195). Having warmed to the concept of retaliation after nearly 200 entries, the code finally proclaims, "If a freeman has destroyed the eye of a member of the aristocracy, they shall destroy his eye" (#196).[4]

This supposedly is the model for the passages in the Bible that read: "If any harm follow, then thou shalt give life for life, eye for eye, tooth for tooth, hand for hand, foot for foot, burning for burning, wound for wound, stripe for stripe" (Ex. 21:23–25; Lev. 24:19–20; Deut. 19–21). Unlike Babylon, where punishments specified under law were actually implemented, the goal of the Mosaic Code was deterrence. The lex talionis is first invoked in Exodus with reference to a pregnant woman and her vulnerable fetus. According to Rabbi J. H. Hertz, chief rabbi of the British Empire, "There is in Jewish history no instance of the law of retaliation ever having been carried out literally."[5]

Rabbinical authorities interpret the expression "eye for an eye" to represent equality before the law. Babylonian society, on the other hand, was rigidly stratified among the *awilum* (patricians), *mushkenum* (free masses), and *wardum* (slaves). Severity of punishment depended upon one's position in society. If a patrician knocked out the eye of a fellow aristocrat, he stood to lose an eye (#196). If he knocked out the eye of a slave that belonged to a member of his own class, he was *fined* half the value of that slave. If, however, he knocked out the eye of a commoner, the patrician would not be mutilated, nor would he be fined a substantial amount. Instead, the penalty would be one silver mina (perhaps $50 to $60). Similar remedies based on class applied whether the offense was knocking out a tooth, striking the cheek of another freeman, or causing a woman to have a miscarriage (#209 and #210). By way of contrast, the Bible recognizes no distinction on the basis of class. All people are to be treated equally before the law, a visionary concept most societies have trouble implementing.

Assyria and the Art of War

Diplomacy is the art of law conducted between nations. The history of man is also the saga of warfare. Once more, it was to be the Middle East that civilization looked for perfection of its war machine. From the Royal Standard of Ur (c. 2700 B.C.) comes the first glimpse of heavy chariots drawn by onagers. The phalanx, that close file of foot soldiers that became the core of Greek military strength, is represented on the Stele of the Vultures dating from the reign of Eannatum about 2500 B.C. One hundred years later, the Semitic king Naram-Sin credited his victories to the moon deity, but actually owed his empire to the recurved composite bow he bears in inscriptions. The Egyptians employed archers and chariots in tandem, festooned their temples and pylons with scenes of cities under siege. From the Hittites came iron weapons that split their enemies' copper and bronze swords. Other refinements in the killing process—ballista, catapults, battering rams, sappers, helmets, bucklers, lances—were added by Kassites, Babylonians, Libyans, Myceanaeans, Minoans, and Assyrians.

It was left to the latter, the Assyrians, to combine the various military advances in a single system. For 300 years (900–612 B.C.), the Assyrian Empire dominated the Middle East. The effectiveness of a system based on terror so impressed other peoples in the Mediterranean basin that many of its principles and weapons were still being employed by Europeans down to the end of the Crusades nearly 2000 years later.

The emergence of the Assyrians, a Semitic people known to northeast Iraq since the middle of the third millennium, was due to a series of historical quirks. Mentioned in the correspondence of Hammurabi in the 18th century and Tell el-Amarna in the 14th, the Assyrians watched as the Hittites and Egyptians battled one another from 1500 to 1100 B.C. The result of this 400-year conflict was the collapse of both empires and the creation of a power vacuum in the Middle East. For a short time (between 1100 and 900), it was possible for independent kingdoms in Israel, Phoenicia and Aramaea to flourish. In this "Era of Small Nations," Tyrian adventurers founded colonies as far off as Tunisia (Carthage) and Spain (Cartagena), and may even have circumnavigated Africa. For Jews, the period is remembered as a golden age. In Syria, Damascus and Palmyra became great centers of trade and culture.

But just as nature abhors a vacuum in a laboratory, so it cannot tolerate one in the realm of politics. Assyria, a nation that barely controlled a 95-mile strip of land along the Tigris at the end of the 10th century, made a concerted bid to fill that void. The ruler credited with this decision was Ashurnasirpal II (884–59 B.C.). His task was not as formidable as it might seem. The Assyrians were not disorganized bedouin. Rather, they were city dwellers who had refined their political and military institutions over a thousand years. They possessed a sense of national unity, common purpose. For 500 years, their small army had raided neighboring territory with some success. Their arsenal included a superior battering ram and composite bow. Conquered foes were harshly treated, as in the reign of Tukulti-Ninurta I (1242–06) who boasted how he deported 10,000 captives from Syria and dragged the King of Babylon to Ashur in chains.[6]

Instead of intermittent raiding parties, Ashurnasirpal took his army into the field every spring and campaigned in every type of terrain. Palace orthostats (wall inscriptions) celebrate the Assyrian army marching through forested regions, scaling the mountains of Elam, portaging swift-flowing rivers, chasing Arabs into the desert. Indeed, the first recorded reference to Arabs comes from an Assyrian document that speaks of Shalmaneser III (858–24) quelling the revolt of "Gindibu the Arabi."

No longer a small standing force, the Assyrian army included every able-bodied male. Soldiers were trained for specific tasks and the same orthostats that proclaim victory reveal a remarkable coordination that existed among different units. From an outer perimeter, archers laid down a barrage of arrows. Nearer the city walls, charioteers were running down the remnants of enemy infantry. Other units wheeled a shielded battering ram into position where it could pummel the city gates. Mobile towers as high as the walls were moved right up to the battlements. As archers in these towers exchanged volleys with enemy troops, additional Assyrians clambered up ladders. Below sappers were tunneling while pickmen pulled away the very stones of the walls. Such techniques of siegecraft would not be surpassed till the advent of gunpowder.

Assyrian Hegemony

By the middle of the seventh century B.C. this war machine provided Assyria with domination over everything from the borders of India to Egypt, including more than 600 vassal kings. It was an empire that prided itself upon cultural achievements. The orthostats cited in the previous section were carved into the walls of great palaces at Ashur, Calah, Nimrud, and Nineveh. The bland inscriptions now on display in the British Museum once were colorful tiles, supported by stone genii, gryphons, and chimera. Archaeologists Austen Henry Layard, Paul Emile Botta, and Hormuzd Rassam retrieved exquisite bowls, delicate pieces of ivory, and amber statuettes, reflecting the prosperity of this great empire.

From the same ruins came 25,000 clay tablets, the library of Ashurbanipal (669–26), the "great and noble Asnapper" of Ezra 4:10, a bibliophile who so impressed the Greeks that they likened "Sardanapallos" to a God. Ashurbanipal's documents constitute the greatest resource of ancient Mesopotamian culture. From the Assyrians come bilingual dictionaries that offer clues to Sumerian records, accounts of mythology (the tale of Gilgamesh, Adapa, Enuma Elish), ancient mathematics (knowledge of cube and square roots), astronomy (the zodiac, phases of the moon, positions of the planets, prediction of eclipses), medicine (what to do when excretion is painful, when one's mouth is swollen, if the skull of a man is seized by the fever demon) geography (clay outlines of mountains, rivers, even a map of the known world), and chronology (the ancient Assyrians named each year after an eponymous official called a *limmu*).[7]

The library of Ashurbanipal reveals instructions for *ashipu* priests (exorcists) whose function it was to rid the body of the fever demon. (A favorite tactic was to place salted meat near the patient and hope that the demon would leap out after it.) The tablets also speak of *baru* priests who could divine the future in various ways. Clay models of livers have been found, replete with cuneiform directions on how to interpret animal entrails. Astrologers wielded great influence in Assyrian society. Their hemerologies transcend time, for it is to the Assyrians that the Western world is indebted for dread of Friday the 13th. Though this particular date was to be feared, Assyrian astrologers gave advice for every day of the year. A list from the month of Tishri (September) warns:

On the first day he (a man) shall not expose himself to the gale of the field.
He must not eat garlic, otherwise a scorpion will sting him.
He must not eat white garlic, otherwise he will suffer a heart attack.

On the second day he must not climb upon a roof, for Adrat Lili (an evil demon)
would find him.
He must not eat roast meat, otherwise he will be covered with sores.

On the third day, he shall have no sexual intercourse with a woman, for the woman
would rob him of his virility.
He shall not eat fish; it is disrespectful and a crocodile would attack him.
He shall not eat dates, for they would give him a stomach illness.
He shall not irrigate a sesame field, for the sesame caterpillar would overcome him.
A woman shall not visit him, for his plan would not succeed.

On the fourth day, he must not cross a river; the fullness of his strength would
depart him.
He shall not go to outlying places, otherwise an enemy would fight with him.
He shall not eat beef, goat's meat or pork, for he would suffer headaches.
He shall not set foot where an ass has walked, otherwise he will develop sciatica.[8]

To the prophets Amos, Isaiah, and Hosea, the Assyrians were instruments of divine wrath, though why the Almighty would have selected them is beyond comprehension. Present-day evangelists who view events through the lens of biblical prophecy liken the Assyrians to the Nazis. Both peoples were led by boorish castes that fancied themselves as cultured. Both favored monumental art, filled with scenes of violence, the hunt, warfare — what can only be termed expressions of *machismo*. Like the Assyrians, Hitler, Himmler, Hess, and other Nazis were extremely superstitious, immovable without the blessing of their horoscopes. Most important, both empires were based on fear and terror.

Ashurnasirpal's conquests could not have been achieved through battlefield tactics alone. It was he who instituted the practice of annihilation of any population that resisted paying tribute. Once a city fell, adult male prisoners of war would be mutilated. Hands and ears cut off, their eyes gouged, the captives were piled in great heaps to perish from their wounds, suffocations, flies and exposure to the sun. Children and women were carried off to slavery or torture. The rebel chieftain was flayed, for the amusement of the emperor, in Nineveh. This grisly policy of mutilation and deportation is vividly portrayed on the bronze gates of Balawat left by Shalmaneser III.[9] Scenes of decapitation, hacking off of legs, impalement through the genitals, and human heads decorating banquet scenes like Japanese lanterns are reminiscent of atrocities perpetrated by the Nazis in World War II. They are there for the viewing, incised on orthostats on display in museums around the world.

Nor did the Assyrian monarchs shy away from trumpeting their deeds in words. Of the town of Kinabu on the Hulai River, Ashurnasirpal declared:

Of the soldiers, I slew 600 with the sword; 3000 prisoners I burned in the fire. I kept no one alive as a hostage. The city king fell into my hands. I piled their corpses as high as towers. The king I flayed and hung his skin on the wall of Damdamusa.[10]

Of his triumph over a coalition of Syrians and Israelites at Karkar in 853, Shalmaneser wrote:

With the august power that my lord Ashur lent me, with the powerful arms accorded me by Nergal who walks before me, I fought against them. From the city of Karkar to Gilgau I routed them. By force of arms I scattered 14,000 soldiers of their army; like the God Adad I rained a deluge upon them; I piled up their corpses. I scattered their numerous troops like seeds over the plain. By force of arms I made their blood to flow in the furrows. The plain was too small to let their corpses fall; the outspread ground was not large enough to bury them; with their bodies I filled the Orontes as with a dam. In this battle I took their chariots, their cavalry, their horses, and their armour.[11]

And in the supposedly peaceful era of the seventh century, Essarhaddon (681–69) told how he disposed of rebels from Sidon and Cilicia:

> Abdi-Milkutti, who fled before my weapons on to the sea, I pulled out of the sea like a fish and I cut off his head.... To give the people an example of the power of Ashur, my lord, I hung the heads of Sandaurri and Abdi-Milkutti round the necks of their most prominent citizens, whom, thus adorned, I made walk in procession along the streets of Nineveh, to the strains of singers accompanying themselves on harps.[12]

The Fall of Nineveh

The object of such brutality was to teach potential rebels a lesson, to compel neighboring cities or peoples to fall into line without having to expend energy creating a permanent provincial administration. Despite constant warfare, this policy of extermination and deportation worked for almost 300 years. Such policies, however, contained within them the seeds of their own destruction. The endless wars sapped Assyria of its own fighters. Just as in Sparta where battlefield attrition reduced the number of warriors, annual campaigns eroded the Assyrian army. Some able-bodied men, living off the tribute of the empire, declined to serve. The Assyrians hired mercenaries— Ionian Greeks— whose commitment to the empire was nowhere near that of native troops.

This warlord empire never earned the trust or affection of its subjects. Fear, cruelty, and arbitrary taxation fostered resentment among the vassals. At the end of the seventh century, these diverse peoples forged an alliance aimed at the destruction of Assyria. Just as the Soviet Union joined forces with Western democracies against Nazi Germany, so Medes, Persians, Egyptians, Lydians, and Babylonians combined with barbaric hordes of Cimmerians and Scythians in the struggle against Assyria.

Confronted with this strange coalition, the ancient Assyrians also suffered a crisis in leadership. Seventh century Assyria produced several ephemeral leaders— Shamashumukin, who attempted to overthrow his brother Ashurbanipal in 652; Ashuretililani, Ashurbanipal's son, who was deposed by an army chief; and Sinsharishkun, grandson of Ashurbanipal. The latter, crowned in 623, witnessed the destruction of his capital, Nineveh, in August 612 following a two-month siege. As the annals of the Babylonian king Nabopolassar tell: "On that day, Sinsharishkun, the Assyrian king was killed. The great spoil of the city and temple they carried off and turned the city into a ruin-mound and heaps of debris." The biblical prophecy of Jonah 3:4 ("Yet forty days, and Nineveh shall be overthrown") was fulfilled. So, too, that of Nahum 3:1, 7, 18:

> Woe to the bloody city!... Nineveh is laid waste: who will bemoan her?... Thy shepherds slumber, O king of Assyria: thy nobles shall dwell in the dust: thy people is scattered upon the mountains, and no man gathereth them.

But in reciting his epitaph for Nineveh, the prophet Nahum may also have uttered a dirge for mankind. Unwittingly, he acknowledged the Assyrians' legacy in war-making when he concluded, "For upon whom hath not thy wickedness passed continually?" (3:19).

7

Ancient Persia: Stability
through Good Government

Herodotus on the Ancient Persians

In the summer of 1972, when a junta of colonels ruled Greece, only government-licensed guides were permitted to lead tourists through historical sites in that country. One such bureaucrat was assigned to a group of Americans trudging up the Acropolis in Athens. Atop the Pnyx, the hill that served as an ancient court, the guide regaled her people with a novel, if inaccurate, interpretation of history. "Here it was," she said, pointing to the ruins of the Parthenon, "2500 years ago that a handful of my countrymen withstood hordes of barbarian invaders. Had the Persians been victorious in 480 B.C., civilization would have been destroyed."

The target of the guide's invective was the ancient Persians, one of the peoples that emerged from the anti–Assyrian coalition to rule the Middle East from 550 to 332 B.C. In the 20th century, when the name Khomeini conjures up images of hostages and child warriors, such a polemic would not be difficult to construct. The original Persian religion was polytheistic, indulging belief in the evil eye, dragons, *daevas* or devils like Aeshma (the demon of drunkenness), Nasu druj (the corpse fiend) and Shaitan (whence our Satan). The pantheon also included Ashir (destiny), Atar (fire), Sraosha (obedience), Vohu Manah (Good Thought), Spenta Mainyu (Holy Spirit), Asha (Righteousness) and Anahita (the mother goddess), all venerated at open-air altars tended by shamans known as Magians. These soothsayers tended eternally burning fires and prepared the mind-expanding *haoma* drink taken during orgiastic rites. The Magians were also responsible for slaughtering bullocks, which served as the epiphany of Mithra, the lord of war and fertility. Devotees of Mithra, a cult favored by the Roman legions, were required to partake of a communal meal of the flesh and blood of their god. Identified with the sun, which was given a special day of the week for religious observance, Mithra's symbol was the cross. Once a year, on the occasion of the winter solstice, his followers celebrated the rebirth of the sun, the *dies natalis invicti solis* (the birthday of the sun), coincidentally on the 25th of December.[1]

Just as there was an obvious connection between Mithraism and early Christianity, so there is a close relationship between Greeks and Persians. Both derived from ancient Indo-European stock who emerged from the steppes of central Russia. The Persians entered the

Iranian plateau and India between 3000 and 2500 B.C., nearly one thousand years before Homer's fair-haired Achaeans settled in the Greek peninsula. Persian gods were gods of nature, controlling agriculture, storms, commerce, war and peace. Like the Greek gods, they were imbued with human frailties. Two Persian deities, Dhu-Pitar and Dyaosh, were actually incorporated in the Graeco-Roman pantheons as Jupiter and Zeus. Persian rituals were no more degenerate than drinking and sexual initiation that typified Orphic and Eleusinian rites.

No less an authority than Herodotus, the Greek chronicler of the Persian Wars, wrote glowingly of this enemy culture. Herodotus praised the simplicity of Persian religion, which required no images, no temples or altars, no libations, flutes or trumpets. The variety of troops arrayed in battle, ranging from lightly armed Bactrian bowmen to bucklered Medes and Egyptians, testified to the adaptability and flexibility of Persian war commanders. Said Herodotus: "There is no nation which so readily adopts foreign customs as the Persians." Impressed with the strict code of etiquette and cleanliness of Persian society, Herodotus noted how equals would greet one another with a kiss on the lips while an inferior would prostrate himself before a lord. He told how Persians frowned on anyone who drank to the point of vomiting, how they would not defile streams or ponds by spitting or washing their hands in the water. The ancient Persians considered lying to be the greatest sin and frowned upon debt slavery. According to Herodotus, all sons in Persia were instructed to ride, draw the bow, and speak the truth.[2]

Ionia: Site of the Ancient Enlightenment

The almost wistful tone to Herodotus' panegyric may be due to the fact that he lived much of his life on the western tip of Asia Minor. This region, known as Ionia, produced many sages that revolutionized civilization, including: Thales of Miletus (640–546 B.C.), almost certainly the first individual to explain phenomena in terms of naturalistic laws of causation; a disciple, Anaximander (610–547 B.C.) whose studies of sea life led to the theory of evolution; Anaximenes, also of Miletus, who refined Anaximander's concept of "the boundless" into "aer," something contemporary scholars identify as dissociated hydrogen gas; Xenophanes of Colophon (d. 570), who offered the cynical view of theology that if cows had hands they would paint their gods as cows; Anaxagoras of Klazomenae (500–428 B.C.), who spent most of his life in exile in Athens pondering the infinite dimensions of the mind; Heracleitus of Ephesus (535–475 B.C.), who argued that all things come into being by a conflict of opposites and that fire was the underlying substance of creation; his opposite, Pythagoras of Samos (c. 580), who maintained that nothing really changes, that immutable numbers were the source of harmony in the universe; and Democritus of Abdera (460–370 B.C.), who reconciled their differences by devising the atom, an "uncuttable" constant that was ever changing through recombination. All of these, like the poets Alcaeus of Lesbos, Simonides of Chios, Archilochus of Paros, and Phokylides of Miletus, as well as the physician Hippocrates of Cos, flourished in a region populated by Greeks, yet ruled by Persians.[3]

Ionia was only one of many territories that fell under Persian domination by the close of the sixth century. Herodotus offers a detailed account of the activities of Cyrus II, the "mule" born of a Median princess and a Persian lord, who created the empire named after his ancestor Achaemenes. From 550, when Cyrus usurped the throne of his grandfather Astyages in Ecbatana, to his death in 530, this resourceful leader added the realms of the

Lydian Croesus (with the sack of Sardis in 546) and the Chaldaean Belshazzar (with the capture of Babylon in 539) to his possessions. Subsequent campaigns by his successors won Egypt, Libya, parts of Afghanistan, Phrygia, Armenia, everything from Lesbos and Cyprus in the west to the fertile lands along the Indus River.

Foundations of the Achaemenid Empire

The Persian government was based on the traditional system of king, council and masses, but it was able to win a unique loyalty from its patchquilt of subjects, experiencing few major revolts in the 200 years before Alexander the Great set out to make himself world conqueror. This quiescent attitude permeates the biblical books of Chronicles and Kings, and may be traced to several factors:

Emancipation of hostage populations and their gods. A year after he fulfilled the biblical prophecy of the destruction of Babylon, Cyrus ordered the reconstruction of the Jewish Temple in Jerusalem (Ezra 6:3–5). So ended the Babylonian Captivity, nearly 50 years of lamentation that followed the destruction of Solomon's temple in 586 and the forced exile of Jews from their homeland to the waters of Babylon. In jubilation, the Jews blessed Cyrus as God's "shepherd" (Isa. 44:28) and as "the anointed one" or messiah (Isa. 45:1).

What the Bible did not note, however, was that redemption of captive populations was part of a general policy practiced by Cyrus. From the start, he sought favor of his subjects by returning them to their homelands. In 1850 a crude foundation brick was retrieved from Uruk that refers to Cyrus as king of Sumer and Akkad, builder of two sanctuaries intended to house Nanna, goddess of Uruk, whose statues had been carried off by the Babylonians. Another cylindrical inscription uncovered in 1879 tells how "the gods of Susa were returned to Elam, those of Ashur to the ancient capital; others from the old debatable land between Assyria and Babylonia equally profited." Babylonian temples that had been neglected by Nabonidus were also restored as Cyrus returned their "captive gods." Other cuneiform inscriptions tell how local administrators in Syria, Phoenicia, Elam, and Babylonia were returned to office and trade resumed throughout the empire.[4]

A provincial system that provided for expressions of autonomy. The ruthless terror practiced by Assyrians and Babylonians was supplanted by a new system of *satraps* ("protectors of the kingdom," provincial governors) whose loyalty to the central government could not be questioned, for the governors were drawn from the royal family. Their posts were hereditary and to guarantee continuity, marriages were arranged among these nobles. The danger of nepotism was more than outweighed by having Achaemenid princes in remote provinces overseeing activities of neighboring governors.

Each satrap was assisted by a secretary, financial officer, and general who reported directly to the king. Within the 31 satrapies, ethnic groups were permitted to designate their own leaders—who could supervise religious affairs, matters of taxation, marriage, divorce, etc.—and serve as intercessors to the emperor. These figures, known as *ethnarchs*, were typified by the High Priest in Judaea who offered his people the semblance of self-pride while he helped to deflect pent-up national frustrations. In rare instances, some towns in Ionia (e.g., Miletus) were even granted autonomy. In Babylon, too, some communities jealously preserved their ancient status as "free cities."[5]

As a last safeguard against peculation and revolt, the emperor annually despatched *missi* ("the king's eyes" or "ears"), inspector generals whose task it was to judge the true state of affairs in the provinces. These dignitaries might be received with great pomp. More often, their travels were made in the guise of a beggar or simple merchant, to ascertain whether the satrap was governing fairly.

Regularity or uniformity of duties of subjects. Unlike the Roman Empire, which practiced tax farming (assigning tax collection to private bidders), the Achaemenids advised their subjects in advance of their taxes. Loans obtained from temple priesthoods could be repaid at 25 percent interest. Grain, meat, oil, dates, wine were all available to the poor at a cost slightly higher than under the Chaldaeans. Though the price of some building materials like baked brick and cypress had risen, copper and iron imported from Cyprus and Anatolia were still surprisingly cheap.

Unlike other powers that swept away the children of their vassals or dragooned soldiers when their ranks were depleted, the Persian military levies were set. Unlike Greek city-states, which jealously maintained their own systems of weights, measures, and coinage, the Persian Empire operated with a single system of measures and coinage based on a gold piece called the daric. Named for Darius, who ruled Persia a decade after Cyrus, this coin typified the monarch's concern for unity. It was Darius who left the heraldic, trilingual inscription at Bogistana 700 feet above the roadway between Ecbatana and Persepolis, proclaiming victory over mutineers and foreign enemies. It was Darius who attempted to link the Mediterranean with the Red Sea by cutting a canal through the desert at Suez. Most important, it was Darius who in 519 B.C. left a code of laws modeled after those of Hammurabi. Herodotus (1:137) tells how one judge was flayed for issuing an unjust decision. Such constancy impressed the ancient prophets, who wrote: "Establish the interdict, and sign the writing, that it be not changed, according to the law of the Medes and Persians, which altereth not." (Dan. 6:8).

Improved communications. The Persians appreciated the importance of improved communications. Two royal highways, roughly paved roads, stretched 1677 miles from Susa to Sardis in the west and a slightly shorter distance from Babylon-Ecbatana to the Indian frontier. A series of inns, customs stations, and guardhouses dotted the highways providing the traveler with a modicum of security.

Specially trained horseman would race along the paths carrying pouches filled with provincial dispatches. These royal messengers (*angaerion*) would relay their communiques to a new set of riders after a day's journey until the information reached the emperor. Of such riders, Herodotus wrote: "Nothing mortal travels as fast as these Persian messengers. And these men will not be hindered from accomplishing at their best speed the distance which they have to go, either by snow, or rain, or heat, or by darkness of night" (8:98). Because of the highway system and the royal messengers, the time required for information to reach Susa from Sardis was cut from 90 days to seven!

Toleration advocated by Zoroastrianism. The Persian empire still might have resembled its predecessors but for the religious reformation caused in the middle of the sixth century by a figure called Zoroaster or Zarathustra ("he who can handle camels" or "one with golden camels").[6] A priest of the old Aryan cult, this man preached a monotheistic message from Ahura-Mazda (the wise lord). For Zoroaster, concepts of wisdom, immortality, good thought, destiny, fire, piety, righteousness and obedience, which men mistakenly had venerated as separate gods, were attributes of one supreme deity. But just as

Judaeo-Christian theology posits the existence of a powerful evil spirit, so Zoroastrianism teaches there is a twin of good attempting to subvert the souls of men. Identified as Ahriman, this demon created bad thought, corruption and the *daevas*. It was Ahriman and his cohorts ("the Sons of the Lie") who brought men the "filthy, intoxicating" haoma drink, fire worship, polytheism, and the nocturnal sacrifices of Mithra. However, the choice between good or evil ultimately was up to the individual. Zoroastrianism stressed free will and direct personal contact between man and god. Where other religions stressed the need for sacrifice and the intervention of a priestly caste before the gods would harken to a man's prayers, Zoroastrians were almost on familiar terms with their god, whom they addressed: "I ask you, tell me truly, oh, Ahura-Mazda."

For the faithful, Zoroaster promised a day of judgment and the coming of a divine kingdom. Sounding much like an Old Testament prophet, he warned of a great cataclysm, a consuming by fire before mankind would stand before a trinity of Ahura-Mazda, his disembodied righteousness, and Zoroaster. A person's conscience would determine his reward in the world hereafter, the wise and virtuous going across the Bridge of the Separator along the Road of Good Thought to the House of Song, the House of Good Thought, where they would abide near the throne of Ahura-Mazda bathed in heavenly light. Fools and liars would travel to the House of Worst Existence, where their fate would be torment, misery and foul food. Some scholars trace belief in heaven, hell, Satan, the end of days and the final judgment to Zoroastrian influence upon a subject Jewish populace. A unique spirit of toleration was fostered in the *Gathas* (hymns), which form the basis of the sacred Zend Avesta and which instruct:

> Grant it for this life and for the spiritual to come that we attain the fellowship with you and with Righteousness forever more. Grant that the warriors long for Righteousness, that the herders be fitted for continuous fellowship, and that they be zealously subservient to us! Thus may the nobles, the peasants, and the priests, with whom we are in fellowship, thus may we all, Mazdah-Ahura, as followers of Righteousness and just, persuade you to grant us what we desire.[7]

Again, in the "Three Prayers," among the oldest documents of that age, believers are taught:

> Righteousness is the greatest good, according to our desires it shall be to us, according to our desires it shall be, Righteousness for the greatest happiness.... Let the longed-for priestly brotherhood come to support the men and women who are taught of Zarathustra, to the support of Good Thought, whereby the conscience may win the precious reward. I pray for the dear prize of Righteousness which Ahura-Mazdah can bestow.

Born under miraculous circumstances (the skies were filled with strange astral phenomena), Zoroaster was harassed, possibly even martyred, by the entrenched magian priesthood. Before his death, however, he won over Atossa, wife of Hystaspes (Vishtaspa), satrap of Parthia and Hyrcania. Soon after, Hystaspes' first son — Darius (Darya-Vohumanah, "who sustains Good Thought") — was born. When Darius, in an ingenious ploy described by Herodotus, ascended to the throne, Zoroastrianism became the state religion of Persia.

Inscriptions left by Darius attribute his success to the god "who made this earth, who made yonder heaven, who made man, who made welfare for man." When Xerxes succeeded Darius, he, too, credited Ahura-Mazda "who created peace for man, who made Xerxes king." Without much success, Xerxes tried to purge the worship of demons, declaring: "Afterward by the favor of Ahura-Mazdah, I destroyed that community of daevas and proclaimed: The daevas you shall not worship. Where formerly the daevas were worshipped, there I worshipped Ahura-Mazda and the holy Arta." The last concept, Arta, synonymous with righteousness, was so important to Xerxes that he named his own son and successor Artaxerxes and left him the instruction: "Worship Ahura-Mazda and the holy Arta. The man who has respect for that holy law which Ahuara-Mazda has established and the holy Arta shall be happy while living and blessed when dead."[8]

Alexander the Great and the End of the Persian Empire

Darius later proved indifferent to the religious changes taking place about him, disappointing Zoroastrian devotees who had expected him to usher in a messianic era. His vacillation is evident in the great legal code which makes reference to Ahura-Mazdah and "the other gods who are [his] strong help." Within two generations after the reign of Xerxes, the backsliding toward polytheism would be complete. Artaxerxes I and Artaxerxes II (one of whom may have been the weakling Ashuerus of the Book of Esther) encouraged the return of the old gods. Once more, the Persian holy writings would redound with hymns of praise to Atar, Anahita, Mithra, and the haoma drinks that "restore us and aid this world's advance."[9]

Grown sotted, the fifth-century descendants of Cyrus indulged in what Professor Olmstead labels "ruinous taxation."[10] Despite their decadence, the Persian monarchs continued to enjoy relative peace for more than another century, to 334 B.C., when Alexander of Macedon launched his campaign of vengeance. Three years later, with the rout of Darius III on the plains of Gaugamela, not too distant from the ruins of Nineveh, the Achaemenid Empire collapsed.

The noble ideas fostered by Zoroaster were not extinguished with political defeat. The sacred writings of the prophet were codefied during the Sassanid era (A.D. 224–640) and elaborated in commentaries issued in the ninth century. To this day, more than 250,000 Zoroastrians remain faithful to the precept that the world is in a struggle between the forces of *Spenta Mainyu* (Bounteous Spirit or Good Thought) and *Angra Mainyu* (Hostile Spirit or Bad Thought) and that the truth and justice of Ahura-Mazda will prevail.

8

The Age of Wonder: Greeks, Romans, Carthaginians

Alexander's Dream of One World

Triumphant from the Adriatic to the Indus Rivers, the Macedonian Greeks were presented with an opportunity of fulfilling the teachings of Plato and Aristotle. People should recognize that they constituted a single family, a great *oecumene* created by a common, supreme power. Acceptance into the *polis*, the Greek city-state, promised political equality even for subject peoples. After all, when asked to what country he belonged, the cosmopolitan Socrates, replied, "I am a citizen of the world." In the end, everyone would benefit from the extension of Greek culture, art, and philosophy. Zeno, the sage from Cyprus (d. 262 B.C.), who was the founder of the school of Stoicism, taught that reason, self-restraint, and wisdom would lead to self-sufficiency, oneness with the universe. *Homonoia* (harmony) would reign throughout the world.

The problem with this romanticized view of a *pax hellenica* is that it ignored the sneering attitude of Greeks toward other peoples. Like the Romans after them, the Greeks categorized non-Hellenes as barbarians. Aristotle rationalized slavery for everyone but his own people, and Delos, formerly a center of devotion to Apollo, god of wisdom and light, became a major slave market trading 10,000 persons per day. Plato's vaunted concept of a republic, in reality a blueprint for totalitarianism, was dismissed by a score of poseurs who succeeded Alexander the Great. By the first century, one-third of Rome's urban population was dependent upon grain distributed by the state. They revelled in gruesome contests between men and animals staged in the arenas. And they endured fires, disease, theft and murder in the *insulares* (crowded tenements) that made this capital city so dangerous. Instead of logic and wisdom, philosophers like Aristippus of Cyrene (d. 360) and Epicurus of Samos (342–270) stressed *hedone* (pleasure) or *ataraxia* (escape from fear). Some, like Antisthenes of Athens (d.370) and Diogenes of Sinope (d.323), founders of the school of Cynicism, went even further, preaching open-air sermons against the follies of civilization.[1]

Many of these problems could be traced to the man identified with ushering in the Hellenistic Age — Alexander the Great. Historians tell how this demi-god slashed the Gordian Knot, peeked into the Holy of Holies in Jerusalem, and chased off to commune with the Oracle of Amon in the Nile Delta, simply because each of these actions was forbidden to normal men. Afghans and Chinese claim his soldiers established dynasties in their lands. Zoroastrians, Buddhists, and Muslims treasure his memory as someone who helped reveal holy writ. Some Jews suggest that Alexander may be the precursor of the messiah, while the French, typically ignoring time and space, speak of him as a knight of chivalry.[2]

Arrian, the first-century historian who wrote the definitive account of Alexander's adventures, concedes that the young king was moved to strike against Persia because of revenge ("Your ancestors invaded Macedonia and Greece ... you sent aid to the people of Perinthus against my father ... my father was killed by assassins whom, as you openly boasted in your letters, you yourselves hired to commit the crime").[3] While Arrian mentions Alexander's "pomp and arrogance" (7:27), he repeatedly points out the Macedonian's commitment to *oecumene*. Alexander's adoption of Persian dress and the proskynesis, his use of the satraps, the enrollment of Bactrian troops, his encouragement of intermarriage with natives are cited as examples of Alexander's one-world vision. Even the great banquet at Opis in 323 is offered up as proof of the importance of *homonoia*. For here, after denouncing his troops for retreating from India, Alexander calls "every man of you ... my kinsman" (Arrian 7:11). To mark the restoration of harmony, he offered a toast and ordered that public sacrifices be jointly made by Persians and Macedonians.

Alexander may well have envisioned a new world order, but it was one that would be fashioned by him, as the unquestioned ruler. Arrian does not fault Alexander's claim to divine origin (7:28). Instead, the Greek historian laments, "Never in all the world was there another like him" (7:30). But that was just the problem. For when Alexander died, following a bout of dissoluteness and gluttony in Babylon in 323, he left no mechanism for succession, no administrative infrastructure, once the living god was gone.

The Diadochi

Alexander's empire-building is another matter. As soon as the Macedonian departed India, onetime vassals acted as if he had never been in that land. Of 18 Iranian satraps appointed by Alexander, two soon died, one retired, two were never heard of again, and the others were either removed for incompetence or executed for murder or treason. His Greek governor in Egypt, Cleomenes, managed to steal 8000 talents (roughly $16 million), while Harpalus, entrusted with Alexander's personal treasury, embezzled another 5000 talents.

Rebellion, intrigue, and betrayal of Macedonian hegemony became even more common after Alexander's death. Among the *diadochi* (Alexander's aides and successors), everyone, it seemed, had a claim to the throne. Few of these had any success in the next half century as the Hellenistic Age came to resemble the last act of a Shakespearean tragedy. Alexander's half brother, Arridaeus, the son of Philip and a Thessalian mistress, was also a half-wit who was executed by Alexander's mother, Olympias, in 317. Olympias committed suicide the next year. Alexander IV, the demi-god's son by the Bactrian princess Roxanne, died at the age of 12 in 310. Perdiccas, who took Alexander's ring, and with it general command of the Greek armies upon the king's death, was assassinated by lieutenants in Egypt in 321. Craterus, keeper of the royal purse and guardian of Philip Arridaeus, was killed in battle in Anatolia by Eumenes, Alexander's secretary, in 321. Five years later, Eumenes was slain near Susa by Antigonus the One-Eyed. In 301, Antigonus, satrap of Phrygia, was killed at Issus. Alexander's confidant, Antipater, Viceroy in Macedonia and one of two leaders who pushed for the boy-king's succession after the death of Philip in 337, waged a two-year struggle against Greek rebels (the Lamian War) before succumbing to old age in 319. Alexander's generals Peucastas, Peithon, and Antigenes were all burned to death in 316. Cassander was ousted from Macedonia in 297, and Lysimachus, onetime lord of Thrace, was killed at Corupedion in 281.

Of all the aspirants, only four may be called successful — Ptolemy, son of Lagus, who won the governorship of Egypt; Demetrius and Antigonus Gonatas, sons of Antigonus the One-Eyed, whose pirate bands seized control of Macedonia; and Seleucus, governor of Babylon, who was able to expand his holdings from Damascus to the Indian border at the expense of Antigonus, Lysimachus and others. Over the next two centuries, Ptolemaic Egypt, Seleucid Syria, and Antigonid Greece would vie with one another for control of the eastern Mediterranean.

Ptolemaic Egypt

Instead of establishing a commonwealth of equals, Ptolemy fused the Egyptian concept of an all-powerful pharaoh with the god-cult of Alexander. Ten million Egyptians were subjected to the rule of a Greek who demanded to be known as *Soter* (savior). The first two monarchs in this dynasty developed the port city of Alexandria with its 400-foot-high lighthouse, parks, gardens and 100-foot wide streets. The city was also home to Alexander's mausoleum and the great library that contained 700,000 papyri from ancient Egypt and Greece. The Ptolemies undertook reclamation of the Faiyyum depression and distributed delta land (*cleruchies*) as payment for mercenaries. Accepting the Egyptian practices of wife-sister relationship and mummification, Ptolemy II Philadelphus instituted the cult of sister worship. The Greeks secured Egypt's borders to the north and east and beautified captured cities with markets, amphitheaters, and educational stoas. Within a century following Alexander's death, Greek became the language of trade in the eastern Mediterranean.

Those Greeks who ruled Egypt down to 31 B.C. (including the fabled Cleopatra) never renounced their absolute power. Pharaoh was the state, able to dismiss troublesome priests, scribes or feudal lords at a whim. He controlled the distribution of land, whether to temples, royal tenants or sharecroppers who paid a rent of 50 percent in kind. He enjoyed a monopoly in the production of olive oil, papyrus and gold from Nubian mines where countless slaves toiled and perished. The Ptolemies instituted an annual census to ease collection of a tax on goods and personal property. Loans carried interest rates of 24 to 36 percent. The people who profited from such a system were the royal family, their Greek friends and merchants, and a bureaucracy loyal to the Ptolemaic dynasty. In the end, these foreign overlords, who dressed and acted like Egyptians, failed to endear themselves to the impoverished peasants, among whom strikes and riots were common.[4]

The Seleucids

Egypt proved easier to administer than the hodgepodge of peoples conquered by Seleucus I and his heirs. Like the Ptolemies, leaders of this second Greek dynasty hoped to win favor with the masses while ruling absolutely. The Seleucids introduced the calendar fixed on Olympiads, then appeased local pride by reviving the art of cuneiform. They embraced local cults and built temples to honor a pantheon that now included the Seleucid kings.

Babylon, the original centerpiece of the empire, was forced to share glory with a network of cities designed to consolidate control from Antioch on the seacoast to Dura-Europos on the Euphrates and Seleucia on the Tigris.

Ultimately, it was not Mesopotamia, but Syria, that would serve as the heart of the Seleucid empire. There were perpetual threats to the monarchy from within and without. In the east, the Seleucids confronted an Indian empire led by Chandragupta Maurya, as well as rebellious Bactrians and Parthians. In Asia Minor, Bithynia, Pontus, Cappadocia, Galatia, Pergamum, and a host of Ionian city-states claimed independence. To the south, Ptolemaic Egypt loomed, powerful and hostile.

In 223 B.C., Antiochus III ascended the Syrian throne, committed to restoring the empire of Alexander. Within a matter of years, this monarch, known as "the Great," suppressed uprisings in Anatolia and Media, reduced the Persians to tributary status, menaced India, and conquered Phoenicia-Palestine. Astute enough to work out an arrangement for sharing tribute with Euthydemus, king of Bactria, and Philip V of Macedon, Antiochus blundered by intervening in the affairs of mainland Greek states that had negotiated alliances with the emerging Mediterranean super-power — Rome.[5]

The Entry of Rome

Simple geography dictated a close relationship between Italy and Greece. Italy's mixed population of Celts, Latins and Etruscans sought grain, wine, and pottery from the east. Between 800 and 500 B.C., thousands of Greek colonists moved across the Adriatic Sea to establish new homes in Magna Graecia and Sicily. By the middle of the third century, these expatriates were conquered by the Romans in a series of wars—the last of which, named after the Epirote king Pyrrhus, proved to be particularly bloody.

As Rome wrestled with its own nemesis in the western Mediterranean — Carthage — it was content to leave affairs drift in the east. A balance of power seemed to operate among the Antigonids, Seleucids and Ptolemids. As long as none of the Hellenistic successor states become too strong, the Romans could focus their attention upon stripping the Carthaginians of their possessions in Sicily, Sardinia, Spain, and even North Africa. Coincidentally, Rome had just defeated Hannibal and the Carthaginians in the Second Punic War when the call for assistance came from its allies in the east.

Rhodes and Pergamum, both important trading depots, complained that Philip V of Macedon was blocking grain access. City-states that belonged to the Aetolian League and the Achaean League in the Peloponnesus also railed against Philip because he was suppressing piracy, their principal source of income. Rome needed no engraved invitation to intervene against Philip, who previously had boasted of helping his ally Hannibal. In one of the more important battles of history at Cynoscephelae in Thessaly in 197, the Roman legions routed the Greek phalanx. The Roman commander Flaminius subsequently reduced Macedonia to the status of "independent ally."[6]

It was now the turn of the Seleucids to experience the process that was Roman imperialism. In 198 and 197 Antiochus the Great humiliated the Ptolemids (a Roman ally) in Palestine and occupied much of the coast of Asia Minor, presenting a new threat to Pergamum. Flaminius warned Antiochus to evacuate Egyptian and Ionian territory. The Syrian monarch rejected the ultimatum, saying the Romans had no right to instruct him. In the abbreviated war that followed, not even the presence of Hannibal on the side of the Seleucids could stave off defeat.

In the peace of Apamea, Antiochus was forced to cede huge tracts of land to Pergamum and pay an indemnity of 15,000 talents to Rome. The Seleucid kingdom would stumble along for nearly another century, picked apart by Parthians, Armenians, and other nations. But it would never attain the glory or power enjoyed under Antiochus III.

There would be two more so-called Macedonian Wars. Perseus, son of Philip V, led an unsuccessful rebellion between 171 and 167 B.C. Following another great battle at Pydna, the Romans punished all of Greece by (a) purging Aetolia of Macedonian sympathizers; (b) deporting 1000 hostages from Achaea to Rome; (c) destroying 70 towns in Epirus and selling 150,000 people into slavery; (d) sacking the city of Corinth; and (e) forcibly reducing the trade of Rhodes by three-fourths. One last uprising in 149 and 148 would result in the reduction of Greece and Macedonia into subject provinces. A little more than a decade later, Attalus III, king of Pergamum, realizing that there was no hope of guaranteeing the independence of his state, willed Pergamum to Rome.[7]

The End of Carthage

There is an epilogue to the conflict that introduced the Romans to the Middle East and it involves Hannibal. This incomparable foe of Rome, whose army lived off the Italian countryside for nearly 18 years, met his death by suicide while commanding a Bithynian fleet in 182 B.C. His beloved home city, located less than six miles from present-day Tunis, was totally razed in 146 after the Romans eliminated any threat from Greece.

For many historians, the disappearance of Carthage is of passing consequence, but this extraordinary city-state also deserves its moment. Founded by colonists from Sidon in Phoenicia some time between 1000 and 800 B.C., Carthage takes its name from the Semitic Kiryat Hadash or Kart Hadash for "new city." Legend has it that Elissa of Tyre, grandniece of the biblical Jezebel and Ahab, came here with 80 priestesses, carrying a fortune from the temple of Melkart, and established a precedent against intermarriage by killing herself rather than marrying a native chieftain.[8]

As their city population swelled to more than 700,000, the Carthaginians tried to maintain a closed society. Scholars have noted how they discriminated not only between themselves and surrounding populations but also among themselves based on social standing, wealth and education.[9] Libyans and Berber Numidians were welcomed into the army as light infantry and cavalry. But Livy points out such supporting troops were held in low esteem, adding that Hanno, one of the Carthaginian commanders at Syracuse during the Second Punic War, was outraged by the suggestion that he consider the advice of the Libyan Muttines, or as Livy says, that he "be taught his business by a half-breed African."[10]

This sense of aristocratic snobbery permeated the operations of government. Like Rome, Carthage had no tradition of kingship. Its constitution, one of the rare ancient charters, provided for a chief magistrate or *sufet*, not unlike the biblical *shofetim* or judges. Only the most important families in Carthage filled this position or that of general, or served in the Senate and its special judicial body known as the One Hundred.

Like Utica in North Africa, Cadiz and Cartagena in Spain, Carthage was established as a colony of the ancient Phoenicians and its culture reflected Semitic roots. The religious cults in Carthage are identical with those of the ancestral homeland, with Baal Hammon, Eshmoun, Melkart, and Tanis-Astarte all figuring prominently. Of the leaders who opposed Rome in the third century, Hamilcar's name means "servant of Melkart," Hasdrubal is "my help is Baal," and Hannibal is "favored of Baal." Cemetery remains from the so-called

Tophet or ritual burial grounds atop the acropolis prove that the Carthaginians, as their kinsmen in Phoenicia, practiced child sacrifice.

For several centuries, Carthage had no major rivals in the western Mediterranean. Its vessels sailed from the colonnaded double harbor known as Cothon to obtain silver from Spain and tin from Cornwall. Carthaginian colonies dotted the southern coast of Sicily. Then Rome completed its expansion across the Italian peninsula and finished off its Greek rivals on the mainland. What followed was the series of conflicts dubbed the Punic Wars (after the purple dye commonly used by Phoenicians).

During the first war (264–41), astoundingly, the land-locked Romans learned to sail and outmaneuver their rivals on the sea, ultimately expelling the Carthaginians from Sicily. Hannibal swore to avenge this humiliation in the Second Punic War (218–01). In a series of spectacular feats, the Carthaginian commander bested Roman allies in Spain, moved across the Pyrenees Mountains and the Rhone River, then repulsed hostile tribesmen in the Alps before descending into Cisalpine Gaul. Over the next decade, Hannibal would rout every Roman general sent against him, while living off the land with a polyglot army. In the end, Rome's superior numbers (its population was 10 times that of Carthage) proved his undoing. Departing Italy with the remnants of his army, Hannibal would finally be defeated, but not pacified, by Scipio Africanus at Zama in August 202.

Hannibal's very existence was a source of concern for the Roman revanchist Cato the Elder, who preached the destruction of Carthage, and the Numidian overlord Masinissa, who sought the city for his own capital. When Hannibal was elected sufet for the year 196, Rome became alarmed and sent a commission to North Africa. Forced out of office by Carthaginian collaborators, Hannibal fled eastward to join Antiochus of Syria, then Prusias of Bithynia in the final struggle against Rome. His legacy endured, for Roman demagogues continued to rave against him long after his death, using the fear of a second Hannibal among other justifications for the Third Punic War that resulted in the leveling of Carthage in 146.

Hannibal: The Question of Race

In recent years, there have been several attempts to assess the racial background of the Carthaginian leader. Some historians have concluded that Hannibal should be portrayed as a black African. The available evidence suggests something different. The Carthaginians, like most Mediterranean peoples, may have been dark or olive-skinned, but two presumed portrait busts of Hannibal now in a museum in Copenhagen and Volubilis, Morocco, show a curly, fair-haired young man who resembles a Roman aristocrat. The same is true of a coin minted at Cartagena, c. 230 B.C., which is regarded as a portrait of Hannibal's father Hamilcar Barca; a silver shekel minted at Cartagena during the Second Punic War showing the head of Hasdrubal Barca, Hannibal's brother; and the figure purported to be Hannibal inscribed upon a silver hexadrachma piece from Spain, struck in 221 B.C., the year Hannibal was appointed general.

It is difficult to believe that the Roman historians would have ignored Hannibal's supposed black African roots. Polybius, one of the earliest writers to stress analysis of sources, makes no mention of this. Nor does Livy, whose bulky tome on the Second Punic War includes page after page of astronomical phenomena, strange births, and imagined tactics and speeches on the field of battle. Livy rails against Hannibal's "inhuman cruelty, a more than Punic perfidy, a total disregard of truth, honor and religion" (30:4), but he, like Polybius, makes no mention of black African origins. This is all the more remarkable because Roman historians did stress the African origins of Syphax, Masinissia, and Jugurtha, rulers of Numidia, and also of the Moor Lusius Quietus who was later raised to consulship by Trajan.

For the racially conscious Romans, the terms *Mauri, Afri,* or *Ethiopian* were generally reserved for peoples of sub-Saharan Africa. Such peoples might be enslaved, but as in Carthage intermarriage was discouraged. The appearance of blacks in battle provoked the Romans at Philippi when the forces of Brutus targeted an Ethiopian in the enemy's front ranks. Says J. P. V. D. Balsdon, "We cannot say in what circumstances the sight of a black man could be inauspicious."[11] How Hannibal could have bedeviled Rome for nearly four decades and no one notice he was black would be one of history's greatest mysteries.

The Hellenistic Legacy

It is possible, as some have done, to wax poetic about the impact of the Hellenistic period, with its call for brotherhood, construction of beautiful cities, introduction of a common language, expansion of women's rights, and promotion of physical as well as mental education. It is equally possible to level a broadside at an age that produced little in science, literature or art . As Henry Bamford Parks gloomily pronounced, "The empire was culturally sterile."[12]

Both judgments are extreme. The Hellenistic Age was not the age of wonder nor were its people on the verge of some great socialist uprising as W. W. Tarn has implied.[13] It was a time when major breakthroughs in science were achieved by the engineer Archimedes, the astronomer Aristarchus (responsible for the heliocentric theory of the universe), the geographer Poseidonius, and the mathematician Euclid. It was a time when primitive physicians discovered the nature of blood circulation and human nerves. Cisterns and aqueducts improved water supplies to cities. Though the concept of big as beautiful replaced the delicate works of Hellenic Greece, few can dispute the glory of the Pharos at Alexandria or the Colossus that spanned the harbor at Rhodes. Learning was encouraged, in Egypt where the priest Manetho reconstructed history back to the Old Kingdom, in Babylon where Berossos did the same for his people, in Rome where Polybius described the governments in his world, even in Judaea where Flavius Josephus attempted an historic telling of the adventures of the Jewish people. It was in Judaea that the many intellectual and religious concepts percolating through the Hellenistic world — Babylonian star worship, Persian Mithraism and Zoroastrianism, Egyptian veneration of the mother goddess Serapis or Isis, Greek stoicism, skepticism, and Gnosticism — would blend with teachings of Judaism to change the course of human history by giving rise to Christianity.

9

The Jews: Historic
Roots and Definitions

Historic Definitions

Of all the peoples of the ancient world only one has manifested its presence on all of the continents at one time or another. For 4000 years, the Jews have moved through history, sometimes as catalysts for progress, more often confounding observers. A "fossilized civilization," Arnold Toynbee once called them. A dangerous, misanthropic people who contributed nothing to culture according to Apion, Cicero, Voltaire, Carlyle, Wagner and Hitler.[1]

It would be more legitimate to say that the Jewish experience reflects universal history. Where bigotry is rampant, Jews have generally been the first victims. In humane societies, Jews have flourished. There are 18 million Jews in the world today, less than one-quarter of one percent of the world's population, yet three of the most influential thinkers of the 20th century—Albert Einstein, Sigmund Freud, and Henri Bergson—were Jews. "Something to conjure with, what this small people has done!" said the artist Marc Chagall. "When it wished, it brought forth Christ and Christianity. When it wanted, it produced Marx and Socialism."[2]

Semite. Hebrew. Israelite. Judaean. Jew. Zionist. Israeli. Each has a specific meaning and by defining them, we may better understand the fabric of Jewish History.

Semites. The Old Testament (Gen. 5:32) states that Noah was 500 years old when he fathered three sons destined to overspread the earth. From Japheth came the people of the north—Gomer, Magog, Tubal, and Ashkenaz. From Ham came: Cush, Seba, Nimrod, Mizraim, Caphtor, Sidon, Canaan and Heth, an arc of tribes encompassing the Egyptians, Philistines, and Hittites. And from Shem came: the people of Elam, Ashur, Aram, Arpachshad, Shelah and Eber, seven generations removed from Abram, the first Hebrew.

The Bible and pseudo-science converged at the end of the 19th century. Scholars trying to classify the world's populations detected peculiarities of language that suggested more than casual contact among peoples located in the same area. The syntax and sound of Hebrew, Arabic, Assyrian, Ethiopic, and Phoenician were so similar that these peoples, believed to be descended from Shem, were labeled Semites. Implied in all of this was a homogeneity of race and culture that was, of course, nonsense.

Anti-Semite. Divisiveness among Semites is evidenced in the controversy surrounding the term *anti–Semite*. Coined in 1873 by Wilhelm Marr, the neologism reflected this German's deep-seated hatred of Jews. Through the remainder of that century, anti–Jewish leagues flourished on the continent under the banner of anti–Semitism. Hitler's supporters were unabashedly anti–Semitic as they sought to exterminate Jews. Unlike other terms that have specially cruel significance for Jews and have since been appropriated by sociologists, anti–Semitism still has only one accepted dictionary definition — animosity toward Jews.

In the wake of the Holocaust, the concept of anti–Semitism has been decried most loudly by those who were its greatest practitioners. Anti-Semitism was banned in the Russian constitution of 1917, but until recently the Soviet government promoted pamphlets, books and cartoons reveling in anti–Jewish stereotypes. The Soviets (as well as Iran and Syria) required Jews to carry national identity cards (though the state denied Jews comprised a separate nationality), prevented them from emigrating, and discriminated against them in education and jobs. Small wonder that tens of thousands seized the opportunity to flee when Gorbachev granted permission in 1989.

Harassment and imprisonment constitute the most blatant forms of anti–Semitism. This bias draws life from a hoary list of canards— deicide (the Jews killed Christ), satanism (they possess demoniacal powers), greed, usury, and unethical business practices, cowardice, disloyalty, double loyalty, and profiteering from wars that kill off the best youth of the white race. Jews have been described as ugly, dirty, pushy, arrogant, stiff-necked, aggressive, offensive, domineering, intransigent. They have been condemned for land-grabbing and sexual activity among Gentiles, for spreading disease, then devising inoculations against these same ailments, for inventing capitalism, communism, then fluoridation, all as part of a scheme to seize control of the world. Anti-Semitism illustrates the vulnerability of a minority. Bigots draw strength from their own numbers and may invent any charge against this perceived enemy.

Hebrew. A descendant of Shem was Eber (Gen. 10: 21–25), whence the word *Hebrew*. Linguists suggest the Semitic root connotes a mixed, unorganized people who crossed rivers, as Abraham did when he came from Syria into Canaan. Six generations removed from Eber, Abraham was the first biblical figure referred to as a Hebrew (Gen. 14:13) who meshes well with the Late Bronze Age culture.

Israelite. Another two generations would pass, during which time God would make a covenant with the sons of Isaac (Gen. 17–19). One of those was Jacob who, with the assistance of his mother, Rebecca, managed to gain blessings intended for his elder brother, Esau. Fearful of what Esau might do, Jacob fled eastward to the ancestral homeland of Haran. Twenty years later, he returned to Canaan with his own wives and children. At a ford of the Jabbok called Peniel Jacob encountered a watersprite or angel. The two wrestled, with Jacob gaining the upper hand. Before releasing the spirit, Jacob demanded another blessing. He was granted a name change, Israel, for "one who has striven with God" (Gen. 32:3–29). From that time, the patriarch's sons— Reuben, Simeon, Levi, Judah, Isaachar, Zebulon, Benjamin, Dan, Napthtali, Gad, Asher, Joseph — were known as Israelites. It remained so between 1750 and 1580 B.C. Enslaved for several hundred years, the Tribes of Israel were emancipated at the instigation of the prophet Moses. They then wandered in the desert for more than a generation before conquering the land of Canaan about 1200 B.C.

Palestine. What some call Palestine has been known by that name only since the Roman period.[3] In ancient times, the Egyptians referred to the eastern littoral of the Mediterranean as Upper Retenu or Kadesh. *Canaan* was one of several biblical terms applied to the land of Jebusites, Kenites, Kenizzites, Kadmonites, Rephaim, Girgashites, Moabites, Perizzites, and Amalekites (Gen. 15:19). Like the ancient Israelites, the Philistines, from whom the term Palestine derives, were latecomers, arriving in this region between 1200 and 1100 B.C. Known as Pulesti, they were part of a migratory band of sea peoples set in motion from their native Crete either by natural calamities or famine. Repulsed from Egypt about 1190, this fierce people established themselves in the cities of Ekron, Gath, Ashdod, Ashkelon, and Gaza. Armed with iron weapons and powerful war wagons, the Philistines continued to vex kings of Israel for the next 400 years. The Greek historian Herodotus was so impressed with their prowess that he dubbed the entire region Palestine.

The Kingdom of Israel. From a tribal confederacy bound together by its monotheistic creed evolved a united government directed first by *shofetim* (judges, warlords like Gideon, Deborah, Samson), then kings (Saul, David, Solomon). With both Hittite and Egyptian empires temporarily exhausted, the ancient kingdom of Israel was able to flourish from Mesopotamia to the Gulf of Akaba. Solomon's mines produced copper in the south, his fleets traded spices and gold with Sheba's empire in Ophir (Yemen), and his diplomats secured cedar from Tyre to grace the great temple in Jerusalem. By 960, however, jealousies in the royal household led to a division into two states—Israel in the north covering the land of 10 tribes and Judaea in the south, incorporating the rocky hills that belonged to Benjamin.

For nearly 300 years, the northern kingdom survived with its capital at Samaria. It was a time when the prophets Amos, Hosea, and Micah criticized the corruption, callousness and sacrilege of Samaria. It was also a time when Assyria dominated the Middle East. Grown haughty and overconfident, Israel confronted the armies of Tigleth-Pileser III and Sargon II in the eighth century. The result was devastation and deportation, leading to the puzzle of the Ten Lost Tribes of Israel. The probability is that those Israelites who were not slain in the Assyrian conquest were fused with other captive populations to make up the Samaritans, a people that clung to quasi-Jewish practices at their cult center of Mt. Gerizim. Though memorialized in the New Testament saga of the Good Samaritan, the Samaritans were denounced by ancient Jewish writers and reciprocated the enmity of their southern neighbors.

Since the destruction of ancient Israel, this region — which was the site of Tekoa (home of Amos), Anata (the birthplace of Jeremiah), Halhul (the grave of Jonah), Bethel (where Abraham erected the first altar to Yahweh), Shiloh (home of Eli, where the Ark of the Covenant was lost to the Philistines), Mizpeh (where Joshua commanded the sun to stand still), and Hebron (with its tomb of the patriarchs)—has been a source of constant unrest.[4]

Judaeans. The destruction of Samaria left the smaller kingdom of Judah. By paying regular tribute to the Assyrians and then courting the strongest successor to Assyrian hegemony (Egypt, Babylon), Judah endured another century before it, too, was laid waste. The Chaldaeans under Nebuchadnezzar ravaged the city of Jerusalem and its 500-year-old temple in a series of raids between 597 and 586 B.C. Most of the Jews were banished for 50 years, a tale recounted in the books of Jeremiah and Lamentations as the Babylonian Captivity. When Cyrus of Persia conquered Babylon in 539, that exile ended. Returned to their land beyond the rivers, the *Yahudim* (people of Judah) were permitted to rebuild their temple and their communal life. Until the arrival of Alexander the Great, they lived quietly within the satrapies of the Persian Empire.

The Maccabees. From 330 to 200 B.C. Judah, or Judaea as it came to be called by the Romans, was a shuttlecock bandied about among the successors of Alexander. First one, then another Greek lord conquered the land that separated Ptolemaic Egypt from Seleucid Syria until 198 B.C. when Antiochus III annexed the land. By this time, the people of Judaea, market places, palaces and temples were made over after Greek models. Greek officials, merchants, settlers, and slaves introduced the Greek language to Judea. Popular names of the period — Theodotus, Menelaus, Aristobulous, Jason, Lysimachus, Alexander, Antigonus — reflected Greek influence. Hellenistic customs and beliefs challenged religious practices that formed the core of Jewish identity.[5]

The crisis came to a head in the reign of Antiochus IV (175–64) who called himself "Epiphanes" (the visible god) and whom Jews labeled "Epimanes" (the madman). Joseph Klausner of Hebrew University called Antiochus "a nervous, fearful degenerate."[6] An impetuous ruler who scandalized the Damascene court by dancing drunkenly at banquets and wandering the streets with what Polybius termed "shady company," Antiochus spent a decade in Rome as a hostage before returning home to usurp the Syrian throne from his nephew. Mindful of Roman power, yet contemptuous toward Ptolemaic Egypt, Antiochus was driven to duplicate the conquests of Alexander. When a major campaign into Egypt in 168 B.C. was blunted by the threat of Roman intervention, he found a convenient scapegoat in the Jews.

Forty thousand persons were purged for alleged pro–Egyptian sympathies as Greek troops razed the walls of Jerusalem and occupied the Temple compound. There followed a series of edicts (*gezerot,* (evil decrees) intended to fuse subject peoples into one. On the Temple mount, sacrifices were offered to Zeus, Dionysius, Athene, Baal, Ashdod, and Astarte. At pagan altars raised about the country, the king's birthday was celebrated each month by the roasting of a pig. Jews were required to partake of this ceremony and encouraged to intermarry. Most ominous, the practice of the Judaism was to be suspended under penalty of death. Ancient documents tell of the burning of Torah scrolls, of parents who had their sons circumcised being cast into pits, of martyrs like the 90-year-old holy man Eleazar, or the mother Hannah who witnessed her seven sons being tortured to death.

Others adopted a more activist response, emulating the priest Mattathias who came from Modiin ten miles west of Jerusalem. Rather than participate in pagan ritual, this grandson of Hasmon seized a weapon and struck down two men who were conducting the service. Mattathias and his five sons (Simon, Eleazar, Judah, Johanan, and Jonathan) directed the rebellion of the Maccabees (a term derived either from the Hebrew word for "hammer" or an acronym for the invocation "who is like unto thee, O Lord"). When their father died a year later, the sons continued to wage guerilla warfare against the Syrians. Then, late in the year 165 B.C., on the 25th of Kislev, they delivered the Temple Mount from the Hellenizers.

Three years to the day of its desecration, the Maccabees rededicated the sanctuary. According to the *Apocrypha* (books not incorporated into formal biblical text), only one cruse of pure oil was available, enough to illuminate the area for a single day, yet the small vessel burned for eight days. In Jewish tradition, the miracle of the lights provided evidence of divine intervention in the small nation's triumph over a powerful foe. For the next several centuries, the festival of Hanukkah became one of the important political-religious dates in the calendar for Jews who remained fixated by their victory. They ignored the fact that the Syrians were occupied with the Romans to the west, the kingdom of Pontus to the north, the Parthians to the east, that the citadel in Jerusalem would not be taken till 161, and that the Hashmonaean dynasty would be plagued with internal cabals for nearly a century until Roman armies entered Judaea in 63 B.C.

Jewish self-government came to an end, if not with the arrival of the Triumvir Pompey, then with the subsequent designation of Herod, son of Antipater, as puppet king in 37 B.C. Although the Herodian line made a pretense at autonomy, actual authority resided with the procurator, a Roman sub-governor responsible to Damascus. Notions of independence were dashed in two rebellions: first in the Great Jewish War of 66 to 70 when Titus, son of the Roman Emperor, sacked the Judaean capital;[7] and second, in the abortive messianic uprising of Simon Bar Kochba between A.D. 132 and 135.[8]

Though the Jewish people, already spread throughout the Roman world from Spain to Babylonia, showed a resilience for survival, their state did not. Perhaps a million residents of Judaea died as a result of warfare, gladiatorial games, or slavery. For the crime of teaching Judaism, a number of sages were flayed, roasted in pans, or pricked with spears. Once more, the sanctuary in Jerusalem was desecrated, converted to the worship of pagan deities. Jerusalem was renamed Aelia Capitolina in honor of the Roman emperor Hadrian, and Jews were denied entry to the city on pain of death. To obliterate the memory of this obstinate, troublesome folk that had resided in this land for more than 1200 years, the Romans renamed Judaea Syria Palaestina, or Palestine, as it has been known in the West.[9]

Zion and Zionism. What sustained a dispersed people through the next 1700 years was Zionism, here defined as the belief that the Jewish people are entitled to a land in the region now called Israel. Rabbis concerned about biblical rights in Judaea and Samaria, as well as anti–Zionists who view modern Israel with scorn, may quarrel with such definition, but the yearning for Jewish freedom in Zion is of ancient origin. In the Old Testament (2 Sam. 5:6–9 and 1 Chron. 11:4), Zion denotes a Jebusite hill fortress conquered by David. Entymology suggests the name comes from the Semitic root *tziyyah* (dry place) or *metzuyyan* (distinguished). In any event, this promontory in southern Jerusalem became more than a shrine for the faithful who believed it to be the resting place of David. Hundreds of years before the Roman destruction of Judaea, Zion came to be identified with the Jewish people. Like Britannia and Columbia, symbols of Great Britain and America, she was personified as a woman. The prophets (Amos 1:2, 6:1; Joel 1:2, 4:17, 4:21; Micah 3:12, 4:2, 4:8, 4:10, 4:11; Zeph. 3:14, 3:16; Zech. 1:14, 2:10, 2:14, 8:2–3, 9:9, 9:13) redound with references to Zion either as a geographical location or as Rachel, weeping for her children. So too Psalms 93, 135, 137, 146, 149, 150; Jeremiah 9:18, Lamentations 1:42, 2:8, 4:2. The most eloquent testimony to the importance of Zion within the Jewish faith, however, comes from the book of Isaiah. Here the distinction between city and people is resolved, for the two really are one. Here Zion appears first as a woman (49:14) or a wilderness (64:9). Her haughty daughters (3:16) are wasted (4:3) as a booth in a vineyard (1:8). Yet God promises an end of her tribulation — "For Zion's sake, I will not hold my peace" (62:1). He tells her to don beautiful garments, diadems, and a crown of beauty (52:1). From the stock of Jesse a redeemer will come to Zion (59:20). And from Zion, this city of justice and righteousness (3:5) shall go the law (2:3) that commands total peace and brotherhood (11:6), and all will call Zion the city of the Lord (60:14).

The importance of Zion to Judaism cannot be overstated. Jews pray toward the east and Jerusalem. Every year at Passover, people in far off lands chant "*L'shana hab'ah b'rushalayim*" (next year in Jerusalem) and hope that if they do not live to see the restoration, then perhaps they might be interred with some soil from the Holy Land. Every year at *Rosh Hashanah* (New Year's) or *Yom Kippur* (the Day of Atonement) Jews pray for the return of God's mercy to Zion as an enduring habitation. Every day, observant Jews who make use of the traditional *siddur* (prayerbook) find reference to Zion in seven prefatory hymns, in the *Kedushah* (veneration of God's name), upon opening the Ark, in blessings after the reading of *Haftarah* (prophetic writings), and most important, the *Amidah*, 18 silent benedictions that form the core of Jewish prayer and which include: "May our eyes behold when thou returnest unto Zion in compassion. Blessed art thou, the Eternal who restoreth his divine glory unto Zion."

In little *shtibls* (synagogues) from Podolia to the Bronx, Jewish aspirations have centered upon Eretz Israel. Marriages have been sealed with the breaking of a glass, commemorating the destruction of the Temple. Homes are left uncompleted, meals lack a course, to remind people how incomplete their lives are in exile. Virtually all Jewish holidays are derived from the Holy Land, whose air, the Talmud advises, "makes one wise." Eight hundred years before Theodor Herzl, the Spanish Jewish poet Judah Halevi rhapsodized, "Zion wilt thou not ask if peace's wing shadows the captives that ensue thy peace, left lonely from thine ancient shepherding. Zion, O perfect in thy beauty." And again: "For my heart is in Zion and my eyes are there." And again: "My heart is in the East and I am at the edge of the West." And again:

> O city of the world with sacred splendor blest.
> My spirit yearns to thee from out the far-off west;
> A stream of love wells forth when I recall thy day,
> Now is thy temple waste, thy glory passed away.
> Had I an eagle's wings straight would I fly to thee,
> Moisten thy holy dust with wet cheeks streaming free.[10]

Despite Roman proscriptions, Jews returned to pray at the Western Wall, the last vestige of their sacred Temple. Despite harassment by Byzantines, Saracens, Crusaders, and Ottoman Turks, they filtered back to create important seminaries in Safed, Hebron, Tiberias, and Jerusalem. Throughout history, they translated their passion for deliverance from the squalor of ghettos and mellahs to support for all manner of Messianic pretenders—an unnamed Cretan who promised to walk across the Mediterranean c. A.D. 400; three aspirants from Abbasid Mesopotamia in the eighth century; two more from Spain in the 12th century; David Alroy, who in 1144 promised to fly them through the night sky from Baghdad; David Reubeni and Solomon Molcho, purged by the Inquisition before 1530; and Sabbatai Zevi, a scoundrel who was forced to embrace Islam before his death in 1676. Sabbatai Zevi excited Jews from Poland (where they recently had undergone a wave of massacres) to Holland and England (where Jews were selling property in anticipation of the return to Zion and where the London Stock Exchange was actually quoting odds of 10–1 against that return). Messianic charlatans were able to exploit the religious passions of Jews against the grim realities of persecution and massacre.[11]

Modern Political Zionism. Three things were lacking for Zionism to achieve success: mobility, money and a heightened sense of consciousness. Despised and degraded, Jews were the pawns of Christian monarchs who regarded them as necessary financial evils. Their stay in any country was temporary, till a pretext for their explusion (religious hysteria, outbreak of plague, over-indebtedness of the lord) could be arranged. So it was that the wandering Jew was ousted from the British Isles in 1290, Bohemia a century later, portions of France in the 15th century, and Spain in 1492. Not until September 1791, two years after the issuance of the Declaration of Rights of Man, were Jews granted civil rights in France.[12] With Napoleon, who literally demolished the gates of Jewish quarters in Italy and the Rhineland, Jews were no longer confined to the ghetto. Encouraged by reforms and tolerance advocated by political leaders like Adolph Cremieux, Benjamin Disraeli, and even Tsar Alexander II, they could move more freely in and out of societies. What had once been only a religious dream, Zionism, might now actually be put into action.

That is where the Jewish philanthropists figured. The age of liberalism spawned the Brodskys in Russia, railroad tycoon Maurice de Hirsch of Munich, British insurance magnate Moses Montefiore, and the house of Rothschild, with centers in the major capitals of Europe. Each of these financiers was committed to helping his people, but in his own way. It might take the form of soup kitchens and blankets for the denizens of Bialystok's attics and coal cellars. De Hirsch's Jewish Colonization Society tried to promote Jewish agriculture in the Pampas of Argentina. Montefiore negotiated in vain with Mehemet Ali for a 50-year rental of more than 100 villages in Palestine in 1839. Shortly after, Edmund Rothschild's agents purchased acreage from Arab absentee landlords as the nexus of a Jewish colony in the Holy Land. Such proposals were flawed, however, because they depended upon the largesse of the philanthropists. Condescension, rather than affection, was the underlying sentiment of such charity. As Theodor Herzl once told de Hirsch, "You breed beggars."[13]

All over Europe, men like Samuel David Luzatto, Moses Hess, Rabbi Zvi Kalischer, Yehudah Alkalai, Shmuel Moghilever, Peretz Smolenskin, Moses Lilieblum, and Dr. Leon Pinsker encouraged Jews to form a great assembly bound for Palestine without waiting for the messiah. In Russia, groups of students calling themselves by the acronym BILU attempted to rouse the Jewish population to follow them to the stony wastes of Palestine. In Poland in November 1884, 35 delegates of *Choveve Zion* (Lovers of Zion), a more respectable alliance of Jewish scholars and political leaders, came together at Kattowice, a few miles from an obsure military settlement that would acquire infamy in the 20th century — Oswiecim — to propose the mass migration of Jews to a land of their own in Palestine. In America, the poetess Emma Lazarus, a member of Choveve Zion, echoed her colleagues, calling for a program of education in Hebrew literature and history and a rejection of assimilation. Because Jews were confronted with blind intolerance and ignorance in virtually every clime, Emma Lazarus concluded, "They must establish an independent nationality."[14]

In 1897, the Austrian journalist Theodor Herzl would convert the aspirations of nearly 100 generations of Jews into reality when he summoned the first Zionist Congress at Basel. That Congress created a modern, mass-based political movement that culminated in the rebirth of the state of Israel in 1948.

Gentile Zionism. Over the course of time, the plight of Jewish homelessness won the sympathy of many Gentiles. Lord Shaftesbury, Laurence Oliphant, Henri Dunant, George Sand, Arthur Balfour, David Lloyd George, John Adams, Harry Truman, William Blackstone, William Moorehead, Dwight Moody, and Billy Graham responded favorably to the concept of Zionism. Some of these were motivated by fundamentalist impulses that the Jews were, as the evangelist Moody declared in 1877, "God's people" and that a restoration of their homeland might presage the messianic era.[15] Some, like the cynical Lloyd-George during World War I, subscribed to the notion that a Jewish state might tip a mythical international Jewish power toward the Allies. Others felt much as Lyndon Johnson when he was asked by Leonid Brezhnev at Glassboro in 1968 why the United States supported Israel.

Reminded that such policy inevitably bred widespread Arab hostility, Johnson said, "We do so because it is right."[16] The president's response was substantially the same as that offered by the British diplomat Mark Sykes to Zionist leader Nahum Sokolow in May 1918. Wrote Sykes:

> Your cause has about it an enduring quality which mocks at time; if a generation is but a breath in the life of a nation, an epoch is but the space 'twixt a dawn and a sunrise in the history of Zionism. When all the temporal things this world now holds are as dead and forgotten as the curled and scented Kings of Babylon who dragged your forefathers into captivity, there will still be Jews, and so long as there are Jews, there must be Zionism.[17]

Israelis. Not all of those who live in the modern state of Israel are Jews, or, for that matter, Zionists. More than 100 ethnic groups—including Poles, Yemenites, Ethiopians, Bokharans, Georgians, English, Turks, Greeks, Hungarians, Romanians, Libyans, South Africans, Russians and Americans—are represented among the nearly six million Jews in the land. A tiny fragment even oppose the existence of the state in which they reside because the messiah has not yet appeared. Within the boundaries of pre-1967 Israel live more than a million Arabs. Most are either Sunni or Shiite Muslims, but Israel's population also numbers 200,000 Christians, including Greek Catholics, Greek Orthodox, Roman Catholics, Maronites, Anglicans, Presbyterians, Baptists, Lutherans, Armenians, Copts, Ethiopic and Syrian Orthodox. Fifty thousand Druze inhabit villages from Mount Carmel to the Golan Heights, and the Baha'i faith maintains its spiritual center atop the bay of Haifa.

Efforts have been made by the Ministry of Religious Affairs and the Department of Antiquities and Museums to safeguard the institutions of these and other sects. The government has responded to attacks on Islamic holy places such as the Dome of the Rock and the al-Aqsa mosque by creating checkpoints manned by Israeli security and military. The shrines are policed solely by Muslims.

No one claims that these national or religious groups live in perfect amity. Discrimination and jealousy among the various Jewish ethnic groups is well chronicled. There are legitimate grievances about gaps in housing, jobs, self-determination that underlie the Arab *Intifada*. On occasion, however, opportunists have attempted to exploit unrest for their own purposes, as in October 1990, when rumors that Jewish zealots intended to restore the ancient priestly worship on the ruins of Muslim holy places led to massive riots involving Arabs and Jews at the Temple Mount. That the modern state of Israel has not succeeded in forging a common identity from dozens of diverse peoples is as much the fault of human nature as the perpetual state of non-peace that has diverted billions of dollars that might better have been applied to irrigation, industry, and education than to implements of war.

10

The Jews and Their Culture

Tradition and Practice in Judaism

The oldest of the monotheistic faiths that came out of the Middle East, Judaism had its roots in the revelations of Moses and the prophets. Since the destruction of Herod's temple and its priesthood, there has been no sacred synod or pope to determine religious dogma for Jews. By tradition, rabbis (literally "teachers") have safeguarded the law (*Halakhah*).

At the beginning of the 18th century, the pietist Israel ben Eliezer, known as the *Baal Shem Tov* (Master of the Good Name) ushered in the age of Hasidism. Despite the opposition of traditionalists, this movement that stressed emotion practically absorbed East European Judaism. Self-proclaimed *tzaddikim* (saints) directed the lives of zealous followers down to the very clothes these sectarians wore. At the same time, modernists in the West were praising the *Haskalah* (the Jewish Enlightenment) that provided opportunities for Jews to free themselves from anachronistic practices and compete with the Gentile world.

For the past 200 years there have been three major branches of Judaism — Orthodox, Reform and Conservative. The Orthodox claim a continuation of the historic traditions of Judaism, namely:

- prayer in Hebrew three times daily
- the keeping of the Sabbath, with abstinence from all forms of work
- segregating women from men during religious services
- the keeping of *kashruth* (dietary and other laws of ritual purity)
- rejection of intermarriage
- reverence before God by wearing skullcaps, earcurls and beards

Reform Jewry, the product of assimilationist impulses in Central Europe after the Napoleonic period, has an opposite thrust:

- prayer should be in a vernacular rather than rote Hebrew
- women and men are equals in prayer services as well as the rabbinate
- in this age of modern hygiene, kashruth is a voluntary concept
- observance of Saturday as a day of rest is a matter of personal choice
- Jews should observe traditional holidays for one, not two days, and dress in contemporary fashion

Between the two stand Conservative Jews, also a product of Bohemia, but attempting to reconcile traditional Judaism with the pressures of a Gentile world. Conservative Jews:

- utilize a bilingual *siddur* (prayer book)
- cover their heads and wear prayer shawls, but permit women to sit together with men in services
- encourage observance of kashruth and Sabbath worship

In Europe, before the Holocaust, Orthodox Judaism predominated. Of those who acknowledge affiliation with a major religious movement within the United States, perhaps one million are Orthodox, 1.3 million Reform, and 1.3 million Conservative. The figures reveal not only a division, but also a disinclination of fully one-third of America's Jews to identify with any religious institution.[1]

Sephardim and Ashkenazim

Since the second century C.E. when Jewish merchants accompanied Roman legions into the Rhineland, Jews have divided into two groups—the *Ashkenazim* (European Jews whose name derives from Gen. 10:3) and the *Sephardim* (Eastern Jews whose name refers to the land of Spain, Obad. 9:20). The Sephardim produced sages like Maimonides in Cordoba, Baruch Spinoza in Holland, and the first American Jewish communities. Merchants, ministers and poets, Sephardic Jews even developed a hybrid Spanish-Hebrew language (Ladino) in the late Middle Ages.

In modern times, it was Jews with Yiddish roots who produced Zionist leaders, scientists and philosophers. Some Western Jews harbored prejudicial views of Jews from Arab lands. Among the Ashkenazim, too, there has always been a tendency to categorize people according to the area from which they came. Thus the *Daytscher* or *Yekke* (modern German) has been contemptuous of his Eastern cousins, whether *Poylisher*, *Litvak*, or *Ungarn*. At the bottom of this social ladder was the *Galitzianer*, poverty-stricken, unworldly and unworthy of intermarriage.

The People Israel

Jews do not constitute a race, nationality, or (according to the U.S. government) an ethnic group. They call themselves *Am Olam*—an eternal people. The term *people* is broad enough to embrace confessional and Marxist Jews, Ashkenazim and Sephardim, Reform and Orthodox. It is valid, for as a people Jews share a common past, common aspiration, common language, and common culture.

The Common Past. Jews have a tradition that they are a Chosen People, but 4000 years of persecution have transformed that concept into an "ol fun yiddishkayt" (yoke of Jewishness, a bearing witness to the frailties of humanity). The 2000 years of homelessness following the destruction of the Judaean state have been especially painful. Labeled by some the *Diaspora*, a Greek word implying a voluntary dispersion, Jews speak instead of the *Galut*, Hebrew for "exile." Under Christianity and Islam, Jews were shut away in ghettos where they were subjected to pogroms. Any telling of the Jewish past must include the following litany of victims in massacres:[2]

1. The Roman Conquest (63 B.C.–A.D. 135)	2,000,000
2. Byzantine-Sassanid persecutions	250,000
3. Arab Conquest	250,000
4. Early Medieval Europe (Visigoths, Franks)	500,000
5. Crusaders in the Rhineland (1095–1300)	50,000
6. European Expulsions (1000–1500)	200,000
7. Ritual Murder/Host Desecration/Well Poisoning	250,000
8. Spanish and Portuguese Inquisitions	50,000
9. Wars of the Reformation	100,000
10. Muslim pogroms to the 20th century	250,000
11. Chmielnicki "Deluge" (17th-century Poland)	500,000
12. Cossack massacres in 18th century	100,000
13. Wars of French Revolution/Napoleon	50,000
14. Pogroms in Western Europe 1815–1848	25,000
15. Russian pogroms in the 19th century	50,000
16. World War I (retreating armies in East)	100,000
17. Independent Ukraine under Petlura (1918–1920)	150,000
18. Interwar pogroms in Romania, Hungary, Poland	50,000
19. Miscellaneous	100,000

What makes this list all the more chilling is that the total murdered in two millennia comes to little more than five million. Between 1933 and 1945, during the Holocaust, the Nazis and their allies succeeded in killing more than six million. In 1939, approximately one of 200 persons in the world was a Jew. One of seven killed in World War II was Jewish. Half the dead in Nazi concentration camps were Jews. Two of every three European Jews were killed, almost 40 percent of all the Jews in the world. An entire generation, perhaps 1.5 million children under the age of 14, was obliterated. All surviving Jews have been permanently scarred by the horrors that occurred in civilized Europe only a generation ago. As Rabbi Herbert Schwartz once said, "Sooner or later, every Jewish child wakes in the middle of the night, screaming, the spectre of those bones before him."[3] The Israeli writer Amos Elon put it into a Middle Eastern perspective when he declared, "Every day we fight the Arabs and win. Every night we fight the Nazis and lose."[4]

The Common Aspiration. What sustained Jews through the years of persecution was Zionism, the belief that the Jewish people were entitled to a land of their own in Eretz Yisrael. The population would be predominantly, not exclusively, Jewish, in a land whose borders were negotiable. Not just religious Jews, but secular ones as well, acknowledged the necessity of restoring dignity to this derelict people. Speaking before the Lemel School in Palestine in February 1923, Albert Einstein said: " This is a great age, the age of liberation of the Jewish soul, and it has been accomplished through the Zionist movement, so that no one in the world will be able to destroy it."[5]

The Common Language. Long before Eliezer ben Yehudah invented words for "postage stamp" or "aeroplane," Jews shared a common language. Hebrew was their means of communication with God and with one another. There were differences in pronunciation between the Sephardic and Ashkenazic, but Hebrew was never a dead, liturgical language. In Spain, during the Golden Age, Solomon ibn Gabirol and Moses ibn Ezra composed love poems in Hebrew. During the bleakest days of Tsarist oppression, Judah Leib Gordon,

Chaim Nachman Bialik, and Saul Tchernichovsky breathed messages of hope through Hebrew. If a Yemenite encountered a fur-hatted Galitzianer in the alleys of Jerusalem, they could still converse in Hebrew. It came as no surprise, then, that with the birth of the political Zionist movement at the end of the 19th century, Hebrew was selected as the formal language of the Jewish people.

The Common Culture. The core of Jewish culture is Judaism. However a Jew identifies himself — by religion, nationality, even cuisine — his connection with his people inheres from a grandparent who may have kept kosher and prayed in a *shtibl* (small synagogue). The basic concepts of this creed are contained in sacred writings, the cycle of holidays, and a value system.

The Sacred Books. *Tanakh* is the Jewish version of the Bible. An acronym for *Torah* (teaching), *Neviim* (prophets), and *Ketuvim* (writings), the Tanakh consists of 39 canonical books. These include Judges, Isaiah, Jeremiah, Ezekiel, the 12 minor prophets, Psalms, Proverbs, Job, Ecclesiastes, Daniel, Ezra, Esther, Samuel, Chronicles, etc. Writings like Tobit and Maccabees, accepted in the Roman Catholic canon, are said to be of dubious authority. The first five books of the Tanakh (Genesis, Exodus, Leviticus, Numbers, and Deuteronomy) are known as the books of Moses or *Torah*. Identical with Christian holy writ, the Torah has been inscribed on rolls of leather or parchment and deposited in a special niche (*aron kodesh*) along the eastern walls of synagogues facing Jerusalem.

Talmud. Comprehension of the written law (*Halakhah*) requires extensive study, hence Talmud, from the Hebrew root *lomed* (study). Because the Torah was so cryptic (there are no specifics for the verse where Moses is instructed by God "thou shalt slaughter," Lev. 1:5), because sections seem to contradict one another, there was a need for an explanation of the written law. Between 200 B.C. and A.D. 500 1000 rabbis offered their opinions on practices that originated in the time of the prophets, laws instituted by Ezra, decrees of the Sanhedrin, scientific and medical information, moral fables, and principles of logic. Their rationale for expounding this "oral" tradition was that God had given these additional ordinances *al pe* (by mouth) to Moses at Sinai and that they were the inheritors of the Mosaic teachings. Regarded as sacrosanct by many Jews, the Talmud obtained its present multi-volume form under the direction of the second-century *posek* (sage) Judah ha-Nasi.

Hukim (Codes). How was the common Jew supposed to know how to behave? That information was supplied by simpler compilations of *Halakhah* stripped of Talmudic argument. The first of these codes, *Halakhot Pesukot*, came from the *gaon* (eminence of the Sura academy in Babylonia) Rabbi Yehudai. Additional instructions were supplied by a number of medieval sages. Rabbi Sholomon Yitzhaki (1040–1105) lived through the horrible epoch of the Crusades. From his home in Troyes, France, Rashi, as he was known, wrote words of encouragement to the Jewish communities of the Rhineland. Rashi's rule that Scripture must be evaluated in both its literal (*peshat*) and common sense (*derash*) remains a standard of rabbinics to the present. It was common to juxtapose his writings next to paragraphs of Talmud and Torah in Hebrew writings. A century after Rashi, Moses ben Maimonides (*Rambam*, 1135–1204) offered consolation to forced converts in Spain and Yemen. His *Mishneh Torah*, a 10-year labor, tried to explain how a wise man behaves. Maimonides' *Guide for the Perplexed* applied Aristotelian logic to questions of the nature of the universe, miracles, the Messiah, prophecy and the soul. Maimonides did not intend this last work for the masses, but Joseph Karo (1488–1575) did have commoners in mind when he issued the *Shulchan Aruch* (prepared table) from Safed in northern Palestine. Karo's work outlined what kinds of food to eat, when to visit the sick, what direction to urinate.

When amended by Moses Isserles of Cracow, the *Shulchan Aruch* became the basic book of conduct for Orthodox Jews to the 20th century.

The Jewish Holidays. The Jewish year, based on the lunar calendar, falls short of the actual solar year by eleven days. Under a system elaborated in the medieval period, seven intercalary months are added every 19 years to synchronize this calendar with that of the West. Apart from the Sabbath, which is to be observed every seventh day, the following are the principal holy days:

Rosh Hashanah (literally "head of the year") ushers in 10 days of religious introspection. It was in the month of Tishri that the world supposedly was created, so new year's was observed at this time of the year. Leviticus 23:24–25 proclaims the day "a holy convocation." From the time the *shofar* (ram's horn) sounds no work may be performed, as Jews are called to affirm their responsibility to God.

Yom Kippur (Day of Atonement) marks the 10th in the Days of Awe. From sunset to sunset (the length of the Jewish day), no one may work, eat, drink, engage in sex, or any other mundane activity. Jews ask forgiveness for sins committed and omitted not only by themselves, but for those too haughty or cynical to pray. It has been said that if all the other days of the calendar disappeared, there would still be Yom Kippur, a day of Judgment.

Succoth (Booths). The Feast of Tabernacles was proclaimed in Exodus 23:16 and Leviticus 23:33–43. During the weeklong holiday in Tishri, Jews were to reside in makeshift shanties, reminiscent of the temporary booths their ancestors used in the flight from Egypt. A thanksgiving that emphasized God's gifts of trees and fruits, Succoth was one of three annual pilgrimages to Jerusalem required in ancient times.

Simchat Torah (rejoicing of the Law). Two days after Succoth, Jews celebrate the reading of the final portion of the Torah. It is a time of gaiety, dancing, flags, and apples, followed by the resumption of Torah reading from Genesis through Deuteronomy.

Hanukkah. The festival of dedication occurs in Kislev, the Jewish month approximating December. A time of gift-giving and lighting of a nine-branched candelabrum, Hanukkah has evoked new interest in Jews who see a parallel in the Maccabean tale and the state of Israel or because the holiday offers an alternative to Christmas.

Purim. The festival of lots in March tells the story of Esther, the Jewish woman who interceded with the fourth-century king Artarxerxes II to prevent a massacre of Jews in Persia. During this celebration, the *Megillah* (Book of Esther) is recited in a single synagogue setting. Children wave *gragers* (noisemakers) to blot out the name of the villain Haman whenever it is mentioned. Purim is supposed to be a happy time for Jewish children, who dress up in costumes of biblical figures, participate in carnivals and eat prune or poppyseed cakes called *hamentaschen*.

Passover. Beginning with the 14th day of the month of Nisan, the first month of the calendar, Jews are required to abstain from leavened bread for seven days, as a reminder of their deliverance from Egypt (Ex. 12:14–20). The second of three pilgrimage festivals, Passover commences with a *Seder* (meal) at which Jews read from the *Haggadah* (a compilation of biblical passages, songs, and prayers). They eat unleavened *matzah*, bitter herbs (as a reminder of slave life), *harosheth* (a mixture of apples, nuts, cinnamon and wine representing the bricks used by Egypt's slaves), greens (suggesting springtime), an egg (evocative of eternal life), and a roasted shankbone (symbolic of sacrifice at the ancient temple), and pray for the redemption of those who are not yet free. It is a grotesque irony that Passover, which emphasizes the immediacy of freedom (Jews give thanks for "all this, which the Lord did for *me* when *I* came out of Egypt"), has been a favorite time for attacks against Jews.

Shavuot. (Feast of Weeks, Lev. 23:15–21). The third of the mandatory pilgrimages in ancient times, Shavuot was associated with the spring grain harvest. Its Christian counterpart is Pentecost. Tradition has it that the Decalogue was given to Moses on Shavuos and the holiday is sometimes referred to as *zeman matan toratenu* (the season of giving of our Torah).

Tisha B'av. The ninth of Ab is one holiday not mentioned in the Torah. It has been described as a Fourth of July in reverse, for some of the worst calamities have befallen the Jews on this summer (August) day. Tradition has it that the Babylonian destruction of Solomon's Temple occurred on the ninth of Ab, 586 B.C. According to Josephus, the forces of Titus entered and burned Herod's great edifice on the ninth of Ab, A.D. 70. Sixty-five years later, Roman legionnaires slew the messianic aspirant Simon Bar Kochba at Betar and effectively ended the Jewish state on the ninth of Ab. In 1492, Ferdinand and Isabella ordered the expulsion of Jews from Spain beginning with the ninth of Ab. And in 1942, Nazi authorities instructed the Jewish Council in Warsaw, Europe's largest center of Jews, that deportations would begin on the ninth of Ab. It is a mournful holiday, one commemorated by Jews who identify with their historical degradation by removing their shoes and reading from the books of Jeremiah and Lamentations.

Tenets of Judaism. The ancient Mosaic Code actually consists of 613 *mitzvot* (commandments), including 365 that begin *lo taaseh* (thou shalt not) and 248 that open with the word *aseh* (thou shalt). Various rabbis have attempted to reduce the tenets of Judaism to their most basic form. For some, the *Shema* (declaration of the unity of God, Deut. 6:4) must be the last words recited by a Jew. Others like Hillel and Rabbi Akiba ben Joseph stressed Leviticus 19:18 ("love thy neighbour as thyself"). It was Maimonides who gave modern Judaism its most concrete statement of faith, the *Yigdal* (from a term praising God.) For Jews, these 13 articles of belief were (1) the existence of God; (2) his unity; (3) God's incorporeal nature; (4) his eternity; (5) his absolute claim on adoration; (6) prophetic inspiration; (7) Moses as the greatest prophet; (8) the divinity of the Torah; (9) the unalterability of the Torah; (10) God's providence; (11) just reward and punishment; (12) the promise of messianic deliverance; and (13) resurrection. Some of these concepts (the immutability of Jewish holy writ and physical resurrection) reflect Muslim and Christian influences of the Middle Ages.

Jewish Ethics. Every society has its own system of values and rules of proper conduct. In the United States, we speak of the Protestant Ethic, the notion that honesty, fair-dealing, thrift will result in success. Like the Ten Commandments, such rules are not always followed. The important thing is that societies have a commitment to them. All Jews, even secular ones, are indebted to the *derech eretz* (the way of the land, straight path) that espouses:

Daat (wisdom). "The People of the Book" have long appreciated that study unlocks mysteries of the universe. Love of learning has been translated to respect for teachers and books. In Europe, the rabbi or *melamed* occupied the seat of highest honor. Among Jews, a frayed prayer book is not discarded or consigned to the trash heap. Because it is a source of knowledge, it must be given a religious burial in a Jewish cemetery.

Emet, Din, Shalom (truth, law, peace). The *Pirke Avot* (sayings of the Fathers) in the Talmud advises that the world stands on three things—truth, justice and peace. Chief among these is peace, from the Hebrew root for "perfection." The Jewish striving after peace is evident in the greeting "Shalom Aleichem" (peace be unto you), in the use of the word three times in the mourners' *Kaddish*, in the *Amidah* (silent prayers) that ask "lasting peace at all times," and in the prophetic teachings (Isa. 2:4) where nations are advised to hammer their weapons of war into ploughshares.

Chesed (piety). In Micah 6:8 we read that three things are required of man — to do justly, love mercy, and walk humbly with God. In Jewish society, the man punctilious in temple attendence and kashrut was accorded great esteem.

Tzedakah. Literally charity, Tzedakah really means a commitment to social justice. Deuteronomy 16:20 states, "tzedek, tzedek, tirdof" ("justice, justice, shalt thou follow"). Amos speaks of justice rolling down as waters and righteousness as a mighty stream (Amos 5:24). The eradication of injustice and oppression are the goals of Rosh Hashanah prayers. From Maimonides came an eight-rung ladder of charity, beginning with people who give grudgingly, moving through those who give less than they should or who puff themselves up with their philanthropy, and culminating with those who give assistance to help others achieve self-sufficiency. The concept of giving is ingrained from childhood when Jewish children at religious school are asked to make tzedakah contributions. From such resources grew community institutions, social welfare agencies, mikvehs (ritual bathhouses), orphanages, old age centers, emigrant aid societies, free loan societies, the *Khevre Kadisha* (volunteers to watch over the dead before burial), job training centers, soup kitchens, the *Vaad Kashruth* (board to administer kosher laws).[6]

Rachmones (compassion). Justice must be tempered with mercy or compassion. The Hebrew term *rachmones* comes from *rechem* (a mother's womb) and suggests a warmth missing from the word *pity.* Judah Halevi likened the Jewish people to the heart of mankind, the organ that feels whenever there is any suffering in the world. For Elie Wiesel, Jews were man's memory. Whatever metaphor is applied, Judaism holds that one cannot truly comprehend the plight of others unless he imagines himself in the other's place.

Tachlis (purpose). Although the book of Ecclesiastes scorns man's achievements as fleeting vanities, he is nevertheless enjoined to rejoice in his work, to make the world a better place (Eccl. 2:21, 3:13, 3:22) "for that is his portion." Rather than meditating upon an eternity of bliss in the afterlife, Jewish tradition is to make meaningful every moment of life.

Naches (joy). No one can live without some joy. Whether it be a spouse, child, song, sport, or vocation, things done in moderation make for a fuller life. Said Maimonides: "Good deeds are such as are equibalanced, maintaining the mean between two equally bad extremes— the too much and the too little."

Hadar (pride). Derived from the Hebrew for "glory" or "splendor," hadar means self-respect, faithfulness, dignity, a sense of worth. Instead of internalizing accusations of bigots and asking what is wrong with themselves, Jews reject the dynamics of discrimination. To those who declaim that Jews have done nothing to foster world progress, they respond that all free peoples can make a contribution to civilization.

Though Jews currently constitute less than one-fourth of 1 percent of the world's population, they have accounted for better than 15 percent of the Nobel laureates. In medicine, the figure is 25 percent. It may even be higher for the field of economics. In the past 30 years, Nobel prizes for literature have been awarded to S. J. Agnon, I. B. Singer, Saul Bellow, Elias Canetti, and Nadine Gordimer. In the same period, Elie Wiesel and Menachem Begin received the Nobel Peace Prize. Nuclear physics has been so dominated by Jewish theoreticians like Albert Einstein, Max Born, Niels Bohr, Lisa Meitner, Leo Szilard, Eugen Paul Wigner, Edward Teller, Isadore Rabi, and J. Robert Oppenheimer that the Nazis denigrated it as *Judenphysik.* The great names in psychiatry — Sigmund Freud, Max Kahane, Alfred Adler, Hugo Heller, Max Graf, Hilbert Silberer — all were Jews. A Jewish immigrant from Germany, Levi Strauss, traveled to the goldfields of California and revolutionized the clothing industry with trousers stitched from denim. In Germany, Siegfried Marcus developed a horseless carriage in Mecklenburg 20 years before August Daimler produced his first automobile. In 1890, again in Germany, David Schwartz secured a patent for the first rigid airship. The English astronomer William Herschel made significant modifications of telescopes in the 18th century. The Italian Cesare Lombroso is called the father of criminology. Isaac Singer invented the sewing machine; Abraham Stern the first calculating machine; and Emil Berliner, the microphone and disc phonograph record. All were American Jews. Six of eight major Hollywood studios (MGM, Universal, Paramount, Columbia, 20th-Century Fox, and Warner Brothers) were founded by Jews. *TIME* magazine once reckoned that 80 percent of the professional comedians in America were of Jewish background. From Jacques Offenbach's "Can Can" to Irving Berlin's "Easter Parade" and "White Christmas," Jews have enriched the musical heritage of countries where they lived.

Since emancipation Jews can point to healers (Elie Metchnikoff, Paul Ehrlich, Bela Schick, Boris Chain, Selman Waksman, Karl Landsteiner, Casimir Funk, Jonas Salk and Albert Sabin), painters (Camille Pissarro, Marc Chagall, Chaim Soutine, Amadeo Modigliani, Ben Shahn), authors (Heinrich Heine, Sholom Aleichem, Franz Kafka, I. L. Peretz, Stefan Zweig, Arthur Miller, Theodor "Dr. Seuss" Geisel, Bernard Malamud), rabbis (Stephen Wise, Abba Hillel Silver, Judah Magnes), political leaders (Chaim Weizmann, David Ben-Gurion, Otto Rathenau, Leon Blum, Pierre Mendes-France, Felix Frankfurter, Judah Benjamin, Henry Kissinger), financiers (the Warburgs, Kuhns, Strausses, Seligmans, Bronfmans, Rosenwalds, and Annenbergs), women reformers (Ernestine Rose, Henrietta Szold, Jessie Sampter, Lillian Wald) and athletes (Hank Greenberg, Sid Luckman, Benny Leonard, Max Baer, Dolph Schayes, Mark Spitz, Vic Seixas and Nancy Liebermann).[7]

It may be just as easy to cite individuals—Dutch Schultz Flegenheimer, Meyer Lansky, Lepke Buchalter, and Bugsy Siegel—who have damaged the reputation of Jews. The latter merely confirm the point that Jews are no more saintly than any other people. By denying Jews the right to settle down or own land in the Middle Ages, non-Jews created a caste of transient money-lenders. By shunting them into squalid sections, Jews became "dirty" and diseased. Yet despite all the adversity and discrimination, the ancient values endured. In 1928, the Austrian Felix Saltzmann penned one of the great books of the 20th century. Ten years later, Saltzmann was arrested by the Nazis because he was a Jew. By then, his book, an allegory of family love, an expression of Jewish values, had been translated into a host of languages. Eventually, Walt Disney would immortalize it in the film version—*Bambi*.

11

Judaism and Christianity

Legacy of Deicide

The major stumbling block for Jews over the past 2000 years has been friction with Christians, who, echoing St. Augustine (354–430), have taught that Jews were "a wicked people," "the children of Satan," "haters of truth" who had "crucified their saviour." For this crime of deicide, the seed of Cain were eternally cursed, doomed to wander the earth without respite. Said Augustine, "To the end of the seven days of time, the continued preservation of the Jews will be a proof to believing Christians of the subjection merited by those who in the pride of their kingdom put the Lord to death."[1]

Many of the early church fathers echoed the polemical bishop of Hippo. Origen (185–259) accused Jews of cannibalism and sexual orgies. Ambrose of Milan called the synagogue "a house of impiety, a receptacle of folly." From St. John Chrysostom, archbishop of Constantinople (344–407), came the admonition that "God hates you." This teaching of contempt was the stuff that pogroms are made of. Wrote Gregory Baum: "The church made the Jewish people a symbol of unredeemed humanity; it painted a picture of the Jews as a blind, stubborn, carnal, and perverse people, an image that was fundamental in Hitler's choice of the Jews as the scapegoat."[2]

Not until Vatican II in 1965 was the charge of Christ-killing formally lifted from the Jews. The much ballyhooed encyclical, *Nostra Aetate*, makes no specific reference to deicide or to prayers for perfidious Jews recited at Easter. Instead, out of deference to Third World sensitivities, the encyclical speaks of Buddhists, Muslims, and other non-Christians before addressing "Abraham's stock" in its final section.[3]

Animosity toward Jews persists even though Jesus, Mary, Paul and all the apostles were Jews. Peter (first bishop of Rome), James (bishop of Jerusalem), along with other Jewish Christians, continued to worship at Herod's temple. Indeed, the Nazarenes were regarded as a Jewish sect until Bar Kochba's revolt in 132 made it impossible for Christians to pay loyalty to two messiahs. At that time, the Jewish Christians, whose numbers had been eclipsed by Gentile Christians, migrated to Perea in Jordan, where they vanished from history.

Ancient Judaea

Once absorbed by the Roman Empire in 63 B.C., Judaea was expected to behave as docilely as Spain, North Africa, Gaul, Britain, Egypt and Greece. Quite the opposite proved true. No people gave more trouble to the Romans than the Jews, who, it seemed, were in a perpetual state of rebellion. There were several reasons for this:

The national humiliation. Only 100 years had passed from the time when the Maccabees restored self-esteem to the Jewish people before the Romans snuffed out the independence of Judaea. Hanukkah was very important to this nationalistic people. Fixated with the memory of a past miracle, they fantasized about a second triumph at the expense of the Romans.

Degradation of the House of Herod. Despite his efforts to ingratiate himself to the Jewish people by marrying Mariamne, the last princess of the Hashmonaean dynasty, and constructing a great temple in Jerusalem, Herod was regarded as an Idumaean pretender. Insecure on his throne, he ordered the mutilation of Mariamne's brothers, Alexander and Hyrcanus, slaughtered Pharisees who opposed his rule, and eventually executed three of his own sons. Brutality and sexual license marked the reigns of his successors—Herod Antipas, Agrippa I, and Agrippa II. Imperial puppets, they supported Rome in its conflict with the Jews and actually rode in the legions' victory parades.

Self-deification of the Roman rulers. Following the reign of Augustus, the Roman empire was ruled by Tiberius (A.D. 14–37), an effete monarch noted for his animosity toward Jews; Caligula (37–41), a monster given to "unnatural relations" with men, women, actors, animals, and the moon; Claudius (41–54), a weakling whose reign was punctuated with suicides and murder; and Nero (54–68), the would-be poet who persecuted Jews and Christians while presiding over the burning of Rome. Each of these degenerates demanded veneration as a living god.

The oppressive nature of Roman taxation. Conquest by Rome brought with it benefits—paved roads, aqueducts, a universal system of law and coinage, secure frontiers. From a Roman standpoint, it was only fitting that provincials pay for the blessings of civilization. No one could object to a *portoria* (customs tax) imposed at every harbor. Greater resistance might be expected to the *stipendium* (a levy for quartering and feeding troops). Periodically, the Romans ordered a census, the counting of heads in their native villages. The Romans also demanded of each household a *decuma*, one-tenth of the annual produce from the soil, rentals, pasturage. Under their practice of farming out taxes to corporations, the decuma often amounted to 40 or 50 percent of a family's income. The rapacity of *publicani* (tax collectors) combined with usurious interest charged by *negotiatores* (money lenders) prompted some freeholders to turn to brigandage.[4]

The incompetence and thievery of Roman procurators. The dozen *procurators* (administrators) sent to Judaea in the first century were not merely thieves, but bumblers. They permitted the public desecration of Torah scrolls and interference with Sabbath worship. In the 20-year period leading up to the Great Jewish War, they shuttled seven men in and out of the post of high priest, appropriated funds designated for temple use, and crucified followers of messianic aspirants. The worst was Pontius Pilate (26–36), described in ancient sources as a vindictive man with "a furious temper" who indulged in bribery, insult, theft, executions without trial—in short "ceaseless and supremely grievous cruelty." Eventually, this tyrant was recalled to Rome to stand trial for his abuse of power.[5]

The messianic expectation. For a thousand years, the Jewish people awaited the coming of a second King David. They read in Isaiah and Ezekiel the promise that idol-worshipping nations would be laid waste. Repeatedly in the inter-testamental period, they turned to figures who, they hoped, would redeem them. Among those who claimed divine inspiration were Judah the Galilean (crucified with 2000 followers in 4 B.C.), the Teacher of Righteousness (a shadowy figure in Essene literature allegedly martyred a generation before Jesus), Theudas (beheaded with his two sons and 400 followers by the procurator Fadus in A.D. 42), an Egyptian who promised to raise the dead from the Mt. of Olives in the prefecture of Felix (c. A.D. 55), another unnamed figure from the time of Festus (A.D. 59–61), Simon Bar Giora and John of Gischala (who led their people to catastrophe between 66 and 70), and Simon Bar Kochba, the only figure in Jewish history to be acclaimed the messiah by rabbinic authorities of his day.

Sectarian Division

Any chance of victory over the Romans was squandered by the division that informed ancient Jewish society. The principal source for that era, Flavius Josephus, has supplied us with in-depth analyses of the major groups:[6]

Sadducees. Taking their name from the priest Zadok in the time of David, the Sadducees constituted the aristocracy of Judaea. Wealthy merchants, landlords, the temple hierarchy, they controlled the Sanhedrin (Council Court of 71), the body charged with implementing Jewish law. Because of their favored position, they brooked no disturbance that might provoke the Romans. Strict constructionists in their interpretation of the Torah, they rejected many Talmudic teachings. For them, messianic deliverance must come from the House of David, but at some future, undetermined moment. Among the three to five million people of ancient Judaea, no more than 10 percent could have been Sadducees.

Pharisees. From the Hebrew *perushim* (separatists), the Pharisees made up the majority who supported the oral tradition. Their concern for minutiae in daily practice and disparaging remarks in the Gospels have given a negative connotation to the word *Pharisee*. In ancient times, however, they were the liberal Jews, insisting upon broadening the spirit of Scripture. From their ranks came critics of temple corruption and the sacrificial cult. Pharisaic inspiration derived from the prophets and was expressed best in the teachings of Hillel, a Babylonian sage who became *Nasi* (president of the Sanhedrin) in 31 B.C. Hillel proclaimed the seven basic rules of hermeneutics, allowing greater flexibility in interpreting the Bible. From Hillel also came a number of aphorisms: "If I am not for myself, who will be? If not now, when? And if I am only for myself, what am I?" "Be of the disciples of Aaron, love peace, love mankind, thus lead them to the law." And one that may have been transmitted to Jesus through Hillel's disciples in Galilee: "Do not unto others that which you would not have them do unto you; this is the whole of the Torah, all the rest is commentary."

Hillel's messiah would be a prince of peace, but there were many Pharisees who espoused self-emancipation from the Romans. One such leader was Shammai, who advised "speak little, but do much and receive all men with a friendly countenance." Stern, irascible, with no tolerance for proselytes, it was Shammai who counseled continuous opposition to Herod and his patrons.

Zealots. The zealots or Kannaim claimed to be an extension of Shammai's activist teachings. A small group, generally identified with Galilee, they regarded obedience to any Roman law — the census, loyalty oaths, payment of taxes — as sacrilege. Some of the more extreme zealots, known as *sicarii* (dagger men) pursued their goals by assassinating Romans, Greeks, and Jewish collaborators on the streets of Judaea's cities. Others were among the doomed followers of the messianic pretender Judah, the Galilean, and the thousand souls who committed suicide following a protracted siege at the hilltop stronghold of Masada in A.D. 72.[7]

Essenes. Josephus wrote at length about these ascetics who resided in monastic communities like Khirbet Qumran, which numbered 2000 men, women and children. Fastidious in personal hygiene, they wore clean white linen, buried their excrement in the soil, and bathed daily in the waters of the Jordan River. The German-Jewish scholar Heinrich Graetz devotes a dozen pages to their communal society, repugnance for vows and wealth, and their reputation for working medical miracles.[8] Since 1947, recovery of a number of ancient documents known as the Dead Sea Scrolls has shed additional light on the practices and beliefs of the group whose name derives from the Syriac for "pious ones."[9]

Christians have been particularly fascinated by these so-called Morning Baptists because of parallels with the early church. Apart from similar rites of confession, sanctification by water, and age limits for bishops and presbyters, both groups were known as "Elect of God," "Sons of Light," "God's Plantation," "the Temple of God." John the Baptist lived the life of an Essene, wearing a simple cloak, eating locusts and honey, and washing in the Jordan. So many of Jesus' teachings — the virtue of poverty, aversion to marriage, rejection of oaths and the temple cult — are so like those of the Essenses that some rabbis have ventured to guess he may have spent years in an Essene commune. In one respect, however, Jesus differed markedly from the Essenes and that was his concern for the *Am ha-Aretz* (the dregs of Judaean society). His association with prostitutes (Mary Magdalene), publicani (Matthew), and lawbreakers (Simon Peter), though consistent with his ministry to all people, would have been regarded by pietists as scandalous.

For those seeking a link between the Essenes and Jesus, translation of the Dead Sea Scrolls provided a boon. The ancient scrolls revealed a figure, the Teacher of Righteousness, who resembled Jesus. The Teacher was a man appointed by God to supplement the old laws with a "new covenant." He was opposed by a high priest (like Caiaphas) who at first "enjoyed a reputation for truth, but who grew arrogant." The Teacher propounded a messianic theory of salvation based upon the sacrificial lamb/suffering servant of Isaiah. Captured and scourged in Jerusalem, he predicted that he would "stand on my watch and post myself on my tower and scan the scene to see whereof he will denounce me." Executed, the Teacher reappeared to his disciples on the Day of Atonement. Eventually, men like vultures came and punished the priest and his minions "because of the mischief he had done to him who taught the law right."

About 40 years would elapse from the death of the Teacher until men would take up arms and "relapse in the company of the Man of Falsehood," precisely the time period between the crucifixion of Jesus in A.D. 30 and the sack of Jerusalem in 70. Back in 1947, some Christians, anxious to discover evidence of an historical Jesus, equated the Teacher of Righteousness with Christ. Today most scholars would disagree. Carbon testing, paleography, and other evidence place the Essene writings at least one generation before the birth of Christianity. The Teacher then would be either an historical character whose unfortunate end was similar to Jesus or a prophetic metaphor offered by critics of the priestly caste.

The Historical Jesus

What do we know of Jesus, his origins, teachings, and end? Was there even an historical Jesus? The question is not as preposterous as it sounds. One scholar who helped translate the Dead Sea Scrolls, John Marc Allegro, lecturer on biblical studies at the University of Manchester, went beyond seeing a mythic counterpart of the Teacher of Righteousness. Allegro contended that Jesus, along with all biblical figures, was nothing but the invention of an ancient fertility cult. Jews and Christians were devotees of the same primitive mysteries known to Athenians and Romans. Where the others drank wine and danced to heighten their religious and sexual experiences, Jews and Christians supposedly employed the *amanita muscaria*. It was this hallucinogenic mushroom that was the core of their religion. To protect this secret, the Old and New Testaments were invented, as codebooks for the initiated. Joseph's coat of many colors, Esau's red hair, the Psalms of David, virgin birth, the twelve apostles were, in Allegro's telling, euphemisms for varieties of the sacred mushroom.[10]

Allegro's theories have been discredited, of course. But he raised an interesting point, one which could never have been discussed a century ago. Apart from the Gospels and the Quran, there are few references to Jesus in ancient sources. Seutonius and Tacitus mention followers of "Chrestos," blamed for the fire in Rome under Nero. Pliny labels members of the new faith "the most misanthropic" of men. Philo of Alexandria, a Jew who recorded events of Pilate's administration, does not mention Jesus. Neither does Justus of Tiberias. Those references that appear in the works of Flavius Josephus are questionable. A passage in Josephus' *Great Jewish War* gives the basic tale of Jesus' divine birth, his ministry and miracles, persecution by Caiaphas, the condemnation before Pilate, and his resurrection offered by the New Testament. Unfortunately this passage, known as the Slavonic Josephus, has been exposed as a medieval fabrication. Experts agree that some unknown Balkan monk, in his eagerness to find reference in historical works, decided to help out Josephus several hundred years after *The Great Jewish War* was written.[11]

Because of that emendation, doubt has been cast over the authenticity of a second reference in *The Annals* of Josephus. There, in the midst of discussion of Pilate's abusive policies, Josephus writes:

> About this time there lived Jesus, a wise man, *if indeed one ought to call him a man*. For he was one who wrought surprising feats and was a teacher of such people as accept the truth gladly. He won over many Jews and many of the Greeks. *He was the messiah*. When Pilate, upon hearing him accused by men of the highest standing among us, had condemned him to be crucified, those who had in the first place come to love him did not cease. On the third day he appeared to them restored to life. For the prophets of God had prophesied these and myriads of other marvelous things about him. And the tribe of Christians, so called after him, has till up to now not disappeared [emphasis added].[12]

The passage is disturbing for many reasons. First, it is virtually identical with the Slavonic Josephus. Second, Josephus was a Sadducee, an aristocrat, hence unlikely to declare that Jesus "was the messiah." Finally, it is impossible to reconcile this single reference with the 20 paragraphs that follow dealing with a minor scandal in the temple of Isis in Rome. Surely, Josephus would not have dismissed the story of the true messiah in such a cavalier fashion. Perhaps Josephus was merely rendering the tale of Jesus in a sarcastic fashion. In 1972, scholars from the Hebrew University in Jerusalem offered a different version of Josephus based on a 10th-century Arabic text:

At this time there was a wise man who was called Jesus. And his conduct was good, and (he) was known to be virtuous. And many people from among the Jews and other nations became his disciples. Pilate condemned him to be crucified and to die. And those who had become his disciples did not abandon his discipleship. They reported that he had appeared to them three days after his crucifixion, and that he was alive; accordingly, he was *perhaps the messiah* concerning whom the prophets have recounted wonders [emphasis added].[13]

The difference between the two versions is slight, but significant. In the second, Josephus does not intimate that Jesus is anything but a man. He credits Jesus with no miracles and says the disciples claimed he returned from the dead. Reporting the tale in its basic form, he adds the major qualifier — "accordingly, he was perhaps the Messiah." Even allowing for editing to fit Islamic perceptions of Jesus, the passage still falls awkwardly in the midst of Josephus' narrative and bears the stigma of illegitimacy associated with the Slavonic Josephus.

There is one other source that specifically mentions Jesus and that is the Talmud. The references are not pleasant — the Nazarene is attacked as a deceiver, a false prophet, a *mesith*— and they are from the late Talmudic period, but at least they appear to confirm his existence.[14] Such negative comments, unfortunately, prompted bigots to consign the Jewish holy book to the flames in the medieval period.

The Nativity Story

Failing any other sources, we have to rely upon the Gospels for details of the life of Jesus. If we accept the traditional account that he was 33 when he was crucified, it appears his life spanned the period between 4 B.C. and A.D. 30. The Jewish lunar calendar should resolve any dispute whether his death came in 29, 30 or 33. Jesus went to Jerusalem to celebrate the Passover and was crucified on a Friday. In the year 30, the holiday began on a Thursday evening (the time of the first seder/Last Supper). Counting back, the most likely year of his birth was 4 B.C. That was the last year of Herod's reign and accords with the slaughter of innocents mentioned in the Book of Matthew. It was also a time of great excitement among the Jews because of the messianic uprising of Judah the Galilean. The chronological error that exists in the Western calendar may be attributed to a sixth-century monk, Dionysius Exiguus, assigned the task of determining when Jesus was born.

By tradition, Jesus' birth date is reckoned as December 25, a time when a great star appeared in the heavens. Astronomers now believe the star of Bethlehem was the conjunction of Saturn, Jupiter, and Mars. The phenomenon occurred, in all probability, some time in the spring. It certainly makes more sense for shepherds to be tending their flocks by night in March. December 25 was chosen by convention because it already held significance for other religions. Devotees of Mithra celebrated the *dies natalis invicti solis* on this date. Hanukkah fell very close by, as did the Roman Saturnalia.[15]

The Nativity story presents several intrinsic problems. There is disagreement among Gospel writers as to the destination of Joseph and Mary after the birth of Jesus. Attendance of Magians, priests of the Persian polytheistic cults, would hardly have been likely, let alone desirable at the manger. Jesus' messianic connection with the house of David is traced back through the line of Joseph. Yet we are told Mary was a virgin, a claim dismissed in the Quran ("Sister of Aaron, your father was never a whore monger, nor was your mother a harlot").[16]

The concept of divine or miraculous birth as presented in the Gospels is commonplace in ancient writings. Zeus literally was the father of the Greeks through dalliances with mortal women. Apart from the Cretans, Heraclids and Athenians, Zeus also sired Alexander the Great. Gilgamesh was two-thirds divine. Noah, Abraham, Apollonius of Malo, and Perseus all supposedly were born of virgins. Romulus and Remus were the illegitimate offspring of Mars and the Vestal Virgin Rhea Silva. Legend has it that Gautama Buddha was conceived when his mother was visited in a dream by a sacred white elephant. Birth came from the right side of his mother as she stood in a garden. Light flooded the world, the blind saw, the deaf heard, and the lame ran to the infant who took seven steps in four directions and announced that this was his last incarnation. About the same time, a series of astral phenomena accompanied the birth of Zoroaster. Centuries later, Muhammad's mother literally glowed when she gave birth. As the babe was born, spotless, with the umbilical already cut and tied, light shone all the way from Mecca to Syria. Earthquakes in Persia extinguished the sacred fires of the Zoroastrians and a calf, about to be sacrificed, spoke, announcing the birth of the seal of the prophets. The Christian Nativity, with its emphasis on the Madonna, may even share elements with the cult of Isis.

What Jesus Looked Like

The years of Jesus' youth prove even more problematic than his birth. Christian writers have dealt awkwardly with James, Joses, Judas, Simon, and two girls who are listed either as the children of Joseph or Jesus' stepbrothers and stepsisters. Following an appearance in the Temple at the age of 12 where he astounded the elders with his knowledge (a feat claimed by Josephus for himself) the next 18 years of Jesus' life are summarized by Luke: "And Jesus increased in wisdom and stature, and in favor with God and man" (Luke 2:52).

When Jesus next appears, he is already committed to the ministry, his years of training with John the Baptist behind him. Amazingly, after 2000 years, we still do not know exactly what he looked like. Over the centuries, certain conventions have been established. Whether in mosaic or on film, Jesus is portrayed as a tall, slim man with a full head of hair and a beard, white-robed and gentle.

Several years ago, the discovery in Jerusalem of a set of bones of a man who had been crucified sparked interest among Christians who wondered whether these might not be the remains of Christ. The controversy was laid to rest when sages assured the public that the bones—from a short, stubby man — did not conform to the structure associated with Jesus. Of course, in searching for his body amid the ruins of Jerusalem, they disregarded the belief that Jesus had been physically taken to heaven.

One object that supposedly gives evidence of the appearance of Jesus is the Shroud of Turin. First displayed in Lirey, France, about 1350, the sacred relic, which measures 4.4 by 1.1 meters, bears an almost photographic image of a bearded man, remarkedly similar to the popular image of Jesus. Markings on the cloth suggest that the man had been scourged. Reddish marks at the scalp indicate some form of barbed cap had been thrust on the head. Similar markings appear below the right eye and along the cheeks. The shoulder areas are blurred due, perhaps, to chafing caused by some heavy weight. The knees are damaged, as if from repeated falls. More reddish marks, perhaps from nails, appear at the wrists and feet. The man's legs are not broken, but another reddish spot appears on his right side. In 1978, a team of scientists from Los Alamos was permitted to examine the shroud and three years later pronounced it "authentic."[17]

Such a declaration was misleading. Not until 1988 did the church permit carbon testing on a fragment of the shroud. These tests indicated that the wrapping was of medieval origin, some time between 1300 and 1500.[18] If there was blood on the cloth, it probably came from an actor who was injured while performing the role of Jesus in a passion play. If the Shroud of Turin is nothing but a clever rubbing or forgery, then, all we know about the appearance of Jesus is the New Testament reference that he was "comely to behold."

Jesus and the Jewish People

The Synoptic Gospels (Matthew, Mark, and Luke) supply a basic understanding of events in Jesus' brief, but meteoric, ministry. Inscribed between A.D. 42 and 66, the Synoptic Gospels (from the Greek for "agreement") were probably derived from an unrecovered testament biblical scholars label "Q." They tell of his preparation for the ministry, his preaching in Galilee, the journey to Jerusalem, and his passion during Holy Week. For the most part, parables (about the blind, rich men and heaven) and miracles (walking on water, raising the dead) are repeated or amplified. So, too, the story of Jesus' temptation, the Beatitudes, the Lord's Prayer. There are also some passages unique to each Gospel, namely the touching Nativity scene recited in Luke 2, Jesus' relationship with his family (Mark 6:3), Herod's slaughter of the innocents (Matt. 2:13–16). There are even some misstatements of Torah. Nowhere in Leviticus or Proverbs does it say "Thou shalt love thy neighbour and hate thine enemy" as in Matthew 5:43, nor does Isaiah say that the house of God will be a "den of thieves" (Matt. 21:13). The reference is from Jeremiah 7:11 and is improperly joined to Isaiah 56:7. With the exception of the tirade offered in Matthew 23 (decrying the Pharisees as iniquitous hypocrites, blind guides, serpents and broods of vipers, and sons of those who killed prophets), there is little to suggest a rupture between Jesus and the Jewish people. As Heinrich Graetz has written:

> Jesus made no attack upon Judaism itself, he had no idea of becoming a reformer of Jewish doctrine or the propounder of a new law; he sought merely to redeem the sinner, to call him to a good and holy life, to teach him that he is a child of God, and to prepare him for the approaching Messianic time. He insisted upon the unity of God, and was far from attempting to change in the slightest degree the Jewish conception of the deity. To the question once put to him by an expounder of the law, "What is the essence of Judaism?" he replied, "Hear, o Israel, our God is one," and "Thou shalt love thy neighbor as thyself. These are the chief commandments." (Mark 12:28.) His disciples, who had remained true to Judaism, promulgated the declaration of their Master — "I am not come to destroy, but to fulfil; till heaven and earth pass, one jot or one tittle shall in nowise pass from the Law till all be fulfilled." (Matt. 5:17).[19]

Jesus and the Sanhedrin

Hosannahed when he entered Jerusalem on Palm Sunday, Jesus struck a responsive chord among the Jewish people. Preaching within the confines of the temple, he boasted how he would cast down and rebuild the great structure in three days to purify the shrine from corruption. When he overturned the tables of money changers during Holy Week, the incident was prompted not so much by concern over the presence of cash in the compound as the connection between money, birds and sheep, sacrifice, and graft. For their part, the temple hierarchy considered Jesus a poorly educated troublemaker from Galilee, that region known for its political ruffians. Worse, this one counted among his closest associates the dregs of Judaean society. Repeatedly, the Synoptic Gospels tell how the chief priests and their scribes wanted to lay hands upon him but "they feared him, because all the people was astonished at his doctrine" (Mark 11:18; see also 12:12, 14:2; Matt. 21:45–47, 27; Luke 19:147–48, 20:19, 22:2).To avoid further repression by Pilate (who had just beaten thousands on the streets), the priests arranged for Jesus' betrayal by Judas. Jesus was arrested by a Roman contingent at the crowing of the cock. What followed was a kangaroo court that violated nearly every rule of ancient Jewish law. Taken into custody on Passover, a festival of freedom, Jesus was marched off either to the house of Annas or Caiaphas. His early-morning trial, which most certainly did not include the full complement of 71 members of the Sanhedrin, did not take place in the Chamber of Hewn Stones (the only place where the Jewish High Court was empowered to sit), but the palace of the High Priest. No runners were sent through the streets, calling for witnesses. With the exception of Judas, one of the two witnesses required in capital cases, those who testified against Jesus were stooges who were quickly dismissed by the priests.

No indictment was presented against Jesus. He simply was charged with threatening to destroy the temple (a distortion of his promise to purify the priesthood), with healing on the Sabbath (there is no prohibition against this kind of activity in Judaism), political insurrection (he had often told his followers to render unto Caesar what was his and to render separately unto God), destroying the tables of the money changers (hardly more than a misdemeanor), claiming to be the messiah and blasphemy. The last two charges were the most serious. It should be noted, however, that claiming to be a redeemer was never construed by the Jewish people as a sacrilege. None of the other messianic aspirants of this period were punished. Indeed, with the exception of the version offered by Mark (14:62), Jesus responds to questions concerning his messiahship with parables (Luke 23:3, John 18:37, Matthew 26:64): "Thou hast said it" or "If I tell you, you will not believe me." As for blasphemy, the Talmud defines this offense not in terms of being the "power" or "son of man," but taking the name of the Lord in vain.

In no version of the Passion do we find Jesus damning God. A small clique in the Sanhedrin was so anxious to dispose of this popular figure they condemned him and pressed for his execution on the same day. By so doing, they violated another principle of Jewish law that required 24 hours to pass between the time of trial and execution in capital offenses. The rationale for such delay was that death is an irrevocable process that should be undertaken only after reflection and the court's seeking additional witnesses.[20]

The Passover Plot

There are historians who believe Jesus was not displeased with his martyrdom. Cecil Roth maintains that Judas betrayed his master when he discovered Jesus was not a zealot who would lead a war of national liberation.[21] Hugh Schonfield attributes Judas' actions to Jesus' wasteful use of oil in the anointing at Bethany. Schonfield goes further, detecting a conspiracy in what he terms a Passover Plot.[22] According to this telling, Jesus deliberately schemed with Joseph of Arimathaea and the Marys to be condemned by the Sanhedrin, crucified, and then reappear miraculously as a fulfillment of the prophecy of the Teacher of Righteousness. To do so required an act that would provoke one of his apostles late in the week. If he were arrested on Friday all the better, for the Romans, out of peculiar solicitude, would not keep prisoners hanging beyond sunset, the beginning of the Jewish sabbath.

The arrest in Gesthemane, hearings before the Sanhedrin, Herod Antipas and Pilate can all be placed within a three- or four-hour time frame. Golgotha, a hillock outside the city walls, was less than a mile from the Roman Praetorium. Jesus could anticipate being on the cross nine hours, which, according to the Gospels, was the case. Schonfield argues that traditional Roman crucifixion did not kill in such a short time. Prisoners were usually lashed to a T-shaped bar where they were left for days, to perish of exposure and starvation. Nails were used as a punitive measure rather than out of any concern to hasten death for the victim. Josephus records how the Romans delighted in nailing fugitives from Jerusalem during the siege of 66–70. On such occasions, the nails were driven through the wrist, not the palms as shown in virtually every church to the 20th century. The hands simply could not support the body on the cross.

It is impossible to know whether Jesus and his two companions were nailed. That the "robbers" with him did not die of crucifixion is evident from the fact that the Romans broke their legs to bring on suffocation before sunset. Jesus' death, on the other hand, coming immediately after being given a drink of myrrh, wine or gall was so suspicious that the Roman centurion pierced his side with a lance before permitting the body to be taken down. When Joseph and the Marys came forward, they sought the *soma* (living body) not the *ptoma* (corpse) of Christ, which they were to whisk away for miraculous recovery in a nearby cave. What none of them anticipated, however, was the fatal wound caused by the Roman soldier's lance.

Schonfield's thesis is disturbing, but flawed. Perhaps Pilate, notorious for his cruelty, did order the use of nails. Jesus may have died from bleeding, shock, the severity of his beating at the hands of Roman guards, despair. Whatever caused his death, the more basic question was this: what could a peaceful messiah have achieved after his staged resurrection? His reappearance would have been a direct challenge to the Sanhedrin, a spark for open rebellion against Rome. If anything, the authorities would have seized him and executed him for all to see a second time.

Responsibility for Christ-Killing

Strange to tell, the one figure who emerges in the Gospels as august, even noble, is Pontius Pilate. The prefect, already noted as a rogue, is portrayed as a reluctant party to an affair of the Jews. When asked by a delegation of the Sanhedrin to render judgment against Jesus, Pilate tells them to take him to Herod Antipas. Upon their return he has the Galilean flogged. Having failed to appease the priests, he agrees to a public trial where a common criminal, Barabbas, is given his release, in preference to Jesus. As the crowd (Matt. 27–20, Mark 15:8) or mob (Luke 23:18) jeers, Pilate washes his hands of responsibility. It is a fascinating tale, and one cut of whole cloth. Chaim Cohn, the Israeli jurist who presided over the trial of Adolf Eichmann, cites many more anomalies in the Gospel story:

1) No Jews, not even High Priests, would be permitted at a hearing traditionally held en camera in the Praetorium;
2) Pilate could not waive jurisdiction over to Herod because Roman governors were under an obligation to adjudicate the case of any man suspected of treason or making preparations for an insurrection;
3) Under Roman law, a prisoner could not be flogged before sentence of death, because scourging was an essential and inseparable part of the crucifixion punishment;
4) The *privilegium paschale* (alleged custom of freeing prisoners at Easter) was never

recorded in Jewish History, but was a phenomenon of the late Roman Empire, limited to the emperor alone and inapplicable to prisoners accused of capital offenses;

5) According to the code of Justinian (9.47.12) *vane voces populi non sunt audiendae* (vain voices of the people may not be listened to), and nowhere in Roman history do we find another court "truckling to the imprecations of the masses";

6) No Roman governor has been recorded as washing his hands in public, a declaration of innocence, as if a mob of subjects were his judges.[23]

Jesus was a victim of Roman imperialism, condemned to death by a Roman governor, scourged and crucified according to Roman practice, all under Roman guard. There were some Jewish collaborators to this crime, but how many? Judaea's population was anywhere from three to five million at the time. Perhaps another five million Jews resided in Rome, Greece, Egypt, and Mesopotamia. According to Samuel Sandmel of Hebrew Union College, the mob that condemned Jesus probably included many of the 71 members of the Sanhedrin, 50 priests, another 100 townspeople — 250 in all, less than one ten-thousandth of the Jewish population in the first century.[24] How then did Jews in every age become responsible for Christ-killing?

The answer comes from the Book of John. Canonized after A.D. 100 when Pauline Christianity had already branched away from traditional Judaism, it is in the Book of John, not a Synoptic Gospel, that the villains are specifically identified as Jews. Because of the miraculous cures Jesus did on the Sabbath "the Jews were more anxious to put him to death" (5:18, Douay translation). Jews at Succoth were concerned about Jesus ministering to Gentiles (7:25). "The Jews" questioned his divinity (8:22), called him a Samaritan and a devil (8:48). During the festival when Jesus claimed to be one with God, "the Jews took up stones again to stone him" (10:31). After raising Lazarus, he was fearful of traveling about openly because of the Jews (11:54). When Jesus is arrested and tormented, the Jews tell Pilate it is not lawful for them to put anyone to death (18:31). The early-morning gathering that howled for Jesus' death at the Antonia was identified by the Synoptic Gospels as a mob or crowd. Faceless and mindless, they could, without fear of consequences, chant as they did in Matthew: "His blood be on us, and on our children" (Matt. 27:25). Only with the Book of John, however, do we learn that those who repeatedly demanded the release of Barabbas, the death of Jesus, the breaking of his legs, were Jews (18:31, 18:39, 19:6, 19:12, 19:13).

From such stuff as this comes the polemics of Augustine and St. John Chrysostom, the hatred of Innocent III and Martin Luther, the massacres of Tsar Nicholas II and Adolf Hitler.

12

The Byzantine Empire

Origins of the Byzantine State

From A.D. 330 to 1453, the center of Christian power in the Middle East was Constantinople. A sprawling metropolis with more than one million Greek, Slav, Jewish, Altaic, Scandinavian, German, and Syrian inhabitants, Constantinople was named after Constantine the Great (306–37), the Roman who promoted Christianity to most-favored status in the empire. Constantinople was superimposed over Byzantium, an ancient town that dated to the 8th century B.C., whence the name of the Eastern Roman state — the Byzantine Empire.

Historians have conjectured why Constantine removed his capital 900 miles eastward. To secure control of the Danubian basis, his predecessor Diocletian (284–305) established a provincial capital in Nicomedia on the Asian side of the Sea of Marmora. The eastern provinces were deemed more important than those in the west because they were more populous, the source of domestic markets and military manpower. Egypt and the Ukraine formed the granaries of the empire, Syria and the Greek cities its mercantile centers. Geographically, Byzantium controlled access between the Black Sea and the Aegean on the one hand, the land routes from Asia Minor to Europe on the other. Its harbor was one of the best in the medieval world. Surrounded on three sides by water and girded by a triple line of walls that stretched 13 miles in circumference, the city was practically impregnable.

According to Eusebius, bishop of Caesarea, the emperor's decision to create a second Rome came as a result of a dream. More likely, a contributing factor was the stubborn adherence of the Roman aristocracy to the old pagan cults. There was no need to invent a story of a dream, for Constantine was surrounded by pro–Christian influences. His father, a Balkan soldier, was already a devotee of "the unconquerable sun," a monotheistic creed linked with Mithraism. His mother, once a Balkan prostitute, most certainly was a convert to Christianity. Later canonized as St. Helena, she was responsible for the establishment of the first churches in Jerusalem.

Of Constantine himself, Lactantius, who served as tutor to the emperor's son, tells how he placed the "Labarum" (the crossed *chi* and *rho* standard of Christianity) on the shields of his men to bring victory in the civil war that ruffled Rome between 306 and 324. Eusebius also tells the story how Constantine, preparing for a crucial battle with his rival Maxentius in 312, was said to have seen a flaming cross in the sky with the inscription *in hoc signe vinces* (by this sign thou shalt conquer). Victorious at the Malvian Bridge, Constantine issued his Edict of Milan a year later, granting Christianity *licet* (legal) status in the empire. When he defeated his last rival, Licinius, in 324, the way was opened to honor the faith that had graced his triumphs. Pressed at court by Hosius of Cordova, bishops of North Africa, Lactantius, and Eusebius to make conversion, Constantine was not formally baptized until he lay on his deathbed in 337.[1]

Legend has it that he had already surrendered imperial authority to the church. Cured of leprosy by Pope Sylvester I, Constantine supposedly designated the bishop of Rome as the leader of all Christians. More, he resigned his throne and humbled himself before Sylvester. In return for this acknowledgement of the new relationship between temporal and spiritual power, Sylvester restored Constantine's crown. This so-called Donation of Constantine became the basis for subsequent coronations in Christian Europe. Less than a century earlier, Decius and Valens had attacked Christians for alleged disloyalty. Four years before Constantine became caesar in 302, Diocletian and Galerius closed churches, banned Christian holy books, and ordered mass executions unless Christians sacrificed to the Roman gods.[2]

The Spread of Christianity

Long before any last-minute confessions from Galerius or Constantine, or a legendary donation of power, Christianity had already spread through the Roman world, challenging the established Jovian, Isis, and Mithraic cults. Its popularity stemmed from several factors:

A base among Jews in the Empire. By some estimates, Jews made up 10 percent of the population in the Roman Empire in the first century. If nationalistic Judaeans were regarded with suspicion, religious Jews enjoyed the rights and privileges accorded a legal sect. Christians, with their clouded origins and potentially mutinous messianism, did not. When Paul traveled from Antioch to Ephesus to Corinth to Rome, he did so under the protection of his Jewish religion. The first place he visited in any of these cities was the synagogue, there to dialogue with and win converts from Jews. Without this receptive base, Christianity might well have withered.

Universality of Christianity. Unlike Judaism, which was restricted to those who accepted the covenant of Jehovah, Christianity was never limited to a single people or class. Under St. Paul, Christianity broadened its message to include all Gentiles, rivaling Mithra for the loyalties of Roman soldiers, Isis for the devotion of Roman women.

Release from Talmudic prescriptions. To accommodate people for whom dietary laws of the Old Testament were meaningless and circumcision barbaric, Paul introduced the concept that Christ's martyrdom had rendered such prescriptions obsolete.

Hope of salvation in a world yet to come. The major advantage that Christian missionaries in the first century enjoyed over their Jewish counterparts was in offering a reward of eternal salvation. Until Maimonides, the Jewish view of life after death was vague. Jews were taught to emphasize improving this world because there was no certainty of anything afterward. Christians, meanwhile, could tell slaves, the poor, and diseased that this world was a shadow of the paradise that would be theirs. Neither Jews nor Neo-Platonists, with their accent on the eternal idea, could match this promise.

Simplicity of the Christian message. Christianity, like Judaism, taught that there was a single, immanent, supreme being who cared about mankind. The message of both religions was one of love and hope, belief that through an ethical life the world could be redeemed. Such ideas were far easier for the common person to accept than elaborate rituals honoring stone idols, deification of degenerates like Caligula and Nero, human sacrifice, or arcane philosophy. As H. L. Mencken once wrote, commenting on the relative merits of two evangelists standing on a street corner in Corinth: if one were expounding the Nicomachaean ethics of Aristotle or a homily by Valentinus the Gnostic and the other the Sermon on the Mount, which would attract the larger crowd?

Syncretistic nature of Christianity. Eager for proselytes, early Christianity displayed little of the arrogance of later missionaries. Thus, where mystical rites were once part of a people's tradition, they were incorporated into a hybrid Christianity. Glossolalia (the speaking in tongues) is still considered legitimate by some Christian sects. Diana of the Ephesians, Isis with the suckling Horus, became the Virgin Mother. The cross, baptism, and eucharist of Mithra all became part of Christian symbolism. To facilitate literacy deemed so essential in early Christianity, St. Cyril invented a script for the Slavs. To the end of the 19th century, in some parts of West Africa people were permitted, temporarily, to blend their native customs with Christian ritual.

Acceptance in official Roman society. The new faith may have made inroads in Roman society even before the death of Caligula. Its teachings may have influenced Zeno and Marcus Aurelius. All that was necessary was for one Roman emperor to accept the faith, legalize Christianity, summon church elders, and guarantee a secure base. The Council of Nicaea in 325 propounded the basic creed of Christianity and agreed upon the mechanics for reckoning Advent, Lent, Easter, and Pentecost. In the process, Jerusalem became a city of churches as did Constantinople.

Constantinople: City of Icons

To give his new capital a genuine flavor, Constantine forcibly transferred masses of the Roman proletariat. The seven districts of Constantinople were deliberately modeled after the seven hill subdivisions of Romulus and Remus. Vendors hawked every conceivable type of fruits, vegetables, pottery and rags at wide gates that opened on to the inner city. These in turn converged upon a series of forums, public squares that doubled as marketplaces. Everywhere could be seen the trappings of the original Rome—basilicas, aqueducts, hospitals, public baths, palaces, amphitheatres.

Each city in the Byzantine Empire had its arena where mystery plays, mock hunts, acrobatics, and chariot racing were performed to appreciative audiences. The most celebrated was the Hippodrome, an elliptical-shaped stadium in Constantinople, 1300 feet long, that could seat 60,000. With its imperial box and special seats reserved for the nobility, its raucous partisans of Green and Blue teams, the Hippodrome was a microcosm of Byzantine society.

The most imposing structures in Constantinople, however, were its churches. The capital contained no less than 500 churches, 67 of them dedicated to the Virgin Mary. Unlike their Western counterparts, the Byzantine sanctuaries had stark brick exteriors with few windows. The dominant feature of these tri-celled structures was a main hall (*naos*) capped with the huge dome. The cupola of the Hagia Sophia, a building that rises 180 feet, was 100 feet in diameter. The hollow spaces below symbolized the emptiness of the tomb of Christ and the triumph of life over death. It took the emperor Justinian five years to rebuild the Hagia Sophia. As he looked upon his handiwork, the Byzantine monarch chortled: "Glory to God who has deemed me worthy of accomplishing such a work. O Solomon! I have vanquished thee!"[3]

Byzantine sanctuaries were bedecked with icons, replicas of holy figures in plaster, marble, fresco, mosaic, ivory triptychs, jeweled reliquaries, silver medallions. Through the centuries, Jesus was shown in a clean gown, draped with purple, a hand lifted in blessing. Peter was an older man with a full head of white hair and a forelock. What was important was not perspective (figures overlap, walk on different planes, tread on each others' toes), but numerology (combinations of 1, 3, 4, 12), color (white associated with purity, purple with divinity), and light.[4]

The crowning achievements of Byzantine iconography were its mosaics. Thousands of tiny cubes of different colored stones were fitted meticulously into wet plaster to make up the image of an apostle or a scene from the New Testament. Scenes of Christ's death and resurrection were placed in the *narthex* (entry), his birth and baptism in the main hall, saints and Old Testament figures in squinches or sidedomes, the apostle at the sanctuary (*bema*), the virgin shielded by a screen behind the altar in the apse, and Christ Pantocrator staring down from the main dome. The hope was that such artwork would be meaningful even to the illiterate man, that he would sense his lowly station and the universal hierarchy that culminated with Jesus.[5]

Art and architecture were among the many contributions of the Byzantines. Medieval social systems would rely heavily upon Byzantine codes of Theodosius (346–95) and Justinian (518–610). Both monarchs dealt with the stratification of society, the rights of slaves, peasants, landholders, punishment of heretics and restrictions of the rights of Jews. Justinian was responsible for recording more than 4600 decrees of his predecessors (known as the Code), a 50 volume collection of jurists' opinions (the Digest), texts for students of law (the Institutes), and his own imperial laws (Novels).The great libraries of Constantinople would be torched by marauding Crusaders in 1204. The formula for Greek Fire, the explosive sulphur-naptha combination that protected Constantinople from invasions, would also be lost. But the Code of Justinian would influence students of law for the next thousand years.[6]

Decline of the Byzantine State

Although the fall of the Byzantine Empire is generally dated from the Ottoman entry into Constantinople in May 1453, the process of decline cannot be attributed to a single event. Following the reigns of Basil Bulgaroctonus (976–1025) and Alexius Comnenus (1081–1118) the empire became a shadow of its former greatness. Circumscribed to Adrianople in the west and the Bosphorus in the east, the population of its capital shrunken to 60,000 desperate Christians, the Byzantine collapse was inevitable for several reasons:

The despotic nature of the Basileus. Initially regarded as an equal to the apostles, the *basileus* (emperor) built upon the Roman tradition of divinity associated with the caesars, ultimately becoming the *mimesis* of Christ. The basileus did not appear at state functions. He materialized from the ceiling, on a throne operated by mechanical winches.

Surrounded by twelve "angels" (eunuchs who were his closest advisers), his meals were supposed to be replicas of the Last Supper. Decked out in white, his face chalked at Easter time, the basileus would sail across the Golden Horn in an imperial barge to symbolize the resurrection of Christ.

A living god, the basileus trucked no difference of opinion, no embarrassment. One autocrat who was bald commanded his courtiers to shave their heads. Another, who dropped a plate, prompting his dinner companions to laugh, ordered this group of "angels" to be blinded, then decapitated. Nothing was to disturb the enjoyment of the basileus. When Constantine Copronymous, attending the chariot races, was notified that his armies had been defeated just 25 miles off, he dismissed the catastrophic news and ordered that the games continue.

As in ancient Rome, the Hippodrome was the scene of the worst excesses in the empire. In normal times, the arena was a riotous place with partisans of the different teams jostling one another. In January 532, groups of Greens and Blues, grown to urban sports militias, had to be suppressed by Justinian. What was known as the Nika Rebellion left 30,000 dead. Drivers of teams not favored by the monarch might be thrown into the Bosphorus. Once, the emperor Phocas (602–10) enticed a crowd to the stadium with an offer of free food. At his signal, nets strung overhead were opened and melons, fish, and poultry were released. As the mob rushed to grab their prizes, Phocas ordered troops onto the floor of the stadium. The entertainment that day was a massacre of spectators.

Few of the icons of Christ ruled undisturbed. Before 1058, there were no less than 65 successful revolutions in the empire. Of 109 Byzantine sovereigns, 65 were assassinated, 12 died in convents or prisons, three were starved to death, and 18 were castrated. The others were mutilated, strangled, or thrown from a column to their death. The punishment meted out to the Basileus Andronicus was not atypical:

> For several days he was chained in the pillory, his head held in place by a great iron collar. The crowd beat him black and blue, broke his teeth with hammers, cut off a hand and hung it on a gallows. Then naked, half dead and starving, he was tied on to a scabby and sick old camel in such a way that his head was under its tail; excrement from the sick animal dripped upon his face. In this way he was paraded through the streets. On the way, a girl emptied a pail of boiling water on his face, women threw the contents of chamber pots over him, and one of his eyes was plucked out. He was still alive, however, and repeated, "Lord have mercy on me! Why do you go on striking a broken reed?" At the Hippodrome he was strung up by his feet and the formal torture began. At last a sword was plunged into his entrails. As he died, he lifted a bleeding stump to his mouth; a nearby wit remarked, "Look! He can't fatten himself on the blood of the people, so he's sucking his own!"[7]

Religious superstition. Religious devotion was carried to an extreme in this empire of icons. Enter a church in Constantinople and behold the adze that Noah used to build the ark, the rod of Moses, one of several heads of John the Baptist, relics of St. Luke, St. Andrew, or St. Timothy, the spikenard used by Mary Magdalene to anoint Jesus' feet, Christ's breadbasket, the linen used to swaddle the infant Jesus, the cloth Veronica used to wipe his face, his blood-stained mantle, the lance which pierced his side, a crown of thorns, numerous nails, and enough wood from the true cross, Erasmus would comment later, to build a ship. If one were ill, impoverished, depressed, all that was necessary was proximity to these sacred objects.

For ascetics who cared little for instant cure-alls, religion was still the answer. St. Simeon Stylite (396–459) and other pillar saints retreated from the cities to caves and hillocks in Cappadocia and Syria, to meditate in hopes of hastening the second coming of

Christ. St. Simeon turned his back on the problems of this world for 30 years, while Arsinos of Damascus and Alypius remained hermits for 40 and 53 years respectively.

The phenomenon of withdrawing from useful labor was only one example of the enervating impact that religion had upon the Byzantine economy. Before the Turkish conquest, one-third of the Byzantine lands, owned by the church, may have been immune from taxation. Still worse, virtually every day on the calendar was a religious holiday associated with a particular saint. Religion was sapping income in favor of churches, monasteries, convents, vestments, and palaces, and returning mumbo jumbo to the faithful.

Internal religious divisions. According to orthodox tradition, the human Jesus perished on the cross, but the spiritual Christ could never die. For many Christians, this miracle was mystifying. Seeking simpler explanations of Jesus' relationship with God the father, they turned to teachings that inevitably were labeled heretical. Perhaps the first was Arianism, a creed formulated by the Alexandrian priest Arius in the age of Constantine. Arianism taught that Jesus was merely a godlike intermediary, on the order of the ancient prophets. Denounced by church councils in 325 and 381, Arianism took root among Visigoths and Vandals.

Closely related to the teachings of Arianism was Nestorianism. In part the result of a feud over authority between the patriarchs of Alexandria and Constantinople, Nestorianism (after Nestorius, patriarch of Alexandria) denied that Mary could be the mother of God, only mother of the human Jesus. In rejecting trinitarian dogma, Nestorianism was declared a heresy by the Council of Ephesus in 431. Its adherents were driven out of the empire, eventually finding refuge among the Sassanid Persians and in Arabia.

If Nestorianism represented the human end of the theological spectrum, Monophysitism constituted its opposite. Certainly this teaching that the human nature of Christ was wholly absorbed in the divine was easier for people to comprehend than the trinity. The simplicity of a divine Christ may account for the spread of monophysitism through Egypt, Asia Minor, and Africa. Despite condemnation by the Council of Chalcedon in 451 and subsequent persecutions, the movement remained strong among Copts, Armenians and Ethiopians.

Donatism and Hesychasm were two lesser heresies that caused disturbance in the empire. The former was a puritanical sect named after a fourth-century North African bishop, Donatus. Victims of polemics from St. Augustine and imperial massacres, the Donatists became an underground church and disappeared after the Muslim conquest of Algeria-Tunisia three centuries later. Hesychasm, a religion-philosophy borrowed from Buddhism, was also opposed by the orthodox.[8]

The most violent upheaval in Byzantine theology was caused by Iconoclasm, a movement that rejected icons as carryovers from paganism. Directed by Leo the Isaurian (717–41), the iconoclasts grew to number six million before the sacred images were restored in 843. Leo's opposition to icons is said to have stemmed from a destructive volcanic eruption he regarded as divine punishment for the idolatrous behavior of the empire. More likely, Leo was pressed by the military to tighten imperial control over the church. By eliminating icons, he could enhance the status of the Eastern Church, which was locked in conflict with Rome, which sanctioned their use. To stamp out this sacrilege, Constantine V Copronymous (741–75) had crude images of carrots, turnips, cauliflower, and other vegetables painted over biblical scenes in the Church of the Holy Apostles. Those who objected to such desecration were blinded, scalped, or had their beards set afire. In the end, however, the monks and commoners who clung to the belief that icons were neoplatonic images won out as the Empresses Irene and Theodora removed all penalties associated with icons.[9]

The Great Schism. The quarrel over icons was only one of several disputes that led to alienation between the Eastern Church and that of Rome. The Byzantines embraced the old Alexandrian notion of *oecumene* and applied it to the Christian world, with the patriarch of Constantinople at its head. This view was resented by the patriarchs of Jerusalem, Antioch, Alexandria, and especially Rome, which claimed primacy on the basis of Petrine succession and the Donation of Constantine. Over the centuries, Rome and Constantinople feuded with one another over diocesan jurisdiction and doctrine. Differences in hair style (western monks shaved their heads, while those in the east wore long hair and beards), celibacy (western priests did not marry), the bread of the Eucharist (unleavened in the west), eating eggs during Lent (permitted in the west), the number and placement of genuflections in the mass, dating of Christmas. Easter, and other holy days (the east favored the Julian calendar) were magnified into life and death issues. When the Roman Catholic church decreed that the Holy Ghost in the Trinity proceeded from the Father and Son (the *filiogue* controversy), Byzantines who held that divine spirit came from the Father were outraged.

Relations between the two religious centers deteriorated when both Rome and Byzantium claimed control over Bulgarian territory. In 860, Phocius, the newly named patriarch of Constantinople, was excommunicated by Pope Nicholas I for attempting a purge of Latin liturgy. Two hundred years later, after the emperor Basil Bulgaroctonus (976–1025) subjugated all Bulgars, the Patriarch Michael Cerularius closed all churches in Constantinople that used western rites. To no avail Pope Leo IX dispatched Cardinal Humbert to negotiate a settlement. When Humbert threw down a ban of excommunication upon the altar of the Hagia Sophia, Cerularius responded by anathematizing the Pope. The Great Schism in the church was thus formalized.

This division was to weaken the Byzantine Empire in several ways. No longer could the emperors count on western support against barbarian invaders. When Seljuk Turks overran Byzantium's eastern border in the 11th century, Pope Urban's call for a Crusade came not so much from concern for the welfare of Constantinople as a desire to reunite the faithful under his authority. The west's contempt for Byzantium was further demonstrated in 1204 when Genoese and Venetians on the fourth Crusade abandoned their stated goal of winning back the Holy Land and sacked Constantinople instead. Perpetually insecure on all its borders, the Byzantines found themselves estranged from the mainstream of European Christianity.[10]

Barbarian invaders from the north. Beginning with the arrival of Germanic hordes late in the fourth century, the Byzantine Empire never knew peace on the north. Visigoths and Vandals, pressed from their central Asian homelands, crossed the Dniester, temporarily taking up residence in Dacia before moving on to Spain and North Africa. In pursuit came the still more barbaric Huns under Attila. When Attila's warlord empire collapsed, the Ostrogoths poured into the Danubian basin, threatening at one time to take over the Byzantine monarchy. A nationalistic purge of these Germans forced them west, where under Odoacer in 476 they were blamed for the fall of Rome. Meanwhile, in the east, more bands from the steppes poured into Byzantine territory. The Bulgars established themselves just to the west of Constantinople in 540. Eight years later, the Sklavenoi, precursors of the Croats and Serbs, sacked cities along the Adriatic. In 559 another Altaic people, the Kotrigurs, were repulsed from the gates of Constantinople by one of Justinian's generals. Shortly after, in 561 the Avars established themselves on the Danube. The ninth century saw the arrival of the Magyars in the Carpathians and the beginning of the Moravian-Czech dynasty in Velegrad (Prague). Soon after, Varangian Norsemen swept through Russia and besieged Constantinople in 860, 907, and 941. Normans and Lombards captured the last Byzantine possessions in Italy in the 11th century. Khazars, Cumans, and Patzinaks detached Byzantine territory north of the Black Sea, preparing the way for more serious ravages of Turks, Mongols, and Tatars.[11]

Four hundred years of warfare with the Sassanid Persians on the east. In many ways, the fortunes of the Sassanid Persian dynasty paralleled those of the Byzantines. Just when it appeared the Persians were ready to sweep through Asia Minor after their capture of the Roman emperor Valerian in 260, they were sent packing by a third force, the Palmyrans. As the Byzantines grew to greatness under Constantine and Theodosius, so the Sassanids expanded to the edge of Anatolia. In the centuries that followed, both empires bolstered their possessions with puppet kingdoms and tried to exploit dissension in enemy territory. When famine led to a violent religious mutiny under Mazdak in the reign of the Persian Firuz (459–84), the Byzantines probed their neighbors' border. When German, Slav and Altaic migrations caused tension for the Byzantines, the Sassanids reciprocated. The two states did exchange wares and ideas, which, instead of bringing them closer, contributed to their alienation. The Byzantines resented the growing economic power of Mesopotamia. They also deprecated the mercantile peoples who figured prominently in the Sassanid capital of Ctesiphon — Jews and Nestorians. The status enjoyed by Nestorian émigrés like Shireen, the wife of Khusrau II, and Yazden of Kirkuk, Khusrau's chief financial adviser, was especially resented.

After a series of minor clashes over the kingdom of Lazica east of the Black Sea, the two empires resumed full-fledged warfare in 540. The conflict would last for nearly 100 years. In the last phase of the war (591–628), Khusrau's son Hormuzd IV was dethroned and his own son Khusrau II forced to seek refuge with the Byzantine monarch Maurice. Restored to his throne by Maurice, Khusrau pursued a policy of peace until the centurion Phocas murdered his patron and usurped the Byzantine throne. Khusrau captured Antioch, the third largest city of the Eastern Roman Empire in 613, carried off the Holy Cross and patriarch of Jerusalem in 614, captured Egypt in 619, and ordered his generals to coordinate an assault on Constantinople with Avars coming from the north. Byzantium was trapped.

In desperation, the Byzantines ousted Phocas and turned to Heraclius, the son of the Armenian Exarch (governor) of North Africa. Taking command of a garrison numbering less than 20,000 men, Heraclius at first contemplated abandoning the capital. When a storm dashed his plans of returning to Carthage, he engaged the enemy beyond the city walls, in its territory. With Caucasian tribesmen and Khazars, Heraclius attacked Persian cities in Azerbaijan, destroying their sacred fire temples and the birthplace of Zoroaster in 623. Four years later, he defeated the Sassanids at Nineveh, not far from where Alexander humbled the armies of Darius a thousand years earlier. The Byzantines were then free to sack Persian estates at Dastgerd. Disgraced, Khusrau was assassinated by his own son Kawad II in 628.

Four hundred years of intermittent warfare had left farmlands despoiled and depopulated. Skilled labor was missing from the cities. When the wars ended, there was little reserve of manpower or willpower from which to draw. Vast amounts of money and energy had been poured into fortifications in the east and north, but the Byzantine Empire's vulnerable territory had been ignored. Eight years after his triumph over the Persians, Heraclius would be defeated by the Arabs.

Losses to the Arabs from the south. Known to its residents as the Jazirat al-Arab, the Island of the Arabs, Arabia has proved to be just that — an island — over the ages. Bounded on three sides by bodies of water (the Persian Gulf, Indian Ocean, and Red Sea), the peninsula was shielded by the Syrian Desert, a quadrilateral measuring 300 miles on each side. Whenever the Arabs wished, they could make forays outside their island, then withdraw behind the safety of sand and water. With the birth of Islam, a new element was introduced into the balance of power of the Middle East. This dynamic force was able to capitalize on the mutual exhaustion of Byzantines and Persians. By 644 the Sassanid Empire existed no more. Blessed with able leaders and a spirit of mission, in very little time the Arabs were able to conquer the Holy Land, Cyprus, North Africa and lay siege to Constantinople on two occasions.[11]

Typical of their victories was the battle fought in the summer of 636 at the river Yarmuk. After tracking their opponents for days, the heavily mailed Byzantine army found itself fatigued, thirsty, at the bottom of a hill (water holes were located at the top), staring into the face of the enemy, the sun, and a gale-force sandstorm. Heraclius could only muse as his forces were annihilated: "Thou hast won, O Saracen. We leave Syria to thee, and a glorious land it is." With Syria and Egypt gone, the sea lanes leading to Constantinople permanently menaced by Muslim corsairs, the economic strangulation of Byzantium had begun.

Discrimination against subject peoples. Many subjects of the Byzantines resented them as foreign interlopers, not withstanding the language they spoke or the number of generations born in the east. Part of the problem stemmed from religious persecution. Native Egyptians, for example, adhered to Monophysite Christianity. Persecuted by the monk-governor Cyrus (who carried out large-scale crucifixions of heretics in Alexandria before 640), Egypt awaited deliverance from Byzantine bigotry.

Economic decay also ate at the Byzantine state. Vast amounts of money were required to sustain the 100,000-man army, churches and monasteries, and the personal quirks of the Basileus. Non-Roman subjects suffered extortion and the worst excesses of tax farming. Diocletian's *annona*, formerly an extraordinary tax for army necessities, became a regular impost upon rural populations. Peasants in Syria saw their taxes trebled in 20 years in the middle of the fourth century. In North Africa Augustine's Berbers were in a perpetual state of rebellion because of taxes. Forced to pay a third of their income to corrupt tax collectors, peasants became serfs to absentee landlords. Socially unacceptable to the Roman Byzantines, harassed for their religious beliefs, and drained economically, Semites and Hamites welcomed the Arab conquest.

Dynastic insecurity. While it is proper to speak of dynasties within Byzantine history (five generations of Heraclids ruled in the seventh century, followed by Isaurians [717–80], Armorians [820–67], Macedonians [867–1025], Comneni [1081–1185] and Paleologues [1259–1453]), the transition of power was never smooth. If the designated successor was a child, as in the case of Constans, the 11-year-old who replaced Heraclius in 641, or girls, like Zoe and Theodora, nieces of Basil Bulgaroctonus, they might rule less than a year.[12]

Between 1025 and 1081, nobles forced the ouster of 17 monarchs. Like other empires bled by incessant warfare, the Byzantines turned to hiring Armenians, Germans, Normans, and Patzinaks for their protection. Placed under the command of a *strategos* (general) these forces often proved unreliable and plundered the very people they were supposed to protect. The defection of mercenary troops cost the Byzantines the battle of Manzikert. The presence of 10,000 Catalans under Roger de Flor in 1302 proved to be so disconcerting that the Emperor Andronicus II expelled them. Forty years later, 6000 Turks dictated the outcome of a dispute between two rivals for the Byzantine throne.

Arrival of the Turks: Manzikert. Despite many shortcomings, Byzantium did last a thousand years. Its survival under incessant attacks of Germans, Slavs, Arabs and Persians defied logic. Periodically, there were novas of revival, under Leo the Isaurian, Basil and John Tzimisces, Alexius Comnenus and Michael Paleologus. What sealed the fate of the empire, however, was the battle of Manzikert, fought on August 26, 1071. On the eastern extremity of Anatolia, Seljuk Turks commanded by Kilij Arslan routed the Byzantine forces of Romanus IV Diogenes. The result was that all of Asia Minor was now opened to the Turks. Within a century, powerful sultanates would be established in Menteshe, Konya, Aydin, Karasi, Hamid, Antalya, Kutahya, and Eskisehir.

Enfeebled and dependent upon the west for military support, its possessions shriveled to a few square miles, the Byzantine Empire waited for one of the so-called ghazi states to produce leaders daring enough to end its existence. With his conquest of Constantinople in 1453, the Ottoman Mehmet Fatih completed a process that had begun hundreds of years earlier.

13

The Arabs and Their Culture

Desert Origins

They speak of a nation of more than 300 hundred million stretching from the Atlas Mountains to Persia, yet they war with one another over boundaries drawn by colonialists. A complex people, controlling the major energy sources for an industrialized world, they are held in awe by international forums. They are the Arabs, a Semitic people that burst out of the Arabian subcontinent in the seventh century, impressing the world with their religion and culture.

The word *Arab* has been traced to ancient roots—*arabha* (dark land), *erebh* (a mixed, unorganized group), *abhar* (to cross)—all of which suggest nomadic origins. More likely, the term implies a "western" origin, not in North Africa or the land of Ethiopia, but in the region bordering the Fertile Crescent that gave birth to Akkadian (2500 B.C.), Amorite (1800), and Aramaean (900) civilizations. Throughout the *Jahiliyah* period (the time of ignorance before Muhammad), Arabs fought in the ranks of Xerxes, traded in the markets of Byblos and Jerusalem, and established city-states and empires. By the time Herodotus wrote his great study in the fifth century, their presence was so well established that the entire peninsula was known as *Jazirat al-Arab* (the island of the Arabs).

The Arab Umma

Northern Arabs in the Hejaz, Najd, and Nabataea traced their ancestry to Joktan (also known as Qahtan), mentioned as the son of Eber in Genesis 10. Bedouins in the south hold Adnan, a descendant of Ishmael, as their progenitor. Ishmael is especially important, for it is through the first-born son of Abraham that Arabs claim a connection with the father of nations. Fifty years ago, the Lebanese historian Philip Hitti intimated they enjoyed a special status when he wrote: "Ethnic purity is the reward of the isolated environment of Central Arabia.... Arabian Arabs, particularly nomads, are the best representatives of the Semitic family, biologically, psychologically, socially and linguistically."[1]

Instead of race or nation, the term most applicable to Arabs is that which Muhammad applied, an *umma* or community, a term similar to the Byzantine *oecumene*, identical with the Jewish *am*. H. A. R. Gibb defined the umma when he wrote: "All those are Arabs for whom the central fact of history is the mission of Muhammad and the memory of the Arab Empire and who in addition cherish the Arabic tongue and its cultural heritage as their common possession."[2] Christian or Marxist Arabs might question the relevance of Muhammad's prophecy, but they could not dispute his political centrality. Unlike other religious leaders (Moses, Jesus, Zoroaster, Buddha), Muhammad's power was not limited to the spiritual. In his lifetime, his followers dominated southern Arabia. Within another generation, holy warriors spread his message from North Africa to Central Asia. Arabs recall *al-Amjad*, that glorious era between A.D. 700 and 1000 when the Islamic world was the center of civilization and long for the time when such grandeur returns to the Middle East.

For members of the umma, the Arabic language is the *lisan al-malaikah*, the noblest of all tongues, given by God to Adam at the beginning of time. Those who read the Quran should do so in Arabic for the divine book is written in this form. The Islamic creed, "There is no god but Allah and Muhammad is his prophet," is rendered only in Arabic. Traditions abound that those who speak and pray in Arabic are the righteous who will have four times the normal reward in the life hereafter. As the 10th-century sage al-Zubaydi instructed:

> Praise be to God who made the Arabic language the most palatable of all languages to utter, the most accurate in its formation, the clearest in the meaning of expression, and the richest in various branches of knowledge.[3]

The Material Culture of the Bedouin

While it is true Arabs no longer constitute a pastoral society (43 percent live in towns or cities as opposed to 10 percent in 1900), the bedouin is not totally a thing of the past. Thousands of Saudis graze their herds in *dirahs*, tribal areas of approximately 50 miles in circumference. Television antenna sprout from corrugated shanties near Beersheba and bedouins wearing designer jeans lead donkeys through the Negev desert. Among some Arabs in Morocco, Libya, and the Sudan loyalties to the *qabila* (tribe), *dawra* (circle) or *qaraba* (people clustered together beyond bonds of blood) transcend loyalty to the nation state.[4]

According to one bedouin saying, the only things necessary for life were *al-aswadan* (the two dark ones), water and food, generally interpreted to mean the *tamr* or date palm.[5] From long-eared sheep and goats came milk, cheese, chalk cakes, meat for stews that with dates, truffles, melons, onions, cucumbers, rice, nuts, eggplant and chicken formed the staples of the Arab diet. Goat's hair and sheep's wool could be stitched together with camel hide to make the 25-foot-long tents that served as portable homes. People dressed in the traditional *dishdasha* or *thawb* (a long cotton smock), *aba* (cloak), and *keffiyah* (headcloth).

The bedouin prized the saluqi, a sleek greyhound used for hunting gazelles and hares. Unlike many mixed breeds that clustered about the campsite, the saluqi was permitted to sleep inside the tent. Nearby were hooded falcons used to hunt down pigeons and other small animals. Camels might serve for caravan traffic through the desert, but for quick raids into enemy territory, the Arabs relied upon the horse. Among the bedouin, the desirable steed was large-ribbed, bay in color, with white fetlocks and hind leg, big nostrils and long ears. Shod with a large flat saucer designed to keep pebbles from bruising its feet, the Arabian was controlled by a halter or head rope looped under its chin. While stallions were tethered with other animals, the mare, a source of foals till she was 20, was permitted inside the bedouin tent.

The Spiritual Culture

Courtesy and respect (*hshumiya*) are social values ingrained in Arab society. The Quran repeatedly advises: "Allah does not love the arrogant and vainglorious" (Surah 31, Luqman) and "Be courteous in speech and do not walk proudly" (Surah 17, Night Journey). Modern Arabs have internalized this and many other concepts from the bedouin such as:

Irdh (family honor) or *sharaf* (personal pride). The Arab world has been dubbed a shame society. A man's pride or dignity is so important that any insult may be deemed permanent. A century ago, University of Pennsylvania archaeologists at Nippur ignored their workers' sensitivities, omitting customary baksheesh. The insulted Arabs not only refused to return to the digs, they attacked the Americans and forced a withdrawal from the locale.[6]

For decades, unyielding pride prevented Arab leaders from sitting down to negotiate with Israel. In 1973, U.S. Secretary of State Henry Kissinger intervened to prevent the annihilation of the Egyptian Third Army. Humiliation averted, Anwar Sadat successfully pressed for Israel's withdrawal from the Sinai.

Asabiyah (loyalty). An Arab saying goes: "*Jaruka, thumma jaruka, thumma jaruka*" (Your neighbor, then your neighbor, then your neighbor). One must be loyal to family, then clan, and tribe. In practice, however, obligations to these groups might not be so neatly sorted out. On one occasion, a bedouin entrusted with the safekeeping of tribal weapons permitted his son to be killed by invaders rather than reveal their whereabouts. In Kuwait in 1912, a shaykh threatened to impale himself unless his son (who had killed a member of the extended family) was punished. More recently, asabiyah was given new meaning by Gamal Abdel Nasser. In his *Philosophy of a Revolution*, Nasser defined loyalty in terms of circles of revolution. At the heart was Egypt, which had to be purged of colonial influences. A broader circle encompassed the Arab world, which he hoped to unite. The outer circle included all Muslims who, with Third-World states, would achieve parity with the two superpowers.

Diyafah (generosity/hospitality). Life in the desert dictates that people share with those less fortunate. Should a wanderer come upon an encampment, he was to wait outside an imaginary taboo zone, perhaps 50 feet off, until he was invited in. He must be invited in and given sustenance for three days. At that time, his host might advise, "My house, of course, is yours, but the mosque is more convenient."

Dakhala (sanctuary). An extension of chivalry shown to prisoners of war, personal safety must be guaranteed even to one's worst enemy. Religious shrines and foreign embassies were supposed to be places of sanctuary, but this has not prevented their being despoiled. The assault on America's Teheran embassy in 1979 and the mutilation of Israeli prisoners of war along the Golan Heights in 1973 demonstrate the discrepancy between the ideal and the real.

Muruwah (manliness or bravery in battle). The national sport of the bedouin has been the *razzia* or raid. Intended to promote stealth and courage, the razzia could take many forms, from a simple nighttime looting of animals and fruit to full-fledged hostilities. A rite of passage for Arab males, the razzia placed a premium on the ability to outwit the enemy. Recklessness or suicidal assaults were discouraged. As another motto instructed: "We take and are ourselves taken."

Insh'allah (fatalism). Even before Islam became dominant in the Arab world, the bedouin developed the belief that much of man's life was beyond his control. The bedouin taught that the sex, life span, vocation and happiness of a child were predetermined.

Taqiya (concealment) and *Kizb* (deception). Fatalism may pose some problems. As F. A. Sayegh and Sania Hamady have noted, mistakes and failures often are ascribed to fate, the devil or imperialism.[7] Concealment of the truth is permitted if revelation might cause harm to an individual. For some, the line between self-preservation and outright prevarication blurs. There is a tale of a Middle Eastern merchant who could not sleep because children were playing outside his window. He cleared them away saying, "Children, they are giving free figs away in the marketplace." After the children ran off, he still could not sleep. "Foolish man," he kept telling himself, "why do you try to sleep when they are giving away free figs in the market?" Of such self-deception, the 11th century-sage, al-Ghazzali commented, "If a lie is the only way of obtaining a good result, it is permissible. We must lie when truth leads to unpleasant results."[8]

Religion in the Jahiliyah Period

Arabia was aswarm with religious ideas during the Jahiliyah period. Iconoclastic pillar saints, Zoroastrians, Nestorian and Monophysite missionaries were active among the Arabs. Jews and Zoroastrians introduced their brand of monotheism to the region long before Muhammad was born. Jews may have been in western Arabia from the time of Solomon. By the seventh century, Jewish farmers, merchants, and smithies controlled the economies of Yathrib (later known as Medina), Tayma, Fadak, Khaibar, and Wadil Qura. Arab poets, singers and prophets like the blind Maslama, who was a contemporary of Muhammad, had begun to speak of one true god.

For the most part, however, the Arabs were polytheists. Some of the gods incorporated superhuman powers of animals. Hence the reverence for Nasr, the vulture deity, and Awf, the great bird. Others resembled gods of Mesopotomia. Wadd, the patron deity of the Minaeans, Almakah, the counterpart of Sin, and Manat, worshipped in the shape of a black stone, were all identified with the moon. Al–Lat, the sun deity venerated in the form of a square white stone, and al-Uzza, identified with Venus and venerated in a sanctuary of acacia trees near Taif, shared power with Manat. From Canaan came Allah (the biblical El of high places), ar-Rahman (the merciful one whose attributes would later be merged with Allah), and Hubal (Baal, god of divination manifested in the form of a red agate figurine).[9]

Initially, these gods were worshipped in portable shrines, much like the ancient ark of the Hebrews. When Arab tribesmen went to battle, their god was in front. When they moved from place to place, their god went with them. The people never developed an organized cosmogeny. Simply put, anything that enhanced life in the desert was a blessing from the gods. Water in the form of wells, springs or oases was sacrosanct. So, too, shady groves, caves, any vegetation. The moon was important, for the moon brought dew and may even have been responsible for shooting stars that crashed to earth. These last objects were regarded as gifts from the gods. People hoping to benefit from divine numena would touch and kiss the meteorite or smear the blood of sacrifice upon it. The sacred object might even be housed in a sanctuary under the care of an established priesthood.

Most Arab temples were rectangular buildings of brick or granite. Because of their peculiar form, they were labeled *kaabas*, from the Greek word for *cube*. At one time there were kaabas in Ma'rib, San'a, Najran, Qudayd, Nakhlah, Taif, and Mecca. The only one that has endured is the kaaba in Mecca. Thirty-five feet by forty feet on the sides and fifty feet high, the kaaba, a black-draped stone-and-brick structure does resemble a cube. At one time, the building contained 360 cult objects, including statues of Jesus and Mary, stone replicas of pagan deities, images of doves and other fetishes, the arrows of Baal, and the sole object that Muhammad allowed to remain, *al-hajar al-aswad* (the Black Stone). Fragmented by people's fondling, the Black Stone is bound in silver and attached to the western entry of the kaaba.[10]

One pre–Islamic tradition holds that the Black Stone, like the *omphalos* worshipped by Greeks at Delphi, was the foundation block of the world. A second explanation holds that it represents the throne of Adam. Expelled from paradise in the east, Adam wandered through the world until he came to the middle of the Hejaz. There, amid the black mountains, he beheld a throne supported by four emerald columns. Beneath lay the stone, which then was a luminous white. A variation of the legend has it that God made a covenant with Adam and that this pact was swallowed by the stone (which originally may have been an angel). On the last day of the universe, the stone, discolored by human sins, will bear witness against mankind.

Ibrahim and Ishmael

The most popular version of the Black Stone's origins comes from the *Qisas al-Anbiya*, medieval stories of the prophets. According to this source, the stone lay buried for nearly 1000 years till it was recovered by Ibrahim (Abraham) and Ishmael. The recovery is recounted in a series of adventures essential to an understanding of Islam.[11]

When Ibrahim was driving his caravans across the bleak stretch near what was to become Mecca, his wife, Sarah, jealous of the handmaiden Hagar who had given birth to a male heir, demanded that mother and infant be abandoned in the desert. As Hagar raced desperately between two hills seeking water, the infant Ishmael uncovered a 140-foot deep spring known as *Zam Zam* (plentiful water). Now shielded by an Arabesque kiosk, the well is venerated for its miraculous powers.

Two decades passed before the narrative resumes. Hagar is no longer mentioned and Ishmael is grown, married to a local tribeswoman. Ibrahim, stricken with remorse, returns to the Hejaz, hoping to make amends. By accident, he finds Ishmael's home, but the latter is out. When Ibrahim asks for food and a place to rest, he is put off by Ishmael's wife who, wrongfully claiming there is nothing in the larder, gives him only water to drink. As Ibrahim rises, he admonishes: "O woman, when thy husband returneth, tell him to cleanse the threshhold of his house." Coming home, Ishmael hears what has transpired and expels his first wife.

Two years pass and Ishmael has remarried. Again Ibrahim stops by his house and again Ishmael is away, hunting. Ibrahim asks for succor and rest from the second woman and she welcomes him heartily, treating him with the respect due a lord. For this, she is blessed as Ibrahim departs: "O woman, tell thy husband to guard the threshhold of his house, for it shall be blessed with a great blessing for this day's work." Ishmael returns, "smells the smell" of his father, races after Ibrahim, and the two are reconciled.

The legend goes on to say that Ishmael accompanied his father for some time, through the plain of Mercy outside Mecca, keeping a respectful few paces behind. When they came to a spot called Muna/Mina, the son was accosted by another man who warned him: "Follow not the footsteps of that wicked old man going before thee, for assuredly he will kill thee on the top of that mountain. Turn thee back that thou may be saved." Angered, Ishmael cursed the stranger and flung seven pebbles at him. Well that he did, for this old man was Iblisu, the devil, bent on preventing Ishmael from fulfilling his destiny.

As Ibrahim and Ishmael scaled Mt. Arafat, a 500-foot-high conical hill 12 miles from Mecca, the patriarch confided: "My son, I saw in my sleep that I have to sacrifice thee." Ishmael's dutiful response was: "My father, thy will is my will, but tie the cords very tight to keep me from trembling and remove my garments lest some of my blood spatter them, and I shall thus lose merit, and lest my wife grieve when she sees them. Also sharpen the blade well, and pull it quickly across my throat so that death may be easier. For, verily, death is a very hard matter. And when you come back to my wife, give her my salaams, and if she so desires, give her my shirt. Perhaps it may comfort her a little."

Both men were weeping as Ibrahim bound Ishmael, kissed him, and put the knife to his throat. Only the instrument could not cut through a sleeve of brass God placed about Ishmael's neck. Again, Ishmael spoke: "O my father, turn me on my face, for when you see my eyes, you are sorry for me and pity takes hold of you and keeps you from doing that which God hath commanded you to do." When Ibrahim tried to put the knife to his son's neck a second time, it turned over in his hand and a celestial voice sounded: "Faithfully done, O Ibrahim, thou art truly my servant indeed." Just as in the biblical tale of Abraham and Isaac (Genesis 22), the binding of Ishmael represents the transition from human to animal sacrifice. For Ibrahim finds a ram entangled in a nearby thicket and substitutes this as his sacrifice. More important, what transpired at Arafat is the underlying test of Islamic faith. Ibrahim is said to have submitted to the will of God. The term *Islam* derives from *aslama* (submission). One who is a Muslim, like Ibrahim, symbolically has submitted to the will of God.

The two men descended from the mountain and were led by a divine whirlwind to the spot where the Black Stone lay. There, in what was to become the sacred city of Mecca, a voice commanded, "Build on me." Ibrahim and Ishmael recovered the stone and constructed the first kaaba. Afterward, Ibrahim proclaimed: "Lord make this a land of peace and bestow plenty upon its people, those of them that believe in Allah and the Last Day. Teach us our rites of worship and turn to us mercifully. Send forth to them an apostle of their own who shall declare of them Your revelations and instruct them in the Scriptures and in wisdom and purify them of sin" (Surah 2, The Cow).

Tradition has it that the kaaba currently standing in Mecca is the same *Bayt al-Atiq* (most ancient house) built by Ibrahim and Ishmael. When Ibrahim was finished, he stood off on a boulder to admire his handiwork. To this day the faithful may view Ibrahim's footprints imbedded in the rock that also has become a shrine. In all probability, the present kaaba dates from seventh-century labors of an Abyssinian lord who used the wreckage of a ship from the Red Sea. But the structure has been attacked so many times it is difficult to say from what century it comes.

Kingdoms in the Sun

It would be a mistake to categorize Arab culture in the Jahiliyah period as exclusively bedouin. Archaeological and literary evidence indicates that kingdoms were emerging in Arabia 1000 years before the time of Christ. Here, as elsewhere in the world, religious shrines proved to be the springboard for empire. As a people secured control of a sacred precinct, it established cities, subjugated neighboring tribes, and expanded control over trade.

In the north, a number of kingdoms emerged before the time of Muhammad. One of the earliest was that of the Nabataeans, descendants of the biblical Edomites, who dominated the region of the Dead Sea from the fourth century B.C. Devotees of the Syrian Zeus-Hadad, these Semites established a number of outdoor sanctuaries atop mountain peaks like ar-Ram, near Aqaba, and Zered, in Idumaea. Their main shrine, however, was at Petra, an exquisite Hellenistic City 55 miles south of the Dead Sea. Here, two miles up from the desert floor, in a vale protected on three sides by steep rock, the Nabataeans carved a number of pillared temples and tombs into the pink-and-purple rock. For nearly 400 years, the Nabataeans preyed off caravans moving between the Hejaz and Palestine before the Roman Emperor Trajan razed their last citadel in the Negev in A.D. 106.[12]

Coincidental with the demise of Petra came the rise of Palmyra (A.D. 130–270), a city-state 130 miles northeast of Damascus in the Syrian desert. Known in biblical times as Tadmor, Palmyra dominated trade routes between Mesopotamia and the Lebanese seacoast. Another marvel of porticos and fora, the city supplied Rome with cavalry and lancers. When the Sassanid Persians disrupted communication with India, Palmyra became even more important. When the Emperor Valerian was seized by the Persian Shapur in 260, the Palmyran prince Odenathus and his widow Zenobia attempted to annex all of Syria, North Arabia, Asia Minor, and Egypt. This Arab empire was shortlived, as Aurelian cleared the Danube of threats from Vandals and Sarmatians, then marched into Syria where he defeated the Palmyrans in two battles by 273. Zenobia was dragged off in chains for Aurelian's triumph in Rome. Palmyra was left a desolate oasis town.[13]

About A.D. 300 a new group of Arabs, the Lakhmids, moved into the Lower Euphrates as clients of the Persians. Hired to protect Sassanid possessions from bedouin, the Lakhmids eventually converted to Nestorian Christianity in the sixth century. According to tradition, there were 20 Lakhmid monarchs, the first of whom was Imru'l-Qays, regarded as the first of the historical Arabs. Among his descendants were Numan the One-Eyed (400–18) who built a legendary castle at Hira, Mundir III (505–54) who raided Byzantine possessions to Antioch, and Amr ibn Hind (554–69) whose court was the birthplace of the *qasida*, chivalrous odes associated with desert warriors.[14] In 602, the Sassanids purged their Lakhmid vassals. The Byzantines also had their border clients. The Banu-Ghassan, or Ghassanids, were moved to Syria to neutralize the Lakhmids. Like their brethren to the south, they converted to Monophysite Christianity and, because they had grown too strong, were suppressed in 584.

The development of kingdoms in South Arabia came much earlier. The region was more populous, richer in natural resources and controlled sea and land routes from Egypt to the Indian Ocean. The first of these empires was that of the Sabaeans (1000–115 B.C.). Familiar to westerners through their queen, who conducted a dalliance with Solomon, the Sabaeans were concentrated in Ophir — the present-day region of Yemen. It was from Sabaea that people in the eastern Mediterranean obtained gold, slaves, spices, frankincense and myrrh. The Sabaean capital was Marib, a tell 60 miles east of San'a. Not far from a modern airport, one may detect the ruins of citadels, a temple to the moon god Almakah, and a huge dam that serviced Ma'rib for nearly 1000 years. The Sabaeans conquered Aden, the Hadhramaut, the Jawf of Yemen, and the Minaeans (700 B.C.–A.D. 200), a sophisticated people whose capital at Qarnaw contained parks with temples.[15]

While the Minaean-Sabaean empire was fending off attacks from the Romans in the second century one of their subject tribes, the Himyarites (115 B.C.–A.D. 300) emerged from the Hadhramaut to dominate South Arabia. Himyarite kings minted coins bearing their images, distributed land to feudal lords, and adopted Graeco-Roman design. Under the Himyarites, San'a became a city of castles, the most prominent of which was Ghumdan. Twenty stories tall, the imperial palace was built of granite, porphyry, and marble.

One of the main problems for the Himyarites came from a group of their own colonists—the Axumites. Sent across the Bab al-Mandab into the land of Cush (Ethiopia), which they renamed Axum, these settlers converted to Monophysite Christianity at the beginning of the fourth century. Between 340 to 378, the Axumites returned to Yemen and imposed their rule and religion over the Himyarites. Although the interregnum was short-lived, the impact of the Axumites was very profound. Yemen was a Christian land, with churches and a cathedral in San'a, and all but one of the restored Himyarite monarchs (378–525) were Monophysite Christians.

The lone heretic was Dhu-Nuwas who, for unknown reasons, hated Christians and converted to Judaism. This king was blamed for a massacre of several hundred Christians in October 523 in what is now the border of Najran. When Dhu-Nuwas compounded this persecution by shutting down churches, the basileus Justin I called for a crusade on the part of the nearest Christian ruler. That happened to be Ela Asbeha, Najashi of Axum, who dispatched an army under his general Abraha. In the first encounter, Dhu-Nuwas was routed from his capitol. When the Axumites departed, he returned to San'a and conducted another purge. Whereupon Abraha returned and drove the Jewish king "into the waves of the sea" where "he was never seen again."[16]

South Arabia again became Christian under the viceroyship of Abraha. From the ruins of Ma'rib, he constructed the magnificent cathedral in San'a called *al-Qalis*. Abraha's armies assisted Justinian in campaigns against the Sassanids and he longed for the opportunity to strike against the remaining pagan cult centers of Arabia. When in 570 two Arabs from Mecca polluted the San'a cathedral on the eve of a festival, he had his justification. For the first time in the history of Arabia, war elephants were introduced into a military campaign. Among Arabs, the year 570 is known as the Year of the Elephant and it is recorded that Arabha's forces were unable to penetrate the sacred harem about Mecca. As they camped in the outskirts of the city, the Christian army was beset with *sijjil* (the pebbles, possibly smallpox) and had to give up the siege. Thus a second significant event occurred in 570 — the sparing of Mecca from almost certain capture and conversion to Christianity. A third major event would take place that year in Mecca — the year of the birth of Muhammad, in 570.

14

Muhammad

Mecca

Had Mecca not been the center of a solar-lunar cult, it still would have been important. Deficient in arable farmland, the city was situated along the principal caravan lanes stretching from Palestine to Yemen, the Persian Gulf to Axum-Ethiopia. The Red Sea lay 45 miles to the west, a chain of rugged mountain ridges and the edge of the Rub'al-Khali equidistant to the east. Their reputation for safety and honesty established by the sixth century, the Meccans were reaping financial benefits from pilgrimage traffic, financial speculation, trade in markets and fairs.

Within the city, leadership inhered to *kabirs* (grandees) of the confederated clans. These men constituted the *mala* (assembly of elders) who were required to act in unanimity. The mala named administrators like the *nasi* (responsible for odering the calendar), *siqayah* (superintendent of water supply), *rifadah* (responsible for housing and feeding pilgrims during the holy month of Rajab), and the *liwa* (given the honor of carrying the war standard).

At various times, Mecca was dominated by the Jurhum, Khazaiah, and Qusayy tribes. By the end of the sixth century, political control had fallen into the hands of the Quraysh, whose principal warrior-statesmen were Abu Sufyan of the Abd Shams clan and Abu Jahl of the Makhzum. Muhammad was born to one of the lesser clans, the Hashim. Today, it is considered an honor to trace one's ancestry back to the Hashemites. But 1300 years ago, the Hashemites had lost whatever influence they once enjoyed. Muhammad's family was so poor they could not obtain the services of a wet-nurse for the infant.

Muhammad

As with all religious reformers, a mystique surrounds the life of Muhammad. Though the Prophet never claimed to be anything but a warner, some tried to transform him into a demigod. People fought for clippings of his hair, his bath water, even his spittle. Legends told how the Prophet could change wooden sticks into swords, feed huge crowds with a small portion of food, and tell at a glance if meat was poisoned. Those who tried to cast stones at Muhammad discovered that their hands dried up, while a handful of pebbles thrust at his enemies decided the outcome of the battle of Badr. Muhammad's birth was miraculous, his death coming at his own choosing after he had been presented with the keys to paradise.

The Quran, the principal holy book of Islam, supplies details from Muhammad's later life, but these are sometimes confused and contradictory. The first actual biography of the Prophet, *Sirat Rasul Allah*, was not completed by Muhammad ibn Ishaq in Baghdad till the middle of the eighth century. Other biographies written by ibn Hisham and at–Tabari, along with *hadith* (oral traditions that have the force of religious law), offer further insight into his life. As with Jesus, we know little of Muhammad's appearance. Because Islam is iconoclastic, we are left with the description that Muhammad was an average-looking man, of average height, with a sturdy build and long arms. Blessed with a full head of hair and a thick beard, he had a hooked nose, dark eyes, and "a pleasant smile." When he walked, he looked as if "he were rushing downhill."[1]

All sources agree that Muhammad was born in Mecca in 570, the Year of the Elephant, on a Monday in April. There had been premonitory signs foretelling his birth. Jesus predicted the coming of an apostle whose name would be Ahmad, and at one point in the Quran, Muhammad is called Ahmad. The Quran also advises that "an unlettered prophet," described in the Torah and Gospel, will show people God's mercy and righteousness. Muhammad's mother Aminah supposedly heard a voice telling: "The son whom you are to bear shall be the ruler and prophet of his people." A Jew in Medina and a calf about to be sacrificed to an idol warned of the coming of the seal of the prophets. When he was born, a divine light shone all the way from Mecca to palaces in Syria. Muhammad's birth is said to have been the easiest ever, as the infant was born spotless, circumcised, with the umbilical already cut and tied.[2]

Muhammad's father either died shortly before the Prophet was born or a few months after. This placed an additional burden on his mother, who may have been deprived of a small inheritance. Later, as hegemon of Arabia, Muhammad would guarantee the rights of widows and orphans. As an infant, he was left to divine providence. The normal procedure was for Meccans to give their children to bedouin women to suckle. Ibn Ishaq recounts how none of the bedouin would take Muhammad, fearing they would not be paid. Finally, a member of the Hawazin clan, Halimah, agreed. This woman barely had enough milk for her own child; her husband's flocks were small and scrawny. Once she took Muhammad, however, her breasts filled with milk and her husband prospered.[3]

As a child, Muhammad faced additional tribulations. His mother died when he was no more than six, his grandfather Abdul Muttalib, the patriarch of the Hashim clan, two years later, and he was raised by an uncle Abu Talib. One story of his childhood tells how he was accosted in the desert by two "Angels" who split his body and extracted his heart, which they cleansed in a basin of pure snow. The two white-robed figures then weighed Muhammad's heart against the hearts of 10 men, 100, 1000. It was heavier than the hearts of all mankind, indicating the depth of his compassion.[4]

Muhammad's religious views were molded while on trading trips with his uncle to Syria. When the boy was about 12, he encountered Christian ascetics living in the desert. According to one tale, Muhammad was constructing a portable altar when Zaid ibn Amir informed him: "Idols are worthless. They can neither help nor harm anybody." The boy never prayed before such images again. In another version of the tale, a monk named Bahira engaged Muhammad in conversation and discovered that the youth already held al-Lat and al-Uzza in contempt. The Christian checked the boy's shoulders and found a birthmark that was the sign of prophethood and told Abu Talib, "Great importance is in store for this, your nephew."[5]

Qadr

In the year 595, Muhammad married a wealthy widow from the Makhzum clan. His bride, Khadijah, previously had assigned goods to the merchant for trade in Syria. Impressed with Muhammad's personality, the 40-year-old Khadijah eventually bore Muhammad six or seven children (historians agree that only one, daughter Fatima, survived) and may have been his first religious convert.

Muhammad's religious reformation began sometime during the year 610, when he experienced *Qadr* (Night of Glory or Night of Power). There is some dispute whether this occurred during February or a summer month. The likelihood is that it was the latter, for Muhammad had gone up to the nearby Hira mountains for *tahannuth* (spiritual exercises), which city-dwellers normally performed during the warm season. Whenever Qadr took place, the Quran states the night was "better than a thousand months," for the angels and spirit of God came down with the heavenly decrees.

Islam teaches that it was from the angel Jibril (Gabriel) that Muhammad received verses of the divine, uncreate Quran. Nothing was of his invention; he served merely as a conduit for the holy book. The Quran tells how Muhammad was instructed: "Recite in the name of you Lord who created, created man from clots of blood! Recite! Your Lord is the Most Bountiful One, who by the pen taught man what he did not know." In a more embellished hadith transmitted by az–Zuhri, Jibril suddenly appeared and hailed: "Oh, Muhammad, thou art the messenger of God." When the angel said, "*Iqra!* Recite!" the Meccan responded, "*Ma aqra'u?* What should I recite?" Jibril gripped Muhammad and squeezed him three times, until he nearly fainted. "Then he said, 'Recite in the name of thy Lord who created.' And I recited."[6]

We are told that Muhammad accepted revelation willingly.[7] Returning home, he revealed to Khadijah what had transpired. She took him to a kinsman, Waraqah ibn Nawfal, described by W. Montgomery Watt as an Arab Christian, by Heinrich Graetz as a Jew. Certainly a monotheist, Waraqah certified the verses were "the *nahmus* (prophecy) of Musa (Moses)."

The Mission

For the next three years, Muhammad continued to experience moments of revelation, which attracted dedicated followers. The *Ashab* (first companions) included Khadijah; a nine-year-old cousin, Ali ibn Abu Talib; his adopted son Zayd ibn Haritha; an elderly business acquaintance, Abu Bakr; and a number of frustrated Meccans. In 613, the Prophet was instructed by Jibril to go public with his message. He was ridiculed as a magician, poet or soothsayer possessed by jinn.

Muhammad constituted a threefold threat to Mecca. His teachings might mean an end to the kaaba as a cult center. Revenue from pilgrimages and religious fairs could be lost. At the very least, the prestige of this new group might force a change in Mecca's political leadership.

To quiet such fears, Muhammad continued to pray before the kaaba. At first, the Quran condoned sacrifice to al-Lat, Manat, and al-Uzza, saying, "These are the swans exalted whose intercession is to be hoped for." Later, the verses were altered to read: "They are but names which you and your fathers have invented: Allah has vested no authority in them." The explanation offered was that in Muhammad's time of trouble, the devil had intervened to confound both him and his followers.[8]

Muhammad's enemies were not put off by these so-called "satanic verses." They taunted him to produce the complete sacred writ or that he resurrect the dead. They challenged his claim to be a warner, pointing out that the only land that produced prophets was Palestine. If he were a divinely inspired messenger, let him travel to heaven and back.

Some time between 613 and 620 Muhammad did enter heaven, if momentarily. The Quran offers a clue in the Surah known as the Night Journey (*Isra*), which reads: "Glory be to Him who made His servants go by night from the *Masjid al-Haram* (sacred temple) to the *Masjid al-Aqsa* (farther temple)." In an embellished version, Muhammad traveled from Mecca to Jerusalem accompanied by Jibril on the back of a celestial horse with a woman's head and a peacock's tail.[9]

They arrived in Jerusalem at the spot now occupied by the al-Aqsa Mosque, then strode several hundred feet to the great rock, which once may have been part of Herod's temple. On the site of what is now the Dome of the Rock, Muhammad made his ascent (*miradj*) to heaven. The great rock tried to follow Muhammad, but Jibril restrained it with three fingers, leaving marks in the stone.

Together, Muhammad and Jibril passed through the seven gates of heaven. At each of these portals, they encountered an historical or religious figure — at the first Adam, serving as a judge of the dead; at the second Yahya and Isa (John the Baptist and Jesus), at the third Yusuf (Joseph); at the fourth Idris (sometimes identified as Enoch, elsewhere as the squire of Alexander the Great); at the fifth Harun (Aaron); the sixth Musa (Moses); and the seventh Ibrahim (Abraham). Each extolled Muhammad. When the Prophet stood before Allah, he was praised anew and told that the number of daily prayers required of Muslims would be reduced from 50 to five.

This story accounts for the development of *salat*, one of the basic practices of Islam. It also explains the emotional connection Arabs have for Jerusalem, a city never mentioned by name in the Quran but the third holiest city of Islam. Unfortunately, it did little for Muhammad.

The principal Meccans instituted a social and economic boycott of Muhammad and his followers. Said Abu Jahl: "You have left your father's religion, although he is a better man than you. We shall make your prudence appear folly, and your judgment unsound, and we shall bring your honor low. By God, we shall see that your goods are not sold and your capital is lost."

Devastated by such ostracism (Abu Bakr's fortune dwindled from 40,000 dirhams to 5000 in two years), 83 of Muhammad's supporters emigrated temporarily to Abyssinia-Axum. For those who remained, the situation worsened in 619 when Khadijah and Abu Talib died, leaving Muhammad without clan protection. Previously, anyone who contemplated assault against the Prophet would have had to reckon with the threat of a blood vendetta. Now the Hashim clan was led by another uncle, Abu Lahab, about whom the Quran says: "May the hands of Abu-Lahab perish! May he himself perish! Nothing shall his wealth and gains avail him. He shall be burnt in a flaming fire, and his wife, laden with faggots, shall have a rope of fibre round her neck!"[10]

Abu Lahab made it clear to Muhammad that there would be no retaliation for any attack against him. Thus, when the Prophet went to pray at the kaaba, men of the Quraysh shouted insults at him and were only prevented from beating him when Abu Bakr intervened saying, "Woe to you, will you kill a man because he says Allah is my Lord?" On another occasion, as Muhammad knelt in prayer at the kaaba, a Meccan came up from behind and struck him with the uterus of a slaughtered camel. At that, Muhammad was more fortunate than an old slave woman, Sumayya, stabbed by Abu Jahl with a lance, or Bilal, the first *muezzin* (caller to prayer) who was buried to his neck in sand in a chain-mail suit — the first martyrs of Islam.

The Quran condemns the "bigotry of ignorance" of those who interfered with the Prophet or barred his way from the kaaba (Victory 48:25–26). At the same time, it denounces bedouin Arabs who because of unbelief or hypocrisy were slow to lend assistance (Repentance 9:90, 97, 101; Victory 48:16; Chambers 49:14). In need of some protection, Muhammad married another widow, Sawdah, of the Adi clan, contacted three bedouin tribes and the people of Taif, and entered into negotiations for sanctuary with the people of Yathrib, Mecca's chief economic rival 250 miles to the north.[11]

Hegira

Yathrib may have been settled first by Jews who came to Arabia in the time of Solomon or after the Roman destruction of Judaea. Over the centuries, this cluster of oases and farms attracted two major Arab tribes, the Aws and Khazraj, who outstripped the Jewish clans in numbers and importance. Squabbles between the Arab tribes impeded success against Mecca.

Early in 620, six emissaries from the Khazraj tribe approached Muhammad, inviting him to assume leadership of the city. The Prophet's response was positive, if guarded. Practically an outlaw in Mecca, he welcomed the opportunity to expand his movement among Jews and non-Jews. For the Aws and Khazraj, a man of Muhammad's prestige, who had no direct ties with either faction, might unite the city's warring tribes.

Negotiations went on for two years as Muhammad had to be convinced that his new hosts were sincere. During the pilgrimage in 622, more than 70 men and women from Yathrib, *ansar* (helpers), came to Aqabah near Mt. Arafat to pledge their loyalty to Muhammad. They vowed to foresake idolatry, theft, adultery, and obey Muhammad "in all good things" and he in turn promised to send them a disciple to instruct them in the Quran. On July 16, 622, the last of his followers in Mecca, *(Muhajirun* exiles), set out for Yathrib. No grand exodus, they moved in small bands resembling caravans. Had the Meccan lords suspected what was happening, the émigrés might have been slain, along with Muhammad. The latter stayed behind, with Abu Bakr and Ali, waiting to learn how his followers were received in the new location. Then, late in August, he set out in a *southward* direction, designed to mislead his enemies. Abu Jahl and Abu Sufyan sent a troop of soldiers in pursuit. Legend has it that as Muhammad and his companions took refuge in a cave, God caused a bush, replete with a dove's nest and a tangled spider's web, to spring up across the cave's entry. Convinced that no one could have entered here, the search party passed by. Thus, the three exiles eluded death and managed to reach Yathrib by September 4, 622.

Muhammad's arrival signaled a name change for Yathrib, which was renamed Madinat an–Nabi (the city of the Prophet). The *hegira* (flight) from Mecca to Medina is so crucial in Arab history that the Muslim calendar is reckoned from 622.

The Maghazi Period

The next eight years marked the transformation of Muhammad from emigrant to hegemon of Arabia. After selecting a mud-brick house in Medina where he would reside, Muhammad lived quietly for a short time, before inaugurating what was called the

Maghazi (raiding) period. His *Dar al-Islam* (house of peace), the umma of true believers, must of necessity be in opposition to the *Dar al-Harb* (house of war), made up of idol-worshippers and pagans. Worst among these were the Meccans whose caravans were subjected to attack from Muhammad's warriors.

Early in 624, one of these raiding parties, consisting of eight men, was sent to observe Quraysh trading activities. At Nahklah, near Taif, they attacked a caravan loaded with raisins, leather and other goods, killing one driver and capturing two others. The raid, during the pagan holy month of Rajab, was condemned by bedouin as well as city-dwellers. Taken aback, Muhammad at first renounced his share of the booty. Later, a Quranic verse (Cow 2:217) would justify the action, saying warfare in a sacred month is a transgression, but "to turn men from the way of Allah and to disbelieve in Him and in the inviolable place of worship and to expel his people thence is worse, for persecution is worse than killing."

The first major encounter between Muslims and Meccans took place six weeks after the incident at Nahklah, in March 624. Unwilling to accept the payment of blood money offered by one of Muhammad's relatives in Mecca, Abu Jahl arranged a trap for the Muslim renegades. A caravan of 1000 camels, carrying goods valued at 50,000 dinars ($100,000) was sent through the Wadi Badr, 11 miles southwest of Medina, accompanied by 70 drivers. Muhammad's forces numbered 305 men, but Abu Jahl had an additional 950 troops secreted beyond a valley ridge. The Meccan lord squandered whatever advantage he enjoyed in numbers by parading his men through the countryside, accompanied by women singers, drummers, and tambourines. Muhammad attacked not the diversionary caravan, but the main force of Meccans. Inspired by their captains Umar and Ali, reinforced by 1000 angels, the Muslims drove directly toward Abu Jahl, who, stabbed in the foot and shoulder, died along with several dozen Meccans.[12]

Almost a year to the day after the debacle of Badr, Abu Sufyan led another army toward Medina. Some 3000 Meccans, 700 of them in coats of mail, marched to the cornfields of Uhud, just outside Medina. This time, the Muslims proved reckless, breaking ranks in the midst of battle to plunder the camp of what they mistakenly believed to be a fleeing enemy. In the fighting, 70 Muslims were killed and Muhammad, who had stayed in a tent praying at Badr, suffered wounds in the leg and face and lost a tooth while leading his men in combat. When it was over, Abu Sufyan and Umar exchanged challenges to meet at Badr in 626.[13]

The war would not be resumed for two years. On March 31, 627, the Meccan army, now grown to 10,000 men, including 600 horses, advanced on Medina. The Quran relates how Muhammad prayed through the night before receiving divine instructions to surround the city with a moat or trench (*Khandaq*). For six days, 3000 men abetted by invisible warriors labored, digging a ditch that made hand to hand combat virtually impossible. In the opening days of the three-week siege, some Meccan horsemen did try to cross the chasm and failed. Wearied by cold weather and windstorms, and unable to obtain fodder, which the Muslims harvested before their arrival, the invaders departed in April. The Meccans lost three men, the Muslims six in the seige of Khandaq.[14]

Within a year, the Meccans lost what enthusiasm they had for the struggle. When Muhammad, therefore, announced his intention of making pilgrimage to the kaaba in 628 (inspired again by a dream), even if it meant storming the city at the head of 2000 warriors, the peace party in Mecca offered to negotiate. At Hudaibiyah, the Muslim camp three miles north of Mecca, the two sides signed a pact that promised: (a) a truce of 10 years, during which there would be no raids or spoilation of property; (b) extradition of traitors;

(c) the right to negotiate alliances with bedouin tribes; and (d) a guarantee of a Muslim pilgrimage in the year 629, during which the Meccans would evacuate the city for three days.[15]

Hudaibiyah is important for several reasons. A divided Meccan aristocracy, fearful that the Muslims might plunder their sacred shrine, caved in when they might have resisted. Their concessions not only acknowledged Muhammad's supremacy in Medina, but also increased his prestige among desert tribes. The truce enabled Muhammad's forces to eliminate Jewish strongholds in Fadak, Khaibar, Tayma, and Wadil Kora. Most important, Muhammad interpreted the pact as a *sulh*, a temporary suspension of hostilities, not a permanent peace treaty. At Hudaibiyah, Muhammad established the precedent that it is permissible to negotiate with an enemy until such time as a people were strong enough to carry out their ultimate goals.

After Hudaibiyah, Muhammad worked to solidify his armed might, forcibly subjugating bedouin tribes, sending emissaries to Sassanid and Byzantine courts demanding tribute of them, and waiting for an opportunity to renew hostilities with Mecca. When Safwan ibn Umayyah, Suhayl ibn Amr, and Ikrimah, son of Abu Jahl, conspired to raise a new army in Mecca, the Prophet had his pretext. In January 630, Muhammad, with 12,000 warriors, attacked Mecca from four directions, routing a small force at Hunain and entering the city he had fled less than ten years earlier as conqueror. The *fatah* or opening of Mecca is noted in the Quranic surah known as Victory 48, which credits Allah with sending his *sakina* into the hearts of Muslims that they might achieve this triumph. With the exception of a few deserters and singing girls, Muhammad decreed a general amnesty for residents of Mecca. Ikrimah, Safwan, even Hind, the wife of Abu Sufyan, who had mutilated corpses at Uhud, were pardoned once they converted to Islam.

The keys to the kaaba having been surrendered, Muhammad walked about the building seven times and proclaimed it sacred. The squat idols inside were smashed, as were images of Manat at Mushallal and al-Uzza at Nakhlah. Approaching the Black Stone, Muhammad touched it with his staff and declared: "No man before me was permitted to injure this sacred place and no man after me shall do it. I myself have only been permitted to do it during a part of one day." Thereafter, all shrines of Allah, but especially the kaaba, were off limits to unbelievers. As the Surah of Repentance (9:28) says: "Let them not approach the Sacred Mosque after this year is ended."[16]

Muhammad and the Jews

Muhammad's triumphs over the pagan Arabs was accompanied by a purge of Jewish tribes in the Hejaz. Two years of appeasing the Jews of Medina in hopes of winning their conversion proved fruitless. Muhammad's first mosque was modeled after a synagogue. Prayers were directed toward Jerusalem, Jewish dietary laws followed, the Fast of Ashura (a replica of Yom Kippur) instituted. The Jews responded by ridiculing him as an illiterate. How could the immutable Quran contain a passage that told that Haman (a fifth-century Persian vizier) was instructed by Pharaoh (probably Rameses in thirteenth-century Egypt) to build the tower of Babel (a Sumerian ziggurat dating to 2000 B.C.)? They took note of Muhammad's 11 wives and innumerable concubines and wondered whether he was more interested in activities of the flesh than the spiritual. When he asked the Jews to lend themselves unto God as a pledge, Pinehas ibn Azura replied sarcastically: "God is so poor that he has to borrow from us?"[17]

The Jews could get away with such effrontery because of their venerable heritage in Medina and because Muhammad's leadership was tenuous. After the battle of Badr, however, that changed. The story is told that an Arab woman was sitting, doing business in the market of the Qaynuqa, a Jewish clan of about 700 persons, famed for their jewelry. One of these played a trick upon the woman, fastening her skirt in such a way that when she rose to leave "a considerable portion of her person was revealed." A Muslim regarded the ensuing laughter as an insult and killed the Jew responsible. When this man was in turn slain, Muhammad instituted a siege of the Qaynuka quarter. After 15 days, the survivors were expelled.[18]

In September 625, following the catastrophe of Uhud, a second Jewish tribe, the an-Nadir, was purged. For some time, the Prophet had been the object of scornful poems composed by Ka'b ibn al-Ashraf of the an–Nadir. When this man returned from Mecca in 625, Muhammad asked, "Who will deliver me from Ka'b?" That same night, five Muslims baited Ka'b into making statements against Muhammad, then beheaded the poet. Ostensibly to prevent a blood feud, Muhammad expelled the other 600 members of the an-Nadir and confiscated their property.

The third Jewish tribe in Medina, the Qurayzah, was made to pay for the conspiracies of the an–Nadir against Muhammad. The Qurayzah believed they were protected by a pact they had signed with the Prophet guaranteeing their security as long as they were neutral in the struggle with Mecca. Whether they offered assistance during the siege of Khandaq is unclear. After the battle of the trench, the Prophet tolerated no more "fence-sitting." The men of the Qurayzah were beheaded, their women and children sold into slavery. Assessing the pogroms, one historian called the attacks "spontaneous and not premeditated," while another incredibly suggested the Qurayzah chose suicide rather than conversion.[19]

The subjugation of the Jews did not end there. Within two years, Muhammad's forces, led by Ali, Umar, and Khalid al-Walid, struck against Jewish communities in Khaybar, Fadak, Wadil Qura, and Tayma, demanding tribute and slaughtering those who did not pay. Their success is recorded in the surah of Confederate Tribes 33:26, which states: "He brought down from their strongholds those who had supported them from among the People of the Book and cast terror into their hearts, so that some you slew and others you took captive. He made you masters of their land, their house, and their goods, and of yet another land on which you had never set foot before."

Death of Muhammad

Muhammad did not enjoy the role of hegemon for long. From Medina came longer revelations that dealt with mundane aspects of life, contracts, usury, the status of women, slaves, prisoners. In 632, the prophet made what is known as the Farewell Pilgrimage to Mecca, ushering in an era of what was supposed to be permanent happiness. Upon his return to Medina, where he stayed with his favorite wife, Aishah (Abu Bakr's daughter), he became seriously ill. Scholars disagree whether he suffered pneumonia, lung inflammation, stomach cramps, or headaches. In one telling, Muhammad was the victim of an assassination plot organized by a Jewish wife, Zaynab, whose family had been massacred at Khaibar. Invited to dine on lamb with Abu Bakr and other Muslim notables, Muhammad took one mouthful and spit it out.[20] Zaynab was, of course, executed. Muhammad gained additional, if temporary, satisfaction by ordering his physicians to drink foul-tasting draughts they brought him during his illness. Finally, on June 8, 632, the Prophet died.

His last words, as he lay with his head in Aishah's lap, were, "No, the friend, the highest in paradise."[21]

Muhammad's body lay untouched for a day as his followers coped with the loss of their charismatic leader. One disciple, Umar, threatened to cut off the hands and feet of anyone who dared say the Prophet was dead. It took the aged Abu Bakr to remind the faithful of the numerous sayings in the Quran (Revelations Well Expounded 41:6, Prophets 21:7, Bee 16:42) noting that Muhammad, like all prophets and apostles, was mortal. Said Abu Bakr: "If anyone worships Muhammad, Muhammad is dead, but if anyone worships God, he is alive and dies not."

Muhammad was 62 years old when he died, with no surviving male offspring. Qasim and Abdallah, his sons by Khadijah, had died. earlier. So too, his son-in-law and adopted son Zayd ibn Haritha, slain in a clash with Byzantine troops near Maan in 629, and Ibrahim, his last son by a Coptic slave woman, who died in January 632. As a result, the Islamic world would be permanently rent between those who believed that Ali, the Prophet's nearest male relative, should be his successor (the *Shiatu' Ali*, "party of Ali," or Shiites) and those who argued for a process based on the tradition of selecting the most qualified man as leader (*sunna*, tradition, Sunnites).

15

The Teachings of Islam

The Quran

Though Islam derives its name from Ibrahim's submission to God at Arafat, in the early Meccan years it was called *Tazakki* (righteousness). The goal of the new religion was the *Shariah*, a path of goodness outlined by Allah at the beginning of time and one that was open to all people. The Quran states that men have called God by many names (Heights 7:180), and all men have been summoned to the true faith (Counsel 42:15). Yet it also advises, "The only true faith in Allah's sight is Islam" (Imrams 3:19) and "He that chooses a religion other than Islam, it will not be accepted from him in the world to come he will be one of the lost" (Imrams 3:85).[1]

The problem for Muslims in Muhammad's day, as well as our own, was how to interpret the Shariah. The principal guide for this divine path was the Quran, an immutable holy text. Scholars have counted the number of Surahs (90 identified as Meccan, 24 Medinan), verses (6239), words (77, 934) and letters (323, 621). Matters were not so precise in the Prophet's lifetime. Muhammad's revelations came upon him unexpectedly. Some verses were recorded on stones, bones, leaves, others in script that left words open to different interpretation. Not until the reign of the third Caliph Uthman (644–51) was the Quran codified. *Ulema* (teachers) who continued to use unauthorized texts did so at their own peril. Even then, not all disputes were resolved, for the sages opted to arrange chapters in order of descending length. Thus long surahs that discuss criminal and commercial law appear at the beginning of a standard Quran, while those that offer Muhammad's first revelations are numbered among the last.

The Quran does not begin with the creation of man and follow through to the mission of Muhammad. Many of its stories are familiar — Noah and the ark, Moses and Pharaoh, Joseph and Potiphar's wife, Solomon and Sheba, Abraham and Ishmael. Such tales are repeated in different chapters, often with embellishment. Thus we learn of Moses striking Pharaoh's captain and fleeing to the Midianites in the surah known as the Story 28:14ff., of his confrontation with the Burning Bush in Ta Ha 20:18, his return and miracles performed with his staff before Pharaoh in the Poets 26:9, the imposition of plagues upon Egypt in the Heights 7:13ff., the destruction of Pharaoh's army in the Red Sea in Jonah 10:89ff., the giving of the commandments at Sinai in the Heights 7:146ff., the creation of the golden calf and subsequent salvation in the desert through manna and quails in Ta Ha

20:87 and the Heights 7:14ff., and the dispatch of spies into Canaan in the Table 5:25. Satan's reluctance to prostrate himself before Adam is likewise recounted in the Surahs of the Cave (18:50), al-Hijr 15:40, the Heights 7:13, Sad 38:65 and the Cow 2:32.

Readers may tire of repeated admonitions of what happened to residents of Thamoud and Aad, sinful towns punished alongside Sodom and Gomorrah. Despite prosaic translations and omissions of major prophets like Amos, Isaiah and Jeremiah, the Quran is much like the Old and New Testament at once, a work of revelation, history, folklore, ethics and law.

The Articles of Belief

Chapter One of the Quran (the *Fatiha* or Opening) reads:

> In the name of Allah, the compassionate, the merciful
> Praise be to Allah, Lord of the creation,
> The Compassionate, the Merciful,
> King of Judgement Day!
> You alone we worship, and to You alone we pray for help.
> Guide us to the straight path,
> The path of those whom You have favored,
> Not of those who have incurred your wrath,
> Nor of those who have gone astray.

Recited at every formal prayer service, this exordium expresses the fundamental concepts of Islam known as the Articles of Belief.[2]

The Unity of God. Worst of all sins in the eyes of Islam is *shirk* (polytheism). The Quran insists that there is only one true God, incorporeal and immanent in the universe. The three-line surah of Unity consists of: "Say Allah is One, the Eternal God. He begot none, nor was he begotten. None is equal to Him" (112:1–4). In Iron 57:3 "He is the first and the last, the visible and the unseen. He has knowledge of all things." The Night Journey 17:111 instructs the faithful to praise Allah "who has never begotten a son, who has no partner in His Kingdom, who needs none to defend Him from humiliation." Those who claim that the Lord of Mercy has sired a son, that he is part of a mystical trinity, "preach a monstrous falsehood" (Mary 19:88), utter "a monstrous blasphemy" (Cave 18:4–5). The "unbelievers" who say "Allah is one of three" must be punished "rigorously" in this life and "Hell shall be their home" (Repentance 9:73).

The Quran relates the tale of Mary's visitation by an angel, her conception and painful birth, Mary's kinsmen disputing her tale until the Christ child spoke from the cradle (Mary 19:1ff.). It also makes clear that Jesus was "no more than a mortal" (Ornaments of Gold 43:59), a "sign to mankind" (Believers 23:50), he and his apostles "helpers of Allah" (Imrams 3:52) and not a son of God. When queried by Allah whether he ever asked mankind to worship him or his mother as gods beside Allah, Jesus is quoted as saying: "How could I say that to which I have no right.... You alone know what is hidden. I spoke to them of nothing except what You bade me.... You are the witness of all things.... You are the Mighty, the Wise One" (Table 5:116).

Allah is all-knowing (Luqman 31:34) and any effort to conceal something from him is useless. According to the surah of Houd: "They cover up their breasts to conceal their thoughts from Him. But when they put on garments, does he not know what they hide and what they reveal? He knows your inmost thoughts." (Houd 11:5). God is "with you wherever you are" (Iron 57:4), nearer to man than the vein in his neck. He is all powerful — he created the heavens and earth in six days, caused the night to pass into day and the day into night (Iron 57:4–6), made water to stream from the sky, set immovable mountains upon the earth and dispersed all kinds of plants and beasts (Luqman 31:10), made milk come from the bellies of cattle and honey from bees (Bee 16:66ff.), and created man from the void (Mary 19:67), a germ (He Frowned 80:19), dust (Cave 18:38), potters clay (Merciful 55:14), clots of blood (Resurrection 75:37, Blood Clots 96:2) or semen (That Which Is Coming 56:58, Event 86: 6–7).

The sole God who created men to test them (City 90:1–3), who knows the term of every man's life (Resurrection 75:1) has an absolute claim on their adoration. (Blood Clots 96:19, al-Furqan 25:60, Heights 7:206, Victory 48:29, Repentance 9:112).

Angels. Islam, just as Judaism and Christianity, allows for immortal helpmates of Allah. Jibril was the divine messenger who imparted the Quran to Muhammad. Every soul has a guardian angel (Nightly Visitant 86:4). In heaven, there are "noble recorders" watching people (Cataclysm 82:10–12), entering their deeds in the *Sidjeen*, the "book of transgressors," and the *Illiyun*, the "record of the righteous" (Unjust 83:1ff.). On the day of judgment, these tallies will be presented for or against each individual. In addition, there are angels who protected Adam, Moses and Jesus, who aided Muhammad at Badr and Uhud, who populate the Garden of Eden — and there are those who frustrate, even punish. The jinn of the desert who cause men to see mirages were created from smokeless fire (Merciful 55:15). Azrad was the angel of death, Satan, a fallen angel whose underworld kingdom is populated with all kinds of demons.

The Inspired Books. The Quran states that "a space of time is fixed for every nation" (Heights 7:34), that "every age has its scripture" (Smoke 13:39). Just as the Torah was given by God to the Jews, and the Gospels to Christians, so Muslims believe in the divinity of the Quran. Skeptics could marshall a number of arguments in opposition. After Muhammad's conquest of Mecca, the *kiblah* (direction of prayer, originally toward Jerusalem) was shifted toward Mecca according to the surah of the Cow, which says "We will make you turn towards a kiblah that will please you" (2:142). Critics could also point to the abbreviated chapter known as Fibre (111), which denounces Muhammad's uncle Abu Lahab and another in the Confederate tribes (33:37) that permitted the Prophet to marry the divorced wife of his adopted son Zayd ibn Haritha as oddities in a divine text.

To those who charged it was an "invented falsehood" or "soothsayer's divination" (Adoration 32:3, Sheba 34:43, al-Furqan 25:4, Pen 69:40–42), the Quran responds, "This is a discerning utterance, no flippant jest" (Nightly Visitant 86:13–14), "no invented tale, but a confirmation of previous scriptures, an explanation of all things, a guide and a blessing to true believers" (Joseph 12:111). If Muhammad claimed to be the author, nothing could save him from God's wrath (al-Ahqaf 46:8) for "this Quran could not have been composed by any but Allah. It confirms what was revealed before it and fully explains the Scriptures. It is beyond doubt from the Lord of the Creation" (Jonah 10:38).

The "best of scriptures" (Hordes 39:23), which must not be doubted (Cow 2:1), the Quran was revealed by Allah to Muhammad (Hordes 39:1) through his messenger Jibril (Star 53:6). Allah intended that revelation should come to Muhammad in sections so he might "recite it to the people with deliberation" (Night Journey 17:106). Because the Prophet's people were Arabs, verses were given in a tongue "that you may understand"

(Joseph 12:1). "Had we revealed the Quran in a foreign tongue, they would have said: 'If only its verses were expounded! Why in a foreign tongue, when the Prophet is Arabian?'" (Revelations Well Expounded 41:44). A Quran in Arabic is "free from all faults" (Hordes 39:28), "there is nothing left out" (Cattle 6:38).

Inspired Prophets. Muhammad's mission was to be a warner (Houd 11:12, Creator 35:20). Like all prophets, he never claimed to be anything but mortal (Revelations Well Expounded 41:5, Prophets 21:42). He was the last and greatest of seven prophets—including Noah, Houd of Aad, Saleh of Thamoud, Abraham, Shoaib of Midian and Moses (Houd 11:25ff.). It is important to note that God's agents have been sent to every nation (Jonah 10:48) and those who reject Muhammad are no different from previous doubters, for "We have sent no apostle to any nation whose message was not denied by those of them that lived in comfort" (Sheba 34:34).

Decrees of God. There will come a time when the earth is rocked in a last convulsion (Earthquake 99:1), when the stars will scatter and oceans roll together (Cataclysm 82:1), when the sun ceases to shine, the sky is rent asunder and reddens like a rose (Noah 55:40), when men become like scattered moths and mountains like tufts of carded wool (Disaster 101:1). On this end of days, the gates of heaven will swing open, revealing Allah, borne on a celestial throne by eight angels. The souls of the dead and living will be resurrected and all must stand in judgment before God for the sins they have committed. On that day, when the earth is a barren waste (Those That Are Sent Forth 78:19), unbelievers will lament (Those That Are Sent Forth 78: 40), and men will try to cheat and lie about their lives (Cheating 64:9). The wealthy and those who have fathered many children will boast about their accomplishments, ornaments of a life that is "but a sport and a pastime, a show and an empty vaunt" (Iron 57:20). All of this is to no avail. The wicked may plead in vain (Forgiving One 40:47), but all slanderers (Slanderer 104:1), blasphemers (Cave 18:5), hypocrites (Hypocrites 63:1), usurers (Cow 2:275), unbelievers (Victory 48:14, Proof 98:7), idolaters, bullies and misers will be branded on the nose (The Pen 62:16). Then, doused with boiling water and fettered with iron chains 70 cubits long that wind from their feet to their forelocks, they will be dragged off to hell (Ya Sin 36:8, Thunder 12:6, Inevitable 69:32).

Sinners will spend eternity in *Jahannam*, an Arabic word borrowed from the Christian concept of Gehenna. That synonym for hell was derived from the Hebrew Gan Hinnom, the vale of Hinnom below the walls of Jerusalem, which was the dumping ground for bones from Canaanite human sacrifice. In ancient Judaea, so much trash was carted out to this perpetually smoldering refuse heap that took its name — the Dung Gate —from its proximity to the valley. Christians and Jews could not have imagined a region more akin to Hell than this garbage pit, which even today reeks.

The damned shall be lashed with iron rods in the pitch-black smoke and blazing fires of Jahannam. Draped with garments of fire, their skins will burn over and over again (Pilgrimage 22:119). Some will be transformed into "detested apes" (Cow 2:65). "The dwellers of Hell will wrangle among themselves" (Sad 38:64), but all they will have to drink will be "boiling water" (Jonah 10:4), "stinking water" (Abraham 14:16), "scalding water, festering blood and other putrid things" (Sad 38:55), which they drink like thirsty camels (That Which Is Coming 56:55). Their only food will be bitter thorns, which "neither sustain them nor satisfy their hunger" (The Overwhelming Event 88:5). The fruit of the "accursed" zaqqum plant (Night Journey 17:60, That Which Is Coming 56:56) is molded in the form of a skull (Those Who Set the Ranks 37:65) and will simmer in the belly like scalding water and dregs of oil (Smoke 44:56).

By way of contrast, *al-Janna* (paradise) is very much like the biblical Eden (Cave 18:32, Battle Array 61:12, Thunder 13:20, Creator 35:33). A lofty garden (Overwhelming Event 88:10) or two gardens with shady trees (Noah 55:46), its rivers flow with fresh milk, delectable wine, and clearest honey (Muhammad 47:15). In the center of this shady grove is a camphor fountain, a gushing spring "at which the servants of Allah refresh themselves" (Man 76:4). Those adjudged to be righteous will enter paradise bedecked with pearls and bracelets of gold and silver (Creator 35:33), wearing garments of fine green silk and rich brocade (Man 76:21, Pilgrimage 22:23). Here, in "goodly mansions" (Repentance 9:72) whose roofs, gates and stairs are of silver (Ornaments of Gold 43:35), they will recline on soft, jeweled couches with green cushions arranged in rows over rich carpets (Man 76:14, That Which is Coming 56:14, Mountain 52:20). The glow of joy on their faces, they will feel neither heat nor biting cold (Man 76:14). All will greet one another with the word "Peace" and, troublefree, they will converse with angels. Boys fair as pearls (Mountain 52:25) will serve them fruits, fowl, meat on silver dishes (Man 76:15) along with a drink in silver goblets that neither dulls the senses nor befuddles the redeemed (The Ranks 37:44). The heavenly nectar is variously described as "ginger-flavored water" (Man 76:15), a cup of "purest wine" (That Which Is Coming 56:15) or "pure wine" from a mixture of musk and water of the Tasnim spring (Unjust 83:20).

Although women are admitted to paradise (Ya Sin 36:55, Ornaments of Gold 43:70), it is in a role subordinate to men. According to one hadith credited to the Prophet by at-Tabari: "They are devout wives and those who with grey hair and watery eyes died in old age. After death Allah remakes them into virgins." In paradise, Allah weds men to these dark-eyed *houris*, bashful, "high-bosomed maidens" (Merciful 55:56, Those that Are Sent Forth 78:33), corals and rubies that neither men nor jinn have touched before (Merciful 44:56ff), chaste as sheltered eggs of the ostrich (Ranks 37:40ff.).[3]

The Five Pillars of Islam

One must not only express belief in the fundamental articles of Islam, but implement them in daily life. Specific rituals known as the Pillars of Islam are the practical means of achieving the Shariah. They include:[4]

Shahadah (Profession of Faith). It is not enough that a true believer accept Muhammad as the "seal" of all the messengers of God. Several times daily he must publicly recite: "There is no god but Allah, and Muhammad is his prophet."

Salat (Formal Prayer). Five times each day (at dawn, midday, midafternoon, sunset and nightfall) Muslims must engage in formal prayer. Allah originally commanded 50 of these exercises, but reduced the number out of respect for Muhammad, after the prophet's ascent to heaven. The individual must be in a state of *taharah* (ritual purity), achieved by washing hands and feet with water or with sand. Then, facing toward Mecca, he will declare that he intends to make so many *rakas* (bowings) or *sujud* (prostrations). The actual service involves a number of gestures, symbolizing the universality of God's message, the brotherhood of man, and the fact that Allah hears man's prayers. Verses recited include the Fatiha, the quatrain known as Unity (Surah 112) and *Allahu akbar* (acknowledgment of God's greatness).

Although a Muslim may pray anywhere on his own, once each week (Friday noon) he is obliged to attend a *mosque* (place of prostration) where an *imam* (leader) will direct his prayers and a speaker delivers a *khutbah* (sermon) on some religious issue. Most Islamic sanctuaries are modeled after Byzantines structures with some modifications. From needle-like towers (minarets) *muezzins* issue chants informing the faithful that it is time for prayer. Within the mosque, Islam makes no distinction as to the rank or station of its adherents. To avoid mix-ups in the direction of prayer a *mihrab* (prayer niche) is cut into the wall facing Mecca.

Zakat (**Obligatory Alms**). As someone whose mother was stripped of her inheritance, Muhammad was very concerned that orphans and widows not be deprived of their property (Women 4:2). One-fifth of war booty was assigned to orphans (Spoils of Wars 8:41, Repentance 9:60). Giving alms willingly is the means by which the good man purifies himself (Night 92:18) for he shall be repaid twofold (Iron 57:18) and shown God's mercy (Light 24:56). Islamic *waqfs* (charitable and religious institutions), including mosques, *medressehs* (schools), orphanages and hostels are dependent upon this obligatory tithing.

Sawm (**Fasting**). When Muhammad first came to Medina, he instituted the fast of Ashura, modeled after the Jewish Day of Atonement. This eventually was replaced by *Ramadan*, identified as the time when Muhammad received his first revelations and also when the battle of Badr was contested. For the length of a lunar month, men are supposed to abstain from food, drink, sex and war, in the hours when they can tell "a white thread from a black one in the light of the coming dawn" (Cow 2:187).

Some believers were exempted from the commandment to fast. Travelers on a journey and those who are ill are granted immunity, provided they vow to make up the fast later on, for "Allah desires your well-being, not your discomfort" (Cow 2:185).

Hajj (**Pilgrimage**). The last of the pillars is pilgrimage to Mecca, commanded in the twelfth lunar month and different from the *umrah* or lesser pilgrimage, which may be performed at any time. In Muhammad's lifetime, the journey to the place where Abraham stood was required every year. As Islam spread through the world, Hajj became a ritual that might be satisfied once in a lifetime. The Surah known as Pilgrimage 22:28 reads: "Exhort all men to make the pilgrimage. They will come to you on foot and on the backs of swift camels from every distant quarter." During the *dhul'l-hijjah* (month of pilgrimage) as many as one million faithful come to Saudi Arabia by boat, airplane and cart, from as far as Indonesia and South America.

For 10 days, pilgrims surrender their passports to a *mutawwif* (guide). Upon arriving at the haram zone of Mecca, an individual must purify himself with water (Pilgrimage 22:29) and change into a white seamless garment known as an *ihram*. Thereafter, the pilgrim must refrain from "sexual intercourse, obscene language and acrimonious disputes" (Cow 2:197), may not scratch or kill an insect, shave or cut his hair, and in the case of women must not be menstruating.

The objective in Mecca is the Great Mosque, the blue marble structure that encompasses shrines associated with Ibrahim and Ishmael. Tens of thousands of the faithful, some on litters, throng the courtyard of *al-Masjid al-Haram* hoping to touch or kiss the sacred Black Stone. To do so they must perform the *tawaf*, circumambulate the kaaba seven times as commanded in the Quran (Pilgrimage 22:30). Experienced guides and armed guards try to ensure that the process goes expeditiously. As one North African observer noted in 1975, people are jostled in the press toward the kaaba's gold and silver door.[5]

Kissing the Black Stone is neither the most important nor final act of pilgrimage. The pilgrim should emulate Hagar's quest for water by passing seven times between the enclosed hillocks of as-Safa and al-Marwah (Cow 2:158–159).

A week later, the pilgrims move out along one of six highways to the campground of Muna or Mina midway between Mecca and Mt. Arafat. Here, in the Plain of Mercy, Iblis is said to have tempted Ishmael. Normally during the year the village numbers only a few caretakers. During the holy month, however, a veritable tent city with 500,000 residents sprouts about three pillars (*jamarat*) identified with the devil. Every pilgrim wants to stone the devil's hide, cast 49 pebbles at these pillars. During his visit in December 1974, *Le Monde* correspondent Tahar Ben Jelloun observed, "On one day alone we counted forty-five dead people in one hospital." Attempting to head off such incidents, the Saudi government surrounded the pillars with a two-tiered structure with a 600-foot-long tunnel leading to the lower level. In July 1990, electricity failed during the pilgrimage. People in the dark and overheated tunnel panicked and by the time authorities restored order they counted 1426 dead at the shrine.[6]

On the morning of the ninth day, the pilgrim leaves his tent city and climbs the hill of Arafat. Here, where the patriarch offered his first-born to Allah, the pilgrim performs the rite of *wuquf* (bearing witness). Through most of the day, he stands on the mountain meditating on the significance of what Ibrahim and Ishmael had done, recalling, too, that it was at Arafat during the Farewell Pilgrimage that God had informed Muhammad he would forgive the sins of pilgrims. This act of identification is the one essential to completion of the Hajj.

Once wuquf has been performed, the pilgrim offers a sacrifice of cattle, camel, sheep or some other animal whose meat should be given to the poor. Said Tahar Ben Jelloun: "It was impossible to find out how many sheep were slaughtered in one morning. I walked through puddles of blood over tons of meat and sheepskins on a particularly hot day...."[7] Just as it has addressed the problem of unruly crowds at Muna, the Saudi government has tried to collect unclaimed offerings and freeze the meat in a nearby packing house for later distribution.

From Arafat, the pilgrim may continue to the tomb of the prophet in Medina.

Jihad (Holy War)

There is a sixth act that has been elevated by some to the level of a pillar and that is *jihad*. Technically the word means any great effort. When the Quran advises the faithful to fight for the cause of Allah (Women 4:73, 74), this could be interpreted to mean an internal struggle for man's soul, a question of conscience, as "he who fights Allah's cause fights for himself" (The Spider 29:6). Among Kharijite and Almohade sects in the Middle Ages, extremists of the Muslim Brotherhood and Hamas today, jihad means war against enemies of Islam.[8] The Quran urges jihad against those who have broken oaths (Repentance 9:13–14), idolaters (Spoils 8:39), those to whom the Scripture was given and do not embrace the true faith of Islam (Repentance 9:29), infidels (Repentance 9:123) and the friends of Satan (Women 4:76).

Jihad must be defensive: "fight for the sake of Allah those that fight against you, but do not attack them first. Allah does not love the aggressors" (Cow 2:190). Believers have an obligation to oppose their enemies: "if you do not fight he will punish you sternly and replace you by other men" (Repentance 9:39). The Quran instructs "when you meet the unbelievers in the battlefield, strike off their heads" (Muhammad 47:4). Or "kill them wherever you find them. Drive them out of the places from which they drove you" (the Cow 2:190). Or "those that make war against Allah and His apostle and spread disorders in the land shall be put to death or crucified or have their hands and feet cut off on alternate sides or be banished from the country" (the Table 5:33).

Those who die as martyrs are assured a place in paradise. They live forever, rejoicing in god's bounty (Imrams 3:170). "He will not allow their works to perish. He will vouchsafe them guidance and ennoble their state; he will admit them to the Paradise He has made known to them" (Muhammad 47:5).

Ethics

There should be no armed clashes among Islamic peoples for believers are "a band of brothers" (Victory 49:11). Further, the surah of Women 4:92 instructs "it is unlawful for a believer to kill another believer except by accident." Within the umma of Islam, blood feuds were abolished, mediation decreed. A clan that had been wronged was to settle for some form of witgelt. Anyone who killed a believer by design "shall burn in Hell for ever" (Women 4:93).

The Quran urges controlled behavior in every situation. A Muslim must ask permission before entering a house (Light 24:27). Once admitted, he must comport himself properly (Confederated Tribes 33:52). He must be courteous in his speech (Night Journey 17:53), showing no arrogance, boastfulness or harsh words (Women 4:36, 148; Bee 16:92). According to the surah known as Luqman 31:18: "Allah does not love the arrogant and the vainglorious." Rather, let your gait be modest and your voice low: the harshest of voices is the braying of the ass."

Muslims are to show kindness to their parents (Spider 29:8), speak for justice, avoid the ignorant and show forgiveness even to their enemies (Heights 7:199) for Islam, like other major religions, has its own variant of the Golden Rule. In Revelations Well Expounded, we read: "Requite evil with good and he who is your enemy will become your dearest friend" (41:34).

True believers may not engage in deceit (Bee 16:92) or create a commotion by obstructing roadways (Heights 7:86). The Quran declares that even idolaters are entitled to asylum (Repentance 9:6), and monasteries, churches, synagogues and mosques to be respected as places of sanctuary (Pilgrimage 22:40).[9]

Status of Women

In his biography of Muhammad, Michael Cook of the University of London writes: "The status of women is extensively treated in the Koran. God's views on this matter are on the whole unfashionable at the present day. Women are not equal, and are to be beaten if they get out of hand. As in ancient Israel, polygamy and concubinage are allowed, and women are easily divorced."[10]

A case can be made that Islam improved the status of women. The Quran forbids burying girls alive (the Cessation 81:8) and other forms of female infanticide (Night Journey 17:31, Cattle 6:152). No woman was to be forced into marriage against her will, and whatever token serves as bridewealth must be given in admiration, not purchase. The actual wedding ceremony takes place publicly, with the signing of a *khatba* before witnesses. If any children ensue from the union, acknowledgement of physical paternity is encouraged. Incest is prohibited, as is homosexuality, but *Bint 'Amm*, cousin marriage, which strengthens families and accounts for more than 40 percent of the marriages among Kurds, is permitted.[11]

The institution of polygamy—a man may take a maximum of four wives, Women 4:3—has been defended by commentators who see it as one way of combating excesses of concubinage, prostitution, and adultery. In a society where men risk dying in combat, there is a possibility that unattached women and indigent widows might seek the companionship of whatever men are available. The Quran does not command that every man take four wives. Only those who can "maintain equality among them" (Women 4:3) and "be impartial" (4:129) may do so. Once fashionable in the medieval world, polygamy is the exception in our own times. If a woman fears ill-treatment or desertion on the part of her husband, she may seek a separation (Women 4:128), for women have rights similar to those exercised against them (Cow 2:228).

The verse goes on, however, to warn that "men have a status above women." Under the *beit al-ta'a* (the traditional law of obedience) women were regarded as subordinate to men and those who sought justification could cite several passages in the Quran. Male authority stemmed from the fact that "Allah has made the one superior to the other" (Women 4:34). Women were frivolous creatures (Bee 16:92). They were "men's fields that they can enter as they please" (Cow 2:223). Ideal women were "submissive, devout, penitent, obedient, given to fasting, both widows and virgins" (Prohibition 66:5). "Good women are obedient. They guard their unseen parts because Allah has guarded them. As for those from whom you fear disobedience, admonish them and send them to beds apart and beat them" (Women 4:34). Men could also obtain a divorce by repeating a simple recitation in public. For women, the process was more complicated.

Because they were carnal creatures (Believers 223:1), girls had to be secluded and compelled to wear the formless *jibbeh* or *chador* when they became nubile. The practice derived from ancient Babylonia, where veiling was a privilege denied harlots and slaves. The Quran commands that to preserve their chastity, females must "cover their adornments (except such are normally displayed), draw their veils over the bosoms, and reveal no finery" except to specific members of the family, and refrain from stamping their feet to ring bells on their anklets (Light 24:31). To curb sexual appetite, some tribes practiced infibulation (female circumcision)—which has been severely criticized.[12]

Much has been made of the changing role of women in the Middle East in the last quarter century. Several women have served as ministers in Iraq, Jordan and Tunisia over the years.

Women supposedly enjoy a much greater influence behind the walls of their own homes anyway. Jehan Sadat, the widow of the assassinated Egyptian leader, was responsible for a law enacted in 1979 that raised the minimum marriage age from 11 to 15 and guaranteed divorced women support for themselves and their children. Similar family codes were enacted in Tunisia in 1956, Iran in 1976 and Algeria in 1982. Unfortunately, all have come under attach from religious fundamentalists who see a conflict with traditional values.[13] Various family reforms instituted by the Shah no longer operate in Iran and Sadat's own daughter was physically abused by her husband before being divorced in the public *talaq* ceremony.[14]

Blacks and Slavery

Islam has a great following in Africa, with perhaps 300 million believers on that continent. Islamic missionaries have also been active among 100 million blacks who reside outside the African homeland. Much of its appeal stems from claims that Islam does not condone slavery and recognizes no color distinctions. Unlike chattel slaves in the Western Hemisphere, Muslim servants were loyal members of an extended family who lived with their masters, dressing alike, eating the same food.

In the medieval world, color did matter. There are numerous tales of miraculous transformations of virtuous blacks who became white and whites being punished for evil deeds by becoming black. Whether known as Ethiopians, Zanj, mawla, Nubians or as-Sudan, blacks were lampooned and stereotyped. Princeton scholar Bernard Lewis has recited a long list of negative attributes ascribed to Africans in two major studies, *Race and Color in Islam* and *Race and Slavery in the Middle East*. Some of the most prominent Islamic scholars (the 10th-century historian al-Masudi, Muhammad al-Idrisi, the Persian Nasir al-Din Tusi, the 11th-century Baghdad physician ibn Butlan, and the 14th-century Tunisian chronicler Ibn Khaldun) repeated racial broadsides. From Basra in the ninth century, al-Jahiz wrote: "The like of the crow among mankind are the Zanj for they are the worst of men and the most vicious of creatures in character and temperament." Like Umar, who was the object of racial derision, al-Jahiz may have been of African descent. Several other black writers who lived through the formative years of Islam engaged in exercises of self-abnegation. Wrote the poet Suhaym, "If my color were pink, women would love me, but the Lord has marred me with blackness." Another, Abu Dulam (d.776), commented, "We are alike in color: our faces are black and ugly, our names shameful."[15] Race affected the nature of the operation preparing slaves for sale as eunuchs. It influenced price at market (the fairer the slave, the higher the price). Once freedom was secured, whites were called by a different name (Mameluke) than blacks (known as Abd) and enjoyed greater access to power.[16]

The existence of slavery in the Islamic world is explicitly acknowledged by various passages in the Quran and other sources. Muhammad encouraged manumission — declaring it to be a righteous act (Cow 2:177; City 90:13) and a penalty for libel or accidental homicide (She Disputeth 48:3, Women 4:92). Muslims were encouraged to turn loose co-believers, though enslavement of non-believers was by no means forbidden (Women 4:25, Cow 2:177, Light 24:32, She That Disputeth 48:3). The Arabian Nights tell of faithful, well-treated slaves winning their liberty through deeds of courage. The medieval world also permitted individuals to achieve freedom through a kind of land contract where a slave made installment payments, or by virtue of conversion to Islam. The last method was not simple, for the prospective convert had to prove before two witnesses that he could pray in Arabic.

Muhammad's admonitions to the contrary, Muslim slavers were trading in sub-Saharan Africa 700 years before the Portuguese rounded the Bight of Benin. From North Africa came Berber and Tuareg tribesmen to purchase slaves in Timbuktu, the fabled entrepot in Mauritania. At Kuka, near Lake Chad, the Bournu people of Central Africa were bound and marched into the desert, where many succumbed to exposure and disease. Slave markets were so numerous in north Somalia that the region across the Red Sea from Jiddah to Hodeida in Asir was dubbed "the Cape of Slaves." In one four-year period (1875–79) more than 100,000 blacks were sold in Khartoum. After the signing of an international convention outlawing slavery in 1926, as many as 30,000 were still being sold each year in the caliphal port of Zanzibar. As in the west, slaves were used for brute labor — in sugar fields and rice paddies, on galleys and caravans. In the Persian Gulf, some were forced into the water to be trained as pearl divers. African slaves carried supplies, but no weapons, for the army. They extracted salt from underground mines. Periodically, like the 300,000 Zanji who lost their lives in Iraq in the ninth century, they revolted against this demeaning servitude.[17]

Dietary Laws

Islam's dietary laws are similar to the Jews: "the food of those to whom the Book was given is lawful to you" (Table 5:5). Muslims may eat no carrion, blood or pork, no flesh of strangled animals, animals sacrificed to idols, beaten to death or mangled by beasts of prey (Table 5:3, Bee 16:115, Cow 2:172). They may eat what trained dogs or falcons catch for them (Table 5:4) and are not bound by certain restrictions imposed upon Jews. For example, animals with undivided hoofs such as camels may be consumed (Cattle 6:147).

In food, as elsewhere, moderation is the rule. The surah of the Heights states: "Eat and drink, but avoid excess. He does not love the intemperate" (7:31). A Muslim may not engage in formal prayer when drunk since he could not "grasp the meaning of your words" (Women 4:43). Whatever value drinking may have for men as an emotional outlet is outweighed by the harm it does (Cow 2:219). For drinking and its inevitable partner — gambling — are abominations devised by Satan. "Satan seeks to stir up enmity and hatred among you by means of wine and gambling and to keep you from the remembrance of Allah and from your prayers" (Table 4:90).[18]

Criminal Laws

What happens to those who gamble or tipple in this world is unclear. A guiding principle of Islamic law is "let your punishment be proportionate to the wrong that has been done you" (Bee 16:126). One punishment prominently mentioned in the Quran is flogging. If adultery is committed by Muslims, both parties are to be given 100 lashes. If someone accuses a woman of adultery and cannot produce four witnesses, the defamer must be given 80 lashes (Light 24:2).

More serious crimes command severe punishment. In theory, a thief is to be punished by having his hands cut off (Table 5:38). Over the years, only the right hand has been removed from a first offender, leaving him to eat with his "unclean" left hand. Recently, there has been a further tempering of this punishment. In Saudi Arabia, a thief will not lose his hand until his third offense. In Pakistan, only the tips of fingers are cut away. Even in Qaddafi's Libya there is some concern for the culprit. His hand is to be removed but only after a surgical operation performed with anesthesia.

The Quran outlines a range of capital crimes. Those who speak ill of Allah, the Prophet, or his holy book, should be branded on the nose then have their heart's vein cut out. Usurers are to be consigned to the hellfire (Cow 2:275) along with those who commit adultery outside the umma, women guilty of lewdness or fornication (Women 4:15), witches, traitors, regicides, and murderers (Women 4:29–30, Table 5:32, Cattle 6:152, Night Journey 17:33).[19]

In sum, the Quran is not merely revealed theology. It is a comprehensive code governing virtually every aspect of a Muslim's life. Rules may be found here pertaining to marriage (Cow 2:221, 235; Women 4:3; Light 24:32) and divorce (Cow 2:226, 230; Women

4:215; Victory 48:2) dowries (Women 4:4,20), and wills (Cow 2:180, Women 4:7), contracts (Cow 2:282) and remission of debt (Cow 2:28), treatment of the feeble-minded (Women 4:5), slaves (Light 24:32) and the *ahl al-Kitab* or Christians and Jews (Table 5:51). No simple text, the Quran is the way for one billion Muslims around the world.

16

The Islamic Schism

The Caliphate

The death of Muhammad precipitated a crisis within Islam that has not been resolved to this day. The prophet predicted that Islam would be splintered among 500 sects, and his failure to appoint a specific successor helped contribute to this division. Tradition dictated that he be succeeded by his nearest male relative, preferably a son, but all three of Muhammad's male offspring died before him. His adopted son, Zayd ibn Haritha, had been slain in an ill-fated venture against the Byzantines in 629.

The Quraysh of Mecca argued that Muhammad was one of them, hence the new leader should come from their tribe. The idea was opposed by the Medinese *Ansar* (helpers) under Abu-Ubaydah, who recalled how Muhammad had been abused by the Quraysh. The *Muhajirun* (emigrants) pointed out that they had been with Muhammad through the difficult times of the Hegira. Some of the original converts (*Ashab*), calling themselves *Shi'at Ali* (the party of Ali, Shiites) stressed that the Prophet's lone surviving daughter, Fatima, was married to a cousin, Ali, who was also Muhammad's nearest male relative.

Ultimately an ad-hoc committee, including the military commanders Abu Ubaydah, Umar ibn al-Khattab, Amr al-As, Ali and Usama, son of Zayd ibn Haritha, would swear allegiance to Atik Abdallah, known as Abu Bekr. Sixty-five years of age, the lean man whose devotion to Muhammad had earned him the nickname of "as-Siddiq" (the upright) had been one of the first converts in Mecca. Abu Bekr endured the economic-social boycott and accompanied the Prophet to Medina. When Muhammad was too ill to conduct prayer services, Abu Bekr substituted and wept with joy when he read from the Quran. According to one hadith, Muhammad said that Abu Bekr's faith outweighed the faith of all Muslims. His daughter Aishah was the prophet's favorite wife. When Muhammad died and Umar went about threatening to kill those who announced the news, it was Abu Bekr who calmed the people, telling them, "If anyone says the Prophet is dead, he speaks the truth, but Allah lives."[1]

Abu Bekr became *caliph*, a term which originally meant successor and which, in the case of the first few caliphs, was exemplified by a simple life style. With the death of each caliph, a *shura* or council of elders was called to select the man best qualified to direct the fortunes of Islam. This principle derived from Arab custom (*sunna*). With the passage of time, notions of democracy would fade away as leaders took on the trappings of hereditary oriental despots.

Sunni Muslims

Sunni Islam employs several means to discern the Shariah.[2] The simplest is the Quran. Of 6000 verses in the Muslim holy book, however, only 200 are legislative in nature. A second source of the divine path were *hadith*, sayings attributed to Muhammad. These oral traditions multiplied after the prophet's death, numbering more than 500,000 by the middle of the ninth century. Many were questionable — derived from people who lived at opposite ends of a century. The task for Muslim scholars was to sift through these adages and determine which were legitimate. The sage Abu Abdullah al-Bukhari (d. 870) listed 7000; his contemporary Ahmad ibn Hanbal, 30,000.

Because the hadith could not provide exact answers for every question, Sunni Muslims devised *qiyas* (analogy, what Muhammad might have done in a similar situation), *ijma* (public consensus, using the entire Muslim community as a barometer) and *ra'y* (personal opinion). Four Sunni sects evolved during the Umayyad period (661–750) and continue to the present:[3]

Hanifite. The largest branch of Sunni Islam was named after Abu Hanifah, who died in Baghdad in 767. Stressing the importance of private opinion as a supplement to the Quran and hadith, Hanafi liberalism was especially attractive to Abbasid and Ottoman caliphs. Considered a "northern" sect, the Hanafis number a half billion adherents from Asia Minor to Pakistan.

Malikite. Founded by Malik ibn Anas of Medina in the eighth century, the Malikite is a more conservative school, ascribing importance to consensus. Because it is nigh impossible to obtain an accurate reading of all Muslims on any issue, the Malikites look to the people residing in the city of Medina. There are 100,000,000 adherents of this "western" school, concentrated mostly in North Africa.

Shafi'ite. Established by the Gaza jurist Muhammad ben Idris al-Shafii, a student of Malik, the Shaf'ite school tried to reconcile differences between the two earlier Sunni sects. Al–Shafii, who taught in Cairo and Baghdad, indicated that if no hadith were available, then consensus and analogy (*kiyas*) were legitimate. This moderate, "eastern" school has perhaps 200,000,000 followers from Palestine, Egypt, East Africa, and the East Indies.

Hanbalite. Extremely conservative, even puritanical in its outlook, the Hanbalite school accepts only sunna found in hadiths as supplements to the Quran. The smallest Sunni sect was the work of Ahmad ibn Hanbal, a student of al-Shafii. Scrupulous attention is paid to laws of *taharah* (purity), separation of sexes, iconoclasm. In the 18th century, the Hanbalite ascetic Muhammad ibn Abdal Wahhab converted the Saud clan of the Nejd to this fundamentalist teaching. Hence the "southern" identity of this school, which numbers 50,000,000, principally in Arabia.[4]

Sufis (Islamic Mystics)

Every religion breeds its mystics, individuals who seek spiritual union with the godhead. Islam always had individuals who encouraged such passionate religious encounters. *Qussas* (story tellers), *qurra* (reciters), *bakka'un* (weepers), *zuhhad* (ascetics) and *majdhubs* (professional mendicants in a perpetual state of trance) borrowed freely from the teachings of other religions, inventing fanciful hadith and ascribing miracles to a host of invisible saints who were responsible for preserving the universe. Prayers to these guardian angels, as well as to a Christlike *Mahdi* or redeemer were approved. People were instructed how to achieve extinction of personal consciousness—*fana,* a term related to the Hindu concept of nirvana.

By the 10th century, this class of self-proclaimed holy men were called *sufis.* The term may derive from the Arabic root *safa* (to be pure) or *suf* (after coarse, woolen garments favored by itinerant preachers). One such mystic was Junayd, a Persian holy man who preached that God created man in his own image, that man could find God in himself. Said Junayd: "I am he whom I love and he whom I love is I. We are two spirits dwelling in one body. If thou seest me, thou seest him and if thou seest Him, thou seest us both." For this heresy, Junayd was crucified in 920. His disciple Hussein al-Hallaj (the woolcarder), upon being condemned for sorcery, was flogged, mutilated, hanged on a gibbet, decapitated and burned.[5]

The safety of Sufi leaders (*shaykhs* or *pirs*) was paramount, for only they knew the ritual (*dhikr*) to achieve fana. Without their leaders, the followers—*faqirs* (Arabic for "poor ones") or *dervishes* (Persian for "disciples")— would be as lost as blind men. For mutual protection, the dervishes banded together in formal groups or orders. These became so powerful that they became major forces in Islamic society. The shaykh commanded absolute loyalty. He explained that the only things needed by men were a book of prayers, a pouch and a begging bowl. And he held the keys to dhikr.[6]

Each dervish order had its own "remembering" process. It might be reciting the 99 beautiful names of Allah with a beaded chain — the *subhah,* which originated in India and was transformed into the Latin rosary. The *Qadiriya* derivishes, whose inspiration was an Iranian mystic; Abdel Qadir al-Gilani, repeated a phrase glorifying Allah in an ever-faster pattern 500 times. The *Rifaiya,* founded by Abdel Qadir's nephew, would scream as they (the howling dervishes) moved together in a circle. The *Sadis,* an offshoot of the Rifaiya, used drums and tambourines. The *Naqshabandi,* named after a painter from Central Asia, sat silently together in the lotus position, eyes shut, hands clenched, painting verses of the Quran on their hearts. The most celebrated group, the *Jibawiya* or whirling dervishes who originated in the 14th century, rotated their bodies slowly at first, then spun about quickly like a graceful skater to induce a trancelike state.

Once fana was achieved, anything was possible. Tales are told of dervishes eating red-hot coals, live scorpions, snakes, and glass. Horses were ridden over bodies, needles passed through hands, spikes into eyes without any permanent damage. Some of this might be ascribed to deliberate illusion, but credible witnesses have attested to feats that cannot be readily explained.[7]

Mutazilites (Rationalists)

If the Sufis represented an emotional extreme of the Islamic spectrum, the Mutazilites were at the opposite end. No formal sect, the Mutazilites were intellectuals who tried to reconcile theology and science. The 8th-century pietist Hasan al-Basri is credited with being the first scholar to reject determinism and stress man's responsibility for his own actions. Some of al-Basri's disciples may have founded *i'tazala* (offshoots of his order).[8]

Whatever their origins, the Mutazilites raised a number of disturbing questions. How could Muhammad be the seal of all prophets if the Mahdi were yet to redeem mankind? How could the throne of an all-powerful god quiver? Why deny the kingdom of heaven to the arrogant when it was open to one who committed the greater sin of robbery? References abound in the Quran to God speaking, moving, lifting his hand. We are told that God created man in his own image, hence the ban on portraits of the prophet or saints. Yet God is said to be non-anthropomorphic, not human in form.

Belief in an uncreate Quran can also lead to confusion. If this work always existed, it is not the product of God. And if it is eternal, it must be another God, on the same level as Allah. Moreover, how is it possible for passages of divine writ to be destroyed (eaten by a goat) or modified by scholars?

A third question of free will/predestination has troubled devotees of all religions. How could a just God, whose powers give him foreknowledge of everything, condemn men to hell? Surely he knows when he creates these defective beings that they would sin. Punishing someone for doing what they were programmed to do is illogical.

The most complete exposition of Mutazilite beliefs is contained in the *Fiqh Akbar* (Great Religious Creed), 29 articles credited to Abu Hassan al-Ashari, who died in Baghdad in 942. Here, it is explained that God is eternal, with no resemblance to man. He does have a face, hands, soul, but it is not legitimate to inquire further. His speech, revealed to the prophets, is immanent in the world. All good and evil were created by God, but it is left for each man to determine his deeds. Whatever the outcome, God cannot be unjust for it is impossible for men to fully comprehend his purposes.[9]

Shi'at Ali (The Shiites)

Although Ali ibn Abu Talib was passed over three times for the caliphate (in 632 by Abu Bekr, 634 by Umar ibn al-Khattab, 644 by Uthman), his supporters never despaired of securing the leadership of Islam for him. All kinds of tales were invented to embellish the claims of this short, bald, corpulent man. Ali was the first *fatah* (warrior) who had fought bravely at Badr, Khadaq and Uhud, receiving 16 wounds in the last battle. Nicknamed *dhu'l-Faqar* (breaker of vertebrae), he had thrashed the enemies of Islam, clearing the Jews from Khaibar and Tayma in 628, leading expeditions to Yemen in 631, killing 523 men on one day, 33 by simply extending his arm. According to one saying, "No sword can match dhu'l-Faqar and no young warrior can compare with Ali."[10]

A simple man who left a fortune of 600 dirhams (roughly $180), Ali's devotion to Muhammad and Islam was as fabled as his military exploits. It was said that to identify with the masses, he fasted for days. At the end of this period of self-mortification, he would turn his bread over to beggars. Ali promulgated four new surahs in 630 (banning polytheists and nudists from the tawaf at the kaaba, as well as defining the time necessary for conversion and entrance into heaven). Ali is credited with 1000 aphorisms, placing him on the intellectual level of Solomon. Muhammad referred to him as his soul, and three months before the prophet's death, during the pilgrimage in 632, he presented Ali to 120,000 people in Mecca, saying: "Oh God, the one who is a friend of Ali, be his friend, and the one who is Ali's enemy, be his enemy."

Some of Ali's followers went so far as to claim that Muhammad was only a prophet while Ali was a saint. In the telling, Jibril mistakenly delivered the Quranic revelations to the wrong individual on the Night of Power. Ali was the *mazhar* (epiphany) of primordial light, the infallible imam or leader of all true Muslims. The concept of election practiced by Sunnis was illegitimate, because such blessing could only be transmitted from one imam to his nearest male relative (in the case of Ali his son Hassan, then a second son Hussein, and so forth).

According to traditional Shiites (*Ithna Ashariya*) there were twelve imams down to the middle of the ninth century, as follows:

SHIITE IMAMS

1. Ali, assassinated in Kufah, 661
2. Hassan ibn Ali, poisoned, 669
3. Hussein ibn Ali, slain on battlefield of Karbala, 680
4. Ali ibn Hussein, d. 713
5. Muhammad al-Baqir, d. 713
6. Jafar as Sadiq, d. 765
7. Musa ibn Jafar, murdered by Harun al-Rashid, 799
8. Ali ibn Musa, poisoned by al-Mamun, 818
9. Muhammad ibn Ali, murdered, 835
10. Ali Naghi, murdered in Iraq, 868
11. Hasan al-Askari, murdered near Samarra, 874
12. Muhammad al-Mahdi, disappeared near Samarra, 880

Each was persecuted by the majority Sunnis and found it necessary to practice *taqiya* (concealment). Shiites faced with torture or execution were to dissimulate when pressed by Sunni authorities. They believed that the last imam — known as Qaim az-Zaman (the imam of all time) or Muhammad Abul Qasim *al-Mahdi* (the rightly guided) disappeared into a cave about 880, and that he will return one day at the end of a century to proclaim the true faith.

Today, Shiites accept only Quranic passages and traditions narrated by a recognized imam. They give greater importance to veneration of "saints" and make pilgrimage to the tombs of Ali and his son at Karbala. There, on the 10th of Muharram, the faithful flog themselves with chains and perform a passion play that recreates the murder of Ali.[11] The Shiites permit temporary marriage, hold to free will, and are scrupulous about hygiene. The last practice, probably derived from India, approaches caste untouchability. It has also been in Shiite territory (Iran and Iraq) that the most extreme decrees affecting the status of Jews and Christians have been imposed.

Like the Sunnis, the Shiites have divided into numerous sects that seem confusing to westerners. Among the more significant are:

Kaisanis (Three'ers). A small group held that Ali had a third son, Muhammad ibn Hanafiyya, who should have succeeded to the imamate before Hassan. One of Ali's servants, Kaisan, was the first to espouse the cause, hence the name.

Zaydis (Five'ers). Taking their name from Zayd, the brother of the fifth imam, these Shiites established a shaykhdom in Yemem that lasted for nearly three hundred years. Following a bloody civil war, in 1962 the Maoist National Liberation Front ousted the last Zaydi Imam Ahmad.

Ismailis (Seven'ers). One of the more fascinating Shiite groups, the Ismailis revered the eldest son of Jafar as-Sadiq as the seventh Imam. Ismail, a profligate, behaved in a manner some Shiites deemed objectionable. His supporters countered that it was impossible for common men to judge an imam. They argued there was something mystical about the number seven. The Quran told of seven speakers who came to enlighten mankind. The universe was organized in seven levels and men could learn divine truth in seven stages. The sect was inspired by the teachings of Persian Abdullah ibn Maimun in the eighth century. Under the leadership of Said ibn Hussein, better known as Ubaydullah, the Ismailis conquered Tunisia and Egypt in the 10th century, establishing the Fatimid dynasty, which ruled from al-Qahirah (Cairo) from 969 to 1171. Prominent in East Africa and India, the Ismailis were once headed by the Agha Khan, a figure who annually received his weight in gold and gemstones.[12]

Qarmatians. Another medieval sect that emerged from the turmoil of the ninth century, the Qarmatians have sometimes been accused of being communist or socialist. They shared property (including wives), created a common treasury and organized workers into guilds. Founded by Iraqi dwarf Hamdan Qarmat, a disciple of the Ismaili leader ibn Maimun, the Qarmatians were a particularly ruthless group. They fomented the rebellion of the Zanjj in southern Iraq between 869 and 883, during which perhaps 300,000 persons died. They attacked Mecca, smashing the Black Stone and destroying the Ka'ba in 929. They taxed pilgrims to the holy city, contending they were the only true Muslims. Although their control over the Hejaz lasted only a few years, some of their settlements existed into the 10th century.

Nusayris (**Eleveners**). Also known as *Alawites* (worshippers of Ali), the Eleveners believe in transmigration of souls and reincarnation. Concentrated in the Latakia coastal region of Syria, they borrow the festivals of Easter and Christmas from the Christians. A minority sect, the Alawites have governed predominantly Sunni Syria since 1970 through one of their adherents Hafez al-Assad and his son.

Druze. A tribal sect that practices strict endogamy (one can only be born into the Druze faith), the Druze live at the intersect of the borders of Lebanon, Syria, and Israel. Founded by the 11th-century Persian missionary al-Darazi, the Druze were taught that God had revealed himself to mankind on many occasions. The last time, apparently, was in the form of al-Hakim, the eccentric Fatimid tyrant who ruled Egypt between 996 and 1021. 300,000 Druze in the world believe that God will ultimately manifest himself in the form of Hamza, the author of all holy books. Till then, they congregate in mountain shrines on Thursday evenings and divide themselves among noble families and the masses or ignorant who aspire to be sages (identified by white turbans).[13]

Assassins. About the same time the Druze came into existence another, more troublesome, sect was founded in the Daylami district south of the Caspian Sea. An Ismaili holy man from Qum, Hasan as-Sabah with 60 or 70 disciples occupied a fortress in the Elburz Mountains. Known as Alamut, the Eagle's Nest, Hasan's bastion would withstand an eight-year siege by the Seljuks. From here, Hasan waged jihad against Turkish sultans, Sunnis Abbasids, even Fatimid Caliphs. Demanding absolute loyalty from his followers, he initiated them into a brotherhood of religious fanatics. The lowly *fedayeen* were to risk their lives to fulfill an order of the Grand Master. Occasionally they were dispatched to kill an enemy in his own palace. Contemporary sources (Arnold of Lubeck, William of Tyre, Marco Polo) maintain the warriors were given women, money, and hashish (hence the name Assassin) as stimulants for suicidal missions. In Hasan's lifetime, 50 martyrs were named to a roll of honor.[14]

For nearly 200 years, the Assassins spread terror through the Middle East. A branch under the command of Rashid ad–Din controlled ten castles in Syria during the 12th century. Crusaders saw them everywhere, confounding Frederick Barbarossa in his campaign at Milan in 1158, killing Contrad of Montferrat in 1192, and fighting Richard the Lion Heart in 1195. It was said that when Saladin was campaigning near Aleppo in 1176, the Muslim chieftain (who twice previously had been targeted by the Assassins) pitched his camp in such a way that it would be absolutely secure. Chalk and cinders were strewn about his well-guarded tent. That night the faint glow of a lightning bug was seen floating over the pure-white perimeter. The next morning, Saladin awoke to find a note pinned to his bed by a poison dagger. It read: "By the majesty of the kingdom! What you possess will escape you, in spite of all, but victory remains to us. We acquaint you that we hold you and that we reserve you till your reckoning be paid." There were footprints in the chalk outside, leading away from the tent.

Alamut was finally razed by Mongol forces under Hulagu in 1256. The Assassins no longer exist, but their order left a worldwide legacy of terror.

Baha'is. Founded by Mirza Ali Muhammad, known as the Bab (the Gate), the Baha'is originated in Iran during the 19th century.[15] When he preached in Shiraz after 1844, the Bab claimed to be the Mahdi who would reveal universal truth. Both the Qajar monarchs of Iran who executed the Bab in 1850 and the Ottoman Sultans who expelled his son Baha'ullah to Acre considered the Baha'is heretics who had to be extirpated. An estimated 20,000 Baha'is were killed in purges between 1844 and 1925 when the Pahlevi dynasty came to power in Iran. In 1933 their literature was banned. Baha'i marriages were deemed illegal — comparable to prostitution — and punishable by prison sentences. Their schools were closed and cemeteries razed. (Baha'is were forced to bury their dead in their own yards.) During the reign of Muhammad Reza Shah II, matters improved somewhat, but the Baha'is were still subjected to denunciatory radio broadcasts by Muslim ulema. Several hundred were slain during the turmoil of Mossadeq's dictatorship (1951–53). There was even economic and religious discrimination after Abbas Hoveida, whose grandfather was a Baha'i, became Prime Minister in 1965.

Despite such persecutions, in 1979 there were still more than 300,000 Baha'is in Iran. With the creation of Khomeini's Islamic republic, they suffered terribly. Baha'i shrines were desecrated. The clay house of the Bab, which had been maintained by the Jews for 130 years, was destroyed and a public square built in its place. The Baha'is National Spiritual Assembly was banned by the revolutionary parliament. Possession of a Baha'i prayer book was deemed a criminal offense. Baha'i telephones were tapped. More than 1000 Baha'is were thrown into prison, 194 executed by December 1984. In desperation, some Baha'is tried to flee over to Turkey. A group of 18 from Tabriz were caught early in 1985, tortured and killed.

The Baha'is have appealed to the Iranian government, the U.N. Human Rights Commission, and the international press, with little success. In 1984, Congressman Tom Lantos of California, himself a survivor of the Jewish Holocaust, chaired a special House Subcommittee that looked into charges of religious persecution by the Khomeini regime. Lantos and other members of the committee were moved to tears by the testimony of one Baha'i refugee. A student told how his mother, sister, and father (an engineer who worked for an oil company) were arrested by the state police. All three were tortured in an effort to get them to abjure their faith. At day's end, the son was called to the police station to view the corpses. His mother's face was so blackened by beatings, he was barely able to identify her remains.[16]

Regarded as heretics by Shiite Iranians, the Baha'is are smeared as agents of America

SUNNIS AND SHIITES IN THE MIDDLE EAST (PERCENT OF POPULATION)			
Country	*Sunni*	*Shiite*	*Christian*
Algeria	99		1
Bahrain	30	66	
Egypt	80	10	10
Iran	5	93	
Iraq	40	55	5
Jordan	95		5
Kuwait	60	30	
Lebanon	15	45	40
Libya	97		
Morocco	99		
Oman	10	75 (Ibadi)	
Qatar	95 (Wahhabi)		
Saudi Arabia	99 (Wahhabi)		
Sudan	75	20	
Syria	74	16	10
Tunisia	95		
Turkey	90	8	
United Arab Emirates	99		
South Yemen	99		
North Yemen (unified)	50	50	

Sources: Azim Nariji, ed., *The Muslim Almanac* (New York: Gale Research, 1995), xxxiv–xxix, and *The Middle East* (Washington, D.C.: Dushkin, 1988).

or Israel. The Turks banished Baha'ullah to remote Palestine. The graves of the first three leaders and the archives of Baha'i reside in a beautiful complex of gardens that overlook Haifa in Israel. The sins of the Baha'is appear to lie not in their abuse of power but in their teachings: Baha'ism teaches that no religion has a claim to absolute truth. God has used prophets like Moses, Muhammad and Jesus at various times. There is a new revelation, according to the Bab, every 1000 years or so, representing successive stages in the spiritual development of human society. The Baha'i practice equality between men and women. Absolute pacifists, they refuse to carry a gun. Their temples are open to all races. They have no priests and are directed instead by a Universal House of Justice, nine men elected by the members of the faith every five years.

BAHA'I LEADERSHIP

The Baha'i leaders since 1844 are as follows:
Mirza Ali Muhammad, the Bab (1844–1850)— slain by Qajars
Baha'ullah (1863–1892)— died in Palestine
Abdul Baha (1892–1921)
Shoghi Effendi (1921–1957)— died in London
Universal House of Justice since 1957

Sunnite-Shiite Division in the 20th Century

Estimates of the number of Muslims in the world range between 700 million and one billion. Seventy percent are Sunnites. Descriptions of Sunnis as more reserved, less emotional than the Shiites are not necessarily valid. Both have been touched by waves of fundamentalism in recent decades— Shiites with Amal and Islamic Jihad in Lebanon, the Taliban in Afghanistan, Sunnis with the Muslim Brotherhoods or National Salvation Parties in Turkey, Syria, Egypt and Algeria. The fairest thing that may be said about the split within Islam is that it probably is permanent, much the same as the breach between eastern and western Christianity.

17

Expansion of Islam

Arab Success

That Islam survived its sectarian battles is wonder enough. One hundred years after Muhammad's death, the faithful had spread the teachings of Allah from Spain to the Punjab. Muslim princes ruled North Africa, Egypt, the Holy Land, Iran and India. Their fleets controlled many of the strategic locales across the Mediterranean — Gibraltar, Sicily, Crete, Rhodes. Merchants, missionaries and holy warriors pushed as far east as the Indonesian archipelago. Arab success may be traced to several factors:

The Sedentary Principle. Four hundred years of warfare between the Byzantines and Sassanid Persians left both empires decrepit. Internal division and corruption placed them at a disadvantage before a people like the Arabs.

Tradition of the Razzia. Many conquests resulted from what were supposed to be simple probes or raids into enemy territory.

Superior tactics/Generalship. Best exemplified by the Muslim triumph at the river Yarmuk in August 636. The forces of Khalid al-Walid occupied the high ground with its water supplies. Meanwhile, the Byzantines, weary from tramping about in chain-mail armor, had to attack — uphill, against the glare of the sun and a dust storm blowing into their faces. The Arabs may not always have been so fortunate, but few enemy commanders could compare to Khalid, Amr al-As, Usama, Muthanna and Said ibn Abi Wakkas.

Unrest in nearby territories. Whether because of religious persecution (Copts in Egypt, Jews in Spain), unfair tax policies in North Africa, or resentment toward the Byzantines and Persians, many subject peoples regarded Muslims as kinsmen who were expelling foreign interlopers.

Success breeds success. Once a movement seems assured of victory, doubters who wavered in support may be converted to the call. The phenomenon occurs in modern political campaigns. Such belated conversions are even more common among religious zealots who find justification in providence.

Leadership of Early Caliphs. Islam was blessed with the creative genius of its first four caliphs—Abu Bekr, Umar, Uthman and Ali. Colleagues of Muhammad in the early years in Mecca (each was related to the Prophet by marriage as well), these men were dedicated to his monotheistic creed. In the two decades after Muhammad's death, they were responsible for codifying the Quran and punishing anyone who challenged caliphal authority. They established the elective principle of the shura, guaranteeing a succession of absolute rulers. Simple men, accessible to their people, they did not use their power for affluence, but rather to serve as role models for Muslims. In the end, however, they paid a price for their devotion. Tradition has it that all four were assassinated.

Abu Bekr and Khalid al-Walid

Known as the Second of the Two, Abu Bekr faced a challenge to his authority when he became caliph in the summer of 632. Once loyal sections of Arabia followed pretenders who claimed to be the rightful successors of Muhammad. In the northern territory of Yamamah, an ascetic named Musaylimah rallied the forces of the Banu Hanifah with those of the sun-worshipping Tamim and defeated two Muslim armies. In Yemen, dissidents followed a "veiled Prophet," in the Hadhramaut a "donkey rider," in Bahrain "al-Aswad."[1]

To eradicate apostasy, Abu Bekr appointed the cavalry commander Khalid al-Walid as his chief general. One of the heroes of the Meccan win at Uhud in 625, Khalid was a late convert to Islam, having undergone a revelation in 629. Few of the original followers of Muhammad liked this impulsive warrior, but none could argue with his results. Commanding 5000 troops, Khalid attacked one Bedouin tribe after another, executing anyone who killed a Muslim in the same manner they had caused a death. On several occasions, he embarrassed even Abu Bekr, marrying the wives or daughters of slain rivals on the battlefield. In one decisive clash at Aqrabah (the Garden of Death), Khalid inspired his men to fight more bravely by dividing them into separate units of Ansar, Muhajirun and desert allies, urging them to compete with one another. When the day was over, more than 1000 of his men lay dead. But so, too, was Musaylima. The *Ridda* (Age of Apostasy) was brought to a close in six months.

Wisely, Abu Bekr declined to sheath his "Sword of Islam." The aged caliph recognized that the men of the Hejaz had been campaigning for 11 years. To demobilize now might create additional tensions in Mecca. A better strategy called for diverting these energies against the outside world. The effete Persian and Byzantine empires appeared tempting. Both had, after all, insulted Muhammad's emissaries when they demanded tribute and both had beaten back earlier probes. Thus, early in 633 two armies, each numbering 20,000 men, were outfitted to strike simultaneously in the east and west. Little more than razzias, they sought to avenge earlier insults and, perhaps, gain territory for Islam.

The first force under Abu-Ubaydah moved into Palestine and bogged down. The other, commanded by Khalid al-Walid, enjoyed success in southern Iraq, routing the Persians from Hormuz, capturing the Lakhmid capital of al-Hira, and penetrating 300 miles up the Euphrates to Firad. In April 634, Khalid al-Walid was ordered to rescue the other Arab column, which had splintered into disorganized bands. Taking 900 men with him, Khalid set out across the Syrian Desert. His negotiation of 1000 miles of wasteland in 18 days is considered by some scholars to be his greatest military achievement. Khalid gorged his camels on water, then tied their lips so they could not ruminate or drool. Periodically, a dozen were slaughtered for his troops. Though guides of the Tayyi tribe despaired of coming out of the desert alive, Khalid and his men eventually arrived at Ajnadayn on the Gaza-Jerusalem road. Here, where David slew Goliath, the Muslims on July 30, 634, routed a Byzantine army numbering 100,000 men.

Nine months later, in March 635, Khalid laid siege to Damascus. There is some question over what actually occurred when that city capitulated in September. Khalid claimed he guaranteed freedom of worship and required only that the residents pay tribute. His position is supported by the Nestorian bishop who wrote that the Arabs "do not war against the Christian religion, rather they protect our faith, respect our priests and holy men and make gifts to our churches and convents." According to another telling, Khalid was enraged when the city was surrendered to Abu Ubaydah, who permitted Christians to flee north. The tale of Khalid pursuing and slaughtering 4000 women and children is more in keeping with his personality. Whether true or not, Khalid consolidated Arab control over Syria by defeating the Byzantines again at the River Yarmuk.

The only prize in the Holy Land that eluded him was Jerusalem, which fell to Muslim forces under Amr al-As between 638 and 640. By that time, the most talented of all Muslim generals had fallen into disgrace. Shortly after his win at the Yarmuk, Khalid al-Walid was accused of mixing wine with his bath water and paying 1000 dinars from army wealth to a poet to create verses in his honor. Condemned by Muslim sages at the court of Abu Ubaydah, he had the right to appeal to the caliph. Abu Bekr, however, was dead, poisoned two years earlier, and Umar ibn al-Khattab was now caliph. A jealous man who had achieved prestige through his own military exploits, Umar granted clemency, but removed Khalid from his command. When Khalid died penniless in 640, surrounded by his many wives and children, he had the satisfaction of knowing that no one had done more in those early years to advance the cause of imperial Islam.[2]

Umar: The St. Paul of Islam

The beneficiary of Khalid's labors was Umar ibn al-Khattab (592–644), designated the next successor by Abu Bekr shortly before the latter's death. Like Khalid, the 42-year-old Umar once had a reputation for sexual excess. Like the warrior whose career he ended, he had once opposed Muhammad. At the height of the Meccan boycott in 616, Umar had beaten a slavegirl convert to Islam, then led an assault against the Muslim quarters in the city. Taunted by one of his victims to cleanse his own house, he searched out and killed his sister as she read from the Quran. In remorse, he went to Muhammad, who welcomed Umar as the 45th convert to Islam.

A puritan, Umar lived on two dirhams per day (60 cents), mending his own clothes. His devotion to Muhammad was such that he was dubbed *faruq* (distinguisher between truth and falsehood). Muhammad also said of him: "If the devil himself were to meet you on the street, he would dodge into a side alley." It was Umar who urged Muhammad to force his way into Mecca rather than negotiate at the time of Hudaibiya, who wanted prisoners of war beheaded, who suggested stoning for adultery and who advocated the prohibition against wine drinking. His own son was convicted of this last offense and flogged so that he was about to die. As the young man cried out, "You have killed me!" Umar responded, "Then go and tell Allah how your father enforces his punishment."[3]

Umar's judgments, imposed with a flick of his riding switch as he strolled the streets, were so harsh that it was said, "Umar's whip is as painful as his sword." The second caliph justified his decrees saying, "The Arabs are like a rebellious camel and it pertaineth to the driver which way to lead it." And again, "Remember all ye people — I have been given the rule over you on the assumption of being the best qualified and strongest among you and the ablest of you to conduct your general affairs."

Umar's contributions, both to the organization of the Islamic religion and the empire, are impressive. It was Umar who instructed the ulema to begin the task of codifying the Quran. He made pilgrimage obligatory once in a lifetime. Recognizing that the caliph could not be everywhere to answer questions of law, Umar instituted the office of *kadi* (judge) in larger cities. Military settlements established at Basra and Kufah in Mesopotamia, al-Ludd and ar–Ramleh in Palestine, Kairuwan and al-Fustat in North Africa evolved into major cities. Taxes were imposed on land, property, slaves. Tribute obtained from the sprawl of conquered territories was funneled into the *diwan* (treasury), then doled out to members of the Islamic community.[4]

Jerusalem fell into Muslim hands and a simple wooden mosque was dedicated atop the temple mount by Umar. When the Umayyad caliph Abdel Malik (685–705) raised a much grander structure over the great rock from which Muhammad supposedly sprang to heaven, the building continued to be known as the Mosque of Umar.

The general credited with the capture of Jerusalem, Amr al-As, soon added an even more impressive conquest. A onetime merchant, Amr knew of Egypt's wealth, its ports, and her internal problems. Native Copts, followers of Monophysite Christianity, were being oppressed by Byzantine overlords. Late in the year 639, Amr won Umar's permission to lead a razzia of 4000 men into the Delta. At the last moment, some of Amr's enemies persuaded Umar to recall the army. A message to this effect reached the Muslim force at El Arish. Choosing to ignore "ambiguous instructions," Amr won a series of engagements against demoralized Byzantines at Pelusium, Bilbays and Ayn Shams. The death of Heraclius in Constantinople in February 641 shattered the will of the remaining Byzantine garrisons. As Muslim reinforcements poured into Egypt, the Patriarch Cyrus negotiated a settlement with Amr in November 641. In offering the Arabs Alexandria, and with it all of Egypt, Cyrus hoped to retain some administrative power in the new order. For his part, Amr sent Umar a cryptic communique that read: "I have captured a city from the description of which I shall refrain. Suffice it to say that I have seized therein 4000 villas with 4000 baths, 40,000 poll-tax paying Jews, and 400 places of entertainment for the royalty."[5]

The Byzantines attempted to recapture Egypt several times in the next decade, actually gaining control of the principal ports for a short time in 646. But Egypt remained in Muslim hands and served as a springboard for further razzias into Cyrenaica and Tunisia, where Berbers felt abused by the Greeks. By the year 699 Muslims were perched at the tip of Tangier ready to cross the straits into the rich Iberian peninsula.

In the east, the Bedouin chieftain Muthanna replaced Khalid al-Walid and enjoyed modest success against the Sassanids in Iraq. Muthanna's successor, Said ibn Abi Waqqas, a veteran of Badr and Uhud, avoided any major confrontation with the Persians until the outcome in Syria was decided. Then, taunted by Muthanna's widow, Said attacked a larger enemy force at Qadasiya on the plains south of al-Hira in May 637. Muslim archers struck a number of Persian war elephants in the eyes, causing these beasts to run amok within their own lines. At the end of four days, the Persians had lost their one able commander (Rustam) and immeasurable wealth on the battlefield. More important, the Persian boy-king Yazdegerd and his court abandoned their Mesopotamian capital of Ctesiphon. When the victorious Arabs entered this fabulous city on the Tigris, they must have thought they entered paradise. The booty from the sack of Ctesiphon may have exceeded $250 million.[6]

Just as Alexander moved relentlessly after Darius, so Muslim warriors won victory after victory — at Jalula in 637; Mosul and Nihavand in 641; Isfahan in 643; Fars, Persepolis and Susa in 649 and 650. By 651 Yazdegerd, run out of his homeland, was appealing for aid from Turkish lords in Central Asia. His death that year at the hands of a Satrap in Merv ended another great Persian empire.

The humiliation of seeing his countrymen paraded through the streets was too much for one slave, Abu Lulua, a carpenter who had been acquired in the conquest of Nihavand. As Umar led prayers in the Medina mosque in November 644, this Persian slave stabbed him six times in the back. A less dramatic version offered by the German scholar Carl Brockelmann suggests Abu Lulua was neither Persian nor a slave, merely a man outraged with Umar over a tax dispute. Whatever his motive, Abu Lulua had slain the caliph who was, to one Pakistani biographer, "Alexander and Aristotle, messiah and Solomon, Tamerlane and Anushirwan [a Persian king], the Iman Abu Hanifa and Ibrahim Adham [a Sufi saint]" all in one.[7]

The Rule of Umar

There was another dimension to Umar. From his deathbed Muhammad had decreed that two religions should not coexist in Arabia. His successors extended restrictions beyond the Hejaz. Under Umar, a code of social conduct was introduced that became the basis of relations between Muslims and other monotheists in the Middle East for the next 1300 years. While some academics maintain the Rule of Umar elevated *dhimmi* (protected people, people of the book) above pagans and idol worshippers, the code, which borrowed heavily from Theodosius and Justinian, served as the basis for institutionalized discrimination.[8] In its simplest form, the Rule of Umar:

- imposed payment of the *jizyah,* a poll tax that ostensibly provided protection to Christians and Jews. Both peoples were supposed to continue paying land taxes (*kharaj)* and taxes on personal property (*ghanimah*) into the state treasury.
- prohibited construction of new churches or synagogues in Muslim cities or the restoration of such buildings if they had been destroyed by Muslim forces. The reality was that buildings could be restored if a bribe were paid. In this case, the structure had to be lower than any mosque in town.
- required a show of courtesy to Muslims passing by. The *dhimmi* were supposed to rise and inquire into the health of the "exalted" guest who would be offered three days of food and lodging.
- forbade touching, reading or teaching of the Quran because it was believed that Christians and Jews, lacking in honor and truth, would distort sacred writ.
- restricted religious ceremonies so they would not disturb Muslim neighbors. Loud singing, the ringing of bells, display of religious articles all were considered offensive.
- barred Christians and Jews from missionary activity or offering sanctuary to runaway slaves or enemies of Islam. The monotheists were also not to approach Muslims in funeral proceedings.
- instituted special dress codes, forbidding dhimmi from wearing clothing, headgear, sandals, even hair styles that resembled Muslims.
- prohibited the sale of wine, the use of saddles, wearing of swords, and the use of signet rings in sealing contracts. No fancy sashes could be worn; only a piece of rope (the *zunnar*), was permitted as a belt.

At borders, Christian and Jewish trades were subjected to higher customs duties than their Muslim counterparts. They were barred from serving as advocates, judges, doctors. Educational opportunities were restricted and the dhimmi were not permitted to serve in the army. Segregated in the seamiest quarters of ancient cities, they were subjected to vilification. The concentration of Christians in specific quarters made it easier for mobs to attack churches in Egypt in the 13th century, the Christian Patriarch of Cairo in 1419, Christians in Aleppo (1850), Nablus (1856), Hasbeya, Rashiya and Damascus (1860), Copts in Egypt (1980–81) and Marionites in Damour (1974).

Professor S. D. Goitein has shown that Jews and Arabs have much in common in ancestry, geography, language, even the religio-legal nature of their creeds.[9] Jewish learning flourished under Islam with such figures as Saadia ibn Yusuf (a ninth-century sage in Mesopotamia), Solomon ibn Gabirol (poet-philosopher in 11th-century Spain) and Moses Maimonides and Judah Halevi (two Jewish sages who flourished in caliphal Spain). Gustave von Grunebaum, however, points out, "It will be just as easy to cite a long inventory of persecutions, arbitrary confiscations, attempts at forcible conversion and pogroms." Saadia was publicly executed for criticizing the Prophet and the Quran. So was ibn Gabirol. Halevi was killed by a Sacacen as he knelt outside the walls of Jerusalem. Josef ibn Nagrela, wazir of Granada, was crucified along with 1500 other Jews on December 30, 1066. Saad Adduala, adviser to the Ilkhan Argun, was purged in 1291. Khalifa ben Waqqasa, chamerlain to Abu Yakub, was murdered in 1301. Aaron ibn Batash, appointed as minister in Fez, was killed with his people in 1465. To avoid such a fate, Moses ben Maimonides, personal physician to Saladin, lived much of his life as a false convert to Islam.[10]

Centuries before the *rouelle* (circular badge) was commanded by Pope Innocent III in 1215, a form of the Yellow Star had become common in the Middle East. Using the *zunnar* as his model, the Abbasid caliph al-Mutawwakil commanded Jews to wear "honey-colored" patches on the breast and back of their garments. Later rulers (al-Muktadir, Abu Shuja and Abdallah) decreed the use of yellow scarves, yellow veils, yellow turbans and armbands. Jews had to wear pointed skullcaps that resembled wizards hats and darb, dark cloaks. In Yemen, Jewish women were required to wear shoes of different colors. In Algeria, as late as the 19th century, they were not to wear any shoes. Hoping to stamp out heresy in his realm, the 11th-century Fatimid caliph al-Hakim ordered Jews to wear tokens of the god they supposedly adored — the golden calf — about their necks. Subsequently, these were replaced by cowbells, then four-pound blocks of wood. When none of these devices sufficiently debased the Jews, al-Hakim ordered a massive purge timed for Passover in 1012.[11]

Persecution at the hands of Idrisids in North Africa actually prompted many Jews to flee to Spain in the 10th century. In 1032, the sons of Afran slaughtered 6000 Jews in their conquest of Fez. The annals of Tlemcen tell of Jewish victims mutilated by mobs in 1275 and 1302. Arab violence in Fez turned that city's Jewish quarter into an abattoir of bodies and bones scattered from desecrated cemeteries in 1465, 1790, 1792, and again in 1820. In Tunis, Algiers, Marrakesh and Tetouan Jewish families were destroyed, women raped, synagogues and Torah scrolls desecrated. The worst atrocities in North Africa are attributed to the Almohades, who swept across the Straits of Gibraltar between 1143 and 1179 destroying Jewish institutions in Seville, Cordoba, Lucena, and Granada and granting Jews a choice between conversion or death.[12]

Conditions were not much better in the east. Following the persecution of al-Hakim, Jews in Alexandria and Cairo were plundered in 1047, 1168, 1265, and 1524. Sultan Baybars in the 13th century blamed them for starting a plague and subjected them to extortion, massacre and expulsion. In Yemen, emirs waged a constant struggle against isolated Jewish communities. In 1474, 1666, 1679, the Jewish quarter of San'a was subjected to pillage and synagogues converted to mosques. Jews in Hamadan were attacked in 1875, in Baghdad in 1877. In Palestine the Muslim population rampaged against the Jews in 809, in 1027, in the middle of the 15th century, during the 1570s, between 1625 and 1627, again at Safed between 1834 and 1838, Jerusalem in 1847, throughout the countryside in 1892 and 1896. When Egyptian nationalists rebelled against the British in the 1880s, their first targets were the Jewish ghettos. Egyptian extremists seized upon the canard of ritual murder, which also served to spark massacres of Jews in Meshed, Iran, in 1839 and Damascus in 1840. The notion of ritual murder was revived by the nationalist press in Cairo between 1903 and 1910, and more recently by the government in Syria, which in 1990 published a scathing anti–Semitic pamphlet, *The Matza of Blood*, on the subject.

The prevailing wisdom among Middle Eastern scholars is to dismiss such incidents as episodic. In the Islamic world, toleration was the rule. Toleration does not connote affection, but sufferance of a minority. The Rule of Umar offered not protection but pain. Princeton's Bernard Lewis concluded that "The golden age of equal rights was a myth, and belief in it was a result more than a cause of Jewish sympathy for Islam. The myth was invented in nineteenth century Europe as a reproach to Christians—and taken up by Muslims in our time as a reproach to Jews."[13]

Uthman

Before his death, Umar tried to provide an orderly transition of power, creating a council of six that would select the next caliph. These notables included Ali, Said ibn abi Waqqas (the conqueror of Iraq), al-Zubayr ibn al-Awwam (who commanded relief troops to Egypt), Talhah ibn Abdullah (an important Meccan lord), Uthman ibn Affah (an associate of Umar's) and Abdel Rahman ibn Awf (a kinsman of Uthman's). In the event of Umar's death, these men were to assemble in the company of 50 armed guards. If after three days they were unable to agree on a successor, they were to be killed. If the selection were not unanimous, the dissidents only were to be slain. If the vote was deadlocked at 3:3, those who voted with Abdel Rahman were to be spared. Umar knowingly had created a system that would once again block aspirations of his rival Ali.

The third caliph was Uthman, a wealthy Meccan merchant, who converted before 615 and who twice was father-in-law to Muhammad. Seventy years old when he came to power, Uthman made one major contribution to Islam. It was in his reign that the Quran was codified. Local *qurra* (chanters of the Quran) who insisted upon preaching from unorthodox texts were purged.

Despite his age, Uthman scandalized the faithful by spending lavish amounts on clothes, his toilet and tonsure, slave girls and poetry. Income that should have been funneled through the diwan to soldiers and descendants of Muhammad's followers was now being diverted by his cousin Marwan to friends of the caliph. Entire regions were carved up as personal fiefdoms, with more relatives designated as governors. The temporary recapture of Egypt by the Byzantines was made possible by Uthman's dismissal of Amr al-As and his replacement with Uthman's semi-competent foster brother Abdallah. Another half brother al-Walid, who once had spit in Muhammad's face, ruled in southern Iraq. From Syria, another cousin, Muawiyah, son of Abu Sufyan, commanded a fleet that patrolled the eastern Mediterranean. Everywhere, it seemed, there was corruption, and, worst of all, control by the very Umayyad clan that had most opposed Muhammad.

In this context it was not difficult for supporters of Ali, Muslims who favored the more austere times of Umar, and other malcontents like Aishah and Said to come together in an organized opposition. Economic problems provided the spark for revolt in the year 656. From Egypt, Muhammad abu Bekr marched with 500 supporters on Mecca. At the time, the holy city was undefended. The caliph was surrounded in his own house and denied water. Hearing that a relief column from Damascus was nearby, Uthman sent a communique ordering his foes to be executed. When his messenger was intercepted in June 656, the rebels broke through the roof of his house and killed Uthman as he read from the Quran. His wife, Nailah, wounded in the ensuing melee, managed to retrieve his bloodied shirt and sacred book, losing three fingers in the process.[14]

Ali and His Sons

Almost immediately, the coalition that had overthrown Uthman came apart. With the blessing of Aishah (long a foe of Ali), Talhah and al-Zubayr raised an army to oppose Ali's succession. On December 9, 656, in the battle of the Camel (so named because the fighting outside Basra centered on Aishah's camel), Ali defeated these dissidents. Talha was killed, Zubayr fled, and Aishah was banished to Medina where she lived another 22 years.

The new caliph was not so fortunate in pacifying another enemy. The column from Syria that Uthman awaited reached not the Hejaz but Mesopotamia in the spring of 657. Fifty thousand men under Muawiyah ibn Abu Sufyan were bent on avenging Uthman's death. To inspire them, the governor of Syria produced the slain caliph's bloodied shirt and his wife's fingers. More than 70,000 warriors perished at Siffin on the western shore of the Euphrates in July 657. On the advice of Amr al-As, Muawiyah called for an end to the bloodshed, hoisting 500 copies of the Quran on lances as an appeal to disputation rather than armed combat as a way of resolving the conflict. Inexplicably, Ali agreed.

The debate on succession took place in January 659. Muawiyah's champion was Amr al-As. Ali designated Abu Musa al-Ashari, a man lukewarm to his cause. By agreeing to debate, Ali gave the impression that the claim of a provincial governor was equal to his own. In the discussions, Amr outmaneuvered Abu Musa. Both men agreed to clear the atmosphere by deposing their respective leaders. After Abu Musa publicly did so, Amr refused to renounce Muawiyah. Abu Musa also conceded that Muawiyah was entitled to avenge his kinsman's death. The beneficiary of this academic exercise was Muawiyah, who claimed to rule as caliph from Damascus.

For his part, Ali retired to Kufah where he spent the last four years of his life with his nine wives and 33 children. His negotiations with Muawiyah infuriated the Kharijites, who held that no one but Allah could designate the leader of Islam. These "Seceders" kept Iraq in perpetual ferment until 659 when Ali defeated their principal force in the battle of Nahrawan Canal. On January 24, 661, the Kharijites had their revenge, when one of their number struck and stabbed Ali in the brain with a poisoned dagger.

Subsequently, Muawiyah approached Ali's eldest son, Hassan, saying: "I admit that because of thy bloody relationship thou art more entitled to high office than I. And if I were sure of thy greater ability to fulfil the duties involved, I would unhesitatingly swear allegiance to thee. Now then ask what thou wilt." Hassan declined to make an issue of succession, opting instead for a harem presented to him by Muawiyah, hence his nickname "the Lecher."[15]

Umayyads: The Empire in Damascus (661–750)

With the creation of the Umayyad dynasty, the power base of Islam shifted from the Hejaz to Syria. The reigns of the Umayyads were relatively brief and contentious. Muawiyah's son Yazid (680–83) was forced to battle and beheaded Ali's second son, Husayn, at Karbala in 680. Muawiyah's cousin Marwan (683–85) defeated an army led by Abdullah al-Zubayr. Marwan's successor, Abdel Malik (685–705), had to reckon with Kalbite rebels in Yemen, Kharijites, Alids and Qaysites near the Euphrates, Mardaites in Lebanon. The challenge to Abdel Malik was so severe (he lost control of Mecca and Medina) that he felt compelled to raise a new sanctuary, the misnamed Mosque of Umar, in Jerusalem in 691 to bolster his prestige.

The wonder is that with so many enemies, the Umayyad caliphate had a significant impact upon Islamic culture. It was during the century of rule from Damascus that the schools of Islamic law evolved and the first critical biographies of Muhammad were written. Aqueducts and canals fashioned after Roman models were constructed. The army was transformed into well-trained units of lancers, heavy cavalry, infantry, and specialists in siegecraft. The navy, employing two-tiered galleys, continued its success against the Byzantines in the eastern Mediterranean.

At the end of the seventh century, the Muslims adopted the architectural style of the Byzantines and joined to it a series of towers for use by muezzins. Inside and out, these domed structures were beautified with arabesque, a design that rejected human forms in favor of calligraphy, floral patterns, and geometric symbols. Archways, cupolas, *minbars* (pulpits) and *mihrabs* (prayer niches cut into the wall facing Mecca) were embellished with mosaics and stalactites. For the Mosque of Umar (built atop the site of the ancient Jewish temple), a copper dome was pilfered from a church in Baalbek. The Cathedral of St. John the Baptist in Damascus was converted to Islam by al-Walid. Other important sanctuaries built in this period included the White Mosque of Ramleh and the al-Aqsa (built over a sixth-century church to the Virgin Mary) in Jerusalem.[16]

The Conquest of Spain

Under the Umayyads, the Sassanid dynasty was finally destroyed in 651. Crete and Rhodes were snatched from the Byzantines between 674 and 680 and three frontal assaults were mounted against Constantinople by 717. The Umayyads were responsible for Muslim penetration to Samarkand, Khiva, Kabul and Hyderabad. In North Africa, Amr al-As established control over Tunis by 670, Algeria in 680. When Musa ibn Nusayr became governor of "Ifrikiyah" in 699, he approved another series of probes across the straits into Iberia, never expecting that these razzias would generate an Islamic civilization that would last nearly 800 years.

Just as Egypt and North Africa, Spain was ripe for conquest. The Visigoths who had settled during folk migrations 200 years earlier proved to be troublesome in many ways. Apart from overtaxing the indigenous Celtic population, the German overlords became increasingly intolerant. When first converted to Arian Christianity (another doctrine that stressed the human aspect of Jesus), the Visigoths acted tentatively. As years passed and they embraced Roman Catholicism, they became more repressive, introducing the inquisition. Their victims included Jews who could trace their lineage in Spain to the Roman era. At the end of the seventh century, thousands of Jews were forcibly converted to Christianity. More (perhaps 250,000) were drowned or "scalped" when they refused to abjure their faith. When the Visigoth lord Roderick seduced the daughter of a Christian noble-man in 709, the latter appealed to the Arabs for assistance.[17]

In July 710, 400 Muslims crossed the eight miles separating North Africa from Spain. They found native Spaniards eager to revolt against a system of feudalism and bigotry, Jews ready to support Semitic kinsmen. In the spring of 711, Musa dispatched a force of 7000 men under the Berber freedman Tariq ibn Zayd. The latter established his base at a moun-tain that came to bear his name — Jebel Tariq (corrupted in English to Gibraltar). Avoid-ing fortified cities and relying upon the dissension that wracked the Visigoth army, Tariq defeated Roderick at the Salado River on July 19. By the end of the year, he controlled half of Spain.

Concerned that too much glory was going to his subordinate, Musa followed quickly with 10,000 men. Then, claiming Tariq had exceeded his orders, Musa deposed his lieuten-ant. Bound in chains, the Berber warrior was sent back to Damascus to stand trial. Musa also returned to the Umayyad capital in September 714, bearing fruits of the Andalusian campaign — princes, slaves, jewels and a wondrous table fashioned (it was said) for Solomon by genii. The table, alas, lacked one leg. When Tariq presented the missing leg, the caliph knew that Musa had wrongly arrogated to himself the conquest of Spain. Tariq was restored to power and Musa died a beggar in Mecca.[18]

Within two years (713) practically all of Andalusia south of the Pyrenees was con-quered. Only a small strip on the Bay of Biscay remained free. Choosing to ignore this rocky plateau, the Arabs struck into France, seizing Narbonne in 718, Avignon in 734, and Lyons in 743. Before 760, however, they had begun to draw back from western Europe. His-torians generally attribute this retreat to the Battle of Tours fought in October 732, a bat-tle that allegedly pitted the valiant forces of Charles Martel against the "barbarian" hordes of Abdal Rahman al-Ghafiki. Here, 12 miles south of Poitiers, the Frankish square repulsed Muslim armies. Edward Creasey lists the battle among the 10 most important in history and tells how for seven days "the nations of the north stood firm as a wall and impenetra-ble as a zone of ice," staying the Arabs with "the edge of the sword." Citing a monk chron-icler, Creasey suggests the Arabs lost 375,000 men, the Christians only 100. Gibbon devotes several pages of his history to Tours and argues if the Muslims had not been checked "per-haps the interpretation of the Koran would now be taught in the schools of Oxford and her pupils might demonstrate to a circumcised people the sanctity and truth of the revelations of Muhammad." Friedrich Schlegel called Tours "a mighty victory" that "saved and deliv-ered the Christian nations of the West from the deadly grasp of all-destroying Islam." Arnold placed the battle above that of Arminius at the Teutoburg Forest as "among the signal deliv-erances which have effected for centuries the happiness of mankind." Even von Ranke called it "one of the most important epochs of the history of the word" when a champion like Charles Martel rose to stop "the threat of Mohammedanism."[19]

In fact, the battle of Tours was anything but a decisive turning point in history. The forces of Abdal Rahman were already more than 1000 miles beyond their principal supply depots when they stumbled across Frankish patrols. There were several cavalry encounters, one where Abdal Rahman was killed, but no major battle was fought and the casualties numbered, at best, in the hundreds. When the Muslims withdrew, they left the field to a brutish horde of fur-clad warriors. One hundred years removed from their desert origins, brandishing steel weapons and riding jewel-encrusted saddles, the Muslims represented civilization at Tours. This may have been their furthest penetration into Europe, but it by no means signaled their departure. They would continue to hold on to sections of the Riviera, Sicily, and Sardinia for another two centuries, Spain until 1492. Rather than a great victory, Tours represents the blunting of a Muslim razzia.

Collapse of the Damascus Caliphate

Not long after Tours, the caliphate in Damascus was overthrown. As the empire expanded, so had the list of groups unhappy with the Umayyads. Fom the start, Shiites insisted that the regime was illegitimate. Non-Arab Muslims (*mawalis* or clients) resented (tax exemptions and diwan payments given to those of Arab stock. The Berbers revolted 20 times in the first 30 years of the eighth century. Pressed to convert, Copts in Egypt and Nestorians in Persia also rebelled. Jews soon realized that dhimmi status left them little better than they had been under the Byzantines or Visigoths. Islamic slavery proved no more humane for blacks or whites than that practiced by Europeans.

What finally brought an end to the caliphate were the personal excesses of its monarchs. Muslim ascetics, the ulema, commoners could only be outraged by tales of dancing girls, banquets, poetry and human portraiture, gambling and drinking, associated with the palace. There were a few proper leaders in the eighth century (Umar II, 717–20, Hisham 724–43.) Generally, though, the last Umayyads emulated Muawiyah's son Yazid, whose reputation for the grape was such that he was dubbed *al-Khmur* (the Wino). Al-Walid II (743–44) supposedly filled a pool with wine, drinking so much that he lowered the level "measurably" as he swam. Of Sulayman, it was said he cared only for his private parts. Umar ibn Abdal Aziz was "a one-eyed man among the blind," Abdal Malik "a tyrant who took no thought of what he did."

The last Umayyad, Marwan II (744–50), known as *al-Himar* (the Ass), proved unable to cope with insurrections in Palestine, Iraq and Iran. In June 747, a Persian convert named Abu Muslim unfurled the black banner of Muhammad at Merv, proclaiming his lord Abul'Abbas caliph. For more than a decade, the Abbasids rallied dissidents from a base in the Dead Sea region, claiming the caliphate on an alleged deathbed transfer from Muhammad to the grandfather of Abu al-Abbas. Following the expulsion of the Umayyads from Khorasan, the black banners of the Abbasids triumphed over the white of their foes at Kufah in 749, on the banks of the Zab in January 750, and finally Damascus in April 750.

With Marwan dead (decapitated at Busiris), Abdullah ibn Ali, the uncle of the new caliph, issued a call for general amnesty. Members of the Umayyad clan were invited to a banquet at Jaffa on June 25. Eighty showed up and were clubbed mercilessly. Thrown to the floor of the hall, where they were covered with leather mats, they died as dancing and feasting went on over their moaning bodies. Umayyads who did not attend were captured, flogged and burned to ashes. According to tradition, all but one were rooted out as the Abbasid caliphate was established in this gruesome fashion.[20]

Umayyad Caliphate of Spain

The lone Umayyad to escape was Abdal Rahman ibn Muawiyah, grandson of Hisham II. When the purge occurred, the 20-year-old noble and his younger brother were being pursued in Mesopotamia. As Abdal Rahman later described it:

Joined by my freedman, Badr, we reached the bank of the Euphrates where I met a man who promised to sell me horses and other necessities; but while I was waiting he sent a slave to find the Abbasid commander. Next we heard a noise of the troop approaching the farmhouse; we took to our heels and hid in some gardens by the Euphrates but they were closing in on us. We managed to reach the river ahead of them and threw ourselves into the water. When they got back to the bank they began shouting, "Come back! You have nothing to fear." I swam and my brother swam.[21]

Eventually, the brother was caught and killed, but Abdal Rahman was able to make his way to Spain, which had not yet been affected by the Abbasid revolution. Gaining the support of other nobles, by 756 Abdal Rahman established the Umayyad caliphate of Cordoba. Until 1031, this city on the Guadalquivir River was the center of Islamic civilization in Spain. With 500,000 people (Paris only had 40,000 at the time), 200,000 whitewashed houses built about airy patios, 700 mosques, 900 public baths, 70 libraries, universities, hospitals, and lighted streets, Cordoba probably was the greatest city of Western Europe. Beyond its three-mile limits in 936 Abdal Rahman III developed a suburb named for his favorite wife az-Zahra. For more than 25 years, 10,000 workmen labored at this city of blooming flowers. Approximately 14,000 people would live in the imperial complex where everything — the pool of quicksilver at the palace entry; the horseshoe arches of the Grand Salon; 4300 marble columns imported from Italy; walls inlaid with ivory, ebony and jasper; a magnificent green marble fountain with 14 statues of different animals encrusted with jewels and pearls — was designed to dazzle the visitor.[22]

Az-Zahra would bask in the shade of fig and citrus trees for no more than 15 years. Another mutiny of Berber subordinates overthrew the ninth and final Umayyad caliph in 976. Once more, Spain was plunged into civil war (*fitna*) with different lords carving out city states (called *taifa*). Toward the end of the 11th century, Seville emerged as the most important under the leadership of al-Mutatid (1042–69) and his son al-Mutamid (1069–91). To combat the united Christian monarchy of Castille and Leon, which had recaptured Toledo in 1085, al-Mutamid invited in Tuareg tribesmen from Morocco. Known as *Almoravids* (from al-Murabitun, those who lived in religious retreats), these Muslim warriors were Malkite fundamentalists described by Neville Barbour as "rough, uncultured and primitive." Instead of helping their co-religionists, the Almoravids established their own hegemony in southern Spain. They caused Moorish culture to stultify as they waged war against the most fabled warrior in Spanish history–Rodrigo Diaz de Bivar, known as *El Cid* (Sayyid). In 1145 the old Islamic lords thought they were delivered when the Almoravids were deposed by another group from North Africa — the *Almohades* (from Tawhid, Asserters of the Unity of God). Again, the remedy proved worse than the sickness.[23]

Founded by holy man ibn Tumart (possibly a Berber) the *Almohades* proved to be more extremist than their predecessors. Ibn Tumart appeared among the Masmuda tribesmen of the Atlas Mountains at the beginning of the 12th century, preaching his own apocalyptic vision and claiming to be the Mahdi. For his followers, he proclaimed simplicity of dress, a strict code of etiquette for women, an end to games and musical instruments. When he challenged the authority of the Almoravid governor of Marrakesh in 1121, the revolt was on. It continued after ibn Tumart's death in 1120, spreading to Spain where, initially, the Almohades were welcomed as deliverers.

Not for long. As they conquered a succession of university towns — Malaga, Granada, Valencia, Seville — the Almohades plundered libraries and destroyed rare documents. Decorations considered offensive were covered up or desecrated. Thousands of Jews were slain, more persecuted, including Moses Maimonides, who was forced to flee to Egypt. The Almohade conquest (1145–1269) seriously crippled Spanish culture. The brutality of the holy warriors toward Christians provided the catalyst that united Spain's lords against the Moors.

By 1300 Islamic Spain would be reduced to a narrow strip below the Guadalquivir River and its center the caliphate of Granada. When the Christian kingdoms of Castille and Aragon were united by the marriage of Ferdinand and Isabella in 1469, the fate of the caliphate was sealed. In 1492, along with Jews, all Muslims were expelled from Spain.[24]

Perhaps 250,000 to 500,000 of these people were driven out, thousands more tortured or converted by the Inquisition in the next century. Seven hundred years of Arab control enriched the land with medieval forts that dot the landscape from Murcia to Olvera. Tile roofs (*azulejos*) favored by Spaniards date to the Arab conquest. So, too, arabesque lattice designs and mosaics favored in window decoration and pottery, and 6500 Spanish words like *alcatraz* (large bird), *alcade* (mayor), *Guadalquivir* (Wadi al-Kabir or Big River Valley) and *olé* (from *wallah*, for God's sake). And they enriched the land with countless Mozarabs and Mudejars, Spaniards descended from Muslims forcibly converted during the 400-year-long crusade that Christians waged to regain the land.

18

Al Amjad:
The Abbasid Caliphate

Al-Mansur and the Founding of Baghdad

The first of 35 Abbasid caliphs, Abu al-Abbas, was dubbed *as-Saffah* (the bloodletter). It was an appropriate title. Apart from the massacre of the Umayyads, as-Saffah's four-year reign (750–54) was marked by incessant purges. Abu Muslim slaughtered 50,000 Kharijite rebels. Shortly after, this warlord, who had the effrontery to place his own name before that of the caliph when recounting his deeds, was hacked to pieces by as-Saffah's brother. Then Abdullah ibn Ali, the uncle who arranged the bloodbath in Jaffa, was buried alive in a house made of salt. Of the Abbasid caliphate, the common folk lamented: "Would that the tyranny of the sons of Marwan return to us; would that the equity of the sons of Abbas were in hell."[1]

Abu Jafar, known as *al-Mansur* (the victorious) gave the Islamic world a relatively peaceful interlude between 754 and 775. During this period, Persian influences became more pronounced. Just as the Umayyads before them, Abbasid Caliphs lived in palaces surrounded by guards, sycophants and their harem.

Al-Mansur introduced other concepts that had their roots in Persian culture: the *wazirate* (prime ministry) to deal with administrative issues; a bodyguard of Turkish converts (*mamelukes*); and an executioner who stood by the throne, axe in hand, ready to dispatch anyone in the act of proskynesis. His greatest achievement, however, was the creation of a new capital in Mesopotamia 300 miles from the Persian Gulf where the Tigris and Euphrates come nearest one another. In August 762, al-Mansur dedicated his Madinat al-Salam (city of peace) on the western bank of the Tigris. The location appealed for several reasons. Kufah in the south was a hotbed of Shiism. The old capital of al-Hashimiyah was not sufficiently regal. Locating near the ruins of Ctesiphon, the former Persian capital, promised access to a quarry of polished stones. The caliph was said to be impressed with the cool nights and absence of mosquitoes in the region. Most of all, he recognized the military and economic importance of the location. The Tigris would, said al-Mansur, "put us in touch with lands as far as China" and the Euphrates would "carry for us all that Syria, al-Raqqah and adjacent lands have to offer."[2]

It took four years for 100,000 laborers to resurrect the city that came to be known as

Baghdad. The circular town was surrounded by walls 150 feet thick, rising to a height of more than 100 feet. Four roads supplied access to the city center, a massive plaza more than a mile across that contained the caliphal palace (a green-domed structure with a golden door) and a 130-foot high mosque. Initially, the common folk clustered in narrow lanes within the perimeter walls of *al-Mudawwarah* (the round city). By the end of the eighth century, Baghdad would count more than 1,000,000 residents, some of them living in homes that rivaled the best in Cordoba. The people entertained themselves with games of chess, backgammon, croquet, falcony, horse-racing, polo, archery. And they traded for paper and porcelain from China, cotton and spices form India, honey and furs from Russia, ivory and slaves from East Africa, grain and linen from Egypt, brocades and metalware from Syria.

Baghdad in the time of Harun al-Rashid (786–809) al-Amin (809–13) and al-Mamun (813–33) was probably the most glamorous city in the civilized world. Powerful enough to exchange gifts with Charlemagne and to wrest tribute from the Byzantine monarch Irene, the Abbasid caliphate is also "blamed" by Henri Pirenne for shutting down commerce in the Mediterranean and ending the Roman Empire.[3]

Guarantors of the Aristotelian Tradition

Far from being destructive marauders who plunged Western Europe into the Dark Ages, the Abbasids promoted learning over the next two centuries. The contributions of Muslims and their vassals in *al-Amjad* (the glorious era) are diverse and many. This was an empire that made a vain effort in the reign of al-Mamun to reconcile all subjects through a state creed of *mutazila*. From astronomical observatories like Jundishapur in Persia came *zijes* (charts for calculating the movement of stars) and the invention of the spherical astrolabe, the celestial sphere and quadrant, all of which improved navigation and made possible the age of exploration. Seminaries like the al-Azhar in Cairo blossomed into full-fledged universities on the order of those in Umayyad Spain.

Thousands of students and teachers flocked to al-Mamun's *Bayt al-Hikma* (house of wisdom), founded in Baghdad in 830 as an archive of precious documents. Here in the Islamic world, not in musty halls of north European monasteries, Graeco-Roman tradition was preserved and amplified for the benefit of future generations. Under the Umayyad Umar II, Masarjawaih, a Jew from Baghdad, laid the foundation for medieval medicine by translating Syriac books into Arabic. A century later, Thabit ibn Qurrah, a Christian physician from Hauran, offered translations of Euclid, Archimedes, and Ptolemy the Geographer. Hunayn ibn Ishaq (809–73), a Nestorian from al-Hirah, surpassed both, pursuing manuscripts all over the Middle East. Hunayn is credited with preserving the botanical studies of Dioscorides, the aphorisms of Hippocrates, Plato's *Republic*, seven books of Galen's anatomy, and 29 titles from Aristotle. The favorite scholar of al-Mamun, it was said that Hunayn was paid the weight of books he translated in gold.

Before Thomas Aquinas, Albertus Magnus or Johannes Duns Scotus, Islamic sages grappled with questions raised by Aristotle, whose writings were accepted as supplements to the Quran. In Kufa in the ninth century, Abu Yusuf al-Kindi authored more than 200 texts that were a mix of neo-Platonism, neo-Pythagorean mathematics, and faith. A century later, the Turk al-Farabi constructed a universal city modeled after the human body, with different organisms playing a hierarchial role. In Spain, Moses ben Maimonides ("Rambam") and Solomon ibn Gabirol ("Avicebron") tried to clarify the nature of the universe.[4]

Muhammad ibn Rushd (1126–98), was a contemporary of Maimonides, and, like him, a native of Cordoba. It was the physician-jurist ibn Rushd (nicknamed "Averroes") who revived the Mutazilite argument that religion and philosophy were not in conflict. What true believers called God was simply Aristotle's prime cause differently defined. People cannot understand the role of God because of the gap in intellect between men and deity. God acts like a great governor, perpetually in motion, allowing some free will to his subjects. When people studied Aristotle, they joined passages of the ancient Greek with clarifications by ibn Rushd known as "the Commentator."[5]

Writing in 1292, Roger Bacon credited ibn Rushd and an earlier Muslim scholar with the preservation and exposition of Aristotle. The second figure was Abu Ali ibn Sina ("Avicenna," 980–1037). A Muslim from Bokhara, Avicenna established a reputation in medicine, mathematics, and theology before he was 20. Like most of his contemporaries, he waited until he was mature enough to deal with philosophical questions. His conclusions (the soul is independent of the body and pre-existent as a part of a universal soul) were not entirely consistent with Aristotelian concepts, but were more palatable to Muslim fundamentalists who burned the works of ibn Rushd in the 12th century.

Avicenna once said he preferred a short life with width to a narrow one with length, and though his span of years was average, his impact was not. Beyond his philosophical meditations, he is known as the author of the *Canon*, a medical text that was in use for 500 years. The *Canon* offered clinical descriptions of a number of diseases (tuberculosis, pleurisy, and psychological disorders, including "love sickness). The book describes 760 drugs and recommends testing on animals before new drugs are used with humans. For cancer, it recommends early and complete surgery. For other ailments, a change of diet, climate, even music are helpful. Most significant, the *Canon* warns of the danger of contagion through contaminated water. Like ibn al-Khatib, vizir in Granada, and ibn Khatima, who lived through the Black Death of the 14th century, Avicenna warned the spread of disease was not the result of fate, but physical contact, and pollution.[6]

Islamic Medicine and Science

Avicenna was not the first Muslim to call for better hygiene or even to compile a medical encyclopedia. Two centuries before, al-Mansur summoned the physician Jurgis ibn Bakhtishu from Iran to Baghdad to cure him of a stomach ache. His grandson would cure one of Harun al-Rashid's slaves of hysterical paralysis and establish the first hospital in Baghdad at the beginning of the ninth century. In Spain, Abul Qasim al-Zahrawi ("Abulcasis," 940–1031) devised procedures for tonsillectomies, tracheotomies, craniotomies, the extraction of cancerous aneurysms, and invented more than 200 instruments (the bulb syringe, tweezers, inhaler, dental forceps) to assist with surgical operations.[7]

The title of first physician of the medieval world, however, belongs to Abu Bakr Muhammad ibn Zakariya al-Razi (865–925), chief physician of the Abbasid caliphate in the reign of al-Muktadir. It was "Rhazes" who selected the location for a new hospital by hanging strips of meat about the city and observing the process of putrefaction. Where the meat spoiled slowest he concluded was the healthiest section of the capital. Myths aside, Rhazes is credited with more than 200 books, including an encyclopedia of medicine. This last work, known as *al-Hawi* (the Comprehensive) offers pathological descriptions of and remedies for colic, psychiatric disorders, skin diseases, measles, kidney stones and bladder infections. No fewer than 14 chapters are devoted to the diagnosis and treatment of smallpox. Like al-Zahrawi, Rhazes devised a number of surgical techniques (sutures, the seaton).

Like Avicenna, Rhazes recommended a balanced diet as a safeguard against sickness, warned against patients swapping doctors, and advocated high standards of education for anyone entering the medical profession.[8]

Before being licensed as a physician or pharmacist, students had to complete a prescribed list of courses at a university. By the middle of the 13th century, ibn al-Baytar (d. 1248) identified more than 1400 drugs. Most of these were innocuous substances consisting of alcohol, camphor, balsam, cassia, or senna mixtures. Some might be doused with opium or arsenic.

In botany, studies of more than 600 plants (fruits, sugar cane, cotton, saffron) improved crop production. In chemistry, Jabir ibn Hayyan (from Kufah, c.776), attempting to discover a universal antidote, stumbled across the processes of filtration, sublimation, evaporation, distillation, and crystallization. "Geber" also prepared crude sulphuric and nitric acids, pure mercury, and waterproof material, and showed steel could be made. Ibn al-Haytham (b. 965 Basra), revolutionized the field of optics. His *Kitab al-Manazir* reversed the theories of Euclid and Ptolemy that held the eye was a transmitter of rays. Said al-Hazen: "It is not a ray that leaves the eye and meets the object that gives rise to vision. Rather, the form of the perceived object passes into the eye and is transmuted by its transparent body." From such a simple assumption came the inventions of Roger Bacon, da Vinci, and Johann Kepler.[9]

Simplicity made possible other important breakthroughs. The best example is Western adoption of what popularly are known as Arabic numerals. To write 999 in Greek required the use of 27 symbols. About A.D. 500, Indian scholars invented the zero. Known in Arabic as the *sunya* (empty, blank), its first appearance in the Islamic world is in a document dated 873. Subsequently, the Arabs modified Sanskrit and Urdu script and transmitted Arabic numerals to the West.

Theoreticians like al-Khwarizmi (750–850) brought together unknowns to match a known quantity (*Hisab al-Jabr wal Muqabala*) and developed the field of algebra. Al-Battani's dabblings in trigonometry were still being used by the Chinese five centuries after his death in 918. The Persian poet, Umar al-Khayyam (1040–1123), offered instruction in cubic and quadratic equations.[10] Scholars like al-Masudi, al-Idrisi (c. 1160), Leo Africanus (c. 1600) and ibn Khaldun (d. 1406) described the spherical nature of the earth, assayed different cultures of Africa and the Mediterranean, and stimulated the age of discovery.[11]

The Thousand and One Nights

Islamic influence in architecture can be seen in archways and buildings from the Alhambra to the Taj Mahal in Agra, the exquisite 17th-century marble mausoleum left by Shah Jahan for his wife Mumtaz. Europeans learned chess and backgammon from the peoples of the Middle East during the Crusades. At the same time, Christians adopted Sufi worry beads (originating like Arabic numbers with the Hindus) and made them into rosaries. The rhythms of Spanish flamenco music, instruments like the guitar, organ and lute are all of Arabic origin. Arabs and Islam played leading roles in the German Grail saga, the French *Song of Roland*, *El Cid*, *Aucassin et Nicolette*, Boccaccio's *Decameron*, Dante's *Divine Comedy*, Chaucer's *Squire's Tale*, Shakespeare's *Othello*, Defoe's *Robinson Crusoe* and Cervantes' *Don Quixote*.

Lovers quote from the *Rubaiyat* of Umar Khayyam. A few aesthetes read Firdawsi's *Shahnamah*. Everyone, though, is acquainted with *Alf Layla wa Layla* (*The Thousand and*

One Nights), a body of literature Arabs assembled from different parts of the world. The opening verses are recited by a Persian princess, Sharazade, whose husband, King Shahriyar, (distrustful of all women since his brother was cuckolded) weds each day and executes his bride after one night. For three years, Shahrazad beguiles the monarch with cliffhanger stories that include a magic horse and prince in Yemen; gorillas and cannibals from East Africa; Aladdin, the good-for-nothing son of a Chinese tailor; and the epic of Sinbad, the world's worst sailor, whose six shipwrecks leave him everywhere from Ceylon to Indonesia.

The first Western edition of *The Thousand and One Nights* was brought back to Europe by Antoine Calland some time between 1704 and 1717. The version compiled by Edward William Lane (c. 1840) is considered the classic translation.[12] More than 1000 pages in length, it is a mix of fable, ethics, and quasi-history. There are Nile boatmen swilling boozah. There are Jews, invariably portrayed as perfidious hagglers and pawnbrokers. There are the caliphs of Baghdad, usually the objects of a moral lesson.

The Thousand and One Nights redounds with reference to flight, the ability to soar from one spot to another on the back of a horse or a bird like the Roc. In these tales, birds speak the Quran and prostrate themselves. Some are actually jinn, immortal creatures made from smokeless fire. Divided into several categories ranging from demons like Iblis to capricious *efrits* and the all-powerful *marids*, they could take the form of birds, cats, snakes, or huge men. The jinn supposedly built the pyramids 2000 years before the time of Adam. They were also credited with the temple of Solomon in Jerusalem. Denizens of isolated regions, deserts, road junctions, the jinn could be warded off by cries of "*Hadeed! Hadeed!* Iron!" It was believed that Solomon gained control of them through the use of this metal. Whether by signet ring or magic lamp, the jinn could still be summoned from the Mountains of Kaf to do one's bidding.

Dabbling in these arts was not without its dangers. The very first tale told by Sharazade dealt with a merchant who killed the son of an efrit with the pit of a date he had just eaten. Three shaykhs intervened to spare the merchant's life. Equally tested were Abu Muhammad the Lazy, who released a marid from the land of Zunj and lost his bride in the process; Prince Bedrbassim, changed temporarily into a bird, and Aladdin, aided by two jinn and beset by two magicians who tried to deprive him of his newfound wealth. Then there was Sinbad, forced to reckon with an irate Roc in the Valley of Diamonds, chased like Odysseus by a horrible giant with tusks in the Mountains of the Apes, and bewitched by the Old Man of the Sea who refused to get off Sinbad's shoulders (after the sailor volunteered to carry him for a short time) until Sinbad gave him a special concoction of pumpkin wine.

Medieval males were obsessed with and repelled by the opposite sex. Possibly because females alone could give birth, men ascribed incredible powers to them. Good or evil, unless women were crones they were invariably beautiful, lustful, superhuman creatures. Queen Lab in the City of Enchanters resembled the Roman Circe with her ability to change men into animals. Jawharah, daughter of the King of the Sea, also possessed this power. The bride of the Young King of the Black Islands turned her husband's lower anatomy to stone as punishment for the death of her lover. The peasant hero Alnaschar was seduced by a beautiful girl, then brutalized by her slaves. Even where a female was admirable, as in the case of Ali Baba's servant girl Marjaneh, she possessed greater wisdom than her master.

This love-hate relationship extended also to slaves, particularly blacks. Arabs, who considered the Zanj inferior, were in awe of their size, strength and sexual potency. The consort of the Young King of the Black Islands debased herself (ate rats) before her black lover in his *kubbeh*. The beautiful girl who tantalized Alnaschar was surrounded by and faithful to blacks. The Polyphemus character that pursues Sinbad was black. So, too, the marid that victimized Abu Muhammad the Lazy. On the Isle of Blacks, Sinbad encountered *suttee* (immolation of women on the grave of their husbands).

Finally, it must be said that the "rags to riches" dream also pervaded this epic. Despite man's disadvantages relative to spellbinding women, physically imposing slaves, and wonder-working jinn, he inevitably won out. Alnaschar, Abu Muhammad, Aladdin, Ali Baba were poor men who, with the blessings of Allah, overcame misfortune to reside in castles filled with divans, curtains, gold, food, and dancing girls.

Even those who appeared beyond hope could be redeemed. The governor of Basra was puzzled by a case involving a handsome young man accused of breaking into the house of an aristocrat. The young man offered no defense but confessed to being a thief and asked that he be properly punished (amputation of a hand with a butcher's knife). Unconvinced, the governor called in the daughter of the aristocrat and learned that the two young people had been lovers. When the man was discovered in the house by the girl's father and brother, he admitted to being a thief in order to shield her honor. In the spirit of an age that may never have been as grand as it sounds, which never may have existed but which has captivated millions of readers and listeners after King Shahriyar, the governor of Basra had the couple married and presented them with 10,000 pieces of silver.

The End of Glory

The sack of Baghdad by Mongols in 1258 signaled the end of the Abbasid dynasty. This was no precipitate collapse. Rather, the once glorious caliphate much as Rome and Byzantium suffered a slow, erosive decline. By the end of the 10th century, internal and external forces combined to reduce the once mighty lords to little more than spiritual figureheads in the Islamic world.

A major factor in the fall of the empire was the decadence of the caliphs. Like the Umayyads before them, the Abbasids preferred an opulent lifestyle. Apart from gilded palaces and silk clothing, the Abbasids lavished huge amounts on public receptions. When al-Muktadir received the envoys of Constantine VII in 917, the palace was draped with 38,000 curtains and 22,000 rugs. One hundred sixty thousand cavalry and footmen, 7000 eunuchs, 700 chamberlains and 100 lions participated in a parade that ended with a performance by automated birds. A century before, Harun al-Rashid celebrated the marriage of his second son, al-Mamun, by showering the wedding couple and guests with pearls and sapphires and balls of musk that contained lists of property given as door prizes to the lucky recipients. To one poet whose verses pleased him, Harun gave 5000 gold pieces, a robe, 10 Greek slave girls, and a horse from the imperial stables. Others received as much as 300,000 dinars ($750,000) for a single work. A caliph whose wardrobe included thousands of kaftans and cloaks, hundreds of swords and turbans, and countless shoes could well afford the stipend as well as his wife Zubaydah's passion for fish tongues. To prepare a one-pound platter of this delicacy, 30,000 pounds of fish were caught and thrown away.[13]

In an empire that annually received $40 million in tribute, corruption was inevitable. Baghdad counted a number of millionaires who had won fortunes in a questionable manner. Chief among them were the Barmakids, a clan that had seen one of its own elevated to wazir by al-Abbas. For three generations, to the time of Harun al-Rashid, the Barmakids laid hereditary claim to the office of chief administrator of the empire and amassed a fortune in property, furniture, slaves, estimated at $75 million.

Harun himself was a profligate given to wine-drinking, boastfulness and sexual license.

Apart from his seven wives and harem, he developed an affection for the son of his chief vizir, Jafar ibn Yahya. To silence whispers about the relationship, the caliph ordered his sister Abassa to marry Jafar. It was to be a marriage in name only. However, when Abassa became pregnant, she fled to Mecca, fearing for the life of her child. Well she might, for when Harun, making pilgrimage to the holy city several years later, met the child and noted the resemblance to Jafar, Abassa, the child, and her slaves were executed. Upon returning to Baghdad, Harun had the Barmakids purged, his lover beheaded. When Jafar's head was brought to his throne room, the enraged monarch cursed, saying the body that had once been his had been betrayed by the head.[14]

Despite the Quranic prohibition against homosexuality, the Abbasids imported *ghilman* (beardless young men) for sexual purposes. Al-Mutawakil had 4000 of these eunuchs, described by Anthony Nutting as not so much a perversion as "a diversion." Earlier, Harun al-Rashid's wife Zubaydah, worried that their eldest son al-Amin had little interest in females, devised a scheme to perpetuate the dynasty. The heir apparent was placed in the company of "page boys." The hope was that proximity might lead to sexual encounters and a surprise for al-Amin. The boys were girls dressed in male clothing.

Disguises, treachery, deceit were important themes in *The Thousand and One Nights* and not without surprise. Few could be trusted in an empire where thousands of peddlers, merchants and physicians were on the caliph's payroll as informers. The postal service opened mail and punished alleged subversives. The brutality of the Abbasids in their purges of the Umayyads, Kharijites, Abu Muslim, Abdullah and various Shiite Imams of the ninth century was notorious. The caliphs practiced fratricide (al-Mamun took the throne from his brother al-Amin) and parricide (al-Muntasir killed his father al-Mutawwakil in 861). Woe also to the poet who backed the wrong figure in a dynastic dispute. Ibn al-Mugaffa, translator of eastern folktales, was executed by al-Mansur. In 783, Abdal Quddus was crucified, Bashar blinded for their literary efforts.[15]

The Fatimids

Victims of their own lechery and intolerance (Harun al-Rashid and al-Mutawwakil both mandated discriminatory garb for Jews), the Abbasids faced constant rebellions. Some of these (the Alids and Zanj in Iraq) were readily suppressed. Control of distant provinces, however, proved more difficult. In 820, Tahir ibn Hussein, a one-eyed general of al-Mamun, declared himself lord in Khurasan. Over the next 300 years, Iran and Afghanistan saw one dynasty after another — Saffarids (867–908), Samanids (847–999), Ghaznawids (961–1168), Buwayhids — toppled as ambitious vassals proclaimed themselves king.[16]

Two years before Harun al-Rashid came to the throne (788), Idris ibn Abdallah established a Shiite dynasty in Morocco. Twelve years later, the governor of Tunisia, Ibrahim ibn al-Aghlab, proclaimed his own caliphate at Kairwan. A mutiny in the reign of al-Mustasim led to the creation of the Tulunid (866–905), then Ikshidid (935–69), dynasties in Egypt. While the Karmatians were ravaging the holy places of Arabia, another band of Shiites, the Fatimids, snatched control of North Africa from the Aghlabids in 909 and, under al-Muizz, conquered Egypt in 969.

Ninth-century Ismaili zealots, the Fatimids owed their origins and ideology to Abu-Abdullah as-Shii, a Muslim holy man from Yemen. Abu-Abdullah inspired a full-blown insurrection in Tunisia with his prophesy that the Mahdi would soon return as an obscure man from North Africa. He even presented such a redeemer in the form of Ubaydullah al-

Mahdi, a merchant who had been imprisoned by the Aghlabids before the Fatimid revolution in 909. In the power struggle between Arabs and Berbers that followed, Ubaydullah and the North Africans won out. Abu-Abdullah was beheaded and Ubaydullah ruled until his death at age 61 in 934.[17]

During his reign, Ubaydullah's fleets attacked Sicily, Tripoli, and Kairwan. Several assaults were also made by his son al-Qaim against Alexandria. His great grandson al-Muizz ultimately conquered Egypt in 969, establishing the Shiite dynasty that also dominated Syria, Yemen and the Hejaz until the age of Saladin. Al-Muizz renamed the ancient fort city of al-Fustat in his own honor—*al Qahirah al-Muizziyah*, Cairo.

Al-Muizz' grandson al-Hakim (996–1021) set a new standard for tyrannical behavior. A puritan who dressed in white wool, al-Hakim forbade the sale of wine or beer, chastised women who went out of their homes without veils, and flogged people who played chess. Shoemakers were forbidden to craft women's shoes. Women were forbidden to visit cemeteries. In al-Hakim's paranoid world, no one could sail past his palace in a boat or ride by on horseback. To ensure this, stirrup makers were executed. Revered by some Islamic sectarians as the true Mahdi, al-Hakim attacked all religious groups. Christians and Jews were compelled to wear the badge or crosses on black garments. Churches and synagogues were razed. Every few days kadis and other religious figures were decapitated or thrown into fire.[18]

The Seljuk Turks

Harun al-Rashid could lacerate Nicephorus of Byzantium as "a dog of a Roman" and dismember the rebel Rafi ibn Lait on his last military campaign. Al-Mamun was capable of leading his armies in the field before succumbing to a stomach full of dates. The next eight Abbasid caliphs, though, were cloistered 60 miles up the Tigris in Samarra, where they were prisoners of their own Turkish bodyguards.

Many rebellions could be traced to these so-called Mamelukes who had been invited into the empire in the reign of Harun. Like Germans in ancient Rome, the Turks soon dominated palace affairs. Their commander, known as *sultan* (one with power), claimed authority equal to, if not surpassing that of, the caliph and it was not unusual to see his throne situated next to that of the Abbasid. Although the caliphate endured until al-Mustasim was forced to eat iron by Hulagu's troops in 1258, a de facto transfer of power had taken place nearly 300 years before. No longer the Arabs, but the Turks were the new lords of the Middle East.

A Turanian people, the Turks claimed descent from Alexander the Great and were also identified with the Hsiung-nu of Attila that had dominated the Eurasian heartland after A.D. 450. Loosely organized in tribal bands that took their names from a supreme warlord, or *kagan*, the Turks were a pastoral people who lived off their herds and plunder. Each spring, the men of the tribe would assemble at a designated spot for an annual military campaign. Before going off to war, veterans and recruits prepared with contests or archery, swords and horsemanship.

As with other migratory folk, the Turkish religion was animistic, dominated by gods of water, earth and sky, chief of which was Tangri, a lord of the heavens not unlike the Hittite Teshub. Communion with this god was possible only through the shaman in a state of trance. The Turks practiced exorcism and ancestor worship. Forced west by the consolidation of Sung power in China in the sixth century, they came in contact with and adopted many of the beliefs of Buddhists, Manichaeans, and Zoroastrians. Some, the Cumans and Pechenegs, entered Byzantine territory as mercenaries. The Khazars who dominated the Crimea for 200 years adopted Judaism for a while.

Other tribes converted to Islam after 970. The chieftain responsible was Seljuk, who lent his name to the horde that usurped Abbasid power.[19] The son of a warrior, Tuquq (Iron Bow), who died in the service of the Khazars, Seljuk was raised at the Khazar court before being banished to Transoxiana. There he defeated the Samanids, converted his people to Islam, and died at the age of 107.

Seljuk had four sons, the names of which (Israil, Yusuf, Musa, Mikhail) reveal his commitment to Sunni orthodoxy. Two of these (Israil and Mikhail) tried in vain to defeat Mahmud the Ghaznawid, whose domains stretched from Khurasan to Lahore. It was not until Tughril Bey, (a grandson of Seljuk) seized control of Bokhara in 1040 that the Turkish advance could resume. Capitalizing on a dynastic dispute among the Ghaznawids, Tughril took Merv, Herat and Nishapur, established a temporary capital at Rayy, and terminated the Ghaznawid dynasty by 1043. Beyond the Caspian, his forces raided Azerbaijan and Armenia, hammered at the Buwayhids in Mesopotamia and Fatimids in the Hejaz. When in December 1055 Tughril stood unopposed before the gates of Baghdad, Caliph al-Kaim had no choice but to admit him to the city and recognize him as sultan.

Tughril had no use for pomp, thrones, and such, and returned to Merv, where he chose to ignore the caliph until his death at age 70 in 1063. His power was inherited by a nephew, Adueddin Alp Arslan, known as "hero-lion." A man of great stature whose mustache was so long he had to tie it into knots to keep from tripping over it, Alp Arslan converted his uncle's warlord confederacy into a great, if short-lived, empire.

Alp Arslan appreciated the malaise that hung over the Byzantine Empire in his day. The death of Constantine VIII in 1025 left two aging sisters, Zoe and Theodora, switching off favorites in Constantinople for more than two decades. When the reign of crones finally ended, the empire passed through several monarchs in rapid order. Michael V (1056–57) was overthrown by the military. Isaac Comnenus I (1057–59) abdicated in favor of his finance minister. Constantine X (1059–64) lost territory in the west to the Normans and alienated foreign mercenaries by instituting austerity measures to cut the size and payroll of the army. Constantine's widow conspired to have her lover Romanus IV Diogenes (1068–71) named basileus. Against this monarch, the Seljuks advanced, taking Caesarea in Palestine, Konya in southern Anatolia, and winning over some of the *akritoi*, Byzantine frontier guards who were of Turkish extraction.

Romanus had no choice but to fight. This clash of the two armies at Manzikert in eastern Armenia on Friday, August 26, 1071, should be marked among the decisive battles in history.[20] Had they heeded a number of omens, the Byzantines would have been wary of the day. It is said the imperial tent collapsed at one of the campgrounds. About the same time, fire ravaged the royal stables. Bari, the last Byzantine possession in Italy, was lost this same year. As Romanus' army marched to Manzikert, they were not cheered by the sight of a previous battlefield littered with the bleached bones of another Byzantine force defeated by the Turks. There were also rumors that mercenaries within their own ranks were unreliable. Inexplicably, Romanus divided his army into three units, each seeking out the Seljuks. When the two forces collided, he was in no position to coordinate an attack. In the midst of battle, contingents of Armenians (long victims of Byzantine intolerance) and Pechenegs deserted. When the basileus called for reinforcements, Andronicus Ducas, commanding the rear guard, refused, claiming all was lost, thereby spreading panic in the ranks. It was Andronicus' way of evening a score with Romanus, who had exiled his father.

Manzikert sealed the fate of the Byzantine Empire. A subcontinent that had been home to Trojans, Hittites and Greeks would henceforth be identified as Turkish. On the battlefield, Alp Arslan asked Romanus what he would have done if their fortunes had been reversed. Replied the hapless basileus, "I would have flogged you to death." Forced to sign a degrading peace (including a ransom of one and one-half on dinars, a guarantee of release of all Muslim prisoners and supply of Byzantine soldiers to the Seljuks for 50 years) Romanus was blinded and imprisoned on an island. He died within the year.

Alp Arslan also lived just one year beyond his triumph at Manzikert. The "Elephant of Ghur" made his capital at Isfahan, never bothering to visit Baghdad, where one of the Abbasids demonstrated the wealness of the caliphate by renouncing his position to an Egyptian Fatimid. In the next 20 years, Alp Arslan's son Malikshah (1072–92) pushed Seljuk domination into Syria and Palestine. Borrowing the institutions of Romans, Persians and Arabs, Malikshah attempted to consolidate the empire. Irrigation canals, sewage systems and cesspools were dug. A network of inns was established at 18-mile intervals along ancient roads to provide travelers with rest. The ruins of some of these small *khans* or more elaborate *caravanserais* with their massive stone walls and honeycombed niches are still visible in parts of the Middle East.

Malikshah revived religious life, building a number of delicate mosques and medressehs and securing the pilgrimage route to Mecca. The simple tent once favored by Seljuk leaders gave way to palaces of pavilions, kiosks and baths. Elegant coronations were added to the hunt and falconry as regular institutions of the empire. It was an exciting age, exemplified by a conference on astronomy that revised the calendar in 1074 and 1075 and the founding of another academy, the Nizamiyah, in Baghdad.

Much of the credit for reform goes to the advisory council that assisted Malikshah. Twenty-four ministers, known as the *diwan*, included military commanders, a chief justice, treasurer, and *Shaykh ul-Islam* (mufti for religious affairs). Most important of these in the reigns of both Alp Arslan and Malikshah was the vizir, Nizam al-Mulk. Once governor in Khurasan, Nizam founded the educational center that bore his name in Baghdad and devised the scheme for subinfeudation, which provided funds for the economic and religious revival of the region.[21]

Possessed of keen philosophical insight, Nizam drew up advisory texts on government. In his *Siyasat Namah* (Book of Administration), he urged the monarch to be wary of placing too much trust in friends or granting a fief for an indefinite period. No Mameluke, he said, should serve as judge, for they were notorious for accepting bribes. Malikshah should prevent too many offices from accruing to another single person, for history demonstrated the propensity of men to rebel once they felt they had sufficient power. Most of all, the Seljuk lord should maintain stringent control of the post and retain a vigilant secret police in order to obtain the most accurate, up-to-date intelligence information.

Malikshah followed Nizam's advice, but to no avail. In 1092, both men were slain by the Assassins, ushering in an era of chaos that Hasan as-Sabah called "the beginning of bliss." It was also the end of the fruitful era in Islamic history known as al-Amjad.

19

The Crusades

The Call for Holy War

The deaths of two great Seljuk leaders marked the onset of the dissolution of the empire. One of Malikshah's sons ruled as sultan in Baghdad. Another held the territory between Aleppo and Damascus. A cousin established the Seljuk sultanate of Rum in Konya. Other members of the family proclaimed independent states in Mosul, Edessa, and Jerusalem.

This fragmentation was not lost upon Europeans who had watched resentfully as the Seljuks, like the Fatimids before them, interfered with pilgrims to the Holy Land and profaned Christian shrines. The time seemed ripe to avenge previous humiliations by ousting the Muslims from Palestine. Here was a way of helping Alexis I Comnenus, the embattled Byzantine emperor, who sat in fear of being overwhelmed from Anatolia. Here a way of showing support for the kings of Castille and Leon engaged in a 500-year-long Reconquista of Spain. Here, too, a way of healing the breach between Eastern and Western Christianity that occurred in 1054.

True believers could argue that fighting a holy war might hasten the second coming of Christ. Academics may debate the significance of millennialism in bringing about the Crusades, but even the simplest peasant knew that it had been more than 1000 years since the first visitation. Europe's population had also doubled between 1000 and 1300. Under feudal primogeniture only eldest sons would inherit land. The growing number of lack-lands demanded relief.

Some of these factors must have influenced Pope Urban II when he addressed 300 cardinals, archbishops, abbots and secular lords at Clermont, France, on November 26, 1095. The Pope was anxious to gain support for the Cluniac reform movement. He wished to enhance his own prestige at the expense of Europe's reprobate monarchs (both Philip I of France and William II of England had been excommunicated for immorality, while Henry IV had his own Pope in Germany). Urban was also aware of the threat to Europe that lay beyond Constantinople. Failure to stop the Turks now could lead to Cumans, Pechenegs, and Seljuks overrunning western Europe. Thus, it came as no surprise when Urban exhorted his listeners:

> O race of Franks! race beloved and chosen by God ... from the confines of Jerusalem and from
> Constantinople a grievous report has gone forth that an accursed race, wholly alienated from

God, has violently invaded the lands of these Christians, and had depopulated them by pillage and fire.... Let your quarrels end. Enter upon the road to the Holy Sepulcher; wrest that land from a wicked race, and subject it to yourselves. Jerusalem is a land fruitful above all others, a paradise of delights. That royal city, situated at the center of the earth, implores you to come to her aid. Undertake this journey eagerly for the remission of your sins, and be assured of the reward of imperishable glory in the Kingdom of Heaven![1]

The cry "*Deus vult!*" (God wills it!) struck a responsive chord among Christians. Over the next 200 years, hundreds of thousands of Franks, Germans, Italians, English and Hungarians would don the cross. Some came willing to sacrifice their lives for Christ. Others were less altruistic. The Pope promised indulgences, release of the soul from wandering in purgatory, to those who made the Crusade. Pirenne argues that the rebirth of medieval cities may be traced to this era of warfare. Still others came lured by adventure, the opportunity to use what was deemed the ultimate weapon. The arbalest, a clumsy crossbow with a wooden stock and hand-drawn winch, was not the most accurate device. Considered inhuman, it was, with the consent of Europe's lords, not to be used against Christians.

The First Crusade

Historians generally count seven offensive campaigns between Urban's call and the fall of Acre in 1291. A number of brigands, however, proclaimed themselves Crusaders in order to justify pillaging. A good example were the followers of the freebooter Emerich who plundered Jewish communities in the Rhineland in 1096. The tradition of *Kiddush ha-Shem* (martyrs to the name of God) originated in the fires of Worms, Speyer, Mainz and Cologne. Church and lay officials stood aside as mobs did God's bidding against the enemies of Christ that were at hand.[2]

Bishops and lords were not so kind toward other bands of impoverished peasants and shepherds. The first wave of these misguided souls set off for the East early in 1096 led by zealots like Peter the Hermit and Walter the Penniless. In a scene reminiscent of Grimms' fairy tales, one group wandered behind a divinely inspired ass and goose. The peasants took what they needed from fields and farms. When they reached Hungary, arguments with merchants left 5000 persons dead. Grown to more than 20,000, the ragtag force was dumped at the doorstep of Constantinople. Alexis Comnenus was stunned that his call for help had been answered by a rabble. Just as quickly as the King of Hungary, the basileus transported these volunteers into Anatolia to do battle with the Turks. Poorly trained, the peasants were annihilated near Nicaea. Only 2000 escaped death or slavery.

The first contingent of bona fide warriors set out for Byzantium in March 1096. They were led by Frankish nobles, although their number included some Italians like Bohemond of Tarento. Among the French knights were Robert of Normandy (son of William the Conqueror), Robert of Flanders, Stephen of Blois, the aged Raymond of Toulouse, the handsome Godfrey of Bouillon (a descendant of Charlemagne) and his younger brother Baldwin of Lorraine. Technically, the entire army was under the spiritual command of Bishop Adhemar of Puy.

Some of the Crusaders marched overland in the path of the unfortunate peasants. Others sailed from Italian ports after making pilgrimage to St. Peter's. Fulcher of Chartres tells of families parting, of Crusaders being pelted with stones as they prayed in Rome, of vessels going down in storms of the Adriatic. When the army assembled, 30,000 strong, at Byzantium by the end of the year, the basileus Alexis was fearful of what he had wrought.

The Crusaders might just be tempted to seize Constantinople as march on Jerusalem. Keeping them from entering the city, he cajoled and bribed their commanders to continue their journey.

A two-week march early in 1097 took the Crusaders past the catastrophic remains of the peasants' battlefield. They captured Nicaea in June 1097, and followed this up with a victory against the Seljuks at Dorylaeum on July 1. As one element under Baldwin veered off to capture Edessa, the main body pushed south through the rugged terrain of Anatolia. Fulcher recounts how the desert heat and dust caused some men to discard their mail and helmets. By the time they entered the mountains, fall rains were flooding the narrow trails. As they crossed the torturous Cilician Gates, Fulcher wrote:

> The diabolical mountain was so high and steep that none of us dared to step before another. There, horses fell headlong and one pack animal pushed over another. Knights beat themselves with their hands for their great grief and sadness, uncertain what they should do about themselves and their arms, selling their shields and their best breast plates, together with their helmets for whatever they could get. Those who could not sell them threw them away.[3]

It was a weary, bedraggled band that stumbled before Antioch in October 1097. What they beheld was a city girded by 12 miles of walls 60 feet high, embellished with 400 towers, and an inner citadel 1000 feet above the rest of the town. The Crusaders could not afford to bypass the impregnable fortress. They encamped and waited, enduring the sight of some of their comrades captured and beheaded. By Christmas, the winter rains had turned their camp into a quagmire. The siege dragged on — as one in seven of the Christians starved to death. People ate dogs, cats, rats, camel hides, and even talked of cannibalism.[4]

Then, a miracle occurred. In a dispatch to Urban, Godfrey wrote: "But God looked down upon his people, whom he had so long chastised and mercifully consoled them. Therefore, he at first revealed to us, as a recompense for our tribulation and as a pledge of victory, his lance, which had lain hidden since the days of the apostles."[5]

The authenticity of this spear, which the centurion Longinus allegedly used to pierce Jesus' side, was later tested in St. Peter's and found wanting. (The man who discovered it died as he ran a gauntlet over hot firewood.) Nevertheless, its discovery inspired the Crusaders to scale the walls of Antioch and capture the city on June 3, 1098. Fulcher explains that an Armenian who converted to Islam betrayed his comrades. The Seljuks tried to recapture Antioch later that summer. Three hundred thousand troops were repulsed after a 28-day siege. Claiming that Christ himself was in their ranks, the Crusaders overran the main Turkish camp. Finding women there, "They did nothing evil to them except pierce their bellies with their lances."[6]

Riven with jealousy and weakened by a typhoid epidemic, the Crusaders could not resume their march on Jerusalem until January 1099. When they finally beheld the sacred city, they fell to their knees in thanksgiving. Such rejoicing was premature. Jerusalem had reverted to the control of the Fatimids, who offered an armistice. When this was rejected by the Crusaders, the Muslim commander Iftikar prepared to defend the city. Though smaller than Antioch (there were at best 40,000 people in Jerusalem), the ancient walls constructed by Hadrian offered comparable protection.

Once more, the Christians faced shortages of food, timber, and especially water. Wood for siege machinery was obtained from a secret cache in a cave near the Old City and from the remains of Genoese ships docked at Jaffa. Water was a more serious problem. The principal supply came from the spring of Gihon, which lay within range of enemy archers.

During this siege, which lasted six months, some Crusaders licked the dew off grass or sucked clumps of mud. Then, on July 15, 1099, divine intervention again preserved the faithful. Wrote Godfrey:

> And after the army had suffered greatly in the siege especially on account of lack of water, a council was held and bishops and princes ordered that all should march around the walls of the city with bare feet in order that he who entered it humbly in our behalf might be moved by our humility to open it to us and to exercise judgment upon his enemies.[7]

Having mortified themselves, carrying banners and pictures of saints, the Crusaders launched a series of human-wave assaults against Mt. Zion, the Citadel of David, and the northeast corner of the city wall. Godfrey directed the overthrow of this last bastion and pursued the fleeing Muslims through the alleys to the Mosque of Umar. Ten thousand Muslims were massacred; 400 Jews who happened to be in the city were also slaughtered in their synagogues. Of the blood-letting, William of Tyre wrote:

> It was impossible to look upon the vast numbers of slain without horror; everywhere lay fragments of human bodies and the very ground was covered with the blood of the slain. It was not alone the spectacle of the headless bodies and mutilated limbs strewn in all directions that roused horror in all who looked upon them. Still more dreadful it was to gaze upon the victors themselves, dripping with blood from head to foot, an ominous sight which brought terror to all who met them.[8]

Godfrey became *Advocatus Sancti Sepulchri*, defender of the Holy Sepulchre, a title he held for only a year before his death in 1100. He would be succeeded by his brother Baldwin, who had been Count of Edessa. Bohemond became Prince of Antioch, Raymond Count of Tripoli, as the once landless lords subinfeudated the conquered territories.[9]

More than 400 years of Islamic rule in the Holy Land was ended and, to ensure that it would never return, the Crusader princes built a number of castles from Beaufort on the Litani to Petra. Some of these, like Saone and Le Moinestre, were carved into rock outcroppings more than a mile high. Massive structures, these circular towers gave peripheral views to a distance of 50 miles. The Roman *portcullis*, an iron grating, slammed down on a bent or angled gateway. *Machicolation*, overhead apertures built in to the walls, enabled defenders to pour oil or molten lead onto attackers. The walls consisted of yard-long blocks of stone assembled to a depth of 80 feet.[10]

Nine hundred years ago, the forts were entrusted to members of three military-religious sects. The Hospitalers, founded by Italian merchants around 1070, were better known as the Knights of St. John. Initially, they maintained hostels for travelers near the Church of the Holy Sepulchre. The Hospitalers eventually moved their headquarters to Rhodes, then Malta before the Ottoman Turks took that island in 1575. The Knights Templar were Burgundian in origin and Benedictine in ritual. Taking their name from their occupation of the Temple compound, the Templars converted the Mosque of Umar into a church and sold chips of the great rock to pilgrims as souvenirs. They also turned the al-Aqsa mosque into a barracks, using its mihrab as a latrine. The third group, the Teutonic Knights, was founded by a German visitor to the Holy Land who wished to offer services comparable to what was being rendered by the Italians and French. Devoted to St. Mary, the Teutonic Knights would immigrate to East Prussia in the 13th century.[11]

These monk-warriors were every bit as fierce as the Assassins and other Islamic zealots. They maintained surveillance and collected taxes in the vicinity of their castles. Some possessed naval units and negotiated on equal terms with European monarchs. Under the direct control of the Pope, they were never to surrender.

Crusader Interregnum

For the next 40 years, the Franks enjoyed supremacy in this region they dubbed "Outremer" (overseas). Settling in, the Crusaders played chess and *Shesh-besh*, bested the Muslims on the battlefield, intermarried and fathered offspring (*pullani*) with native women. Bulky clothing gave way to loose, embroidered robes, upturned shoes, and kaffiyehs. Mutton and pilaf replaced pork and sugar honey, and pita bread became the staple, as old eating habits gave way to new ones. Said Fulcher of Chartres:

> Now we who were Westerners have become Easterners. He who was Italian or French has in this land become a Galilean or a Palestinian. He who was a citizen of Rheims or Chartres is now a Tyrian or an Antiochene. We have already forgotten our birthplaces. Most of us do not know them or even hear of them. One already owns home and household as if by paternal and hereditary right, another has taken a wife not a compatriot, but a Syrian, Armenian, or even a baptized Saracen woman.... He who was an alien has become a native, he who was immigrant is now a resident.... For those who were poor there has God made rich here. Those who had a few pence there have numberless gold pieces here; he who had not a village there possesses with God as giver a whole town here. Why then return to the West, when the East suits us so well.[12]

A better reading of the popular contempt Turks and Arabs felt for the Crusaders comes from the writings of Usama ibn Munqidh of Damascus (1095–1188). His autobiography (*Kitab al-Itibar*, Book of Instructions) offers numerous anecdotes about the Franks. Whether introduced with an aside ("this is an example of Frankish barbarism, God damn them!") or a more polite statement that "the Franks are without any vestige of a sense of honour and jealousy," Usama's hatred was apparent.[13]

Usama ridiculed the European predilection for "pig's flesh." He was outraged when one of the Templars seized him in the al-Aqsa and twirled him about, joking, "That is the way to pray!" But two entries revealed his aversion for the conquerors. In one tale he related the curious medical practices of the Crusaders. A knight who was suffering an abscess in his leg was taken to a Frankish doctor. The latter informed him that the leg would have to be removed. As Usama watched, the physician flailed away with an axe until "the marrow spurted out of the leg and the patient died instantaneously." The doctor then went on to treat a women who, he said, was possessed. To remove the demon, he slashed her skull with a razor and rubbed part of her brain with salt. This patient also died. Wrote Usama: "At this juncture I asked whether they had any further need of me and as they had none I came away, having learnt things about medical methods that I never knew before."[14]

The other story was a lampoon of Christian marital fidelity. As Usama tells it, a Frank living in Nablus returned home one day to discover his wife in bed with a stranger. When he demanded to know what was going on, the stranger responded, "I was tired and so I came in to rest." Why this bed? "I found the bed made up and lay down to sleep." But his wife was in the bed. "The bed is hers. How could I prevent her getting into her own bed?" To which the master of the house replied naively, "I swear if you do it again I shall take you to court!"[15]

Islamic resentment would find more than a number of champions in the 12th century. One of these, Imad al-Din Zangi, was a blue-eyed Turkish officer whose father had served Malikshah as Chamberlain. Having distinguished himself in combat with the Crusaders at Tiberias in 1121, Zangi was given an estate at Basra by the Seljuks. Six years later he became governor of Mosul and mounted a series of assaults against Christian positions in eastern Syria. A harsh overlord who never repeated an order, Zangi flogged subordinates who trampled crops or abused women. Disobedience he punished with crucifixion. Just as ruthless with the enemy, he was dubbed *Sanguineus* (Bloodletter) by the Franks after his destruction of Cerep, a Crusader fort near Aleppo in 1130. Over the next decade, Zangi consolidated control in the northern arc of the Fertile Crescent. His seizure of Edessa in 1144 is said to have prompted Bernard of Clairvaux to call for the Second Crusade. Zangi was not around to confront Louis VII and Conrad III. In September 1146, three of his slaves stabbed him in the heart as he lay in a drunken stupor at castle Jaabar near the Euphrates.[16] His son Nurredin continued to rule from Damascus (conquered in 1154) until the Zangids, Fatimids and Crusaders encountered a greater foe at the end of the century — a Kurd named Saladin.

Saladin

Salah al-Din Yusuf ibn Ayyub, "Rectitude of the Faith" (1139–93), was the greatest leader produced by Islam during the Crusader interlude. Raised in Baalbek where his father was one of Zangi's top aides, Saladin's youth was spent in leisure, polo matches and chess, wine-drinking and wenching. Later, he acquired such a reputation for Quranic devotion that it was said he wept when he studied the holy book. A brilliant man who discussed philosophy with Maimonides, he lived simply, foreswearing 4000-room palaces for a small house where he could meet with and answer the problems of his subjects. Married to one woman (they had 16 children), when he died Saladin's fortune consisted of one dinar, 47 dirhams (approximately $20), the rest having been given to the poor.[17]

No one better personified the chivalrous knight, courageous in battle, willing to spare enemies who pledged never to take up arms upon their release. Saladin received his first combat experience in 1164 when he accompanied an uncle Shirkuh on an expedition into Egypt. That land was a hopeless tangle in the middle of the 12th century. Ruling in Cairo was the Fatimid caliph el-Adid, a 13-year-old Shiite who was unable to control two warring nobles, Shawar and Dirgham. Having temporarily gained the upper hand, Dirgham appealed to Nureddin in Damascus for assistance. The latter, a Sunnite whose loyalties were to the Abbasid caliph in Baghdad, dispatched the force that included Saladin. Four years would pass before the conflict was resolved in January 1169. Neither Shawar nor Dirgham emerged victorious. Rather, Nurredin's vassal Shirkuh was now serving as vizir for the Fatimids. His death, from over-eating, elevated Saladin to the high post in March 1169.

Just 30 years of age, Saladin was deeply resented by colleagues who tested his authority. In July 1169, Nejah, the chief black eunuch at the Fatimid court, incited a revolt of 30,000 blacks. Although Saladin quelled the uprising (Nejah was beheaded), his lieutenants had to deal with additional troubles in the Sudan for the next five years. In November 1169, Amalric, the king of Jerusalem, attacked the Delta. Some 220 ships struck against Damietta in what proved a disaster because of poor planning and foul weather. Saladin never forgot this Christian assault. He had said, "When God gave me the land of Egypt, I was sure he meant Palestine for me also." The ill-fated siege of Damietta would help justify jihad against the Franks.

When el-Adid died in September 1171, 200 years of Fatimid rule in North Africa came to an end. Saladin saluted the Abbasid caliph al-Mustadi in Baghdad. Meanwhile, he set about beautifying Cairo with mosques, seminaries, aqueducts. Order was established in the city where, according to one saying, "there was not so much as the butting of two goats." Saladin rebuilt Cairo's walls and constructed a citadel on the city's southeast corner in 1176.

The 30-foot high walls and circular towers of the complex supposedly were built of stones taken from Menkaure's pyramid at Gizeh.

The popularity of the young governor was not lost upon Nureddin. Just as Khalid al-Walid and Tarik, Saladin aroused the jealousy of his lord. More astute than his predecessors, Saladin refused to respond when Nureddin summoned him to court. Nureddin died in May 1174, and his domains were fragmented among relatives. The only Muslim figure powerful enough to emerge from the internecine fighting over the next six years was Saladin. Withstanding three attempts on his life by the Assassins, he occupied Damascus in the summer of 1182 and finished off the remnants of the Zangid clan in Mosul in February 1186.

Saladin was now sultan of an empire that stretched from Mesopotamia to Sudan with one important exception — Palestine. The sacred land lay exposed before a giant Islamic nutcracker. The enthusiasm of the monastic orders for warfare was said to be flagging. The Frankish lords had never ceased feuding among themselves. Amalric's death in 1183 resulted in the accession of his 16-year-old son, Baldwin V, as king of Jerusalem, but not for long. An unfortunate youth, afflicted with leprosy and a right arm that had been immobilized by an earlier test of valor, Baldwin was ousted in 1186 by his brother-in-law, Guy de Lusignan.[18]

The Third Crusade

Guy's coup was just the last in a number of provocations for war. Apart from desiring revenge for the humiliation of 1099, Saladin recalled Amalric's invasion of Egypt in 1169. Eight years later, in the course of his campaigns against the Zangids, Saladin captured Ashkelon in Palestine, but was routed at Ramleh by a smaller Crusader force. In 1183, Reginald of Chatillon, a knight based at Kerak, launched a land-sea invasion against the Hejaz, expressing the desire to destroy the tomb of "the accursed camel driver" at Medina and the kaaba in Mecca. It was another catastrophe for the Crusaders. Egyptian forces intercepted their fleet, sending the prisoners tied to camels off to Mecca where they were used for sacrifice during the month of pilgrimage. The same Reginald repeatedly broke truces, attacking caravans, including one in 1186 that bore one of Saladin's sisters. Taunted Reginald: "Since they trusted in Muhammad, let Muhammad come and save them."

As soon as the weather turned mild in April 1187, Saladin did just that. Moving south from his Syrian capital, he struck at both Kerak and Acre. Then, veering inland, he seized Tiberias. Hearing that the citadel in Tiberias was under attack, the 15,000-man Christian army reacted. Hot and weary from a 20-mile forced march in mail, visor and heavy equipment, the Crusaders stumbled across Saladin's force at a spot five miles west of the Sea of Galilee. Having seized the principal water holes, the Muslims set fire to the scrub, creating a wall of irritating smoke. Saladin's cavalry enveloped their opponents, nudging them back and up on to an oddly shaped hill known as the Horns of Hittin.

As Crusaders rallied around the True Cross, they were picked off by a hail of arrows from Saladin's archers. (It was said that the rain of arrows were so thick an ant could not have escaped.) When the battle ended, Guy, Reginald, the Grand Master of the Templars, and hundreds of knights were prisoners. Guy was ransomed on his word (later renounced) that he would never fight again. Reginald to the end acted presumptuously and was slain by Saladin himself. In an uncharacteristic action, Saladin also permitted the brutal execution of many prisoners by Sufi fanatics.

What transpired at Hittin horrified Muslim observers. Of the many carcasses "shrugged off by Hittin," one Arab historian wrote:

I passed by them and saw the limbs of the fallen cast naked on the field of battle, scattered in pieces over the site of the encounter, lacerated and disjointed, with heads cracked open, throats split, spines broken, necks shattered, feet in pieces, noses mutilated, extremities torn off, members dismembered, parts shredded, eyes gouged out, stomachs disemboweled, hair coloured with blood, the praecordium slashed, fingers sliced off, the thorax smashed, the ribs broken, the joints dislocated, the chests smashed, throats slit, bodies cut in half, arms pulverized, lips shriveled, foreheads pierced, forelocks dyed scarlet, breasts covered with blood, ribs pierced, elbows disjointed, bones broken, tunics torn off, faces lifeless, wounds gaping, skin flayed, fragments chopped off, hair lopped, backs skinless, bodies dismembered, teeth knocked out, blood spilt, life's last breath exhaled, necks lolling, joints slackened, pupils liquefied, heads hanging, livers crushed, ribs staved in, heads shattered, breasts flayed spirits flow, their very ghosts crushed; like stones among stones, a lesson to the wise.[19]

The road to Jerusalem now lay open to Saladin. The remaining Crusader strongholds—Belfort, Safed, and Tyre—lay north of the holy city and could be of little assistance. As Saladin's army approached Jerusalem in September 1187, panicked residents of Gaza, Ashkelon and Ramleh swelled the city's population to 70,000. Hoping to avoid a battle, Saladin sent Balian of Ibelin, a knight captured at Hittin, into the city to persuade the Christians to capitulate. There is some confusion whether Balian went back on his word and urged the Christians to resist. While negotiations meandered on for five weeks, Saladin placed his siege machines in position near the Damascus Gate and waited. When Christians demanded safe conduct away from the city, he is said to have replied: "We shall deal with you just as you dealt with the population of Jerusalem when you took it in 1099, with murder, enslavement and other savageries." Informed by Balian that the Christians were prepared to raze the city and slay 5000 Muslim POWs, Saladin agreed to ransom the inhabitants. Those who could pay (10 gold pieces per man, two for a woman, one for a child) were free to leave with what they could carry. When the exodus took place on October 2, Muslim guards watched as the disheartened populace, some shorn of hair in penance, followed the patriarch of Jerusalem, who carried gold plate from the Church of the Holy Sepulchre. Behind stayed 15,000 persons who could not pay and were thus enslaved. The fate of the refugees was not much better. After straggling along the coast to Tripoli in Syria, they were attacked and robbed by their co-religionists.

Saladin permitted no sack of Jerusalem. Rather, he took pains to remove traces of Crusader desecrations. The cross atop the cupola of the Dome of the Rock was knocked away. Within the mosque, icons and an altar were removed and sale of chips from the great stone banned. In the al-Aqsa, Saladin personally purified the mihrab with rose water and censers of perfume. The Citadel of David near the Jaffa Gate he took as his headquarters. Several churches were converted to medressehs, but the most important Christian sanctuaries (the Church of the Resurrection, Holy Sepulchre) were merely locked for the time being.[20]

Saladin believed his victory over the Franks to be so complete that it was followed up with only token attacks against the remaining enemy strongholds. Such policy was a mistake, for Tyre, which lay close to Palestine, would serve as a conduit for 300,000 Christian warriors who flocked eastward in the Third Crusade between 1189 and 1192. Ironically, the fighting centered neither around Jerusalem nor Tyre, but Acre, the port in the bay of Haifa that had been captured after the battle of Hittin. In the fall of 1189, Crusaders surrounded the city, which was garrisoned by a few thousand Muslims, with a network of trenches. Too late, Saladin, who had been off attacking Belfort Castle, tried to relieve the city by besieging the besiegers. Winter rains turned the terrain beyond the Carmel Ridge into a swamp. Saladin could only marvel as each passing month brought a never-ending supply of manpower to Acre. Early in 1190, the followers of Frederick Barbarossa arrived (the Holy Roman German Emperor had died in Asia Minor). They were joined that spring by 10,000 men under the command of Henry of Champagne. Frederick of Swabia brought 1000 more in October, about the time the first British ships docked at Tyre. Then in 1191 the combined armies of Richard the Lionheart of England and Philip Augustus of France moved into position for the final push against Acre. Saladin exhorted his comrades within the city to persevere, but overpowered by the Crusaders' battering rams, mobile towers, mangonels, catapults and sappers, they capitulated on July 12, 1191. The Muslims were to be ransomed for 200,000 dinars. Whether Saladin failed to act quickly enough or the Crusaders were acting out of duplicity will never be known. In any event, all of the captives were put to death by lance or sword.[21]

The war dragged on for another year before both sides, realizing that neither could obliterate the other, agreed to an armistice. For their part, the Crusaders were not anxious to undertake another siege of Jerusalem. A scheme to snatch Cairo instead fell apart as a result of squabbles among the royal leaders. Saladin, too, lost prestige with Crusader victories at Acre, Ashkelon and Arsuf. The peace of Jaffa signed in September 1192 ceded control of the coastal strip from Acre to Jaffa to the King of England. Ashkelon, a potential entry point for Crusaders, was to be demolished. Jerusalem would remain in Muslim hands, with all faiths guaranteed access to their shrines.

Saladin died six months after signing the pact of Jaffa on March 4, 1193. Afterward, legends about him cropped up everywhere. It was said that he and Richard tested one another in battle, that the British king, upon hearing that Saladin had a horse shot from under him, sent a steed to his enemy because "it was not right that so brave a warrior should have to fight on foot." Richard supposedly offered knighthood to Saladin and suggested a marriage alliance between their two families. Christians were so fascinated by the character of this great lord, they could not let him die a Muslim. They told how on his deathbed Saladin called for a basin of water and spoke several words in French. Then, making the sign of the cross, he baptized himself. Such stories were no more believable than the tale that traced the outbreak of the Second Crusade to Saladin's alleged seduction of Eleanor, wife of Louis VIII. When this dalliance supposedly occurred, Saladin would have been eight years old.

Impact of the Crusades

The contest for control of the Holy Land continued for another century after the death of Saladin. In 1229, one of his successors, Sultan al-Kamil, relinquished control of everything except the Haram esh-Sharif and Bethlehem to Frederick II Hohenstaufen. Denounced by Christian clerics for not claiming these sites as well, the German prince left the city after one week. Over the next 15 years, Jerusalem and its walls disintegrated as rival mobs plundered each other's neighborhoods. The Templars returned to restore order for a short interlude (1241–43), but in 1244 the end came to Frankish Jerusalem. Muslims looted the Holy Sepulchre, the Church of the Dormition, Armenian churches, the tomb of Mary in the Valley of Kidron, and the tombs of Hashmonaean kings.

A Fourth Crusade mounted by the Genoese in 1204 opted to plunder Constantinople rather than continue on to Palestine. Hungarian King Henry's Fifth Crusade, designed to capture and swap Damietta for Jerusalem in 1219, bogged down in the mud of Nile flooding. Frederick II's plan to repopulate Jerusalem with Christians in the Sixth Crusade failed when the bishop of Casearea placed the city under ban of interdict. The Seventh Crusade, marked by Louis IX's diversionary assault against Egypt was aborted in 1249 when a plague swept the Christian ranks. Not even the fall of Antioch in 1268 — with churches set ablaze, 16,000 persons killed and 100,000 enslaved —could prompt a European consensus. Louis IX tried to mobilize a united force in 1270, but only got as far as Tunis, where he died of dysentery. Seljuks, Ayyubids, Mamelukes picked off the remaining Christian strongholds— Marqah in 1285, Acre in 1291— and the era of Europe's offensive campaigns against the Muslims was at an end.[22]

The legacy of that romantic era can still be felt in the Middle East. Apart from the rugged castles that dot the landscape, the warlord mentality of the Crusades prevails in Lebanon where armed bands control specific areas of the countryside. Animosities between sects date to fabled ancestors who dueled with pickaxe and halberd. French imperial policy was based, in part, upon fancied connections with the Frankish Crusaders. According to another popular myth, Israel, too, should be measured against the Crusader model. Foreigners, lacking land and driven by religious zeal, entered the region. Having won a number of victories through superior technology, foreigners occupied land and oppressed the native population. Territory seized in both instances could be superimposed on one another, stretching 200 miles in length, 50 in width, from the Lebanon mountains to the Negev. Though both peoples abandoned European ways for a Middle Eastern lifestyle and had children who knew no other land, they were rejected by their neighbors. The invaders' presence was maintained by elite military units. Jerusalem, the object of their holy war, came into their possession.

Whether it takes 200 years, as was the case for Crusaders, or a century, as with the French and British, the Israelis will also be dislodged. Sooner or later, another Saladin will arise to oust them. It is no coincidence that the principal training bases for anti–Western terrorism in Lebanon are located in Baalbek, the very town that was once home to Saladin.

There are, of course, significant differences between the Crusader states and Israel. The Franks were Germanic people who never resided in the Middle East, whose sole connection with the region was spiritual. Jews are Semites who originated in the Middle East and had maintained a state for more than 1000 years. Despite harassment from Muslims and Christians they continued to reside in the region, develop religious institutions, and speak of *hazarah* (a return). Many who came to Israel were induced to do so by desperation, the product of the Holocaust, an event without precedent in history. The Frankish states were several, feudal, and disunited. The modern state of Israel may be fragmented politically, but only a few extremist parties are committed to its dismantling. The Crusaders could count on an almost limitless supply of manpower, hundreds of thousands of troops who volunteered in the 11th, 12th, and 13th centuries. A single defeat would destroy the Israeli state.

There is one last problem with the equation of Israel with the Crusaders. In the Middle Ages, Muslims could wait a century for a Saladin, 200 years for the ultimate defeat of the crusaders. In our age, when weapons quickly become obsolete and where missiles have replaced the tinker toys of yesterday, the question is whether civilization can afford the luxury of 200 years of warefare.[23]

20

Mamelukes, Mongols, and Delhi Sultans

Baybars

The Ayyubid dynasty established by Saladin was short lived. By the middle of the 13th century, family feuding resulted in a transfer of power to the Mamelukes, a motley band of Turks, Mongols and Circassians who ruled from Egypt to 1517. The average reign of 47 Mameluke sultans was less than six years. Some were Muslims in name only; some were illiterate, several were drunkards, and some were lunatics. One had an alchemist blinded for failing to turn iron into gold, another executed a physician who was unable to cure his malady. When locusts and a low Nile combined to create famine, the Mamelukes introduced new taxes on crops and instituted state monopolies on sugar, spices, and pepper. While the population of Egypt dwindled by two-thirds as a result of the Black Death in the 14th century, these lords constructed more mosques for personal glory.

According to Sir William Muir, history offered no parallel for their two centuries of "slavish," "cruel," "barbarous" and "treacherous" dominance. "The wonder," wrote Muir, "is that a foreign yoke so feared and hateful was not long before destroyed." More wondrous when one factors in other qualities that Muir imputes to Mamelukes: (a) rigid faithfulness to a single leader; (b) their imperfect sense of hereditary title; (c) the many monuments, pious endowments and schools they established; and (d) the "few and far between" just rulers they produced.[1]

The exception was the fourth Mameluke Baybars (1260–77). In his reign, sweeping domestic reforms were attempted. Canals and harbors that had not been upgraded in a century were improved. Regular postal service (four days) was established between Egypt and Syria. Religious instruction was overhauled (four kadis supervised the operations of the major sects of Sunni Islam) and the pilgrimage to Mecca was made safe again. Diplomatic relations were established with Christian monarchs in Byzantium, Sicily and Aragon. During this time, also, the Crusaders suffered the loss of Antioch.

All of this was achieved by a Kuman Turk who once served in the ranks of the Mongol army. Captured near Crimea, Baybars al Bandukdari was sold into slavery in Damascus for 800 drachmae (less than $100). Subsequently this one-eyed hero was given the responsibility of checking the advance of the Locust People, the Mongols.

The Mongols

Starting from a base near Lake Baikal at the beginning of the 13th century, the Mongols carved a swath of destruction from the Pacific to the Mediterranean. Another of the fierce, migratory peoples from Asia, the Mongols were led by Genghis Khan. Originally called Temuchin, the supreme leader (khan) summoned 95,000 horsemen to his standard. Outfitted with leather helmets and fur coats, each of these men was trained in the use of saber, lance and bow. Undaunted by poor weather, the Mongols preferred winter campaigns since ice provided passage across rivers and their horses usually could find stubble under the snow.[2]

Inspired by the blessings of the gods of the Eternal Blue Sky and his ancestors, the Gray Wolf and the Doe, Genghis Khan struck first at the rulers of China. Fifty years before, the Chin Dynasty had expelled his ancestors to the wasteland of Mongolia. In 1211, the Mongols pierced the Great Wall and captured most of northern China. Four years later, Peking fell. When in 1218 Mongol ambassadors were abused by the shah of Khwarizm, Genghis Khan marched west into Turkestan, destroying mosques and Islamic libraries. In 1227, after victories in Bukhara, Samarkand, Merv, Nishapur and Hamadan, the Great Khan was killed in a fall from a horse.

The death of Genghis Khan did not halt the Mongol advance. His son, Batu, routed the forces of Kaikhusrau II at Kozadagh in 1243, ending the Seljuk sultanate of Rum. Another Mongol unit swept into Russia and created the khanate of the Golden Horde between the Dnieper and Volga Rivers. About the same time, grandson Hulagu moved out of Karakorum at the invitation of the Abbasid caliph Nasir, to rid the world of the Assassins.

Initially, the Mongols encountered few problems with the Assassins, whose master Jalal ad-Din was the first Muslim ruler to pay tribute to Genghis Khan. Jalal ad-Din's successor, Aladin Muhammad, however, was an unstable leader who vacillated between bouts of alcoholism and depression. Aladin's son Rukn ad-Din may have been responsible for his father's death in December 1255. Simultaneously, Hulagu had begun to penetrate Persia, the destruction of Assassin fortresses as his principal objective. Some Persian princes welcomed the Mongol lord who threatened to destroy the Assassins "down to the children in the cradle."[3]

Rukn ad-Din attempted to appease Hulagu by dismantling several castles, even sending his own seven-year-old son as a hostage. Nothing mollified the Mongols, not even the surrender of Rukn ad-Din and his royal retinue. Alamut was besieged for what medieval chroniclers claim was three years and what more likely was a year. When the Mongols overran the Assassin sanctuary, they torched the buildings, leveling them to the foundations, and, in the process, destroying the secret writings of the once powerful sect. Rukn ad-Din and his family were murdered while in transit to Karakorum.[4]

The Mongols now presented themselves before Baghdad and the descendant of the very Abbasids that had invited them into Persia. Hulagu demanded that the reigning caliph, al-Mustasim, offer tribute and open the gates of his capital. To which the caliph responded: "You ask what will never be given. Do you not know that from west to east all who hold the true faith are my servants? Did I wish to do so, I could make myself master of the whole of Iran, but I have no wish to conjure up war. Walk, therefore in the paths of peace and return to Khorasan."[5]

Dismissing al-Mustasim's warning (and that of his own seer) that the sun would cease to shine and rain to fall if he attacked Baghdad, Hulagu laid siege to the city. The Mongol leader offered immunity if al-Mustasim would surrender. Accompanied by his court, al-Mustasim went out to the Mongol army, which slaughtered them all, sparing only the caliph. For him, the pagan Hulagu reserved a special punishment. Because al-Mustasim had been unwilling to part with his treasures, Hulagu ordered that he be given nothing to eat, save an ingot of gold. When the starving ex-caliph protested that no one could eat gold, Hulagu retorted, "If you knew that, why did you not send it to me? Had you done so, you would still have been eating and drinking peacefully, and without a care, in your palace."[6]

Leaderless, Baghdad capitulated. For one week, in February 1258, the glorious city of Harun al-Rashid was given over to plunder. Mongols torched virtually every building save the churches (one of Hulagu's wives was a Christian). They filled sacks, boxes, even scabbards with gold, jewels and pearls. They also killed more than three-fourths of the city's million inhabitants. The stench from rotting corpses was so great that Hulagu was forced to withdraw his army from the city.[7]

The Abbasid caliphate that had existed since 750 was now ended. With all the tugs at its prestige by various sultanates, there had been few challenges to its religious leadership. Muslims took comfort knowing there was an Abbasid caliphate, however weak, sitting between the major population centers of Egypt and Syria and the barbarian hordes on the steppes. Now that buffer was gone and thousands of Muslims were dead as the Mongols swept through Damascus, Aleppo, and Sidon.

The Battle of Ayn Jalat

There seemed little chance that the Mamelukes could stop the Mongols. The slave dynasty had only come to power in Egypt in 1252 with the ouster of the last descendant of Saladin, a six-year-old boy. For the next seven years, power was wielded mainly by a woman, Shajar al-Durr, widow of a Mameluke, who shuffled lovers like Catherine the Great. When surviving Abbasids taunted the Egyptians that they had no men to rule them, a warlord from Khwarizm, Sayfaddin Kutuz, tried to rally true believers against the Asian invaders.

Threatening to bastinado Muslims who evaded the call to service, Kutuz recruited a force of more than 100,000 men. To finance his new army, he rigorously collected land, property, and protective taxes, and confiscated fortunes of his enemies. The next step was to appoint a competent general. That was the one-time slave from Crimea known as Baybars. Promised the governorship of Aleppo, Baybars introduced a new form of warfare to the Middle East. He ordered the burning of any vegetation that might provide forage for the Mongol horses. A stretch of land from Syria into Mesopotamia was devastated, trees fallen, bushes burned. This scorched-earth policy proved successful. By the time the two armies met at Ayn Jalat (Goliath Wells) near Jerusalem on September 3, 1260, the Mongols were a tired, thirsty, overextended band of warriors.

The battle itself was somewhat anti-climactic. Hulagu was not present, having to attend to affairs of a deceased brother back in Asia. His own general, Ket-Buka, fell for Baybars' trap. Believing the Muslim army was fleeing, Ket-Buka pushed his forces into a cross fire from which most never returned. The remnants fled beyond the Euphrates.[8] In the aftermath, Kutuz rewarded all of his underlings except Baybars. Fearing his general would exploit his success as a step toward becoming sultan, Kutuz reneged on his promise of a governorship. In return, Baybars arranged the murder of Kutuz during a Muslim festival in Egypt.

Like all usurpers, Baybars set out to win approval of his subjects. That same year, he invited the uncle of al-Mustansir to Cairo as caliph, a feat carried out with great pomp and the participation of Christian and Jewish leaders. In Palestine he instituted a ban on non-Muslims at the Cave of Machpelah in Hebron. By skillfully playing off the Mongols against the Franks, Baybars was able to chase most of the Christians out of Palestine. Then, manipulating the friendship of Bereke, the khan of the Golden Horde, and the Byzantines, before his death in 1277 he was able to lay claim to the ancestral lands of the Arabs in Iraq. With Baybars, the region was granted a temporary respite from Asian invaders.[9]

Some historians argue that it has taken centuries for the Middle East to recover from the destruction of the Locust People. Sydney N. Fisher, for example, has written:

> The devastation wrought by the Mongols is only now in the twentieth century being mended. Millions of peoples perished; cities vanished; government disintegrated; civilization foundered; and life returned to the bare essentials. Through the previous ages conquering armies and peoples had come and gone — Medes, Persians, Sassanids, Greeks, Romans, Byzantines, and Arabs — and customs, religions, knowledge and culture had been modified, developed and altered. But through all this time, the Middle East had never suffered such a cataclysmic and paralytic shock as it received from the Mongol invasion.[10]

A more restrained appraisal has been offered by Bernard Lewis. "The destruction which they (the Mongols) wrought in the lands they conquered has been much exaggerated," says Lewis. "Most of it was purely strategic, not willful. It ceased after the campaigns of conquest of which it was a part, and in Persia under Mongol rule a new period of economic and cultural development began."[11]

Fisher's apocalyptic view ignores a number of factors that contributed to the regional malaise. We have already mentioned climatic changes, plagues of locusts and disease, over-reliance upon capricious water systems. To these, add centuries of poor agricultural techniques, indolence, ignorance and fatalism on the part of farmers. Repeated sallies of Arab or Turkish armies left irrigation channels in constant need of repair. Tribes like the Beni Hillal and Beni Sulaym in the 11th century plundered stretches from Egypt to Tunisia, where no Mongols had trod. The scorched-earth policies of Baybars, while successful in beating back the Mongols, hastened the economic decline of the region. When Vasco da Gama circumnavigated Africa, returning to Portugal with a load of Indian spices, he sealed the economic fate of the Middle East. No longer would the region profit as middle man in trade between Europe and the Orient.

The Moghuls

The Abbasid caliphate in Baghdad may have ended, but until 1517 the caliph of Islam would rule from Egypt. Elsewhere, Mongols behaved much like the Sassanids, Persians and Greeks, settling down, intermarrying and converting to Islam. In Russia, the khanate of the Golden Horde held sway for 200 years from Sarai, a city of several hundred thousand residents. In Isfahan and Samarkand, Muslim Ilkhanates built delicate, turreted mosques and embellished walls with arabesque designs. A glorious chapter was added to Persian poetry when Maulana Jalaluddin Rumi, Saadi of Shiraz, and Kamal of Isfahan flourished alongside Firdawsi and Umar al-Khayyam. In China, Marco Polo was dazzled by the court of the Mongol Kublai Khan.[12]

And there was the fabulous land of India, touched and transformed by many cultures, including Muslims and Mongols. Arab invaders were lured to the peninsula in the eighth century. They were followed by Turks, Ghaznawids and Afghans, who seized Baluchistan, the Sind, Punjab, and Deccan by 1206. These warlords, known as *rajputs*, faced perpetual rebellion. Their castles and libraries were also ravaged by the Mongols and Tamerlane. Yet from the ashes of Delhi rose a society that was the synthesis of Islamic and Asian cultures—the Moghuls.[13]

It was Babur, a descendant of Genghis Khan, who established the dynasty that would confront European imperialists. Originally called Zahiruddin Muhammad, Babur achieved victory over the Delhi sultans at Panipat in 1526. Babur despised the Indian climate, food, its people, even Hinduism. So it was left to his grandson Akbar (1556–1605) to carry out the major reforms that symbolize Moghul civilization. An illustrated history of this ruler's career, the *Akbarnama*, tells of his feats in battle defending himself at age 18 by pitching a conspirator off the parapets of a castle, gaining victory over an impregnable city in nine days. Akbar reorganized the political divisions of the country, establishing the system of *rajahs*, *maharajahs*, *nawabs*, and *nizams*, familiar to the West. Most important, this Sunni Muslim tried to establish toleration throughout his realm. Married to a rajput princess, Akbar abolished the jizyah. In 1579, he issued a decree of infallibility, giving him the right to decide matters of religious conflict. Three years later, in 1582 he proclaimed a new monotheistic creed, *"Din Illahi,"* that, he hoped, would fuse his subjects into one people.[14]

Akbar offered prizes to poets and encouraged painters and architects to express themselves. The poetry of Amir Khusrau, Hasan of Delhi, and Urfi of Shiraz as well as the city of Fatehpur Sikri near Agra, the Shalimar Gardens in Kashmir, mosques in Lahore and Delhi, the red forts at Delhi and Agra, the Humayun tomb at Delhi all testify to the greatness of this Golden Age. More wondrous yet was the mausoleum built by Akbar's grandson Shah Jahan for his wife Mumtaz who died in 1631. The Taj Mahal took more than 22 years to build and when it was completed, the white marble structure represented a perfect fusion of Islamic and Mongol civilizations.[15]

To suggest the Mongols caused civilization to stultify is simplistic and inaccurate. One of their later dynasties did, however, provide a second shock to the Middle East. The Timurids, Muslims who took their name from their leader Tamerlane, exploded out of Turkestan at the end of the 14th century, causing widespread destruction and fear.

Tamerlane

The man who came to be known as Tamerlane was born to a Tatar tribe in Transoxiana in 1336. His people were a blend of Turkic-Altaic and Mongol stock who fancied they were descended from Alexander the Great. Since the 10th century, the Tatars had been Muslims and their principal cities—Samarkand and Bokhara—that lay astride the caravan routes from Central Asia to Cathay, were famed centers of Islamic culture.

It is said that Tamerlane's father was inspired to call him Timur because he was reading from the Quran and had just come to the word *tamurru* (shock) when his son's birth was announced. Tamerlane's Turkish and Persian enemies called him Aksak-Timur (Limping Timur) or "Timur-i-lenk" (Timur the Lame), which Europeans corrupted to Tamerlane. A white-haired commander with an unstable disposition, he walked with a pronounced limp and sometimes had to be borne to battle upon a litter. According to one tale, as a youth Timur attempted to prod his horse across a gorge. The animal plummeted to its death, but the rider managed to leap to safety, injuring himself in the process. More likely, Timur was handicapped by wounds sustained during the initial phase of his military campaigns.

When Tamerlane was growing up, two rivals, Kuzgan the One-Eyed and Toghluk, khan of Kashgan, vied for control of the region. Some time after 1360, Tamerlane led a band of 40 followers into the mountains, hoping one day to match the exploits of his fabled

Macedonian ancestor. In 1369 he won the support of the 7000-man Jagatai Mongol army and installed himself as lord in Samarkand.[16]

A restless soul who could not sleep in the same place on consecutive nights, Tamerlane was confronted with challenges to his authority. His response was always swift and brutal. When in 1380 the people of Khurasan refused to pay tribute, he descended on Sabzevar and sealed 20,000 villagers in their huts to die. Immediately after, he looted the town of Sistan, carrying off everything "to the nails of the doors," as legend holds, and killing everyone from babes to centenarians.

A few years later, relations with Tokhtamish, khan of the Golden Horde, deteriorated. Tokhtamish now made the mistake of demanding tribute from the Tatar chieftain whom he addressed as "my son." The two clashed also over tribute from Georgia and Kurdistan. Finally, in 1392, Tamerlane led 100,000 men across the Khirgiz Steppe toward Sarai. There, on the banks of the Volga in June a major battle was fought, in the middle of a blinding snowstorm. Six days later, the Tatars celebrated their triumph in the ruins of the Mongol capital.[17]

Tamerlane next turned his attention to Persia. The various khanates of Astrakhan, Crimea, and Khazan were panicked into paying tribute. Not, however, the shah of Isfahan. While Tamerlane was occupied with Tokhtamish, a garrison of 3000 Tatars had been killed. Tamerlane now retaliated against the people of Khwarizm and Khuzistan, ordering his troops to raze the city of Shiraz and bring back 70,000 human heads from Isfahan. Henceforth, the practice of stacking pyramids of human skulls became standard procedure when dealing with rebels.

Baghdad was spared Tamerlane's wrath momentarily in 1393 only because he decided to plunder India first. Moving across the Hindu Kush mountains, he ordered the massacre of 100,000 slaves because they were slowing the advance of his army. Rajput India proved as rich and soft as he anticipated. Within two years, most of the northwest territory of the subcontinent was under Tatar control. Each of Tamerlane's soldiers possessed more slaves, cattle, and jewels, and there were 80,000 skulls stacked at Delhi.

The lords of the Middle East realized that it was only a matter of time before Tamerlane would resume his westward march. Sultan Ahmed of Mesopotamia ("a living morsel of flesh with two eyes" Tamerlane called him before he fled to Egypt in 1393) conspired with Bayezid Yilderim, chief of the Ottoman Turks, to crush Tamerlane. When Tamerlane demanded the surrender of his enemies, Bayezid responded in an insulting letter that read: "Know, bloodthirsty hound named Tamerlane, that the Turks are not wont to refuse asylum to friends or to shun battle against foes."[18]

An enraged Tamerlane responded swiftly, leaving pyramids of 20,000 heads at Aleppo, 90,000 at Baghdad, 40,000 at Takrit. Even those cities, like Damascus, that opened their gates to his army were not spared. Only hospitals, mosques and schools escaped the fury of the Tatars.

The Battle of Ankara

The unpredictable Tatar chieftain then veered into Anatolia at the head of an army reckoned at 800,000. His opponent, Bayezid, was a cruel pederast who engaged in drunken orgies with his grand vizir. Nicknamed "Yilderim" (Lightning) because of victories over Christian knights in the Balkans, Bayezid was crude, arrogant, and gout ridden. After a series of minor clashes, their two armies collided at Ankara in July 1402. Demoralized by irregular pay, desertions and thirst, weakened by a fruitless hunt for game, and outnumbered 4 to 1, the Ottomans were routed. Bayezid was taken captive after a courageous defense offered by Serbian auxiliaries and Janissaries. Placed in a metal cage for Tamerlane's amusement, he witnessed the rape of his queen at a banquet. According to one telling, the Ottoman committed suicide by bashing his head against the bars of his cage. Another version speaks of Bayezid living for another eight months, after which Tamerlane made a stool of his skin. Whatever the truth, the outcome was that Ottoman sultans refused to acknowledge any woman as their wife for more than 100 years, to prevent a recurrence of this shame.[19]

After Ankara, Tamerlane tarried on the coast of Anatolia for another year. In Smyrna, he slaughtered thousands and piled up more pyramids of skulls. Before he captured Ephesus, he ordered his men to trample children who had come out of the besieged city singing songs of praise. The Ottoman sultanate was crushed. So, too, the dynasties of India and the khanate of the Golden Horde. The house of Dmitri Donskoi in Moscow, the Byzantines in Constantinople, and the Mamelukes in Cairo all braced for what they anticipated would be further onslaughts from the invincible Tatars.

Then, inexplicably, his forces only days march from the Aegean, Tamerlane struck east. He intended to march 4000 miles across mountain and desert, to smash the Ming Dynasty in China. The great Tatar only got as far as Otrar on the Jaxartes River where, on February 18, 1405, he died.

Timur's legacy was one of terror and destruction. There is no great art associated with this man who fancied himself a connoisseur. His empire was based on fear, and soon after his death it fragmented among a number of short-lived dynasties in Uzbekistan, Hindustan, Merv, and the Oxus River. His destruction of the khanate of the Golden Horde created a power vacuum in Russia that enabled an obscure vassal state, the Grand Duchy of Muscovy, to rise to prominence under Ivan III. His emotional instability provided Byzantium and Mameluke Egypt with yet another century of political independence. And what should have been a major victory at Ankara proved of fleeting importance. For from that humiliation rose the empire that was to dominate the Middle East for the next 500 years—the Ottoman Turks.

21

The Ottomans

Ghazi Warriors and the Crusades of South Slavs

In the wake of devastations wrought by Crusaders, Seljuks, Mongols, Mamelukes and Tatars, the Ottoman Turks emerged as the dominant force in the Middle East. A mix of Turkish nomads, Greek, Catalan and Mongol renegades, the Ottomans had been assigned a frontier strip at Sogut in north central Turkey by the Seljuk Sultan of Rum, around 1230. Their name came from Osman, son of Ertoghrul, the chieftain of a band of *ghazi* (frontier) warriors. Known as Kara Osman (Black Osman, because of his dark hair, beard and eyebrows) or Osman the Bonebreaker (his arms were huge and powerful), this devout Muslim adopted the vulture as his emblem and was ruthless in battle. When he died in 1326, his conquests included Brusa and Nicaea and much of Anatolia to the Sea of Marmara.[1]

For more than a century after Osman's death, able successors—Orkhan (1326–60), Murad (1360–89) and Bayezid "Yilderim" (1389–1402)—pushed into Europe. Byzantium sent out the call for help and Christian Europe responded in what is known as the era of the Crusades of the South Slavs. These were holy wars designed not to win back the sepulcher of Christ, but to blunt the onslaught of the Turks into Europe.

The century produced fascinating legends. According to Bulgarians, Shishman III, decapitated on the plains of Samakov in 1371, still rides headless through the Rhodope Mountains. Another legend revolves around Janos Hunyadi, a warrior whose defense of Belgrade in 1456 won him the title of "the White Knight of Transylvania."

Perhaps the greatest legends are the tales of one of Hunyadi's contemporaries, the Romanian Vlad Tsepes, who struck at all enemies, real or imagined. When two Turkish ambassadors refused to doff their turbans in his presence, he nailed the bonnets to their heads. When two priests insisted that Vlad was not the greatest Christian lord, they were lowered into vats of boiling water. Another time, 50 Gypsies were invited to his Targoviste Castle for a feast. Forty sat down at the table and midway through dinner, they were informed that they were eating the other ten. At Easter, Vlad invited the local populace to a celebration. Three hundred showed up and were dragged off to work at his new castle in Poenari. Heretics, Jews, Hungarians, Catholics, Orthodox, even a mistress, suffered at the hands of the man the Germans called *Wütrich* (bloodthirsty monster). But it was the Saxons—Germans living in Hungary—who suffered most. An estimated 100,000 were impaled, in geometric patterns, while this strange man sat dining. Vlad "the Impaler" is best remembered by the Romanian word for his symbol — the dragon — as Drakul or Count Dracula.[2]

Ottoman expansion coincided with a century of European weakness. When not facing one another in the Hundred Years War, England and France were wracked with peasant revolts. Confessional Catholics found their allegiance strained by three claimants to the papacy sitting simultaneously in Rome, Pisa, and Avignon. Earthquakes devastated the walls of Gallipoli and opened Thrace to the invaders. Between 1348 and 1350, the Black Death raged through Europe, wiping out an estimated 30 million people.[3]

Undeterred by disease or natural disaster, the Turks moved across Bulgaria, Wallachia and Moldavia, inspired by ghazi enthusiasm and forceful leadership. The younger of Osman's two sons, Orkhan, induced Jewish and Christian craftsmen to settle in his domains by forming *akhis*, guilds that strengthened the economic base of the empire. Orkhan also improved the Ottoman military system. Previously the core of the army had been *spahi*, cavalry rewarded with land grants. Armed with the Turkish longbow, a weapon deadly at 300 yards, the spahi were required to serve until a campaign was concluded.

To these knights and the mass of raw, untrained foot soldiers (*bashi-bazouks*), Orkhan added *yeni cheri* (new troops). Kidnapped from Christian populations, branded, then forcibly converted to Islam, the *janissaries*, as they were known, became the first professional soldiers since the Roman legions. Forbidden to marry or learn a trade, their function was to make war — with scimitar, dagger, hatchet, and musket. Distinguished by blue uniforms; red, yellow or black boots; and long feathered caps, the janissaries lived and ate together, their standards the kettles from which they took their communal mess. It was said one janissary could lead 10,000 by a thread. Failure to obey an order resulted in flogging, desertion by death.

In the Ottoman scheme, the janissaries could be counted on in the rear ranks as the bashi-bazouks were sacrificed up front. The strategy worked, as impetuous bands of Christian knights plunged into the masses of raw recruits at the river Maritza in 1363 and Nicopolis in 1396, only to find themselves arm weary before the best soldiers in Europe.[4]

Perhaps the most disastrous defeat occurred on August 27, 1389, at Kosovo, the Field of Blackbirds, near the border of Serbia and Bosnia. There a combined force of Serbs, Albanians, and Bosnians was routed by the Ottomans, destroying a Serbian kingdom that had existed since the ninth century. The establishment of an independent Serbian, in the 19th century did not satisfy irredentists who believed their ancestral homeland had not been fully restored. When Austria annexed Bosnia in 1908, radical Serbs, under the banner of the Black Hand, plotted revenge. In the summer of 1914, they struck, killing the Archduke Ferdinand at Sarajevo. Few soldiers who died in World War I had an inkling that the conflict had its seeds in the little known Field of Blackbirds.[5]

The only serious setback the Ottomans sustained in that first century of expansion came at the hands of Tamerlane. Following the debacle of Ankara in July 1402, it appeared the Ottoman Empire might break into a number of smaller principalities, much as the regimes of the Seljuks and Zengids. With Tamerlane out of the way in China, however, one of Bayezid's sons, Mehmet I, restored order.

The Fall of Constantinople

Having bypassed Constantinople in their dash to the Balkans, it was inevitable that the Turks would turn their attention to this city. By the middle of the 15th century, the

Byzantine Empire consisted of little more than 30 square miles. The capital, sealed off by Turkish forts on either side of the Bosphorus, counted less than 70,000 inhabitants. When Mehmet II laid siege to Constantinople in April 1453, there were 8000 fighting men in the city, a number bolstered by the arrival of 700 Genoese under the command of Giovanni Giustiniani. Byzantium's last Christians placed their faith in God and city's walls that withstood 20 previous attacks.

Against the city, Mehmet arrayed 100,000 troops, including 12,000 janissaries, 125 ships, and a host of siege machines: catapults whose 16-foot arms could sling 100-pound loads of stone; steel-tipped balista; and 60-foot long counterpoised trebuchets that could hurl dead horses, prisoners of war, even manure, at the enemy. The Turks also employed Europeans to cast bronze cannon for their assault. In the siege of Constantinople the Turks used 14 huge cannon and 56 smaller ones. One weapon, known as the Basilic or Royal One, was dragged into position by 100 pair of oxen. Its 1500-pound ball took two hours to load and made a crater six feet deep when it impacted. One after another the walls of Constantinople were pounded into rubble.[6]

On May 29, 1453, waves of bashi-bazouks burst through the St. Romanus gate, beating, raping and killing the hapless remnant in the city. Kritovolos, a Greek renegade in Mehmet's service, recounted the death throes of Constantinople, telling how soldiers were permitted to terrorize the people of the city. "Like wild and ferocious beasts," he wrote, men with swords ("their hands bloodstained with murder") leaped into houses, murdering residents and dragging away well-born girls and boys. Bodies of nobles and prelates were tossed from their resting places in cemeteries. Churches were looted of icons, reliquaries and chalices. In their quest for gold or jewels, looters deliberately smashed goblets of lesser value. The victorious Turks ripped apart embroidered robes and paneled shrines, trampled holy books, and tossed other priceless objects into the fire.[7]

It is said that fish frying in a pan leaped into a nearby pool when the Turks entered the city. (That supposedly is why there are fish in the region today whose scales appear singed.) It is also said that the priest who was leading the final mass in the Hagia Sophia disappeared through a wall bearing the holy chalice of Christ. He supposedly will return on the day when the church reverts to Greek control.

Historians, too, have fed legends surrounding the fall of Constantinople. One assessment holds that the fall blocked trade routes to the East, thereby forcing the age of discovery. Another view holds that refugee monks carried so many manuscripts to Italy that they initiated the Renaissance of the 15th century. Without Byzantium, goes another argument, the Turks faced no serious barrier to conquest of the Balkans. Of course, the Byzantine Empire had been powerless for 100 years while the Ottomans dealt with Bogomils, Albanians, Magyars, Greeks, Serbs, Venetians, and Russians. The latter would propagate their own myth that the marriage of Ivan III and Zoe Paleologus invested Moscow as the third and final Rome whose destiny was to regain control of Tsargrad (Constantinople).

Mehmet Fatih (Mehmet the Conqueror) would not permit this strategic city to languish for long. Thousands of Christian peasants from as far off as Trebizond were resettled in the lighthouse district of Phanar. To allay their fears, Mehmet confirmed George Scolarius as patriarch of the Orthodox Church. The walls of the city were refurbished and shops and medressehs opened about the Hagia Sophia, which remained the cultural center of Constantinople. Only now the city was renamed Istanbul and the church was reconsecrated as a mosque. Mehmet himself stopped the pillaging of the great sanctuary, but permitted the stripping of icons and crosses from other churches. Constantinople was now a Muslim city.[8]

Organization of the Ottoman Empire

Mehmet also started the Topkapi Saray, a complex of tiled pavilions, marble kiosks and pillared halls that housed the leaders of the Ottoman state. Ten thousand people, advisors, concubines, slaves and soldiers, lived in this great palace that covered 300 yards to the Golden Horn. From windows in the two-storied Great Gate, residents of the Topkapi looked upon commoners going about their business. At least one sultan used the location to snipe at his subjects with real bullets. Beyond the arched first gate lay an expanse of grass and cypress where peacocks strolled and the sultan reviewed his janissaries.[9]

To the right of this Second Court were kitchens and storehouses. To the left, were stables and quarters of the sultan's *baltajis* (halberdiers) selected from the levies of janissaries. Depending upon intellect, some of these might be assigned menial duties—fueling steambaths or serving as gatekeepers. Others, perhaps as many as 2500 dubbed *bostanjis* (gardeners), tended flowers and protected the sultan's intimacy. Among their duties was the drowning of concubines who had lost favor with the sultan.

The brightest of the new draftees were rewarded with a spot in the *enderun* (palace school). Numbering 340 in Mehmet's day, more than 1000 under Suleiman the Magnificent, these pages were taken at age 18 and subjected to a stringent academic and social discipline. Under guard of eunuchs, they were drilled in language, law, mathematics, history, geography and competitive sports. The future statesmen of the empire were instructed in proper etiquette: each was to have a manicure and bath every week, a haircut once a month; noses were to be blown discreetly, into a clean handkerchief; there was to be no belching or flea-picking in public. And though the young men were sequestered from females for nearly a decade, no homosexual activity was permitted.

The enderun produced the *seferli odasi* (intellectual bodyguard) that accompanied the sultan; the *kiler odasi* (pharmacists) who tasted his food, prepared aphrodisiacs and antidotes; the *hasna odasi*, sword bearers and treasurers; and the elite *has odasi*. From the latter came the *chorbaji-bashi* (janissary commander, known as the head soup distributor) and the *kapudan pasha*, admiral of the Ottoman fleet commanding more than 300 vessels. They also included ambassadors, viziers and judges, who met twice weekly in a room empty but for a row of couches set along the walls. A carry-over from the Sassanids, the members of this *diwan* (cabinet) propped their feet up on small stools (*ottomans*) as they conducted the business of state. The sultan could evaluate their performance from a latticed screen above the room.

Beyond the diwan was the sultan's *selamlik*, his private quarters, populated with mutes, dwarfs, jesters and 300 red-coated bodyguards. Here also the harem was monitored by 40 black eunuchs. As many as 200 girls vied with one another, bribing the *kizlar aghasi* (chief black eunuch) for the opportunity to bed down with the sultan. When, after the humiliation suffered by Bayezid Yilderim, the sultans again took wives, the goal of women in the harem was to produce an heir and become one of the four *kadins* (legal wives) permitted under Islamic law. If a woman's son succeeded to the throne, she would be honored as *sultana valideh* (mother of the sultan) with her own ornate chambers. This unofficial position also carried undefined but ominous powers.[10]

Complementing this mass of *kullar* (once slave) officials who made up the administrative system were hundreds of free Muslims who advised the Ottoman ruler on religion. With the transfer of the caliphate from Egypt to Istanbul after the battle of Marj Dabik in 1517, Muslim charitable and religious institutions were administered by the Ottomans. Dervishes, muftis, sayyids and sharifs (descendants of the Prophet) resided at the Topkapi.

Religious questions were decided by the sultan-caliph assisted by his personal *hoja* (teacher) and the *shaykh ul-Islam* (the highest ranking theologian in the empire). These men stood at the ruler's side when he received ambassadors at the Gate of Felicity leading to the gardens of the Third Court. It was this "Sublime Porte" that gave the Ottoman Empire the nickname by which it was known to the European world.[11]

The Greatest Empire in the World

By the middle of the 16th century, the Turks arguably possessed the greatest empire in the world. In a master stroke prompted not so much by altruism as avarice, Bayezid II *Sofi* (the Mystic) welcomed 100,000 Jewish refugees from the Spanish Inquisition. Blacksmiths, gold artisans, weavers, glassmakers, printers, moneylenders, statesmen and physicians flocked to Salonika, Adrianople, Smyrna and Istanbul where the sultan esteemed the *haham bashi* (chief rabbi) over the patriarch.

While European Jews were tormented through the Reformation, their kinsmen enticed them eastward with tales of economic and social opportunity. The situation was not idyllic. Hans Dernschwam, a Bohemian traveler around 1555, noted that Jews were "despised in Turkey as they are anywhere else," that they "live on top of one another" in "miserable, stinking" houses.[12] They also were subjected to the *jizyah*, the Rule of Umar, and periodic outbursts of violence.

As for Bayezid, he was occupied with various rivals in the Middle East. His brother Djem flitted from one European court to another, seeking support for rebellion until his death in 1494. A five-year war with the Mamelukes ended disastrously with cession of much of Syria to Egypt. When a Persian dynasty headed by Ismail known as *Kizilbash* (Red-Hat) began to push into eastern Anatolia, the day-dreaming Sultan was deposed by his own son Selim in April 1512.

A tall, dark warrior, titled *Yavuz* (the Grim), Selim was an intense individual, addicted to opium. His coronation was celebrated with the strangulation of five nephews, then the strangulation of two brothers, Korkud and Ahmed. During Selim's eight-year reign (1512–20), seven vizirs were beheaded, along with the commander of the janissaries who had the audacity to request gifts "normally" distributed by a new monarch.

Following an exchange of insulting letters, Selim struck against the Shiite dynasty in Iran. The Safavids supposedly had given refuge to the last surviving son of his brother, Ahmed. At Chaldiran in northern Azerbaijan on August 23, 1514, the Persian forces marched into battle without armor, chanting verses that supposedly would immunize them, and were promptly neutralized by Ottoman artillery.

The same cannon proved decisive in the renewed struggle with Egypt. The 70-year-old Mameluke sultan, Kansuh al-Ghuri, held that only the sabre and bow were weapons worthy of true Islamic warriors. When Selim's forces again penetrated northern Syria, Kansuh dispatched an envoy accompanied by an armed guard to warn them off. Selim's response was to scalp the envoy and murder the guards. He did the same with two subsequent Egyptian missions. The result was another clash at Marj Dabik, a plain near Aleppo. Here on August 2, 1516, and again at Ridaniya outside Cairo on January 22, 1517, Ottoman cannon decimated the Mamelukes. In the second battle, 25,000 are said to have perished, 50,000 more when the Ottomans put down a rebellion within the Egyptian capital.

Selim could not be troubled with personal administration of the newly won land. Assigning a garrison of 5000 men to Cairo, he left Egypt without even visiting the pyramids. What he brought back with him was more important than sight-seeing or even the annual tribute of 80,000 ducats. Amid the booty were the standard and cloak that belonged to Muhammad and the keys to the kaaba in Mecca. The Ottomans were now guardians of the Islamic holy places. With the capture of the Abbasid heir Muhammad, the caliphate was transferred to Istanbul where the institution was formally merged with the Ottoman sultanate in 1774.[13]

Suleiman the Magnificent

Selim's son, Suleiman the Magnificent (1520–66) maintained the status quo with the Safavid Persians. His main interest, however, was pressing the Ottoman advantage into Europe. Belgrade fell after a three-week siege in the summer of 1521. A year later, the island of Rhodes, a perpetual thorn in the side of Islam, surrendered to a Turkish armada. A relatively brief battle at Mohacs on August 27, 1526, gave the Ottomans control of central Hungary. Jealousy and dissention among Magyar nobles, the inept leadership of King Louis plus the sheer weight of numbers (it is said the Ottomans rallied 300,000 men against 30,000) worked in favor of the Turks.

When the city of Buda was torched and its inhabitants massacred, Christian lords temporarily gave up slaughtering one another to confront a greater, common threat. "The anti–Christ," "Satan loosed from his prison," "the worst of nations"—so Martin Luther scored the Ottomans. As the Turks marched into central Europe, Luther urged all Christians to obey their temporal masters and unite in a holy war against the Turks, whose holy book, he alleged, was nothing but "a collection of sermons," "a devilish patchwork" of Jewish, Christian and heathen beliefs.[14]

By September 1529, the Turks were camped in the southern suburbs of Vienna. As his sappers tunneled into the city's bastions, Suleiman boasted that he would breakfast in the Austrian capital. Repeated assaults against the walls on October 9, 11, 12, and 14, however, were unsuccessful. This time the Turks were without their gigantic cannon, which had been lost to muddy Balkan trails. With casualties mounting and winter rains threatening to cut them off from supplies, the janissaries pressed for withdrawal. Upon the advice of his vizir Ibrahim, himself a Greek convert, Suleiman reluctantly agreed, rationalizing that the siege was no longer necessary since his nemesis, the Hapsburg Ferdinand, was no longer in the city.

Suleiman would go on to more triumphs, directing 13 campaigns that gave him control of Iraq, Armenia, Georgia and Aden. Most of the ancient capitals and religious centers (Athens, Cairo, Jerusalem, Mecca, and Constantinople) were under his control. Ottoman corsairs operated from Gibraltar beyond Egypt to Yemen. Suleiman's chief architect, Sinan Pasha, beautified Constantinople with more than 300 structures. Of those buildings, 81 were mosques, including the Shezade Mehmet complex dedicated to Suleiman's heir-apparent in 1543; the blue Mihrimah mosque distinguished by a single minaret; and Sinan's finest achievement, the Suleimaniye. The latter covered three hills with *turbes* (small mausoleums), gardens, baths, arcades. Most imposing was the sanctuary named after the Sultan-Caliph with blue-tiled minarets stretching 220 feet in height; entry doors of bronze inlaid with pearl, ivory and ebony and overhung with delicate stalactites; a 170-foot square interior decorated with red, blue, green, and gold marble; and a 60-foot dome buttressed by two exposed arches.

Suleiman counted 50 million people as subjects, nearly 10 times the number who pledged loyalty Henry VIII. Forty-eight million dollars poured annually into the treasury. The vaults of the Topkapi overflowed with gilded ceremonial thrones, bassinettes, robes, turbans, even arrows and quivers.

Though he ruled another 37 years after the siege of Vienna, Suleiman would never come as close to changing the course of world history as he had in the fall of 1529. A victory over the 16,000 Austrian troops in that city might have laid all of Central Europe open to Islam. As it was, when Suleiman died, Ottoman glory also passed. A century later, the Ottoman Empire would be derided as the "Sick Man of Europe."[15]

22

Ottoman Decline

The Sick Man of Europe

When representatives of the European powers convened at Berlin in the summer of 1878 to discuss the fate of the Middle East, it was a very different Ottoman Empire that held their attention.[1] No longer was there any threat from a Muslim presence in the Balkans. The Turks had been repulsed from Hungary by 1699, the Crimea by 1774, Greece in 1829, Serbia in 1856, Romania in 1887. That same year, the Ottomans lost another war with Tsarist Russia. Chunks of North Africa had been lost to private warlords, or, as in the case of Algeria, Tunisia, Egypt, and the Sudan to Western colonialism. One billion dollars in debt, Turkey agonized as the Europeans forced her to grant autonomy to Bulgaria, cede Austria-Hungary administrative control over Bosnia, recognize Russia's gains in Bessarabia, give Cyprus to Britain and reaffirm international control over the straits connecting the Black Sea with the Aegean.

The Ottoman Empire had sunk to this sorry state as a result of a number of factors.

Incompetent leadership, the product of the harem and cage system. Suleiman *Kanuni*'s image was so imposing that for three weeks following his death in September 1566, his corpse was propped up on the throne, messages delivered at its feet, and it was taken for rides in the royal carriage. Not one of the 10 men who ruled Turkey between 1566 and 1687 possessed Suleiman's charisma or ability. Products of the harem system, these men grew up ignorant of world affairs and terrified that their lives might suddenly be snuffed out. A new sultan secured his throne by having all of his male siblings strangled by a bowstring. After 1600, a more "humane" policy was instituted—the brothers were now deposited in the *Kafes* (Cage), a closely-guarded two-story structure in the Topkapi, where their only companions were mutes and a few concubines. One of them might be needed if the ruling sultan died without a son.

Within the harem, wives and mothers schemed for power. Suleiman was manipulated by his first kadin, Roxelana, who managed to eliminate all rivals for her son, Selim. The widow of Selim, Nur Banu, arranged for the succession of Murad III as well as the assassination of a grand vizir. Murad's wife, Baffo, a Venetian blonde, had passing influence, in contrast with her successor, Kossem (Moonface). The latter, the daughter of a Greek priest, handpicked three sons as consecutive sultans and dominated the court for nearly four decades until she was purged. Not surprisingly, the royal products of such intrigues were pathetic figures.

Selim II (1566–74) was a fat lecher who had little use for statecraft. During his reign poets sang praises of the grape until Selim, nicknamed "the Sot," was killed in an accident. (While touring a new palace bath, the monarch downed a bottle of Cypriot wine, slipped on the wet tile floor and cracked his skull.) Murad III (1574–95) was an epileptic, an opium addict, and a miser who stashed ducats and jewelry under his bed, until he succumbed to concoctions of meat, soup, sheep's and sundry aphrodisiacs. Mehmet III (1595–1603) was a burly, feeble-minded man with a vicious temper who ordered 19 of his siblings to be strangled and women in the harem branded on their breasts. Ahmed I (1603–17) was more mellow. Although he suffered from smallpox and tuberculosis, he introduced tobacco to the court and confined his brothers to the Kafes. Mustapha (1617–18, 1622–23) was a grinning idiot who gave money away in the streets before being deposed on two separate occasions. Osman II (1618–22) came to the throne as a boy of 14, only to be murdered by the janissaries four years later.

Murad IV (1623–40) was a fabled warrior whose fundamentalism was matched only by his cruelty. Much like the Fatimid al-Hakim, he would go through the capital at night, visiting taverns and ordering the execution of anyone caught smoking or drinking. A doctor who prescribed opium, a Venetian accused of spying on the harem, a French interpreter who offended Murad were all impaled. A group of women who made too much noise in a nearby meadow were taken away and drowned. A boat that came too near the seraglio was sunk by royal batteries. Murad also ordered his concubines into a swimming pool where he shot at them with cork bullets. Worse, he sat by the main gate of the palace and shot at passersby with real bullets. (It is said he averaged 10 hits per day.)

Murad's successor, Ibrahim (1640–48), was little better. A product of the Kafes, where he had lived since the age of two, he refused to leave this sanctuary when soldiers informed him that his brother was dead. Only after Murad's body was stretched out beneath his window did Ibrahim come out and dance jubilantly. Ibrahim's reign was marked with excess. His beard was studded with diamonds, curtains were drenched with ambergris, mirrors placed on the walls of his bedroom, and pet cats cloaked with sable furs. His penchant for virgins (one daily) eventually cost him his throne. In debauching the daughter of the Shaykh ul-Islam, he forced an alliance between religious and military leaders. The result was another coup that led to the rule of Mehmet IV (1648–87), a weak-eyed psychotic who was a puppet of the janissaries.[2]

Obscurantism in religion, military planning and economics. At the moment the West was undergoing one of the most creative surges in history (the 17th century produced the likes of Descartes, Locke, and Newton), the Ottomans stultified, refusing to accept new ideas or permit experimentation. The Turks maintained the world dangled like a ball from a chain from one of seven heavens and that the sun was created solely to give light and heat to the earth. Though the Abbasids were responsible for transmitting paper to the West in the eighth century, the Ottomans to the 18th century refused to allow printing presses in their territory. In later times, bicycles, autos, telephones similarly were discouraged as the devil's handiwork.[3]

Ottoman armies, once the scourge of Europe, clung to sabre and harquebus, when European soldiers were being drilled with pikes and Jaeger rifles, carbines, and flintlocks—weapons with greater range and accuracy which could be reloaded more quickly. Lumbering Ottoman cannon were dragged into combat where they assumed stationary positions and fired at great intervals and little accuracy. By way of contrast, the Europeans developed mobile mortars (*mordschlage*) that could be wheeled quickly from place to place.

European naval commanders welcomed the opportunity to fight an enemy that would not change. An example of obscurantism on the high seas was the battle of Lepanto, fought off the coast of Greece in October 1571. Three hundred Ottoman galleys clashed with an equal number of vessels from the Holy League (Austria, Spain, the Vatican, Genoa, Venice). The forces of Selim the Sot were convinced they would triumph because their commander was flying a pennant inscribed 29,000 times with the name of Allah. The standard had never been lost. Nor had another talisman — the right canine tooth of Muhammad encased in a crystal ball. The Ottomans' slave-powered galleys, however, proved no match for Christian innovation. Six Venetian galleasses — high-powered battleships with armored sides and huge rams — decimated the Turkish fleet. When the battle was over, the Ottomans had lost 260 ships, 30,000 men. Selim, failing to appreciate that a revolution had taken place in naval warfare, merely refitted another 250 galleys within a few months and sent them out to sea where they continued to lose.[4]

The commercial revolution and age of exploration. For centuries, the Middle East had been a conduit for trade conducted between Europe and the Far East. Porcelain, tea, silks and furs had passed through Istanbul and Damascus. More important were the spices of India — pepper, clove, ginger, sage, thyme — needed to preserve meat in a time before refrigeration. When the Portuguese circumnavigated Africa at the end of the 15th century, they wittingly or otherwise doomed an empire that would not adapt to new patterns of trade. In Britain, France, and Holland groups of investors banded together creating joint stock companies that risked common funds in ventures to the East or West Indies.[5] Capitalism was born in the West, while the Ottoman masses continued to scratch at the earth and haggle in the bazaar.

The rise of feudalism and oppressive tax farming. Expansion of trade created a dynamic middle class, burghers, bourgeoisie who demanded rights and a stable government that would protect them. Allegiance to a central authority supplanted loyalty to barons. Over the next several hundred years, England, France, Germany, Italy all would consolidate into modern nation-states. Local principates and duchies were replaced by kings, backed by modern armies and sectioned by some form of council or assembly.

In the Ottoman empire, the process was reversed. Where Europe was turning away from feudalism after the 16th century, the Turks could envision no other means of controlling their newly won domains. Originally the idea had been to reward *spahi* (feudal cavalry) with *timars* (plots of land given for military service). These were converted to freeholds (*chiftlik sahibi*) held by lords who had neither the intention nor ability of mounting up to do battle for the sultan. Two absentee landlords sitting in Beirut owned much of the land in northern Palestine.

Instead of bolstering the regime, the policies of feudal lords did much to weaken it. Where *rayas* or peasants once enjoyed more rights than their European counterparts (hereditary use of the land, no eviction unless the land lay fallow for three years, lighter taxes and corvee), the opposite was now true. Tenant farmers were converted into serfs. Runaways were returned to their masters 15 years after they had escaped. Two-thirds of a peasant's annual produce was given over to the feudal lord. Taxes were "farmed" arbitrarily by the government. Appeals to local officials who had secured their pashaliks through bribery were useless. People who refused to accept these conditions could be evicted from their homes, or, as in the case of many Greeks, Serbs, Klephts, Hayduks, Uskoks, and Jelalis, would retreat to the mountains where they survived as freebooters.[6]

Some districts of the Ottoman Empire were enrolled under waqfs and became exempt from taxation, while others, like Thrace, were required to pay over $1 million in gold tribute each year. Peasant revolts were common and military commanders who were less than diligent in suppressing unrest were summarily executed. When the call went out for cavalry in time of war, only a handful of the feudal lords responded.

Meanwhile, travelers passing through fertile, picturesque regions of the Balkans found cemeteries in place of cities that had long since disappeared. There was not a trace of human life, by day or night. The seeds of nationalism, planted by Ottoman victories in the 14th and 15th centuries, were being nurtured by brutal, insensitive economic policies.

Decay in the morale and function of the janissaries. Like the Spahi, the janissaries had been a factor in the expansion of the Ottoman Empire, and like their counterparts in the cavalry, they played a key role in its decline. Designed to be professional warriors and nothing else, the janissaries won a number of concessions from the sultans. They were permitted to learn trades, to marry, and by 1568 even to enroll their sons in the corps. The levy or *devshirmeh* that was supposed to bring new faces into the ranks was abolished in 1637. About the same time, Mehmet Küprülü (1656–61), once a cook, then master of horse, became grand vizir and established a dynasty within the dynasty. Through the janissaries, the Küprülüs controlled the Ottoman Empire to the end of the 17th century.

Every janissary was given a ticket that entitled him to a guaranteed income from the state. In 1740, they won the right to transfer these documents. Aging warriors sold their paybooks to speculators for a lump sum or bequeathed the certificate to their families. Thousands of names were added to the rolls, none subtracted, and when they were called upon to fight, these paper regiments produced five or six able-bodied men. Numbering more than 135,000 by 1826 (nearly 10 times their original number), the janissaries resisted changes in weaponry or the creation of new military units. Periodically they staged revolts that menaced the sultan.

On three separate occasions, the behavior of the janissaries seriously compromised imperial goals. The first time was at Vienna in the fall of 1529 when their recalcitrance cost Suleiman the Magnificent an opportunity to overrun Central Europe. The second gaffe occurred at Vienna in the summer of 1683. This time a huge Turkish force, reckoned at between 275,000 and 500,000 men, marched toward the Austrian capital under the direction of Kara Mustapha. Instead of making a direct assault on the outmanned city, the Turks nestled in for a protracted siege. Kara Mustapha, an affable leader with a weakness for brandy and women, hoped to enjoy the spoils intact. As his soldiers lazed about the camps, making little effort at sanitation, the Turkish commissariat sold supplies to the beleaguered Austrians within the city. Resentful of a tax imposed on booty, the janissaries made no attempt to fortify their own positions. The Ottoman lines were so exposed that when the Polish King Jan Sobieski arrived with relief troops, he marveled at the general of an army who "had neither thought of entrenching nor concentrating his forces, but was encamped as if he were one hundred miles from home, is predestined to be beaten."[7]

The janissaries had one more opportunity to alter the course of history. The grand duchy of Muscovy was casting covetous eyes upon the Crimea, the Black Sea and ultimately Istanbul. When Peter the Great went to war against Sweden in the Great Northern War, the Turks, irritated by Russian raids into their territory, joined the side of Sweden. In July 1711, the Ottomans surrounded Peter's forces at the Pruth River in Bessarabia. They had it within their power to snuff out the growing threat from the north. Inexplicably, they released their captives. Some historians contend the Turkish commander, Baltaji Mehmet Pasha, was persuaded to release the Russians on their promise that they would demolish forts along the border. Perhaps he was fearful of a Russian suicide assault, perhaps impressed with the character of Peter. The story is also told that the grand vizir was concerned about the unreliability of his janissaries in battle. As a result, the Ottomans broke off, but only after being rewarded with jewels offered by Catherine I. Turkey would pay for this bribe for the next 200 years in the form of constant warfare with Russia.[8]

Efforts to replace the janissaries in 1768, 1793, and 1808 all proved unsuccessful. In November 1808, the corps and its supporters rampaged through Istanbul, burning 5000 homes and killing 10,000 people. Finally, in June 1826, Mahmud II felt confident enough to send loyal troops against the janissary barracks. When they refused to abide by an edict to reduce their numbers by one-third and reorganize along modern military lines, they were hit with an artillery barrage. As 6000 were killed and 13,000 survivors banished, the 500-year-history of these warriors came to an ignominious end.[9]

Abuse of the millet system. Twice betrayed by policies that seemed beneficial (feudalism, the janissaries) the Ottomans were also victimized by their own toleration. Never enthusiastic about non-Muslim population, the Turks nonetheless encouraged these people to enter their territory and band together in commercial associations. Apart from these *akhis*, the Turks also recognized the special status of various nationalities. Designated *millets* (nations), such people were permitted to use their own languages, collect taxes, maintain marriage, divorce, adoption customs, develop educational and religious institutions, and operate courts for offenses other than those involving public security. What determined a millet was religion, the Turks believing that it was inappropriate to hold other sects to the standards of the Shariah. Instead of fostering loyalty to the state, however, the various millets (Greek Orthodox, Armenians, Dönmeh, Roman Catholics, Jacobites, Greek Catholics, Jews) regarded their autonomy as a stepping stone to greater liberties, even independence. The millets fed passions of nationalism that flourished in the 19th century.[10]

Capitulatory treaties that contributed to economic bankruptcy. Before that time, however, European powers, too, had begun to exploit advantages inherent in the millet system. If, for example, it was improper to adjudicate a civil case involving Jews according to the Quran, how justify the use of Islamic law in a matter involving a Venetian or a German merchant? As early as 1503, Bayezid II reached an agreement with Venice permitting a *bailo* (consul) to reside in the empire for three years for the purpose of deciding cases among Venetians. Soon after, the principle of extra-territoriality was extended to Hungarians, Austrians, Englishmen and Portuguese.

Several interim agreements with the French culminated in a treaty in 1740. The 82 articles or Capitulations of this pact became a model for European powers. French subjects were granted the right to travel and trade in the empire. French goods were immune to taxation except the normal import-export duties. Frenchmen could not be arrested or tried without knowledge of a consul. Roman Catholics in the empire were enrolled and protected under the flag of France. And anyone who so desired — whether Sicilian or Turk — could secure a *barat*, a certificate from a French consul indicating he was a French subject. For a small fee, therefore, people who had never been to France might obtain immunity from taxation.[11]

Having granted special privileges to the French, the Turks were bullied by Catherine the Great into making similar concessions to the Russians in 1774. Along with trading privileges, consuls, and the right to enroll the Orthodox, the Turks also granted the Russians the right to protect the holy places of Christendom in Palestine, the same concession given the French in 1740. The result was that for the next century in Bethlehem and Jerusalem Orthodox and Roman Catholic clerics waged a veritable civil war. There were constant arguments over which group was entitled to the keys of the shrines, what kind of cross, what kind of star should be placed at the Church of the Nativity. Bearded monks armed with brooms fought on the square outside the Church of the Holy Sepulchre or lashed out with gigantic crucifixes as they collided along the Via Dolorosa at Easter. Eventually, their European benefactors were swept into an emotional conflict resulting in the Crimean War of 1854–1856.

The rise of modern nation-states in Europe. It was only too clear that Turkey's failure to check the rise of Russia in 1711 was a mistake, for the Tsarist state waged war incessantly against the Ottomans. The results were generally the same — costly defeat. By 1875, Turkey was bankrupt, $1 billion in debt. Once the richest empire in the world, its annual income was $80 million, of which three-fourths went toward interest on the debt. With the creation of a Council for the Administration of the Ottoman Debt (a form of international receivership with a staff of Europeans managing Turkish finances for the next two decades), its humiliation was complete.

Mutual mistrust among Europeans was the only thing that prevented a partition of the Ottoman state. The Russians did propose this very idea, but the British, fearing Tsarist advances into Southwest Asia and the Aegean, rejected the notion. For their part, the Russians resented Austrian claims upon the Balkans. And the French, seeking *gloire* everywhere, were suspicious of any proposal that did not reward them.[12]

Smoldering nationalist movements. The millet system had one last, unexpected impact — the rebirth of nationalism. People defeated by the Turks never really lost their sense of national pride and shame. Depending on their distance from the center of an empire hampered by corrupt administrators and weak lines of communication, they might attempt rebellion. In the 16th century, Berbers in North Africa severed all but ceremonial ties with the sultan-caliph. In 1769, another band of Mamelukes took control in Egypt. Twenty years later, Ali Pasha made himself tyrant in Epirus. In 1800, the Hejaz was lost temporarily to Wahhabi fundamentalists. When the Ottomans suppressed these rebels, their own generals turned against them. Such was the case with Mehemet Ali, an Albanian commander sent against the Mamelukes. Successful in Egypt, he soon added the pashaliks of Sudan, Arabia, Crete and Palestine. When Mehemet Ali also demanded Syria in 1831, his forces were superior to those of Mahmud II. Only the intervention of French and British troops sent him packing back to Egypt.

In the hilly sections of Moldavia and Wallachia from 1711 *hospodars* (Romanian lords) refused to pay taxes. The Serbian Church and figures like Dmitri Obradovich and Vuk Karajich inculcated a spirit of resistance to Turkish domination. With the onset of the Napoleonic Wars, Karageorge Petrovich and Milosh Obrenovich, misreading promises of aid from Russia, staged unsuccessful Serbian uprisings between 1807 and 1813.

Of all the subject peoples, none had suffered as long or as much as the Greeks. Romantics like Lord Byron embraced their struggle for independence. The Greeks, after all, had been victimized by feudalism, tax-farming, absentee landlords, even massacres. Their treasures atop the Acropolis had been devastated in wars between the Venetians and Turks. In the 18th century, Greek intellectuals traveled about Europe and imbibed theories of Rousseau and Locke. They returned home committed to changing the system, by force if necessary. Adamantios Koraes, Rhigas Pheraios, and Nicholas Skophas helped organize the *Philike Hetaeria* (Friendly Society), a student group not unlike nationalistic organizations springing up in Germany and Italy. Prompted by this spirit of nationalism sweeping the continent, bolstered by support given by European intellectuals, and building upon the sense of separateness fostered by the millet system, the Greeks revolted in 1821. Without the intervention of British and French sea forces at Navarino, however, it is unlikely that the Greeks would have won their independence in 1829.[13] Inspired by the success of the Greeks, every group that could fancy itself a nation clamored for autonomy, then independence, in the next 75 years.

Failure of Tanzimat

By the end of the 18th century, some Ottomans were committed to stemming the erosion of their power through a program of *tanzimat* (reform).[14] Abdul Hamid I (1773–89) initiated the process by exchanging military missions with the French before their revolution. Abdul Hamid's nephew Selim III (1789–1807) expanded the relationship, welcoming French experts who served as instructors in schools, translated military manuals, built ships, forged cannon for new forts, and redesigned the saddles for Ottoman cavalry. Selim also attempted to create a modern army. His *Nizami-Jedid* were given new uniforms, bayonets, and drilled along European lines. Unfortunately, this "New Organization" had to contend with the rivalry/jealousy of the janissaries until that corps was dispelled by force in 1826. Even then, the Turkish army continued to be an embarrassment on the battlefield, whether advised by the French in Syria in 1830, the English in the Crimea in 1856, or the Germans in World War I.

Mahmud II (1808–39) was the sultan who bombarded the janissaries. Hailed as another Peter the Great because of his commitment to westernization, Mahmud proclaimed massive changes for his empire. Turbans gave way to the fez. The government bureaucracy was overhauled, salaries raised, merit recognized, "parasites" like "the Keeper of Nightingales, Parrots and Heron's Plume" ousted, and a government gazette published for the first time. Inspector generals were sent into different districts to end arbitrary confiscations, executions without trial or appeal. Lighthouses and bridges were built, sanitation reforms attempted, a census taken, coinage minted with the image of the sultan, and a tariff adopted.

For all his effort, Mahmud was powerless to halt the decline of Ottoman power. His successor Abdul Mejid (1839–61) inaugurated his rule by issuing a decree, the *Hatti Sharif* (Noble Words), that was supposed to demonstrate that the empire was embracing the modern epoch. Drafted by the grand vizir, Reshid Mustapha Pasha, the decree called for tax reforms in the provinces, abolition of capital punishment, abolition of preferential favors at court and nepotism, the end of property confiscation, and the guarantee of life, honor, and fortune for all people in the empire. That the decree did not work wonders is evidenced by the issuance of a second decree by Abdul Medjid in 1856. The *Hatti Humayun* (Imperial Words) outlawed discriminatory practices against non–Muslims and called for mixed tribunals, mixed schools, guarantees of security for Christians and others, for an imperial budget, bank reform, road-building, an end to corporal punishment. As ever, it came late.[15]

When Abdul Mejid died, the worst nightmares of the reform leaders were realized. Not since the 17th century had the empire produced a set of bunglers like the sultans who occupied the throne. Abdul Aziz (1861–76) was a 230-pound glutton who downed a dozen eggs at a sitting, increased the number of concubines from 300 to 900, and lavished millions on gold dinner service and palaces paneled in mother-of-pearl. A lover of music, he strapped pianos to the backs of slaves who, thus adorned, accompanied him on strolls through the Topkapi. Abdul Aziz decreed that no other person might use his name. Schoolbooks were rewritten, deleting reference to Turkish defeats. A crude, superstitious man whose favorite kadin was 16 years old, Abdul Aziz was responsible for the massacre of 12,000 Bulgarians in April 1876. The pogroms plunged the empire into another war with Russia. His death in June, called a suicide, was probably the result of a palace coup.[16]

The new sultan, Murad V, the eldest son of Abdul Mejid, was hailed as a reformer. In reality, Murad was a physical and mental wreck, an alcoholic who had lived his life in terror of the bowstring. Drunk when he was notified of his appointment, Murad was deposed three months later after a specialist from Vienna and the court physician testified that he was insane.

Last and Worst: Abdul Hamid II

The throne now passed to a second son of Abdul Mejid, Abdul Hamid II (1876–1909). Like his father, Abdul Hamid gave indications at the start of his reign that he was committed to reform. On December 23, 1876, he issued the first Ottoman constitution, providing for a cabinet and parliament with proportional representation for all nationalities. The constitution affirmed equality for all subjects, guaranteed freedom of religion, education, press, and equal taxation. Every year the Ottoman state yearbook made reference to this remarkable document. Unfortunately, constitutional monarchy operated on paper only. With the outbreak of the Russo-Turkish War in May 1877, the first parliament (a noisy, disruptive affair) was prorogued and was not called back until 1908.[17]

Abdul Hamid, who some labeled "the worst, the least, and hopefully the last" of the Ottoman sultans, adapted to the role of despot. A small, dark man with a large nose and ears, he looked the part. As Zionist leader Theodor Herzl once commented:

> I can see him before me now, the Sultan of this declining robber empire. Small, shabby, with his badly dyed beard touched up apparently once a week for the *selamlik*, the hooked nose of a Punchinello, the long yellow teeth with a big gap to the right in the upper set, the fez pulled low over his doubtlessly bald head, his stuck-out ears serving, as I say to my friends, as a pants protector — to keep the fez from slipping down below his waist, the feeble hands in their white over-size gloves and the loud-colored cuffs that don't match his suit, the bleating voice, restraint in every word and fear in every glance. And *this* rules![18]

Like many of his predecessors who were second sons, Abdul Hamid had grown up uneducated. America's minister to the Porte, General Lew Wallace, observed that the sultan was fascinated with the Wild West, Indians, clocks, telescopes, and mousetraps. Beyond that, his knowledge of the world was negligible. A comment made as a youth is especially telling. To an Armenian architect working on the Dalma Bagsh palace who refused to work on Sunday, the young Abdul Hamid snorted: "You heathen dog, you Armenian. *If* I grow up and some day become a Sultan, I will force all the Armenians to break the Sabbath and if they do not, I will order the soldiers to kill them all" [emphasis added].[19]

The comment reveals Abdul Hamid's deep-seated hatred for Armenians, which stemmed from a palace rumor that the Sultan was himself the illegitimate son of an Armenian cook. It also says something of the nervousness that marked the Sultan's life. Haunted by the thought of assassination, Abdul Hamid hired thousands of spies to watch other spies. When building another palace, the Yildiz Kiosk, he constructed a number of secret passageways, for escape if necessary. He never slept in the same room on consecutive nights. A chain smoker, Abdul Hamid ordered the least expensive cigarettes, believing these would be more difficult to poison. His food was sampled by the chief chamberlain, milk brought in sealed cans from cows that were closely guarded. Afraid that his clothes also might be poisoned, he ordered another half brother to warm them for 30 minutes before he put them on. Suffering from dyspepsia, he downed stomach pills from hundreds shaken in a bag.

With Abdul Hamid, the Turkish experiment at reform came to a halt. Others conspired to keep the idea of Tanzimat alive. Exiles in Paris, students at the Imperial Medical College, young army officers, Jews, Arabs, Armenians, organized in secret societies. Calling themselves by a variety of names—*Vatan* (Fatherland), Congress of Ottoman liberals, Ottoman Society of Liberty—these groups shared a common goal: the democratization of the Ottoman Empire. Especially important was the Committee of Union and Progress (*Ittihad*) founded by Ibrahim Temo in 1889, which absorbed the other groups in 1907. A year later, with Macedonian army units grumbling about poor conditions and arrears in pay, the dissidents struck. Using a popular Arab officer, Mahmud Shevket Pasha, as their front man, they issued an ultimatum to Abdul Hamid: convene a popular assembly or face a march on Istanbul.

The nervous monarch caved in temporarily and even issued a speech from the throne welcoming the creation of this parliament in December. All the while, he continued to work for its undoing, promoting publications that opposed the constitution and rewarding agents for attacks on his political enemies. When, in April 1909, harassment of troop commanders and officials of the CUP became so severe that Abdul Hamid's opponents were forced into hiding, units under Mahmud Shevket Pasha descended upon the capital. Abdul Hamid was deposed, the national assembly reinstated under control of the Committee of Union and Progress.[20]

Whatever exuberance the revolutionaries may have felt was dissipated as Turkey continued to suffer one diplomatic setback after another. In the week of October 5 to 12, 1908, Bulgaria proclaimed its independence, Crete declared union with Greece, and Austria-Hungary (trading upon a secret agreement with Russia that sanctioned the eventual takeover of Istanbul and the Straits) annexed Bosnia. In 1910, Turkey failed to suppress Albanian national aspirations. The following year, its army bogged down in a hapless struggle with Italy. (Forced to cede control of Libya, the Turks retaliated by boycotting macaroni.) Between October 1912 and September 1913, the empire became embroiled in a series of Balkan wars. Initially the Ottoman Empire was the object of a combined assault from Bulgaria, Greece, Serbia and Montenegro. Ultimately it emerged as an ally of these same nations against Bulgaria. Whichever side it favored, the results for Turkey were the same: more loss of territory. Then in 1914 the Ottomans made a last mistake—going to war on the side of the one European nation that had offered economic and military assistance without taking land in return. Turkey's fate was now tied to that of the German Empire.

23

World War I

Turkey Stumbles into War

When the forces of imperial jealousy exploded into a world war in the summer of 1914, it was inevitable that the Ottoman Empire would be dragged into the conflict. The question was which side would be unlucky enough to be burdened with Turkey. Since the assassination of Mahmud Shevket Pasha, real power had been vested in a triumvirate—Ahmed Jemal Pasha, minister of marine; Mehmed Talaat Bey, the one-time brawler who became interior minister; and Enver Pasha, the dapper minister of war. Hopelessly backward in industry and agriculture, its army poorly supplied and trained, Turkey was, in the words of the German ambassador to Constantinople, Hans von Wangenheim, "without any question a worthless ally."[1]

The Turks themselves were split over whom to favor at the start of World War I. Most wanted an end to the degrading Capitulations, return of the Aegean islands and Balkan territory, and a guarantee of their eastern borders. Considering historic problems with Britain, France, Italy, and Russia, an alliance with the Entente seemed unlikely. Considering Allied war goals, which included protection of the Suez Canal and oilfields, seizure of the Straits and Holy Land, and a final partition of Middle Eastern lands, it was more expedient for Turkey to join the Central Powers.

United only in 1871, Germany played no role in the conquests that stripped Turkey of North Africa, Egypt, Cyprus, Crete or any of the Balkan states. Germany preferred economic penetration, with a view toward striking a not so subtle blow at Britain's Indian empire. Between 1870 and 1900, German goods to Turkey increased 350 percent while Turkish exports to Germany (tobacco, chromium, iron, oil) increased 700 percent. Posing as the patron of Muslims, Kaiser Wilhelm visited Constantinople and Jerusalem and pushed for the completion of a Berlin-to-Baghdad railway system that supposedly would serve religious pilgrims.

Impressed with German success on European battlefields, Ottoman sultans repeatedly appealed to the Prussians to upgrade their forces. Helmuth von Moltke trained the army of Mahmud II that was routed by Mehemet Ali in 1839. Later, General Colmar von der Goltz spent 13 years in Turkey (1883–1906) laying the foundations for disasters in the Balkans and Libya. Undaunted, Ittihad leaders—particularly Enver who had spent time in Berlin as a military attaché—requested additional advisors. By 1914, General Liman von Sanders controlled the Ottoman army with the rank of field marshal, General Fritz von Schellen-dorf headed up Turkey's military intelligence, while Admiral Wilhelm Souchon commanded the two greatest vessels in the navy—the *Sultan Selim Yavuz* and the *Midilli*. Both were manned by German crews and, until August 10, 1914, had been known as the *Goeben* and *Breslau*, two of the most important ships in the kaiser's fleet.

A secret protocol with Germany dated August 2 promised that if Russia attacked Austria, Turkey would assist Germany. Publicly, Enver and his cronies infuriated the Allies by abolishing the Capitulations on September 9. By the end of September, General Reinhardt Weber closed the Dardanelles to merchantmen bound for Tsarist Russia, reducing trade to that state by 50 percent. When German invasion plans in the West faltered, Admiral Souchon was ordered into action in the Black Sea. On October 28, elements of the Turkish navy, led by the two ersatz Ottoman cruisers, bombarded Sevastopol, Odessa and Novorossisk in the Crimea. Undismayed, Russia, Britain and France declared war on Turkey a week later. In return, on November 14, the sultan called for a jihad.[2]

Offensive Debacles

Trench lines in Western Europe remained relatively unchanged over the next three years. In the Middle East, too, strategies that appeared brilliant in map rooms failed when translated into action. For example:

Turkey's attack against Suez. Hoping to rouse the Egyptians to rebellion, Jemal Pasha sent 22,000 men against the Suez Canal in January 1915. British aircraft monitored the advance of the Ottomans across the waterless Sinai. On February 2, 16,000 stragglers who survived the two-week journey were routed by 100,000 colonial troops dug in to receive them.[3]

Britain's attack on Gallipoli. The brainstorm of Naval Minister Winston Churchill, the scheme was tantalizingly simple. British forces would seize control of the Dardanelles, then Istanbul, opening the Black Sea and linking up with the Russians. The British assembled 250,000 troops at Imbros and Tenedos, early in 1915. Their armada proceeded to the Straits in March, bombarding targets for two weeks before the first landings were attempted. Then everything went wrong. British vessels could not pass the gauntlet of Ottoman cannon, ships, and booms stretched through the narrows of the Straits. The Allied barrage failed to dislodge von Sanders' troops from positions in the hills above Gallipoli. Allied soldiers were easy targets as they tried to come ashore. Those who did land found limited shelter in the sand and bush. Before a pullback was ordered in December, more than 500,000 men, Turkish and Allied, lost their lives to enemy fire, dysentery, and exposure in the siege of Gallipoli.[4]

The British invasion of Iraq. Designed as a companion pincer to Gallipoli, the invasion of Iraq in 1915 was to secure oilfields in Mosul-Kirkuk. British commanders led Sikh and Gurkha forces on what they believed would be a parade up the Tigris-Euphrates. After taking Kut, however, the Allies found themselves besieged by a Turkish army. In the next six months, 24,000 men lost their lives. Of the 9000 who surrendered early in 1916, few survived the death march to Baghdad. A survivor recalled the brutality of their guards:

Men were dying of cholera and dysentery and often fell out from sheer weakness. Enteritis, a form of cholera, attacked the whole garrison after Kut fell. A man turned green and foamed at the mouth. His eyes became sightless, and the most terrible moans conceivable came from his inner being.... They died, one and all, with terrible suddenness. We saw officers and men lying uncovered from the sun on stretchers covered by thousands of flies.... One saw British soldiers dying, with green ooze issuing from their lips, their mouths fixed open, in and out of which flies walked.... Officers were deliberately starved to death.... Groups of men were left for the Arabs to play with, torture, and mutilate.[5]

Russia's invasion of the Caucasus. Between August 1914 and the end of 1916, an estimated 13 million men were called up by the Tsarist government. Nearly half of these were killed or wounded. The Grand Duke Nicholas' defense of Galicia in 1915 resulted in two million casualties. General Alexis Brusilov's assault against Bukovina in the spring of 1916 cost another million. Almost lost in these staggering figures was the attack directed by General Nicholas Yudenich into the Armenian highlands during November 1914. Designed to wrest away control of Turkey's eastern provinces as well as pose a threat to Istanbul, the invasion was stymied by Izzet Pasha at Kara Killessee on November 8. Tens of thousands of light-armed Russian troops were destroyed by Turkish machine guns and cannon concealed in mountain passes.[6]

Turkey's invasion of the Caucasus. Jubilant at his victory over the Russians, Enver launched a retaliatory strike into the Caucasus in December 1914. His goal: to conquer Russian Armenia and sweep into Central Asia, uniting all Turanian peoples against the British. Enver marched 150,000 light-clad troops into mountain passes in the middle of winter. This time, though, the Russians were fighting for their own soil and they were assisted by blizzards that devastated the Turkish ranks. By January 5, 1915, more than half of Enver's army was destroyed, 30,000 frozen corpses visible on the ground at one location. As General Yudenich took to the offensive again, it was left to one of Enver's aides, Mustapha Kemal, to block the Russians. By war's end, an estimated 26 of 52 Turkish divisions— more than 300,000 men —had been lost in eastern campaigns.[7]

Forgotten Genocide: The Armenians

Unwilling to accept responsibility for his mistakes, Enver blamed the Russian disaster on Turkey's traditional scapegoats— the Armenians. What ensued was a policy of deliberate dehumanization and killing that some have dubbed the forgotten genocide of the 20th century.[8]

Once the ruling dynasts of the Byzantine Empire, the Armenians endured a precarious existence after the arrival of the Turks in the 11th century. Nestled mainly in the eastern quadrant of Anatolia about Mt. Ararat, these Monophysite Christians had kin as far south as the bay of Alexandretta and north in Russia Azerbaijan. An industrious, mercantile people, the Armenians were hated as much for their business acumen as their religion. Despite harassment, intermittent attacks, and institutional discrimination from Muslims, the Armenians retained their cultural identity and grew to more than four million in number by 1900.

Inspired by other nationalities who clamored for self-determination, the Armenians grew restless. Students agitated for reform at schools from Tiflis to Marsivan. Their peaceful protests were suppressed by Abdul Hamid II. Shamed in combat and forced by the

European powers (especially Britain) to grant independence to Serbs, Romanians, and Bulgars, Abdul Hamid vowed never to yield to the Armenians—the group he regarded as the wards of the hated British.[9] Whenever the Armenians demonstrated, Abdul Hamid directed bands of thugs to murder and pillage. Between May 1894 and July 1896, more than 3000 villages were attacked, anywhere from 25,000 to 100,000 persons killed.

Statistics do not tell the horrors of what happened in Van, Trebizond, Sassun, or Mush. Eyewitnesses, including the American nurse Clara Barton, told of seeing priests tortured, of children hacked limbless, of pregnant women having their stomachs ripped open, of men being flayed, doused with kerosene, or crucified. Despite universal protests, including those from Tsarist Russia, persecution of the Armenians continued, with severe outbreaks in 1904 and 1908. In response, some Armenian intellectuals embraced violence and nihilism.

Enver could rationalize his defeats in the very existence of Armenians. After all, there were more than a million living in Russian Armenia along with the Catholicos, the head of the Armenian Church. The latter had blessed the Christian war against Muslims, and some Armenian civilians had attacked retreating Turkish troops. Another 150,000 responded to promise of independence made by Foreign Minister Serge Sazanov in February 1915, by enlisting in the Tsarist army. Although 250,000 Armenians were already fighting for the Ottomans, on February 18, 1915, the Ittihad ordered the transfer of its Armenian soldiers to "labor battalions," a euphemism for forced labor and death.

At first the men disappeared in ravines, where they were shot. Villages were denied food supplies and starvation became widespread. The same hoodlums that had preyed upon Armenians before the war now attacked orphanages, raped women, and mutilated prisoners. On March 9, 1915, Interior Minister Talaat gave the order to deport the allegedly disloyal populations. Accompanied by Kurdish and Turkish guards, the Armenians left their homes for unknown destinations. Some were bayoneted and dumped into wells. Others were taken on rafts to the middle of the Black Sea where "a clean expeditious job [drowning]" was done in minutes.[10] Through the summer of 1915 reports from Arnold Toynbee, American travelers, the Italian Consul at Trebizond, Viscount Bryce, and the Russian Foreign Office told of convoys of half-naked men, women, and children being driven through the desert by soldiers who shot anyone who fell out of line.[11]

A German Jew, Franz Werfel, would immortalize their suffering in his book, *The Forty Days of Musa Dagh*. Written in 1932–33, on the eve of the Nazi takeover in Germany, *Forty Days* is the story of resistance of 4000 Armenian villagers in the Suedia district near the bay of Antioch. Led by pastors Dikran Antreassian and Abraham Kaloustian and political activists Moses Der Kalousdian, Anania Viravorian, and Hagop Karageozian, the Christians abandoned their towns and took up positions on the slopes of the 2000-foot high peak of Musa Dagh in August 1915. Pelted by rain, short of supplies, and despairing of survival, the Armenians were rescued by a French cruiser, which saw their distress signal while passing near shore in September.

Others were not so fortunate. Oral testimonies tell of men separated from their families in Konia, only to be bayoneted. Lice-ridden children were alternately exposed to cold or blistering sun. Old people who could not keep up with the lines of deportees were shot where they fell.[12] Werfel detailed these brutalities in an extraordinary, painful passage:

> A shifting carpet woven with the threads of blood-stained destinies. It is always the same. After the first few days on the roads all the young men and the men in the prime of life get separated off from the rest of the convoy. Here, for instance, a man of forty-six, in good clothes, an engineer. It needs many cudgel blows to get him away from his wife and children. His youngest

is about one and a half. This man is to be enrolled in a labour battalion, for road-making. He stumbles in the long line of men and shuffles, gibbering like a half-wit: "I never missed paying my bedel ... paying my bedel." Suddenly he grips hold of his neighbour. "You've never seen such a lovely baby..".. A torrent of sentimental agony. "Why, the girl had eyes as big as plates. If only I could, I'd crawl after them on my belly like a snake." And he shuffles on, enveloped in his grief, completely isolated. That evening they lie down to rest on a hillside. Long after midnight he shakes the same neighbour out of his sleep. "They're all dead now." He is perfectly calm.[13]

The destination of the Armenians was Deir ez-Zor, a limitless concentration camp in the Syrian Desert described by Werfel as "a horrible cloaca of death." Here survivors of the death marches tried to survive by chewing grass or picking oat grains from horse dung. Some of the living skeletons drank dirty water mixed with animal urine. Others, their bellies bloated with edema, were chained together and forced into caves where they were burned alive by guards. The pathways to Deir ez-Zor were studded with human skulls and no less a personage than U.S. Ambassador Henry Morgenthau Sr., basing his actions on information supplied by missionaries, Samuel Ussher and Johannes Lepsius, offered a stern protest to the Ittihad in April. It was rejected by Enver, who noted, "Mr. Morgenthau is a Jew and Jews fanatically are on the side of minorities."[14] Again, Franz Werfel:

> The most horrible thing that had been done was, not that a whole people had been exterminated, but that a whole people, God's children, had been dehumanized. The sword of Enver, striking these Armenians, had struck Allah. Since in them, as in other men, even unbelievers, Allah dwells. And who so degrades His dignity in the creature, degrades the creator in his victim. This, then, is God-murder, the sin which, to the end of time, is never forgiven.[15]

To this day, the Turkish government denies that its predecessors engaged in a deliberate policy of genocide. When Hollywood flirted with the idea of producing an epic on the Armenians in 1935, Ankara warned of the dire consequences such a film would have upon the U.S.-Turkish relations and the MGM project was "postponed indefinitely." When Holocaust scholars planned a conference on genocide at Tel Aviv that would include a panel on the Armenian tragedy in the summer of 1982, the Turkish government let it be known if the Armenian archbishop appeared, Turkey would no longer guarantee the safety of its 25,000 Jews or escape routes to Jews fleeing Syria and Iran. Under duress, many participants to the conference withdrew.

In 1986 the Turkish government issued a lengthy report that explained how concern for security mandated the removal of some populations during the First World War. The report denied the existence of any orders calling for the death of Armenians and stressed how Ottoman civilians assisted the Armenians. The Turks argue that there are always civilian casualties in wartime, that the suffering of the Armenians was unfortunate, unforeseen, and unplanned.[16] And indeed it was difficult to corroborate the existence of orders to exterminate — until a young Armenian scholar located one such copy in Russian Armenia in 1986.

The validity of that order may be debated, but there is no debating the proofs offered by the Ottomans' chief allies when these acts were taking place. On June 10, 1915, the German Consul at Mosul wired Hans von Wangenheim of Armenian bodies clogging the Tigris River. Eight days later the German Consul at Erzerum reported on 25,000 women and children massacred in a gorge near Erzinjan. On October 8, German missionaries at Erzinjan offered grisly testimony of victims drawn and quartered, hacked to death with hatchets. Ambassador Wangenheim himself reported to Berlin in May 1915: "I think we ought to mitigate the form the hardships take but not to attempt to prevent them on principle. The work of the Armenian undermining, nourished by Russia, has assumed dimensions which menace the existence of Turkey." Then, for a German newspaper, von Wangenheim observed: "I think that the Turks are entirely justified. The weaker nation must succumb."[17]

No one knows for certain how many Armenians were slaughtered during the pogroms and deportations of World War I. Figures like 500,000, 800,000 and 1,000,000 victims have been bandied about. What is remarkable is the response of reputable historians. Sydney Fisher, for example, dismissed the aspirations of the Armenians as "hallucinations of independence" and stated, "No doubt certain deportations were required, but the total action was entirely inconsonant with the need."[18] William Yale's assessment was even more cavalier. Of the massacres perpetrated by Abdul Hamid, Yale has written:

> nineteenth-century writers thought in terms of the humane and beneficent civilization of the Christian West; they had not experienced two world wars, the first commencing with an assassination at Sarajevo and the second ending with the destruction of Hiroshima by an atom bomb. Who now, having participated in these world conflicts, would dare to cast a stone at Abdul Hamid for the massacre of a few thousand resulting from the pursuit of policies based on his ideologies.[19]
>
> ...A more balanced perspective of these events is possible if one calls to mind the slaughter by hanging, crucifixion, decapitation, and drowning of 100,000 Paulician Christian heretics by the Christian Empress Theodora of the Byzantine Empire or in more recent times the slaughter of 6,000,000 Jews in the heart of Christian Europe.[20]

Yale's observations on the Armenian atrocities in World War I — "In 1915 and 1916 people had not yet accepted mass slaughter as a legitimate means of warfare" and "Let he who is without sin cast the first stone"[21] — are equally unacceptable. Not just to this writer, but to the Armenians themselves, who hunted down and assassinated both Jemal Pasha and Talaat Bey after the war, and to the government of Woodrow Wilson, which was so moved by Morgenthau's reports that it considered taking a protective mandate over Armenia at Versailles. Some scholars even suggest that the failure of the civilized world to react to the plight of the Armenians helped convince the Nazis that genocide could be attempted and concealed.[22]

The Collapse of Ottoman Turkey

In the summer of 1916, the Germans prodded their Ottoman allies to make another attack against British positions in Egypt. Once more, an offensive operation, *Yilderim* (for Lighting) proved futile. On paper, everything seemed to be in place, but the German-Turkish forces were routed from Suez by a new British general, Sir Edmund Allenby. Unlike his predecessor, John Maxwell, or General S. F. Maude, the victim of the Kut campaign, Allenby was one commander whose tactics did succeed. His forces were better supplied than the enemy, which by this time was practically exhausted. His intelligence, drawn from friendly Arabs operating in the Holy Land, was superior as well. Striking in the spring of 1917, Allenby divided his troops into several columns and outflanked Turkish gun emplacements. In December, he won a striking victory at the plains of Megiddo and went on to secure Jerusalem before Christmas. Rather than pursue the collapsing Ottomans, Allenby settled in for the winter, reinforcing his own armies before renewing the attack in Jordan and southern Syria in the summer of 1918.[23]

With no victories to speak of in the Balkans, Russian-Persian forces hammering at Iraq, and Arab units entering Damascus on the 30th of September 1918, more than one million men killed or wounded and a public debt of more than $10 billion, Turkey's ruling military clique reached a decision. On October 7, the Ittihad resigned and its leaders went into exile. Three weeks later, on October 30, 1918, Turkey agreed to terms aboard the battleship *Agamemnon* anchored at Mudros. Under this "armistice" Turkey would cease fighting, surrender all war material and permit the Allies to occupy any point in the Ottoman Empire, including the six Armenian vilayets. Two days later, the other Central Powers capitulated. On November 13, 1918, British ships entered the Golden Horn. The Capitulations were restored and four occupation zones (British, French, Italian and American) were established in Istanbul.

24

Republican Turkey

Turkey Humiliated

World War I brought about the collapse of an empire that had been tottering for two centuries. Turkey suffered one million combat deaths, 20 percent of its able-bodied men. By 1918 the public debt had quadrupled to more than $10 billion. Stripped of 770,000 square miles in peace treaties, the Turks were dependent upon occupation forces for food. When the Allies ordered the surrender of weapons, Turkish military units presented themselves like robots, leaving no more than 40,000 men under arms by the spring of 1919.

The Turks were relieved that they were being punished by the British, Americans, and French, and not the hated Russians. Such idealism vanished on May 15 when thousands of Greek troops stormed ashore at Izmir (Smyrna). Greek Prime Minister Eleutherios Venizelos had made a case at Versailles for the return of ancestral lands in the Aegean Sea and Ionian coast. Greece was promised the territory when it joined the Allied cause in October 1915; 26,000 of its soldiers died fighting in the Balkans. More than a million Greek kinsmen lived in squalor under the Turks. Evidently Venizelos' call for self-determination resounded with Woodrow Wilson, for on May 6 the American president, recovering from a bout of influenza, joined with George Clemenceau and David Lloyd-George in approving the Greek landing in Anatolia.[1]

For 16 hours, Greek soldiers raced through Turkish sections of Izmir, looting, raping and killing. Even if there had been no sack of the city, the very presence of these ancestral enemies would have been sufficient to prompt Turks to resistance. As people flew black flags of mourning, the puppet cabinet in Istanbul offered its resignation. Elsewhere, General Mustapha Kemal, commanding what was left of the Third Army at Sivas, halted the disarmament process and rallied the people to "the Association for the Defense of Turkish Rights in Europe and Anatolia."

Kemal Ataturk

Born Mustapha ibn Ali in Macedonia in 1880, the man who would modernize Turkey was the son of a bureaucrat in the Ottoman Debt Administration. Sent to school to become a merchant or priest, he was transferred to a military cadet school in Salonika. Unpopular with his fellow students, Mustapha was dubbed Kemal (perfection) by a teacher. In 1900, while attending the General Staff College in Istanbul, he organized a secret society, *Vatan* (Fatherland). He opposed Ittihad policies, which sacrificed poorly trained soldiers to wars in North Africa and the Balkans, yet he fought courageously in these losing ventures. He opposed the alliance with Germany, yet he became von Sanders' most effective aide during the Gallipoli and Balkan campaigns. Frequently bed-ridden with social diseases, Mustapha resented his younger rival, Enver Pasha, yet he accepted the appointment as inspector general of the last autonomous Ottoman army unit at Sivas. Years later, as dictator, he would take the surname of Ataturk (father of the Turks).[2]

In the summer of 1919, the survival of an independent Turkey was in doubt. Some political leaders rallied to Kemal hoping he would achieve a fair postwar settlement. On September 4, the nationalists wired the sultan from Sivas, informing him that they had adopted a new constitution, the National Pact. Many of the signatories traveled to Istanbul, expecting to oust the vizir and, occupation forces. Instead, Mehmet VI declared a holy war against the rebels. Some were exiled to Malta. Others, including Kemal, were condemned to death in absentia. On March 15, 1920, the Allies moved from military camps about Istanbul and occupied the capital.

Kemal's response was to summon the remnants of the nationalist movement to the provincial town of Ankara. There, on April 23, 1920, Muslim leaders countered with fetwas of their own and Kemal was named president of a provisional government. A day later, the new regime astonished the world by signing a mutual defense pact with Russia. Desperate for military supplies and realizing that the Bolsheviks were also pariahs, Ataturk ignored the traditional animosity that existed between the two nations. To Western diplomats gathered at San Remo to work out a preliminary distribution of Ottoman spoils, the Russo-Turkish alliance confirmed the necessity of dealing a final blow to the upstart Turkish nationalists.[3]

The Greek War

By June 1920, Kemal was ready to launch a formal assault on Istanbul itself. The Allies countered by unleashing the Greeks against him. All of the major European powers had problems of their own (France with Syria; Britain in Ireland, India, and Iraq; Italy torn with domestic unrest). America, suffering political paralysis with a sick president, had just undergone a year of anti–Red hysteria. The Greeks, with the largest army in the region, seemed perfect policemen to force Kemal to accept terms of San Remo.

What followed was 14 months of Greek rampage from Adrianople to Eskisehir. Kemal tried to draw enemy forces into rugged terrain where their supply lines would be stretched and where Turkish peasants could make guerilla attacks. Kemal recognized that some Greek officers were unpopular or incompetent. (General Giogios Hadjianestes insisted he was made out of glass or dead.) Kemal was aware of Bolshevik and pacifist agitators working among opposing troops. He also knew that he no longer had to reckon with the two most popular Greek leaders. Venizelos was voted out of office in November 1920, a month after King Alexander died when he was bitten by a monkey in his palace zoo.[4]

The royal house of Greece was of German lineage, and some of its leaders sympathized with the Central Powers during the great war. One such figure was Constantine, who had been living in exile since 1917. When he succeeded Alexander, French and Italian support for the effort in Anatolia waned. To curry favor with the inevitable government in Turkey, the Italians turned over supplies when they evacuated Antalya in March 1921. The French, convinced by a Turkish victory at the river Sakarya in September 1921, secretly offered Kemal arms. Strengthened by their newfound friends, the Turks finally pierced the enemy front in August 1922.

As the Greeks retreated, only the British and Lloyd George expressed support. In the panic that followed, both sides perpetrated atrocities. Hundreds of Greeks drowned or were stampeded at the wharf as 40,000 of their number fled Izmir on September 11. They feared that the Turks would retaliate for what they had done when they burned mosques and crucified Muslim children. Kemal did stand by as the city was torched and Greeks and Armenians were brutalized. And then, at the end of the month, he wheeled his troops into position, surrounding the British at Chanak, a tiny garrison on the Asian side of the Dardanelles.

The British vowed that the Turks would not be permitted to cross the Straits and they backed up their rhetoric with the dispatch of a fleet to the Sea of Marmora, seven battalions of troops, and some fighter planes. As tensions mounted, the French and Dominion nations informed Lloyd George that they would not support a confrontation. The British caved in, acknowledging that Kemal had won control of Turkey, and arranged for an armistice at Mudanya.

The Peace of Lausanne

Less than two months after Chanak, diplomats from 10 nations gathered at Lausanne, Switzerland, to arrange terms of a Middle East peace treaty. There would be no dictate this time as Ismet Pasha represented the interests of a revitalized Turkey. Among the provisions of the pact signed on July 24, 1923 were:

• Eastern Thrace and Edirne were assigned to Turkey.
• The Aegean Islands were distributed with Tenedos and Imbros going to Turkey, the Dodecanese to Italy, the rest to Greece.
• Territories with predominantly Arab populations were separated; Turkey's southern border with Syria was to be arbitrated; so, too, its eastern frontier with Iraq and the award of Turkish Petroleum.
• Neither Armenians nor Kurds were granted independence, but Turkey would honor minority guarantees outlined by the League of Nations.
• Capitulations and foreign privileges were abolished.[5]

Perhaps one of the most significant terms of Lausanne was the provision for the exchange of populations. In an effort to stabilize the region, one and one-half million Greeks who lived under Turkish sovereignty were exchanged for 500,000 Turks living in Greece. The population transfers began in the summer of 1923 and lasted until 1925. Unquestionably, they wrought hardship upon many people. As Lewis Thomas and Richard Frye have noted:

> The spectacle of large numbers of people painfully being sorted out and relocated in this way, in a sort of hectic international game of musical chairs, is most dismaying, especially as one appreciates the human suffering and sadness involved in plucking simple people from their traditional homes and possessions, and plumping them down in what is still a strange land.[6]

Executed by one side and in the guise of "ethnic cleansing," as in Yugoslavia in 1992 and 1993, population exchange may seem brutal, inhumane. The Greek-Turkish exchange, however, like that of 12 million Hindus and Muslims on the Indian subcontinent in 1947, was arranged by the international community and has proven to be workable.

Turkey under Ataturk

Until his death of cirrhosis of the liver on November 10, 1938, Mustapha Kemal was dictator of Turkey. Ataturk surrounded himself with former comrades in arms who gushed: "You are the greatest soldier of the world and of all history. You are like the sun, a sun that fills the world and lights up every facet of our lives." These sycophants knew well with whom they were dealing, for during the Greek War, Ataturk had said: "I mean that I will have everyone to do as I wish, carry out what I command. I will have no criticism or advice. I will have my own way. All, and you too, shall do as I wish absolutely and without question." Later, he put it more succinctly: "I am Turkey. To destroy me is to destroy Turkey."[7]

Philosophically, Ataturk was a disciple of Ziya Gökälp (1876–1924), one of those critics of the sultanate who had been banished after the Sivas Congress of 1920. Gökälp was convinced that glory had faded from the Middle East because the Ottoman Empire failed to embrace modern technology. A 20th-century nationalist, he urged the Turkish people to abandon notions of empire and concentrate on forging a modern nation state. The key word was *modern*, for Gökälp advocated the substitution of modern commercial and civil codes for theocracy. He believed in emancipation of women, industrialization, patriotism and rejection of alien ideologies like communism.[8] It was left to the soldier-statesman Ataturk to implement Gökälp's teachings in what has come to be called Kemalism.

Kemalism

Republicanism. When Mehmet VI, the 37th Ottoman, was deposed and sent to Malta by the Grand National Assembly on November 1, 1922, Ataturk did not replace him as sultan. Rather, he opted to become president of the kind of state envisioned by Gökälp. Article 1 of the Turkish Constitution, adopted in April 1924, provided that the Turkish State was a republic. The constitution spoke eloquently of sovereignty residing with the Turkish nation and of all Turks, without distinction to race or creed, being free and equal before the law. Like ukases issued during the time of Tanzimat, the constitution guaranteed freedom of speech, press and travel. The constitution outlined the new political apparatus (Grand National Assembly, presidency, Cabinet) that was to govern Turkey.

And yet there was no such thing as constitutional democracy in Turkey. Ataturk invoked press censorship for 10 years. Elections were rigged. Generally, only one slate of names, those of the *Čümhüriyet Halk Firkasi* (Republican People's Party), Ataturk's party, was submitted to the voters. Ataturk was the sole candidate for the presidency in 1927, 1931, and 1935. Debates in the Grand National Assembly were perfunctory, with the president glaring down on so many puppets. Each time Ataturk experimented with creating a loyal opposition he wound up having to suspend the constitution and imprison party activists who had strained his patience. Although his close friend, Ismet Inönü, who served as prime minister through much of the period, offered platitudes about the rule of the people, Ataturk summed up Republican Turkey when he said: "I govern."[9]

Secularism. For more than a year and a half after the expulsion of Mehmet VI, Ataturk put up with the charade of Vaheddin Abdul Medjid acting as caliph, the spiritual leader of all Muslims. Kemal made no secret of his atheism. He blamed the ulema for obscurantism that had made Turkey weak and one occasion chased the Shaykh ul-Islam from his office, hurling a copy of the Quran after him. He recalled that in the postwar struggle, he had been anathematized by various shaykhs while the British were supported by the Agha Khan, the Ismaili chief. "Islam," he said, "this theology of an immoral Arab, is a dead thing.... A ruler who needs religion to help him rule is a weakling. No weakling should rule.... All our troubles come from the misuse of religion in the state.... Was it not for the Caliphate that, for Islam, for the priests and such-like cattle, that for centuries the Turkish peasant has fought and died in every climate?"[10]

Finally, on March 3, 1924, Ataturk abolished the caliphate. This was followed by the dissolution of Shariah law courts and the creation of a new law school in Ankara to teach western law. The following year, the Grand National Assembly adopted the Swiss civil code, Italy's penal code, and a commercial code based on that of Weimar Germany. The year 1926 saw the introduction of the Gregorian Calendar, Friday became a compulsory day of rest and the so-called *Vikend* that corresponded to the two-day sabbath normally enjoyed in the West. Religious instruction was taken from the schools, mosques were converted to barns or museums, and all public officials ordered to take oaths on their honor, instead of the Quran.

The purge of religious power was not accomplished without opposition. Members of dervish sects, officially disbanded by presidential decree in 1925, refused to abide by Ataturk's order and were hanged by the dozen. Five years later, in December 1930, the dervish leader Shaykh Mehmed of Menemen proclaimed himself the Mahdi. After four months, Ataturk prevailed, declaring martial law, arresting more than 1000 of the ringleaders, and publicly hanging many from the Galata Bridge in Istanbul.

Populism. Although Article 69 of the Turkish Constitution abolished pre-existing privileges and proclaimed equality before the law for all individuals in Turkey, Ataturk was no Jeffersonian. The instrument vital to promote equality was education. According to a 1927 census 90 percent of the Turkish people were illiterate. Better than 80 percent lived in villages. To resolve the problem, Ataturk mandated primary school education to the fifth grade. In a period of 15 years, 10,000 schools were built, guaranteeing every village a school of its own. Bright graduates were encouraged to obtain teaching certificates and return to their hometowns. The aged, too, were brought into the educational process through a system of *halkevis* (community centers) where reading was promoted along with patriotism and recreation. No prisoners would be released from jail unless they could demonstrate an ability to read. Apparently the program worked, for illiteracy was reduced to 40 percent in one decade.

Nationalism. As dictator, Ataturk tried to boost Turkey's prestige in the international community, instituting soccer as the national game, sending entries to the Balkan and Olympic games, upgrading an army that once been a laughingstock. For Ataturk, a major barrier to a revival of Turkish pride was the Arabic language. Early in 1928, he summoned a group of notables to Istanbul where, before a blackboard, he lectured them on the necessity of replacing the Arabic script with Latin letters. Turkish was the pure language from which all others derived. For Turks to enjoy their proper place in the modern world, they would have to purge their speech of foreign corruptions. A Turkish Quran would have to replace the Arabic, with the word *Tanri* substituted for *Allah*. Streetcars would have to change their markings. No books could be published in the old script. The government would not reply to correspondence in Arabic. And while the decree led to some anomalous situations (53 bags of Finance Ministry documents were sold to Bulgaria in 1931 as scrap paper), the reform took hold; Turkey is the only Muslim nation in the Near East that does not use of the Arabic script.

Statism. Ataturk believed that Turkey's future was not in agriculture, but industry. Somehow, the majority of its people, utilizing wooden plows and cattle dung to fertilize farms of 10 acres or less, should be directed toward the exploitation of vast reserves of coal, chromite, and iron ore. This required extensive government activity, not unlike the corporativist programs of Mussolini. Ataturk established a set of national banks—the Central Bank of the Turkish Republic to act as a mint; the Commercial Bank of Turkey, comparable to a Federal Reserve; the Eti Bank for mining; the Sumer bank for everything from textiles to steel; the Credit Foncier for real estate loans; and the Bank of Agriculture to expand services to farmers. A series of four- and five-year plans enabled him to obtain multimillion-dollar loans from Russia and Germany. These, in turn, were converted into railroads, tractors, model farms, irrigation projects, electricity, clothing, cement, chemicals and other light industries, all protected by government monopoly, but designed to benefit the people.

Reformism. Finally, to be strong and independent, Turks had to reject the old patterns of the Ottomans. They must advocate change for change sake, even as the Ottomans had embraced obscurantism. Some of these reforms took on amusing dimensions. When Ataturk commanded that all Turks adopt surnames, some became Biyikliogu (son of a man with a mustache), Ustundag (mountaintop), and Kirkagaclioglu (son of a man with 40 trees). Later, he ordered diplomats to learn social dancing (foxtrots, the waltz) as a mark of sophistication.

Kemal encountered stiffer opposition when he ordered the adoption of Western dress. At Kustamuni on the Black Sea in 1925, he banned the use of pantaloons, robes, and the fez. Resplendent in a broad-brimmed Panama hat, he declared: "If we will be a civilized people, we must wear civilized, international clothes. The fez is the sign of ignorance."[11] Muslim fanatics were prepared to make of this headdress an issue of life and death. In Sivas, Erzerum, and Marash, dervishes argued that it would be impossible to pray properly with a peaked hat or fedora. Ataturk's response was to arrest, bastinado and hang the ringleaders. Some fundamentalists preferred suicide. The majority, when confronted with an ultimatum to replace the fez by a certain date, panicked and grabbed whatever they could find—bowlers, caps, straw boaters, feathered women's hats—to stay out of prison.

Reformism carried with it benefits for women and children. Polygamy was abolished in 1926. Civil marriage and divorce supplanted the old rites about the same time. Though never formally banned, use of the veil was discouraged in cities. Women obtained the right to vote in 1934 and moved into previously restricted fields like medicine, law, banking, publishing, even flying. Like most enlightened nations, Turkey passed laws regulating employment of children. Hospitals, harbors, streets, sewage systems, skyscrapers, parks, and statues were built in Turkey's revitalized cities. Turkey was welcomed to the League of Nations, regained the right to fortify the Straits through the Montreux Conventions of 1936, and joined the Saadabad Defense Pact (with Iran, Iraq and Afghanistan) as Ataturk fulfilled his promise to restore national pride.

The Meaning of Ataturk

In the space of a few years, Mustapha Kemal transformed his homeland from the rotting joke that the Ottoman Empire had been. Turkey managed to avoid entangling itself on the side of the Axis during World War II, emerging instead as a charter member of the United Nations. In 1947, with the Soviet Union menacing Greece and the Straits, Turkey accepted $100 million in military and economic assistance under the Truman Doctrine.

Between 1950 and 1953, Turkish armed forces distinguished themselves during the Korean War. Despite its membership in NATO, Turkey sent 40,000 of its soldiers into Cyprus in 1974 and 1975, ostensibly to protect the Turkish minority on that island. The Turkish Republic of North Cyprus proclaimed in November 1983 has to this day been recognized only by Ankara.[12]

Since Ataturk, Turkey's army has been the force periodically called upon to stabilize a shaky political system. Three times in recent years, the military has staged coups to prevent the collapse of the nation. Reacting to widespread corruption and police abuse, General Cemal Gursel intervened in May 1960. Leaders of the ruling right-wing Democrat party (Celal Bayar, Adnan Menderes, Fuad Kuprulu, and Refik Koraltan) were purged and the 1924 constitution was replaced with one that promised more freedom. Reconstituted as the Justice Party of Suleiman Demirel, the conservatives regained power in 1965 and plunged the nation once more into unemployment, inflation, and university unrest. The result was that the generals imposed martial law in March 1971. Four years later, in the midst of the Cyprus crisis, Demirel was back as prime minister. Again he proved incapable of dealing with foreign debt, internal strikes, and ethnic violence. In September 1980, General Kenan Evren engineered a third coup and reformed the constitution, permitting only three political parties.[13]

Under the lackluster leadership of Evren and his successor, Turgut Ozal, Turkey drifted in the 1990s. By the time voters went to the polls in October 1991, its trade deficit was more than $6 billion. Unemployment was at 25 percent, inflation close to 70 percent and the giant labor union DISK was unable or unwilling to check the anger of workers whose per capita income was 7 percent that of the United States. More than a million Turks emigrated to Europe where they encountered racial hostility. Those who stayed behind had to deal with surging nationalism of Armenians and Kurds, both of whom adopted militant positions in the 1980s. Ataturk's vaunted populism now meant repression of the Kurdish language culture, imprisonment of thousands of Kurds— even a member of Parliament whose crime was that he declared "I am a Kurd. There are Kurds in Turkey." While the world shrugged, between 1984 and 1988 thousands of Kurds were slaughtered in the eastern provinces, not of Iraq, but Turkey.[14]

Under Ataturk's successors, reformism stultified, secularism was reversed. Fewer women were admitted to government posts or professions. The police were granted more power. Imams were granted power in schools, mosques were opened, and the pilgrimage to Mecca was encouraged. Out of deference to growing influence of fundamentalist groups like the National Salvation Party and the National Action Party, the 1982 constitution acknowledged Turkey's Islamic roots. For the first time, in 1980 mass demonstrations were held at Konya on behalf of the PLO.

For some, Turkey is the model for what a developing nation may do for itself. Ataturk, however, would hardly be delighted with the current state of affairs in his country. In 1991 the Turkish electorate gave its overwhelming approval (292 seats of 450 in the National Assembly) to the right-leaning True Path Party and its leader, Suleiman Demirel. Astoundingly, Demirel, the man who twice before had been ousted by generals because of his inability to govern, was returned to the presidency on the basis of a simplistic pledge of "a home and car for everyone."[15]

To those who invoke his name in a revolutionary cause, Ataturk once said: "There are no oppressors, nor any oppressed. There are only those who allow themselves to be oppressed. The Turks are not among these. The Turks can look after themselves. Let others do the same." And to those who see in an increasingly reactionary Turkey a potential ally in the anti–Western, anti-modern struggle, this unique man said: "I am neither a believer in a league of all the nations of Islam, nor even in a league of the Turkish peoples. Away with such dreams and shadows."[16]

25

The Renaissance
of Arab Nationalism

A Majority That Did Not Rule

By the end of the 19th century, a familiar pattern had developed among subject peoples within the Ottoman Empire. Serbs, Greeks, Bulgars, Armenians developed national consciousness through contact with Western missionaries and academics. Deprived of what they deemed their rightful place in history, these people turned to self-proclaimed liberators whose revolutions inevitably ended in failure. Intellectuals, banding together in cultural societies, attempted to politicize the masses in support of movements calling for autonomy. The Ottomans reacted by outlawing these seemingly innocuous student or scientific groups. Driven underground, the intellectuals reconstituted themselves in secret societies committed to total independence.

The Arabs were not immune to the virus of nationalism. For nearly 700 years, this once great nation endured the insult of Turkish caliphates. Its fellaheen tilled the soil for absentee landlords. Its young men were dragooned for military service in far-off lands. Few were valis, pashas, or sanjakbeys (governors). Although scholars write of an Arab Awakening, these people never stopped hoping for a restoration of that glorious era between A.D. 700 and 1000 when the Middle East constituted the center of world civilization.

The Wahhabis

The Arab world experienced spasms of independence for nearly 200 years. One of the earliest movements was spearheaded by Muhammad ibn Abdal Wahhab, an 18th-century Sunni from north Arabia. An iconoclastic kadi who preached a literal interpretation of the Quran and a return to *salaf* (the life of Arab ancestors), Shaykh Muhammad viewed the Ottomans as idolatrous and sinful. In 1747, he convinced Muhammad ibn Saud, chieftain of the Nejd, that Islam's sacred cities must be purified. In the next half century, the Wahhabis threatened Baghdad, Kerbala, Mecca, Medina, Damascus and Aleppo before being defeated by forces loyal to the caliph at Deraa in 1818. Chased back into the desert, the fundamentalists continued to rule in the Najd until Abdal Aziz ibn Saud added the Hejaz to his domains in 1926 and renamed the region Saudi Arabia.[1]

Mehemet Ali

The man responsible for defeating the Wahhabis was an Albanian whose father had been a tobacco vendor in Macedonia. This did not prevent Mehemet Ali from claiming to be the champion of the Arab people once he arrived in Egypt at the head of a punitive expedition in 1798. An ambitious, unscrupulous man, Mehemet Ali was rewarded by Mahmud II with the title of pasha of Egypt in 1805. In the next two decades the governor slaughtered hundreds of Mamelukes, extended Islamic control into the Sudan, and defeated the Wahhabis. When asked to pacify the piratical Ali of Janina, to clean out Greek rebels on Crete or to assist the caliph at Navarino, Mehemet Ali responded quickly and efficiently. Each time, however, there was a price — another pashalik. When Mahmud refused to transfer control of Syria to Mehemet Ali, a showdown was inevitable. The week of June 24, 1839, the Ottoman Empire lost its army, navy and sultan. Only the intervention of British Lord Palmerston, who despised and distrusted Mehemet Ali, prevented the breakup of the Turkish empire at that point. Beaten back by the Allies, within two years Mehemet Ali was reduced to rule over Egypt.[2]

Abdel Kader

Palmerston sought cooperation of France in chastising Mehemet Ali. At the time, the French were occupied elsewhere. For hundreds of years, the Barbary states of North Africa exercised a stranglehold over commerce in the western Mediterranean. Ships bound for Gibraltar were subjected to raids by Muslim raiders. Civilians might be kidnapped and held for ransom. Merchants who negotiated with the Beys or Deys were unable to collect on debts. Governments, including that of the fledgling United States, were forced to pay extortion to guarantee safe passage of their vessels.

In 1830, the French, angered by insults of Hussein, Dey of Algiers, dispatched an armada of 600 ships across the Mediterranean. This invasion, while relatively successful in the costal towns, aroused fanatical desert tribesmen. Among the Kabyles, jihad was preached by an aged holy man from Mascara, Muhyi ad-Din. His 22-year-old son, Abdel Kader, assumed the lead of what was to be a heroic guerilla war. For 16 years, Abdel Kader led the French on an exasperating chase across gorges and deserts from Morocco to Tunisia. When it was over, Abdel Kader was locked up in a Toulon fortress and Algiers, Oran, and Constantine incorporated "permanently" as departments of France.[3]

Said, Ismail, and the Suez Canal

French colonial aspirations were not limited to the Maghreb. Egypt, with its great population and natural granary had great allure. When Mehemet Ali tried to streamline his army or to stamp out cholera or introduce new crops and factories he turned to French experts. One of these, Ferdinand De Lesseps, championed the idea of a canal linking the Mediterranean with the Red Sea. Such a Suez Canal would have been dug in virtually the same location where the ancient pharaohs had linked the Nile to the Bitter Lakes. Before de Lesseps, several engineers (the Englishman Thomas Waghorn; Prosper Enfantin, a disciple of the Utopian socialist Saint-Simon; and Jean Baptiste Le Pere, who traveled with Napoleon) had written on the feasibility of such a scheme.

Egypt's first khedive was personally opposed to the notion of a Suez Canal, favoring instead the construction of an trans-isthmian railroad. His successors, Said (1854–63) and Ismail (1863–79), were persuaded by de Lesseps that whoever constructed a canal would be regarded as immortal, alongside the pyramid builders. This appeal to ego cancelled out harping from the British, who objected that the project was financially impossible, would require slave labor, and that once completed the higher (by 30 feet) Red Sea waters would flood the Delta. In fact, the British regarded a canal as a dagger pointed at India.

Undaunted, de Lesseps obtained a 99-year concession from Said on November 30, 1854. Two years later, with studies estimating the cost to be $8 million, de Lesseps' Compagnie Universelle du Canal Maritime de Suez offered 400,000 shares of stock to the public. Fifty percent were sold at $100 a share to French subscribers. The Egyptian lord retained 177,000. A glowering Britain rejected the opportunity to buy in for 80,000 shares.

After many delays, the canal was formally opened on the morning of November 17, 1869. The night before, 4000 persons attended a lavish dinner party hosted by Said's nephew Ismail at a cost of more than $7 million. Among the dignitaries invited to the opening ceremonies of the Canal were the French Empress Eugenie, Franz Joseph of Austria, the German Crown Prince Wilheim, Prince Henry of the Netherlands, Emile Zola, Henrik Ibsen, Abdel Kader, and the patriarch of Jerusalem. Ismail also commissioned Giuseppe Verdi to commemorate the event by writing *Aida*.

All the pomp and bluster could not conceal the fact that Egypt was bankrupt. Mismanagement (the canal ultimately cost over $50 million, twice the original estimate) combined with unrealistic optimism over the future of Egyptian cotton prices (which skyrocketed during the American Civil War) resulted in Egypt's national debt climbing to more than $450 million by 1876. In that year a desperate Ismail was forced to sell off his nation's shares. The only buyer was the very nation that had vehemently opposed the project — Great Britain. When a representative of Prime Minister Disraeli sought emergency capital to guarantee the purchase which gave the British government control over the canal, the loan was approved by Lionel Rothschild of the Jewish banking house of Rothschild.[4]

Ahmed Urabi

Having gained controlling interest in the Suez Canal, the British sought to protect their investment by intervening in the domestic affairs of the Egypt. Ismail, who had proven unable to check his own extravagance or that of Muslim nobles, was replaced by his son Tawfik in June 1879. At the same time, France and Britain established the offices of dual controllers, imperial agents who supervised Egypt's finances. Salaries of bureaucrats were slashed, positions eliminated. Circassians, deemed more reliable, were given top ranks in the military. Some native-born Egyptians who had never been enthralled with Mehemet Ali's dynasty resented these last indignities. In 1882, Colonel Ahmed Urabi, the son of a village shaykh, decided to do something. As minister of war, Urabi commanded perhaps 5000 troops. In February 1882, promising personal gain to landowners and junior officers, he deposed Tawfik and declared an end to the dual controllers.

Once more, France, which was bumbling through its own domestic crisis (the Boulanger Affair), was unable to respond. Protection of imperial interests was left to the British. On June 11, 1882, a dispute in Alexandria between a Maltese British subject and an Egyptian donkey driver resulted in a riot with more than 100 Christians slain. Within the month, the British sent warships to Alexandria, ostensibly to conduct maneuvers with the French. As more foreigners were attacked in the city, the British demanded that the Urabi government refrain from strengthening coastal defenses. On July 10, the fleet laid down a 10-hour bombardment and two days later marines occupied Alexandria. The actual conquest of Egypt was not accomplished until September 13, 1882. Then, General Garnet Wolseley sailed with 20,000 soldiers to Port Said and made a strike against Urabi's camp at Tell el-Kebir. In the nighttime rout, thousands of Egyptians were bayoneted. Urabi was arrested and exiled to Ceylon. Tawfik was restored to the khedivate and for the next 50 years real authority in the Egyptian protectorate was exercised by the British ambassador, euphemistically known as "the British Agent."[5]

Muhammad Ahmed, the Mahdi

About the same time Ahmed Urabi was staging his unsuccessful coup, another Muslim leader attempted to purge foreign influences from the Sudan. In December 1881, Muhammad Ahmed, the son of a Nile boat builder, proclaimed himself the Mahdi, that Shiite figure who promised to return one day to purify the world. An ascetic from Kordofan, Muhammad Ahmed gathered about him more than 200,000 followers. According to Quranic law, thieves were punished with the loss of a hand or foot. People who drank alcoholic beverages, smoked tobacco, or engaged in dancing were flogged. In this society, all men supposedly were equal and were to dress after the fashion of the Mahdi, who wore a simple woolen *jibbeh*.

In point of fact, all men were equal, with the exception of the Mahdi, whose word was to be obeyed on pain of death. All men were to live simply except the Mahdi who, dressed in linen and silk, reclined on cushions of gold brocade while slaves cooled him with ostrich feathers or rubbed incense into his feet. People fought to drink the wash water of this messiah, who had his choice of any female past the age of five. This movement, which screeched the sanctity of freedom, was steeped in the tradition of chattel slavery. Muhammad Ahmed might have played out his life as a minor shaykh but for the efforts of Charles "Chinese" Gordon, a British officer who with Egyptian troops stopped the Sudanese slave trade between 1874 and 1879.

By March 1884, the Mahdist forces, were strong enough to isolate Khartoum. Gordon, who had been sent back to the Sudanese capital by Prime Minister Gladstone to conduct an orderly withdrawal, decided against a retreat. He also refused to surrender to what he termed "a feeble lot of stinking dervishes." As the siege of Khartoum continued, Britain's Parliament debated the merits of sending reinforcements. In September, Gladstone yielded to pressure from Queen Victoria and authorized a relief mission. That force was only a few miles from Khartoum when on January 281, 1885, the Mahdi's army broke through the mud ramparts near the Nile and overran the city. Thousands were massacred, including Gordon, whose beheaded body bore traces of 1000 stab wounds.

Muhammad Ahmed did not enjoy the fruits of victory for long. Five months later, in June 1885, he died, the victim of a life of dissolution. His dream of conquest of Egypt, then the world, was taken up by his successor Abdullahi, known as the khalifa. The khalifa had to deal with rivals among the Mahdi's inner circle who disputed the messianic mantle. There was also the matter of a Christian monarch in neighboring Ethiopia that required a jihad in 1889. Bad weather and famine caused food shortages between 1889 and 1892. And the question of racial differences between blacks in the Bahr al-Ghazal and Kordofan Arabs surfaced repeatedly after the Mahdi's death.

Finally, in 1896 the khalifa felt secure enough to move against Egypt proper. But the passing decade had enabled the British to strengthen their positions with railway lines, forts, and better-trained troops. The *sirdar* (commander) of the khedive's forces was Horatio Herbert Kitchener, a no-nonsense imperialist who appreciated the value of the Maxim machine gun. In a methodical campaign that saw the khalifa's forces annihilated at Firket and Atbara, the British and their Egyptian allies moved into position outside the Mahdist capital of Omdurman. There, on September 2, 1898, 50,000 Arabs and Nilotic Sudanese, believing incantations would protect them from bullets, charged Kitchener's lines. In a matter of minutes, the fight was over. The Muslims lost 11,000 dead and 16,000 wounded, the British 48 dead, 382 wounded. Although the khalifa remained at large for more than a year, the Mahdist movement was effectively silenced. Sudan would be governed as an extension of Egypt (the so-called Anglo-Egyptian Sudan) to 1956. Of Omdurman, General Kitchener observed, the British had given the enemy "a good dusting."[6]

The Philosophy Behind Arab Nationalism

It would take more than Abdullahi or Ahmed Urabi to mobilize Damascenes and Cairenes. Arabs had to be reminded what it was that once made theirs *the* dynamic culture in the world. Ironically, that ideological foundation was supplied in the 19th century by missionaries and educators from the United States.

Americans were not the first to express a paternalistic interest in the Levant. The French built railroads, ports and harbors in Syria-Lebanon. This was the region with the largest concentration of Christians. Its silk and tobacco trade was directed westward, its people considered the most sophisticated in the Middle East. Since the time of the Crusades, French religious orders (Jesuits, Marians, Dominicans, Franciscans, Trappists, and Benedictines) operated colleges and hospices. A Lazarist school for boys at Aintura flourished between 1728 and 1773 and was reopened in 1834.

The year 1834 was a year of many important events. It was the year that Mehemet Ali's son Ibrahim decreed compulsory primary education. It was the year that the first Arabic printing press was brought to Beirut from Malta by the American Presbyterian Missionary Society, which was in direct competition with the Roman Catholics. It was the year that Eli Smith opened a school for girls in Beirut. Smith was assisted by Dr. Antoine Clot, a medical aide to Mehemet Ali, Dr. Cornelius Van Dyck of Jefferson Medical School, and the Reverend Daniel Bliss, who served as president of the Syrian Protestant College, later known as the American University of Beirut. Within 25 years, these men helped create 33 schools with 1000 students.

The American presence prompted sages at the al-Azhar to open a traditional college in Beirut as a reaction against this new presence. But it also served as a catalyst for political action among Arab intellectuals. The first of these were Christian Lebanese. Nasif Yazeji (1800–71) was a small-town bureaucrat who vowed never to speak a language other than Arabic. Combing remote monasteries, he copied rare manuscripts and developed books on grammar and logic that were used in American missionary schools.

Another Christian, Butrus Bustani (1819–83), who studied with Smith and Van Dyck, was fluent in eight languages. Bustani was responsible for a two-volume dictionary of Arabic in 1870, another six-volume encyclopedia of Arabic culture. Following a series of bloody sectarian riots that left 11,000 Christians dead in Damascus in 1860, Bustani founded the first political weekly in Beirut. In 1863 he established his own nationalist school, stressing "patriotism as an article of faith." By the end of the century, a third Christian (Najib Azuri, onetime deputy governor of Jerusalem) concluding it was impossible for Arabs to remain tied to the Ottomans, urged a separation into two states—a northern, secular one of Turks, and a southern territory ruled by an Arab caliph.

Such ideas appealed to Muslim Arab ideologues. Abdul Rahman Kawakebi (1849–1903) was a talented journalist from Aleppo. A critic of Turkish decadence and weakness, he traveled through Egypt, East Africa and the Hejaz calling for a separation from the Ottomans. In the first of two books, *Umm al Qura*, published anonymously in Egypt, Kawakebi wrote of a gathering of 22 fictitious scholars. Islam could only be regenerated with the selection of a descendant of the Quraysh as caliph in a Mecca. Once Muslims rejected obscurantism and tyranny, Arab greatness would be restored. Kawakebi would pay for his teachings by serving 10 years in a Turkish prison.[7]

Sayyed Jamaluddin al-Afghani (1839–97) shared Kawakebi's fate. An Afghan Muslim who opposed Great Britain's intervention in his country, Jamaluddin was expelled to Istanbul in 1868. Three years later, the Turks chased him to Cairo. Then, in 1879, he was again ousted for political reasons and wandered to India, England and France before returning to Istanbul, where he spent the last five years of his life virtually under house arrest. Before that capitulation, however, al-Afghani earned a reputation as the greatest pan-Islamic polemicist. His sole published book, *The Refutation of the Materialists,* was a rejoinder to the French historian Renan who, viewing the low state of Arabs in his world, had said Islam was the incurable enemy of reason. For al-Afghani, not Christianity, but Islam was the religion of reason. Muslims understood that the first duty of the Quran was to spread knowledge, that there was no incompatibility between science and religion, that even Darwinism could be reconciled with Quranic teachings of the origins of man. Where men had failed was in their interpretation of the Quran. *Taqlid* (conformity) operated everywhere, in government as well as religion. For al-Afghani, the answer was in the democratic principle of the *shura*. Let representatives responsible to the people interpret the laws. Let the people express themselves freely through multiple parties and constitutions. If corrupt mullahs, monarchs, or assemblies did not accede to the wishes of the masses, then al-Afghani urged the people to engage in tyrannicide or revolution.[8]

With the help of American missionaries in 1847, Yazeji and Bustani formed the first Arab Society of Arts and Sciences in Beirut. Three years later the Jesuits organized their own Oriental Society and in 1857 Christian Arabs created *al-Jamiya al-Ilmiya al-Suriya* (the Syrian Scientific Society). When these groups were suppressed in 1875, the first Arab secret society calling for outright independence was organized by five men at the Syrian Protestant College.

Believing the rhetoric of the Young Turks, Arabs supported the revolution in 1908 and 1909. A host of organizations—*al-Arabi al-Uthmani al-Ilkha* (The Ottoman Arab Fraternity), *al-Muntada al-Adabi* (the Literary Club), *Hirzb al-Lamarkaziya al-Idariya al-Uthmani* (Ottoman Decentratization Party)—advocated religious freedom, autonomy and proportional representation in the Ottoman Parliament. Instead, Arab activists were arrested or exiled, their organizations driven underground. They reconstituted themselves *al-Qahtaniya* (after one of the Arabs' legendary ancestors), *al-Fatat* (Youth), and *al-Ahd* (the covenant). Their program basically amounted to a call for *Ausgleich* on the order of Austria-Hungary. The Arabs demanded decentralization in every Arab province, limitation of military service to the Arabian peninsula save in extraordinary circumstances, recognition of Arabic as an official language, and extensive economic reforms. The Young Turks found these terms unacceptable.[9]

Perhaps the most charismatic leader of the new generation of Arab nationalists was a young Egyptian army officer, Major Aziz Ali al-Misri (b.1880). A veteran of campaigns in Yemen and Libya, early in 1914 Aziz Ali promoted a conspiracy to establish an Arab regime in North Africa. Arrested and tried en camera by the British, he was sentenced to death. General Kitchener, bowing to threats of massacre if Aziz Ali were harmed, ordered the death sentence revoked and the major exiled on April 21. Aziz Ali would return to promote Axis collaboration in World War II.[10]

The Pledge That Was Not a Pledge

On July 14, 1915, the British agent in Cairo Sir Henry McMahon received a communiqué from Hussein ibn Ali, sherif of Mecca, that expressed the aspirations of the submerged Arab nation. In this Damascus Protocol, Hussein called upon the British to recognize his dominion over Palestine (including Jordan), Lebanon, Syria, Mesopotamia, and all of Arabia with the exception of Aden. In return, the new Arab state would withdraw its support from the Ottoman Empire and accord Great Britain strategic and economic privileges. There followed, through January 1916, an exchange of eight diplomatic notes. In the eyes of the Arabs, the Hussein-McMahon correspondence constituted a British commitment to self-determination in the territories designated in the Damascus Protocol.

The proposal was not totally unexpected. Before the outbreak of the First World War in February 1914, one of Hussein's sons, Abdullah, initiated contact with General Kitchener, pointing out the advantages of submarine bases in the Hejaz. For their part, the British recognized the tenuous nature of supply lines through the Suez Canal. Twenty million Arabs serving as cannon fodder for the Turks might disrupt the flow of oil. Muslim leaders in the Middle East might encourage co-religionists in India to join their jihad against the democracies. Much better it would be to reward Arabs grousing under Turkish rule to become allies of Great Britain. In September 1914, Kitchener responded to Adbullah's overture, suggesting that the British might welcome "an Arab of truth" assuming the caliphate in Mecca, so that "good may come out of all this evil."[11]

Neither Hussein nor McMahon should have been misled about the other's capacity to assure promises. McMahon was a cautious, even timid, individual who had never been authorized by London to alienate a region vital to its interests, let alone those of a close ally, the French. Concurrent with negotiations with Hussein, the British were drafting a blueprint with the French outlining postwar domination in the Middle East. This Sykes-Picot Treaty called for European spheres of influence in the very territories promised Hussein. Yet, there was no outcry against British duplicity made by Hussein when the terms of this treaty were made public in April 1916.

The British never had any illusions about the man with whom they were dealing. Hussein ibn Ali only controlled the Hejaz, with a population of 600,000 Arabs. Within Arabia itself, he enjoyed little prestige among the shaykhs of Kuwait, ibn Saud of the Nejd, the amirs of Muscat, Muhammarah, or Asir. As late as December 1913, he was not even listed as among figures invited to a congress of Arab notables. Hussein was, as Imam Yahya of

Yemen declared, "a piece of vileness left by the Turks in Mecca." Appointed guardian of the Holy Places of Islam in 1908, Hussein owed his selection over the better qualified Ali Haydar of the Dahawu-Zayd clan to his very mediocrity. During the 18 months he was negotiating "in good faith" with the British, the sherif promised the Turks that he would raise an Arab legion of 70,000 men, sent his son Faisal to Istanbul to pledge undying fealty, accepted subsidies from the Germans in exchange for naval bases and radio stations along the Red Sea. It is doubtful that Hussein would have approached the British at all had the Turks not extended the Hejaz railroad to Medina—an act designed to facilitate pilgrimage traffic, but one that the sherif construed as unfriendly.

After the war, and especially at a major conference held in London in January 1939, the Arabs would claim they had been deprived of their rightful patrimony in several areas, notably Lebanon and Palestine. In actuality, McMahon's first letter to Hussein on August 30, 1915, taking note of French interests in the region, warned against "premature" promises of independence. Later, on October 24, the British declared that "portions of Syria lying to the west of the districts of Damascus, Homs, Hama and Aleppo cannot be said to be purely Arab and should be excluded from the limits demanded." While Hussein protested that the vilayets of Aleppo and Beirut were purely Arab, on February 18, 1916, he assented to the British reservations.

Arab nationalists were incensed that Palestine was excluded from lands to be granted independence. British diplomats issued statements clarifying what they had meant, what they thought the Arabs understood, why they had not mentioned Palestine by name, the importance of rail lines, and other convoluted explanations. There was also some confusion between the parties over the exact meaning of administrative terms. In November 1915, Hussein himself referred to the vilayet of Mersin (there was no such Turkish province) when he meant district. At that time, there was no legal territory known as Palestine. As late as July 1919, a congress of Arab leaders in Damascus were insisting that the region should be known as Southern Syria. Under the Ottomans, the Holy Land consisted of the vilayet of Beirut extending through the Sanjaks of Acre and Nablus to Jaffa and the independent sanjak of Jerusalem, which was joined to the vilayet of Syria. By his subsequent silence when the British issued the Balfour Declaration, Hussein conceded the rest.[12]

The Revolt in the Desert: Lawrence of Arabia

Still, the Arabs would claim that they offered the necessary consideration to force execution of a pledge of independence for all territories, including Palestine. Through the so-called Revolt in the Desert, under the direction of Captain T. E. Lawrence, the Arabs rendered invaluable assistance to General Allenby in his campaigns of 1917 and 1918, thereby shortening the war in the Middle East. Maybe, maybe not. Of these sporadic attacks Pierre Van Paassen once wrote: "The revolt in the desert may have been the most hilarious, whacking, yelling, bubbling, colorful, gun-firing Fourth of July jamboree that ever moved through the wilderness, but ... its military value had been well-nigh zero."[13] Van Paassen continued: "After two years of shouting, riding, and quarrelling in the course of which the throats of some isolated Turkish patrols were cut, the tribesmen did not have to their credit the capture of a single place that the Turks decided to hold and defend."[14]

Officially, the Arab Revolt began on June 5, 1916, when Hussein, acting upon British promises, issued a *fetva* in Mecca deposing the Ottoman caliph and proclaiming the independence of his Arab state. Thousands of tribesmen rallied to his cause, receiving rifles and a monthly stipend from the British. Hussein's forces seized Mecca, Taif, Jidda, and a few minor ports like Rabegh and Yanbo, less major setbacks than irritants to the Ottoman war effort. By September, the novelty of war had worn off and desertions riddled the ranks of the Hejazi Arabs. In Cairo, the group of experts commanded by Brigadier General Gilbert Clayton assigned a young officer the task of rekindling the revolt.

Thomas Edward Lawrence (1888–1935) was the illegitimate son of an Irish baron. A short man (5'6") who bore little similarity to the actor who portrayed him in Hollywood's epic (6'2" Peter O'Toole), Lawrence was a complex man. Educated at Oxford, he proved a talented linguist and archaeologist in the pre-war years. Because of a unique ability to relate to workmen, Lawrence was selected to restart the Arab revolt. A true imperialist, a Francophobe, Lawrence had no affection for either an Arab state or the Hejazis. A propagandist with a flair for exaggeration, if not outright lying, he once claimed to have read all the books in the Oxford Union by going through six per day for six years. (Elsewhere, he offered four embellished versions of a tale of shooting, bandaging and befriending an Arab intruder into his camp at night.) Less than competent in military affairs, on one occasion he misplaced $146,000 in subsidies. Another time, while leading a camel charge, he shot his own beast in the head and was catapulted into the enemy's trenches. And in November 1917, while on a mission to Deraa at the Syrian-Jordan border, he was captured and abused by the Turks.

Lawrence's first objective was to disrupt communication from Jordan to the Turkish garrison which held Medina until January 1919. At one point in his 700-page *Seven Pillars of Wisdom*, he claims that *his* forces blew up 79 bridges along the Hejaz Railway.[15] Because of these attacks, the Turks supposedly diverted 15,000 men to guard the line. In another spot in his memoir, however, Lawrence notes the sense of futility that confronted him during every operation. From behind a ridge, he would watch as a dynamite explosion derailed a train. His troops would rush forward, shooting and looting. Afterward, they could not be found for days. The effectiveness of this railroad campaign was brought into question when David Lean, scouring the region for site locations for his film in 1964, discovered the tracks virtually unscathed.

Each of Lawrence's vaunted triumphs was tainted. His forces greatly outnumbered the few Turks at Wejh. No more than 30 Turks defended the Taggart forts at Mriegha and Waheida, perhaps 50 were squeezed in the two stone buildings at Atwi facing 3000 Arabs. A victory at Ghadir el-Haj, south of Maan, early in 1918, was achieved over a small desert patrol guarding 2000 sick baggage camels. The Arabs played no role in the repulse of the Turks from Suez or in Allenby's capture of Gaza, Jerusalem, Megiddo, Jericho, or Amman. With the exception of Aqaba, their sole claimed conquest was of Damascus, taken during the first days of October 1918. As the Turkish army disintegrated before the British, Lawrence persuaded the Australian General Chavel to permit Faisal to make a symbolic first entry into the Syrian capital.

Lawrence conceded that the Revolt in the Desert was "a sideshow of a sideshow." Brigadier General Guy Dawney seconded that assessment, saying, "To claim that these spasmodic and comparatively trifling efforts had any serious bearing on the war with Turkey, let alone the greater war beyond, is absurd." Richard Aldington is even more blistering toward Lawrence's "overwritten, self-conscious" memoirs. The "Arab Army," says Aldington, failed to make the slightest interruption of the main line of Turkish rail communication, nor was it capable, after Aqaba, of storming a town held by the Turks. "All this bravura of desert heroes and flaring about on camels had resulted in what? The wrecking of a train with few Turkish casualties." Concludes Aldington:

Indeed the whole objection to the "Arab War" as expounded by Lawrence after Akaba is simply that it was a political demonstration, that militarily its aid was negligible, while time and time again it failed to achieve what Lawrence promised. And one cannot escape the conviction that much of the "history" of the Arab war was simply political propaganda designed to prove that "the Arabs" had captured certain areas and towns and therefore were obliged under "British promises" to be ruled by Lawrence's friend Feisal independently though perhaps not unsubsidized, though in fact all the real work was done by English, Scottish, Anzac and Indian troops.[16]

When the war ended, 5000 heavily subsidized Arabs were still in the ranks of the Allies. Perhaps they had killed 5000 and captured 8000 of the enemy.[17] To the end, their loyalties and those of their leaders— like Auda Abu Tayeh, the hawknosed desert chief who assisted at Aqaba while still receiving money from the Turks, and Faisal who in April 1918, informed Jemal Pasha that the Arabs would break their alliance with the British for a larger sum — were negotiable. Yet it was the same Faisal who would travel to the Peace Conference at Versailles the following winter, demanding fulfillment of pledges given his father on the basis of Arab sacrifices made during the Revolt in the Desert. At Versailles, Arab nationalists would discover the full extent of contradictory promises made by the Allies.

26

Political Zionism

The Versailles Peace Conference

No more disparate group could be imagined than the peacemakers who convened at Louis XIV's country palace in January 1919. They came from all over the globe — Japanese, French, Chinese, English, Italians, Greeks, Americans— each with their own agendas and few showing a willingness to compromise. The babel of tongues was compounded by the presence of delegations claiming to represent Arabs, Koreans, Khirgiz, Kurds, Armenians, Vietnamese and Jews, all hoping to achieve Woodrow Wilson's promise of self-determination.[1]

The Arabs, led by the Emir Faisal, were armed with what they considered ironclad guarantees of independence. There was the 12th point in President Wilson's Fourteen Points declaring that all nationalities within the Ottoman Empire be given "an undoubted security of life and an absolute unmolested opportunity of development." There was the Hussein-McMahon correspondence and the resulting Revolt in the Desert. Britain and France reaffirmed the promise of establishing "indigenous governments" in the Middle East in a declaration to seven Syrian leaders on June 16, 1918 and again on November 7, 1918.

What the Arabs did not understand was that neither Britain nor France had any intention of divesting control of an area that was crucial in postwar geopolitics. Under terms of the Sykes-Picot Agreement, any postwar settlement would cede Britain an arc of land including northern Palestine, present-day Jordan, and Mesopotamia. France would receive Lebanon and Syria into Iraq. Tsarist Russia's dream of controlling the Straits and the Black Sea would also be satisfied. As for Palestine, the Holy Land, listed in official documents as the "Brown Zone," would be governed under an international condominium.

Sykes-Picot was a classic example of Allied duplicity. Signed on April 26, 1916, while the British were negotiating with Sherif Hussein of Mecca, the treaty came as no surprise to the Arabs, who learned of its contents following the Bolshevik revolution of 1917. A basic policy of the British during the First World War was to promise the same thing to more than one ally. The treaties of London in 1915 and St. Jean de Maurienne in 1917 contained contradictions as far as Turkish land masses. With respect to Palestine, however, one betrayal was not enough.

Birth of Political Zionism

For 1800 years, Jews lived in exile, subject to massacre and expulsion. American and French Revolutions raised hopes that biblical ideals of justice and equality might be extended to them. Some Jews, like Ludwig Börne and Heinrich Heine in Germany, Judah Leib Gordon in Russia, and Isaac Mayer Wise in the U.S., sensing the dawn of an age of brotherhood, advocated assimilation, blending into the greater national culture. This meant a renunciation of Zionism, reduction of Jewishness to a religion. Other visionaries regarded the new freedom as an opportunity to fulfill Zionist dreams. In 1834, Rabbi Yehudah Alkalai called for a tithe from Jews around the world in order to purchase land for the "Great Assembly" of Jews who would return to Palestine. Twenty-five years later, Rabbi Zvi Kalischer from Posen agreed that a society funded by philanthropists should encourage Jewish emigration to the Holy Land.

Perhaps the most articulate statement on Jewish self-determination in that early period came from German-born Moses Hess. A onetime Marxist and an internationalist, Hess returned to his people when revolutionary slogans were not matched with deeds of kindness. Writing in *Rome and Jerusalem* (1862), Hess noted massacres that occurred at Damascus in 1840 and the Rhineland in 1848. He charged that bigotry was endemic, though not limited, to Germany. Warned Hess: "The old framework of European society, battered so often by storms of revolution, is cracking and groaning on all sides. It can no longer stand the storm."[2]

Within a few years, Hess was proven correct. Fifty thousand Jews perished in state-organized pogroms that ravaged 167 communities and left 100,000 families beggared in Tsarist Russia in 1881 and 1882. Assimilationists like Moses Lilienblum now agreed with Hess and the younger scholar Peretz Smolenskin that Jews were an eternal people, bound by 4000 years of religion and history. In the wake of renewed assaults, Jewish students calling themselves BILU (an acronym for "House of Jacob Let Us Go") attempted to settle in Palestine. Other intellectuals rallied to the banner of *Choveve Zion* (Lovers of Zion).[3]

In 1882, at the height of the Russian pogroms, Leon Pinsker proclaimed the failure of assimilation in a 30-page pamphlet with the self-explanatory title *Auto-Emancipation*. A physician/lawyer from Odessa, Pinsker found few positives in Christian-Jewish relations. Jews were treated like a shuttlecock, tossed from one land to another. Such dehumanization could only be compared with that of black slaves and women. But Jews were especially hated, in part because the Jews remained a spectral people without a land. The hatred was also pathological. Argued Doctor Pinsker: "Judaeophobia is a psychic aberration. As a psychic aberration it is hereditary, and as a disease transmitted for two thousand years it is incurable."[4]

In November 1884, Dr. Pinsker was named chairman of an international conference that met in Upper Silesia. This conference, which hoped to impress the world with the urgency of the Jews' plight, took place in Kattowice, just a few miles from Oswiecim — a Silesian town that would gain infamy in the 20th century as Auschwitz. Thirty-five delegates from Russia, Rumania, Germany and England, representatives of Choveve Zion, came together to endorse Pinsker's program of a national congress, a stock company, and Palestine land purchases. Pinsker died in 1891, just a few years before Theodor Herzl transformed the Zionist movement into a viable political force.

Theodor Herzl

In *Der Judenstaat,* his 1896 work that served as the manual for modern Zionism, Theodor Herzl suggests that if a people is endangered, a *negotiorum gestio* — a person acting on behalf of affairs not strictly his own — may intercede. For the Jewish people, exposed and powerless at the end of the 19th century, Theodor Herzl was that gestor. No less likely champion could be imagined.[5]

Born to a liberal Jewish family in Budapest in 1860, young Herzl received a basic training in Judaism (Sabbath services, some Hebrew, bar mitzvah). In 1878, his family moved to Vienna, one of the most anti–Semitic cities in Europe and a town where Herzl grew accustomed to hearing the cry "*Saujud*" (Jewish pig). Six years later (1884) Herzl earned a degree in law. His interest, however, lay in writing, where he earned acclaim for plays and short stories. Although Herzl married in 1889, the union was a stormy one and just two years after the wedding he welcomed the opportunity to go off to Paris as correspondent of *Die Neue Freie Presse.*

Much has been made of Herzl's impressions of France, the street life and cabarets, the free spirit of artists and striking workers. Yet bawdy, republican France was groping with its own inexperience with democracy. Newspapers exposed corruption in government and the defunct Panama Canal Company, stressing the prominence of Jewish bankers in these scandals. One journal, Eduard Drumont's *La Libre Parole,* was especially venomous in its denunciations of Jews who comprised less than percent of the French population. On November 1, 1894, Drumont's paper bannered "Jewish Traitor Under Arrest." Captain Alfred Dreyfus, the only Jew on the French military staff, had been arrested and charged with relaying secrets to the hated Germans. For the next decade, the Dreyfus Affair rent the unstable republic from within.[6]

Historians debate how all of this may have affected Herzl. His disillusionment with France was clear when he wrote: "In France, in republican, modern, civilized France, a hundred years after the Declaration of the Rights of Man. Until that time most of us believed that the solution of the Jewish question was to be patiently waited for as part of the general development of mankind. But when a people which is in every other respect so progressive and so highly civilized can take such a turn, what are we to expect from other peoples which have not attained the level France attained a hundred years ago?"[7]

Where Alkalai, Kalischer, Pinsker and others had written of the need for philanthropists to volunteer sums for a Jewish haven, Herzl decided to confront the millionaires directly. In June 1895, he had an audience with railroad magnate Baron Maurice de Hirsch. The latter had already contributed more than $40 million to the Jewish Colonization Society, whose goal it was to transform Jewish immigrants in Argentina into farmers. The meeting did not go well from the moment Herzl reproached de Hirsch for breeding beggars. When Herzl spoke glowingly of the intellectual potential of a free Jewish people, de Hirsch, fearful of an anti–Semitic backlash, terminated the conversation with a quip, "We have too many brains."[8]

De Hirsch died in 1896, so Herzl turned his attention to the philanthropist who was committed to Jewish colonization in Palestine — Baron Edmund Rothschild. In July of that year, Rothschild agreed to a meeting. Accompanied by two bodyguards, he listened as Herzl outlined a scheme for mass migration of Jews to the Holy Land. For the sum of 10 million marks, Rothschild could serve as the "Doge" of a republic modeled along the lines of medieval Venice. After listening to the proposal, Rothschild asked how Herzl would control 150,000 schnorrers. How prevent "unfortunate incidents"? How obtain guarantees from the Turks? Admonished the baron: "One must not have eyes bigger than one's stomach." To which Herzl rejoined in his diary: "The house of Rothschild is a national misfortune."[9]

Undaunted, Herzl decided to assemble Jewish leaders from all over the globe. Such a gathering would be a first of its kind since Napoleon convened a European Sanhedrin in 1807. With his trusted aides—Dr. Max Nordau, a Paris physician, and David Wolffsohn, a merchant from Cologne—Herzl issued a call for this first Zionist Congress. The program for this Congress was already outlined in his pamphlet, *Der Judenstaat.*

Der Judenstaat

This 96-page pamphlet was published in February 1896, when Herzl still hoped to win favor of the major Jewish philanthropists. It was no remarkable breakthrough in scholarship; Chaim Weizmann once remarked of *Der Judenstaat*, "Fundamentally [it] contained not one single new idea for us." Herzl began by ploughing familiar ground—the universal nature of anti–Semitism. Wherever there were Jews, they were despised—by religious zealots for allegedly having killed Christ, by a competitive bourgeoisie, and by an ignorant peasant class. Assimilation and intermarriage had failed. Said Herzl, "We are a people— one people" whose enemies wanted them out of Europe.[10]

To solve this Jewish question, Herzl proposed that the Jews purchase a piece of land, preferably in Palestine. Toward that end, he envisioned the creation of a Jewish Society, possibly headquartered in London, that was to amass £50 million from private subscription and bank loans. A second agency, the Jewish Company, would then negotiate for a cession from the Ottoman Turks. All of this would be done legally, since territory could no longer be seized as 500 years before. The Jewish Company would liquidate Jewish holdings in Europe and transport Jews to the Holy Land. Those Jews who emigrated would have their dignity restored. Those who remained would profit from a reduction in anti–Semitism.[11]

While personally favoring "democratic monarchy" or "an aristocratic republic," Herzl called upon the Jewish Society to summon a council of state jurists to devise the best possible constitution. No theocracy, "above and before all we shall make room for the immortal band of our freethinkers, who are continually making new conquests for humanity."[12] Priests and rabbis would be kept within the confines of their temples "in the same way as we shall keep our professional army within the confines of their barracks."[13] Noting the absence of toleration in Europe, Herzl urged: "Every man will be as free and undisturbed in his faith or his disbelief as he is in his nationality. And if it should occur that men of other creeds and different nationalities come to live amongst us, we should accord them honorable protection and equality before the law."[14]

Herzl glossed over the details of mass migration of Jews to Palestine in *Der Judenstaat.* But in his diaries and a later novel, *Altneuland* (1899), he offered elaboration. The people were to come as communities, from Ukrainian shtetls and Rhenish ghettos, with their neighbors and rabbis to minimize homesickness. They were to travel abroad ocean liners specially outfitted with bands of entertainers and singers. There would even be "coffin ships" to bring the Jewish dead back home.

Once in the old-new land, the government would act to ensure that "no member of the Jewish State will be oppressed, every man will be able and will wish to rise in it." Although Herzl favored Yiddish as a common language, he believed that Jews could retain their native dialects and/or Hebrew, much like multi-lingual Switzerland. Land, which

belonged to all the people, would be distributed to the poor. Cities, linked by modern rail-
ways, would be planned about parks and gardens with detached homes, not tenements.
Electricity for the cities and irrigation water for farming would come from power stations
and dams tapping into a Mediterranean-Dead Sea Canal. The state would provide vocational training, full employment, free education, sick benefits, life insurance, retirement
homes for all, and ask in return two years of public service. Jews were to do all the labor
in this society, where women were to enjoy absolute equal rights and from which profiteers
were expelled. At a time when American miners, steelers, and seamstresses fought to have
their hours reduced from 12 or 14 to 8, Herzl advocated a seven-hour working day and even
incorporated the concept into a national flag in the form of seven Stars of David.[15]

The World Zionist Congress

Herzl's was a bold, progressive program. And yet he was lampooned as a Jewish Jules
Verne, another Sabbatai Zevi, a chimera. All kinds of objections were offered to his proposal for a Zionist Congress in Munich. Herzl was compared with Mordecai Noah, an
American Jew who in 1825 tried to entice Jews to Grand Island near Buffalo. Where was it
written, inquired Orthodox Jews, that a 36-year-old Viennese should be the messiah? Why,
asked American Reform rabbis, encourage anti–Semites who believed in an international
Jewish conspiracy? Why, asked the Jews of Munich, did Herzl have to choose their city,
thereby drawing into question Jewish loyalties? With Jewish millionaires cool, the clergy
in London and Vienna opposed, Herzl and his colleagues now managed to secure a new
site for August 29, 1897 — the Opera House in Basel, Switzerland.

Two hundred ninety-four delegates, including 15 women with voting rights, attended
this meeting. In keeping with the solemn nature of the occasion, delegates wore formal
attire. Doorways were draped with biblical colors, blue and white, the same colors that were
integrated in the flag of the Zionist movement. The Congress selected a poem by Naphtali
Herz Imber, *Hatikvah* (The Hope) as the anthem of the Jewish people. Herzl, apprehen-
sive about balancing so many "eggs" (the ego of Rothschild, his newspaper job, the tenuous status of Jewish communities in Eastern Europe, opposition from assimilationists),
accepted the presidency of the World Zionist Organization.[16]

After heated debates among socialists and cultural Zionists, the delegates agreed upon
three essential points: (a) Zionism sought a publicly recognized, legally secured home for
the Jewish people in Palestine; (b) it encouraged settlement of Jewish agricultural workers, laborers, and artisans; and (c) it hoped to strengthen Jewish self-awareness and national
consciousness. The platform adopted at Basel was essentially Herzl's. As he declared: "At
Basel, I created the Jewish State."[17]

Herzl's Last Years

Herzl devoted his energies to winning approval for the Zionist scheme from every possible source. Somehow, he would have to gain influence with the Ottoman sultan Abdul
Hamid, the despot who would not be receptive to cutting off another important chunk of
his empire. Herzl sounded out King Milan of Serbia, Prince Ferdinand of Bulgaria, Victor
Immanuel III of Italy, the Austrian foreign minister, and volunteered medical assistance to
the Turks in their losing war with Greece in 1898, all to no avail.

Then, in October 1898, Herzl obtained an audience with the one European leader who might influence the sultan — Kaiser Wilhelm II of Germany. This meeting, arranged by two Zionist sympathizers, William Hechler (chaplain of the British legation at Vienna) and Philip zu Eulenburg (grand duke of Baden), took place at the Yildiz Kiosk in Istanbul. The kaiser was making a pilgrimage to the Holy Land. Although Wilhelm and his aides punctuated their remarks with anti–Semitic asides (dismissing the Dreyfuss Affair as of little consequence, referring to pogroms as "this Russian thing," and quickly agreeing that Jews had "plenty of money"), Herzl was not dismayed. Instead, he rushed ahead to Palestine to prepare a reception for the German ruler.[18]

What followed on October 28, 1898, must go down as one of the most surrealistic moments in history. A few miles outside Jaffa, on the road to Jerusalem, at the entry to one of Lord Rothschild's colonies, Herzl and a group of Jewish children greeted the kaiser with a chorus of *Heil Dir im Siegerkranz* (the German national anthem). On November 2, the two men met again in Jerusalem to pour over maps Herzl had brought out with him, hoping to impress Wilhelm with the prospect of a German protectorate. At first, Herzl was encouraged by the Kaiser's attitude. As he jotted in his diary: "He didn't say yes, and he didn't say no." In fact, the Kaiser had no intention of championing Jewish nationalism. Instead, he told Abdul Hamid: "The Zionists are not dangerous to Turkey, but the Jews are everywhere a nuisance we should like to be rid of." Later, Herzl would express relief that Jews had not been enrolled under German protection, for "we would have had to pay a most usurious interest."[19]

Between 1899 and 1901, Herzl tried a direct approach to Abdul Hamid. A meeting with the sultan on May 17, 1901, arranged by Professor Armin Vamberry, a Jewish apostate to Islam, went rather well. For his part, Herzl promised to erase the billion-dollar Ottoman public debt. In return, Abdul Hamid awarded him the Grand Cordon of the Order of the Mejidje and a sampling of Turkish cigarettes. While Herzl appealed for funds from Nathan Rothschild, Sir Thomas Lipton, Cecil Rhodes, Andrew Carnegie, and the French Pereire family, Abdul Hamid privately confirmed he had no intention of alienating land that had been won by Turkish blood.[20]

In frustration, Herzl turned to Great Britain. Abdul Hamid's worst enemy, this imperialist nation seemed able to do what it wanted anywhere in the world. Besides, the concept of a Jewish state appealed to both the British government and the Jewish aristocracy, which were increasingly concerned about the mass of Jewish immigrants crowding London's East End. In October 1902, Herzl discussed the problem with Colonial Secretary Joseph Chamberlain. The British were unwilling to talk about Cyprus, Australia, or any other spot in the Empire "inhabited by white settlers." Chamberlain did approve a survey of the Sinai and El Arish that winter, a study strongly opposed by Lord Cromer in Egypt.[21]

At Easter 1903, a new wave of pogroms, sparked by the slaughter of 42 Jews in Kishinev, erupted in Eastern Europe. Desperately, Herzl sought what he called a *nachtasyl* (night haven) for his people. He appealed to Portugal for space in Mozambique. He asked the Belgians for the Congo, Italy for Tripoli, and he negotiated with the Russian ministers, Wenzel von Plehve and Serge Witte, promising mass emigration if they would control violence against the Jews. Against this background, in August 1903, Britain's Chamberlain made what he considered to be a humanitarian offer: the Jews could come to Uganda. In reality the Mau Mau escarpment of what currently is Kenya, the misidentified Uganda Plan split the Zionist movement. While Herzl approved of the idea, cultural Zionists agreed with Achad Ha-Am who said, "*lo zeh ha-Derech*" (that is not the way). In two meetings that year, the very Jews who were to benefit — Russian Jews led by Menachem Ussishkin — opposed the British offer.[22]

Herzl recanted his position in a letter dated November 11, 1903, where he wrote: "For me there is no other solution to the great problem which is called the Jewish problem other than Palestine." On January 26, 1904, Herzl met with Pope Pius X in Rome. Once more, he tried to impress a world leader with the plight of the Jews. To which Pius replied: "The Jews have not recognized our Lord, therefore we cannot recognize the Jewish people.... And so, if you come to Palestine and settle your people there, we will be ready with churches and priests to baptize all of you."[23]

Six months after this audience in the Vatican, Herzl would be dead. Worn down by his travels, suffering from pneumonia and heart problems, he died on July 3, 1904. At great personal cost, he had set in motion the process for the political rebirth of his people. Herzl foresaw the deterioration of Jewish-Christian relations in Europe ("Things cannot improve, but must get worse — until the massacres. Governments can no longer prevent it even if they wanted to.") He predicted the benefits of a new Jerusalem, a new state ("Let the craven, assimilated converted Jews remain behind. We will even benefit them — they will eventually boast of their kinship with us as now they blush at it.) And he encouraged the Jews: "If you will it, it is no dream."

The Yishuv

In the decade after Herzl's death, a steady stream of pioneers infiltrated the Holy Land. Known as the "Second Aliyah," this group was responsible for developing the "Yishuv" (Jewish settlement) in Palestine. The settlers followed the lead of Russian-born Eliezer ben Yehudah, who believed that Hebrew should become their daily parlance. More than 20 religious and technical schools were opened. Communities like Herzlia, Natanya and Nahalal came into existence and in 1909 a metropolis, Tel Aviv, began to take form along the sand dunes outside Jaffa. At the same time, the people, inspired by Aaron David Gordon and Nachman Syrkin, embraced a cooperative system of labor, for both farming and industry.[24]

In 1912, the first professional nurses were sent to Palestine at the urging of Henrietta Szold, the founder of Hadassah, the women's Zionist organization. Four years later, a larger unit of American volunteers arrived as the core of what would become *Mogen Dovid Adom*, the Jewish counterpart of the International Red Cross. Doctors and nurses operated out of clinics housed in shacks, treating patients without distinction to nationality or religion. From these rustic beginnings, there eventually grew a modern hospital atop Mt. Scopus and the *Kupat Holim* medical service. A score of diseases endemic to the Middle East — malaria, cholera, leishmaniasis, schistosomiasis — were eradicated. Infant mortality rates plummeted and the life expectancy for all inhabitants of Palestine nearly doubled as a result of Zionist efforts.[25]

Trumpeldor and Jabotinsky

There were 90,000 Jews in Palestine by 1914. Among the newly arrived immigrants from Eastern Europe were the Hebrew poet Chaim Bialik, future president of Israel Itzhak Ben Zvi, and David Green of Plonsk, who changed his name to Ben-Gurion. They were joined by Joseph Trumpeldor, a Jew who lost a hand in combat during the Russo-Japanese War of 1904 and 1905. Trumpeldor came to Degania in 1911 and impressed fellow kibbutzniks with his physical strength and ideological commitment. When the war broke out, he was among 7000 Jews expelled from Palestine as security risks. In a refugee camp outside Alexandria, Egypt, Trumpeldor met Vladimir Jabotinsky, another Russian émigré dedicated to the revival of a Jewish state. Together, they plotted to impress the British with an armed legion of Jewish volunteers that would liberate Palestine.[26]

The British were decidedly cool toward the creation of what Field Marshal Allenby termed "freakish regiments." The best they would allow was a unit of Jewish auxiliaries to supply regular troops with water and ammunition. Jabotinsky rejected the concept, but Trumpeldor accepted a commission in what came to be known as the Zion Mule Corps. In April 1915, 600 Muleteers shipped out with the fleet to Gallipoli. Six of their number were killed, 55 wounded (including Trumpeldor), and three Distinguished Conduct Medals awarded over the next seven months. Of their valor, General Ian Hamilton declared: "They toiled quietly with their mules under heavy fire, showing thus an even higher form of courage than is required of soldiers in the front, because they were not infected with the excitement of the fighting that enthuses the latter." Jabotinsky agreed, conceding his mistake: "Trumpeldor was right. Those 600 Muleteers actually opened up a new avenue in the development of Zionist possibilities. The Mule Corps reminded the world that Zionism was part of actuality."[27]

Another year and a half would follow before the British agreed in July 1917 to the creation of a legitimate Jewish legion. Nearly 11,000 men, including Ben-Gurion, Ben-Zvi, and Moshe Shertok, joined the Royal Fusiliers. Decorated with insignia that read "*Kadima*" (Forward), these troops participated in Allenby's attacks against Gaza, Lydda, Jerusalem, Jericho, es–Salt, and Damascus. They were part of a greater mass of Jews, including three Congressional Medal of Honor winners from the United States, who contributed to the Allied war effort. Ironically, Joseph Trumpeldor, the man most responsible for the arming of the Judaeans, was rejected for combat duty because of his disability.[28]

Chaim Weizmann

At the same time Jabotinsky and Trumpeldor were pressing Lord Denby for a Jewish fighting force, an equally important political struggle was taking place in the British cabinet. Already in 1915, Home Secretary Herbert Samuel circulated a memorandum proposing the annexation of Palestine and the creation of a Jewish state. The note caused a sensation in Jewish circles, many of whom opposed it for the same reasons they had opposed Herzl. The Orthodox wanted no part of a Jewish army or a British protectorate. Assimilated Jews like Lord Edwin Montagu (secretary of state for India), Lord Bertie (ambassador to France), and David Alexander of the Board of Deputies of British Jews raised objections based upon the old canard of double loyalties.

One Jew who worked ceaselessly to obtain a favorable statement from the British was Dr. Chaim Weizmann (1874–1952).[29] From Motl in western Russia, where his father imbued 15 children with a love of Zion, Weizmann obtained a doctorate in chemistry at the University of Freiburg in 1898. He met Theodor Herzl that same year, and debated Lenin, Trotsky and Plekhanov when he took a job in Geneva shortly thereafter. In 1904, Weizmann came to the University of Manchester where he was introduced to Zionist businessmen Simon Marks and Israel Sieff. He also met C. P. Snow, editor of the *Manchester Guardian*, Henry Wickham Steed of the *London Times*, and then prime minister Arthur Balfour. The last three were Gentile fundamentalists who believed that through reconstituting the Jewish national home they might hasten the second coming of Christ.[30]

Still, it is unlikely Weizmann would have made much headway with the government without making a substantial contribution to the British war effort. In the fall of 1914, the admiralty approached him to devise a method of synthesizing acetone, an ingredient vital to the production of cordite smokeless powder for naval shells. Previously, the compound has been obtained through the destructive distillation of wood, a process impaired by U-boat attacks upon Allied freighters. Weizmann solved the problem within a few months, using acorns.

Weizmann's work eased the munitions problems faced by the British and may in its own way be compared with the development of the Atom Bomb in World War II. Yet Herbert Samuel's proposal for a Jewish state languished in the cabinet two more years until other factors forced its release.

By November 1917, British casualties in the war numbered more than one million. Romania and Italy had been routed and the French were still clinging to trenches. The arrival of American troops at the front was still weeks away and would more than be outweighed by the capitulation of war-weary Russia. The British needed manpower, any kind of manpower. British politicians, including Minister David Lloyd-George, believed that Jews in America wielded such financial influence that they might expedite the shipment of troops. Perhaps, reasoned Whitehall, a pro–Zionist declaration might win favor with the new Bolshevik regime in Russia, which included a disparate number of born Jews. And if nothing else, such a statement ought to neutralize sympathies of Jewish populations on the continent, many of whom were serving in the armies of the Central Powers.

The Balfour Declaration

On November 2, 1917, British Foreign Secretary Arthur Balfour sent the following letter to Lord Walter Rothschild, scion of the banking house of Rothschild and president of the British Federation of Zionists:

> Dear Lord Rothschild, I have much pleasure in conveying to you, on behalf of His Majesty's Government, the following declaration of sympathy with Jewish Zionist aspirations which has been submitted to, and approved by, the Cabinet: "His Majesty's Government view with favour the establishment in Palestine of a national home for the Jewish people, and will use their best endeavours to facilitate the achievement of this object, it being clearly understood that nothing shall be done which may prejudice the civil and religious rights of existing non–Jewish communities in Palestine, or the rights and political status enjoyed by Jews in any other country." I should be grateful if you would bring this declaration to the knowledge of the Zionist Federation.[31]

This was no treaty between two sovereign peoples, merely a promise from a government not yet in possession of land to a people in dispersion. Despite statements of agreement promptly issued by the French and American governments, Balfour did not have the force of law when it was incorporated into the League of Nations Mandate for Palestine on July 24, 1922. The reference to a Jewish "national home," the term that Herzl had employed at Basel, was deliberately vague. Herzl intended the Jewish state to be a sovereign nation, but the British Cabinet in its debates and subsequent statements made it clear a "homeland" would be something different. The Zionist idea of *all* of Palestine being reconstituted as a Jewish national home was whittled away to *some* of Palestine.

With tears in his eyes, Lord Montagu demanded protection for Jews who did not want to associate themselves with the Zionist movement. There was equal solicitude for the more than 700,000 non-Jews resident in Ottoman Palestine, though no one could explain how their status could not but be altered by the arrival of large number of Jews. Finally, there was the British pledge to assist with the development of the Jewish homeland, a pledge that the imperialists never intended to honor.

Comité des Délégations Juives

As if all the wartime pledges did not complicate matters sufficiently, there were also two separate Jewish delegations at Versailles. The Assimilationists were represented by Ambassador Henry Morgenthau Sr., the champion of Armenian self-determination. When it came to Jews, Morgenthau was more timorous. He submitted a petition signed by prominent American Jews (the banker Jacob Schiff, Mayer Sulzberger of the *New York Times*, and Louis Marshall, head of the American Jewish Committee) warning of dangers arising from the creation of a Jewish state.

Most Jews favored the program carried to Versailles by the Comite des Delegations Juives. A multi-national group committed to making all of Palestine and parts of the Sinai into a Jewish state, the Comite included Chaim Weizmann, Leo Motzkin, Rabbi Stephen Wise, Harvard law professor Felix Frankfurter, and U.S. Supreme Court Justice Louis D. Brandeis. The participation of Brandeis was a major coup. Brandeis was the great reformer of the Progressive Era. Champion of unions in the bloody Homestead Strike of 1892 and the ILGWU Strike of 1910, author of the sociological brief in *Muller vs. Oregon* that ultimately paved the way for the end of racial segregation in America, Brandeis was won over to Zionism by Jacob de Haas, Herzl's onetime secretary, in 1912. Two years later, he accepted the chairmanship of the American Committee for General Zionist Affairs. It was Brandeis who drafted the Pittsburgh platform in May 1918, calling for political and civil equality, free education for all inhabitants of Palestine, public ownership of land and cooperative development of its resources. Brandeis headed up the Zionist Organization of America, with 190,000 members, until 1921.[32]

The Zionists had every reason to believe that their proposals would be favorably received at Versailles. As Wilson said to Frankfurter in May 1919: "I never dreamed that it was necessary to give you any renewed assurance of my adhesion to the Balfour Declaration, and so far I have found no one who is seriously opposing the purpose which it embodies." Shortly after, Britain's Lord Curzon declared: "Zionism, be it right or wrong, good or bad, is rooted in age-long traditions, in present needs, in future hopes, of far profounder import than the desires and prejudices of the 700,000 Arabs who now inhabit that ancient land."[33]

The Jewish Delegation also had reason to believe that a Semitic entente might be reached with the Arabs. At a December 1918 meeting with Weizmann arranged by Lawrence, the Emir Faisal stated: "No true Arab can be suspicious or afraid of Jewish nationalism. We are demanding Arab freedom and we would show ourselves unworthy of it if we did not now, as I do, say to the Jews—welcome back home and cooperate with them to the limit of the Arab state."[34] In another statement to Reuters, he declared: "Arabs are not jealous of Zionist Jews and intend to give them fair play." At Paris on March 1, 1919, Faisal wrote Frankfurter:

We Arabs, especially the educated among us, look with the deepest sympathy on the Zionist movement.... We will do our best in so far as we are concerned, to help them through; we will wish the Jews a most hearty welcome home.... We are working together for a reformed and revived Near East, and our two movements complete one another. The Jewish movement is national, and not imperialist; our movement is national and not imperialist, and there is room in Syria for both of us.[35]

Most significant was an agreement between the Arab spokesman at Versailles and Weizmann dated January 3, 1919. This nine-point document opens with a statement of goodwill. Affirming the Balfour Declaration, it calls for Jewish immigration and economic development in Palestine. The sanctity of religious shrines is guaranteed and disputes are referred to the British for arbitration. Arabs insist that the document is of no value since Faisal appended a reservation declaring the terms void if independence were not approved by Great Britain by the 4th of January. Which, of course, they were not.[36]

It is hard to imagine Weizmann signing an agreement that required the acquiescence of a third party within 24 hours. It is equally difficult to imagine Weizmann signing an agreement, then permitting Faisal to append such a reservation in Arabic. If anything, the agreement, along with Faisal's other pro–Zionist statements (to the Council of Ten in February 1919, to Churchill in January 1920) showed how quickly the Arabs mastered the game of diplomacy.

No Jewish state was created at Versailles. Wilson withdrew his own concept of self-determination from the draft of the League Covenant, submitting instead a report from Secretary of State Robert Lansing that warned of "perpetual agitation for boundary changes all over the world." The Allies also dismissed the report of the King-Crane Commission, a board appointed by Wilson in the summer of 1919 to gauge sentiments of the people of Syria, Lebanon, and Palestine. The overwhelming consensus of residents (most of whom were Arabs) was that Greater Syria (including Palestine and Lebanon) should be preserved as a unity and that Zionist proposals should be curtailed. The Commission report also contained a gratuitous aspersion suggesting that Jews could not be trusted to protect Muslim and Christian holy places.

The peacemakers at Versailles finally settled on something that was the handiwork of South Africa's Jan Christian Smuts. On December 16, 1918, Smuts proposed that territories formerly belonging to Russia, Austria, and Turkey be placed under a "mandate." In this novel arrangement, developing peoples would be placed under Allied tutelage until they were deemed sufficiently mature to handle their own affairs. Of course, the caretaking power, together with a League of Nations Mandates Council, would determine when that occurred. On April 28, 1919, Wilson gave his assent to the mandate concept as Article 22 of the League Covenant. A year later, with the American president seriously impaired, the British and French carved up the Middle East at San Remo.[37]

27

The Middle East
between World Wars

The Old Imperialism Revived

France and Great Britain had no intention of living up to grand promises made at the peace conferences. Mandates became little more than a guise for the old imperialists to intrude into the affairs of developing nations, sending troops to police the streets and loyal proconsuls to control spokesmen for independence. Britain and France were repeatedly censured by the League of Nations Mandates Commission for manipulating sectarian, cultural, and political divisions within their respective spheres. And while the allies should have been working in concert with one another, their policies often clashed.

Ungovernable Syria

A good example of duplicity among the partners was Syria. When the First World War ended, no one seemed able to define what constituted Syria or what to do with it. Faisal was at Versailles lobbying to be recognized as king of Greater Syria, including Palestine. Some Syrian nationalists wanted no monarch, Palestine nationalists wanted no part of Syria, and the Zionists wanted no part of an Arab state. The King-Crane Commission was urging autonomy for Lebanon. For historic and cultural reasons, France had been promised Syria as part of the Sykes-Picot Agreement. But the British army had physical control of the region and General Allenby did not conceal his contempt for the French. In military parades, French troops marched last. Ports were closed to French supplies. Use of the French language was discouraged and there was no effort to censor Arab newspapers that attacked Britain's ally. While British diplomats in Europe feigned concern for French sensitivities, Lord Milner confessed he intended to "diddle the French out of Syria," or, as T. E. Lawrence put it, "to biff the French out of all hope of Syria."[1]

It made little sense to antagonize the French with so many problems from India to Egypt, and the deal with Syria was confirmed at San Remo in 1920. As British troops were withdrawn from Syria and replaced by French, a humbled Faisal traveled to Paris in December 1919, to acknowledge Clemenceau's authority. Three months later (March 7, 1920) Faisal reversed himself, agreeing to head a united, independent state proclaimed by a General Syrian Congress.

When Arab nationalists continued harassment of the French, General Maurice Gouraud issued an ultimatum on July 14, 1920, calling for the formal adoption of the Mandate. Faisal refused and Gouraud's forces moved on the capital. On July 26, Damascus was taken, and Faisal expelled from Syria. As Clemenceau told Pierre van Paassen:

> I was perfectly well aware that Faisal was a puppet of those gentlemen in Cairo and Jerusalem and of their plot to throw us out of Syria and rob the Jews of their birthright at the same time. So I took the decision to throw the Arab out (of Damascus) at the first opportunity.... I forced the British government to notify Faisal that changes in the status of the Near Eastern countries could only be made by the peace conference. When the king therefore still hesitated, I ordered the army into Damascus and chased the fool back to his old father, that still greater fool in Mecca. All that those gentlemen could do for him after that was to send a guard of honor to salute him at the railway station of Lydda when he passed through on his way to senile pappy.[2]

In the next decade, Syria was governed by a series of marginally competent high commissioners (Generals Gouraud, Maxime Weygand, Maurice Sarrail, and Maurice Gamelin). In a county where nearly half the population was illiterate, the mandatory power required instruction in French. The French divided the land into several administrative districts (Latakia, the Jebel Druze, Aleppo-Alexandretta, Damascus, and Lebanon). Syrian nationalists could only look on as the Maronites in Lebanon declared their independence in May 1926. Not until 1943 would the French renounce special privileges related to control of railroads and ports. As for Alexandretta, this territory was turned over to Turkish troops in the fall of 1939, prompting a flight of thousands of panicked Armenians.

As Philip Hitti warned:

> Syria itself presented well-nigh insurmountable difficulties. It was at perhaps the lowest ebb in its history politically, economically, socially, and spiritually. It had no developed institutions for self rule, no proper implementation for democratic procedure, and its people had no experience in parliamentary affairs or modern civil service. The mandatory was from the outset confronted with the task of literally creating administrative and judiciary organs of state, repairing roads, establishing public education on a systematic basis and developing the natural resources.[3]

Many of their troubles, the French believed, stemmed from the British who were fomenting rebellion to force their ouster from Syria. Said General Sarrail: "I knew as far back as 1924 that the revolt was coming. I had been forewarned. No less a person than Abdullah, the Emir of Trans-Jordan, a British puppet volunteered the information that officials of the Colonial Office and certain British officers in Palestine were trying to make trouble for us in Syria."[4] General Gamelin, Colonel Charles Henri, and Druze chieftain Sultan Atrash agreed that the British supplied rifles, ammunition, food, and money to the Druze to embarrass their onetime allies.

Confronted with an ungovernable mess, the French did not grant Syria its own constitution until 1930. Even then, the high commissioner retained veto power over legislative actions. In the 25-year history of the Mandate, only three elections were held (1928, 1932, 1936) resulting in the formation of *al-Kutlah al-Wataniyyah* (the National Bloc). Organized by Taj al-Din, chief judge of Damascus, the Kutlah agitated for an end to the Mandate, internationally supervised elections, and the restoration of all Syrian territory, including Palestine. Its leaders (Hashim al-Atassi, Shukri al-Kuwatli, Jamil Mardam, and

Faris al-Khouri) would guide Syria into the League of Nations in 1939, negotiate independence in 1941, and dominate Syrian politics into the 1950s.[5]

Iraq: An Invention of the British

In all of Mesopotamian history, there never had been a nation known as Iraq. When the First World War ended, the territory was ill-defined. Its population included Kurdish nationalists in the north; Shiiite fundamentalists in the southern holy cities of Karbala, Kufah and Najah; and veterans of the Ottoman army hopeful of capitalizing on the riches of Mosul-Kirkuk oil, all bent on expelling a British occupation force under the command of Lt. Col. Arnold Wilson, who had no intention of ceding control of this strategic land. Colonel Wilson, however, found himself at odds with officials in London who gave off contradictory signals about Iraq. Since San Remo, it seemed Britain intended to remain in Iraq. Yet early in 1920 Curzon buoyed nationalists by calling an Arab consultative assembly. Then Colonial Secretary Churchill cut Wilson's troop complement to 3500.

The result was another bloody revolt. From the ancient hills of Assyria to the Shatt-al-Arab, Anglo-Indian units were isolated, then massacred. Britain rushed 65,000 soldiers to Iraq to pacify the situation. At least 10,000 people would die, $100 million would be spent in another fiasco traceable to Colonial Secretary Churchill. The redoubtable Churchill shifted blame to Colonel Wilson, who was replaced by Sir Percy Cox. Arab notables were informed that Britain intended to implement its mandate. Iraq would have a Council of State and a king designated by the British.

In March 1921, Churchill convened a summit of Middle East advisers at Cairo. The gallery included T. E. Lawrence, General Walter Congreve (commander of British forces in Egypt and Palestine), Sir Herbert Samuel, Cox, Arnold Wilson (representing Anglo-Persian Oil), and Gertrude Bell (one of the few bureaucrats who had devoted a lifetime of study to the region). The experts agreed that it would be more efficient to deal with a king who would be indebted to His Majesty's government. None of the candidates (Ibn Saud, the Agha Khan, Said Abdal Rahman al-Gailani) had an advocate like the Emir Faisal. T. E. Lawrence reminded the group of Faisal's contribution to the war effort and the shabby treatment the emir received in Syria. Lawrence had spoken with Faisal in Switzerland and found him receptive to taking the throne of Iraq. Faisal's brother Abdullah (designated king of Iraq by Arabs the same day Faisal became king of Syria) would be compensated with another fiefdom carved from two-thirds of the Palestine Mandate — Trans-Jordan.[6]

Colonel Wilson had polled the leading shaykhs of Iraq in January 1919 and found them opposed to the introduction of an Hejazi prince as their sovereign. When several Iraqis voiced their displeasure in April 1921, they were deported to Ceylon. Meanwhile the bureaucrats also eased the way for Faisal. Gertrude Bell arranged meetings with tribal chiefs, even designed a temporary flag of state. On August 23, 1921, Faisal was installed as king. Subsequently, in a plebiscite on his monarchy he won 96 percent of the vote. There were no other candidates.

The special position of Great Britain was formally outlined in a treaty imposed upon this puppet government in October 1922. The terms of that pact and others signed in 1926, 1927, and 1930 were basically the same: Iraq agreed to a military alliance, yielding control over foreign policy, police functions, (seaports, air bases, railroads and oilfields), to the Mandatory power. British nationals obtained trading privileges, not unlike those in the hated Ottoman Capitulations.

In return, Iraq was promised a constitution and eventual independence. On paper, at least, Britain seemed to honor both pledges. A constitution calling for a two-house parliament was promulgated in 1924, but none of the 20 cabinet coalitions that sat between 1925 and 1939 served a four-year term. The situation was not helped when Britain granted titular independence to Iraq in 1932. Just as in Syria, frustrated members of the nationalist *Istiqlal* (Independence), National Democrat, National Brotherhood, and Progressive parties bickered with one another over their inability to oust the occupying imperialists.

Faisal's death in 1933 merely complicated matters. For three years, Iraq foundered under one cabinet after another until General Bakr Sidki engineered a coup in October 1936. The man who hoped to be another Ataturk or Reza Shah had been responsible for carrying out massacres of "Assyrian" Christians (Nestorians scattered through northwest regions). Within the year, Bakr Sidki antagonized socialists, members of the Chamber of Deputies, and his army colleagues. On August 11, 1937, he was assassinated during another putsch. To the outbreak of World War II, Iraq was an unstable British protectorate.[7]

The British in Egypt

Egyptians also seethed under a sham independence. The British had no intention of abandoning this precious choke-point. Under the supervision of the British agent or high commissioner, descendants of Mehemet Ali shared power with a legislative assembly. Egypt had little experience with, less affection for, representative government. Late in 1914, when several ministers were assassinated, the Khedive Abbas Hilmi, suspected of pro–Turkish sentiments, was deposed and martial law was declared.

Until Allenby's invasion of the Holy Land in 1917, Egypt served mainly as a military campground. As the war neared an end, Egyptian nationalists were buoyed by the rhetoric of American President Wilson. Their leader, Saad Zaghlul, one-time minister of education, received permission from British High Commissioner Reginald Wingate to lead an Egyptian delegation (*Wafd al-Misri*) to Versailles. London countermanded that order and Zaghlul and several colleagues were detained at Malta.[8]

By treaty, on February 28, 1922, Britain granted "independence" to Egypt. The ruler, Fuad, became king, with powers to summon a parament and veto its acts. Election procedures for the legislature were outlined in a new constitution promulgated in April 1923. There was no mention of the British in the constitution, but as in Iraq the Resident controlled foreign policy, the Sirdar was the actual commander in chief of Egypt's armed forces, and British troops were responsible for security in the cities, the canal zone and the Sudan.

Zaghlul's Wafdists won every election between the wars (188 of 215 seats in September 1923; 166 of 232 in the summer of 1936). Because of their strident nationalism, they also were blamed for anti–British incidents. On November 19, 1924, the sirdar, Sir Lee Stack, was assassinated on the streets of Cairo. Several Wafdists, including two cabinet members were involved. The British demanded that Prime Minister Zaghlul punish the guilty and issue an apology within 24 hours. Additionally, the Egyptians were to withdraw troops from the Sudan, stop agitating against the British, and endorse additional irrigation projects for the Gezira district. Finding this ultimatum unacceptable, Zaghlul resigned.

Zaghlul died in August 1927. In the next decade, a number of nationalists (Ismail Sidki, Muhammad Mahmud, and Mustafa Nahas Pasha) would continue opposition to the British presence in Egypt. When the British, reacting to Mussolini's invasion of Ethiopia in 1935, moved headquarters of their Mediterranean fleet from Malta to Alexandria, Egyptians were outraged. Relations deteriorated when, following the death of King Fuad in April 1936, the British imposed a new mutual defense pact upon his teenaged successor, Farouk, and his chief adviser, Nahas Pasha. Egypt agreed to a 20-year military alliance, where British troops were permitted to intervene at any time to maintain the safety of the canal and territorial integrity of the land. In return, British trading privileges would be abolished. The 1936 treaty merely confirmed their view that the British considered Egypt a chunk of the empire and had no intention of leaving.[9]

Palestine: The Focus of Anti-Colonialism

During the interwar period, the French suppressed a Rifaiya revolt led by Abdel Krim in Morocco, the Neo-Destour party of Habib Bourguiba in Tunis, and emerging anti–Colon agitation in Algeria. In Libya, desert tribesmen attacked Italian transports that ventured along the Benghazi-Tripoli highway. Arab dissidents may have differed on whether the British, Italians or French were worse. But the one thing they could agree upon was their inveterate opposition to the Zionist settlement in Palestine.

Arab leaders expressed their solidarity with Palestinian Arabs and endorsed calls for an economic and social boycott of any company that did business with Jews. They took their inspiration from Haj Amin el-Husseini, the soft-spoken figure who was named Grand Mufti of Jerusalem, guardian of Islamic institutions, by the British in 1921. Disowned by nationalists and virtually ignored by historians today, the mufti of Jerusalem was one of the most charismatic Arab leaders in the 20th century.[10]

As the war with the Central Powers ended, the British knew they were facing serious trouble in the Holy Land. The Arabs resented Zionist settlements that fenced off communal grazing land while denying the native inhabitants employment or loans. Haj Amin, scion of one of the wealthiest feudal families in Palestine, took the lead in staging anti–Zionist demonstrations early in 1919. He was emboldened by British Mandatory officials like Sir Louis Bols, chief administrator for the country, and his aide Sir Ronald Storrs, who complained of Zionist aggressiveness. Harold Ashbee, civil adviser to Storrs, noted: "The Jew is unthinkable without the bargain; he bears the brand of that mean fellow Jacob upon his brow."[11] Added Gertrude Bell: "The Arabs have enough to do, if they will only believe it, in organizing what they have got, and if they will be patient (which they never will!) whatever else they deserve will drop into their laps, and not all the gold of the Hebrews in the world can prevent it."[12]

Storrs, Bols, Allenby, Ernest Richmond, Harry Keith-Roach, and most high commissioners for Palestine were not enamored with the idea of a Jewish state bordering Suez. In the spring of 1919, they winked at the creation of Arab liberation societies like *an-Nadi al-Arabi, al-Akha wal-Arab,* and *al-Fedaiyeh* that interfered with Jewish pilgrims coming to Jerusalem. They did nothing to protect Jewish settlers in the Galilee from Arab attacks.[13] Despite warnings of violence in Jerusalem from Intelligence Chief Richard Meinertzhagen, mandatory officials withdrew policemen from the Old City before the Nebi Musa festival in April 1920. Crying *"adawlah ma'ana"* (the government is with us), Arab mobs pillaged Jerusalem for three days, leaving nine persons dead and more than 200 Jews injured. The following year, in May 1921, another series of anti–Jewish riots in Jaffa, Hadera, Rehovot, Petach Tikveh and Kfar Saba resulted in the deaths of nearly 100 people. The Wailing Wall riots of August 1929 resulted in more than 500 casualties. Seventy-four men, women and children were slashed to death in Hebron as British soldiers stood by. As a consequence of

these attacks, this ancient town became *Judenrein*.[14] Palestine suffered another violent eruption on the eve of World War II. Between 1936 and 1939 another 2287 Arabs, 450 Jews, and
140 British subjects were killed, in what some historians label civil disorders.[15]

The Role of the Mufti

The instigator of much of this violence was Haj Amin el-Husseini, who seemed
immune to punishment. Following the Easter riots of 1920, the British administration
feigned a clampdown on troublemakers, ordering the arrest of both Haj Amin and the
leader of Jewish self-defense — Zev Jabotinsky. Jabotinsky was manacled in Acre prison, then
given a 15-year prison sentence (reduced to exile) for illegal possession of firearms. By way
of contrast, Haj Amin avoided arrest by fleeing to Jordan. Given a 10-year sentence, he never
spent a day in jail. On the promise of good behavior, High Commissioner Samuel issued
a pardon and named Haj Amin grand mufti of Jerusalem over four more qualified candidates in May 1921. Reacting to this appointment, Meinertzhagen wrote Churchill: "He (the
Mufti) is ambitious, unscrupulous, dishonest. Sooner or later his appointment will be
greatly regretted by us."[16]

Blessed with the prestige of his new office, Haj Amin aspired to be king of Palestine,
if not caliph of all Islam. He directed the Arab Executive, the political body calling for a
renunciation of the Balfour Declaration. He helped create the Supreme Muslim Council,
the religious body that administered the $2 million annual income. In 1934, he fused both
groups into the Arab Higher Committee, the shadow government responsible for the revolt
between 1936 and 1939. Though the British tried to appease Palestinian nationalists by sev-
ering two-thirds of the Mandated territory (35,000 miles of which became Trans-Jordan
in 1921), restricting Jewish immigration (no more than 16,500 during the 1920s), and limiting land sales (slices of the Beit Shean and Huleh districts were declared off limits to Jews,
even before a 1940 ordinance practically foreclosed all of Palestine), it was not enough. The
mufti, reacting to the placement of stools and benches for the aged at the Wailing Wall,
charged that the Jews were attempting to take control of the Mosque of Umar and charged
his followers to attack in 1929. The mufti, reacting to the arrival of refugees from Hitler
during the 1930s (as many as 65,000 in one year) charged that Jews were "flooding" the
country. The mufti rejected the Peel Commission report in July 1937 that called for the partition of Palestine, with most of the land going to the Arabs. He established contacts with
fascist agents, securing arms, money, and propaganda that transformed disorders in 1936
into a bloody assault upon his own people, who endorsed co-existence with the Zionists.
Between 1936 and 1939, a number of Nazi leaders, including Baldur von Shirach and Adolf
Eichmann, visited the Middle East and saluted the efforts of the Palestinian nationalists.
Pursued by the British, Haj Amin took refuge in the Mosque of Umar, then magically
escaped to Lebanon in 1936. From exile in Beirut (until the French heaved him over the
border into Iraq in 1939) the mufti continued to champion mayhem against the British
and the Jews.

The British and the Zionists

In contrast with Egypt and Iraq, where the British dealt ruthlessly with the political
opposition, the performance of the Palestine government "looked like that of a figure in a

dressing gown and slippers pathetically padding along in the dusty wake of the Arab Higher Committee."[17] Some bureaucrats were troubled by the romanticized legacy of Lawrence. Some wanted to keep Palestine as pristine as it had been when Christ walked the land. Some, like the effete, mustachioed high commissioners who succeeded Samuel — Lord Plumer (1925–28), Sir John Chancellor (1928–30), Sir Arthur Wauchope (1930–38), Sir Harold MacMichael (1938–44) — were cloned from an imperial mentality that held that only what was good for the mother country mattered. And some merely wanted to keep Arab and Jew at each other's necks in order to justify the permanent occupation of Palestine.

Deferent toward the Arabs, the British were much harsher in their dealings with the Zionists. Dr. Weizmann, who had settled into his research institute at Rehovot, found government officials less receptive to him once the world war was over. The Zionist shadow government (*Vaad Leumi*) under David Ben-Gurion was responsible not only for its developmental projects, but was taxed disproportionately (85 percent for the defense and welfare of the Mandate). The Zionists drained swamps, created electrification systems, planted settlements with little British support. Organized self-defense was discouraged, even after Orde Wingate arrived in Palestine in 1936 and trained the first units of what was to become the *Haganah*. Zionists like Jabotinsky, who demanded admission of millions of Europe's imperiled Jews and retaliation against the mufti's gangs, were banished. For establishment Zionist groups as well as the British, Jabotinsky seemed to be a renegade out of control. Calling himself a "revisionist" (a Zionist who opposed collectivism and who defined the Jewish homeland in biblical terms), Jabotinsky declared:

> In the world of today, in particular among the younger generation, the dream of a dictator has become epidemic. I use this opportunity to state once more that I am an implacable enemy of this dream. I believe in the ideological patrimony of the 19th century, the century of Garibaldi and Lincoln, Gladstone and Hugo. Today's ideological fashion is that a human being is in his essence dishonest and stupid, and he should not therefore be given the right to govern himself; freedom leads to perdition, equality is a lie, society needs leaders, orders and a stick. I don't want this kind of creed: better not live at all than to live under such a system.[18]

Jabotinsky died in exile in New York City in 1940. His disciples, David Raziel and Menachem Begin, who led the militant Irgun, and Abraham Stern, founder of the terrorist Stern Gang, were all hunted down or imprisoned by the CID.

The Bi-Nationalists

British imperialists and Arab extremists chose to ignore one small, but important group of Zionists. Labeled bi-nationalists, these idealists were disciples of Achad Ha-Am. Members of *Brit Shalom* (the Brotherhood of Peace) or *Ihud* (Unity), they called not for a modern state ("like all the other nations") but for a Palestine based on equal political rights for Arabs and Jews, a land that would be a spiritual hub for Jews, yet a land that would be federated with Jordan and other states in a regional union of free peoples. To achieve peace, everything was negotiable, including immigration and land purchase. The bi-nationalists included Henrietta Szold (founder of Hadassah), Rabbi Judah Magnes (president of the Hebrew University of Jerusalem), Martin Buber (the philosopher who had been expelled from Germany), Arthur Ruppin and Hayyim Kalvarsky. All believed that a Zionist state imposed by force would face the perpetual antagonism of its neighbors. To Mahatma Gandhi (who suggested the Jews should resist Hitler with civil disobedience) Buber wrote: "We love this land and believe in its future. Such love and such faith are surely present on the other side as well. Where there is faith and love, a solution may be found even to what appears to be a tragic opposition."[19]

Instead of encouraging the bi-nationalists, the British forbade expressions of solidarity between Jews and Arabs. They barred the two peoples from belonging to the same labor unions, going to meetings together, and even prohibited the publication of a Jewish paper printed in Arabic. In a moment of despair, Arthur Ruppin conceded that the underlying cause of troubles in the Holy Land is "that we (Jews) exist."

Each time there were incidents, the British reacted in a dilatory manner. In 1929, outnumbered police were supplemented with Jewish supernumeraries (some of whom were then detained for bearing arms illegally). In 1937 the British deployed 50,000 soldiers and tanks along barbed wire at the border of Lebanon in a feeble effort to stem infiltration by Arab raiders. The homes of suspected terrorists were also destroyed. Each wave of pogroms was followed by a commission of inquiry. These invariably absolved Mandate officials of culpability and eroded commitment to the Balfour Declaration. Colonial Secretary Churchill visited the region following the disturbances of 1921. His White Paper, issued in June 1922, stated that Jews were in Palestine as of right, not sufferance, but cautioned that they should not conceive of the whole territory being transformed into a Zionist state.

Nine years later, in the wake of the Wailing Wall riots, two reports (from Sir Walter Shaw and Sir John Hope-Simpson) and the Passfield White Paper (drafted by the Fabian socialist Sidney Webb) concluded that the soil of Palestine was inadequate to sustain a larger Jewish population and that immigration ought be curbed. Basically the same conclusions were reached by the Woodhead Commission of April 1938 and Colonial Secretary Malcolm MacDonald, who called Arab and Zionist leaders to a summit in London in January 1939. Although Egypt, Iraq, Transjordan, Saudi Arabia, Yemen and the mufti sent representatives, the Arabs refused to sit with Dr. Weizmann, Ben-Gurion or Miss Szold. (Jabotinsky and the Revisionist Zionist were barred by the British.) As the so-called Round Table Conference foundered, MacDonald admonished Weizmann that the Jews were in Palestine "as of sufferance, not of right."[20]

The Peel Commission and the 1939 White Paper

The only panel that made sense in this whole period was the one headed by Lord William Peel, former secretary of state for India, which issued its 404-page report in July 1937. The Peel Comission concluded that Arab grievances concerning Jewish immigration and land acquisition were not legitimate. Quite the contrary, the Zionist settlement through its anti-malarial work, swamp reclamation and rural health clinics had "a general fructifying effect" on the life of the country. According to the Commission, "The Arab charge that Jews have obtained too large a proportion of the good land cannot be maintained. Much of the land now carrying orange groves was sand dunes or swamp, and uncultivated when it was purchased.... There was land available and a general willingness to sell ... [once] satisfactory financial arrangements could be devised."

The Peel Commission noted that more than 80 percent of 3271 claims of family displacements by Zionist land purchases had been rejected. Between 1922 and 1931 Arab populations had shown marked increases in cities with mixed populations (Haifa, 86 percent; Jaffa, 62 percent; Jerusalem, 37 percent) as compared with purely Arab towns (Hebron and Nablus, 7 percent; Gaza, 2 percent). Thousands of Arab immigrants had also entered Palestine from neighboring countries enticed by higher wages (160 percent those in Egypt), education expenditures (200 percent those of Jordan), agricultural productivity (191 percent that in Syria), food consumption (166 percent that of Iraq), and life expectancy (49.5 years as opposed to 38.5 in Egypt).[21]

Nevertheless, the Peel Commission concluded that no mutual understanding was developing between Jews and Arabs. Because of the "irrepressible conflict," the Mandate was unworkable. Arab demands for a state under the grand mufti were unacceptable because there were no guarantees of safety to 400,000 Jews. Equally untenable was the Revisionist call for a state whose boundaries encompassed both sides of the Jordan. As a compromise, the Commission recommended a partition. The bulk of Palestine (including all of the Negev) would become an Arab state united with Transjordan. A tiny enclave along the coast into the Galilee (2000 square miles) was to be awarded to the Jews—provided that £2 million compensation was paid to the Arabs and immigration limited to 50,000 in the next five years. Strategic sites—the ports of Jaffa and Aqabah, Lydda airport, the Jaffa-Jerusalem highway, and Jerusalem itself—would remain under British control.[22]

Partition was probably the only sensible way of resolving the Arab-Jewish conflict. It was the mechanism adopted by the United Nations 10 years later. In retrospect, a Zionist state, however truncated, might have served as a life raft for thousands of Jews trapped in Europe. In 1937, however, the concept was rejected by Jabotinsky, by Zionists at the 20th Congress in Zurich, by the grand mufti, who complained that too much land was being awarded to the Zionist state, and by 500 delegates at a Pan-Arab Congress in Bludan, Syria, who echoed Haj Amin's call that Zionism must disappear. King Abdullah, who was slated to become king of Palestine, and members of the Nashashibi clan, traditional rivals of the Husseinis, endorsed the Peel Plan. So, belatedly, did the general Zionists.

Fed up with Jews and Arabs and facing a greater threat in the form of Adolf Hitler, the British issued a White Paper on the Palestine problem on May 7, 1939. Jewish immigration was curtailed — no more than 75,000 over the next five years, only 75,000 if the country could absorb that number, and all Jewish immigration to be halted after five years unless the Arabs agreed to more. Jews were to constitute no more than one-third of the population and their purchase of land was to be severely regulated by the high commissioner (as outlined in a land ordinance promulgated in 1940). After five years, the British would no longer be under any obligation to facilitate further development of the Jewish national home. Within 10 years, the British promised the establishment of an independent Palestinian state.[23]

Here then, on the eve of World War II, was a renunciation of the Balfour Declaration. An angry House of Commons rejected the White Paper 268 to 179. Calling the document "another Munich," Winston Churchill suggested that the government "file a petition in moral and physical bankruptcy."[24] Added Lt. Commander Fletcher: "I think what we have seen in the White Paper is another instance of how the government get out of their difficulties by sacrificing the easiest victims. The government are now joining in the hunt of the Jews which is going on in Europe. Last year, to get out of a difficulty, they did not hesitate to sell the Czechs down the river. This year we see them prepared to sell the Jews down the river."[25]

In June 1939, the League of Nations Mandates Commission meeting in Geneva observed that Great Britain had "turned the Mandate upside down."[26] It was not the first time Britain had been censured by outside observers. Three U.S. senators declared in 1936 that "prolongation of terror in the Holy Land is due to a manifest sympathy for the vandals and assassins displayed by many British officers." Two years later, members of the Mandates Commission accused the British of being "the conscious and deliberate fomenters of trouble in Palestine," of betraying the Jews and "to say otherwise was insulting the intelligence of the members of the Permanent Mandates Commission."[27]

As Jews demonstrated against the White Paper on the streets of Tel Aviv, Malcom MacDonald told Chaim Weizmann that the British government did not agree with the document. Yet Palestine was made off limits to Europe's Jews, not merely by the Chamberlain government, but his successor, Churchill, after Nazi Germany invaded Poland in September.

28

World War II

The Battle of El Alamein

Some of the most bitter fighting of the Second World War took place in the Middle East and North Africa between 1940 and 1943. For nearly a decade, Germany and Italy had been subsidizing subversion and beaming propaganda in the region. One blow to the economic jugular of the British Empire and the Arabs would rise in revolt. The man designated to deliver that strike was Field Marshal Erwin Rommel. Rommel came to North Africa early in 1941 to rejuvenate another failed Italian campaign. Just as Mussolini's attempt to overrun Greece had miscarried, so his September 1940 onslaught against Egypt ended in disaster.

After a few weeks in the desert, the Italians panicked for the safety of Libya. By the time the Germans arrived, nearly 130,000 Italians had been captured. Rommel's Afrika Korps, some of Germany's most elite units, had no intention of retreating further. On March 24, Rommel launched a counter attack that would take him deep within Egyptian territory. His attack faltered, however, during the siege of Tobruk, where the gritty garrison held out until June 1942. With Tobruk out of the way, the Afrika Korps settled in at El Alamein, less than 100 miles from Alexandria.

On October 23, 1942, the British Army retaliated. Rommel was away in Germany recuperating from wounds, but rushed back to the front. Not even his leadership, though, could compensate for British air supremacy and the enemy's bigger, faster tanks. Ignoring Hitler's orders to fight to the death, the German line broke on November 2 and once disciplined troops fled across the same paths etched by their Italian allies two years earlier.[1]

El Alamein is one of the turning points in World War II. Between November 18 and 23, 1942, the Red Army launched a counter attack at Stalingrad that resulted in the destruction of Germany's Sixth Army. Of more immediate concern to Rommel was the American invasion of Morocco and Algeria on November 8, 1942. Vichy French contingents opposed the Americans at the very moment the Nazis seized the rest of mainland France.

Before the Afrika Korps capitulated on May 7, 1943, 500,000 German troops had been funneled into North Africa. They were to win one major battle with the Americans—at the Kasserine Pass in Tunisia in February 1943.

Myths of Assistance

In November 1974, Yasser Arafat addressed the General Assembly of the United Nations. Bedecked in his checkered keffiyah, pistol in side holster, Arafat paid homage to Washington, Lincoln, and Wilson. Then he told the General Assembly: "While we (the Arabs) were vociferously condemning the massacres of Jews under Nazi rule, Zionist leadership appeared more interested, at the time, in exploiting them as best it could in order to realize its goal of immigration to Palestine."[2]

The theme of Zionist perfidy against their own people found currency among some historians. Anthony Nutting referred to the extermination of the six million Jews as "a trump card of the Zionists who used every trick and artifice to bring in illegals."[3] Philip Hitti also noted that the persecution of "German Jews" aroused new and wider sympathies for Zionist plans.[4] William Yale accused Palestinian Jews of creating a "dangerous subversive movement" against the British in World War II, thereby jeopardizing the lives of their brethren in Europe.[5]

Of 135,000 Jews in Palestine who volunteered for duty, 32,000 were inducted into the British armed forces. Some conducted suicide missions against the Italians in Bardia or served as ferrets against Rommel at Tobruk. Jewish civilians maintained radar installations, harbor facilities, pipelines, and hospitals. During the battle of El Alamein, Jewish leaders in Palestine developed the Carmel Plan, a scheme that would enable the British to flee eastward while the Jews fought delaying skirmishes on the hills outside Haifa. When the tide of war turned and the British in 1944 created a Jewish Legion, Palestinian and stateless Jews distinguished themselves in Crete, Greece, Abyssinia, Iraq, Italy, the Low Countries and Austria. Adolf Hitler was so incensed by Jewish resistance in North Africa that he issued a rare written order (to Rommel) urging the "ruthless destruction" of all Jews in the battle zone in June 1942.[6]

Arabs also contributed to the war effort, but not to the degree suggested by their partisans. Algerian and Moroccan troops fought alongside the French, but like thousands of Muslims from the Indian sub-continent, they were dragooned into the conflict. Resentment of the Allies was a basic tenet for organizations like *Misr el-Fatat*, the Green Shirts of Ahmed Hussein and Hasan al-Banna's Muslim Brotherhood in Egypt; the Syrian National Party of Antun Saadah, *An-Nadi al-Arabi*, the National Bloc, the Council for the Defense of Arab Palestine; the Istiqlal Club, and the Iron Shirts of Lebanon and Syria; the *Futuwwa* and Golden Square in Iraq. In May of 1941, when the British were fighting virtually alone, the Iraqi government of Rashid Ali al-Gailani declared war against Great Britain.

Jordan's Brigadier John Bagot Glubb Pasha lamented, "Every Arab force previously organized by us mutinied and refused to fight for us, or faded away in desertions."[7] In Palestine, 12,455 Arabs were recruited by the British, a number reduced by 50 percent due to discharges and desertions before the war's end. Wrote Pierre Van Paassen, 1943:

> Had one German division set foot on the Syrian or Palestine shores, the British command would have had a conflagration at its back running from the Persian border to the Hadhramaut and Aden. As it was, almost as many British troops were required to patrol the doubtful Arab areas and cities, especially in Egypt as there were actually facing Rommel's Afrika Korps in the Libyan Desert.[8]

As Rommel's tanks rumbled eastward in the summer of 1942, the situation in Egypt seemed hopeless. Mobs were preparing a welcome for the Nazis in Alexandria and Cairo. King Farouk refused to invoke terms of the Defense Treaty and was placed under house arrest by the British. Farouk's father-in-law Zulfikar Pasha, his uncle, the ex-khedive Abbas Hilmi, publicly expressed sympathy for the Germans. Unnerved by plots among young officers in the Egyptian army and the attempted defection of Aziz Ali al-Misri and Defense Minister Ahmed Saudi Hussein, the British removed Azzam Pasha from his post as chief of Egypt's Territorial Army.[9] Writing in those gloomiest of times, Van Paassen declared:

> The truth is that the so-called Arab world — that is to say, the princes, potentates, imams, mullahs and emirs— were yearning to stab Britain in the back. King Ibn Saud who was suddenly to declare himself an ally of Britain and America, had not a word to say and could not spare a single trooper, camel or donkey when Rommel stood at Alamein. The imam of Yemen had to be watched constantly.[10]

After the British repulsed the Germans, they convened a summit of Arab leaders at Cairo in August 1943 to discuss the future of the Middle East. Guests included members of the Palestinian Arab Higher Committee, the prime minister of Iraq, and kings of Jordan, Saudi Arabia, and Egypt. No Zionists were invited. According status to the Arab Higher Committee, the creation of Haj Amin el-Husseini, was a concession of the immense influence the grand mufti of Jerusalem wielded in the Islamic world.[11]

For more than 40 years, through appearances at international conferences at Karachi and Damascus in the 1950s and his creation of a Palestine Liberation Army under the auspices of Abdel Karim Kassem in 1960, Haj Amin el-Husseini was *the* spokesman of Palestinian nationalism. He may well have been the most celebrated Arab nationalist leader before Gamal Nasser. Yet for professional historians he has become a veritable phantom.[12]

A self-proclaimed Palestinian patriot and "the leader of all Northern Arabs," Haj Amin later would claim that he never spoke out against the United States or the Allies, that he had never espoused the idea of destroying Jews. None of this was true. The mufti was one of the most respected individuals in Iraq prior to the Gailani coup in 1941. Supported by state tithes, he was secretly being paid by the Italians and Germans in the amount of $500,000. The mufti served as liaison between Nazi Ambassador Franz Grobba and the Iraqi prime minister. As British intelligence observed: "The ex-Mufti commenced his political activities without check from the first day of his arrival in the country. In these activities, he was encouraged by the reception he was accorded on all sides, including parties given by responsible ministers and Nuri Pasha."[13]

In July 1940, the Iraqi foreign minister carried a letter from the mufti to Franz von Papen, the German ambassador in Istanbul, offering "sincerest felicitations" to Hitler for victories in Western Europe. Shortly after, the mufti offered to negotiate an alliance with the Axis. The proposed treaty would have given Germany and Italy preferred economic status in newly independent Arab states. In return: "Germany and Italy [would] recognize the right of the Arab countries to solve the question of the Jewish elements in Palestine and other Arab countries in a manner that conforms to the national and ethnic interests of the Arabs and to the solution of the Jewish question in the countries of Germany and Italy."[14]

In January 1941, the mufti assured the "great Führer" of the "friendship and admiration" of the Arab people. As he put it, Arab peoples everywhere were prepared to act as is proper against the common enemy and to do their part in the well deserved defeat of the Anglo-Jewish coalition.[15] Haj Amin was receptive to Hitler's offer in March 1941 of a German volunteer legion that would be parachuted into Iraq. He proclaimed Iraq's declaration of war in May 1941, a jihad. And when that revolt was snuffed, the mufti incited a pogrom in Baghdad that left 110 Jews dead.[16]

After the failure of the Gailani coup, the mufti fled to Iran, where he encouraged Reza Khan to oppose the British and Russians. When the allies jointly occupied Persia in August 1941, he fled to Italy, claiming that he had no place else to go. On November 20, 1941, the mufti was granted a 90-minute audience with Adolf Hitler at the latter's Wilhelmstrasse residence. He sought a blessing from the Nazi leader for the creation of a proposed Arab state. Hitler replied it was premature to speak of boundaries. He did, however, promise that Haj Amin would have the decisive voice in Arab affairs once the war was concluded. "You will be the man to direct the Arab force," said Hitler.[17]

For the duration of the war, the mufti was housed in two elegant villas and subsidized to the sum of 75,000 marks per month for heading a special *Buro des Grosmufti*.[18] Its three-fold function: (a) espionage (training of saboteurs), (b) propaganda (public broadcasts on Muslim holy days),[19] and (c) recruitment of 500,000 troops for the Waffen SS.[20] Although the numbers never reached such size, dozens of his recruits were charged as war criminals in Bosnia, Croatia, Serbia and Lithuania.[21]

The Mufti and the Jews

During the war, the mufti repeatedly volunteered his expertise on the Jewish question. He praised the Führer as a descendant of the Prophet, "the savior of Islam," and called upon Arab Americans to rise up against the Allies, to create a Fifth Column to "stop FDR and his Jewish ambitions." He reminded his listeners that the Jews were an immoral people, "incapable of being trusted," "the most evil-minded toward Muslims." From Berlin on the anniversary of Muhammad's birthday in March 1943, he warned Muslims around the world that the Jews, bolstered by gangsters from Chicago, had designs on the holy places in Jerusalem. America's invasion of North Africa was nothing more than a subterfuge for the creation of a second Jewish state that would be populated by European Jews and Negroes. When the Institute for the Study of the Jewish Question convened "scholarly meetings" at Frankfurt in April 1943, and Cracow in 1944, the mufti lectured on "Palestine: A World Center for Jewish Domination Plans."[22]

From one principle, the mufti never wavered: the expulsion of all Jews from Arab lands. On the anniversary of the Balfour declaration, he asked for and received anti–Zionist pledges from Nazi Foreign Minister Joachim Ribbentrop in 1942 and Heinrich Himmler in 1943. According to a Luftwaffe report from March 1944, Haj Amin urged the bombing of Tel Aviv, the Dead Sea Potash Works, the Jewish Agency in Jerusalem, the Rutenberg Electric Works and the harbor at Haifa. Such attacks would have been of little strategic importance and might have caused extensive casualties among Arab civilians. But Haj Amin told one Nazi official: "The Jewish national home must disappear and the Jews get out. They are free to go to Hell."[23]

Whenever one of Hitler's puppets contemplated negotiation with the Allies to rescue Jews, the mufti presented a stumbling block. Thus, when King Boris indicated a willingness release 4000 Jewish children for Palestine in May 1943, the mufti protested that the children "present a degree of danger to Bulgaria whether they remain in Bulgaria or be permitted to depart from that country." Later that month, the mufti reacted against a proposal of the government of Ion Antonescu that would have permitted 80,000 Jews to flee Rumania. At the same time, he demanded that Italy and Hungary rescind permission for Jewish emigration and suggested that if Jews left these countries they should be sent to Poland "where they are under active supervision." The German Foreign Office applied pressure to its satellites on behalf of Palestine, which "was an Arab country," and few of the refugees escaped.[24]

At a time when the Nazis were transporting Jews to killing centers in Poland, Haj Amin declared, "The Arab nation awaits the solution of the world Jewish problem by its friends, the Axis powers." He knew what the Nazis meant by *Endlosung*. As Dieter von Wisliceny, one of Adolf Eichmann's aides, reported: "The grand mufti has repeatedly suggested to the Nazi authorities, including Hitler, Ribbentrop, and Himmler the extermination of European Jewry. He considered this a comfortable solution to the Palestine problem."[25]

Even as the military situation deteriorated for Germany in the last 18 months of the war, the mufti found himself drawn closer to his Nazi associates. He exchanged photographs with Himmler and pledged cooperation for common goals. He urged Ribbentrop to commemorate Balfour Day with a statement denouncing the British promise of a Jewish homeland. And he made it very clear that when the time was appropriate, he would call upon the "best saviour of the Arabs"—Adolph Eichmann—to apply his expertise in shuttling Jews to death camps. Eichmann had met the mufti in the Middle East in 1937 and later testified that he had been instructed to open all filed on Jewish Question to the affable Arab.[26]

According to Nazi hunter Simon Wiesenthal, Haj Amin not only met Rudolf Hoess (commandant of Auschwitz), Franz Zereis of Mauthausen, Siegfried Seidl (Theresienstadt) and Joesf Kramer (Belsen), he may have witnessed mass killings before returning to the Middle East in 1945.[27] After several vain efforts to win diplomatic recognition for his Palestinian entity at the United Nations, Haj Amin faded into obscurity till his death in 1974.

Palestine: A Land Off Limits

Mindful of widespread anti–Jewish attitudes of populations from Morocco to Yemen, the British cleaved to policies outlined in the White Paper of 1939, limiting Jewish immigration to Palestine. Fewer than 40,000 legal refugees were admitted, as Mandatory authorities suspended Jewish immigration during the winters of 1939 and 1940. Withal his indignation against the White Paper of 1939, it was Churchill who ordered the repulse of shipload after shipload of "illegal" Jews (among them the *Salvador, Liesel, Rim, Tiger Hill,* and *Sakarya*) from the shores of Palestine. Some of these passengers were ultimately admitted. Others, like the 254 passengers aboard the *Patria* in Halfia Harbor in 1940 and the 769 passengers aboard the *SS Struma* that sank in the Black Sea in February 1942, were killed.[28]

British diplomats at the Bermuda Conference on Refugees, which met during the death throes of Warsaw Ghetto in April and May 1943, would not permit Palestine to be discussed as a refuge, for fear of Arab recriminators. After the British created the Middle East Relief and Refugee Administration, they admitted 40,000 Yugoslavs, Greeks, and Poles—but no Jews—to come to the Egyptian Delta, Sinai, and Cyprus.[29] And when Joel Brand of Budapest *Vaad* (Jewish Council) made his way to Egypt in the spring of 1944, carrying Eichmann's offer of 1 million Jews for equipment, the British locked him up for the duration.[30]

The U.S. also proved solicitous of Arab feelings. In the immediate wake of Pearl Harbor, when the Afrika Korps was on the move and when every supporter was precious, officials in the Roosevelt administration encouraged Jews to "make any sacrifice" to the "Jewish Haven." Noting the strategic importance of Palestine Navy Secretary Frank Knox told a group of American Zionist leaders in January 1942, "Palestine ... is a thorn in the flank of Hitler."[31] But here, too, as the Allies experienced good fortune, the importance of Jews and their haven in the Middle East waned. Throughout 1943, discussion of Palestine was practically taboo in Washington. Even though it was public record by this time that the Nazis were engaged in a full-scale genocidal program against the Jews of Europe (protest rallies at Madison Square Garden heard Rabbi Wise speak of poison gassings, smaller informational groups in Cleveland were mimeographing accounts of death camps, the British House of Commons actually took a moment of silence to acknowledge the plight of the Jews), the U.S. remained mute. Between May 1942 and April 1943, Under Secretary of State Sumner Welles offered a host of speeches to rally support for the war. In these addresses, Welles paid tribute to 28 nations joined in the fight for liberty. He mentioned 19 Latin republics, the Chetniks of Yogoslavia, patriots in Poland, Czechoslovakia, Luxemburg, and France who murdered daily. And just as Winston Churchill saluted virtually every ethnic group in Europe but one, Welles made no reference to Jews.[32]

When Allied troops "liberated" North Africa, U.S. intelligence recommended retention of anti–Jewish decrees in Algeria and Morocco, ostensible to forestall an Arab uprising that might disrupt military operations. To American Jews who were outraged by this action, Secretary of State Cordell Hull declared: "You will readily realize that no measure is practicable unless it is consistent with the destruction of Nazi tyranny; and that the final defeat of Hitler and the rooting out of the Nazi system is the only complete answer."[33]

Chaim Weizmann had heard talk like this before. Even as they were turning the Palestine mandate on its head in the summer of 1939, British officials advised the Zionist leader to "save up" entry permits to Palestine "for your best people." In the midst of the maelstrom, October 1943, Weizmann lamented that 150,000 to 200,000 Jews had died "in torment" because of British enforcement of the 1939 White Paper on Palestine.[34]

The Arabs Declare War upon the Axis

In February 1945, King Ibn Saud met with Franklin Roosevelt aboard the cruiser *Quincy*, anchored at the Bitter Lake of Suez. The American president, returning from his meeting with Stalin at Yalta, was exhausted, but he later informed Congress: "I learned more about the whole problem, the Muslim problem, the Jewish problem, by talking with Ibn Saud for five minutes than I could have learned in the exchange of two or three dozen letters."[35]

The image of righteous commitment from a valued ally was enhanced when Saud's son Faisal participated in the opening ceremonies of the United Nations in San Francisco in April 1945. The Arabs could point out that Jordan, Iraq, Egypt, Saudi Arabia and Lebanon were all charter members of an organization formed to fight fascism, that Yemen was the first state admitted to the U.N. at the war's end.

Jordan did declare war against the Axis in 1939 — the only Arab state that joined the fray that early — because its king was subsidized by the British crown, its army officered by British soldiers. Iraq became the second Arab state to declare war against Germany, in January 1943. The rest of the Arab nations remained neutral until the last week of February 1945, when an Allied victory was assured. To secure charter membership in the international organization of nations, they had to declare war by the first day of March, a deadline that prompted Argentina to declare war upon its longtime friend Germany.

At no time, in any Arab country, did any leader, party or group protest the Nazi policy of extermination of the Jews. Among people given to street demonstrations, there were no demonstrations on behalf of Jews. Quite the contrary, Jewish refugees from Syria, Iraq,

Egypt and North Africa recall the hostility of their neighbors when an Axis victory seemed imminent. In 1942, John Gunther reported that "the greatest contemporary hero is probably Hitler." In Palestine, the peasants were being told by their mukhtars and mullahs: "Now go and sell your land to the Jews and be quick about it, for in a month Hitler will be in Jerusalem and you will not only have your land back but everything the Jews possess! Let the knives be sharpened! The great day is about to dawn!"[36]

29

Postwar Palestine:
Two Refugee Questions

The End of World War II

Before his death in April 1945, President Roosevelt promised a postwar world based on self-determination, freedom of conscience, and access to raw materials and markets. Unfortunately, the defeat of Hitler did not generate a spirit of altruism among the imperial powers. American troops helped install the French once more in North Africa. French cannon did the job in Hanoi and Damascus in 1945. The British sent forces to India, which was wracked with sectarian violence; to southern Iran, which also was in a state of civil war; to Iraq, which had been occupied in 1941; to Palestine, Egypt, Cyprus and Greece. Their major cities blitzed, their industry crushed, the British insisted upon clinging to the scraps of their crumbling empire.[1]

After two world wars, little had changed for the masses in the Middle East. Iraqi peasants were living in mud wattle huts and, like their Sumerian ancestors, were at the mercy of the annual floodwaters. Children were still being bought and sold during the month of pilgrimage in Saudi Arabia. Half the children in Egypt died before their fifth birthday. In a region where the per capita income was less than $60, *fellaheen* earned 10 cents for a 12-hour working day.[2] The British and French tolerated, but did not listen to, politicians like Nahas Pasha in Egypt, Nuri es-Said in Iraq, Shukri al-Kuwatli in Syria, and Riad as-Sulh in Lebanon. They controlled the monarchs, from Morocco's doughty King Hasan to Yemen's Imam Yahya. Abdullah needed, and feared, his 10,000-man Arab Legion, trained and staffed by British officers. Faisal, the boy king of Iraq, was little more than a figurehead. Farouk, the rotund playboy who "ruled" Egypt, busied himself with assorted currencies (his collection included 1776 U.S. Continentals and Czarist medals), pornography (photos, statuettes, and kodachromes) and comic books.

The Muslim Brothers and the Ba'ath

Just as in 1919, attempts to organize resistance against foreign occupation were quashed, agitators arrested. In Egypt, Hasan al-Banna, a hefty teacher from Ismailia, organized the

Society of Muslim Brothers in 1928. A religious zealot who roused his neighbors for morning prayer by banging on their doors in the pre-dawn hours, Hasan preached holy war against the British ("confound, disperse and punish them"). He called for a fundamentalist society based on obedience, censorship and the Shariah. By 1946 the Muslim Brotherhood counted more than two million members, another six million sympathizers in the Nile Valley. In 1951, the Brotherhood won 80 percent of the student vote in Egypt's university elections. To achieve their goals, the Brotherhood embraced terrorism, killing Egyptian Prime Minister Nokrashi Pasha in December 1948. Hasan al-Banna was assassinated two months later.[3]

The Muslim Brotherhood collided with another nationalist ideology that had its roots in the Second World War. In 1940, three Syrian dissidents meeting in Damascus created the Arab Socialist Resurrection Party (*Ba'ath*). Zaki al-Arsuzi contributed notions of a single Arab leader-liberator and racial purity. The Sunni school teacher Salah al-Din al-Bitar stressed passion over reason. Paris-educated Michel 'Aflaq, a Greek Orthodox Christian, devised the basic tenets of the movement: (a) unity of a single Arab nation stretching from the Atlantic Ocean to the mountains of Persia; (b) freedom from "colonialism, Zionism, and exploitation"; and (c) socialism, a vaguely-expressed concept that promised protection of people's rights. Driven underground by the French, the Ba'ath emerged as Syria's second strongest party in 1954.[4] The movement spread to Iraq and in 1963 Baathists staged successful coups in both countries.

Palestine: The Heart of the Arab Nation

Palestine is the "heartland of the Arab world" say Ba'ath ideologues. The intrusion of the "Zionist entity" is a dagger in the body of Islam say the Muslim Brothers. In virtually every Muslim country in the Middle East Zionism is regarded as a crime, the loss of Palestine defined in textbooks as "the disaster."[5]

When World War II ended, it was clear that the Labor government of Clement Attlee, which had been so critical of Churchill's position on Palestine, intended to implement the same policies. British Foreign Minister Ernest Bevin tried to prevent European Jews from reaching Palestine. Destroyers from the Mediterranean fleet, RAF patrol planes, and 100,000 British soldiers scoured the coastline of Palestine in search of illegal Jewish immigrants. Between April 1945 and January 1948, only five of 63 primitive scows bearing DPs made it through the gauntlet. Numbers, however, do not give an accurate reading. When the British attacked the *President Warfield*, renamed *Exodus 1947* in July 1947, world opinion was outraged. Four thousand five hundred Holocaust survivors stuffed on an old Chesapeake Bay river boat were bombarded by the British, then returned to barbed-wire encampments in Germany.[6]

Smarting from diplomatic condemnations, the British resorted to their favorite tactic—sending a commission. If nothing else, another commission would legitimate their continued presence as referee between feuding Jews and Arabs. Since war's end, Palestine had been the subject of several reviews. In April 1946, an Anglo-American Commission recommended abolishing the White Paper, ending land purchase restrictions, and the admission of 100,000 Jewish refugees yet in Displaced Persons camps. That same figure (100,000) was suggested by U.S. Immigration commissioner Earl Harrison to President Harry Truman in August 1945. It was also included in the report co-authored by Henry Grady of the U.S. State Department and Herbert Morrison of the British Foreign Office. All of these recommendations were rejected by the Arabs.

In February 1947, a United Nations Special Commission on Palestine (UNSCOP), representing 11 nations, toured the DP camps in Europe and the Middle East. Their hosts, the British, made them feel uncomfortable, offering poor food and accommodations. And though the Arabs made it clear that they wanted no part of a Zionist settlement, UNSCOP submitted a plan calling for the end of the mandate by October 1948 and the partition of Palestine into two states, one Arab and one Jewish. Each of these would consist of three interlocking triangles, which for the Zionists included part of the upper Galilee, the coast from Haifa to Jaffa, and much of the Negev.[7]

Partition was unacceptable to the Arabs in 1937. It was unthinkable now — to the mufti, who was waiting to return home in triumph; to Abdullah, who entertained notions of leaving Amman for Jerusalem; for Farouk, who fantasized about a new Egyptian empire; to the Saudis only recently removed from the Middle Ages. Unthinkable because the British themselves were turning over arms and strongpoints to the mufti's army in the hope that they might return to Palestine with Abdullah's Jordan Legion. Unthinkable because of the makeup of the Palestinian U.N. delegation at Lake Success: Jamal Husseini, Emil Ghouri, Rassem Khalidi and Wasef Kamal, all of whom participated in pro–Axis activities during the war.[8]

Partition was unthinkable because the plan required two-thirds approval of the members of the General Assembly. On November 29, 1947, Arab spokesmen pleaded with their colleagues to reject a partition that was "smirched with blood." The delegate from Iraq queried whether the map was drawn in a madhouse and warned that the plan, "guarantees chaos and disorder." In this, he was seconded, by delegates from Pakistan, Ethiopia, China, even Canada.[9]

There were 54 members in the United Nations. The Arabs could count on their own bloc (Egypt, Iraq, Lebanon, Saudi Arabia, Syria, and Yemen) plus Muslim states (Afghanistan, Iran, Turkey) and those with exposed minorities (Greece, India) to vote no. Britain and several other countries (China, Ethiopia, Yugoslavia, Mexico, Honduras, Chile and Argentina) would, for a variety of reasons, abstain. The U.S., Latin America and Western Europe could be dismissed as a lost cause because of domestic Jewish influence.

Partition depended on the vote of the Soviet bloc. Historically, the communists, from Marx through Lenin and Trotsky, opposed Zionism. When the Byelorussian delegate voted yes in the roll call, it was clear that Czechoslovakia, Poland, the Ukraine, and USSR would follow. To this day, scholars dispute why Stalin took this action. Perhaps it was prompted by a moment of madness, perhaps the misguided notion that left-wing parties in Israel might serve as a springboard for communist penetration of the Middle East. At the very least, a Jewish state would stir anti–Western sentiment.

When the vote was counted, it was 33 to 13 in favor of partition, with eight abstentions. Two "Third World" states, Liberia and the Philippines, supported partition. The only surprise negative came from Cuba, ruled by dictator Fulgencio Batista.[10]

Israel's War for Independence

Celebrations on the streets of New York and Tel Aviv proved premature. From Arab notables came anger and threats. Syrian President Shukri al-Kuwatli said, "We live or die with Palestine." His prime minister, Jamil Mardam, added: "Stop talking my brother Moslems. Arise and wipe out the Zionist scourge." From Ibn Saud: "There are fifty million Arabs, what does it matter if we lose 10 million people to kill all the Jews. The price is worth it." In Egypt, Azzam Pasha, late of a detention camp, declared: "This will be a war of extermination, a momentous massacre which will be spoken of like the Mongolian massacres." Hassan al-Banna agreed: "All Arabs shall arise and annihilate the Jews. We shall fill the sea with their corpses." Of all those who welcomed the conflict, Haj Amin el-Husseini put it most succinctly. Said the friend of Hitler and Eichmann, "I declare a holy war, my Muslim brothers! Murder the Jews! Murder them all!"[11]

In 1947 and 1948, such threats loomed very real to people who had just seen six million of their own murdered. Jews believed the chants of hatred because terrorists were translating words into action. In December 1947, Arabs at the Haifa oil depot attacked Jewish co-workers with knives, leaving 41 dead. In January 1948, several Jews were burned alive at the settlement of Ein Zeitun near Safed. Between January and May, 300 defenders of the Kfar Etzion complex (south of Jerusalem) were overrun by 2000 volunteers of the mufti's Arab Liberation Army. Many who surrendered were machine-gunned. Twenty girls were blown up in one house. On January 16, 1948, 35 students (including one young woman) bound for Kfar Etzion as a relief column were ambushed on the Jerusalem road. The men's bodies were found sexually mutilated. The girl's body was never recovered. On February 1, 1948, a bomb planted at the *Jerusalem Post* building killed one and injured 20. Three weeks later, another explosion rocked the Ben Yehuda market, killing 46 and wounding 130. On March 12, a third device killed 14 and wounded 40 at the Jewish Agency building."[12]

The attacks did not abate when the British departed Palestine on May 15. Overnight, the *Vaad Leumi* (the Jewish National Council) declared the independence of Israel. (The U.S. offered de facto recognition minutes after David Ben-Gurion made his announcement in Tel Aviv. De jure recognition came from Russia the next day.) As contingents from seven Arab armies (Egypt, Jordan, Syria, Lebanon, Iraq, Saudi Arabia and Yemen) attacked the new state, atrocities generated more hatred. On April 14, a convoy of 105 patients, doctors, and nurses winding its way to Mt. Scopus hospital was slaughtered in revenge for the massacre of Deir Yassin (see following). The same month, Egyptian soldiers were captured on Palestinian soil, carrying matches and razor blades to be used in burning and castrating Jews at Kfar Darom. In May, the settlements of Ramat Rachel (near the tomb of Rachel at Bethlehem) and Yad Mordechai (made up of survivors of the Warsaw Ghetto) were overrun. On May 28, the Jewish Quarter in the Old City fell and 5000 Jews, most of them noncombatants, many of them tracing their roots in this section back generations, were expelled. The Arab Legion pummeled synagogues and hospitals at point-blank range. Thirty-five religious institutions, including the venerable Hurve, Rambam and Sephardi Istanbuli synagogues, the Porat Yosef yeshiva, and the Sephardi hospital were gutted. Building blocks and tombstones from the Mt. of Olives were stripped to provide fortifications, latrines, even garden walls of the Intercontinental Hotel overlooking the ancient Jewish cemetery.[13]

The killing went on—at Nitzanim, where several Jewish females were disemboweled in June 1948; at hill 69 in the Negev, where Jewish defenders were routed by Egyptian tanks; and at El Auja in December 1948, where several Jews were bayoneted as they crawled toward water holes. As ghoulish as they may sound, it is necessary to recite these atrocities because few, if any, of the principal texts on the Middle East mention them. The standard procedure is to lament wrongs that were committed by both sides, then detail one incident perpetrated by the Zionists—Deir Yassin.

Deir Yassin and the Arab Refugees

A sleepy village of apricot orchards and olive groves four miles west of Jerusalem, Deir Yassin was attacked by elements of the Stern Gang and Irgun on the morning of April 10,

1948. Before the day was over, 250 Arabs lay dead and Palestinians would be convinced that Deir Yassin was the model for what would result from a Zionist victory. In this telling, Deir Yassin caused the flight of 600,000 Palestinians from their homes.[14]

In reality, Deir Yassin was less an atrocity than a bungled military operation. Later disavowed by Ben-Gurion's government-in-waiting, the attack was sanctioned by David Shaltiel, *Haganah's* commander in Jerusalem. By April, the situation for 100,000 Jews in the vicinity of Jerusalem had become desperate. Ammunition, petrol, water, milk, and food were all in short supply. The steep, narrow highway through the *Shaar ha-Gai* was littered with the rusted hulks of trucks that failed the gauntlet west of Jerusalem.

Zionist militants hoped to build a small airstrip for Piper Cubs to give Jerusalem some relief. Deir Yassin was selected because of its location and because its villagers allegedly had participated in pogroms in 1929 and 1937. The attackers claimed they merely wanted to frighten the villagers away. To accomplish this, they were going to use a loud speaker mounted on a truck. But as dawn broke on the morning of April 10, the truck skidded into a ditch and could not be moved. Armed sentries at village checkpoints refused to permit the intruders and gunfire broke out.

Arab runners were sent to Kawukji's camp at Ein Karem and to the Mosque of Umar in East Jerusalem where thousands of Palestinians were mourning the death of one of their military leaders, Abdel Kader el-Husseini. Though the fighting in Deir Yassin continued for more than eight hours, neither the Arabs nor Mandatory authorities attempted to intervene. Meanwhile, the raiders, angered by the resistance they encountered, were using grenades against the villagers. At nightfall, officials of the International Red Cross arrived on the scene and condemned the carnage. Haganah's commander Shaltiel disavowed responsibility and Ben-Gurion, trying to save face, repudiated the action in an apology to King Abdullah.[15]

Deir Yassin was not the cause of the Palestinian exodus, but rather another manifestation of that flight. Israelis maintain that even before Deir Yassin the grand mufti had broadcast warnings that any Arab who remained in Zionist territory would be treated as a collaborator. Over the winter of 1947 and 1948, Western journals were telling of "fat effendis in tasseled tarbooshes and double-breasted business suits streaming from Jerusalem in new American sedans that swayed under the load of rolled-up Turkish rugs and bundled household goods."[16]

More Arabs fled their home cities when the Arab Liberation Army proved incapable of stopping the Zionists. When British troops withdrew from Tiberias on April 18, the local mufti urged 6000 Arabs to flee. On April 20, Amin Izzedin, the ALA commander in Haifa, went off to Beirut. Within a week 40,000 Arabs left the seaport city. Pitched battles were fought between Jew and Arab in Jaffa during the last week of April and when it was over, the Muhktar Abdel Bari urged 65,000 Arabs to go to Gaza. Claiming that the Jews were using the atom bomb (actually a homemade mortar nicknamed the Davidka), two ALA commanders abandoned Safed on May 10. In some instances, the Arabs were urged by Jews in these communities to stay. In Haifa, Arab-Jewish trade councils plastered walls with appeals for calm — to no avail.[17]

There was one last wave of emigration, in July 1948. A contingent of Israeli troops under Moshe Dayan occupied Lydda (July 10) and Ramleh (July 12). The two towns were left unprotected by Abdullah, who did not want to risk losing Jerusalem by spreading his forces too thin. The townsfolk in Lydda attacked and killed five Israelis posted at the Dahmash mosque. Fighting lasted nearly a day. When it was over, 30,000 people (including George Habash, who later created the Popular Front for the Liberation of Palestine) were given three hours to leave.[18]

1949: The Rhodes Accords

The first Arab-Israeli conflict lasted through most of 1948. There were two pauses in the summer as mediators worked for a cessation of hostilities. The first truce, in June, cost the life of Count Folke Bernadotte, assassinated by Zionist extremists for advocating a plan that would have deferred Israel's independence. The second, in July, resulted in the expansion of Zionist territory at Lydda-Ramleh and parts of the Galilee.

Finally, at the end of February 1949, U.N. Envoy Ralph Bunche negotiated a series of agreements among the major belligerents (Egypt, Syria, Jordan, and Israel). These Rhodes Accords guaranteed the right of all states to security and freedom from attack. The signatories renounced the use of para-military forces and pledged their assistance to the U.N. secretary general in facilitating the transition to a permanent peace.[19]

For the Zionists, the Rhodes Accords seemed to be the fulfillment of Herzl's dream. In their eyes, Israel's triumph was as miraculous as that of the ancient Maccabees. Six hundred thousand people had withstood the challenge of 100 million Arabs and even Great Britain (which in December threatened to intervene in the Sinai). Some partisans argue the adversaries were never so unfairly matched as the Zionists claim. In this telling, the Zionists were able to mobilize 100,000 troops, many of them veterans of World War II, against ragtag elements of the mufti's army. The Zionists received shipments of arms from American sympathizers and the Czechs in the summer of 1948, while poorly trained forces of Egypt and Syria tried to make do with rifles that backfired.

Neither scenario is accurate. Nothing prevented the Arabs from gaining military experience with the British in World War II. The one contingent that trained in such a manner, the Jordan Legion, distinguished itself during the 1948 War. Arab supplies were defective because of graft and corruption in their own capitals. Arab morale was poor because their leaders— the mufti, Abdullah, Farouk — rarely coordinated plans and entrusted command to incompetents like Fawzi al-Kawukji. Perhaps the most significant factor in determining the outcome of the war was the attitude of the resident population of Palestine itself. Arab refugees fled their homes in panic after Deir Yassin because of projected fears of what the Jews might do to them. Despite suffering a string of bloody massacres, Jews stayed because there simply was no place else to go.

Palestine and Refugees

In 1969, Israel's Prime Minister Golda Meir asked disparagingly, "Who are the Palestinians?" Meir's comments were directed to descendants of Canaanites, Samaritans, Amorites and Assyrians who occupied portions of the land in the pre–Christian era; Greeks and Romans who remained after their empires crumbled; Arabs who founded camp cities in the seventh century; Tulunid Egyptians who brought Turkish and Black African slaves with them in 868; Fatimids who introduced Berber, Slavic, and Kurdish mercenaries; Persian troops granted leaseholds in Galilee and Sidon by Saladin; the Mongol hordes of Hulagu and Tamerlane; 18,000 Yurate Tatars from the Euphrates valley; 20,000 Ashiri Tatars and 4000 Moulai Mongols who occupied the Jordan Valley in the 14th century; legions of Mamelukes, Georgians and Circassians; Moghrabiyeh Muslims who moved to the Holy Land once North Africa passed under European control in the 19th century; Maraba tribesmen from Libya who brought Sudanese slaves with them to the Negev; landless Egyptian *fellaheen* who fled to Jaffa and Acre in 1829; bedouin from Arabia who moved to the Beisan and Nablus to avoid paying extortionate levies to their shaykhs; and thousands more, between 40,000 and 250,000, who were attracted to Palestine in the 1920s by economic opportunity.[20]

In addition to Jews, the Palestinian population included Bosnians, Kalmucks, Turkomans, Kharmazians, Maronites, Ethiopians, Gypsies and Armenians. Many of these people could only trace their lineage back one or two generations. In a feudal empire, most did not own the land they farmed. And, as William Ziff relates: "As long as these masses have lived side by side, they have been at each others throats. Tribe hated tribe, city man hated fellah, Bedouin despised both, sect cursed sect, and even family disdained family as unworthy scions of an inferior race."[21]

Refugees did flee their homes as a result of the fighting in 1948, but they did so identifying not so much as Palestinian nationals as Arabs. They were powerless to prevent Egypt from occupying the Gaza Strip or Jordan from annexing the West Bank and claiming Jerusalem as its new capital. The Arab refugees were confident that they would soon return to their homes. It was a confidence born as much of United Nations resolutions as the bluster of Arab governments.

On November 19, 1948, the U.N. General Assembly adopted a resolution to provide temporary care for the refugees. A year later (December 8, 1949) the United Nations Relief and Works Agency for Palestinian Refugees in the Near East (UNRWA) was created. Its charter was to run only until December 31, 1950. Experts like Clarence Pickett of the American Friends Service Committee and Henri LaBouisse (director general of UNRWA between 1954 and 1958) repeatedly urged that the refugee problem be peaceably resolved. Yet UNRWA's mandate was extended to 1952, then 1955, 1960, etc., and the number of refugees enrolled in its $100-million annual budget climbed from 711,000 in June 1949 to 879,667 in June 1951, and more than 1.5 million by June 1967. As Ralph Galloway, onetime head of the UNRWA office in Jordan, put it: "Arab leaders don't give a damn whether the refugees live or die."[22]

Meanwhile, the refugees festered in unspeakable conditions. The fortunate ones found shelter in churches or monasteries. Most were housed in leaky tents, caves, or stone huts. Western observers told of four persons sharing a single blanket. Two hundred persons daily died of exposure or diseases like measles, diphtheria, dysentery, and malaria. Before volunteers from the Red Crescent, Red Cross, Catholic and Lutheran charities became involved, food consisted of dates and flour and little else. The intercession of UNRWA, raising the daily food ration to 1500 calories, also helped sustain the refugees. Nothing could assuage their sense of loss.[23] From camps in Lebanon, the West Bank, or Gaza, they heard tales of how Israelis reclaimed the Jezreel and Negev. They resented the apartments and universities that sprang up in Haifa and Tel Aviv and other Israeli settlements which, they claimed, were planted atop the ruins of their own towns.

Over the years, Palestinian refugees became one of the better educated groups in the Middle East. But as Edward R. Murrow once observed, the substance of that education was questionable. An anti–Western generation proclaiming itself the *Jil al-Naqma* (the generation of revenge) was reared on history texts that praised Pharaoh and denounced the Jews as false Semites.[24]

Although the Arabs claim Israel has attempted genocide against the Palestinians, their numbers multiplied to more than 4 million by 1978. In the West Bank, 400,000 persons who had never left their homes were declared eligible for UNRWA assistance in April 1950. Not all of those enrolled by UNRWA were bona fide refugees. Already in 1952, the U.N. agency stated that refugees were passing newborn babies from family to family and failing to report deaths in order to increase their food rations. When U.S. Senators Albert Gore, Sr. (D-Tenn.) and Gale McGhee (D-Wyo.) held hearings on the refugee problem in 1959, they were told by George Vinson, UNRWA field eligibility officer: "We are fully aware we have tens of thousands of non-existent people with ration cards." In 1965, State Department spokesman Phillips Talbot informed the House Foreign Affairs Committee that a considerable number of the 876,000 persons drawing rations were self-supporting, dead, or the product of fraudulent registrations. Another State Department spokesman added on June 14, 1966, that perhaps as many as 200,000 of the 450,000 cards issued for Jordanian camps had fallen into the hands of speculators. When the Israelis occupied the West Bank in 1967, they found 228,000 fewer persons in the camps. UNRWA's official 1966 report noted a gap between actual refugees and those being assisted. On May 9, 1988, Dr. Magnes Ehrenstrom, an international authority on refugees, conceded that "Many, many on the rolls were dead people."[25]

Wherever they have gone in the Middle East, the Palestinians have faced discrimination. It is virtually impossible for them to obtain citizenship, let alone vote, in Libya, Syria, Egypt, or Lebanon. They have been confined to shanty towns and compelled to carry identity cards listing them as refugees. No Arab state permits them to become a minister or hold rank in the police or military. Palestinians receive unequal pay, are subjected to quotas in education, and face religious discrimination (if Christian), even in Jordan where 60 percent of the population is Palestinian.

The Forgotten Refugees: Jews from Islamic Countries

Before the creation of the state of Israel, more than a million Jews lived in Muslim countries. There were 80,000 in Yemen and Aden with ties to the land dating back to Solomon; 100,000 Egyptian Jews could trace their ancestry back to mercenaries who came into the upper nomes in the fifth century B.C. The Jews of Iraq, perhaps 150,000 in number, looked back to the Babylonian Captivity; 50,000 lived in Syria and Lebanon since the time of David. Some of the 40,000 Libyan Jews were troglodytes. Five hundred thousand in the Maghreb (Tunisia, Algeria, Morocco) claimed descent from Jews who traded with the Carthaginians and pre–Christian Berbers. Some 80,000 lived in Iran, and 75,000 in Turkey.

Today there are fewer than 1000 Jews in Yemen-Aden; perhaps 500 in Egypt, Iraq and Lebanon combined; 2500 in Syria; less than 20 in Libya; 3000 in Tunisia; 300 in Algeria; 10,000 in Morocco; 27,000 in Iran; and 24,000 in Turkey. Many left their homelands for Western Europe, Canada and the United States. Many more went to Israel in airlifts like "Operation Magic Carpet," which ferried 75,000 Yemenites between 1948 and 1950, and "Operation Ali Baba," which brought another 125,000 from Iraq in 1950–51.[26]

In the postwar period, these exposed communities experienced waves of brutality associated with the fight for Palestine. Pogroms went unchecked in Tripoli, Lebanon, where 14 persons were killed in November 1945; in Aleppo where the great synagogue was looted and torched the same month; in Cairo where 10 people were killed and 350 injured on Balfour Day 1945 and another 50 in the ghetto were killed in bomb blasts in the summer of 1948; in Libya where vandals did $3 million damage to Jewish institutions; in Baghdad where Jews were accused of ritual murder in May 1947; in Aden City where $4.5 millions in damage was done in December 1947; in Beirut where the main synagogue was bombed back in 1939; and in Damascus where 12 persons were killed and 26 injured when a bomb rocked the great synagogue in August 1949.[27]

In Lebanon, rabbis were required to pay a special tax for every religious service. Synagogues were closed (including 25 houses of worship in Baghdad) or converted into tourist attractions (as was the ancient Ben Ezra synagogue in Cairo). Jews were ousted from schools and jobs. Where education was compulsory, as in Lebanon, Jews wore shirts with distinctive blue and white stripes. In Iraq, Jewish teachers were dismissed from schools, Hebrew and Jewish history were forbidden, and Arab headmasters were put in charge of community schools.

Jews were stripped of civil rights, denaturalized, as every state emulated Iraq, requiring Jews to carry identity cards stamped "Yahudi" or "Mousawi." Zionism was equated with atheism, anarchism and Nazism and was punishable either by 15 years in prison or death. Anyone attempting to travel to Israel or send a letter to that country could be arrested and tortured. Jews were sent off on labor details from which they never returned. The simplest solution, though, was to hang them. In September 1948, Shafiq Ades of Basra, denounced as "a founder of Zionism," was publicly lynched, leaving the Iraqi government $20 million richer.

Such confiscations proved lucrative as governments encouraged Jews to leave while freezing bank accounts and denying them the right to take more than a handful of possessions. In this manner, it is estimated that Nuri es-Said enriched Iraq by $120 million in Jewish bank accounts and $300 million in sequestered properties. When Egypt expelled 20,000 Jews in 1956 Nasser permitted the emigrants to take one outfit of clothing and some pocket money. In August 1971, the Association of Jewish Victims of Egyptian Persecution in Tel Aviv estimated their total losses at more than $1 billion.

Jews forced to flee Arab lands endured harassment, sickness and starvation in their journeys. As one nurse reported of the Yemenite exodus:

> They camped in the open. I found men, women and children disintegrating, dying a slow death, minute by minute, lying on the ground with swollen bellies, others with open wounds. No doctors were allowed to go out to them, but a hundred and fifty thousand Paludrine pills were eventually sent, only they could not take place of food. There was no one to help them, only the savage sun looking down. I get sick when I remember some of the scenes I saw. Worms crawling in the festering wound of a man, eating his flesh. Men in pain pleading with me: "Cut off my leg." I estimate that four or five hundred died in those two places alone in a few weeks. I don't know how may perished in other places.[28]

As more "Oriental" Jews arrived in Israel, tensions among the different nationalities grew. Lacking decent housing and denied job opportunities, militant refugees, calling themselves "Black Panthers," demonstrated in 1958 and 1961.[29] The government tardily acknowledged that major problems existed for immigrants from Arab lands. Few of the Sephardic refugees could read or write, fewer still possessed technical skills. Personal hygiene, cleanliness in the home, pre- and post-natal care had to be improved. Despite spending 40 percent of its annual budget on defense, Israel developed a host of social welfare programs to aid the refugees. Histadrut, the giant labor union that embraces most of Israel's workers, set aside sums for elementary education and university scholarships. The Association for Working Mothers and *Kupat Holim* (the national health service) sent volunteers to instruct refugee women in cooking, contraception, and care of their children. Youth organizations, adult centers and *Zahal* (Israel's army) worked to upgrade literacy. According to Yehuda Dominitz, onetime head of Israel's Immigration Agency, the cost of integrating refugees from Islamic lands by 1990 topped more than $11 billion.[30]

Most of the money came from the Israeli government assisted by individual Jews around the world. The American Joint Distribution Committee has spent $150 million in

Muslim countries since 1914 and the U.S. State Department budgets $12 to $25 million annually through its Refugee Programs Bureau for Jews from "countries of distress" such as Iran, Iraq, Syria, Yemen, Russia, and Ethiopia. By way of contrast, in 1987 the U.S. continued as the largest donor to UNRWA with a contribution of $67 million.

In April 1954, the U.N. defined a refugee as "a person who ... owing to a well-founded fear of being persecuted for reasons of race, religion, nationality, membership in a particular social group or political opinion, is outside the country of his nationality and is unable, or owing to such fear, is unwilling to avail himself of the protection of that country."[31] Arabs argue that Jews do not qualify as refugees because they left of their own volition and have been naturalized in Israel. Apparently the international community accepts this position. Although the United Nations High Commissioner for Refugees is responsible for the welfare of 12 million persons it has never included Jews from Islamic countries.

Solutions That Were No Solutions

Over the years, a number of proposals have been advanced for the resolution of the Palestinian refugee question. In January 1952, the United Nations devised a three-year, $250-million master plan for relief and re-integration of the Palestinians. By 1955 only $10 million had been spent, fewer than 8000 persons made self-sufficient. In 1953, the U.S. government proposed a Jordan River Authority that would create 200,000 farms and practically resettle the whole lot of 600,000 refugees. Through 1953 and 1954, Israeli diplomats Moshe Sharett and Gideon Raphael expressed their country's willingness to readmit 100,000 refugees, provided those returning promised to live in peace. In the fall of 1954, Raphael went so far as to propose compensation for refugees, access to the port of Haifa, and a land-link between Gaza and the West Bank in exchange for non-aggression pacts. All of these schemes were rejected by Arab states.[32]

Since World War II, the world has resettled more than 50 million refugees. Nine million East Germans and three million Sudeten residents fled into the Federal Republic of Germany. Some 400,000 Karelian exiles have been integrated into Finland. Throughout Africa, states have welcomed victims of civil war, famine and tyranny. The U.S. has helped with millions of displaced persons— 500,000 Hungarian refugees, another 500,000 refugees from Fidel Castro, and tens of thousands from Asia and Central America. Fifteen million Hindus and Muslims were exchanged by Pakistan and India in 1947 and 1948.

Acknowledgment that there were two refugee questions generated by the Arab-Israeli war of 1948 and that it simply is not feasible to repatriate two refugee peoples might have gone a long way toward defusing an interminable wound in Middle Eastern affairs. Unfortunately, such a concept requires a commitment to peace from both sides, and as Azmi Nashashibi of the Jordanian-Israeli Mixed Armistice Commission once told his Israeli counterpart: "The difference between us is that you are interested in resolving the disagreements between us, and we are not."[33]

30

Egypt: Nasser's Philosophy of Revolution

1952: The Ouster of Farouk

Arab state blamed Arab state for the "Palestine disaster," as the defeat in 1948 was called. With the passing years, a myth was invented, one given new life during the Anglo-French invasion of Suez in 1956, that Britain always favored the Jews, that America had actually sent troops to aid the Zionists. In this atmosphere of rage, murder became synonymous with political opposition — in Egypt where Prime Minister Nokhrashi was assassinated in 1948, in Jordan where King Abdullah was shot dead on the steps of the Mosque of Umar in 1951. Another generation was preparing to take power, one that took inspiration from Mohammed Mossadeq's nationalist upheaval in Iran.

In Egypt the revolutionaries had been trained at the Royal Military Academy and blooded in war against Israel. One of these, the son of a postman from Upper Egypt, was Gamal Abdel Nasser (1918–70). Wounded and captured in the Negev fighting of 1948, Nasser blamed the British and their political lackeys for pushing Egypt into a war for which it was unprepared. His list of villains included Abdullah, who was "sitting on the sidelines laughing at us" and the "shiftless" Palestinians. Said Nasser, "If ever I should occupy an official position, I shall think a thousand times before dragging my men into war. I would only do so when the honor of the Fatherland was threatened and its future at stake; when nothing but the fire of battle could save the situation."[1]

The Palestine debacle was only one humiliation that caused Nasser and his comrades in a clique known as the Free Officers to seethe. Negotiations between Egypt and Great Britain on the issue of complete independence merely resulted in the withdrawal of British troops to the Canal Zone. In October 1951, the Wafdist government abrogated the treaty of 1936 and gave its blessing to the "liberation" of Suez. For several months, the British were besieged by Muslim fanatics. On January 22, 1952, they attacked the headquarters of auxiliary police in Ismailia killing 45 Arabs. The following day, "Black Saturday," police abandoned their posts in protest, and dozens of foreigners were killed in hotels, clubs and businesses.[2]

As Egypt stumbled through four prime ministers in six months, Nasser's Free Officers plotted to put an end to the monarchy and inept parties like the Wafd. Fearing their youth would work against them, the Free Officers tried to enroll Aziz Ali al-Misri, the icon of Egyptian nationalism, to serve as a figurehead in the new government. Aziz Ali was flattered, but declined, leaving titular command of the revolution to Major General Muhammad Naguib, a 51-year-old hero of the 1948 war whose grandfather had fought with Gordon at Khartoum.[3]

According to Kermit Roosevelt, U.S. intelligence operatives promoted the scheme and even helped draft Egypt's new constitution once the revolution took place on July 23, 1952.[4] Three days after the bloodless coup, Farouk abdicated his throne and went into exile. A sham regency was abolished in June 1953. By order of the new ruling elite, the Revolutionary Command Council, political parties were dissolved. Elections were promised for 1956. Until then, the affable Naguib would serve as president and prime minister, the somber Nasser as deputy prime minister.

Disagreements between the two men resulted in a flurry of resignations and counter-resignations. Naguib quit on February 25, 1954, and Nasser succeeded him. Two days later, demonstrations in Cairo forced Naguib's recall as president. On March 9, Nasser resigned as prime minister but retained his post in the Revolutionary Command Council. When Naguib tried to repeal the ban on political activity, Nasser again assumed the prime minister's portfolio on April 18. In the next few months, he exploited the threat of the Muslim Brotherhood and terms of an October treaty negotiated by Naguib with the British over Sudan to expand his influence in the junta and the army. Finally, on November 14, 1954, Nasser forced Naguib to resign a second time. The senior officer was placed under house arrest in Cairo. Nasser was now supreme ruler of Egypt.

Nasser

This self-proclaimed Saladin was a moderate when he engineered Egypt's 1952 revolution. Abdul Karem Kassem of Iraq, Libya's Qaddafi, and a host of other Arab militants paid tribute to him as the inspiration for their own brand of revolution, yet he was no profound thinker.

"Nasserism" was articulated in Nasser's *Egypt's Liberation: Philosophy of a Revolution.*[5] In this pamphlet (ghost-written by Muhammad Heikal), Egypt's war lord likened himself to a figure from Luigi Pirandello's *Six Characters in Search of an Author.* He had been thrust into the role of champion of his people. But Nasser recognized that his obligations extended beyond Egypt to a number of peoples described in a series of concentric circles. The first and most important circle was that of the Arabs, all of whom must be delivered from "the hooves of the invaders' steeds." The second was that of 200 million Africans who needed guidance from Egypt because "we are *in* (sic) Africa." The third circle spans oceans and continents and unites "brothers in faith," the Muslim peoples."[6]

Nasser's proposed charter borrowed freely from Baathist verbiage. The goals of Arab nationalism were (a) freedom; (b) socialism; and (c) unity, precisely the tenets outlined by 'Aflaq. Freedom was defined as independence for the nation and individual liberty. The enemy of freedom was imperialism. Socialism, the redistribution of wealth through state control of production and modern science, was the way to freedom. Unity meant solidarity with other Arab leaders, ultimately the reconstitution of a single, united Arab state. Freedom, socialism and unity were embodied in one political organization — Nasser's National Unity Party (endorsed by 99.9 percent of the people in a 1956 referendum), ousting Copts and Jews from commerce, nationalization of banks, and unions with Syria, Yemen, and

Libya. Nasserism meant boosting national pride by having the president photographed alongside India's Nehru, Yugoslavia's Tito, and Indonesia's Sukarno at Bandung in the spring of 1955, where the non-aligned Third World force was proclaimed.[7]

Unable to deal with chronic domestic problems that have plagued Egypt since the time of the pharaohs (food shortages, lack of arable land, disease, illiteracy, poverty, and one of the highest birth rates in the world) Nasser resorted to a favorite tactic of tyrants— xenophobia. Britain was damned for refusing to budge from Egypt's one great potential source of income, the Suez Canal. Though technological and economic assistance was asked from the United States, it was vilified for its support of the Zionist state. Israel was simply condemned for existing.

The Suez War 1956

Nasser based his regime on hostility toward Israel. Every scheme for the resettlement of the Arab refugees or regional development was rejected. Instead, Nasser expanded the mufti's boycott of Jews and invited armed confrontation with Israel. Planes bound for Israel were not permitted to enter Egyptian airspace. In violation of the 1888 Constantinople Convention that promised freedom of movement through the Suez Canal, Egyptian warships intercepted 103 ships of 13 nations bound for Israel between 1950 and 1956. Egyptian gunners at the Straits of Tiran also attacked ships sailing from Israel.

The Rhodes Accords prohibited all forms of para-military activity between Israel and its neighbors.[8] Nasser converted the Gaza Strip into a training ground for *fedayeen* (commandos) and encouraged their forays into Israeli territory. A four-story papier-mâché statue of a man with a gun graced Suleiman Pasha Street in the middle of the Egyptian capital. Radio Cairo warned: "Cringe and fear, O Israel, for your future, night and day, and watch out for death at any time. The fedayeen are with you everywhere. Repent in the land which will be your grave." Said Nasser: "The Fedayeen, the Palestine Army, which I started as a small force of 1000 men is today greater in number, training and equipment. I have faith in the strength, the ability, the loyalty and the courage of this army. Its soldiers will be responsible for taking revenge for their homeland and people."[9]

Between September 1, 1954, and February 1, 1955, Egypt was condemned 27 times by the Mixed Armistice Commission. On January 21, an Egyptian army unit hit an Israeli post, killing two men and wounding two others. On January 27, commandos crossed the border and ambushed farmers at Ein Hashlosha. Despite warnings from the MAC, attacks increased in frequency. In the last week of February, fedayeen raided government offices at Rishon Le-Zion, 30 miles inside Israel and killed a cyclist near Rehovot. With 50,000 nervous Jewish settlers in the Negev, Israeli strategists decided that they would respond to the next Egyptian incursion.[10] That is precisely what occurred on February 28. Egyptian troops, some of them from the Muslim Brotherhood, struck across the border and were stunned when the Israelis chased them back to their barracks in Gaza, killing 38 and wounding three.[11]

If the raid was intended to chasten Nasser or bring him to his senses, it failed. Quite the contrary, the Egyptian leader exploited the U.N.'s condemnation of Israel. The raid, just as the botched Lavon Affair of 1954 (where Israeli spies were to stage a series of bombings in Cairo), increased international sympathy for the Egyptian president. It expedited an arms deal with the U.S.S.R. (200 Mig aircraft, 200 heavy tanks, artillery, troop carriers, minesweepers, even subs) that had been in the talking stage for several months.

It contributed to a growing estrangement from the United States. And ultimately it embold-ened Nasser to exorcise his imperialist demons.

Egypt could not hope to pay for Soviet arms out of profits from cotton sales. Where would it obtain the $2 billion for a proposed Aswan High Dam project that would bring nearly 15,000 square miles of land under cultivation? The answer was the Suez Canal, which generated annual revenues of $100 million. Nasser had never been enthusiastic about the pact Naguib negotiated with the British in October 1954. Under these terms, British troops were to leave the Canal Zone by June 18, 1956, but British technicians would continue to direct operations until 1969, the expiration date of their concession. And while the 1936 mutual defense treaty was terminated, the British were granted the right to intervene in the canal zone in the event of attack "from outside the Middle East."

Britain's Prime Minister Anthony Eden and U.S. Secretary of State John Foster Dulles deluded themselves that economic assistance might tame Egypt's budding radicalism. Rela-tions cooled with the British over the winter of 1954 and 1955. The Americans experienced similar frustrations through much of 1955, when Nasser extended diplomatic recognition to communist China. Even though the Egyptian strongman had already promised the Rus-sians the Aswan project as part of his 1955 arms deal, he teased Dulles and the World Bank with the notion that he might permit the Americans to build the 400-foot high dam.[12]

Matters came to a head in the summer of 1956. As promised, on June 18, the last British troops left Suez. On June 30, the deadline passed for acceptance of America's initial grant of $56 million. After waiting nearly three weeks, on July 19, Dulles announced that the U.S. was withdrawing its loan proposal for the Aswan Dam. A week later, on July 26, Nasser informed a mass audience in Cairo that he was nationalizing the Suez Canal. He was confident that the Western allies would not be able to agree on any effective response.

While specialists in international law debated the merits of the seizure, Egyptian pilots and troops remained in position from Port Said to Ismailia. When a humbled Dulles pro-posed a conference to oversee operations, Nasser ridiculed the idea as tantamount to war. As the world's attention was diverted to anti–Soviet uprisings in East Germany, Poland and Hungary, Anthony Eden seethed. The British prime minister likened Nasser to Mussolini or Hitler and wanted no part of a second Munich. A preferable historical lesson was that taught to Mehemet Ali by Palmerston in 1839 and 1840. In this, Eden would have the sup-port of French Prime Minister Guy Mollet, smarting from Nasser's shipments of arms to FLN rebels in Algeria. With or without American support, the allies hoped to strike a blow that would regain control of Suez and finish off Nasser.

The Israelis, coincidentally, had reached the same conclusion. Bolstered by the arrival of Soviet arms shipments, Nasser moved 45,000 troops into the Sinai and stepped up feday-een raids. New airfields and ammunition dumps were carved out of the desert in anticipa-tion of an attack on Israel scheduled for April 1957. Early in October 1956, Iraqi troops began filtering into Jordan in violation of the 1949 Rhodes Accords. That same month, Egyptian General Amer visited Amman to establish a unified military command among the Arab states. As casualties from armed incursions from Egypt continued to amount (more than 101 dead, 364 wounded according to Abba Eban), Israel's limits were reached when feday-een attacked Sde Boker, David Ben-Gurion's kibbutz in the Negev.

"Operation Kaddish," Israel's intended death blow to Nasser, was scheduled for November 1956. Israeli intelligence learned that the British and French were planning their own independent action. On October 23, at a time when Hungarian nationalists were still hopeful that demonstrations would force the Russians from Budapest, Ben-Gurion met with Christian Pineau and Selwyn-Lloyd at Sevres. Two days later, the French transferred jets and gunboats to Israel. On October 29, Israeli paratroopers jumped into the Mitla Pass, cutting off the main body of the Egyptian army, which was shredded simultaneously by tanks and aircraft. The next day Britain and France warned belligerents to stay 10 miles away from both sides of the canal. The meaning of this communiqué was clear, if not imme-diately, then at dusk on the afternoon of October 31, when a joint detachment of British and French bombers flattened Egyptian airfields and the city of Port Said.

In the ensuing U.N. debates, Selwyn-Lloyd justified the intervention under terms of a Tripartite Declaration (American, British, French) in 1950 guaranteeing the territorial integrity of all states of the Middle East. The British also claimed the right of intervention under terms of the 1954 pact with Egypt. Confronted with threats of Russian "volunteers," the same kind of brute force that killed 16,000 Hungarians in the first days of November 1956, the British and French backed down. They had hoped for the U.S. to be supportive. But the Eisenhower administration, re-elected for a second term, indicated through Dulles that it would do no more to assist its NATO allies than it had for the stone-throwers of Budapest.

The 100-Hour War came to an end with a truce on November 5. The human toll was 180 Israelis dead and four captured; 3000 Egyptians dead and 7000 prisoners. After much cajoling from the United States and promises from the U.N. that an effective United Nations Emergency Force would replace UNTSO border patrols, Israel agreed to pull out of the Sinai on March 16, 1957. By that time, the British and French had long since left the Canal Zone. Eden and Mendes-France both were shamed into resigning. Ironically, the only figure who profited from the carnage was Nasser. Just as he had done with the Gaza Raid of Feb-ruary 1955, he transmuted the 1956 disaster into a "strategic withdrawal." In speeches, arti-cles and films, the Egyptian people were commended for their resistance against the imperialists.[13]

A Decade of Non-Peace

Nasser waited, calculating the moment for revenge against Israel. He viewed with con-tempt American efforts to shore up anti-communist alliances in the region. The brain-storms of Dulles, the Baghdad Pact (U.S., Britain, Iraq, Jordan) and CENTO (Iran, Afghanistan, Pakistan, Turkey) would be gone within the decade. Nasser took comfort watching the French and British roll up the rugs of their African empires. The Arab League gained strength from the French withdrawal from Morocco and Tunisia in 1956 and Alge-ria in 1962. Algeria's independence was especially gratifying. Nasser supported the rebels through their eight-year civil war, knowing that FLN leadership would ultimately repose in a hard-lining radical like Chadli Boumedienne.

In February 1958, Nasser and Shukry al-Kuwatli of Syria agreed to merge their two states. The so-called United Arab Republic was approved by a vote of 99.8 percent in a March plebiscite. That same spring, Syria and Egypt tried to exploit the sectarian crisis in Lebanon. Nasser's agents incited riots in Beirut, Tripoli, and among the Druze. Radio Cairo vilified the Lebanese-Christian leader Camille Chamoun, Jordan's King Hussein, and Faisal, king of Iraq. Between May and July, 1400 persons lost their lives in Lebanon as no one, not even U.N. Secretary General Dag Hammarskjold, could bring an end to the fighting. Finally, responding to a request from Chamoun, President Eisenhower sent an American force to Beirut during the last week of July. Ten thousand Marines stabilized the situation sufficiently for elections to be held and General Fuad Chehab to take office as president of Lebanon.[14]

What prompted the American intervention was a pro–Nasserite military coup in Iraq on July 14. This time, however, the revolution was not bloodless. Mobs bent on spilling blood ran through the streets of Baghdad screaming, "We are your soldiers, Gamel Nasser!" The bodies of 23-year-old King Faisal and his uncle Abdul-Illah were torn apart. Nuri es-Said, Iraq's most respected politician, was impaled and hanged from a lamppost, some foreigners decapitated in the violence. The leader of the coup was Abdel Karim Kassem, an avowed disciple of Nasser who would rule over the neutralist republic till February 1963, when he and his closest associates were killed in another revolt directed by Deputy Prime Minister Abdel Salam Aref.[15]

Nasser's first union with Syria lasted three years. A second, federated state with Syria and Iraq in 1963 ended in disagreement after a few months. A third merger with Qaddafi's Libya in 1969 was never more than a pipedream. Unable to achieve a united *umma* from the Atlantic to the Indian Oceans, Nasser employed ruthless methods to extend his influence. In 1962 he sent 85,000 Egyptian troops to Yemen to aid in the overthrow of the Zaydi dynasty. The International Red Cross accused his forces of using poison gas during the six-year conflict in Yemen.[16] At the same time, Egypt's air force helped suppress anti-government rebels in Southern Sudan.

Riding the crest of popularity, Nasser convened an Arab summit in Cairo in January 1964. Other nations had pressed for such a meeting for several months. The cause of their concern: the impending opening of Israel's national water carrier. Unable to secure an agreement with any of its neighbors on the sharing of Jordan River waters, the Israelis proceeded with construction of a pipeline that arched around the West Bank and delivered water necessary for development of the Negev. In a region jealously guarded about water supplies, Israel's project was seen as an act of provocation.

Despite having refitted his war machine, Nasser realized that the time was not right to challenge Israel. As he said: "We will not liberate Palestine today, but time is on our side. We shall liberate Palestine by building up our strength and our armies.... We shall enter Israel not on a red carpet, but on fields of blood." At Cairo, Nasser again proposed coordinating Arab armies under General Abdel Hakim Amer. He also called for the creation of a Palestine Liberation Organization, a political movement that would embrace different factions sponsored by Egypt, Kassem, the mufti, and other dissidents. This new PLO would play a role as a fighting force for its own homeland.

On May 28, 1964, the first PLO Congress met in East Jerusalem. Superimposed on a huge map of Palestine was the slogan "We Shall Return!" After swearing an oath "that we shall sacrifice our blood for your liberation," 350 delegates selected Ahmed Shukeiry as their spokesman. The stoutish, one-time assistant secretary-general of the Arab League was introduced as the official spokesman of the Palestinian people. In fact, he, like the Palestine Liberation Army he allegedly directed, was nothing but a device of Nasser. Even Shukeiry's rhetoric ("After waiting 17 years for justice, we are morally entitled to take the law into our own hands and wage war against Israel. We know Israel will never yield our rights except at the point of a bayonet. We will sacrifice much blood, but we will win.") was a reflection of his Egyptian controller.[17]

The Six-Day War

Hoping to emulate Viet Cong successes in Southeast Asia, young Palestinians renewed fedayeen raids against Israel. *Fatah* (an acronym for *Harakat Tahrir Falastin*, Movement for the Liberation of Palestine) and its elite wing *Assifah* (storm) struck against Beit Jibrin on January 18, 1965. Before January 1967, the PLO would kill 11 Israelis and wound another 58 in more than 70 incidents. The raiders were encouraged by Nasser, who possessed a $2-billion war machine that now included 1200 tanks, 550 airplanes, SAM-2 missiles, and his own al-Zafir missile, an offensive weapon with a range of 175 miles, developed by German scientists.

In February 1966, the Baathist Party seized control in Syria and almost immediately the Syrian Air Force confronted Israeli planes above Mt. Hermon. The U.N. Security Council passed resolutions calling upon member states to desist from the hostile actions against one another. But whenever Israel or the U.S. called for specific condemnation of Arab provocations, the Soviet Union vetoed the measure.

The crisis reached a flash point in May 1967. Having been pummeled in the air, the Syrians claimed that the Israelis were mobilizing troops in the north for an invasion. Two U.N. inspections concluded the charge was baseless. However, Secretary-General U Thant reported on May 11 that Palestinian commando activity had been stepped up. Five days later, Nasser reacted to Syrian taunts that he would never face down the Israelis. On May 16, he asked Indian General Rikhiye, commanding the 1800-man United Nations Emergency Force, to withdraw from the Sinai and Sharm el-Shaykh. On May 18, U Thant ordered UNEF forces out even though the secretary-general conceded "it inevitably restores the armed confrontation of the UAR and Israel and removes the stabilizing influence of an international force up along the boundaries between the two nations." This was an astounding statement from the man charged with maintaining peace in the Middle East. U Thant's precipitate action violated personal pledges made to Israel's Golda Meir by John Foster Dulles and Dag Hammarskjold. It was illegal because the original charge for UNEF required discussions in the General Assembly before it could be terminated. But U Thant had not made any promise and he reasoned that the continued presence of a U.N. force depended upon "the consent and cooperation of the host country." In a particularly disingenuous gesture, he suggested that the UNEF troops might be transferred within Israel's borders to protect it.[18]

On May 22, Israeli Prime Minister Levi Eshkol called for a mutual troop reduction. Two days later Egyptian guns closed the straits of Tiran to Israeli traffic. Apologists for Egypt contend that the straits, just 500 yards wide, were within Egyptian territorial limits. Egypt's claim to Sinai, however, had only been recognized by Great Britain and the U.S. since 1949 and was based on a specific promise that Egypt would not interfere with peaceful shipping. Even if Egypt claimed the Sinai peninsula on the basis of links with the ancient pharaohs, a long-standing principle of international law was that "gulfs and bays enclosed by the land of more than one littoral state, however narrow their entrance may be, are nonterritorial."[19] When American Vice President Hubert Humphrey visited Europe urging U.S. allies not to cave in to Egyptian threats, no shipper risked running the gauntlet of Sharm el-Shaykh in the last week of May. Nasser's blockade of the Straits of Tiran was effective. In international parlance, a blockade once effective is an act of war.

Some historians claim Nasser's threats were nothing but bluster designed to assuage the Syrian militants. Without offering evidence, they contended Nasser was prepared to withdraw forces from the Sinai when Israel launched a pre-emptive strike on June 5. The issue of who actually started the so-called Six-Day War became moot as of May 29, when PLO units attacked the settlement of Nahal Oz and Egyptian Ambassador El Kony declared publicly that a state of war existed between the two nations. For Israelis and Jews all over the world, the atmosphere at the end of May was horrifyingly familiar. Once more the airwaves crackled with threats of Jewish extermination. Once more no nation, no international peace-keeping body, was prepared to intercede.

Monday morning, June 5, Israeli aircraft struck a series of devastating blows to airfields in the Sinai. In a matter of minutes, 410 Egyptian planes were destroyed. Air supremacy established, the Israelis recreated the 1956 drop of paratroopers into the Mitla Pass and hammered at Egyptian front line positions with tanks. Nasser charged that forces from the American Sixth Fleet had participated in the surprise attack and called upon all Arab states for assistance. Jordan, Syria and Iraq quickly responded. Jordan's artillery bombardment from Jenin proved to be self-destructive. In less than 50 hours, Israeli troops pounded their way through the West Bank to the Old City of Jerusalem. There on Wednesday, June 7, an emotional scene was enacted as soldiers joined with rabbis at the Wailing Wall. For the first time in 19 years, Jews were permitted to return to their most sacred shrine. The same day, Israeli troops began the torturous march uphill toward Syrian bunkers on the Golan Heights. By sundown of Friday, June 9, those guns were also silent.[20]

During the first hours of the war, the United Nations procrastinated. But when it became clear that the Israelis were winning, the Soviet Union demanded a cease-fire. As the Security Council worked late into the night, casualties continued to mount—more than 6000 Jordanians dead, 2500 Syrians, perhaps 20,000 Egyptians. The death toll also included 34 Americans aboard the *USS Liberty*, an intelligence-gathering vessel that was attacked by Israeli aircraft in the war zone on June 7.[21]

His dreams of empire shattered along with $2 billion in Russian equipment, Israeli soldiers cavorting on the East Bank of the Suez Canal, a canal blocked with vessels he had ordered scuttled, Nasser offered his resignation as president of Egypt. His behavior was identical with actions taken after the 1955 Gaza raid and the Suez War. Responding to public outcry, within six hours Nasser was back at his post, propagating the myth of collusion between the United States and Israel. On August 29, he attended a meeting of Arab heads of state at Khartoum. While Prime Minister Eshkol of Israel was suggesting the time was ripe for a true reconciliation in the Middle East, the protocol from Khartoum committed the Arabs to no negotiations with Israel, no recognition, no peace.

Two months later, Nasser and other Arab leaders gave their assent to U.N. Resolution 242. The text of this Security Council draft, adopted November 22, 1967, called for (a) withdrawal of Israeli armed forces from territories occupied in the recent conflict; (b) termination of belligerency and recognition of the right of every state in the region to live in peace within secure and recognized boundaries; (c) freedom of navigation through international waterways; (d) a just settlement of the [Arab] refugee problem; and (e) establishment of demilitarized zones. All of this would be accomplished under the aegis of the U.N. secretary-general. In style and substance, the peace plan differed very little from promises made at Rhodes in 1949 and again by Hammarskjold and Dulles in the winter of 1956 and 1957.

The Death of Nasser

As illusions of a peace settlement dictated by its victorious army faded, the Israelis dug into bunkers, dubbed the Bar-Lev line, along the eastern banks of the Suez Canal. Nasser, meanwhile, was mending his image as a strategist. Three times he had faced the Israelis and three times he had been routed. Nevertheless, there simply was no one else who could galvanize opposition to Israel. Stubbornly, he rejected peace plans proposed by U.S.

Secretary of State William Rogers and U.N. Special Envoy Gunnar Jarring, both of whom were favorable to Arab interests. Instead, reinforced by massive arms shipments from the Soviet Union, Nasser committed Egypt to a new variation of hostilities—the so-called War of Attrition. Over the next four years, Egyptian missile batteries and aircraft caused some casualties in the hope of wearing the Israelis down.

Nasser was not around for the Yom Kippur War of October 1973. His health broken (he was suffering from diabetes, leg pains, and a nervous rash), he died of a heart attack in September 1970. The peasant son who failed five grammar school grades had achieved extraordinary things in his 52 years. Graduate of the Royal Military Academy, leader of the Free Officers Corps, where his code name was "Jimmy," Nasser became *the* symbol of nationalism for a generation of Arabs. He never achieved his dream of a single Arab state, but millions mourned him from Morocco to Iran. Nasser resisted Aziz Ali's instruction to "kill and kill and kill" enemies of the Egyptian revolution, but he did not fulfill expectations as a peacemaker. That task would be left to his heir-designate Anwar Sadat. Perhaps the best assessment of this Egyptian leader came from P. J. Vatikiotis, who said of Nasser:

> The man therefore who, in less than a generation, became the oracle of Egypt's destiny and of Arab revolution at mid-century, was a soldier by chance, a politician by instinct and a conspirator by ability and inclination. He contributed little to soldiering or politics. But he elevated the more native art of conspiracy to new technical heights. At the end of the day, however, he was by formation, tradition and force of circumstances an Egyptian despot. The monstrous structure he controlled—the Egyptian state—tends to transform any well-intentioned ruler into a tyrant, *unless he is prepared to limit its and his own powers* (original italics).[22]

31

Egypt: Sadat and Mubarak

Anwar Sadat

Nasser's successor was even more of an enigma. An amiable, pipe-smoking man, Anwar Sadat may have done more to redeem his nation's honor than anyone since the pharaohs. It was Sadat who made the return of captured soil his main objective. Sadat who expelled the Russians from Egypt in 1972. Sadat who, dealing from a position of confidence, became the first Arab leader to visit Israel in 1977 and then subsequently agree to the Camp David Accords in 1979. Sadat, the recipient of a Nobel Peace Prize, who was so beloved in the West. And yet at the time of his funeral in October 1981, there were no crowds cheering his name or mourning his loss in Cairo or any other city in the Islamic world.

Nothing in Sadat's early life suggested he would become the dapper cosmopolitan of his last years. Born in a small town in the Nile Delta in 1918, he was a fierce nationalist from his youth. His heroes were Mustafa Kamil, Saad Zaghlul, Aziz Ali al-Misri, Hasan al-Banna, and an obscure Egyptian martyr, Zahran of Denshway. A 1938 graduate of the Royal Military Academy, Sadat claims to have been the organizer of the Free Officer clique at the base of Manqabad the following year. During the Second World War, Sadat conspired with other Egyptian officers who believed a Nazi victory was the only way to achieve independence. For his overtures to Field Marshal Rommel, he was jailed by the British.

Although he would later portray himself as a victim of imperialist cruelty, Sadat's admiration for Hitler exceeded the bounds of a normal Egyptian patriot. In his two auto-biographies, *Revolt along the Nile* and *In Search of Identity*, he describes how he was dazzled by the Nazi seizure of power in 1933. Such references might be written off to youthful indiscretion. Sadat had more problems dismissing a later paean to the Führer. In September 1953, a report cropped up in the wire services indicating that Hitler had actually survived the war and was living in South America. Asked by a Cairo newspaper to comment, the 35-year old Sadat congratulated Hitler "with all my heart." He praised Hitler for splitting Churchill and his allies from "the devil" (presumably atheistic communists), suggested there would be no peace until Germany was reunited, and closed with a benediction: "You are forgiven on account of your faith in your country and people. That you have become immortal in Germany is reason enough for pride. And we should not be surprised to see you again in Germany, or a new Hitler in your place."[1]

Some writers have argued that Sadat intended no approval of genocide, merely the efforts that a nationalist had made for his country.[2] Through the 1970s, however, the statesman Sadat made no effort to recant. Instead, he repeatedly harped on Jewish, not Israeli, faults. On Muhammad's birthday in 1972, he railed against the mean, treacherous, conspiratorial behavior of the Jews. During a Washington visit in 1975, he defended the 1974 U.N. resolution equating Zionism with racism, noting that Jews once tried to control the Egyptian economy. During a 1977 radio interview with a Tunisian journalist, he stressed that Jerusalem was an Arab city and "no Jews should live in it." A year later, the Cairo magazine *October* quoted him saying Jews were "stiff-necks," "intransigent," "clever tradesmen" who had alienated the world with their self-serving plans and complaints of persecution.[3]

On the run or in jail for most of the period between 1942 and 1950, Sadat missed the 1948 war with Israel and was only reinstated to the rank of captain in January 1950. His role in the 1952 revolution was so minor that he considered emigrating to Lebanon six months after Farouk was deposed. Ever the good bureaucrat, he served where Nasser wanted — as editor of the party newspaper *al-Gumhurriah* in 1953, secretary-general of the Islamic Congress, minister of state without portfolio, speaker of the National Assembly, and finally as vice president and heir-designate in December 1967.

Nasser trusted Sadat implicitly. He took him along to Moscow in 1965 to help persuade the Soviets to write off 50 percent of Egypt's £400 million debt. Sadat was the one who convinced Nasser that he was indispensable to Egypt following the Six-Day War. He supported Nasser's purge of generals blamed for the June 1967 debacle. He was at Nasser's side when the latter hosted an Arab summit at Cairo, days before Nasser's death in September 1970. Following that traumatic moment, Sadat moved swiftly to consolidate his own hold on government, eulogizing Nasser, emphasizing that he was Nasser's hand-picked successor, and squelching any possible mutiny in the army.

Years later, Sadat would be much harsher upon his predecessor. Nasser, he charged, had left a "crassly stupid" economic legacy. Egypt was bankrupt, in part, because of its commitment to an amorphous concept of socialism that frightened away private investors. Nasser's political legacy was equally pitiable.[4] Egypt was isolated because of an over-reliance upon the Russians. According to Sadat, Nasser alienated the U.S., his Arab kinsmen and Iran, leaving him no friends apart from the Soviet Union: "This deprived him of all freedom of movement, particularly as the way in which the Soviet Union treated him could never be described as either generous or dignified, and that consequently had an adverse effect on his health."[5]

As president, Sadat expanded trade with India and Iran, and entertained notions of union with Libya and the Sudan. He announced his own peace initiative in February 1971 (the "year of decision" he called it), and expelled 15,000 Soviet military technicians from Egypt in July 1972. While many experts in the West hailed the last move, Sadat subsequently explained: "The Soviet Union, the West and Israel misinterpreted my decision to expel the military experts and reached an erroneous conclusion which in fact served my strategy, as I had expected — that it was an indication that I had finally decided not to fight my own battle.... It was precisely what I wanted them to think."[6]

The Yom Kippur War

From the moment he came to power, Sadat was motivated by the desire to erase the shame of 1967. Arab derision of his failed peace plan fed his revanchism. Under the cover of Soviet protection, he waged his two-year War of Attrition preparing for the moment when

Egyptian forces could recross the Suez Canal. The departure of the Russians signaled the likelihood of full-scale hostilities between Israel and Egypt.[7] There now was no third force separating the belligerents. As in 1967, Egypt and Syria coordinated their plans when Assad made a secret visit to Cairo in April 1973. Unlike 1967, however, Egypt was facing a foe that had been warned that the U.S. government would not tolerate a preemptive strike.

Twice during the year 1973, in May and August, Israel reacted to what it regarded as a real threat and mobilized at the cost of $10 million. That was exactly what Sadat wanted. Egyptian and Syrian forces attacked on October 6, 1973, a date selected because it was Yom Kippur, the Jewish Day of Atonement. This attack on the most important Jewish holy day caused barely a ripple of outcry from the onlooking world. Muslims pointed out that the war was being fought during their holy month of Ramadan and that the timing of the initial assault was "strategic."

At first, IDF Commander Benjamin Elazar sounded like Fawzi Kawukji in 1948, promising that his forces would "break the enemy's bones." In fact, the Bar-Lev line on the eastern bank of Suez was being bludgeoned daily and reports of mutilation-murders of captured Jewish soldiers on the Golan Heights were causing shudders in Israel. On October 15, day nine, General Ariel Sharon directed a counter-attack, cutting off Egypt's Third Army Corps in Sinai. As a result of the fighting, 18 African states (among them Ethiopia, Liberia, Kenya, Ghana) severed diplomatic relations with Israel.

The $6 Billion War dragged on till October 27 when U.S. Secretary of State Henry Kissinger mediated a cease-fire. The Arabs had not achieved their goals. Syria wanted the Golan Heights returned and even boasted of having captured all of Mt. Hermon. Instead, Israeli attacks so panicked Baathist leaders, they prepared to flee Damascus at the end of the second week. Only a sliver of occupied territory was returned in subsequent negotiations. Sadat narrowly escaped Nasser's fate of provoking a fight and losing. He proved just as nimble, however, at reconstructing his own view of history.

All the Arabs had wanted, said Sadat, was to regain their lost territory. His troops had been well on the way to doing so until the Americans blocked his victory, through the use of spy satellites and supplies. Still, his Egyptian soldiers had fought the Israelis to a standoff. That restoration of Egyptian pride was worth the struggle. Subsequently, Sadat would construct a set of monuments to his soldiers at Nasr (Victory) City in the outskirts of Cairo.

Sadat's narrative was self-serving and inaccurate. The forces that struck across the Suez were hardly inferior in weapons or numbers to the Israelis. Egypt had 1000 artillery pieces in place, 10 times the number of guns on the Bar-Lev line. Protecting the fortifications were the most modern radar-jamming devices, more than 1000 SAM-2s, 3s and 6s that had proven so effective in Vietnam, and Frog ground-to-ground missiles. From Russia came 300 MIG 21s and MIG 23s, faster and more maneuverable than any jet fighter in the Israeli arsenal, and another 90 all-weather bombers with a range of 500 miles. Sixty thousand men, many of them trained for months in commando operations, were ferried across the canal on modern landing craft, transport helicopters or prefabricated pontoon bridges. It took these five divisions four days to dislodge the 436 men and one tank brigade defending the Bar-Lev line.

In the greatest tank battles in history, the Arabs lost 1270 Stalin IIIs, T-54s and T-55s, some of the most sophisticated equipment in the Russian arsenal (comparable to three and a half years of U.S. tank production) while Israel lost 420. The Arabs lost 387 aircraft to Israel's 115. The ratio of air-to-air combat was even more remarkable — 334 Arab aircraft lost to 3 Israeli. According to *Aviation Week and Space Technology*, Israel's losses amounted to one per 1000 sorties, surpassing the 4:1000 ratio of the Six-Day War. Together, Egypt and Syria lost 25,000 men killed, 80,000 wounded. Israel's toll was 2500 dead, 8000 wounded. Unquestionably, Israel benefited from U.S. assistance. But that was late in coming. Every member of NATO save Holland refused U.S. aircraft the right of overflight, even after the Soviet Union threatened to send volunteers into the region and President Nixon put American bases around the world on a state of alert.[8]

The Peace Process

The fourth round of Arab-Israeli hostilities did produce one positive result. Exaggerated perceptions of their military accomplishments enabled Egyptian generals to sit as equals at a negotiating table with their Israeli counterparts in the winter of 1973 and 1974. The mediation of Secretary of State Henry Kissinger led to full-fledged disengagement on September 1, 1975. To safeguard mutual security, a buffer zone manned by U.N. troops was expanded. Two hundred American civilians were sent to surveillance posts in the desert. The two adversaries were enticed with American economic assistance ($800 million to Egypt, $2.3 billion to Israel). Sadat's prestige benefited from the reopening of the Suez Canal and the return of the Sinai with oilfields that had been developed by the Israelis since 1967. For Israel, the beginning of the first serious dialogue with an Arab state was worth the sacrifice of the Abu Rudeis fields that had supplied the Jewish state with nearly 100 percent of its petroleum needs.[9]

The peace process seemed to suffer a setback with the election of Menachem Begin, a hard-liner from the Herut-Likud faction, as prime minister of Israel in the spring of 1977. In reality, Begin proved to be more flexible than his Social Democrat counterparts. While critics of Israel fretted, the staged withdrawal of Israeli troops and dismantling of Jewish towns in the Sinai proceeded, with minor incidents.

Perhaps the most incredible event in this period occurred when Anwar Sadat flew to Jerusalem on November 19, 1977. The Egyptian president had repeatedly expressed his willingness to talk anywhere to Israeli officials and Begin had responded in kind. Romanian President Nicolae Ceausescu offered to arrange a meeting, but the whole thing sounded like political puffery. Then in the fall of 1977, Israeli intelligence passed along information that Libya's Muammar Qaddafi intended to assassinate Sadat for betraying the Arab cause. Bravely or defiantly, Sadat made his pilgrimage to the Knesset in Jerusalem.[10]

It was a heady time, when the U.S., enjoying the euphoria of a bicentennial, elected Jimmy Carter president. As in the age of Wilson and FDR, there was talk of human rights. Egypt, which had been expelled from the Arab League, was receptive to American overtures to broker an Egyptian-Israel peace. In September 1978, a preliminary framework was worked out at Camp David, Maryland. The actual treaty, known as the Camp David Accords, was signed by Sadat, Begin and Carter in ceremonies at Washington on March 26, 1979.[11]

For the first time, an Arab nation recognized the territorial sovereignty of Israel and agreed that the state of war was terminated. Disputes between Egypt and Israel would be resolved peacefully, in accordance with the United Nations Charter. Israel promised to evacuate Egyptian soil within three years. In return, Egypt guaranteed the borders of Israel, renounced para-military attacks, and guaranteed freedom of passage through international waters, including the Mediterranean, Suez, and Straits of Tiran. Signed annexes promised normalization of economic and cultural relations, including freedom of movement between the two countries, and "cooperation for development."

On one question, there was no real agreement. Sadat was committed to Palestinian rights and had Carter's support. Israel agreed to open negotiations on the future of the West Bank and Gaza within a year after the exchange of formal documents. There also was discussion concerning a five-year transitional period before the Palestinians would be granted autonomy. But the issue of Palestinian rights was never outlined, let alone mentioned in the formal treaty or annexes. No one offered a sensible mechanism for discussions between Israelis who refused to recognize the PLO and the PLO, which continued to preach the destruction of Israel as part of its program.

Although Sadat privately considered the treaty a *sulh* (a tactical agreement on the order of Muhammad's pact at Hudaibiyah, not a true peace), he was reviled throughout the Arab world. Adored in the West, he became increasingly estranged from his own people. Just as the shah in Iran, he miscalculated the impact of modernization upon a traditional society. Thirty years after the 1952 revolution, the annual per capita income in Egypt was only $400. Farmers displaced by irrigation projects were clustered in shantytowns. There were riots by minorities who believed they had been unfairly treated. Fifteen hundred Copts were killed or jailed in 1981. Muslim clerics resented the prominence of Sadat's wife Jihan and legal reforms granted to women. From Cairo's al-Azhar, the blind imam Keshk preached a blend of rage and fundamentalism, not unlike that of the Ayatollah Khomeini in Iran. His cassette tapes reached Islamic dissidents in the military, some of whom formed a holy band called *Gihad*. On October 6, 1981, a group of these fanatics gunned down Sadat as he was reviewing a military parade celebrating the eighth anniversary of the Yom Kippur War.[12]

The civilized world reacted to Sadat's death with shock. But in Damascus, Tripoli, and Beirut there was dancing in the streets. Former Presidents Nixon, Ford, and Carter attended his funeral along with Begin, German Chancellor Helmut Schmidt, French President Francois Mitterand and Prince Charles of England. Only three Arab states (Sudan, Oman and Somalia) sent representatives. As one writer put it, "In Egypt, 43 million people went on with the celebration of *Id al-Adha*, the Feast of the Sacrifice, as if nothing had happened."[13]

Sadat was not as great as he or his Western admirers imagined. There is much appeal, however, in his denunciation of totalitarianism. "A man's humanity is inevitably lost," he wrote, "as he ceases to be an individual worthy of the responsibility and the vocation entrusted to him by God. The holy torch which he was created to bear and to use in lighting the way both for his fellow man and for posterity is then extinguished."[14] Sadat may be criticized for shifting policies, dictated as much by vanity as expedience. But there is no denying his commitment to peace. "For the sake of peace," he said, "I believe that for peace man may, even should do everything in his power. Nothing in this world could rank higher than peace."[15] Like so many other decent men and women in the Middle East, Sadat sacrificed his life for peace.

Mubarak

Hosni Mubarak was practically an unknown in the West when he succeeded Sadat. Commander of Egypt's Air Force during the Yom Kippur War, he is not even mentioned in Walter Laqueur's study of the 1973 war, *Confrontation*. Subsequently promoted to the vice presidency, Mubarak remained obediently in the background while Sadat won laurels. Mubarak was a military man and his diplomatic naiveté was evident in a rare interview granted to Lebanese-American journalist George Nader less than two months before Sadat's assassination. Libya, Syria, Algeria and South Yemen were, he contended, all "mini–Soviet states." PLO leadership was "not mature and honest enough to represent the Palestinians." As for Iran, "I don't think they will have a big effect on the Middle East."[16]

Back in 1981, Mubarak did say one thing that made sense. He cited an Arab proverb: "As long as there is life, you cannot be pessimistic. Once you become pessimistic, it is the beginning of the end of life. Therefore, you should always be optimistic and hope for the best." Since succeeding Sadat and being ratified in a plebiscite by 98 percent of Egypt's voters, Mubarak has attempted to give meaning to that Arab bromide. In Egypt, he moved swiftly to suppress further fundamentalist outbreaks, arresting members of *Al Takfir Wal Hijra* (repentance and flight from sin) and executing five of their leaders. At the same time, he met with Islamic leaders to assure them of his commitment to the special place of religion in Egypt's society. He ended Sadat's economic policy of *Infitah* ("opening" Egypt's business), freeing the economy from socialist restrictions.[17] While some Egyptian entrepreneurs became millionaires, most Egyptians benefited little. Food and clothing were in short supply. Most housing was substandard. A nation that was once the breadbasket of the Middle East was now forced to import as much as 60 percent of its food requirements.

Mubarak tried to rectify these problems by increasing the minimum wage, expanding social security and subsidies for clothing, fuel and food. For many years, construction for his Cairo metro, a costly boondoggle, snarled traffic in the capital. But once completed it gave the nation a sense of pride that this ancient land also had its modern underground transit system. Mubarak addressed the dislocation in agriculture through reform of water management, crop quotas and prices. He also gave Egypt its first free elections in 1984. Mubarak was elected to a six-year term as president while his National Democrats won 73 percent of the seats in the People's Assembly.[18]

Despite revenues from the Sinai oilfields, as late as 1985 Egypt's trade balance was negative $6 billion. Without American aid ($2.4 billion in 1989), Mubarak might emulate the fate of his predecessor. Somehow, the competent soldier has proved to be an astute administrator. He has maintained a unique relationship with the Americans without jeopardizing Egypt's position in the Arab world. Mubarak not only managed to have Egypt welcomed back to the Arab League in November 1987, but he took the lead in calling an Arab summit to deal with Iranian provocations. He released political prisoners, including the leader of the Christian Copts who had been persecuted by Sadat. Mubarak has attempted to influence the PLO to renounce terrorism and recognize Israel. In March 1989, arbitration removed a thorn in Egyptian-Israel relations with the return of the Sinai resort settlement of Taba to Egypt. In 1990, Mubarak sent troops to the Gulf region to help protect Saudi Arabia. The following year, longtime Egyptian diplomat Boutros Boutros-Ghali was designated secretary-general of the United Nations.

Egypt under Mubarak seemed to be entering a phase where it was a responsible player in the international arena. Some critics wondered, however, whether this was all the product of wishful thinking. Could Mubarak hold together a nation of more than 60 million people, most of them impoverished Muslims, only 40 percent of whom could read or write? Could Egypt survive alienation from other Arab states or internal stresses caused by radical terror cells?

Despite being a partner in the international war gainst terror, Egypt neither guarantees nor tries to ensure the protection of foreign tourists, whatever their background. Any hope of Egypt and Israel achieving a true peace has long since dissipated in the one-way tourist and trade traffic between the two nations. In the past decade, Cairo's major newspapers have waged a vicious campaign against Israel. Jewish leaders are caricatured in anti–Semitic editorial cartoons. Israel has been charged with persecution, use of bacteriological weapons, and genocide against the Palestinians. Welcomed back to the Arab League, Egypt presents one face to the U.S., but champions anti–Zionist resolutions at international conferences and threatens war if Israel continues its "racist" behavior. A political chameleon, Mubarak has demonstrated extraordinary staying power. Considering the increasingly harsh rhetoric of Egyptian journalists, Islamic shaykhs, and university students, the possibility exists that Egypt's future may belong to someone more sympathetic to religious radicalism.[19]

32

Israel and the Palestinians

Israel: A Strategic Ally

Were Martians to visit this planet, they might, by watching the nightly news, conclude that Israel was one of the largest nations on earth. Born in the violence and rancor that binationalists like Buber and Magnes warned against, the state of Israel has endured. It has not faded away like the medieval Crusader principalities, in part because American presidents have deemed the state worthy of friendship, help and protection. Israel came into existence primarily as a result of political assistance rendered by the Truman Administration. Such assistance derived, in part, from horror and guilt at what had transpired during the Holocaust.

Since 1948, Israel has served as a strategic ally in the Middle East, welcoming the American Sixth Fleet to facilities in Haifa, supplying the U.S. with information on the Soviet arsenal (tanks, SS-21s, fighter aircraft) and developing weapons (Arrow, Harpy, Popeye missiles) that benefit the West.[1] Despite a wartime economy, the Jewish state has pioneered breakthroughs in solar energy; drip-hydration agriculture; burn, heart and cancer treatment; space technology; child psychology; and contributed a Nobel laureate in literature (S. J. Agnon). Even those who do not like the Zionist state cannot deny its cultural and scientific importance.

Since 1948, Israel's Jewish population has grown from 600,000 to over six million. Some of these are Arabs, 500,000 who remained in their homes in the Galilee and Negev during the fighting in 1948. Many are Christians, who continue to maintain the holy places in Bethlehem, Jerusalem, and Nazareth. The overwhelming majority are Jews, from 100 different countries—Bokhara, Romania, the United States, Ethiopia, Australia. In 1959, scholars at Yad Vashem (the institute devoted to the study of the Holocaust) estimated that 400,000 Israelis were survivors of Europe's ghettos and death camps.[2]

Since 1948, another 800,000 refugees, Sephardic Jews from Islamic countries, have returned to Israel. With *Sabras* (Jews born in Israel), they constitute two-thirds of the population. Sephardic Jews tend to vote in greater numbers for conservative parties. They support the Orthodox position in religious affairs, such as the definition of who is a Jew. This last issue, raising questions about the Law of Return, (originally framed to give every persecuted Jew a sanctuary) has threatened a rift between the Jews of Israel and those in Diaspora, particularly in America.[3]

The arrival of several hundred thousand Jews from the defunct Soviet Union and its East European satellites has clouded the picture. Some pundits believe that their past experiences will prompt them to reject any party that smacks of "socialism." Other analysts suggest that ultimately Russian Jews will favor concessions to achieve the peace that eluded them in Europe.

Israel may be a victim of its own commitment to democracy. Representation in its 120-seat *Knesset* (assembly or parliament) has been open to any political group that captures 1.5 percent of the vote. Until 1977, the prime ministry belonged to Labor, Social Democrats like David Ben-Gurion, Moshe Sharett, Levi Eshkol and Golda Meir. The Likud Party of Menachem Begin, Yitzhak Shamir and Ariel Sharon claims descent from Jabotinsky's free enterprise philosophy. Arab delegates have sat in every assembly, some expressing anti–Zionist positions along with communist colleagues. Several years ago, Rabbi Meir Kahane's *Kach* faction (a small group that advocates the expulsion of Arabs from Israeli territory) was banned by a law denying representation to racist groups. The shifting allegiance of voters mandates coalition government and gives more influence to religious parties and fundamentalist agendas.

Sacrifice and Intransigence

Three times in the past 50 years (1949, 1957, 1975–77), Israel has withdrawn victorious armies from Egyptian soil on the promise of improved relations with its neighbors. In pulling out of the Sinai the last time, it did what no other nation has done in this century: it not only returned conquered territory larger than the home nation itself, it also sacrificed energy self-sufficiency.

Despite such sacrifices, Israel has still been scored in the Western press as intransigent. One reason may be its actions in the West Bank and Gaza. Since 1967, several hundred settlements have been created in what Israelis call Shomron and Judaea. Some were established by the military in strategic locations. Some were restored over the ruins of Jewish communities plundered in 1929, 1936, or 1948. Many, however, were founded by religious zealots (*gush emunim*) who based their claims on biblical connections with sites like Ai, Bethel, Kiryat Arba, Tekoa, Mizpeh, Shiloh, Beth Horon, and Jericho. Responding to the needs of residents of the West Bank, the Israeli government built roads, brought in electricity, and modernized water systems. As a result, water supplies in the Hebron area increased nearly 400 percent in 20 years.

Arabs benefited in other ways, as well. Many were shifted from refugee shanties to new apartments. Females attended schools or universities and voted for the first time. Every day, new autos queued up at Gaza checkpoints as Arabs drove into Israel to work. They wore Western clothing, owned Yamaha keyboards, and prayed at new mosques like one constructed at Hebron in 1989. But there were other concerns.

Jerusalem was formally annexed (an act recognized by no other nation) and the capital transferred to the town where the Knesset had always sat. Israel tried, without much success, to cultivate village councils. At no time, however, did the Israelis offer citizenship to the more than one million Arabs of the West Bank. Arabs who worked with the government were regarded as collaborators, shunned or killed by other Arabs. In return, mayors of Nablus, Hebron and Ramallah who railed against Israel were attacked by Jewish fundamentalists. Over the years, the settlers became increasingly belligerent. They paraded through Arab villages, retaliated for any assault, and made it clear that they had no intention of leaving the land — until Ariel Sharon, making his own bid for a place in history, commanded that withdrawal in 2005.[4]

The Palestine Generation of Revenge

For their part, the generation of Arabs reared under Israeli occupation looked increasingly to their own militants for inspiration. The 1967 debacle produced a younger group of leaders in the Palestine Liberation Organization. In place of discredited muftis and tired diplomats came the *Jil al-Naqma*, the generation of revenge — men like George Habash, leader of the Popular Front for the Liberation of Palestine; Nayef Hawatmeh, who created the Maoist Popular Democratic Front for the Liberation of Palestine; Ahmed Jibril, founder of the PFLP-General Command; and Yasser Arafat. Some were educated in the halls of German universities, others seethed with hate in the refugee camps.[5]

This new leadership disavowed connections with its corrupt predecessors. Yet Arafat epitomized a kind of continuity with traditional Palestine leadership. Born in Cairo, Egypt, in 1929 (not Jerusalem as he claims), Arafat was a cousin of the grand mufti. His father Rauf Arafat al-Qudwa al-Husayni was a prosperous merchant who settled in Egypt in 1927. Before Israel declared its independence, Arafat volunteered to fight with Abdel Kader el-Husseini's forces in the Jerusalem area. A gun-runner, in one embarrassing incident, he shot himself in the thigh. Afterward, Arafat returned to Egypt where he obtained a degree in civil engineering, worked for a time in Kuwait, then served in the Suez war of 1956. A member of the Muslim Brotherhood, in 1964 Arafat and 20 colleagues created the al-Fatah group that ultimately dominated the Palestinian movement.[6]

Under Arafat, PLO combat units held their own in clashes with Israeli tanks at Karameh, Jordan, in 1968. The PLO executed a number of strikes against air carriers, notably the hijacking of three planes of Pan Am, TWA, and BOAC blown up on the tarmac of Cairo and Zerqa, Jordan on September 6, 1970. Arafat was cheered as a statesman by the U.N. General Assembly in 1974 and the PLO was accorded observer status with the international body. The United Nations pledged itself to protect their "inalienable rights" and authorized funding for a film on the subject. In the General Assembly, women's conferences, scientific meetings, and third-world congresses, Zionism was flogged as racist. And every Arab summit, from Khartoum in 1967 to Rabat and Tunis in 1988, continued to champion the PLO cause.

At the same time, there were down moments for the movement. Embarrassed by how the PLO was using his territory as a base for skyjacking operations and fearing a coup from Arafat's forces, King Hussein of Jordan instituted a purge in September 1970. Ten thousand commandos were killed, al-Fatah dispersed to Lebanon. The Black September attack upon Israeli athletes at Munich in 1972 also backfired. The world reacted with disgust at such incidents as that and the Kiryat Shimona (1974) and Maalot (1975) massacres. The PLO was not heartened by Sadat's peace overture to Israel. Its attempt to subvert southern Lebanon prompted the Israeli invasion of 1982. By 1988, Palestine splinter groups were fighting one another as well as Israelis. Their issue, it seemed, was no longer accorded top priority by Muslim nations. When representatives of the Arab League met at Amman in November 1987, the burning issue was the Iran-Iraq war.

The Intifada

Something had to be done to rekindle interest in the plight of people living within the West Bank and Gaza. The answer came in the form of the *Intifada,* the uprising that has continued intermittently since December 1987. According to 7000 journalists who flocked to the occupied territories, rock-throwing Palestinian children and women were Little Davids pitted against the Israeli Goliath. As the death toll mounted — more than 1000 by September 1993 — the Intifada became clouded with mythology.

Arafat and the PLO claimed responsibility for sparking the uprising. In unrelated incidents in November 1987, four members of al-Fatah were killed by Israelis in a shoot-out in Gaza, while another contingent from the PFLP-General Command killed six Israeli soldiers along the Lebanese border. Then, early in December, several Israeli citizens in Gaza were attacked. When four Arabs in that city were killed following a traffic collision with an Israeli truck on December 16, Gaza's population ran amok, blocking roads with burning tires and throwing stones at moving vehicles. While some Israeli intelligence reports initially blamed the troubles on the PLO, it was evident as the uprising spread from village to village, that this was a spontaneous response to Israeli occupation. For 20 years the Israelis had been occupiers and the people in the West Bank and Gaza wanted an end to it.[7]

Rejuvenated by the outpouring of sympathy, the Palestine National Council convened in Tunis in December 1988 to declare the creation of a government in exile. A number of states from the Third World and Eastern blocs accorded recognition to Palestine and unofficial legations were upgraded to embassies. Eager to curry favor with the U.S. government, Yasser Arafat declared that the Palestinians were prepared to acknowledge the existence of two states— a Jewish state and an Arab state — in what was once Palestine. He was also prepared to meet face to face with Israeli leaders.[8]

Since Faisal met with Chaim Weizmann at Versailles in 1919 until Anwar Sadat flew to Jerusalem in 1977, the official position of Arab governments was exactly what had been outlined at Khartoum in August, 1968 — no public meetings with Jewish leaders, no recognition of the Zionist state, no peace. Arabs refused to accept the terms of the Peel Plan in 1937, refused to sit at the same table with Jews in London in 1939, declared war rather than negotiate in 1948, and reluctantly agreed to armistices at the close of each war since then. The Arabs refuse to negotiate water rights, repatriation and resettlement of refugees, boycotted U.N. sessions dealing with regional problems of labor, health and food. In 1986, King Fahd of Saudi Arabia exhorted his fellow Muslims to liberate Palestine from "Zionist usurpers and aggressors." Said Fahd: "We will never recognize Israel. We don't have to recognize anyone we don't want to recognize."[9]

Terror and State Terrorism

Arafat expressed a willingness to renounce terrorism as an instrument of PLO policy. Some Westerners argued that Arafat was no worse than Shamir, who had been a member of the terrorist Stern Gang, responsible for the assassination of Lord Moyne in Cairo in 1944 and U.N. mediator Count Folke Bernadotte in 1948. Moreover, the argument went, Israeli's retaliatory raids and incursions into Lebanon, Jordan, even Uganda in 1976, constituted state terrorism.[10]

Terrorism may be defined as the use of fear for political purposes. This would include attacks against undifferentiated victims, like Israeli school children murdered along the Lebanese border in 1969 or teenaged victims of suicide bombers in discos or pizzerias. Those who decry "state terrorism" would probably cite any bombardments that injure civilians, like Israeli assaults against PLO refugee camps in Lebanon. By this standard, every American bombing raid against Hamburg or Tokyo in World War II or Kabul in 2001 could be labeled terrorist because of "collateral" civilian casualties. Whether the Allies desired this may be debated, but there is no question that the PLO used non-combatants as shields. Tanks were placed in churches, artillery and machine guns in hospitals. A PLO operational order dated May 28, 1981, declared that "residential areas" make "excellent shelter, perhaps the best possible cover for troops and vehicles." As the Lebanese journal *al-Nahar* declared in January 1982: "Western Beirut controlled by the PLO and the Moslem left is flooded with armed people carrying heavy and medium size weaponry ... in every house there is either a recoilless launcher, a heavy-machine gun or a mortar."[11]

Arafat's renunciation of terrorism did not extend to the disturbances within the West Bank and Gaza. Since December 1988, knives, automatic weapons, and bombs laced with nails have replaced rocks in the hands of assailants. More than 400 Israeli farmers, rabbis, women and school children have been slain in the name of national liberation. At the moment of his no-terror pledge, Arafat proved unable to restrain the PFLP-General Command from bombing Pan Am 103. He proved unwilling or unable to check assaults by masked members of the Muslim fundamentalist group Hamas against hundreds of Palestinian civilians accused of collaborating with the Israelis.[12] To maintain his own image of constructive confrontation, Arafat refused to check attacks of his own PLO commandos across the Israeli border from Lebanon or Jordan.

The roots of PLO terrorism, it has been argued, stem from the same frustrations that motivated Shamir, Begin and other Zionists in the 1940s. Palestinian spokesmen have often made the comparison, adopting terms that have specific meaning in Jewish history, speaking of a Diaspora, ghettoization and genocide. Arafat himself made the point when he laid a wreath in 1983 at the memorial to the fighters of the Warsaw Ghetto. There really is no equivalence between the desperation of Jews in 1943 and Palestinians today. Sixty years ago Jews were fighting for their lives against a movement that was attempting to exterminate every one of them. Six million died while the world remained mute. By way of contrast, the Palestinians, bolstered by propaganda and military support of 21 Arab states, have quintupled in numbers. Palestinians have been welcomed to international conferences, their plight noted by the papacy. It was hardly appropriate to say terror was the only alternative when every peace proposal was rejected by the PLO.

There is another significant difference between Zionist actions and those of the PLO. During World War II, terror was adopted by Jews not to destroy the British Empire, but to force the British to open Mandatory Palestine to people who were fleeing the death camps of Europe. Israel under Golda Meir may have denigrated a Palestinian nationality, but it did not deny the existence of these people or call for their extermination.

The Palestine National Covenant

The Palestinian National Covenant was adopted by the Palestinian National Council at Cairo in July 1968. The 33 articles of this document superseded a previous charter adopted in 1964. To alter "the fundamental law" of the PLO, a vote of two-thirds of the members of the PNC is required. The National Covenant is a constitution, and until legally amended, this document, not some private aside, remains the operative law of the PLO. As Abu Iyad, number two in the PLO hierarchy, stated in December 1988: "There is no intention to amend the Palestinian Covenant and the matter had not even been brought up during the meeting of the Palestine National Council."

What the Covenant says about Jews is anything but pleasant. Article 20 defines what is a Jew: "Judaism, in its character as a religion or revelation, is not a nationality with an independent existence. Likewise, the Jews are not one people with an independent personality." Having presumed to tell Jews what they are, the Covenant also defines Zionism as "racist, fanatical, aggressive, expansionist, colonialist, fascist and Nazi" (Article 22). Israel, the product of imperialism, is an illegitimate state and a threat to world peace. Palestine is the "homeland of the Palestinian Arab people" and an integral part of the Arab nation (Article 1). The Arab claim rests upon material, spiritual and historical ties with the land, all of which are "permanent realities" (Article 7). Palestinian Arabs possess the legal right to exercise self-determination according to their will (Article 3). Jews living in Palestine until "the beginning of the Zionist invasion" may be considered Palestinians (Article 6). The Balfour Declaration, British Mandate and the partition of Palestine are null and void (Article 19). The liberation of Palestine is a national duty and an act of self-defense (Article 18 and 15). The Palestinians have mobilized their human, material and spiritual resources in the only way open to them — armed struggle (Article 9).

The covenant has been formally clarified twice. In May 1970, the Unified Command Planning Board of the PLO declared that "the object of the Palestinian struggle is the liberation of the whole of Palestine." Four years later, in June 1974, the PLO adopted a transitional program that again embraced irredentism and violence. In 1977 PLO Foreign Minister Farouk Khaddoumi rejected any thoughts of compromise with Israel, warning: "The Palestine Revolution would continue its military struggle and the Palestinian gun would remain in use until the achievement of our national goal which is to liberate our entire national soil." Khaddoumi underscored that hard line in August 1979, when he told Bonn television: "The PLO will never recognize Israel, even if Israel recognized the PLO." Speaking over PLO Radio from Beirut in 1981, a confident Arafat warned:

> We are marching through a dark tunnel. However, at the end we can already see the vast land with the mosques and churches of Jerusalem. Like the Vietnamese farmer marching from Hanoi to Saigon, will our people wave the flag first over Jerusalem, the west Bank and Gaza, and then over Nazareth and the Negev.... Our brothers in the Galilee, in the Triangle, Haifa, Jaffa, Ashkelon, Rafiah, Khan Yunes, Hebron, Ramalla, Nablus, Jenin, and in the entire occupied land. That people is alive. Our people is the essence of the land. The land is Arab and it will remain Arab.

Asking self-determination for the West Bank and Gaza was only the beginning. Once that was conceded, the PLO would raise the question of the 1947 partition and Israel's "illegal" expansion into territory promised to an Arab state in Palestine. In this "incremental" scenario, the entire land area of Palestine (at least west of the Jordan) would be fused under one government dominated by Arabs. As refugees flocked back to join their fellow Arabs, they ultimately would select which Jews might remain and which would have to leave.

That the eradication of Israel remained the ultimate goal of the PLO was clear from statements not merely of Arafat's opponents within the organization, but from his intimate comrades as well. Said Abu Iyad in Kuwait in October 1988: "There is no way that we will recognize our enemy's right to any parcel of Palestinian soil." From Dr. Nabil al-Shaath, Arafat's advisor on international affairs: "We will continue all forms of struggle within the borders of historical Palestine." And Jawad al-Bashiti, senior commentator for the PLO journal *Falastin a-Thawra*: "There is no Palestinian or Arab document that sees the West Bank and Gaza as the ultimate geographical basis of the Palestinian state."[13]

In the wake of the Gulf War of 1990 and 1991 and the collapse of the Soviet Union, American diplomats labored ceaselessly to nurture what popularly was called "the peace process." At Madrid, again in Oslo, they coaxed control of Gaza, Jericho, and Ramallah away from the Israelis in return for promises that a Palestinian Authority would check armed assaults. However grudgingly, every prime minister (Yitzhak Shamir, Yitzha Rabin, Shimon Peres, Benjamin Netanyahu) yielded to American pressure. Discussions mediated by Bill Clinton at Camp David in the fall of 2000 revealed the futility of such efforts. Ehud Barak, then Israel's prime minister, offered Arafat control of 90 percent of the lands in the West Bank and Gaza, permission for the PLA to organize its government offices in a Jerusalem neighborhood, titular control over the Muslim holy places in Jerusalem, permission for a number of refugees to return to their homes in Israel and the right to seek compensation for lost property all in exhange for an end to terrorism that had erupted in Jerusalem the previous fall. While disavowing any connection with actions of Islamic Jihad or Hamas, a confident Arafat rejected the proffer.

There is an old Talmudic expression that asks "Can a goat and a tiger live in the same barn?" The answer was clear to Henry Kissinger, who remarked in August 1982: "How can we deal with an organization dedicated to the destruction of a friend and ally. Its refusal to recognize not borders but Israel's right to exist tells more of the nature of the organization which has been dedicated to the overthrow of the Israeli state."[14] The intent of the PLO was clear to civil rights leader Bayard Rustin, who in August 1979 labeled it "an organization; committed to the bloody destruction of Israel — indeed of the Jewish people." Added Rustin, "Looking back on the history of the PLO, one thing has become abundantly clear; the PLO from the day of its creation in 1964 has never once uttered a word in support of any form of nonviolent resistance, peaceful relations between Israelis and Palestinians, or a political solution to the complex problems of the Middle East. Instead, it espouses violence, hatred and racism, scorns reconciliation and exalts the sword that kills."[15] When Yasser Arafat died in 2004, he left a legacy of violence and hatred that continues to blight Palestinian nationalism.

33

Lebanon: Good
Intentions Gone Awry

The Concept of Territorial Integrity

For nearly 30 years, Lebanon was a nation especially close to the hearts of Americans. This stemmed, in part, from the fact that many of the 2.6 million Arabs in the U.S. were hyphenate descendants of Lebanon. Because a sizable portion of the country's population were Christian Maronites, Lebanon did not suffer from the stereotypes Americans ascribed to Muslim Arabs. Many Lebanese-Americans preferred to claim Phoenician, rather than Arab, descent. Lebanon had been a center of American missionary activity, and the 75-acre American University of Beirut offered testimony to the intellectual achievement of the people. Visitors rhapsodized about the beauty of the country — its wondrous cedar trees, the Graeco-Roman ruins at Baalbek, casinos that illuminated the bay above Jounieh, the modern hotels and shops of Beirut. In that "Golden Age," Lebanon was likened to the United States as "a haven for wave upon wave of immigrants, who despite differences, did rock along in friendship and peace."[2]

With 17 identifiable ethnic and religious groups, Lebanon's fabled political stability was a mirage. According to the National Pact of 1943, the president was to be a Maronite, the prime minister a Sunni and the speaker of the legislature a Shiite. The system was based on 1942 census figures, when Christian and Muslim numbers were relatively equal and, incidentally, the last time Lebanon conducted a true population count. Over the years, few people in command gave much thought to the economic and political disparities suffered by a Muslim population that had, by 1974, doubled the size of its Christian neighbors.[3]

Arrival of the Palestinians

Politically, Lebanon played the role of moderate in the international arena. Lebanese delegates attended Arab League conferences on Palestinian unity between 1946 and 1948. Beirut hosted the grand mufti of Jerusalem until his death in 1975 and Lebanon opposed partition of Palestine. But Lebanon's contribution to the war effort in 1948 was one feeble assault against Malkiyah. For more than 25 years, it was said that Lebanon would be the

second Arab state to conclude a peace treaty with Israel.[4] The border between the two countries was relatively quiet. Charles Malik, a Lebanese statesman at the U.N., flatly declared
that the basic stumbling block to peace in the Middle East was the Arabs' refusal to recognize the state of Israel.[5]

One of Lebanon's prime ministers, Riad as-Sulh, was assassinated for advocating overtures to Israel. Between 1946 and 1958, 10 ministries failed to complete their term of office.
Sectarian violence and Nasserism posed such threats to the republic by summer of 1958
that Eisenhower sent Marines to restore order. Most Lebanese ignored the proliferation of
some 100 radical organizations, each with its own militia, in the 1960s. Government leaders blundered on November 3, 1969, when they signed the Cairo Agreement with Yasser
Arafat, permitting Palestinian commands to operate against Israel. Lebanese president
Charles Helou submitted to Egypt, Libya, Iraq, and Syria, all of which promised to supply
arms, and money.[6]

Helou did not anticipate the transformation of southern Lebanon into an armed Palestinian state. As he noted, "On 3 November 1968, the number of *fedayeen* did not exceed
some ten units, and we were dealing with the problem, when suddenly they began to pub-
lish propaganda against us and today there are several thousand of them."[7] Beirut became
the center of planning and publications for al-Fatah and the Popular Front for the Liberation of Palestine before King Hussein of Jordan chased Palestinian commandos from his
country in September 1970. Ten thousand Palestinians were killed by Hussein's forces that
month. The remnants fled to Lebanon where they were embraced by compatriots.

In the two years preceding Black September, Palestinian terrorists attempted to hijack
El Al, TWA, Lufthansa and BOAC aircraft. Bombs were planted at Jewish stores in London, a school in Teheran, the Jewish community center in Berlin, an old-age home in
Munich. PLO commandos failed to assassinate David Ben Gurion in Copenhagen, but they
did plant a bomb aboard a Swissair plane leaving Zurich on February 21, 1970. Forty-seven
passengers and crew were killed in that incident.[8]

Members of the PFLP, PFLP-GC, Saiqa and the Palestine Armed Struggle moved into
the Rushdiya, Chatilla, Sabra, and Ein el Hilwe refugee camps. Villagers in Shoba, Bariya,
Rashiya al Fakher, Einata, Arkub, Hasbeya, Dir el Ashir, al Mazraa, and al-Suriya were
ousted and their homes converted into forward bases for attack against Israel. Following a
Katyusha rocket barrage that killed 12 children in a school bus near Avivim on May 2, 1970,
Israeli forces entered "Fatahland," bulldozed roads and announced the creation of a security belt two miles deep inside Lebanon. The Israelis were welcomed by Christians living
in the region. It was the beginning of a close relationship between Israel and its own buffer
militia headed by Major Saad Haddad.

In the next decade, Lebanon's shaky government coalition was unable or unwilling to
control the PLO, as it carved out a state within a state in the south. In May 1972, three
members of the Japanese Red Brigade, aligned with the PLO, opened fire with machine guns
at the Lod Airport in Israel, killing 24 persons and wounding 80. Four months later, members of al-Fatah's Black September group were responsible for the deaths of 11 Israeli athletes at the Munich Olympic Games. Palestinian incursions into the Galilee continued. The
result in 1974 and 1975 was Kiryat Shimona, where 28 persons in a single apartment building were slaughtered; Maalot, where 26 Israeli schoolchildren were killed in gunfire; and
Nahariya and Shamir, each resulting in the deaths of three Israelis.[9]

Having failed to gain control of Jordan, the PLO attempted to topple the Lebanese
government in the spring of 1975. The nation, by this time, was clearly on the verge of collapse. In Parliament, Baathist, Nasserite, Druze and Islamic spokesmen were advocating

contradictory programs. Gangs of sectarian militia outnumbered the unreliable 17,000-man Lebanese army.[10]

No Civil War

Full-scale hostilities broke out on April 13, 1975, when a bus filled with Palestinians passing through Ayn al-Rummana, south of Beirut, was attacked by right-wing Phalangists and 27 persons were killed. The so-called Lebanese Civil War would go on for more than 15 years. Every major nationalist volunteered his direction, including the Christian leaders Camille Chamoun, Bashir Gemayel, and his brother Amin; the quixotic Suleiman Franjieh and Elias Sarkis; Druze chieftains Kamal and Walid Jumblatt; and Muslim spokesmen Rashid Karami and Imam Fadlallah. Publicly, all agreed that Lebanon should be evacuated by foreign troops, so its people could determine their own fate. Unfortunately, there never was any agreement on how this might be achieved and Lebanon became a dysfunctional country where 152,000 people died, another 400,000 were injured, and perhaps as many as 750,000 made refugees.

Initially, the conflict pitted the Christian Right against Palestinians and Leftist Muslims. Battles erupted in the Muslim Karantina and al-Maslakh districts of Beirut and Christian towns of Achrafieh, al-Dawi, Enfi Amchit, and Chekka. Then, in the last week of January 1976, an incident occurred that had long-range consequences. Following a five-day mortar and rocket barrage, a force of Palestinians and Muslims occupied the town of Damour, just south of Beirut. Once there had been 28,000 persons, most of them Christian, living in what had been a well-to-do community. After the assault, Damour was a burning ruin. An estimated 1000 persons died in Damour, some of them beheaded. Another 7000 were expelled by Palestinian militiamen who boasted to foreign journalists: "From now on there will be no more forgiving. The rightists used to say that Lebanon would be a graveyard for the Palestinians. Now it's a graveyard for them."[11]

Such cockiness prompted concern on the part of Syria, a state that had been aiding the leftist militants. Confronted with the prospect of anarchy in Lebanon, Syrian President Hafez al-Assad ordered his troops to assist the embattled Christians in April 1976. Thus, the conflict entered a second phase, where the Syrians tried to pacify the very forces they previously had armed. More than 70 Muslims were massacred on December 6 ("Black Saturday") and subsequently the Druze leader Kamal Jumblatt (who had boasted of skinning Christian heads) was machine-gunned by assassins linked to the Syrians.[12]

Representatives of the Arab League meeting at Riyadh on October 16, 1976, agreed to the creation of a multi-national Arab Deterrent Force in Lebanon. Most of these troops, 30,000 Syrians, were already in place. Instead of promoting peace, the Syrians reversed themselves, giving arms to the Palestinians and supporting the Druze and Muslims against the Christians. In March 1979, Robert Basil, president of the American Lebanese League, declared: "For four months last year [1978] the regular Syrian Army engaged in the heaviest sustained saturation artillery bombardment of civilian areas since the Soviet shelling of Berlin in World War II. The objective clearly appears to have been widespread devastation of civilian areas (hospitals, homes, apartments) in an attempt to kill or forcibly displace the Christian population from East Beirut, thus controlling the entire city. These military operations indeed resulted in over 1000 civilians killed, several thousand wounded, and over 500,000 displaced into the mountains, church monasteries, schools and other make-shift shelter under poor conditions."[13]

Wrote Notre Dame Professor Elias el-Hayek: "As foreign armies occupied Lebanese territory, the alien in Lebanon became the master, and the Lebanese citizen became both alien and refugee in his own country. The invaders imposed a dictatorial rule and the citizens of Lebanon suddenly lost their freedom. The population was exposed to kidnapping, killing, torture and mutilation."[14] Syrian bombardments in 1977 and 1978 destroyed the hotel districts of Tripoli and Beirut. More than half of East Beirut was destroyed in actions that former president Camille Chamoun labeled "genocide against 600,000 Lebanese."[15]

From Damascus, Hafez al-Assad prodded the Palestinians to acts of terror against the Israelis. In March 1978, a PLO group came ashore at Tel Aviv and commandeered a bus along the costal highway. In the ensuing shootout, 33 persons lost their lives, many consumed by flames. The Begin government retaliated, sending troops to the Litani River as a warning to the Lebanese government, the Palestinians, and the Syrians. The drawing of this Red Line 25 miles north of Israel's border did little good. Condemned by the United Nations and the Carter Administration in the U.S., the Israelis withdrew in favor of a United Nations Interim Force in Lebanon (UNIFIL).[16]

In the next four years neither the United Nations nor UNIFIL could safeguard the residents of West Beirut, let alone 60,000 Israelis living in Galilee settlements like Avivim and Keren Ben Zimra. A generation of Jewish children went to bed every night in underground shelters. Between 1968 and 1982 over 1000 Jewish civilians were murdered, 4250 were wounded as a result of PLO attacks. In a single year (1981–82), the toll along the Lebanese border was 29 Israelis dead, 271 wounded. With Syrian blessings, the PLO established bases in Sidon, Ras-A-Shek, Zharan, Nabatiye, Aichiye, Rachaya el-Quadi, Marjayoun) and even penetrated the demilitarized zone at Tyre and Qana. Ten thousand men, including volunteers from Egypt, Yemen, Bangladesh, Turkey, Pakistan, India, Iraq, Morocco, Somalia, Niger, Ceylon, Brazil, Canada, Saudi Arabia, and Mauritania, were assembled as the vanguard of an invasion force. Stored in underground caverns of South Lebanon were rocket launchers, 130-mm. and 160-mm. cannons, anti-aircraft guns, tanks, thousands of light arms and ammunition worth more than $250 million.[17]

Operation Peace for Galilee

Captured documents indicated that the multi-national force intended to step up attacks against Israel in the summer of 1982. The attempted assassination of Shlomo Argov, Israel's Ambassador to England, on June 3, followed by a 1000-shell bombardment against 23 settlements the next day, triggered an Israeli response. On June 6, 1982, Defense Minister Ariel Sharon announced the beginning of Operation Peace for Galilee, whose declared purpose was the pacification of a 25-mile strip of Lebanon. Israel's latest retaliation was again denounced in international forums. Some critics charged that Israel wanted to annex Lebanon. Others claimed that houses, churches, and hospitals destroyed in seven years of internecine warfare had only recently been gutted. Deluded by the ease of its army's advance and the reception extended by Shiite Arabs, Israel pushed beyond its original goals—to Beirut.[18]

On June 7, one day after the Israel invasion began, President Reagan dispatched special envoy Philip Habib to press for a cease-fire. Two days later, Israeli aircraft downed 22 Syrian jets in a clash over the Bekaa Valley. By June 14, land forces encircled West Beirut and were prepared to finish off the military infrastructure of the PLO. For whatever reason the Reagan Administration demanded that the Israelis not enter West Beirut. Washington offered something to all sides — the PLO fighters could withdraw by sea to another land. Israel would be permanently rid of their threat and also would withdraw. Lebanon would be protected by a multi-national peace-keeping force and an emergency grant of $50 million. Late in August, 800 American Marines and French paratroopers arrived in Beirut as the last of the PLO commandos departed the city.

In its first free election in years, Lebanon had a new president, Bashir Gemayel. Although decried as a fascist, Gemayel appeared to be what Lebanon needed, a strong man respected by Israel and feared by his enemies, who was ultimately a Lebanese patriot. Said Gemayel, "As far as we are concerned, we are looking for the liberation of our country — we are looking that all the foreigners get out — Syrians, Palestinians, and Israelis, and even the UNIFIL — we don't need any foreign armed presence in this country. As Lebanese, as a strong central government, as a strong central army, as once again the nation reunited, we will take care of our own country."[19]

The Massacres of Sabra-Chatilla

There were some in the American administration who questioned the wisdom of these policies. Secretary of State Alexander Haig favored a free hand for the Israelis and was replaced by George Schultz during the crisis. Many PLO fighters, including Arafat, merely sailed to the port of Tripoli, which was in Syrian hands, there to re-enter the country and rejoin the fight. On September 10, Secretary Schultz having declared a "break-through" in negotiations, the first elements of the multi-national peace-keeping force began their withdrawal from Lebanon. Four days later, September 14, 1982, a 500-pound car bomb exploded outside Phalangist Party headquarters, killing President Gemayel. The next day, Israeli tanks entered West Beirut, turning responsibility for patrolling the Sabra and Chatilla refugee camps over to Christian militiamen under Josef Edde, Elias Hobeika, and Fadi Frem. In the next three days, 1000 Palestinians would die in those camps as the world decried an atrocity perpetrated "under the aegis of Israel."[20]

Israeli commanders should have anticipated a reprisal by the Phalangists for the murder of their leader. Some of the perpetrators were veterans of Major Haddad's forces; some came to the camps to pay back the murders in Damour. To this day, none of the Phalangists have been punished. Amin Gemayel, Bashir's brother, spoke before the U.N. General Assembly later that month and was accorded a standing ovation. Few observers noted that there were still 2000 PLO fighters among the 60,000 men, women and children in Sabra-Chatilla. They attacked with carbines and machine guns when the Phalangists entered the camps. And while scores of articles and documentaries were written about the new Palestinian tragedy, there was passing reference to an equally bloody incident that took place on the anniversary of Sabra-Chatilla. On September 7, 1983, the *Washington Post* reported a massacre of Christians by Druze militiamen in the city of Bhamdun on the Damascus-Beirut highway. Many of the victims had been wired by the neck to trucks and dragged to their deaths. "'I think we killed a good 800 of them,' said a bleary-eyed American-educated youth with savage glee."[21]

From the start, many Israelis questioned the wisdom of the 1982 invasion, likening it to America's involvement in Vietnam. The deaths of 300 young men in the first weeks of fighting and the thought of a protracted occupation of another country while the West Bank and Gaza were still "occupied territories" were difficult to accept. But Israeli involvement in a massacre, no matter how indirect, was unbearable. Days after the news of Sabra-

Chatilla became public, 400,000 people, one-tenth of Israel's population, marched in the streets of Tel Aviv, as a protest against the tragedy perpetrated in the camps. No comparable demonstration against terrorism has ever been held in any Western or Muslim land.

A Province of Syria

Since 1982 Lebanon has been less a state than an idea. Palestinian forces returned to the south and resumed attacks across the border. In principle, the Palestinians were supported by a range of militant groups like Nabbi Berri's *Amal* (Arabic for "hope"), Islamic Jihad, Ibrahim Qoleitlat's Nasserite Murabitun, Ina'am Ra'ad's National Syrian Socialist Party, Mohsen Ibrahim's Organization of Communist Action in Lebanon, Kassib al-Khatib's Arab Democratic Party (known as the Arab Knights), Suleiman Franjieh's pro–Syrian Marada Brigades, and Walid Jumblatt's National Salvation Front. These groups have been unable to defeat the Phalangists or their splinter elements, al-Tanzim and the Guardians of the Cedars. They cannot get along with one another. In 1988, while the world's attention was riveted to riots in the West Bank and Gaza, more than 1000 Lebanese and Palestinians were killed in bombings and retaliatory attacks by one Muslim group against another in the streets and refugee camps of Beirut.

The militants intimidated the Western world by seizing hostages. Businessmen and professors have been snatched from the campus of the American university. Some, like American journalist Terry Anderson, were held for seven or eight years. Concern over nine hostages prevented the Reagan Administration from carrying out raids into the Bekaa Valley during the hijacking of the *Achille Lauro* or TWA Flight 847 in 1985. Hostages factored in negotiations between the U.S. and Iran for arms shipments and other bribes during the Iran-Contra affair. While the West negotiated, the KGB responded to the kidnapping of two Soviet citizens by killing several Muslim radicals. There were no further anti–Russian incidents until Chechneyan rebels joined an international jihad in 1990.[22]

The one glimmer of peace in Lebanon, a 1983 treaty sponsored by the U.S. and calling for the withdrawal of Israeli troops, failed ratification by an increasingly hostile Lebanese regime. Amin Gemayel served as a figurehead as his country unraveled before petty war lords. The Israelis attempted several withdrawals, only to find that it was necessary in 1991 and 1992 to pummel terrorist bases again. In April 2000, Ehud Barak simply pulled back Israeli forces and prayed for the best, relying on armed patrols and barbed wire to protect the border. Despite a few rock-throwing incidents in the first days of disengagement, the region was relatively quiet.[23]

In October 1990, Syria's President Hafez el-Assad shifted troops from the Bekaa Valley into Beirut with the sanction of Shiite, Druze and Palestinian leaders. Amazingly, the move prompted no outcry from the U.S. State Department or the United Nations, not even after 800 Phalangist prisoners (among them Dany Chamoun) were shot dead with their hands tied behind their backs. Fifteen years later, Assad is gone and the new regime in Syria promises to cooperate in the war against terror. Recent actions in Lebanon (approval of supervised elections, limited troop withdrawals, suppression of the opium trade) supposedly confirm this. The assassination of Prime Minister Rafik Hariri in 2005, however, gives a different view to the continued Syrian presence. Until the Syrians fully withdraw their armed forces, Lebanon is nothing but a puppet state.[24]

34

Modern Iran

The Qajars: Pawns of Imperialism

Persia has endured the lash of many tyrants, but none so terrible, we are told, as Muhammad Reza Pahlevi, who ruled this land between 1941 and 1979. At best, his critics charged, the soft-spoken monarch was "a boss-boy for Anglo-Iranian Oil and the C.I.A." In his final days, the shah was likened to a combination Adolf Eichmann and Tsar Nicholas and charged with heading "one of the most violent regimes in the history of mankind."[1] His crimes, which allegedly surpassed anything attempted by Hitler or Stalin: (1) the killing of 65,000 Iranian patriots; (2) theft of $25 billion; (3) betrayal of the nation; and (4) suspension of every single human and civil right.[2]

Reza Khan, father of the notorious shah, seized control of the Iranian government in a military coup in 1921 and established his own dynasty in 1926. This power play was just one chapter in Persia's tragic history. Unable to consolidate the empire of Alexander the Great, feuding Greek lords were ousted by the Parthians, fierce warriors who vexed the Romans for 400 years. They, in turn, gave way in A.D. 264 to the Sassanids, Zoroastrians who contended with the Byzantines for control in the Middle East. Like their Christian rivals, the Sassanids ultimately were conquered and converted by the Arabs.

Through the Middle Ages, Tahirid (821–73), Saffarid (879–1400), Ghaznawid (961–1186), Seljuk (1039–1194), Timurid (1370–1506) and Safavid (1500–1722) dynasties never wavered from their devotion to Islam. Despite momentary bursts of brilliance — the poetry of Umar Khayyam, the astronomical observatory at Jundishapur, and the exquisite mosques of Tabriz and Isfahan—centuries of warfare left the land in ruin. By the time the red-capped Qajars emerged from the western desert to establish their empire in 1779, Persia had reverted to a primitive state. Much of its land lay untilled, its irrigation channels in ruin. Persia's people were impoverished, illiterate and diseased, barely able to fend off the neighboring Ottoman Empire.

In the 19th century, Great Britain dictated treaties to various Middle Eastern shayhk-doms, reducing them to subsidized dependencies. When imperialists in St. Petersburg induced the Romanovs to expand across the Urals into Asia and the Middle East, England moved into central Asia, ostensibly to protect the flank of India. The threat appeared serious when Russia, in a series of successful wars with the Qajars, grabbed Georgia in 1801, Daghestan (1805), Erivan and Nakhichevean (1826), Tashkent, Samarkand, Bokhara and Khiva (1864–68) and Merv (1884).

Russian and British financiers competed with one another for privileges in factories, telegraph and railroad lines, tobacco, salt, and exploration of oil and minerals. Economic penetration might have resulted in partition but for the ability of the Qajars in playing off one foreign power against another.[3]

Yielding to popular clamor, Shah Muzaffar al-Din convened a National Consultative Assembly in December 1906. Nine months later, his son Muhammad Ali Shah was forced to accept a special treaty dictated by Great Britain and Russia. The pact gave the Europeans the right to intervene in Persia to guarantee its territorial integrity. In effect, the pact divided Persia into spheres of influence, the Russians taking the arc along the Caspian Sea from Tabriz to Meshed while the British "protected" a smaller territory abutting West Pakistan. Khuzistan and Shiraz were to be "neutral," though not for very long, as British extraction of oil would begin within the year.[4]

Reza Khan

When World War I placed demands upon the Allies for fresh supplies of manpower, Persia proved a handy source. One recruit from a small village in the Elburz Mountains was General Reza Khan, a man trained by the Russians to head up a Cossack brigade. At war's end, Reza Khan was named commander in chief of armed forces for a revolutionary government that sat in Teheran in February 1921. From that point, until the spring of 1926, when he formally deposed Ahmad Shah, the last Qajar monarch, and assumed the Peacock Throne, Reza Khan was the strong man of the state, which he insisted be called Iran (land of the Aryans).

The new shah drew inspiration from Kemal Ataturk, the leader responsible for the reconstruction of Turkey. Like Ataturk, Reza Khan adopted a family name — Pahlevi — after his home town. Like Ataturk, Reza Khan favored a reduction in power of the Muslim clergy. The traditional veil was dropped and Western dress became compulsory. Primary school education was mandated and women were admitted to the new University of Teheran. All teaching was to be in Persian and no foreign ideology (i.e., communism) would be permitted. Like Ataturk, Reza Khan favored a strong central government.[5] Restrictions were enacted against foreigners purchasing Persian land or controlling monopolies in certain products. From taxes on tobacco, sugar and tea, the shah built railroads and highways linking Iran's cities. And like Ataturk, Reza Khan dabbled at parliamentary democracy, permitting four parties to function in the fledgling *Majlis*.

Less ruthless than Ataturk, Reza Shah could not duplicate the success of his idol. Instead of giving the people a republic, he perpetuated the monarchy. Neither Reza Shah nor his son appreciated the depth of religious passions in Iran. The elder dynast also failed to anticipate the reaction of Britain and the Soviet Union when he warmed to overtures made by Italy and Germany on the eve of World War II. Guided by the mistaken notion that the fascists might be more generous than the old imperialists, the shah declared Persia neutral when Hitler invaded Poland in September 1939 and again in June 1941 when the Nazis abrogated their alliance with the Russians. Teheran became a center of intrigue for more than 700 German agents, including the grand mufti of Jerusalem.

As groups of black-shirted Persians took to the streets calling for the ouster of British forces and control of Iran's oilfields, pro–Western officials became targets of assassination. With Rommel's armies slicing across North Africa toward El Alamein and another hundred German divisions moving toward Stalingrad, the beleaguered allies took a desperate step. On August 26, 1941, Russian troops crossed the border into Azerbaijan while the British entered Iran from Iraq and decimated the Iranian fleet. What justified this invasion: the treaty of 1907, which permitted intervention to uphold the territorial integrity of Iran. The result of such action: a memorandum of demands delivered to Shah Reza Pahlevi on August 30, and his abdication and exile in favor of his son Muhammad on September 16, 1941.[6]

Muhammad Reza Shah II and the Crisis of 1946

For the remainder of the war, the Swiss-educated, 21-year-old monarch was virtually ignored by the Allies. His people suffered shortages of food and severe inflation, while the Allies (including the U.S., which sent 30,000 troops to Iran in 1942) channeled millions of dollars in economic assistance to the Soviet Union. One of the rare achievements in the young Shah's early reign was the signing of a Tripartite Treaty with the Soviets and British on January 29, 1942. Little more than an acknowledgment of Allied hegemony, the pact included a stipulation that all foreign forces would be withdrawn within six months after the close of war with Nazi Germany.

The date agreed upon for departure was March 2, 1946. Both the Americans and British were gone by that date; not so the Russians. During the war, they promoted secessionist elements in Azerbaijan and Kurdistan. Over the winter of 1945 and 1946, these nationalists, with the backing of Russian troops and Iranian communists (*Tudeh*), proclaimed a pair of "independent" republics. In reality nothing but Soviet satellites, these republics fomented revolution in Khuzistan and other parts of Iran. When the central government appealed to the U.N. Security Council, that body did little. Finally, Iranian Prime Minister Ahmad Qavam negotiated a direct agreement with the Soviets which called for their withdrawal before the end of summer 1946.

It is doubtful, however, that the Russians would have agreed to anything, but for thinly veiled threats issued by the United States.[7] Of the 65,000 "victims" of Shah Muhammad Reza Pahlavi's regime, 25,000 to 40,000 died in this civil war prompted by Soviet interference. But for military and economic aid from the United States, Iran probably would have disintegrated into a number of mini-states in 1946.

Mohammed Mossadeq: Nationalist and Demagogue

The ouster of Russian troops did not signal an end to subversion. The Tudeh Party was outlawed following an unsuccessful attempt on the shah's life in February 1949. Two years later (March 1951), another assassin would succeed in killing Prime Minister Ali Razmara. The fifth prime minister in five years, General Razmara was attempting to address the most important issue in his country—relations with Anglo-Iranian Oil.

Since 1933 (when the oil company won a 50-year concession from the old shah), Anglo-Iranian had succeeded in creating its own separate state within the state, employing 50,000 people in a region of 38,500 square miles. Impoverished Iran received one-fourth of the revenues generated by its own resources. Religious fundamentalists, neo–Nazis, and socialists, together with elements of the Tudeh, coalesced in a National Front. The leader of this movement was a wealthy landowner, Dr. Mohammed Mossadeq. A long-time foe of the monarchy, Mossadeq championed nationalizing the oil industry. A demagogue who would faint or weep while delivering a speech, Mossadeq likened his opposition to British domination to that of Gandhi in India and took to wearing pajamas in public. Born in 1880, he was, in all likelihood, too old to sit in the Majlis (Iran had an age limit of 69). Yet in the turmoil following Gen. Razmara's assassination and the passage of a resolution calling for a national takeover of Anglo-Iranian oil, Mossadeq was named prime minister by the Majlis on April 29, 1951.

Two days later Mossadeq announced the nationalization of the oil industry. In reply, the British offered several mediums of negotiation — the U.N. Security Council, the International Court of Justice at the Hague, the International Bank, mediation by the U.S. government — to no avail. When Iran, lacking technicians to operate the oilfields, requested assistance from France in October 1952, Britain severed diplomatic ties. As the situation deteriorated, the United States, fearful of repercussions upon oil-rich nations in the Gulf, sided with Britain. Leftist support for Mossadeq coupled with increased trade with the Soviet Union, seemed to indicate that the old leader was a stooge for the communists.

Far from it, Mossadeq was craftily accruing power for himself, not some foreign state. By July 1952, he became minister of war as well as prime minister. That same year, he forced the passage of acts that allowed him to decree martial law, prohibit strikes by government employees, arrest newspaper editors, and restrict movement of Iranians and foreigners through oil-producing areas. Mossadeq could suspend operations of the Iranian Supreme Court, the Senate and Majlis. In April 1953, he replaced the minister of the Imperial Court with one of his own aides. Three months later, with the connivance of 35 National Front deputies who resigned from the Majlis, he managed to destroy the quorum necessary for parliamentary government to operate. With the support of the Tudeh Party, anti-shah riots were orchestrated in July 1953, and Mossadeq seized command of the army on the 21st of that month. When the shah went into exile on August 13, it appeared that Mossadeq and his nationalists had won control of Iran.[8]

It was not to be. From Iraq, the shah issued a *firman* (decree) naming Gen. Fazlullah Zahedi to replace Mossadeq as prime minister. On August 19, a million people took to the streets of Teheran shouting "Long live the Shah!" Mossadeq and his cronies were placed under house arrest. In what critics of American policy refer to as a counter-coup, the shah was restored in a relatively bloodless power play by the army. Without doubt the CIA had a hand in rallying support for the shah.[9] But no amount of Bondsian machinations could have succeeded without the support of the military along with crowds of shopkeepers, peasants, and bureaucrats, who filled the streets in August. Within the year, election for a 19th Majlis was held and by August 1954 a 50-page agreement on the transfer of ownership of Anglo-Iranian Oil was signed by representatives of Iran and the companies comprising the Anglo-Iranian oil consortium.

The White Revolution

Iran's constitution had been preserved and the goal of nationalization achieved, but extremists and Western apologists could only see American frustration of nationalist goals. In their view, Iran was reduced once more to lackey status, forced to sign the anti–Soviet Baghdad Pact in October 1955, then serving as the linchpin of John Foster Dulles' CENTO Pact in 1959. The shah subscribed to the Eisenhower Doctrine of 1958 (which opposed communist penetration of Lebanon) and its 1972 corollary, the Nixon Doctrine (which held that Middle East surrogates should maintain the interests of the free world in the Persian Gulf).

In the process, the shah was becoming one of the most important men in the region. He became an inspiration for developing nations, having launched his so-called White Revolution of land reform, education, and health care after 1960. Smallpox, plague and malaria were eradicated, cholera checked by 1964. The life expectancy of an Iranian exceeded that of neighboring Afghanistan, Iraq, Jordan, Saudi Arabi, Syria, Turkey, Yemen, or Pakistan. For 25 years, the shah banned production of the opium poppy. To combat illiteracy, the government in 1974 mandated free education through the eighth grade. Vocational training was free, as was college for those who would return two years of government service for each year of college study. By 1970, the shah's government had created eight universities, 69 teacher colleges, and hundreds of technical schools. For the first time in history, women could share these educational opportunities, studying beside men in medical and law schools. Women could own property, operate businesses, dress in the latest fashions and (as a result of the Family Protection Act of 1975) be protected against arbitrary divorce and polygamy.[10]

In the last four years of his regime, the shah committed more than 36 percent of the annual budget to social programs. His ministers attempted to meet the needs of low-cost housing with the construction of 800,000 units for the poor. Price controls were instituted and more than 1500 persons daily were charged in the shah's courts as violators. The Ministry of Labor ordered that bonuses equal to 100 days' pay be given to workers, even when industries sustained losses in 1975 and 1976. And in 1977 and 1978, the Amuzegar cabinet ordered some industrialists to sell 49 percent of their stock to workers.[11]

The shah attempted to preserve Iran's sparse vegetation by nationalizing forests in 1962. That same year, he followed up on an earlier measure of his father and ordered the redistribution of estates to lackland peasants. By 1969, nearly 2.5 million families benefited from these reforms. To provide more irrigation water, his government built a number of breakwaters like the Pahlavi Dam on the Dez River.

Generally, religious minorities were treated fairly by the regime. At no time while Muhammad Reza Shah II ruled did Iran's 30,000 Zoroastrians or 70,000 Jews complain of discrimination. According to Kurdish Liberation Front sources in Washington, the shah's government offered sanctuary to 500,000 Kurds chased from their homes in Iraq between 1961 and 1975. The Shah also earmarked one billion dollars for an international fund to help developing nations hardest hit by the energy crisis between 1973 and 1975. One group that was not enthusiastic about his rule, however, were the Baha'is. During the first years of the Pahlevi dynasty, Iran's 100,000 Baha'is felt the lash of persecution. Literature was banned, cemeteries confiscated, schools closed. During the 1950s, Shiite mullahs continued to incite violence against the Baha'is. There was even discrimination when Amir Abbas Hoveida served as prime minister in 1965 (because Hoveida had to prove he was not descended from Baha'is).[12]

Under the shah, Iran was a force for stability in the Middle East. Through the placement of IBEX radar equipment, Iran enabled the U.S. to monitor Soviet missile development. Iran's military helped put down a Soviet and Yemeni-sponsored revolt against Oman. It bolstered Faisal of Saudi Arabia when his regime was menaced by his own air force in 1969. It aided Pakistan in suppressing a Baluchi revolution. During the Yom Kippur War, Iran was the sole Middle Eastern nation to deny the Russians overflight of its air space. The shah was crucial to negotiations between Israel and Egypt in 1974, guaranteeing the Jewish state oil in exchange for return of the Abu Rudeis fields in Sinai. Virtually alone among Middle Eastern leaders, the shah endorsed the Camp David Accords and denied the PLO embassy status in his country.[13]

During a visit to Iran in 1977, Jimmy Carter lavished praise upon Muhammad Reza Shah II, saying, "Under your leadership, Iran is an island of stability in one of the more troubled areas of the world." Yair Hirschfeld and Aryeh Schmulevitz of the Shiloah Center of Middle East Studies in Tel Aviv reported that hundreds of written and mimeographed letters of complaint were printed in Iranian newspapers in 1976 and 1977. These included petitions from Haj Seyyid Javadi (former co-editor of the newspaper *Khayan*), historian Ibrahim Khajenuri, some 64 leading attorneys, 40 members of the writers union, former ambassador Feerydun Adamiyat, and others. Opposition leaders from Mossadeq's old National Front continued to sit in the Majlis.[14] The only party that was outlawed was the Tudeh, and according to Fred Halliday, the shah was promising free elections for the summer of 1979.[15]

Fiercely proud of his nation's accomplishments, the shah constructed a special memorial, the Shahyad Tower, at the entry to Teheran to celebrate the 2500th anniversary of Persian monarchy in 1971. Four years later, in the fall of 1975, his government hosted an international symposium at Persepolis on "Iran: Past, Present and future." The conference was a harbinger of revolution that was to bring about the collapse of the Pahlevi dynasty.

Causes of the Revolution of 1979

For the shah, 1979 seemed to be a recreation of 1953. Once more, he was opposed by a charismatic figure claiming to represent the spirit of nationalist reform. Again, he was caricatured as a royal villain sustained by imperialists. As the army wavered, waiting to see what Iran's allies would do, the shah emulated his earlier action by going into exile after naming a transition government headed by Shapur Bakhtiar. Unfortunately, Muhammad Reza Shah discovered that history does not repeat itself. In 1979, the United States was led by a timorous president. The CIA, haunted by debacles in Cuba, Viet Nam, Angola, and Lebanon, and impaired by Congressional restraints, was equally indecisive. Most significant, the Iranian people who had filled the streets in 1953 cheering the shah were now overwhelmingly alienated.

Several factors help explain why the Khomeini revolution of 1979 was successful: (1) the inherent instability of government in the Middle East; (2) torture and other human rights violations; (3) opposition of the mullahs; (4) idealism of students; (5) grievances of so-called moderates; and (6) modern propaganda techniques.

Inherent Instability in the Region. John Laffin has recounted in his *Rhetoric and Reality* how violence, not democracy, is a way of life in the Middle East.[16] In this region, if people do not like their leaders, they remove them by force. Witness the axe murders of King Faisal, his uncle Crown Prince Abdul Illah and Prime Minister Nuri es-Said in Baghdad in 1958; the machine-gun slaughter of the man who engineered that coup, Abdel Karim Kassem, in 1963; the death of Iranian premier Hassan Ali Mansour in January 1965; the assassination of Jordanian prime minister Wasfi Tal in Cairo on November 28, 1971; the murder of U.S. Ambassador cleo Noel, U.S. chargé d'affaires George Moore and Belgian chargé d'affaires Guy Eid in Khartoum in March 1973; the shooting of King Faisal of Saudi Arabia by his nephew in Riyadh in February 1975; the killing of Kamal Jumblatt, Lebanese Druze chieftain, near Beirut in March 1977; the death of former Iraqi premier Abdul Razak al-Naif in London in July 1978; the assassination of Anwar Sadat in Egypt in October 1981; the murder of Lebanese president Gemayel in September 1982; or the shooting of PLO representative Dr. Issam Sartawi in Portugal in April 1983. What happened in Iran in 1979 was another example of people voting with the fist and the gun.

Torture and human rights abuses. The most convenient charge for critics of the shah's regime was that of government terrorism. The possibility of detention and torture by the SAVAK coupled with indiscriminate killing on the streets by government troops was enough to set people against the monarchy. No one knows how many Iranians were murdered in SAVAK prisons or in the riots of 1963 and 1978, but tales of martyrdom were embellished among eager listeners. Even the shah's worst critics, however, concede brutality was on the wane by the end of 1977. In February of that year, the shah ordered prison authorities and the SAVAK to halt torture. Three months later, a political trial of 11 accused communists was for the first time held in public. In May, an appeal was heard and sentences reduced. That same spring, a Red Cross delegation inspected 20 prisons holding 3087 persons. This was followed by visits from newsman of the Belgian paper *LeSoir* and the BBC. At the time of the revolution, the Majlis was discussing laws to guarantee the rights of political dissidents, requiring trials or release within 24 hours after arrest, guaranteeing the right of civilian prisoners to their own lawyers, and permitting them to inspect prosecution dossiers. With all the criticism of Iran's legal policies, the nation under the shah was far more humane than any of its Muslim neighbors.

Opposition of the mullahs. In 1935, 100 persons in Meshed were killed protesting against land confiscations of the first Pahlevi who intended to help the poor. Similar riots in June 1963 catapulted the Shiite ayatollah of Qum, Ruhollah Khomeini, to prominence. Khomeini and other Muslim leaders were incensed by "anti–Islamic" laws that extended suffrage to women, established a literacy corps, nationalized forests, and redistributed tracts of land once under the control of the waqfs. Charges of licentiousness, alcoholism, risque movies, and immodest dress could also be cited by an embittered Khomeini who lost one of his sons to SAVAK agents while in exile.

Idealism of Students. While the Pahlavi regime allegedly was salting away $25 billion in Swiss banks, Hollywood mansions, and Rolls Royces, it was also subsidizing the studies of more than 50,000 Iranian youths at foreign universities. Such education was designed to train technicians so the nation might one day enjoy autarchy. These students came into contact not only with principles of electrical engineering, they also imbibed theories of Locke, Mill, Veblen, Marx and Fanon. Through the 1970s, campuses in France and the United Stated hosted demonstrations staged by students who, fearing their own safety, donned Halloween-style masks. Those who returned home stirred up an already restive population.

Grievances of moderates. The shah might withstand the barbs of mullahs and academics, but not from his base among the workers and the middle class. By 1979, most elements of Iranian society seemed disaffected. Shopkeepers in the bazaar and laborers on the Farhzbad housing project were upset at inflation running 30 percent per year. Women were demanding more rights and somehow believed Khomeini would deliver them. Commuters fighting two-hour traffic jams in and out of Teheran every day cursed the government. And all Iranians blamed the government for its slow response to earthquakes in 1975 and 1978 that left more than 25,000 dead.

Modern propaganda techniques. Radio, television, and tape recorders spread the ayatollah's message. At first, Khomeini was ill-disposed toward Western inventions (except air-conditioning, autos, the airplane, modern surgery). When he arrived in Paris in 1976, his advisors seized the occasion to make him into a media celebrity. With the blessing of French authorities who subsequently limited access for anti–Khomeini leaders like Abul Hassan Bani-Sadr and Shapur Bakhtiar, the ayatollah regularly held court for the press at his suburban Paris villa. Rarely did an evening go by until his triumphant return to Iran in April 1979 without a clip of Khomeini on the evening news in the United States. Aides explained his commitment to democracy, religious freedom, human rights. Meanwhile, in Iran, tape recordings of the ayatollah were circulating among the faithful and disenchanted. The grandfatherly, bearded face became a symbol for all who wanted change in Iran.

The Devil and the Devil's Grandmother

In this imperfect world, people are often forced to choose their leaders from among the ignoble. The Abe Lincolns and Jesus Christs in history are rare. More often, the choice is between the devil and the devil's grandmother. In 1979 good-intentioned, yet naive souls in America believed the people of Iran were opting for the lesser of two evils. Not much later, in October 1983, Abdel Rahman Ghassemloo, chairman of the Kurdish Democratic Party, told the French newspaper *LeMatin*: "What is going on today is much worse than what happened under the old regime. The Shah's dictatorship, in spite of everything, respected certain rules." To which Hossein Khomeini, grandson of the ayatollah, added, Iran was "governed by fascists more dangerous than the founders of fascism," with revolutionary courts dispensing "more brutality than the Mongols did."[17]

Comparisons between Khomeini's *wilayet i-faqih* (rule of Islamic justice) and the shah's regime are instructive:

Nature of the ruler. The shah was said to be a throwback to the days of Louis XVIV, whose title of King of Kings an exiled Khomeini once charged was the most hated title in the sight of God. Khomeini would not settle for this in the 10 years he ruled Iran before his death in June 1989. God had given him all the rules on human conduct, he told ABC News' Tim O'Brien in November 1979, and during that month Khomeini began calling himself Imam (the leader). Not the imam or Mahdi (the deliverer promised the Shiites), just the *Faqih*, the agent of the messianic redeemer, ruler for life, whose power over a 73-man Islamic Council of Experts, a 12-man Council of Constitutional Gluardians, and the majlis was absolute.[18]

Form of government. The shah allegedly violated the constitution that antedated his father's coup. Yet Khomeini dictated a new charter, telling its framers: "You are here to create a constitution that is 100 percent Islamic. Not a single clause, not a single phrase can be devoid of the Islamic spirit." To no one's surprise, in a plebiscite where votes were cast publicly, Khomeini's rule received a resounding endorsement of 99 percent of the electorate. The transfer of power to his hand-picked successor, Hashemi Rafsanjani, went equally well when the ayatollah died in June 1989.

Operations of parliament. The shah's majlis was said to be a rubber-stamp assembly. Under Khomeini and his successors, Iran has had no independent legislature, no political opposition, even of a token sort. According to Khomeini's older brother, Ayatollah Sayyed Morteza Pasandeedeh, the ruling Islamic Republic Party used "deceit, intimidation ... mass imprisonment, and murder" to ensure victory in the 1980 parliamentary elections.[19] The charade of democratic government ended with the departure of interim prime ministers Bakhtiar and Bazargan, the shuffling of "moderate" revolutionaries Ibrahim Yazdi and Abulhassan Bani-Sadr out of office, and the 1982 execution of onetime foreign minister Sadegh Gotbzadeh. Two years of civil war between *Pasdarans* (fundamentalist street thugs) and *Mujahedeen* (Marxist revolutionaries) left 6000 dead and Mujahidin leader Massoud Rajavi in exile.

Freedom of the press. The shah suppressed free speech and censored newspapers when he held power. In Khomeini's first year, 44 newspapers, including the liberal *Ayandegan*, a journal openly critical of the shah, were shut down. Early in 1980, Yousef Ibrahim, writing for the *New York Times*, reported that political opponents of the Islamic regime were being executed and dissenting publications banned. The imam justified his actions to journalist Oriana Fallaci, saying:

> You presume I would permit the plots of those who want to bring the country to anarchy and corruption as though freedom of thought and expression were the freedom to plot and corrupt. I say: For those who did not think as we do. We understood they were taking advantage of our tolerance to sabotage us, that they did not want freedom, but the license to subvert, and we decided to stop them and when we discovered that, urged on by the former regime and foreign forces, they were seeking our destruction with other plots and other means, we shut them up to avoid further problems.[20]

That Khomeini and his followers did not restrict their understanding of free speech to Iran was evident in their reaction to the publication of Salman Rushdie's *The Satanic Verses* in 1989. This satire loosely based on the life of the prophet Muhammad was roundly condemned in the Islamic world as sacrilegious. But it was only from Iran that a call went out for the assassination of Rushdie, only Iran promised to pay a bounty for the deed. As a result, Rushdie and his wife went into hiding. Though Khomeini has since died, in June 1991 the Special Branch of British intelligence warned Rushdie that the bounty has not been withdrawn.[21]

Operations of law. Under the shah, there were complaints by Muslims that traditional values and powers of the mullahs were being impinged. In fact, the Islamic calendar was reintroduced in 1978, casinos were closed, some films banned, in an effort to mollify the teachers. Rule by the imam meant an end to legal rights as they are known in the West. Mullahs serve as prosecutors, judges, jury, and there are no appeals. Judgments are final and punishments "rendered swiftly," according to Quranic law. Public flogging may be administered to a dishonest merchant (50 to 80 lashes), one who drinks alcohol (80 lashes), or an unmarried adulterer (100 lashes). Married adulterers, along with traitors to the state, are condemned to death. According to Mansour Farhang, once Iran's ambassador to the United Nations, and Hossein Montavalli, "thousands of Iranians" have been arrested and publicly whipped for listening to music, playing cards, or playing chess.[22]

When Oriana Fallaci interviewed Khomeini, she asked him about people being shot for adultery, prostitution, and homosexuality. The imam replied: "If your finger suffers from gangrene, what do you do? Do you let the whole hand, and then the body become filled with gangrene or do you cut the finger off? What brings corruption to an entire country and its people must be pulled up like the weeds that infest a field of wheat." When

Fallaci asked about the execution of a boy charged with sodomy, Khomeini's response was "Corruption, corruption. We have to eliminate corruption." When she asked about the death of a pregnant 18-year-old shot in Beshar for adultery, he added, "Lies, lies. Lies like those about cutting off the breasts of women. In Islam, these things do not happen. We do not shoot pregnant women in Islam." When Fallaci insisted that Iranian newspapers reported the story, that a debate was held on television because the girl's lover was only given 100 lashes, Khomeini, wearying of the interview said, "If that is true, it means she got what she deserved."[23]

Women's rights. More than a decade after the shah opened the franchise to women, years after the International Year of Women proclaimed equality of the sexes, there is no freedom in Iran for women who supported the revolution. Feminists who rushed into Iran to link arms in street demonstrations were hustled out on the next available aircraft. Under Khomeini, women were arrested for not wearing headcoverings in public or donning "immodest" bathing suits in their own backyards. Females were segregated in schools, barred from law schools. Voices of women singers were banned from the radio. The Family Protection Act of 1976 was repealed. Prostitutes have been stoned to death. It is all part of a policy to return women to their traditional, subservient status.

Education. The irrational behavior of the Iranian regime prompted the flight of thousands of doctors, engineers, economists and teachers before the end of summer 1979. That brain drain has been slowed by rules abrogating the right of emigration. The promise of change betrayed, Iran's universities remain in disarray. As Mansour Farhang and Hossain Montavalli noted in 1984:

> Most fields in the social sciences, humanities, literature, art and music have been abolished because the Islamic Republic considers secular study to be unnecessary at best, blasphemous at worst. Books deemed contrary to Islamic doctrine have been destroyed or removed from libraries and bookstores. One young teacher was executed after Revolutionary Guards found works by Marx, Flaubert, Rousseau and Zola in her home.[24]

Religious toleration and minority guarantees. When he came to power, Khomeini promised religious freedom, in keeping with the Persian tradition dating to Zoroaster, Cyrus and Darius. Within three months, the Associated Press reported that Baha'i shrines (including the home of the sect's founder) had been ravaged. Regarded as schismatics, the Baha'is saw 140 of their people shot, another 700 imprisoned under threat of the death penalty by 1984.[25] Iran's 30,000 Zoroastrians have sought protection from the United Nations and the editorial columns of the *New York Times*. Iran's Jews, shrunken to less than 30,000 terrified individuals, witnessed the public lynchings of Habib Elghanian (head of the Teheran Jewish Central Committee) and eight others for the crimes of "contact with Israel, Zionism and the Devil." Communication with the outside world is discouraged and some Iranian Jews worry that the day may return when they will again be accused of ritual murder, suffer harassment or ghettoization. The imam's discourses, published as *Islamic Government*, charge Jews with perverting Islamic texts, abusing Palestinian Arabs, and "plotting against Islam and preparing the way for the Jews to rule over the entire planet."[26]

Khomeini's bigotry did not end with Jews or Baha'is. In 1994, Bishop Haik Hovsepian Mehr, leader of the tiny Assemblies of God Church in Iran, was found stabbed to death on a road near Teheran. Bishop Mehr had denounced a death sentence handed down against a member of his church who converted from Islam.

Under the revolution, there has been no autonomy, no political freedom for the millions of Baluchis, Arabs of Khuzistan, the Azerbaijanis who make up 20 percent of Iran's population, or four million Sunni Kurds who struggled against the shah and the fundamentalist Shiites. Khomeini once promised the Kurds "a feast of blood" when he took power. And while Iran has not proved to be as brutal as Iraq in dealing with the Kurds, perhaps as many as 10,000 of these people have been murdered since 1978.

Stability. Because of its many ethnic, religious, and political divisions, revolutionary Iran was perceived by its neighbors as weak and inviting. Thus in September 1980, Iraq's dictator Saddam Hussein attempted to wrest control of the Shatt al-Arab waterway. An earlier adventure in the Straits of Hormuz in 1975 had been rebuffed. But Saddam, exploiting the ancient animosity between Arabs and Persians, envisioned a short, happy war that would result in the partitioning of Iran and his recognition as a new Nasser.

Most Western experts believed the conflict would be protracted and that is exactly what transpired. Following initial successes that brought Iraqi forces to the outskirts of Khorramshah and Abadan, Iranian resistance stiffened, partly as a result of religious zeal, which hurled thousands of boys against the Iraqis in human-wave assaults. As both sides continued to preach jihad, more than 100 neutral ships were attacked, three million people were displaced, one million killed. And through it all, the battlelines did not shift more than 20 miles.

To date, Iran's state-controlled radio directs incendiary broadcasts throughout the Middle East. The gutted ruins of American chancelleries in Islamabad, Lahore, Izmir and Beirut testify to the spillover effect of the Iranian revolution.[27] Shiite fanatics were responsible for the 1979 seizure of the Grand Mosque in Mecca, though Khomeini blamed that incident on an American-Egyptian-Zionist conspiracy against Islam. There may have been a connection between Khomeini's revolution and the assassination of Egyptian leader Anwar Sadat, who once declared, "This is not Islam, this is Khomeini."[27]

Iranian Fascism and the Future

Twenty-five years after its glorious revolution Iran is a nation wracked by inflation — nearly 100 percent per year. Two-thirds of its people endure an annual income of less than $100. Some 21 million suffer from malnutrition. According to James Bill, "People are disillusioned. The masses who hoped their lives would improve with the revolution are still waiting."[28] Instead of confronting its problems honestly, the reactionary claque that rules Iran expropriates property, sponsors international terror, and aims to humiliate the Western world. It is a threat to the stability of the Persian Gulf, the economic stability of Japan and Western Europe, perhaps even to parts of Russia. It is a land dominated by the image of one man — the imam. His stern, larger than life visage may be seen everywhere. Once, a word from him and a million Iranians filled the streets chanting well-practiced slogans. A word from him and American hostages were freed after 449 days. Iran endures under non-socialist, statist economic control. Thought control is conducted through the use of propaganda. Enemies of the state are eliminated. Ethnic minorities are suppressed and that hoary staple of bigots, the international Jewish conspiracy, has been resurrected. Threats of force, terror, and aggression have been broadcast to Iran's neighbors. Finally, there is the great myth of self-righteousness, impregnability, ultimate victory.

The Random House Dictionary of the English Language defines fascism as "a governmental system led by a dictator having complete power, forcibly suppressing opposition and criticism, regimenting all industry, commerce, etc., and emphasizing an aggressive nationalism, and often racism." The description fits Iran's fundamentalist regime. The connection was not lost to Oriana Fallaci, who, wearing a chador, referred to Khomeini as "the new boss, the new master, the new dictator, who inspires not admiration but fear." Added Fallaci:

> But you frighten people. And even this mob which calls your name is frightening, all of them sitting for hours, being shoved about, suffering, just to see you for a moment and to sing your praises. By fascism I mean a popular phenomenon, the kind we had in Italy, when the crowds cheered Mussolini, as here they cheer you, and they obeyed him as they obey you now.[29]

Shah Muhammad Reza Pahlavi died in exile in 1980, and with him perished the dreams of a dynamic Iran that might serve as a model for emerging nations. The Ayatollah Khomeini died nine years later, but he left behind a corps of grim disciples dedicated to the belief that the problems of a 20th-century world would best be solved by a 14th-century mentality.

35

The Radical Arab States

The Neutrals of North Africa

From the arrival of the first GIs in North Africa in the fall of 1942, American policy-makers have tried to balance the interests of France against nationalist impulses of the native Berber-Arab populations. The United States was cheered when France granted Morocco its independence on March 2, 1956, and followed by freeing Tunisia less than three weeks later. In both instances, though, the French tried to hold onto their colonies, even if it meant imposing martial law, exiling Morocco's King Muhammad V or jailing Tunisia's most popular leader, Habib Bourguiba. In the end, the French had to concede it was to their advantage to divest themselves of Tunisia occupied in 1881, Morocco between 1900 and 1912. Parting under friendly terms gave France first option on natural resources like manganese, iron ore, and oil.

The reign of Habib Bourguiba as president of Tunisia until the aging statesman was forced to step down in 1986 stabilized that nation. Because of its willingness to negotiate with Israel and because it supplied haven to the PLO after it was expelled from Lebanon in 1982, Tunisia gained a reputation as a moderate in world affairs. Morocco, too, under-went a difficult maturation process. There were no less than three attacks by Morocco's air force against planes carrying King Hasan II in 1971 and 1972. Yet Morocco was one of the few Arab states to formally endorse the Camp David peace process.[1]

The last of France's North African possessions, Algeria, was a different matter. Conquered between 1830 and 1846, Algeria was integrated into the French political system in 1871. As a Department, it was as much a part of France as Texas or Arizona were parts of the United States. Although a governor-general presided over the territory, Algeria's elected representatives sat in the National Assembly in Paris. Two hundred fifty thousand of its people were drafted to fight in both world wars. Frenchmen enticed by the warm clime and cheap land flocked to Algeria. They modernized and renamed cities, built railroads and schools, and made French the required language of all residents. By 1954, these *colons* numbered more than one million. Many, who traced their roots in North Africa three generations, knew no other home. As a gesture of their permanent attachment, the colons celebrated a grand centennial in 1930.[2]

Native Algerians were less sanguine. During the 1920s and 1930s, the *Jeunes Algeriens* movement cut across ideological and racial boundaries with its message of independence.

Messali al-Hajj, a journalist with a Marxist orientation, and Druze leader Shakib Arslan forged an unlikely alliance with Algerian communists and Muslim ulema. Abdal Hamid Ben Badis, meanwhile, was committed to a union of the Berber and Arab peoples under Islam. More temperate was the program of Ferhat Abbas, a pharmacist, who believed in something called "association" with France. During the Second World War, Abbas replaced that concept with the call for "federation."

No French politician, not even DeGaulle, was willing to renounce a portion of the empire during the Second World War. On May 8, 1945, an incident at Setif, south of Constantine, rekindled nationalist fury. What was supposed to be a parade celebrating the victory over Nazi Germany turned into an anti-colonial demonstration. Muslims, Arabs and Berbers carried placards denouncing a system where one-sixth of the population dominated politically and economically. They also carried green-and-white banners associated with the 19th-century hero Abdel Kader. Ninety-seven Frenchmen were killed, houses were burned as rioting spread throughout Algeria. By the time the police restored order, between 1165 and 50,000 Muslims had been killed, and the nationalists had another date to add to their martyrology.[3]

As in Egypt, soldiers trained by the French waited for the moment when they could stage a coup. A former sergeant, Ahmed Ben Bella created the OS (Secret Organization), a group dedicated to the principles of Messali Hadj. Ben Bella fled to Egypt in 1952 when his revolutionary network was exposed by French intelligence. In his absence, the moderate Ferhat Abbas wrested token concessions from the French. The government budgeted monies for upgrading Arab agriculture, granted Muslims more influence in municipal councils, and took the extraordinary step of permitting Muslims to become French citizens.

None of this mollified the nationalists. Elections were rigged. The disparity in lifestyle between European shopkeepers and Arabs in shantytowns was too great. In the middle of All Saints' Night, November 1, 1954, elements of Ben Bella's OS, reconstituted as the *Front de Liberation Nationale* (FLN) and rearmed by Nasser, attacked government buildings, communications centers and French military posts throughout Algeria. Just as Dien Bien Phu in Vietnam, this coordinated attack was intended to shatter French confidence.[4]

France may have been willing to bail out of a misbegotten territory halfway around the globe, but not Algeria. Hoping to placate the moderates, in 1955 the Mendes-France government sent Jacques Soustelle to restore order. Later identified as a hard-liner, Soustelle came to Algeria with a reputation as a progressive. The key word of his plan: "integration" of Algeria as a French province, but with electoral equality for two peoples. It was a classic case of too little, too late. Following the example of the Mau Maus who butchered English settlers in Kenya, the FLN executed Frenchmen at Ain Abid and al-Halia. The French countered with reprisals. By the end of the year, the issue of Algeria (which the French insisted was an internal matter) was being debated in the United Nations.[5]

The year 1956 brought with it a new government in Paris, that of socialist Guy Mollet. This was the regime that collaborated with England and Israel in attacking Suez. More than 400,000 French troops were tied up in Algeria trying to pacify a rebellion whose roots and support could be traced to Cairo. In their anger and frustration, the French behaved more and more like their World War II enemy. To ferret out the 6000 rebels sponsored by Nasser, the French moved 2 million people into regroupment camps whose barbed-wire enclosures resembled concentration camps. The torment of the common people was dramatized in book (Franz Fanon's *The Wretched of the Earth)* and film (*Jamila*, about a young woman whose husband refuses to reveal the names of his compatriots under torture). As

French casualties reached 1000 per week by 1958, the estrangement between the colons and any moderates left in Algeria was complete.

Colons welcomed the announcement in June 1958 that Charles DeGaulle, the war hero, an advocate of union, was taking power in France. Like Eisenhower visiting Korea, the imperious DeGaulle came to Algiers, uttered an enigmatic, "*Je vous ai compris*," and returned to Paris. At first he offered the Arabs citizenship with full respect for Muslim law and tradition, the very dualism the Algerians had been rejecting since 1850. In September 1959, DeGaulle proposed an association or federation with France. That might have worked in 1940, but the Algerians already had formed a government in exile under Abbas. The French president then agreed to negotiate with Algerian leaders at Evian.[6]

French settlers understood that the meetings at Evian could have only one outcome. Riots and counter-riots erupted in Algiers and Oran as early as January 1960. The following year, Generals Salan, Challe and Jouhaud created their own Secret Army Organization (OAS). Its goals: to eliminate DeGaulle (by assassination, if necessary); to oppose any plan that would give Arabs control of Algeria; and, as a last resort, to proclaim an independent, French-controlled Algeria. Now it was their turn to plant bombs in schools and hospitals, to kill people on the streets.

The French army remained loyal to DeGaulle, however. Leaders of the OAS were arrested and tried for mutiny. The Evian Conference ended in March 1962 with a promise of a plebiscite on Algeria. In April, the mainland French voted overwhelmingly for self-determination. On July 1, the Algerians voted 99.7 percent in favor of independence.[7] The colons boycotted an election they regarded as little more than appeasement. They voted, instead, with their feet. Within two years, 800,000 colons, nearly all of Algeria's skilled workers, bureaucrats, technicians, and professional class had fled the country.

As the time approached for Algeria to gain its independence in the spring of 1962, Western experts were promising that this emerging nation would be a model of responsibility and moderation. The French legacy of reason, parliamentary fairness, education, the guardianship of DeGaulle, and the leadership of Ferhat Abbas guaranteed there would be no postwar bloodlettings. Having suffered so long at the hands of colonialists, Algeria would honor cultural and religious rights of all its minorities. Moreover, Algeria would be the first Arab state to appreciate the Jewish national aspiration and treat fairly with Israel.[8]

In retrospect, the Algerian revolution was a classic case of zealots wresting control from moderates, then turning on their own. Ferhat Abbas may have been a very decent man, but he found himself at odds with FLN leadership and was imprisoned after resigning the presidency in 1963. His colleague, Yusuf Ben Khedda, the first prime minister, also described as a moderate, was replaced by Ahmed Ben Bella in April 1963. Another of Ben Bella's FLN associates, Muhammad Khider, fled the country and was hunted down and killed in Europe in 1967. The same fate befell Kabyle chieftain Belkacem Krim who was murdered in 1970.[9]

The FLN never had any intention of sharing power with other political parties. Indebted to Nasser, it emulated the Egyptian system of one-man rule, Arab unity, socialism, and Islam. Ben Bella himself was purged by Defense Minister Colonel Houari Boumedienne in June 1965. Until his death in 1978, Boumedienne ruled as president, prime minister, and commander of the armed forces. The constitution, which he had drafted in 1976, declared that Algeria was a socialist state. The nature of that socialism was evidenced in the widespread confiscation of colon landholds and business in 1962 to 1965, in arms shipments, virtually all of which came from the Soviet Union, and Algeria's voting record in the General Assembly where in 1989 and 1990 it disagreed with the United States on 93 percent of the votes, a figure higher than Cuba, Russia, or any of the Soviet satellites.[10]

Algeria is committed to Arab unity. Under Boumedienne and his successor Chadli Benjedid, this meant the conversion of signs, journals, government correspondence from French to Arabic. After all these years, the constitution of Algeria declared Islam to be the official state religion. That meant a betrayal of the rights of women, many of whom were among the most courageous fighters of the FLN. As one Algerian feminist, Fadela Mrabet, has noted, Algerian women continue to be treated like chattel. The revolutionary heroine Jamila Buhrayd speaks of the secondary role that women must play in building the nation.[11]

Final proof that Algeria's experiment with Western socialism has failed was supplied early in 1991 when the army intervened, canceling elections that gave a majority in Parliament to Islamic radicals. Muslim Councils banned Western music, co-educational schools, and even threatened Western journalists and travelers with death if they did not leave Algeria. Since 1992, the ruling military junta has killed 10,000 of its own people to maintain order.

Promises of academics notwithstanding, Algeria has been a steadfast opponent of Israel. It supported Arab belligerents in the 1967 and 1973 wars, participated in punitive, anti–Western oil embargos, denounced Sadat's peace overture. Far from being the moderate intermediary that helped end several jet hijackings, Algeria has lent economic and military assistance to the PLO, given warnings to terrorists of Western plans for their capture. Its hostility toward Jews does not end with a pro forma declaration that Zionism is a crime. All but a handful of Jews have fled the country because of a deliberate program of persecution which, for Algeria, was all too familiar.

Jews served as convenient targets for Algerian nationalists. In May 1897, a synagogue in Mostaganem was sacked. The incident sparked pogroms in other towns. Thereafter, Arab mobs rallied to the cry *a bas les Juifs* (down with the Jews) as they struck against what they perceived to be agents of imperialism. On August 5, 1934, Muslims killed 25 Jewish civilians. They were abetted by French anti–Semites who marched in Algiers and killed a Jewish soldier in that city in 1936. Vichy fascists repealed the Cremieux Decree in 1940 and set up concentration camps for Jews before the Allied landing. When the FLN declared full-scale warfare, Jewish shops were boycotted and individuals threatened that the enemies of the Algerian revolution would be treated to "fire and sword." Anti-French riots in Algiers, Oran, and Tlemcen degenerated into pogroms. Synagogues were burned (in some instances more than once) and people were beaten on the streets.

By 1961, the Algerian Provisional Government was on record as opposing Jewish emigration to Israel. Once in power, the FLN deprived Jews of constitutional protection. By 1965, the Algerian Supreme Court sanctioned a formal boycott of Jewish businesses, declaring that Jews were no longer under the protection of the law. The following year, a Jew was executed on Rosh Hashanah for economic crimes. On the eve of the Six-Day War, in May 1967, 13 persons were injured when a terrorist threw a hand grenade into a Jewish cafe in Constantine. Synagogues everywhere became targets following Nasser's defeat at the hands of the Israelis.

Before the FLN brought France to its knees, Ferhat Abbas had promised Algeria's ancient Jewish community that "everybody is equal before the law."[12] Today there are only 300 Jews left in Algeria, mostly elderly people who have difficulty putting together a prayer service. In January 1977, the one synagogue of Algiers was burned and looted. Although 12 youths were apprehended, they were given suspended sentences. A 1983 survey by the American Jewish Committee revealed that the Algerian Jewish community is practically dead. Its cemeteries have been desecrated, its synagogues either taken over by the state or destroyed.[13]

An exponent of pan-Arabism, Algeria has not hesitated to foment trouble for its own kinsmen. For nearly 15 years, the Boumedienne-Benjedid junta has quietly underwritten a bloody civil war in the Western Sahara. Morocco's King Hasan claimed the phosphate-rich region on the basis of geography, Spanish cession, and the fact that his own family originated in what some have dubbed the Polisario. Morocco's attempt to occupy the region was resisted by Mauretania (which claimed its own historic right), Algeria and refugees from the Western Sahara who constituted themselves in exile as the Sahrawi Arab Democratic Republic. Algeria continues to support the separatist insurrection that has taken at least 10,000 lives since 1975. Though rival groups contend for leadership, Algeria continues to take pride in its leadership role in anti–Western African, Arab, and Third World blocs.

Taming of Outlaw Nations: Libya

Algeria can be labeled a moderate state only when contrasted with another of its neighbors—Libya. Ruled by Colonel Muammar Qaddafi, Libya is the heir of a 500-year-old tradition of piracy. Since the 16th century, the Berber and Arab rulers of Morocco, Algeria, Tunis and Tripoli preyed on ships sailing through the Mediterranean, kidnapping crewmen and passengers, stealing cargoes, and insisting upon tribute. The mercantile nations did not like the policy of extortion, but they were unable to do much about it. Britain, with the greatest fleet in the world, appeased the dey of Algiers with barrels of coin and gunpowder. The United States also, at a time it was refusing to pay "one cent in tribute" to ministers of France, was paying upwards of $1 million in bribes to the Barbary states. When Thomas Jefferson became president that policy changed. Gunboats were sent to the shores of Tripoli in 1804 and 1805 and again in 1915 and 1916, but the corsairs of North Africa would not be subdued until the French conquest in 1848.[14] So long as North Africa remained under colonial rule, there was little threat to international stability. With the ouster of the French and Italians, however, the old anti–Western piratical instincts were rekindled. Not so much with Tunisia and Algeria, the lawlessness is much more obvious in the case of Libya. Once a backward stretch of sand that served as a battlefield in World War II, Libya became a postwar ally of the United States. Under King Idris, it became one of the 10 leading producers of oil in the world. Then, in 1969, Colonel Qaddafi staged the coup that ended the monarchy.[15]

The son of an illiterate shepherd, Qaddafi has been called many things—mercurial, charismatic, unstable, insane. Anwar Sadat once called him "100 percent sick and possessed of the devil." A fervid pan-Arabist and disciple of Gamal Nasser, he championed the union of his nation with Egypt, and even threatened to open his borders so thousands of his countrymen could flood into Egypt as a gesture of friendship. A devout Muslim, he decreed the return of Islamic law as the basis for criminal punishment in Libya. Dependent upon the Eastern bloc for arms, Qaddafi rejected alignment with the Soviet Union as well as the free world. Instead, he imagined himself a profound thinker who has come up with a unique system of government

As postulated in his three-volume *Green Book*, his new form of government was a babble of Rousseau, Jefferson, and Marx. This *gumhuriya*, or people's government, has no political parties, because the party system splits societies and aborts democracy. There are no elections because all voting is a fraud. There can be no representatives because no one should presume to supplant the people. How then does such a system operate? Through committees, first at the trade and professional level, then a series of vaguely defined people's committees, on to a People's Congress, and finally through the head of state, who has no title but is simply their spokesman. This leader, whose will cannot be questioned, is Colonel Qaddafi.[16]

In the quarter century that he has ruled, Colonel Qaddafi has been a disruptive force in the Middle East and beyond. He has purged opponents in Libya and assassinated dissidents as far off as England arguing "my people have the right to liquidate opponents inside and outside the country even under broad daylight." He supplied troops to destabilize regimes in Chad, the western Sahara and the Central African Republic and gave sanctuary to the mass murderer Idi Amin when he was expelled from Uganda. He supported the Sandanistas, the Irish Republican Army, the Japanese Red Army, as wall as revolutionary brigades in El Salvador, Uruguay, Colombia, Peru, and Turkey. He has also supplied arms, money, and diplomatic channels to international terror gangs that have targeted Americans and Jews as their victims.

A virulent anti–Zionist, Qaddafi opposed negotiations with the state of Israel and has been on record for more than a decade offering $1 million to anyone who would supply him with an atomic bomb. Failing that, in 1987 and 1988, Qaddafi proceeded with plans for a German-built poison-gas factory. The object of this factory was clear — Israel. A staunch supporter of the PLO, in 1972 Qaddafi welcomed three of the murderers of 11 Israeli athletes to Libya and permitted the notorious Abu Nidal to operate out of offices in Tripoli. He cheered the atrocities of Maalot and Kiryat Shimona in 1974, the bus bombing that left 28 dead along the Tel Aviv highway in 1978. U.S. intelligence sources linked him with the 1982 bombing of a Pan-Am jet from Tokyo to Honolulu, the April 1986 bombing of a TWA jet that cost the lives of four persons, and an explosion that decimated a West Berlin disco injuring 230 persons, also in April 1986.[17]

The Reagan Administration struck back at Libya twice — in April 1986 and December 1988. Though critics denounced the violation of Libyan territorial sovereignty and resulting casualties, Qaddafi seemed cowed. He offered journalists interviews in which he spoke in subdued tones about the prospects for peace with the Bush Administration. The illusion was shattered in December 1988, when a Pan-American jetliner bound from London to New York exploded in the skies over Lockerbie, Scotland. Two hundred sixty persons perished in this atrocity, which experts attributed to the combined efforts of Ahmed Jibril's Popular Front for the Liberation of Palestine-General Command and the governments of Iran, Syria, and Libya.

In November 2001, Colonel Qaddafi and his son Seif publicly condemned acts of international terror. Libya agreed to pay families of Lockerbie victims compensation. And more recently, Qaddafi, fearing possible invasion of his country by the second Bush administration, agreed to scrap his fledgling nuclear program.

Operation Desert Storm: Iraq

In retrospect, Reagan's punitive expeditions against Libya seem miniscule when contrasted with the international chastening of Iraq between January and March 1991. The roots of Operation Desert Storm may be traced back to the overthrow of Iraq's Hashemite dynasty in the summer of 1958. In a nation that was oil-rich, the people were suffering from poverty, disease, and illiteracy. A monarchy planted by foreigners and sustained by corrupt politicians was following the lead of imperialists, accepting Point Four Aid from the Americans in 1951, joining the Baghdad Pact, and contemplating federation with Jordan in the spring of 1958. Inspired by Egypt's Nasser, a band of army officers led by General Abdel Karim Kassem overthrew the Iraqi government in what was one of the bloodiest coups in Middle East history. Following another massacre conducted by Colonel Abdel Aref in February 1963, Iraq became the first Arab nation to fall under the rule of the Baathists. Three years later (April 1966), an even more radical faction from the city of Tikrit led by General Ahmad Hasan al-Bakr assumed power. The real strongman in this group was a streetbrawler named Saddam Hussein.

Like a second Stalin, Saddam exploited party loyalties and eventually replaced the ailing General Bakr in July 1979. Lacking any military experience, he proclaimed himself a great strategist, general and admiral, and plunged Iraq into the decade-long war with Iran. For most of the 1980s, Saddam was favored by the West, which supplied him with some of his armaments (the Soviets remained Iraq's main source of military hardware), nuclear capabilities (through the French), long-range cannon (British technology) and poison gas (the Germans later claimed they were unaware Saddam was stockpiling tons of nerve gas and biological weapons).[18]

A patron of Palestinian extremists, Saddam tolerated no criticism of his dictatorship. A health minister, a brother-in-law, and a cousin who directed the Republican Guards were all purged for alleged mistakes. He created five security services and conducted mass arrests of enemies in cities like Kerbala, Najaf, and Basra in 1982. Three years later, more than 300 children between the ages of 10 and 14 were taken hostage in the town of Sulaimaniya. Annual reports of Amnesty International and Human Rights Watch accused Saddam's jailers of torturing victims with rubber truncheons and electric shock. Trials were held on camera and the death penalty meted out to anyone who was a Zionist, Communist, or Kurdish independence fighter. Between 1988 and 1990, at least 500 Kurdish villages came under assault from chemical weapons.[19]

When the war with Iran finally ended in 1989, Iraq was exhausted. Approximately 500,000 of its young men were dead. The nation was now $70 billion in debt. From Saddam's perspective, the oil-rich Arab nations of the Gulf owed him something. Saddam was especially upset with Kuwait, which was the likeliest target for Iranian-backed revolutionaries. In his eyes, he was Nebuchadnezzar reincarnate and this shaykdom was an imperialist invention on Babylonian soil, blocking access to the waterways of the Shatt al-Arab. He believed the Kuwaitis were tapping into oilfields that belonged to Iraq.

Iraq's dictator could only be emboldened by strange signals he was receiving from American leaders at that time. There had been no outcry against his massacre of the Kurds. A senatorial delegation to Iraq in April 1990 returned to Washington singing his praises. Then in July 1990, America's acting ambassador to Baghdad, April Glaspie, let it be known that the U.S. would not intervene in disputes between Arab nations. To Saddam Hussein, such a statement seemed a green light. Though Kuwait, at the last moment, offered to write off much of Iraq's debt and even pay for the lease of a disputed island in the gulf, Saddam ordered an invasion of his neighboring country on August 2, 1990.[20]

Outraged, the Bush Administration called upon the United Nations to condemn Iraq's aggression and to assist in protecting Saudi Arabia and other Gulf states. Critics of Operation Desert Shield, as the deployment of military personnel to the Gulf was called, warned the U.S. was risking another Vietnam by its actions. Cynics also questioned whether the U.S. would have done anything if Kuwait, like Yugoslavia, had no oil.

As more than 500,000 American troops poured into the region, congressional critics called for economic sanctions instead of military action. How a trade embargo could have hurt Iraq, whose main exports were oil, sulfur, phosphates, and cement, no one bothered to explain. How any embargo that would permit the passage of "humanitarian" goods like food and medical supplies could be effective was also ignored.

The question of sanctions became moot when Allied aircraft began the bombardment of Iraqi cities on January 16, 1991, and Operation Desert Shield became Operation Desert Storm. Viewers around the globe were transfixed by nighttime images of green tracers over the Baghdad skyline. Disputes raged over whether a destroyed milk factory was what it claimed to be or a poison gas plant. Air raid sirens howled in Dhahran and Tel Aviv and civilians scurried to safe rooms (rooms that might supply some protection against poison gas) as SCUD missiles added a new terror. While Navy Seals practiced sallies against the Kuwaiti coast, Iraq committed a new act of ecological terrorism, dumping 100 million barrels of oil into the Gulf. Then on February 27, Allied forces launched the land invasion of Kuwait and Iraq.

In less than a week, the fighting was over. Not surprisingly, Saddam's army was routed. Kuwaiti jubilation at being liberated was tempered by widespread destruction and looting of this prosperous nation. Saddam's army departed Kuwait after igniting virtually every oilwell and plunging the landscape into an eerie twilight.[21]

After two years the wellheads were capped and much of the cleanup in Kuwait was completed. The "legitimate" regime in Kuwait was restored. Yet many people wonder whether the war was worth it. Promises that the Sabah monarchy would be more responsive to the will of the people have not been fulfilled. Kuwaiti officials have been exposed as the source of false atrocity stories designed to arouse the American public against Iraq. In a position to press Arab states like Saudi Arabia and Kuwait for concessions, the U.S. instead forgave Jordan its open support of Saddam Hussein, and cancelled billions of dollars in debts owed by Syria and Egypt.

In Iraq, Bush's hoped-for goal of the ouster of Saddam Hussein by some native Iraqi faction did not materialize. No one had the ability or audacity to strike him down. Not the Americans, who did not want to risk creating a still worse nationalist leader in Iraq. Not the Shiites in Basra, who attempted a short-lived rebellion in the heady days after Desert Storm. Not the Kurds in mountainous regions near the Turkish border, who lived a tenuous existence protected only by American air cover against the revived army of Saddam. Saddam Hussein rebounded, much like Nasser after the 1956 Suez debacle, and became a greater hero to many Iraqis.[22]

The Fedayeen State: Syria

Libya, Iraq and Iran are the first nations that come to mind when observers list the renegade states that sponsor terrorism. There is a fourth Middle Eastern state that has been deeply involved in terrorist activities and which enjoys a surprising immunity from retaliation — Syria.

Syria has always maintained its position as a confrontationist state with Israel. Its violent encounters on land and in the air led to the resumption of full-scale warfare in 1967 and 1973. Since the Baathists seized power in 1963, and especially since the coup in November 1970 that brought Hafez al-Assad to power, Syria has been *the* training ground for all kinds of terrorists. In September 1971, Assad boasted how the fedayeen had freedom of movement on the Syrian front, how "we encourage and stimulate them." He added, "If it had not been for Syria, there would not have been any fedayeen action."[23]

Of 14,000 commandos in Arab lands in 1972, 9000 were based in Syria. A number of Palestinian organizations— including the PFLP-General Command, al-Fatah, National Front, Democratic Front, Abu Nidal faction, and the Palestine Liberation Army— maintained central military commands and annual conferences in Damascus. Like the soldiers of Saiqa, the PLO strike force organized by the Ba'ath, and the forces of the Islamic Jihad, Hezbollah, and AMAL, Lebanese fundamentalists based in the Bekaa Valley, these men received their military training, weapons, supplies, from the Syrians. From Damascus and Deraa, Syria offers daily propaganda broadcasts, scoring its enemies in Iraq and Jordan, but reserving special rebuke for the Israelis who are likened to Adolf Hitler and the Nazis. Syria quietly recruits volunteers supplies them with diplomatic papers and/or the necessary explosive devices, and then sends them out on suicide missions.

Assad's government was implicated in all of the following atrocities:

May 24, 1982: Beirut, French embassy compound; 12 persons killed, dozens wounded as a result of a car bomb.

August 23, 1982: Beirut; Bashir Gemayel, president of Lebanon, killed as 500 pounds of explosives detonate outside Phalangist Party Headquarters.

April 18, 1983: Beirut, U.S. embassy; 57 killed, 120 wounded in suicide bombing.

October 23, 1983: Beirut, U.S. Marine barracks and French military compound; 241 American and 58 French troops killed by vehicle bomb.

September 20, 1984: Beirut, U.S. embassy; 14 killed, 70 injured by car bomb.

April 12, 1985: Madrid; 18 killed, 82 injured in restaurant bombing.

June 24, 1985: TWA Flight 847 from Rome to Athens hijacked for two weeks; U.S. Navy Seal Robert Stethem beaten to death.

September 25, 1985: Larnaca, Cyprus; three Israelis on yacht murdered at Rosh Hashanah.

October 14, 1985: Italian cruise ship *Achille Lauro* seized in Egypt; 69-year-old passenger Leon Klinghoffer shot and pitched overboard in his wheelchair.

November 23, 1985: Malta; Egyptian airliner skyjacked by members of Abu Nidal; two passengers killed before Egyptian commandos storm plane, 58 more passengers killed in ensuing gunfight.

December 27, 1985: Rome and Vienna airports; grenade and machine gun attacks kill 20, wound 120.

March, 1986: West Berlin, German-Arab Friendship Society; 9 wounded in bombing.

April, 1986: Athens-Rome airliner; Explosion in cabin results in two persons being sucked out of plane.

April 17, 1986: London; El-Al guard finds Syrian-made bomb planted in luggage of pregnant Irish woman. If the bomb had gone off, 300 persons would have died.

September 5, 1986: Karachi; 21 killed, 100 wounded in commando assault on hijacked airliner.

September 6, 1986: Istanbul; 22 Jews killed, three wounded in machine-gun assault against a synagogue during a Saturday-morning service.

September 8–16, 1986: Paris; a series of bombings in the Jewish quarter kill 10, wound 160.

December, 1988: Lockerbie, Scotland; Western intelligence links Syria with the bombing of Pan-Am Flight 103 through Ahmed Jibril's PFLP-GC group.

International experts agree that Syria is a key center of terrorism. Says Ariel Merari, director of Tel Aviv University's Project on Terrorism: "There is no doubt that the general policy of sponsoring terrorist activity in Western Europe is done with Assad's approval and probably his initiative." Adds Daniel Pipes: "Syria is the only state where terrorism has been used as an effective tool of state on a consistently long-term basis."[24] According to Brian Jenkins of the Rand Corporation: "Qadhafi's terrorism is hot; Assad's terrorism is cold. For Qadhafi, terrorism is like a banner; for Assad, it's as quick and silent as an assassin's bullet." Sequestered in his presidential palace that looms over Damascus like a Crusader fortress, Assad designated specific targets for the military or the *Muhabarat* (state police). Thus in February 1982, to prevent a coup by the Muslim Brotherhood, he destroyed their center, the town of Hama. Nearly 30,000 persons were killed in a combined aerial-tank blitz. Troops loyal to Assad piped cyanide gas into the ruins of buildings. Hama was left like Berlin in 1945. Few visitors, no journalists, no photographs were permitted on the streets of this devastated city.[25]

Assad has been equally brutal toward a powerless segment of his people. Four hundred Jews, the remnant of a once thriving community of 40,000, are hostages, bargaining chips for Israel's return of occupied Syrian territory. Conditions have improved since 1970 when Jews could be beaten or raped on the streets, but they are still denied political and civil rights. No Jews serve in the government, as elected officials or bureaucrats. Their role in the economy is severely restricted. No Jews engage in banking or foreign trade. The Muhabarat monitors religious observances, censors texts sent in from the West. Until 1993, Jews were denied the right to emigrate, a rule that violated the International Declaration of Rights of Man and the U.N. Charter. Families of those who have eluded border patrols forfeit all claim to property. Those who are intercepted trying to flee, like six men who were apprehended in the fall of 1987, are tortured and sentenced to an indefinite period in prison.

Jews have been in Damascus, Aleppo, and Qamishli since the time of David. Their quiet persecution is symbolized in the tale of a young couple with four children who tried to escape in 1978. Part of a group that was escorted by smugglers to Turkey, they were betrayed somehow by an informer. Syrian army units opened fire as they tried to cross the border. The mother, a 27-year-old woman, tried to shield a daughter from the crossfire and was hit in the spine. At first, it was believed the woman would die. Paralyzed from the waist down and in great pain, she was permitted to go for surgery in Italy. From there, she went to Israel and the United States. Her husband tried a second time to leave Syria illegally and was caught. Finally in 1982, just before the woman was to undergo surgery in the United States, a bribe was paid to the Muhabarat enabling the family to leave. At the Damascus Airport, the father was stopped by police and told that he could take only two of his four children with him.[26]

The man responsible for this cruelty was Hafez al-Assad.[27] Assad intervened in the Lebanon Civil War, at first to help the Palestinians, then turned his troops against them, the Maronites, Shiites and anyone else that opposed his design for chaos in the coastal region of Greater Syria. While the rest of the world was transfixed by the Gulf crisis in 1990, Assad occupied and put an end to independent Lebanon. For nearly a decade, he profited from traffic in heroin and opium that originated in the Bekaa Valley. Assad's saving grace: his intermittent war of words, cannon and assassination with brother Baathists in Iraq since 1975.

Shrewd though he was, Assad was not immortal. His death through heart attack in 2001 resulted in a surprisingly peaceful transfer of power to his son Bashar. Western educated and a physician, the younger Assad seems less the ideologue than his father. He still relies, however, upon the same Baathist advisers: Chief of Staff Hikmat Shihabi, Defense

Minister Mustafa Tlas, and Foreign Minister Abdal Halim Khaddam. No one can predict the course of Damascus in the next decade. Whatever happens, the words of Henry Kissinger ring true. Said the onetime secretary of state, "There can be no war without Egypt, no peace without Syria."[28]

36

The Middle East
in the 21st Century

Islamic True Believers

As the new century progresses, the greatest threat to peace comes not from an ideology devised in thatched-roof communes of 19th century Russia, beer halls of Munich, or the shantytowns of South Africa. Rather, a spirit of intolerance has been rekindled by religious zealots, cut from the same mold as monks of the Inquisition. Acting as if there has been no passage of time since the holy warriors of Khalid al-Walid spread the word of Islam, Muslim radicals and their allies in the hybrid Baathist parties have demanded that the world take note of their movement. Inspired by the Ayatollah Khomeini, the Mujahideen have directed Iraq, Libya, Saudi Arabia and Syria to the bottom of nations listed as not-free by Freedom House in New York. They have eroded freedom in Bahrain, Oman, Tunisia, and the United Arab Emirates. They plan to do the same in Turkey, Egypt and North Africa. Willing to offer themselves as human sacrifice for what they perceive as truth, they have declared war on all foreigners, businessmen or tourists in Algeria and Egypt. Peace with Israel is unacceptable. They aspire for a league of states including the breakaway republics of Kazakhstan, Turmenistan, Uzbekistan, and Tadzhikistan.[1]

A host of scholars (Adeed Dawisha, R. Hrair Dekmejian, John Laffin, Emmanuel Sivan, Menachem Friedman and Daniel Pipes) have commented on this disturbing trend.[2] In this mindset, compromise with Westerners is unthinkable. The new generation of True Believers has contempt for scholars or diplomats who offer "understanding" or "consideration" of Islamic fundamentalism. The traditional ways hold the answer to every question. As Fouad Ajami noted in his *Arab Predicament*: "To [the Arab nativist] the whole world should be in the Arab world, instead of the Arab world in the whole world. To him the Arab world must be the self-completed world. It is a great pain to every people who had once lived in a self-completed world to admit that their world is nothing other than a small part of the whole world."[3]

The Iranian revolution and the seizure of the American embassy by "students" in November 1979 ushered in this era of melancholy. For the next 444 days, the world watched as the United States proved incapable of rescuing its diplomatic staff. Hostage-taking became institutionalized among militants in Lebanon like AMAL, Hizbollah, and Islamic Jihad, all of which were linked to Iran. Although the numbers of their captives were small (no more than 20 Westerners were in captivity at any time) the radicals prized the leverage these lives gave them. Thomas Jefferson sent Marines to Tripoli when the Barbary pirates disrupted trade in the Mediterranean. Eighty years later, Teddy Roosevelt demanded the freedom of one woman or the head of Raisuli, a North African bandit. In 1987, the Reagan Administration was unable to free a handful of captives even when its agents offered bribes through intermediaries to Iran. Only when Islamic extremists deemed the moment provident (after the deaths of Khomeini and the Soviet Union) were the hostages released.[4]

Moderate Friends and Satanic Verses

One of the most shameful rationalizations for fundamentalist brutality came in 1980. American public television announced plans to broadcast a documentary titled *Death of a Princess*. Based on the story of Misha, a 19-year-old member of the royal family of Saudi Arabia, the hour-long program was a tale from the *Arabian Nights*. Here was a vivacious girl, married against her will to an older cousin. While in England, she fell in love with a young Saudi. The two continued their illicit affair when they returned to Arabia. Discovered, they tried to flee the country. Instead, the man was publicly beheaded and Misha was stoned to death. When the government of Saudi Arabia learned that PBS planned to tell the story, it complained to the State Department and to oil companies that did business in the region. The United States government did nothing, but Mobile Oil, one of the chief underwriters for public television in this country, took out full-page advertisements in the major American newspapers, expressing regret for any embarrassment the program might cause to Saudi Arabia.[5]

The Saudis were also involved in another incident that demonstrated a willingness on the part of the industrial world to appease. Early in 1989, the Saudis declared a jihad against 66 writers, one of whom was the Pakistani-born novelist Salman Rushdie. Rushdie's *Satanic Verses* was a 600-page chronicle of good and evil, a dream of sequences and exploding aircraft over Scotland. A satire that exposed some of the hypocrisy of Christianity and inferiority complexes of Judaism, *Satanic Verses* revolved about the adventures of a man named Mahoun. This hero cynically fabricated a road-show religion, feigned contact with angels, slept with whores, and generally lampooned the founder of Islam.[6]

There had been advance publicity on the book for several weeks. Once it appeared, however, Muslims reacted strongly. Twelve states, including Saudi Arabia, Egypt and Turkey, banned it. In Pakistan, several dozen people were killed and wounded in rioting attributed as much to chauvinist opposition to the naming of Madame Bhutto as the first female head of state in the Islamic world as the writings of native son Rushdie. And then came word from Ayatollah Khomeini: the *wilayat al-faqih* decreed that Rushdie had blasphemed. Under Quranic law, he was an outlaw who should be punished with death. Khomeini offered a reward ($2 million to any non-Muslim, $5.6 million to any Iranian) who would kill Rushdie.[7]

In the furor that followed, American Muslims demonstrated against Rushdie and demanded that bookstores not sell his work. Initially, two major chains, fearing the safety of their employees, caved in and indicated that they were removing *Satanic Verses* from their shelves. That resulted in another uproar, as a number of celebrated authors, led by Norman Mailer, declared such action a violation of the First Amendment of the U.S. Constitution. The writers held their own demonstrations outside bookstores, had public readings of Rushdie's book, contributed op-ed essays to major newspapers, and even appeared en masse on *The Phil Donahue Show*.

Rushdie was also bolstered by the British government, which withdrew its ambassador from Iran, and by several other European nations that announced their intent to go ahead with translations of his book. But such support was not unqualified. Quite soon, the caveats and apologies began to appear. The British foreign secretary equivocated, noting that he could understand how Muslims might be offended by the book, but that calling for death of an author was unacceptable. President George Bush and ex-president Jimmy Carter made virtually the same statement. The writers who boldly positioned themselves before Rushdie on American television proceeded to turn the affair into a recitation of their own grievances. Somehow the threat against Rushdie's life was lost amid debates dealing with blacklists in the McCarthy era, sexism, racism homophobism, etc.

From a hiding place in Britain, Rushdie tried to calm the situation by issuing a statement of regret. It was, apparently, insufficient for Khomeini, who repeated the bounty. A summit of Muslim nations rejected Iran's formal call for assassination. *Satanic Verses* rushed to the top of the *New York Times* bestseller list. Late-night television programs invented skits about Rushdie and Khomeini. The debate continued among scholars, writers, and diplomats. But it was no longer academic in nature. Early in March 1989, Abdullah Ahdal, a Muslim cleric living in Belgium, stated on French television that while Rushdie's book was offensive, the author did not merit death. On March 29, 1989, Ahdal, director of the Muslim World League in the Low Countries, was shot to death on the streets of Brussels.[8] The assault on freedom of expression was renewed in February 2006 following the publication in a Danish journal of a series of editorial cartoons deemed offensive by Muslims across the world.

The Proper Step into Darkness

Ahdal was deemed a traitor, punishable by death, by Muslim extremists, just as with Muhammad Shaaban, one of Yasser Arafat's top aides in the PLO. On September 21, 1993, less than one week after the signing of a preliminary accord between representatives of the PLO and Israel, Shaaban was gunned down by hooded men after he delivered a speech in defense of the agreement in Gaza. Shaaban's death also symbolized the dangers faced by those who work for peace and reconciliation instead of war and hate in the Middle East.

In 1993, the Soviet Union and its cynical machinations in the Middle East were fading memories. For many Israelis and Palestinians, a century of animosity and six years of fruitless deaths and retaliations were enough. In an event every bit as extraordinary as Anwar Sadat's trip to Jerusalem, PLO Chairman Yasser Arafat and Israeli Prime Minister Yitzhak Rabin journeyed to Washington to publicly recognize the legitimate interests of one another's people. More than a handshake, the 16 articles and annexes at long last provided a timetable (five years or 1998) for the transfer of power in Gaza and the West Bank to Palestinian authorities. The agreement was fraught with all kinds of unanswered questions. What would be the ultimate disposition of East Jerusalem? Or of 100,000 Jewish settlers on the West Bank? Who would decide the flow of precious waters in Samaria? How could Palestinians move from one self-governing sector (Gaza) to the other (Jericho/Ramallah) on Israeli highways? Who would be responsible for curbing violence on the part of extremists on either side (Hamas, the PFLP, Jewish militants)? What of jurisdictional conflicts between Palestinian police and Israeli military units in the region? Would the Golan Heights be returned to Syria? What impact would the agreement have for refugees living outside the Holy Land? What impact upon bordering states like Jordan and Lebanon?

Would it finally signal a new era of responsibility and peace on the part of other Arab and Muslim states in the Middle East? However flawed the negotiations, it was as one Israeli lawyer said "the proper step into darkness."

The fragile state of negotiations was illustrated in March 1994 when an American-born zealot, Dr. Baruch Goldstein (allegedly motivated by the recent killing of a pregnant Jewish woman), slaughtered 29 Arabs at prayer in the shrine of Abraham at Hebron. In swift retaliation, somebody set off a bomb that killed nine Maronite Christians in southern Lebanon. Hamas fundamentalists bent on becoming martyrs attacked Jews in Gaza and Jaffa. Terrorists detonated a car bomb in Afula, killing seven and wounding 52. A group calling itself *Ansarallah* (Partisans of God) claimed responsibility for the bombing of the Jewish Community Center in Buenos Aires, Argentina, which left 96 dead in July 1994. That same month, Ansarallah blew up an airplane flying over Panama, killing 21 Jewish businessmen. Though Israeli governmental officials were joined by rabbis and Jewish masses in their public denunciation of the Hebron massacre, Syria, Jordan and the PLO temporarily broke off negotiations with their traditional enemy.

Despite the death of hundreds of innocent Arabs and Jews (including Yitzhak Rabin — assassinated by a Jewish zealot in 1998), talks resumed between the two sides. Hopes for peace that burned so brightly in 1979 were rekindled at Madrid and Oslo in the wake of the Gulf War. There was even more optimism when President Clinton squeezed a series of extraordinary concessions on territory, Jerusalem, and the status of refugees from Israeli Prime Minister Ehud Barak in the summer of 2000. All of that good will evaporated in September when Ariel Sharon visited the Temple Compound and Arab rejectionists proclaimed a new intifada on behalf of al-Aqsa. As Islamic propaganda likened Jews to pigs and monkeys who deserved to die, self-proclaimed holy warriors strapped with dynamite sacrificed themselves and dozens of little girls and old men at discos, pizzerias, bus stations and bat mitzvahs in Israel.

9/11

September 11, 2001, was one of those early fall days that makes one glad to be alive. Trees had just begun to take on color. Skies were clear from Maine to Missouri. Children had returned to school, and the National Football League had just opened its season. Americans were coming to grips with the reality that George W. Bush, a man of middling intellect, was president — not by popular vote, but by decree of five justices of the Supreme Court. America had seen worse days (the interregnum of Nixon, Ford and Carter) and better (the heady times following the collapse of the Soviet empire when pundits were crooning that peace was breaking out all over the world).

In New York City, Battery Park was crowded with families making their way to ferries that would take them to Ellis Island or the Statue of Liberty. Just to the north of the Battery, the financial district was aswarm with more tourists and aspiring brokers bound for the top floors of the Marriott and the twin towers of the World Trade Center.

Amid the bustle, members of a French video crew shooting a documentary noticed an aircraft flying dangerously close to the skyscrapers.

At 8:45 A.M. American Airlines Flight 11, carrying a complement of 93 (82 passengers and a crew of 11) bound from Boston to Los Angeles, slammed into the North Tower of the trade center. As news commentators struggled to determine if this disaster were akin to the crash of a jumbo airliner into the Empire State Building in 1945, United Airlines

Flight 175, bound from Boston to LAX with 65 persons aboard, crashed into the other tower at 9:03 A.M. The deliberateness with which this second plane maneuvered into position for its suicidal run dispelled any doubts as to whether the crash was intended. Forty minutes later (9:43 A.M.) a third jetliner, American Airlines Flight 77 flying from Washington to Los Angeles with 64 persons, struck the Pentagon Building in the District of Columbia. As national security alerts were sounded along the East Coast, leaving military authorities to ponder how many more aircraft had been seized and what their destinations might be, a fourth jet, United Airlines flight 93, crashed in the fields of Somerset County, Pennsylvania, following a desperate effort on the part of its passengers to wrest control of the aircraft from five hijackers.

At 10:05 A.M. the South Tower of the World Trade Center collapsed quietly, almost gracefully, in a scene evocative of a Hollywood science fiction epic. The North Tower came down 23 minutes later. Before the day was out more than 3000 persons would be dead in what was the worst attack upon America in its history. Some economists reckoned financial losses from this single terrorist act in the billions. The dead included men, women and children of every age and description, from countries all over the world.

Critics of the new administration would ridicule President Bush for sitting seven minutes in a Florida kindergarten class as snippets of information were relayed to him by his staff. Three years later, a bi-partisan committee would fault the President for inaction after he received a CIA memorandum warning of an "imminent" but unspecified attack on the U.S. in August 2001. In his State of the Union address of that year, however, Bush acknowledged that the free world faced a new enemy, one more insidious than the Soviets. He spoke of a war against terrorism, a war that might last a hundred years. And he cautioned that the U.S. would evaluate all states by their behavior as either "with us or against us."

Osama bin Laden and al-Qaeda

In the fall of 2001 it was clear who the villains were. They included Taliban warriors in Afghanistan, fundamentalist tribesmen armed and trained by the CIA for resistance against the Soviets. Like the Assassins of Alamut, they imposed a medieval code upon their own society and recruited volunteers from the disaffected for suicide missions against onetime allies.

Not surprisingly, 15 of the 19 hijackers on September 11 came from a single country — America's good friend Saudi Arabia. Following the conclusion of the Gulf War, Osama bin Laden, a Saudi import/export investor with $50 million in the al-Shamal Islamic Bank of Sudan, took up residence in Sudan, linking forces with a radical group called *al-Qaeda al-Sulhah* (the solid base). Created in Peshawar, Pakistan, in 1979 by Palestinian exile Abdallah Azzam, al-Qaida consisted of small terror cells dedicated to fighting the enemies of Islam. These included the Philippines government, Russians in Afghanistan and Chechnya, and the United States, which had committed sacrilege by supporting Israel and sending troops to the Islamic Holy Land. Because of his financial resources and organizational skills, bin Laden was designated leader. His top assistant and ideologue was Egyptian physician Dr. Ayman al-Zawahiri, the head of Gihad, the group that murdered Sadat.

Operating from safe houses, college dormitories, mosques and training camps as far flung as Kabul, Hamburg, Fort Lauderdale and Newark, al-Qaeda planned methodically — not for minor incidents that took two or five lives in Israel. Its actions were designed for maximum shock and loss of life. Thanks to the cooperation of several intelligence services, a number of schemes were foiled. These included plans to murder Clinton and Pope John Paul II during the winter of 1994 and 1995, an attack against Mubarak when he visited Ethiopia six months later, the bombing of LAX Airport targeted for December 1999, the planned bombing of NATO headquarters in Belgium in September 2001, two assaults against the U.S. embassy in Sarajevo, and a mass murder planned for millennium festivities in Jordan. Sadly, the list of Qaeda's "achievements" is equally long:

December 29, 1992: Aden, Yemen; two persons killed when hotel housing transient American servicemen was dynamited.

February 26, 1993: New York City; six murdered, hundreds injured when bomb detonated in basement parking facility of World Trade Center.

October 3–4, 1993: Mogadishu, Somalia; al-Qaida implicated in massacre of 18 American troopers by gangs of Mohammad al-Adid.

November 13, 1995: Riyadh, Saudi Arabia; car bomb kills five American and two Indian soldiers.

June 25, 1966: Dhahran, Saudi Arabia; explosives shear facade away from Khobar Towers, killing 19 U.S. military personnel, wounding hundreds.

August 7, 1998: Dar es-Salaam and Nairobi, East Africa; bombs explode simultaneously at US embassies in Tanzania and Kenya, killing 12 Americans and 200 Africans.

October 12, 2000: Aden, Yemen; suicide vessel collides with *USS Cole*, killing 17, wounding 30.

September 11, 2001.

Like his father, George W. Bush encountered little opposition from the international community as he fashioned a coalition against the Taliban and al-Qaida in Afghanistan. Within days of the World Trade Center atrocity, American Special Forces were on the ground in East Asia. They would be joined soon by token elements from more than two dozen countries. A popular tribal chief, Hamdan Karzai, was installed as head of a provisional government and bin Ladin and his cronies were chased to the caves of Bora Bora. As coalition forces played the futile game of Where in the World is Usama?, Bush learned the lesson Afghans have taught every would-be conqueror from Alexander the Great to the redcoated Lieutenant Favisham: Afghanistan is rock, cave and impregnable.

Another Little War in Iraq

When the U.S. and Great Britain, constituting virtually all that was left of the coalition, struck against Iraq in the spring of 2003, it was as much in frustration as humanitarian concern for Kurds or Shiites, Iraqi oil, or weapons of mass destruction. Saddam Hussein had been teasing Allied aircraft and playing his own game with U.N. weapons inspectors for a decade. If they could not finish off a disturbing gnat like bin Ladin, Bush, Blair, et al, reasoned they would rid the Middle East of the man who issued checks to Palestinian families whose children offered up themselves as suicide bombers.

The Second Gulf War went pretty much as expected—few casualties, a race to capture Baghdad, celebrations in Basra and Mosul, bitterness in the so-called Sunni Triangle that was Saddam's base, capture and arraignment of the haggard warlord, and a moment of puffery as the U.S. president landed a fighter jet aboard the USS *Abraham Lincoln* and proclaimed the "mission accomplished"—i.e., an end to major war operations in Iraq.

And then it all went badly. No weapons of mass destruction were found—no great arsenals of poison gas, no missiles, no nuclear weapons, no anthrax. Al-Qaida operatives emerged to mine the subways of Madrid in the midst of national elections to force Spain from the coalition. Similar terrorist actions—kidnappings, bombings and beheadings—caused the withdrawal of troops from Bulgaria, Poland, the Philippines and South Korea. As gangs of "insurgents" congregated in Falluja under the banner of Abul Musab al-Zakarwi for a showdown battle with the Americans, bin Ladin reappeared on al-Jazeera television to advise Americans how they should behave.

Coalition forces led by U.S. marines and soldiers (including some Iraqis trained by the Allies) won control of Falluja in two days in November 2004. In doing so, they vindicated current strategy, which held that it is better to fight the war on terror in the Middle East than have it erupt in the subways of Philadelphia or the supermarkets of Columbus. At the same time, critics charge that failing support of China, Russia, France and Germany, there can be no resolution of the war on terror.

A decade ago, the *Economist* warned that the world must prepare to confront "the hooded man with a gun," the angry fanatic who feels he can only accomplish his goals through bloodshed. Look around the world and that seems to be the case. Palestinian teenagers blow themselves up in an Israeli disco or the market of Beersheba. Iraqis decapitate terrified foreign workers on television. Hate-inspired crowds dip their hands into the blood of frontier guards and smear racist slogans on the stuccoed walls of a police station in Ramallah. Pakistani medressehs continue to preach bigotry, and clerics in Iran and Saudi Arabia urge their faithful to renewed holy war. Fanatics claiming justification from God use machetes to hack women and children to death in Ivory Coast or Darfur. Australians are murdered in Bali. Bombs kill dozens of tourists in an Egyptian hotel in Sinai. Serbian shrines are desecrated in Kosovo, those of the Baha'is are flattened in Iran. Hindus are attacked in Pakistan, Jews in France, and schoolchildren are taken captive by Chechen rebels who murder dozens. Children hiking through the desert are pelted to death with stones, like the ones flung at our bus as we drove through Gaza in the spring of 1986. And the president of Iran (a state that is developing its own atomic bomb) calls for the eradication of the State of Israel.

If there is one truism that may be sounded as we enter a new century it is that the world has become a more dangerous place even as it has become a smaller place. The peoples of the Middle East have no need of xenophobes preaching hatred and death, the use of biochemical weapons and nuclear arms.

We opened this book with reference to a fable involving Yitzhak Rabin when he was prime minister of Israel back in the 1970s. It is appropriate to end by quoting Rabin from the White House ceremony in September 1993: "Let me say to you, the Palestinians: We are destined to live together, on the same soil in the same land. We, the soldiers who have returned from battle stained with blood, we who have seen our relatives and friends killed before our eyes, we who have attended their funerals and cannot look into the eyes of their parents, we who have come from a land where parents bury their children, we who have fought against you, the Palestinian — we say to you today in a loud and clear voice: enough of blood and tears. Enough."[9]

Chapter Notes

Preface

1. On objectivity, see Jacques Barzun and Henry Graff, *The Modern Researcher* (New York: Harcourt, Brace, Jovanovich, 1985), 183–85.

2. Arnold Ages, "Israel's Case in the Court of Public Opinion," Reconstructionist, 31 (January 21, 1966): 7–16.

3. Critics like Nat Hentoff, Martin Kramer, and Daniel Pipes accused Columbia University of regimenting Middle East Studies when Edward Said flourished on that campus. See "Columbia's Own Middle Eastern War," New York (January 17, 2005: "There Is More to Be Explored in Columbia University's Middle East Studies Than Israel," Village Voice (December 28, 2004). Similar criticisms have been leveled at other Ivy League institutions and major state schools that have accepted endowment monies from oil shaykhdoms.

4. Anatole France, *Penguin Island*, trans. A.W. Evans (New Haven: Leete's Island Books, 1981), vii.

1. An Introduction

1. *Bulletin of World Health Organization*, vol. 56, no. 4, 1978.

2. *Plain Dealer*, July 4, 1984, p. 10E.

3. *USA Today*, August 8, 1983, p. 9a.

4. *New York Times*, September 20, 1970, p. 76.

5. *Bulletin of World Health Organization*, vol. 59, nos. 1, 2, 4, 1981; vol. 60, nos. 2, 3, 4, 5, 1982; vol. 61, 1984. For l994 country-by-country statistics, see William Spencer, ed., *The Middle East* (Guilford, Conn.: Duskin, l994).

6. *United Nations Statistical Yearbook 1981*, pp. 590–601.

2. The Dry Land

1. George Cressey, *Crossroads: Land and Life in Southwest Asia*, (Chicago and New York: J. B. Lippincott, 1960), p. 521.

2. Ismail Nawab, Peter Speers and Paul Hoye, eds., *Aramco and Its World: Arabia and the Middle East*. (Dhahran: Aramco, 1981), pp. 30–31, 104–05, 111, 114.

3. See Daniel Hillel, *Negev, Land, Water and Life in a Desert Environment* (New York: Praeger, 1982); Troy Pewe,

ed., *Desert Dust: Origin, Characteristics and Effect on Man.* (Boulder, Col.: Geological Society of America, 1981).

4. Richard Bulliet, *The Camel and the Wheel* (New York: Columbia University Press, 1990); Daniel Streeter, *Camels!* (New York: Putnam, 1927).

5. More than 70 persons were reported dead, 150 missing, 3000 made homeless in these floods. See *New York Times*, March 12, 1966, p. 24 and March 13, 1966, p. 10. See also Nelson Glueck, *Deities and Dolphins: The Story of the Nabataeans* (New York: Farrar, Straus, and Giroux, 1963).

6. Thorkild Jacobsen, "Mesopotamia," *The Intellectual Adventure of the Ancient Man*, ed. Henri Frankfurt, (Illinois: University of Chicago Press, 1946); Jacobsen, *Oriental Institute Discoveries in Iraq, 1933–34.* (Illinois: University of Chicago Press, 1935).

7. *New York Times*, January 27, 1954, p. 5. See also U.S. State Department Bulletin, vol. 29, December 28, 1953, pp. 891–93; M. A. Garbell, "Jordan Valley Plan," *Scientific American* 212 (March 1965): pp. 23–31.

8. *New York Times*, January 18, 1964, p. 5.

3. The Blessings of Oil

1. Samuel Eaton, *A History of the Oil Region of Venango County, Pennsylvania* (Philadelphia: J. P. Skelly, 1866).

2. Allan Nevins, *John D. Rockefeller: The Heroic Age of American Enterprise* (New York: Scribner, 1940); *Study in Power: John D. Rockefeller, Industrialist and Philanthropist* (Scribner, 1953).

3. Fouad al-Farsy, *Modernity and Tradition: The Saudi Equation* (London: Kegan Paul Intl., 1990).

4. For the developing oil embargo of 1973 and 1974 see *New York Times*, May 14, p. 1; May 16, p. 6; July 15, p. 1; October 7, III, p. 1; October 8, p. 14; October 16, p. 1; October 17, p. 16; October 18, p. 1; October 19, p. 1; October 2, p. 1; October 21, p. 28; October 22, p. 1.

5. On the *ABC Evening News* of September 19, 1977, Howard K. Smith reported that if Arab states suddenly withdrew some $50 billion on deposit in Western banks, they might destroy the West's economic system.

6. *Plain Dealer*, October 7, 1976, p. 6A.

7. Edward Sheehan, "The Epidemic of Money," *New York Times Sunday Magazine*, November 14, 1976, pp. 31, 116–21, 124–36.

8. Sheehan's follow-up article in the *New York Times*, November 14, 1976, VI, p. 31. Similar conclusions were reached by Thomas Ferris, March 25, 1979, VI, p. 23; and Daniel Pipes, November 8, 1979, p. 23.

9. John Laffin, *The Dagger of Islam* (New York: Bantam, 1981), pp. 122–23.

10. Jacqueline Ismael, *Kuwait: Social Change in Historical Perspective* (New York: Syracuse University Press, 1982); Harry Winstone and Zahra Freeth, *Kuwait: Prospect and Reality* (New York: Crane, Russak, 1972); Alison Lanier, *Kuwait* (Yarmouth, Me.: Intercultural Press, 1985).

4. The Cradle of Civilization

1. Seton Lloyd, *Mesopotamia* (London: Lovat Dickson, 1936); *Foundations in the Dust* (Harmondsworth: Penguin, 1953).

2. A. Leo Oppenheim, *Ancient Mesopotamia* (Illinois: University of Chicago, 1964), p. 365.

3. Erich von Daniken, *Chariots of the Gods*, trans. M. Heron (New York: Putnam, 1968).

4. John Marshall, ed., *Mohenjo Daro and the Indus Civilization* (London: Arthur Probstbain, 1931); Mortimer Wheeler, *Civilizations of the Indus Valley and Beyond* (New York: McGraw-Hill, 1966); Stuart Piggott, *Prehistoric India to 1000 B.C.* (Penguin, 1950); Walter Fairservis, *The Roots of Ancient India* (Illinois: University of Chicago, 1975).

5. The Greeks also credit a mortal, Prometheus, with having civilized man through the theft of fire from the gods.

6. Andre Parrot, *Sumer*, trans. Stuart Gilbert and James Emmons (London Thames and Hudson, 1960).

7. Samuel Noah Kramer, *Cradle of Civilization* (New York: Time-Life, 1967), pp. 41–49.

8. James Mellaart, *Earliest Civilizations of the Near East* (New York: McGraw-Hill, 1965), pp. 21–32.

9. Ibid., pp. 77–102.

10. Kathleen Kenyon, *Archaeology in the Holy Land* (New York: Praeger, 1970), pp. 39–66.

11. Similar developments were proposed by Henri Pirenne in *Medieval Cities*, trans. Frank Halsey (Garden City, N.Y.: Doubleday, 1956).

12. On Menes see Alan Gardiner, *Egypt of the Pharaohs* (New York: Oxford University Press, 1966), pp. 400–13, 429–31; I. E. S. Edwards, "The Early Dynastic Period in Egypt," *Cambridge Ancient History*, vol. 1, part 2 (Cambridge University Press, 1971), pp. 11–15.

13. Theodor Gaster, *Thespis: Ritual, Myth and Drama in the Ancient Near East* (New York: Harper, 1961); E. O. James, *The Ancient Gods* (New York: Capricorn, 1970).

14. Henri Frankfurt, *Ancient Egyptian Religion* (New York: Harper, 1948), pp. 43–58; Margaret Murray, *The Splendor That Was Egypt* (New York: Praeger, 1969), p. 121.

15. Leonard Woolley, *The Beginnings of Civilization* (New York: New American Library, Mentor, 1963).

16. John Wilson, *The Culture of Ancient Egypt* (Illinois: University of Chicago Press, 1957), pp. 55–58.

17. Edward Chiera, *They Wrote on Clay* (Illinois: University of Chicago Press, 1938); P. E. Cleator, *Lost Languages* (New York: Mentor, 1962).

5. Foundations of the Bible

1. Alexander Heidel, *The Babylonian Genesis* (Illinois: University of Chicago, 1942 and 1951).

2. Samuel Noah Kramer, *The Sumerians* (Illinois: University of Chicago, 1963), pp. 314–15.

3. Georges Roux, *Ancient Iraq* (Harmondsworth, English: Penguin, 1966), p. 131.

4. Cyrus Gordon, *The Common Background of Greek and Hebrew Civilizations* (New York: Norton, 1962), pp. 89–90.

5. Samuel Noah Kramer, *History Begins at Ur* (Garden City, N.Y.: Doubleday, 1959), pp. 139–42.

6. Ibid., pp. 222–23.

7. Alexander Heidel, *The Gilgamesh Epic and Old Testament Parallels* (Illinois: University of Chicago, 1946, 1949); James Pritchard, ed., *The Ancient Near East: An Anthology of Texts and Pictures* (New Jersey: Princeton University Press, 1958), pp. 40–75; R. Campbell Thompson, "The Influence of Babylonia," in *Cambridge Ancient History*, vol. 3, pp. 226–32.

8. Cf. Heidel, *The Gilgamesh Epic*, pp. 51–54, and Pritchard, *The Ancient Near East*, pp. 42–45.

9. Heidel, *The Gilgamesh Epic*, pp. 37–39.

10. *Ibid.*, pp. 43–51.

11. Cf. Heidel, *The Gilgamesh Epic*, pp. 51–54, and Pritchard, *The Ancient Near East*, pp. 51–55.

12. Cf. Heidel, *The Gilgamesh Epic*, pp. 59–63, and Pritchard, *The Ancient Near East*, pp. 56–61.

13. Cf. Heidel, *The Gilgamesh Epic*, pp. 72–74 and Pritchard, *The Ancient Near East*, pp. 63–64.

14. Cf. Heidel, *The Gilgamesh Epic*, pp. 78–86, 224–69, Pritchard, *The Ancient Near East*, pp. 65–70, and Gordon, *The Common Background of Greek and Hebrew Civilizations*, pp. 75–83.

15. C. Leonard Wooley, *Ur of the Chaldees* (New York: Norton, 1965), pp. 17–33.

16. John Gray, *Archaeology and The Old Testament World* (New York: Harper, 1962), p. 34.

17. Chaim Bernant and Michael Weitzmann, *Ebla: A Revelation in Archaeology* (New York: Times Books, 1979).

18. Cyrus Gordon, *The Ancient Near East* (New York: Norton, 1958), pp. 115–25.

19. See generally Nahum Sarna, *Understanding Genesis* (New York: Schocken, 1978); R. K. Harrison, *The Archaeology of the Old Testament* (New York: Harper, 1963), pp. 23–29.

20. C. J. Gadd, "The Dynasty of Agade and the Gutian Invasion," in *Cambridge Ancient History*, vol. 1, pp. 417–18.

21. Yigael Yadin, *The Art of Warfare in Biblical Lands* (New York: McGraw Hill, 1963), vol. 1, pp. 176–81.

22. Pritchard, *The Ancient Near East*, pp. 225–26.

23. *Ibid.*, pp. 12–15.

24. Sigmund Freud, *Moses and Monotheism* (New York: Knopf, 1939).

25. Adolf Erman, *The Ancient Egyptians* (New York: Harper, 1966), pp. 14–29.

26. James Henry Breasted, *A History of Egypt* (New York: Bantam Reprint, 1967), pp. 350–53.

27. Robert Silverberg, *Akhnaten: The Rebel Pharaoh* (Philadelphia: Chilton Books, 1964); Cyril Aldred, *Akhenaten, Pharaoh of Egypt* (New York: McGraw Hill, 1969).

28. Wilson, *The Culture of Ancient Egypt*, pp. 227–28.

29. Spyridon Marinatos, *Crete and Mycenae* (New York: Abrams, 1960); Ian Wilson, *Exodus* (New York: Harper and Row, 1985).

6. The Origins of Law and War

1. C. J. Gadd, "The Cities of Babylonia," in *Cambridge Ancient History*, vol. 1, pp. 139–43.

2. Kramer, *History Begins at Sumer*, pp. 51–55.

3. Kramer, *The Sumerians*, pp. 336–40.

4. Pritchard, *The Ancient Near East*, pp. 138–66.

5. Dr. J. H. Hertz, ed., *Pentateuch and Haftorahs*, (London: Soncino Press, 1969), pp. 404–05.

6. Roux, *Ancient Iraq*, pp. 261–66.

7. Sidney Smith, "The Age of Ashurbanipal," in *Cambridge Ancient History*, vol. 1, pp. 89–112, and "Ashurbanipal and the Fall of Assyria," in *Cambridge Ancient History*, vol. 1, pp. 113–31; Roux, *Ancient* Iraq, pp. 322–38.

8. On divination, see H. W. Saggs, *The Greatness That Was Babylon* (New York: Hawthorn Books, 1962), p. 319; Georges Contenau, *Everyday Life in Babylon and Assyria* (New York: Norton, 1966), pp. 281–90.

9. Yigael Yadin, *The Art of Warfare on Biblical Lands in the Light of Archaeological Study*, vol. 2, trans. M. Pearlman (New York: McGraw-Hill, 1963), pp. 396, 397, 399, 406–07.

10. D. D. Luckenbill, *Ancient Records of Assyria and Babylonia*, vol. 1, (Illinois: University of Chicago, 1926), p. 146.

11. *Ibid.*, pp. 222–24.

12. L. Delaporte, *Mesopotamia: The Babylonian and Assyrian Civilization*, trans. V. Gordon Childe (New York: Barnes and Noble, 1925), pp. 276–78.

7. Ancient Persia: Stability

1. H. J. Rose, *Religion in Greece and Rome* (New York: Harper, 1959), pp. 284–89.

2. Herodotus, *The Persian Wars*, vol. 1, trans George Rawlinson (New York: Modern Library reprint, 1942), pp. 73–78.

3. Benjamin Farrington, *Greek Science* (Penguin Books, 1941), pp. 33–78.

4. A. T. Olmstead, *History of the Persian Empire* (Illinois: University of Chicago Press, 1948), pp. 51–52.

5. I am indebted to Professor William McDonald of Ohio State University for this assessment of the system of checks and balances that operated in the Persian empire.

6. James Moulton, *The Treasure of the Magi: A Study of Zoroastrianism* (New York: AMS Press, 1972).

7. Olmstead, *History of the Persian Empire*, p. 475.

8. *Ibid.*, p. 232.

9. *Ibid.*, p. 234.

10. *Ibid.*, p. 298.

8. The Age of Wonder

1. See Robert Pfeiffer, *History of New Testament Times* (New York: Harper, 1949).

2. W. W. Tarn, *Alexander the Great* (Boston: Beacon reprint, 1966), pp. 125–26, 138–40.

3. Arrian, *The Life of Alexander the Great*, trans. Aubrey de Selincourt (Harmondsworth, England: Penguin, 1962).

4. W. W. Tarn, *Hellenistic Civilization* (New York: World, 1961), pp. 177–209.

5. *Ibid.*, pp. 126–176.

6. H. M. D. Parker, *The Roman Legions* (New York: Oxford University Press, 1928); Moses Hadas, *Imperial Rome* (New York: Time-Life Books, 1965), pp. 98–101.

7. Arthur Boak and William Sinnigen, *A History of Rome to A.D. 565* (New York: Macmillan, 1969), pp. 127–140.

8. B. H. Warmington, *Carthage* (London: Robert Hale Ltd., 1960); Donald Harden, *The Phoenicians* (New York: Praeger, 1962).

9. Leonard Cottrell, *Hannibal: Enemy of Rome* (New York: Holt, Rinehart and Winston, 1960), p. 67; Gavin De Beer, *Alps and Elephants* (New York: E. P. Dutton, 1967), p. 87.

10. Livy, *The War with Hannibal*, vol. 25, trans. Aubrey de Selincourt (Baltimore: Penguin, 1965), p. 40.

11. J. P. V. D. Balsdon, *Romans and Aliens* (Chapel Hill: University of North Carolina Press, 1979), p. 218.

12. Henry Bomford Parkes, *Gods and Men: The Origins of Western Culture* (New York: Vintage, 1959), p. 332.

13. Tarn, *Hellenistic Civilization*, p. 124–25.

9. The Jews: Historic Roots

1. Any bibliography on anti–Semitism should include works by Leon Poliakov, George Hosse, Nora Levin, Luey Dawidowicz, Peter Pulzer, Howard Sachar, Malcom Hay, and Simon Dubnow.

2. A. Werner, "Chagall's Gifts to Humanity," *American Zionist* 62 February 1972, pp. 27–29; Werner, "Chagall at 90," *Midstream* 23 June/July 1977, pp. 43–48.

3. *Encyclopædia Britannica* (1967), 27: p. 155.

4. S. Friedman, *Land of Dust: Palestine at the Turn of the Century* (Washington: University Press of America, 1982), pp. 157–58.

5. See Tcherikover, *Hellenistic Civilization and the Jews*; Abraham Schalit, ed., *The Hellenistic Age: A Political History of Jewish Palestine from 332 to 67 B.C.* (New Brunswick, N.J.: Rutgers University Press, 1972).

6. Joseph Klausner, *The Messianic Idea in Israel* (New York: Macmillan, 1955).

7. Josephus, *The Jewish War*, trans. G. A. Williamson (Hardmondsworth, England: Penguin, 1939).

8. Yigael Yadin, *Bar Kochba* (New York: Random House, 1971).

9. Cassius, *History*, vol. 69, pp. 12–14.

10. T. Carmi, ed., *The Penguin Book of Hebrew Verse* (Harmondsworth, England: Penguin, 1981), pp. 347–51.

11. On Sabbatai Zevi, see Jacob Marcus, *The Jew in the Medieval World* (Philadelphia: Jewish Publication Society, 1960), pp. 261–70. For other pseudo-messiahs, see *Ibid.*, pp. 225–26, 247–55, 279–84.

12. Arthur Hertzberg, *The French Enlightenment and the Jews* (New York: Columbia University Press, 1968).

13. *Diaries of Theodor Herzl*, ed. and trans. Marvin Lowenthal (New York: Grosset and Dunlap, 1962), p. 16.

14. Emma Lazarus, "The Jewish Problem," *Century* (February 1883), pp. 609–10.

15. D. Rausch, *Zionism within Early American Fundamentalism 1878–1918* (New York: Edwin Mellin Press, 1979), pp. 155–57.

16. Friedman, "Telling the World," *Jewish Frontier* 42 (August/September 1975), p. 21.

17. Nahum Sokolow, *History of Zionism* vol. 1 (New York: Ktav, 1969), p. 62.

10. The Jews and Their Culture

1. *USA Today*, March 17, 1983, D1; See also Morris Kertzer, *What Is a Jew* (New York: Macmillan, 1977).

2. Leon Poliakov, *The Aryan Myth: A History of Racist and Nationalist Ideas in Europe* (New York: New American Library, 1974); George Mosse, *Toward The Final Solution: A History of European Racism* (New York: Howard Fertig, 1978).

3. Friedman, *Amcha: An Oral Testament of the Holocaust* (Washington: University Press of America, 1979), p. XI.

4. *The Israelis*, CBS News documentary (October 1973).

5. *Voice of Giants*, PBS documentary (May 1988).

6. Mark Zborowski and Elizabeth Herzog, *Life Is with People: The Culture of the Shtetl* (New York: Schocken, 1952); Diane and David Roskies, *The Shtetl Book* (New York: Ktav, 1975).

7. Jacob Katzman, *The Jewish Influence on Civilization* (New York: Bloch, 1974); Cecil Roth, *The Jewish Contribution to Civilization* (London: East and West Library, 1956); Dagobert Runes, *The Hebrew Impact on Western Civilization* (New York: Citadel Press, 1965).

11. Judaism and Christianity

1. See Augustine's reply to Faustus the Manichaean in Philip Schaff, ed., *Nicene and Post Nicene Fathers*, vol. 4 (Grand Rapids: Eerdmans, 1956), pp. 186–87; see commentaries on the Gospel of St. John in *Ibid.*, vol. 6, pp. 421–34; see commentaries on Psalm 44 in *Ibid.*, vol. 8, pp. 264–65.

2. Friedman, *The Oberammergau Passion Play: A Lance against Civilization* (Southern Illinois University Press, 1984), p. 119.

3. Arthur Gilbert, *The Vatican Council and the Jews* (Cleveland: World, 1968), pp. 262–280.

4. Michael Rostovtzeff, *The Social and Economic History of the Roman Empire* (Oxford: Clarendon Press, 1926).

5. Philo, *De Legatione ad Gaium*, vol. 10, pp. 299–305.

6. Josephus, *De Bello Judaico*, vol. 2, pp. 8, 2–14.

7. Yigael Yadin, *Masada* (New York: Random House, 1966).

8. Graetz, *History of the Jews*, vol. 2, pp. 23–31, 100, 145, 219ff.

9. Millar, Burrows, *The Dead Sea Scrolls* (New York: Viking, 1955); Cecil Roth, *The Dead Sea Scrolls* (Philadelphia: Jewish Publication Society, 1962); Geza Vermes, *The Dead Sea Scrolls: Qumran in Perspective* (Cleveland: Collins-World, 1977); Hershel Shanks, et al, *The Dead Sea Scrolls after Forty Years* (Washington: Biblical Archaeology Society, 1991).

10. John M. Allegro, *The Sacred Mushroom and the Cross* (New York: Bantam, 1971).

11. On the Slavonic Josephus, see Josephus, *The Great Roman-Jewish War* trans. D. S. Margoliouth (New York: Harper, 1960), pp. 309–10.

12. Josephus, *Antiquities*, bk. 1, 3:3.

13. *New York Times*, February 13, 1972, p. 24.

14. Although there are passing references to Jesus in Sotah 47a and Gittin 56b, the most offensive passages are in Sanhedrin 43a–43b and 61b where Jesus is marked down as a deceiver.

15. Jack Finegan, *Handbook of Biblical Chronology* (New Jersey: Princeton University Press, 1964); *The Archaeology of the New Testament: The Life of Jesus and Beginning of the Early Church* (New Jersey: Princeton University Press, 1969).

16. Mary 19:28.

17. Ian Wilson, *The Shroud of Turin* (Garden City, N.Y.: Doubleday, 1978).

18. *Skeptical Inquirer* vol. 6 (Spring 1982), containing essays on the Shroud of Turin by Marvin Mueller (15–34), Walter McCrone (35–36), and Steven Schafersman (37–56).

19. Graetz, *History of the Jews*, vol. 2, pp. 155–56.

20. Friedman, *The Oberammergau Passion Play*, pp. 67–74.

21. Cecil Roth, *History of the Jews* (New York: Schocken, 1954), p. 140.

22. Hugh Schonfield, *The Passover Plot* (New York: Bantam, 1966).

23. Chaim Cohn, *The Trial and Death of Jesus* (New York: Harper and Row, 1971), pp. 145, 158, 166–67, 171–73, 181, 267–69.

24. Samuel Sandmel, *Anti-Semitism in the New Testament?* (Philadelphia: Fortress Press, 1978); Ellis Rivkin, *What Crucified Jesus* (Nashville: Abingdon Press, 1984).

12. The Byzantine Empire

1. Eusebius, *History of the Church from Christ to Constantine*, bk.10 (New York University, 1966), pp. 380–400. See also *Constantine and Eusebius* (Cambridge, Mass.: Harvard University Press, 1981), pp. 222–23.

2 Norman Cantor, *Medieval History: The Life and Death of a Civilization* (New York: Macmillan, 1963), pp. 42–43.

3. Speros Vryonis, *Byzantium and Europe* (New York: Harcourt, World and Brace, 1967), p. 51; A. H. M. Jones, et al, *The Cities of the Eastern Roman Provinces* (Oxford: Claredon Press, 1971).

4. D. A. Miller, *The Byzantine Tradition* (New York: Harper & Row, 1966), pp. 77–78.

5. Philip Sherrard, *Byzantium* (New York: Time-Life, 1966), pp. 101–11.

6. H. J. Roby, "Roman Law," in *The Cambridge Medieval History*, vol. 2, H. M. Gwatkin and J. P. Whitney, eds. (Cambridge University Press, 1967), pp. 53–103; Charles Diehl, "Justinian; The Imperial Restoration in the West," in *Ibid.*, pp. 1–24; "Justinian's Government in the East," in *Ibid.*, pp. 25–50.

7. Rene Guerdan, *Byzantium: Its Triumphs and Tragedy*, trans. D. L. B. Hartley (New York: Capricorn, 1957), p. 39.

8. Vryonis, *Byzantium and Europe*, p. 38.

9. Edward Martin, *A History of the Iconoclastic Controversy* (New York: AMS Press, 1978); Leslie Barnard, *The Graeco-Roman and Oriental Background of the Iconoclastic Controversy* (Leiden: Brill, 1974); Jaroslav Pelikan, *Imago Dei: The Byzantine Apologia for Icons* (New Jersey: Princeton University Press, 1990).

10. Louis Brehier, "The Greek Church: Its Relations with the West up to 1054," in *Cambridge Medieval History* vol. 4, J. R. Tanner, et al, eds. (Cambridge University Press, 1927), pp. 246–73. See also Paul Alexander, *Religion and Political History and Thought in the Byzantine Empire* (London: Variorum Reprint, 1978).

11. J. M. Hussey, *The Byzantine World* (New York: Harper, 1961), p. 49.

12. Steven Runciman, *Byzantine Civilization* (Cleveland: World reprint, 1967), pp. 37–45.

13. The Arabs and Their Culture

1. Philip Hitti, *History of the Arabs from the Earliest Times to the Present*, rev. ed. (New York: St. Martin's, 1968), p. 8. (Hitti's magnum opus was first published in 1939, a time when people were defining race loosely.)

2. H. A. R. Gibb, *Mohammedanism* (New York: Oxford University Press, 1953).

3. See "Arabiyya," in *The Encyclopedia of Islam*, vol. 1, H. A. R. Gibb, et al (London: E. J. Brill, 1960), pp. 561–602; Anwar Chejne, *The Arabic Language* (Minneapolis: University of Minnesota Press, 1969).

4. Dale Eickelman, *The Middle East: An Anthropo-*

logical Approach (Englewood Cliffs, N. J.: Prentice-Hall, 1981), pp. 76–80.

5. H. R. P. Dickson, *The Arab of the Desert* (London: Allen and Unwin, 1952).

6. H. V. Hilprecht, *The Excavations in Assyria and Babylonia* (Philadelphia: University of Pennsylvania Press, 1904), p. 289ff.

7. Sania Hamady, *Temperament and Character of the Arabs* (New York: Twayne, 1960), p. 43; F. A. Sayegh, *Understanding the Arab Mind* (New York: Organization of Arab Students in the U.S., 1953), p. 28.

8. Laffin, *Rhetoric and Reality*, p. 91. Eickelmann is much harsher, suggesting the *kizb* represents institutionalized lying (*The Middle East* 190–92). Even Hitti concedes the problem, saying, "What a people believes, even if untrue, has the same influence upon their lives as if it were true" (History of the Arabs).

9. Hitti, *History of the Arabs*, pp. 96–108. See also "Allah," in *Encyclopedia of Islam*, vol. 1, pp. 406–17; Joseph Henninger, "Pre-Islamic Bedouin Religion," in *Studies on Islam*, ed. Merlin Swartz, (New York: Oxford University Press, 1981), pp. 3–22.

10. G. R. Hawting, "The Origins of the Muslim Sanctuary at Mecca," in *Studies on the First Century of Islamic Society* (Carbondale: Southern Illinois University Press, 1982), pp. 9–22; D. S. Maroliouth, *Mohammed and the Rise of Islam* (New York: Putnam's, 1905), pp. 1–44.

11. Dickson, *The Arab of the Desert*, p. 293. See also W. R. Smith, *The Religion of the Semites* (London: A. C. Black, 1927).

12. See Glueck, *Deities and Dolphins*; Browning, *Petra*; and Avraham Negev; *Nabataean Archaeology Today* (New York: Oxford University Press, 1986).

13. Michael Rostovtzeff, *Caravan Cities*, trans. D. and T. Talbot Rice (New York: AMS Press, 1971).

14. C. H. Becker, "The Expansion of the Saracens," in *The Cambridge Medieval History*, vol. 2, eds. H. M. Gwatkin and J. P. Whitney (Cambridge University Press, 1967), p. 331.

15. Robert Playfair, *A History of Arabia Felix* (Salisbury, N.C.: Documentary Pubs., 1978); James Montgomery, *Arabia and the Bible* (Philadelphia University of Pennsylvania Press, 1934).

16. "Dhu Nuwas," in *Encyclopedia of Islam*, vol. 2, pp. 243–45.

14. Muhammad

1. Tor Andrae, *Mohammed: The Man and His Faith* (New York: Harper, 1960), pp. 186–90. See also Al-Damiri's description in Arthur Jeffrey, *A Reader on Islam* (The Hague: Mouton, 1962), pp. 330–31.

2. Andrae, *Mohammed*, p. 35.

3. W. Montgomery Watt, *Muhammad at Mecca* (Oxford: Clarendon Press, 1952), pp. 33–35.

4. Alfred Guillaume, *Islam* (Harmondsworth, England: Penguin, 1966), pp. 24–25.

5. Alfred Guillaume, *The Life of Muhammad: A Translation of Ishaq's Sirat Rasul Allah* (New York: Oxford University Press, 1967), pp. 79–81.

6. Qadr 97:1 and Blood Clots 96:1.

7. Ibn Ishaq, *The Life of Muhammad*, vol. 3. For Muhammad's mental state atop the mountain see also Turkish illustrations in Desmond Stewart, *Early Islam* (New York: Time-Life, 1967), p. 23.

8. The Star 53:23.

9. Night Journey 17. See also Ibn Ishaq, *Life of Muhammad*, pp. 181–87; al-Ghaiti in Jeffrey, *Reader on Islam*, pp. 621–40.

10. Fibre, 3: pp. 1–3.

11. Ibn Ishaq, *The Life of Muhammad*, pp. 221–28. See also W. Montgomery Watt, *Muhammad: Prophet and Statesman* (New York: Oxford University Press, 1961), pp. 83–101.

12. The Spoils 8:7–19. See also Ibn Ishaq, *The Life of Muhammad*, pp. 289–314; "Badr," *Encyclopedia of Islam*, vol. 1, pp. 867–68.

13. Ibn Ishaq, *The Life of Muhammad*, pp. 370–91; W. Montgomery Watt, *Muhammad at Medina* (Oxford: Clarendon Press, 1956), pp. 21–29.

14. The Constellations 85:1 and the Confederate Tribes 33:10. See also Ibn Ishaq, *The Life of Muhammad*, pp. 456–61.

15. Ibn Ishaq, *The Life of Muhammad*, pp. 499–504; Watt, *Muhammad: Prophet and Statesman*, pp. 182–89.

16. Victory 48:1 and Repentance 9:18.

17. Ibn Ishaq, *The Life of Muhammad*, pp. 242–70; Exile 59:2.

18. Watt, *Muhammad: Prophet and Statesman*, p. 130; Margoliouth, *Mohammad and the Rise of Islam*, pp. 309–37.

19. Watt, *Muhammad at Medina*, p. 217; Guillaume, *Islam*, p. 47.

20. Graetz, *History of the Jews*, vol. 3, p. 84.

21. Ibn Ishaq, *Life of Muhammad*, pp. 682–83; Margoliouth, *Mohammed and the Rise of Islam*, pp. 444–72; Andrae, *Mohammed*, p. 172.

15. The Teachings of Islam

1. Cf. Marmaduke Pickthall, *The Meaning of the Glorious Koran* (New York: Mentor, 1953) and George Sale's richly annotated, *The Koran* (London: Frederick Warne, n.d.).

2. Philip Hitti, *Islam: A Way of Life* (South Bend: Regnery Gateway, 1970), pp. 30–34. See also "An Islamic Catechism: The Ajwiba," in Jeffrey, *A Reader on Islam*, pp. 457–519.

3. Andrae, *Mohammed*, pp. 56–57.

4. Guillaume, *Islam*, pp. 66–73; Hitti, *History of the Arabs*, pp. 128–36; John Esposito, *Islam: The Straight Path* (New York: Oxford University Press, 1991), pp. 89–94.

5. Tahar Ben Jelloun, "The Rocky Road to Mecca," *Atlas* 22 (April 1975), p. 21.

6. *Plain Dealer*, July 5, 1990, p. 12A.

7. Ben Jelloun, "The Rocky Road to Mecca," p. 21.

8. "The Five Pillars of Islam," Films for the Humanities and Sciences (Princeton, New Jersey, 1984).

9. Levy Reuben, *The Social Structure of Islam* (Cambridge University Press, 1965); William Graham, *Divine Word and Prophetic Word in Early Islam* (The Hague: Mouton, 1977).

10. Michael Cook, *Muhammad* (New York: Oxford University Press, 1983), pp. 49–50.

11. Eickelman, *The Middle East*, pp. 129–31.

12. According to Raqiy Haji Dualeh, vice minister of the Somali Ministry of Health, the practice led to "chronic infections, painful menstruations, complicated childbirth, sexual fear, and pain." According to the World Health Organization at least 30 million women in the Middle East and Africa in 1979 had experienced "Pharaonic" or "Sudanese" circumcision (*Plain Dealer*, July 30, 1985). In 1990, Professor David Belasco, whose doctoral research just two years previous dealt with economic conditions in the Nile Delta, informed an audience at Kent State University that the practice was commonplace, unsanitary and harmful to Eyptian fellaheen.

13. Nadia Hijab, "The Changing Role of Women," *The*

Cambridge Encyclopedia of the Middle East and North Africa, exec. ed. Trevor Mostyn (Cambridge University Press, 1988), pp. 124–31. See also Louis Beck and Nikki Keddie, *Women in the Muslim World* (Harvard University Press, 1980); Fatima Mernissi, *Beyond the Veil: Male-Female Dynamics in a Modern Muslim Society* (New York: John Wiley, 1975). For different views on the status of women in the Middle East, see Dr. Nawal al-Sadawi, *Women and Sex* (Cairo: Arab Institute for Studies and Publications, 1973); Dr. Ian Young, *The Private Life of Islam* (London: Allen Lane, 1970); Abdal Rahman al-Darbandi, *The Contemporary Iraqi Woman* (Baghdad: Dar al-Basri Press, 1970); and Jean Sasson, *Princess: A True Story of Life Behind the Veil in Saudi Arabia* (New York: Morrow, 1992).

14. Said Camelia Sadat, "The wife is, according to Islam, the servant of her house. She is the one who the husband is always putting a lot of pressure on. But she shares life responsibilities with him. She shares in everything with him. She is a very strong, very tough Egyptian woman, but in the house he is the master. He decides alone for the good of the family. God gave him the right to decide for them, care for them and make the right decision for them" (*USA Today*, November 21, 1985, llA).

15. Bernard Lewis, *Race and Color in Islam* (New York: Harper Torch, 1970), pp. 11–13, 34, 37, 38, 99, 209. See also Lewis, *Race and Slavery in the Middle East* (New York: Oxford University Press, 1990), pp. 46–52; Lewis, *Islam from the Prophet Muhammad to the Capture of Constantinople*, vol. 2 (New York: Harper Torch, 1974), pp. 2, 210–11; *Race and Color in Islam*, pp. 11–13; Akbar Muhammad, "The Image of Africans in Arabic Literature," in *Slaves and Slavery in Muslim Africa*, ed. John Willis (London: F. Cass, 1985), pp. 48–51.

16. The economics of slavery are outlined in Patrick Manning, *Slavery and African Life* (Cambridge University Press, 1990), pp. 86–109, and Allan and Humphrey Fisher, *Slavery and Muslim Society in Africa* (Garden City, N.Y.: Doubleday, 1971), pp. 121–28. See also Martin Klein, "Women and Slavery in Western Sudan," in *Women and Slavery in Africa*, Clair Robertson and Martin Klein, eds., (Madison: University of Wisconsin Press, 1983), p. 67; James Kritzeck and William Lewis, *Islam in Africa* (New York: Van Nostrand, 1969); I. M. Lewis, ed., *Islam in Tropical Africa* (University of Indiana, 1980).

17. A. M. H. Sherif, "The Slave Mode of Production along the East African Coast, 1810–1873," in *Slaves and Slavery in Muslim Africa*, vol. 2, ed. John Willis (London: F. Cass, 1985), pp. 161–81. See also Beachey, *The Slave Trade of Eastern Africa*, pp. 8–11, 17–23, 38–40, 89–92, 121–26; John Laffin, *The Arabs as Master Slavers* (Englewood, N.J.: SRS Publ., 1982); Frederick Cooper, *Plantation Slavery on the East Coast of Africa* (New Haven, Conn.: Yale University Press, 1977).

18. Carl Brockelmann, *History of the Islamic Peoples* (New York: Capricorn, 1960), pp. 43–44; Sale, *The Koran*, p. 137.

19. Esposito, *Islam*, pp. 76–85. See also N. J. Coulson, *A History of Islamic Law* (Edinburgh University, 1964); Joseph Schacht, *Origins of Muhammadan Jurisprudence* (Oxford: Clarendon Press, 1950).

16. The Islamic Schism

1. Hitti, *The Arabs*, 74. See also "Abu Bakr," in *Encyclopedia of Islam*, vol. 1, pp. 109–11.

2. On the process of reason, see Fazlur Rahman, *Islam* (Garden City, N.Y.: Doubleday Anchor, 1968), pp. 44–74.

3. *Ibid.*, pp. 75–95.

4. Hitti, *Islam: A Way of Life*, pp. 42–53. See also George Makdisi, "Hanbalite Islam," in *Studies on Islam*, pp. 216–74; Mahmoud Shaltout, "Islamic Beliefs and Code of Laws," in *Islam — The Straight Path*, ed. Kenneth Morgan (New York: Ronald Press, 1958), pp. 87–143.

5. Najib Ullah, *Islamic Literature* (New York: Washington Square Press, 1963), pp. 150–52.

6. "Dhikr," *Encyclopedia of Islam*, vol. 2, pp. 223–26; J. Spencer Trimingham, *The Sufi Orders in Islam* (New York: Oxford University Press, 1971); Philip Hitti, *Islam and the West* (Princeton, N.J.: D. Van Nostrand, 1962), pp. 125–30; Rahman, *Islam*, pp. 153–202.

7. Rahman, *Islam*, pp. 184–94.

8. Guillaume, *Islam*, pp. 128–42; A. E. Affifi, "The Rational and Mystical Interpretations of Islam," *Islam — the Straight Path*, pp. 144–79.

9. "Al-Ashari," *Encyclopedia of Islam*, vol. 1, pp. 694–95.

10. For Muhammad's blessing upon Ali, see Mahmoood Shehabi, "Shi'a," in *Islam — the Straight Path*, p. 187; Hitti, *History of the Arabs*, pp. 247–50; "Ai b.Abi Talib," *Encyclopedia of Islam*, vol. 1, pp. 381–86; "Dhul Fakar," in *Encyclopedia of Islam*, vol. 2, p. 233.

11. Gustave von Grunebaum, *Medieval Islam* (Illinois: University of Chicago Press, 1954), p. 192.

12. Bernard Lewis, *The Origins of Ismailism*, (Cambridge University Press, 1940).

13. Philip Hitti, *The Origins of the Druze People and Religion* (New York: Columbia University Press, 1928).

14. Bernard Lewis, *The Assassins: A Radical Sect in Islam*, (New York: Oxford University Press, 1967). Also "Alamut," in *Encyclopedia of Islam*, vol. pp. 2, 352–54.

15. Ruth Afnan, *The Revelation of Baha'ullah and the Bab* (New York: Philosophical Library, 1970); "Bahai," in *Encyclopedia of Islam*, vol. 1, pp. 915–18.

16. *The Baha'is in Iran: A Report on the Persecution of a Religious Minority* (Bahai International U.N. Office, 1982); House Subcommittee on Human Rights, *House Subcommittee on Religious Persecution of Baha'is in Iran*, video, May 2, 1984 (Washington: Government Printing Office, 1988).

17. Expansion of Islam

1. Hitti, *History of the Arabs*, pp. 140–41.

2. Laura V. Vaglieri, "The Patriarchal and Umayyad Caliphates," *Cambridge History of Islam* (1970), P. M. Holt, Ann Lambton and Bernard Lewis (eds.), vol. 1, 58–62; Anthony Nutting, *The Arabs* (New York: Mentor, 1964), pp. 33–34, 47–51; and I. M. Lapidus, "The Arabic Conquests and the Formulation of Islamic Society, "*Studies on the First Century of Islamic Society*, G. H. A. Juynboll (ed.), 49–72.

3. Philip Hitti, "Umar ibn al Khattab: Founder of the Moslem Empire," *Makers of Arab History* (New York: St. Martin's Press, 1968), pp. 20–37.

4. "Diwan," *Encyclopedia of Islam*, vol. 2, 323–337.

5. Hitti, *History of the Arabs*, 160–62. See also A. J. Butler, *The Arab Conquest of Egypt and the Last Thirty Years of the Roman Dominion*, (Oxford University Press, 1902), pp. 310–327.

6. Hitti, *History of the Arabs*, 156–57. See also Michael Morony, *Iraq after the Muslim Conquest*, (Princeton University Press, 1984).

7. Hitti, *Makers of Arab History*, pp. 41–42.

8. For a recounting of Jews as "protected people" under Islam, see Bat Y e'or, *The Dhimmi: Jews and Christians under Islam*, trans. David Maisel, Paul Fenton and David Littman (London and New York: Farleigh Dickin-

son, 1985); Norman Stillman, *The Jews of Arab Lands* (Philadelphia: Jewish Pulication Society, 1979); and Saul Friedman, *Without Future: The Plight of Syrian Jewry* (Westport, Conn.: Praeger, 1989).

9. S. D. Goitein, *Jews and Arabs: Their Contacts Through the Ages* (reprint, New York: Schocken, 1974).

10. Saul Friedman, "The Myth of Arab Toleration," *Midstream* 16 (January 1970), p. 57.

11. For al-Hakim, see P. M. Holt, Ann Lambton, and Bernard Lewis, eds., *Cambridge History of Islam* (Cambridge University Press, 1970, vol. 1, pp. 186–88, and Lewis, *Islam* (New York: Harper Torch, 1974), vol. 1, pp. 46–59.

12. Heinrich Graetz, *History of the Jews* (1894; reprint, Philadelphia: Jewish Publication Society of America, 1956), vol. 3, pp. 357–61.

13. Bernard Lewis, "The Pro-Islamic Jews," *Judaism* 17:4 (1968), p. 401.

14. Nutting, *The Arabs*, 62–64; Hitti, *History of the Arabs*, 176–78; and Vaglieri, "The Patriarchal and Umayyad Caliphates," 67–70.

15. Hitti, "Muawiyah: Architect of the Arab Empire," *Makers of Arab History*, pp. 43–47.

16. Carl Brockelmann, *History of the Islamic Peoples*, (New York: Capricorn, 1960), pp. 71–106; Vaglieri, "The Patriarchal and Umayyad Caliphates," 73–103; Hitti, *History of the Arabs*, 189–287; Philip Hitti, *Syria: A Short History*, (New York: Collier Books, 1959), 115–41; and Bernard Lewis, *The Arabs in History*, (New York: Harper Torch, 1960), pp. 80–98.

17. Graetz, *History of the Jews*, vol. 3, pp. 41–52.

18. Francesco Gabrielli, *Muhammad and the Conquests of Islam*, (New York: McGraw-Hill, 1968), 189–95; Bernard Lewis, *Islam*, (Harper, 1974), vol. 1, pp. 110–18; and Hitti, *History of the Arabs*, 493–97.

19. Edward Creasy, *Fifteen Decisive Battles of the World*, (London: Colonial Press, 1899), pp. 88–89. See also Hitti, *History of the Arabs*, 500–01.

20. Hitti, *History of the Arabs*, 279–87.

21. Tor Eigeland, "The Golden Caliphate," *Armaco World Magazine* (September-October, 1976), vol. XXVII, p. 13. See also Anwar Chejne, *Muslim Spain: Its History and Culture*, (Minneapolis: University of Minnesota Press, 1974) and "The Legacy of Al-Andalus," special edition of *Aramco World Magazine* (January-February, 1993), LXIV.

22. Eigeland, "The City of al-Zahra," *Armamco World*, (1976), p. 17.

23. Roger Le Torneau, *The Almohad Movement in North Africa in the Twelfth and Thirteenth Centuries*, (Princeton University Press, 1969) and Abdal Wahib al-Marrakushi, *The History of the Almohades*, ed. Reinhart Dozey (Amsterdam: Oriental Press reprint, 1968).

18. Al Amjad

1. Hitti, *History of the Arabs*, pp. 288–96.

2. Lewis cites as his source al-Yaqubi, *Islam*, vol. 2, pp. 64–78.

3. Alfred Havighurst, ed., *The Pirenne Thesis: Analysis, Criticism and Revision* (Lexington: D. C. Health, 1976).

4. S. Pines, "Philosophy," in *Cambridge History of Islam*, vol. 2, pp. 741–79. See also W. Montgomery Watt, *Islamic Philosophy and Theology* (Edinburgh University Press, 1962); F. E. Peters, *Aristotle and the Arabs* (New York University Press, 1969).

5. Hitti, "Ibn Rushd: The Great Commentator," in *Makers of Arab History*, 219–37.

6. Hitti, "Ibn Sina: Prince of Physicians and Philosophers," in *Makers of Arab History*, 202–18; Soheil Afnan, *Avicenna: His Life and Works* (London: Allen and Unwin, 1958).

7. John Badeau, et al, eds., *The Genius of Arab Civilization* (London: Phaidon, 1976), pp. 170–72.

8. Ibid., p. 166. See also A. H. Arberry, *The Spiritual Physick of Rhazes* (John Murray, 1950).

9. *The Genius of Arab Civilization*, pp. 133–39.

10. Hitti, *History of the Arabs*, 373–82; A. I. Sabra, "The Scientific Enterprise," in *World of Islam*, ed. B. Lewis (London: Thames and Hudson, 1976), pp. 181–200; G. Anawati, "Science," in *Cambridge History of Islam*, vol. 2, 741–79.

11. Hitti, "Ibn Khaldun: First Philosopher of History," in *Makers of Arab History*, p. 238–56.

12. Richard Burton, *The Book of the Thousand and A Night* (New York: Heritage Press, 1934); Edward Lane, *Thousand and One Nights* (New York: Tudor, 1927). See also Isle Lichtenstadter, *Introduction to Classical Arabic Literature* (New York: Schocken, 1976).

13. Muhammad Ahsan, *Social Life under the Abbasids* (London: Longman, 1979); N. Abbott, *Two Queens of Baghdad* (Illinois: University of Chicago Press, 1946); Guy LeStrange, *Baghdad under the Abbasid*; and at-Tabari, *The Crisis of the Abbasid Caliphate* (Albany: SUNY Press, 1985).

14. Nutting, *The Arabs*, pp. 117–18.

15. Hugh Kennedy, *The Early Abbasid Caliphate: A Political History* (Totowa, New Jersey: Barnes and Noble, 1981); Jacob Lassner, *The Shaping of Abbasid Rule* (New Jersey: Princeton University Press, 1980).

16. Richard Frye, *The Golden Age of Persia* (London: Weidenfeld and Nicolson, 1975); Said Amir Arjomand, *The Shadow of God and the Hidden Imam* (Illinois: University of Chicago, 1984); C. E. Bosworth, *The Ghaznavids* (Edinburgh University Press, 1963).

17. Hitti, "Ubaydullah al-Mahdi: Founder of the Fatimid Empire in Africa," in *Makers of Arab History*, pp. 95–115. See also W. Ivanow, *The Rise of the Fatimids* (London: Oxford, 1942).

18. Bernard Lewis, "Egypt and Syria," *Cambridge History of Islam*, vol. 1, pp. 186–88.

19. B. Spuler, "The Disintegration of the Caliphate in the East," in *Cambridge History of Islam*, pp. 149–59. See also Tamara Rice, *The Seljuks in Asia Minor* (London: Thames and Hudson, 1961).

20. Gen J. F. C. Fuller, *A Military History of the Western World*, vol. 1 (New York: Funk and Wagnalls, 1954), pp. 389–405; Osman Turan, "Anatolia in the Period of the Seljuks and the Beyliks," in *Cambridge History of Islam*, vol. 1, pp. 231–34, 243–44.

21. Spuler, "Disintegration of the Caliphate," 150–51. See also Carla Klausner, *The Seljuk Vezirate: A Study of Civil Administration* (Cambridge, Mass.: Harvard University, 1973); Claude Cahen, *Pre-Ottoman Turkey: A General Survey of the Material and Spiritual Culture and History 1071–1330* (New York: Taplinger, 1968).

19. The Crusades

1. D. C. Munro, "Speech of Pope Urban II at Clermont 1095," *American Historical Review*, vol. 11 (1906), pp. 231–42.

2. Edward Synan, *The Popes and the Jews in the Middle Ages* (New York: Macmillan, 1965), pp. 66–82.

3. Fulcher of Chartres, *A History of the Expedition to Jerusalem 1095–1127*, vol. 1, trans. Frances Ryan (Knoxville: University of Tennessee, 1969), pp. 76–91.

4. Quoted by Franc Shor, "Crusader Road to Jerusalem," *National Geographic* 124 (December, 1963), p. 824.

5. James H. Robinson, ed., *The Origin and Deeds of the Goths* (Boston: 1904), pp. 325–29.

6. Fulcher of Chartres, *A History*, vol. 1, no. 26, p. 106. See also *The First Crusade: Chronicle of Fulcher of Chartres and other Chronicles*, Edward Peters, ed. (University of Pennsylvania Press, 1971).

7. *Ibid.*, vol. 1, no. 26, p. 122.

8. William of Tyre, *A History of Deeds Done Beyond the Sea*, trans. Badcock and Krey (New York: Columbia University Press, 1943); William Stevenson, "The First Crusade," in *Cambridge Medieval History*, vol. 4, ed. J. M. Hussey (Cambridge University Press, 1967), pp. 265–99.

9. D. C. Munro, *The Kingdom of the Crusaders* (New York: Appleton-Century, 1935); T. S. R. Boase, *Kingdoms and Strongholds of the Crusaders* (Indianapolis: Bobbs-Merrill, 1971); Charles Kingsford, "The Kingdom of Jerusalem, 1099–1291," *Cambridge Medieval History*, vol. 4, pp. 300–19.

10. Robin Fedden, "The Castles of the Crusaders," *Armaco World* 21 (May/June, 1970), pp. 20–25; Fedden and J. Thompson, *Crusader Castles* (London: 1950).

11. R. C. Smail, *Crusading Warfare (1097–1193)* (Cambridge University Press, 1956); G. A. Campbell, *The Knights Templars* (New York: AMS reprint, 1980).

12. W. B. Stevenson, *The Crusaders in the East* (Cambridge University Press, 1907); William Miller, *The Latins in the Levant: Essays on the Latin Orient* (Cambridge University Press, 1921); E. J. Passant, "Effects of the Crusades upon Western Europe," in *Cambridge Medieval History*, vol. 4, pp. 320–33.

13. Usama ibn Munquidh, *Autobiography*, in *Arab Historians of the Crusades*, ed. Francesco Gabrielli, trans. E. J. Costello (Berkeley: University of California, 1969), pp. 73, 79.

14. *Ibid.*, pp. 76–77.

15. *Ibid.*, pp. 77–78.

16. Stanley Lane-Poole, *Saladin and the Fall of the Kingdom of Jerusalem* (New York: G. P. Putnam, 1898), 41–58.

17. Baha al-Din, *Life of Saladin*, trans. C. R. Conder, in *Arab Historians of the Crusades*, pp. 87–113. See also Bernard Lewis, "Egypt and Syria," in *Cambridge History of Islam*, vol. 1, pp. 201–07; "Ayyubids," in *Encyclopedia of Islam*, pp. 796–807.

18. Nutting, *The Arabs*, pp. 176–85; Hitti, *History of the Arabs*, pp. 645–47.

19. Ibn al-Athir, cited in *Arab Historians of the Crusades*, pp. 119–39.

20. *Ibid.*, pp. 139–74.

21. *Ibid.*, pp. 182–307.

22. Richard Newhall, *The Crusades* (New York: Holt, Rinehart and Winston, 1966); Stephen Runciman, *History of the Crusaders* (Cambridge University Press, 1951–1954).

23. Friedman, "Arab Irrealism," *Jewish Spectator* 33 (April 1968), pp. 9–11.

20. Mamelukes, Mongols, Sultans

1. William Muir, *The Mameluke or Slave Dynasty of Egypt* (New York: AMS Reprint, 1973), pp. 215–20. See also Stanley Lane-Poole, *A History of Egypt in the Middle Ages* (London: Frank Cass, 1968).

2. On Genghis Khan, see Paul Ratchnevsky, *Genghis Khan: His Life and Legacy*, trans. T. N. Haining (Oxford: Blackwell, 1991); Bertold Spuler, *History of the Mongols: Based on Eastern and Western Accounts of the Thirteenth and Fourteenth Centuries* (Berkeley: University of California Press, 1942); Harold Lamb, *Genghis Khan: The Emperor of All Men* (Garden City, N.Y.: Doubleday, 1927).

3. Michael Prawdin, *The Mongol Empire: Its Rise and Legacy*, trans. Eden and Cedar Paul (New York: Free Press, 1967), p. 307.

4. Lewis, *The Assassins*, pp. 77–95.

5. Prawdin, *The Mongol Empire*, p. 308.

6. *Ibid.*, p. 309.

7. Hitti, *History of the Arabs*, pp. 486–89; Nutting, *The Arabs*, p. 94.

8. J. J. Saunders, "Islam and the Mongols: The Battle of Goliath's Springs," *History Today* 11 (1961), pp. 843–51.

9. Muir, *The Mameluke or Slave Dynasty of Egypt*, pp. 13–32; Bernard Lewis, "Egypt and Syria," in *Cambridge History of Islam*, pp.211–15; "Baybars," *Encyclopedia of Islam*, vol. 1, 1124–26; Abdul Aziz Khowaiter, *Baibars the First: His Endeavors and Achievements* (London: Green Mountain Press, 1978), pp. 20–23.

10. Sidney N. Fisher, *The Middle East: A History* (New York: McGraw-Hill, 1990 edition), p. 125.

11. On the assimilation of the Mongols, see Bernard Lewis, *The Middle East and the West* (Harper Torch, 1964), p. 36. On the exaggeration of their destructiveness, see Bernard Lewis, *The Arabs in History* (Harper Torch, 1960), p. 154.

12. *Marco Polo: The Description of the World*, trans. A. C. Moule (New York: Paul Pelliott, AMS, 1976).

13. See S. M. Ikram, *Muslim Civilization in India* (New York: Columbia University Press, 1964); Mirz Haydar, *A History of the Moguls of Central Asia* (New York: Praeger, 1970).

14. Abul Fazl, *The Akbar-nama: History of Akbar*, trans. H. Beveridge (Calcutta: Asiatic Society, 1907).

15. Lucille Schulberg, *Historic India* (New York: Time-Life Books, 1968), pp. 143–54.

16. Jean du Bec-Crespin, *The Historie of the Great Emperor Tamerlan* (Amsterdam: De Capo Press, 1968); Rene Grousset, *The Empire of the Steppes*, trans. Naomi Walford (New Brunswick: Rutgers University Press, 1970); Hilda Hookham, *Tambourlaine the Conqueror* (London: Hodder and Stoughton, 1962); Edward Sokol, *Tamerlane* (Lawrence, Kan.: Coronado Press, 1977.

17. Charles Halperin, *Russia and the Golden Horde: The Mongol Impact on Medieval Russian History* (Bloomington: Indiana University Press, 1985). See also Sokol, *Tamerlane*, pp. 107–18.

18. Prawdin, *The Mongol Empire*, p. 491.

19. Sokol, *Tamerlane*, pp. 165–88; Halil Inalcik, "The Emergence of the Ottomans," in *Cambridge History of Islam*, 278–79.

21. The Ottomans

1. Halil Inalcik, "The Emergence of the Ottomans," in *Cambridge History of Islam*, pp. 266–69. See also Paul Wittek, *The Rise of the Ottoman Empire* (London: Royal Asiatic Society, 1938); Herbert Gibbons, *The Foundation of the Ottoman Empire* (London: Frank Cass, 1968).

2. Raymond McNally and Radu Florescu, *In Search of Dracula* (Greenwich, Conn.: New York Graphic Society, 1972).

3. Michael Dols, *The Black Death in the Middle East* (New Jersey: Princeton University Press, 1977).

4. Lord Eversley and Sir Valentine Chirol, *The Turkish Empire from 1288 to 1914* (New York: Howard Fertig, 1969), pp. 41–43, 60–61, 101–04, 117–18. See also Lord Kinross, *The Ottoman Centuries: The Rise and Fall of the Turkish Empire* (New York: Morrow, Quill, 1977), pp.

297–310; Halil Inalcik, "The Heyday and Decline of the Ottoman Empire," in *Cambridge History of Islam*, pp. 377–78.

5. Kinross, *The Ottoman Centuries*, pp. 61–63.

6. *Ibid*, pp. 94–110. See also Steven Runciman, *The Fall of Constantinople, 1453* (Cambridge University Press, 1965); Inalcik, "The Rise of the Ottoman Empire," in *Cambridge History of Islam*, pp. 295–308.

7. Guerdan, *Byzantium*, 219. See also Ducas, *Decline and Fall of Byzantium to the Ottoman Turks*, trans. Harry Margoulias (Detroit: Wayne State, 1975).

8. Kritovoulos, *History of Mehmed the Conqueror* (New York: Greenwood Press, 1954), part 1, section 239–45, pp. 72–74.

9. Fanny Davis, *The Palace of Topkapi in Istanbul* (New York: Scribner, 1970).

10. Barnette Miller, *The Palace School of Muhammad the Conqueror* (Havard, 1941); N. M. Penzer, *The Harem* (London: 1936 reprint).

11. Norman Itzkowitz, *Ottoman Empire and Islamic Tradition* (New York: Knopf, 1972), pp. 49–61.

12. Marcus, *The Jews in the Medieval World*, p. 413.

13. Kinross, *The Ottoman Centuries*, pp. 166–71. See also P. M. Holt, *Egypt and the Fertile Crescent 1516–1922* (Ithaca, N.Y.: Cornell Press, 1966).

14. Robert Schwoebel, *The Shadow of the Crescent: The Renaissance Image of the Turk 1453–1517* (New York: St. Martin's Press, 1967); Stephen Fischer-Galati, *Ottoman Imperialism and German Protestantism 1521–1555* (Cambridge, Mass.: Harvard University Press, 1959).

15. Roger Merriman, *Suleiman the Magnificent 1520–1566* (Cambridge, Mass.: Harvard University Press, 1954); Albert Lyber, *The Government of the Ottoman Empire in the Time of Suleiman the Magnificent* (Cambridge University Press, 1913).

22. Ottoman Decline

1. On the Berlin Conference, see Sir Charles Eliot, *Turkey in Europe* (London: Crep, 1900, 1965); Charles Swallow, *The Sick Man of Europe: Ottoman Empire to Turkish Republic 1789–1923* (London: Ernest Bevin, 1973).

2. Noel Barber, *The Sultans* (New York: Simon and Schuster, 1973), pp. 36–137; Halil Inalcik, "The Heyday and Decline of the Ottoman Empire," in *Cambridge History of Islam*, pp. 342–53.

3. L. S. Stavrianos discusses obscurantism in *The Ottoman Empire: Was It the Sick Man of Europe?* (London and New York: Holt, Rinehart and Winston, 1957), pp. 25, 33.

4. On Lepanto, see Gen. J. F. C. Fuller, *A Military History of the Western World*, vol. 1 (New York: Funk and Wagnalls, 1956), pp. 556–78.

5. L. S. Stavrianos, *The Balkans Since 1453* (New York: Rinehart, 1958), pp. 413–543. See also Charles Issawi, ed., *The Economic History of the Middle East 1800–1914* (Illinois: University of Chicago, 1966); Y. Hershlag, *Introduction to the Modern Economic History of the Middle East* (Leiden: E. J. Brill).

6. Itzkowits, *Ottoman Empire and Islamic Tradition*, pp. 38–49.

7. See Stavrianos, *The Balkans Since 1453*, pp. 171–72; Thomas Baker, *Double Eagle and Crescent, Vienna's Second Turkish Siege and Its Historic Setting* (Albany: SUNY, 1967), pp. 194–96; and J. Stoye, *The Siege of Vienna* (London, 1964).

8. B. H. Sumner, *Peter The Great and the Ottoman Empire* (Oxford: Blackwell, 1949).

9. Eversley, *The Turkish Empire*, pp. 265–66; Uriel Heyd, "The Later Ottoman Empire in Rumelia and Anatolia," in *Cambridge History of Islam*, p. 365.

10. Stavrianos, *The Balkans Since 1453*, pp. 384–88; Kinross, *The Ottoman Centuries*, pp. 112, 117, 320, 527.

11. Sevket Pamuk, *The Ottoman Empire and European Capitalism, 1820–1913* (New York: Cambridge University Press, 1987).

12. Elizabeth Latimer, *Russia and Turkey in the Nineteenth Century* (Chicago: McClurg, 1893); J. A. R. Marriott, *The Eastern Question* (Oxford, 1947); M. S. Anderson, *The Eastern Question 1774–1923* (New York: Macmillan, 1966).

13. William St. Clair, *That Greece Might Be Free: The Philhellenes in the War of Independence* (New York: Oxford University Press, 1927); E. M. Forster, *A Short History of Modern Greece* (New York: Praeger, 1957).

14. Roderic Davison, *Reform in the Ottoman Empire 1856–1878* (New Jersey: Princeton University Press, 1963). See also Heyd, "The Later Ottoman Empire in rumelia and Anatolia," in P. M. Holt, Ann Lambton, and B. Lewis (eds.), *Cambridge History of Islam*, vol. 1 (Cambridge University Press, 1970), pp. 364–73.

15. Stavrianos, *The Ottoman Empire*, pp. 41–43.

16. Eversley, *The Turkish Empire*, pp. 320–23; Kinross, *The Ottoman Centuries*, 518–20; Stavrianos, *Balkans Since 1453*, pp. 364–66.

17. Sir Edwin Pears, *The Life of Abdul Hamid* (New York: AMS reprint, 1973); Alma Wittlin, *Abdul Hamid: The Shadow of God* (London, 1940).

18. *The Diaries of Theodor Herzl*, trans. and ed. Marvin Lowenthal (New York: Grosset and Dunlap, 1962), p. 351.

19. Kinross, *The Ottoman Centuries*, pp. 554–63.

20. E. F. Knight, *The Awakening of Turkey: A History of the Turkish Revolution* (Boston: J. B. Millet, 1910); E. E. Ramsaur, *The Young Turks: Prelude to the Revolution of 1908* (New Jersey: Princeton University Press, 1957).

23. World War I

1. Howard M. Sachar, *The Emergence of the Middle East 1914–1924* (New York: Knopf, 1969), p. 24.

2. Frank Weber, *Eagles on the Crescent: Germany, Austria and the Diplomacy of the Turkish Alliance 1914–1918* (Ithaca, N.Y.: Cornell University Press, 1970).

3. George Antonius, *The Arab Awakening* (New York: Capricorn, 1946).

4. Trumbull Higgins, *Winston Churchill and the Dardanelles* (New York: Heinemann, 1963); Alan Moorhead, *Gallipoli* (New York: Harper, 1956); Robert James, *Gallipoli* (New York: Macmillan, 1965).

5. Pierre Van Paassen, *The Forgotten Ally* (New York: Dial Press, 1943), p. 68.

6. Michael Florinsky, *Russia: A History and an Interpretation* (New York: Macmillan, 1963), pp. 1353–79.

7. W. E. D. Allen and Paul Muratoff, *Caucasian Battlefields* (London: Cambridge University Press, 1953); F. Kazemzadeh, *The Struggle for Transcaucasia 1914–1921* (New York, 1951).

8. Gerard Chaliand, *The Armenians: From Genocide to Resistance* (London: Zed Press, 1983); Stanley Kerr, *The Lions of Marash: Personal Experiences with American Near East Relief 1919–1922* (Albany: SUNY Press, 1973).

9. Akaby Nassibian, *Britain and the Armenian Question 1915–1923* (New York: St. Martin's Press, 1984).

10. *Living Age* 288 (February 15, 1916), pp. 370–73.

11. Herbert Gibbons and Herbert Adams, *The Blackest Page of Modern History: Events in Armenia in 1915* (New York: Tankian, 1916, 1975).

12. Donald and Lorna Touryan Miller, *Survivors: An Oral History of the Armenian Genocide* (Berkeley: University of California Press, 1993), pp. 80–100.

13. Franz Werfel, *The Forty Days of Musa Dagh* (New York: Carroll and Graf, 1933, 1983), pp. 155–56.

14. Henry Morgenthau, *Ambassador Morgenthau's Story* (Garden City, N.Y.: Doubleday, 1918).

15. Werfel, *The Forty Days of Musa Dagh*, p. 673.

16. *Armenian Allegations: Myth and Reality* (Washington, D. C.: Assembly of Turkish American Associations, 1987).

17. Sachar, *Emergence of the Middle East*, p. 105.

18. Fisher, *The Middle East, A History*, pp. 331, 366.

19. William Yale, *The Near East: A Modern History* (Ann Arbor: University of Michigan Press, 1958), p. 101.

20. *Ibid.*, p. 125.

21. *Ibid.*, p. 229, 231.

22. Kevork Bardakjian, *Hitler and the Armenian Genocide* (Cambridge, Mass.: Zoryan Institute, 1985).

23. Brian Gardner, *Allenby of Arabia* (New York: Coward-McCann, 1966); William Massey, *Allenby's Final Triumph* (London: Constable, 1920).

24. Republican Turkey

1. Harry Howard, *The Partition of Turkey* (Norman: University of Oklahoma Press, 1931, Fertig reprint, 1969).

2. Lord Kinross, *Ataturk: The Rebirth of a Nation* (London: Weidenfeld and Nicolson, 1964); Ray Brock, *Ghost on Horseback: The Incredible Ataturk* (New York: Duell, Sloan and Pearce, 1954).

3. H.C. Armstrong, *Gray Wolf: The Life of Kemal Ataturk* (New York: Capricorn, 1933), pp. 122ff.

4. David Walder, *The Chanak Affair* (New York: Macmillan, 1969); C. F. Abbott, *Greece and the Allies, 1914–1922*.

5. Marian Kent, ed., *The Great Powers and the End of the Ottoman Empire* (London: Allen and Unwin, 1984).

6. Lewis Thomas and Richard Frye, *The United States and Turkey and Iran* (Cambridge, Mass.: Harvard University Press, 1951), pp. 69–74. See also Dmitri Pentzopoulos, *The Balkan Exchange of Minorities and Its Impact upon Greece* (The Hague, 1967).

7. Armstrong, *Gray Wolf*, p. 227.

8. Ziya Gökälp, *Turkish Nationalism and Western Civilization*, trans. Niyazi Berkes (London: Allen and Unwin, 1959).

9. Armstrong, *Gray Wolf*, p. 264.

10. *Ibid.*, pp. 178, 201–05.

11. *Ibid.*, pp. 241–43.

12. Dankwart Rustow, *Turkey: America's Forgotten Alley* (New York: Council on Foreign Relations, 1987); Polyvios Polyviou, *Cyprus: Conflict and Negotiation 1960–1980* (New York: Holmes and Meier, 1980).

13. Walter Weiker, *The Modernization of Turkey from Ataturk to the Present Day* (New York: Holmes and Meier, 1981); Metin Heper and Ahmet Evin, eds., *State, Democracy and the Military: Turkey in the 1980s* (Berlin and New York: Walter de Gruyter, 1988).

14. Robert Olson, *The Emergence of Kurdish Nationalism and the Sheikh Said Rebellion 1880–1925* (Austin: University of Texas Press, 1987); Stephen Pelletiere, *The Kurds: An Unstable Element in the Gulf* (Boulder, Colo.: Westview Press, 1984).

15. Scott MacDonald, "Turkey's 1991 Elections: Condemned to Relive the Past?" *Middle East Insight*, 8 (January/February 1992), pp. 25–31.

16. Armstrong, *Gray Wolf*, p. 178.

25. Arab Nationalism

1. Ameen Rihan, *Ibn Saud of Arabia* (London: Constable, 1928).

2. Henry Dodwell, *Founder of Modern Egypt: A Study of Mohammed Ali* (Cambridge University Press, 1931); Afaf Marsot, *Egypt in the Reign of Muhammad Ali* (New York: Cambridge University Press, 1984).

3. W. J. Blunt, *Desert Hawk, Abdel Kader* (Paris: Presses Universitaires de France, 1947).

4. Lord Kinross, *Between Two Seas: The Creation of the Suez Canal* (New York: Morrow, 1969); Benno Avram, *The Evolution of the Suez Canal Status from 1869 to 1956* (New York: Doctoral Dissertation, 1956).

5. See Elie Kedourie, *England and the Middle East* (London: Bowes and Bowes, 1956).

6. Sir Reginald Wingate, *Mahdism and the Egyptian Sudan* (London: Macmillan, 1891); Rudolph Slatin, *Fire and Sword in the Sudan* (London and New York: Edward Arnold, 1896).

7. Antonius, *Arab Awakening*, pp. 45–50.

8. Elie Kedourie, *Afghani and Abduh* (London: F. Cass, 1966); Nikkie Keddie, *Sayyid Jamal al-Din "al-Afghani"* (Berkeley: University of California Press, 1972).

9. Antonius, *Arab Awakening*, pp. 51–56.

10. *Ibid.*, pp. 118–20, 122–23, 159–61.

11. See Shlomo Moskowits, "The Pledge That Was Not a Pledge: The Hussein McMahon Correspondence" (master's thesis, Youngstown State University, 1972); J. C. Hurewitz, *Diplomacy in the Near and Middle East: A Documentary Record*, vol. 2 (New Jersey: Princeton University Press, 1956); *Correspondence between Sir Henry McMahon and Sherif Hussein* (London: HMSO, Cmd. 5957, 1939).

12. See Antonius, *Arab Awakening*, pp. 249–58; Leslie Shane, *Mark Sykes: His Life and Letters* (London: 1923); W. W. Gottlieb, *Studies in Secret Diplomacy during the First World War* (London: Allen and Unwin, 1951); C. Ernest Dawn, "The Amir of Mecca al Husaynibn Ali and the Origin of the Arab Revolt," *Proceedings of the American Philosophical Society*, vol. 10 (April 1960), pp. 11–34.

13. Van Paassen, *The Forgotten Ally*, p. 80.

14. *Ibid.*, p. 75.

15. T. E. Lawrence, *Revolt in the Desert* (London: Jonathan Cape, 1927); *Seven Pillars of Wisdom* (London: Jonathan Cape, 1935).

16. Richard Aldington, *Lawrence of Arabia* (London: Colliers, 1955), p. 198.

17. Antonius, *Arab Revolt*, pp. 195–200.

26. Political Zionism

1. H. W. V. Temperley, *History of the Peace Conference* (London: British Institute of International Affairs, 1920–24); David Lloyd-George, *The Truth about the Peace Treaties* (London: Gollancz, 1936); Miles Copeland, *The Game of Nations* (London: Weidenfeld and Nicolson, 1969).

2. Edmund Silberner, ed., *The Works of Moses Hess* (Leiden: Brill, 1958).

3. Nahum Sokolow, *Hibat Zion* (Jerusalem: R. Mass, 1935).

4. Pinsker, "Auto-Emancipation," in David Vital, *Origins of Zionism* (New York: Oxford University Press, 1946), p. 78.

5. Theodor Herzl, *The Jewish State* (New York: American Zionist Emergency Council, 1946), pp. 136–40.

6. Alex Bein, *Theodor Herzl: A Biography* (Phila-

delphia: Jewish Publication Society, 1941); Jacob De Haas, *Theodor Herzl: A Biographical Study* (Chicago and New York, 1927); Joseph Adler, *The Herzl Paradox: Political, Social and Economic Theories of a Realist* (New York: Hadrian Press and Herzl Press, 1962).

7. Bein, *Theodor Herzl*, pp. 115–16.

8. *The Diaries of Theodor Herzl*, trans. and ed. Marvin Lowenthal (New York: Dail Press, 1956), p. 18.

9. *Ibid.*, pp. 184–90, 193.

10. Herzl, *The Jewish State*, pp. 85–92. See Weizmann, *Trial and Error* (New York: Haper & Bros., 1949), p. 43.

11. *Herzl*, pp. 92–100, 118–22.

12. *Ibid.*, p. 133.

13. *Ibid.*, p. 146.

14. *Ibid.*, pp. 146–47.

15. *Ibid.*, pp. 101–07. See also Bein, *Theodor Herzl*, pp. 396–405.

16. *Diaries of Theodor Herzl*, pp. 221–29; Bein, *Theodor Herzl*, pp. 226–42.

17. Bein, *Theodor Herzl*, pp. 238–42.

18. *Diaries of Theodor Herzl*, pp. 261–94.

19. *Ibid.*, pp. 298–300.

20. *Ibid.*, pp. 144–72, 323–58.

21. *Ibid.*, pp. 372–84.

22. *Ibid.*, pp. 406–15.

23. *Ibid.*, pp. 428–30.

24. S. Tolkowsky, *The Jewish Colonisation in Palestine* (London: Zionist Organization, 1918).

25. Marvin Lowenthal, *Henrietta Szold: Life and Letters* (New York: Viking Press, 1942).

26. Vladimir Jabotinsky, *Story of the Jewish Legion* (New York: Ackerman, 1945).

27. See Elias Gilner, *War and Hope: A History of the Jewish Legion* (New York: Herzl Press, 1969); J. H. Patterson, *With the Judaeans in the Palestine Campaign* (New York: Macmillan, 1922); Joseph Schechtman, *Rebel and Statesman: The Vladimir Jabotinsky Story, the Early Years* (New York: T. Yoseloff, 1956), pp. 261–88.

28. When Alexander Kerensky called for the creation of ethnic divisions to fight the Germans, Trumpeldor tried to rally 100,000 Jews to battle their way through the Caucasus to the Holy Land. That scheme ended with the Bolshevik Revolution in November 1917.

29. Chaim Weizmann, *Trial and Error* (New York: Schocken, 1966).

30. Barbara Tuchman, *Bible and Sword: England and Palestine from the Bronze Age to Balfour* (New York: Minerva Press, 1956, 1968).

31. L. Stein, *The Balfour Declaration* (London: Valentine, Mitchell, 1961). See also Esco Foundation for Palestine, *A Study of Jewish, Arab and British Policies* (New Haven, Conn.: Yale University, 1947).

32. See Ben Halpern, *A Class of Heroes: Brandeis, Weizmann, and American Zionism* (New York: Oxford University Press, 1987).

33. Sachar, *Emergence of the Middle East*, 384.

34. Emir Faisal, letter to Felix Frankfurter, Paris, March 1, 1919.

35. Walter Laqueur, *The Israel-Arab Reader* (New York: Bantam, 1968), pp. 21–23.

36. *Ibid.*, pp. 18–20.

37. *Parliamentary Papers*, Cmd. 1785 (1922), pp. 1–11.

27. Between World Wars

1. Sachar, *The Emergence of the Middle East*, p. 187.

2. Van Paassen, *The Forgotten Ally,* p. 144. See also Robert Morris, *The Hashemite Kings* (New York: Faber and Faber 1959).

3. Phillip Hitti, *Syria: A Short History* (New York: Collier, 1959).

4. Van Paassen, *The Forgotten Ally*, pp. 145–54.

5. Stephen Longrigg, *Syria and Lebanon under French Mandate* (London: Oxford University Press, 1958); Albert Hourani, *Syria and Lebanon* (London: Oxford University Press, 1946).

6. E. Burgoyne, ed., *Gertrude Bell: From Her Personal Papers, 1914–1926* (London: Barzau, 1961).

7. Stephen Longrigg, *Iraq, 1900–1950* (London: Oxford University Press, 1953); Reeva Simon, *Iraq between the Two World Wars* (New York: Columbia University Press, 1986); A. S. Stafford, *The Tragedy of the Assyrians* (London: Allen and Unwin, 1935).

8. Lord Cromer, *Modern Egypt* (London: Macmillan, 1908); Robert Tignor, *Modernization and British Colonial Rule in Egypt 1882–1914* (New Jersey: Princeton University Press, 1966).

9. Lord Lloyd, *Egypt since Cromer* (London: Macmillan, 1933–34); Janice Terry, *The Wafd, 1919–1952: Cornerstone of Egyptian Political Power* (London: Third World Center, 1982); Afaf Marsot, *Egypt's Liberal Experiment 1922–1936* (Berkeley, 1977); Marius Deeb, *Party Politics in Egypt: The Wafd and Its Rivals, 1919–1939* (London: Ithaca Press, 1979).

10. Joseph Schechtman, *The Mufti and the Fuhrer* (New York: T. Yoseloff, 1966); Maurice Pearlman, *Mufti of Jerusalem: The Story of Haj Amin el Husseini* (London: Victor Gollanez, 1947); Eliahu Elath, *Haj Mohammed Amin al-Husseini* (Jerusalem, 1968).

11. Malcolm Hay, *The Roots of Christian Anti-Semitism* (New York: Freedom Library Press, 1981), pp. 285–87. See also Sir Ronald Storrs, *Orientations* (London: Nicolson and Watson, 1937).

12. Van Paassen, *Forgotten Ally*, p. 125.

13. Trumpeldor was killed, defending the outpart of Tel Hai in March 1920.

14. Naomi Cohen, *The Year after the Riots* (Detroit: Wayne State University Press, 1988).

15. See William Ziff, *The Rape of Palestine* (New York: Longmans, Green, 1938).

16. Richard Meinertzhagen, *Middle East Diary, 1917–1956* (London: 1959), p. 98.

17. Howard Sachar, *Europe Leaves the Middle East, 1936–1954* (New York: Knopf, 1972), pp. 37–39, 66–71.

18. Joseph Schechtman, *Fighter and Prophet: The Vladimir Jabotinsky Story*, vol. 2 (New York: T. Yoseloff, 1961), p. 162.

19. Arthur Hertzberg, *The Zionist Idea* (New York: Atheneum, 1969).

20. Sachar, *Europe Leaves the Middle East*, pp. 97–102.

21. Three excellent studies on Palestine in this period are Fred Gottheil, "Arab Immigration into Prestate Israel: 1922–1931," in American Professors for Peace in the Middle East, *Middle East Information* Series 25 (Fall 1973), pp. 13–22; Moshe Aumann, "Land Ownership in Palestine 1880–1948," in *Ibid.*, 5–12; Frederick Kisch, "Arab-Jewish Contacts in Palestine, 1923–1931," in *Ibid.*, pp. 23–26.

22. *Palestine, Royal Commission Report*, Cmd. 5479 (London: HMSO, 1937). See also Kenneth Stein, *The Land Question in Palestine 1917–1939* (Chapel Hill: North Carolina Press, 1984).

23. *Palestine: Statement of Policy (White Paper)*, Cmd. 6019 (London: HMSO, 1939).

24. Van Paassen, *Forgotten Ally*, pp. 282–83.

25. *Ibid.*, p. 285.

26. Oscar Janowsky, *Foundations of Israel* (Princeton, N.J.: D. Van Nostrand, 1959), p. 142.

28. World War II

1. Jan Playfair, *The Mediterranean and the Middle East: Official History of the Second World War* (London: H. M. Stationery Office, 1954); George Kirk, *The Middle East in the War* (London: Oxford University Press, 1953).

2. "Palestine Lives: Address by Mr. Yasser Arafat, November 13, 1974" (Washington: Free Palestine, 1974), pp. 19–20.

3. Nutting, *The Arabs*, p. 327.

4. Philip Hitti, *A Short History of the Near East* (Princeton, N.J.: D. Van Nostrand, 1966), p. 236.

5. Yale, *The Near East: A History*, p. 396.

6. See Gerald Fleming, *Hitler and the Final Solution* (Berkeley: California Press, 1984), pp. 37–38; Van Paassen, *Forgotten Ally*, pp. 175–236.

7. Quoted in Howard Sachar, *The Course of Modern Jewish History* (Cleveland: World, 1958), p. 461.

8. Van Paassen, *Forgotten Ally*, p. 180.

9. Jean Lugol, *Egypt and World War II*, trans. A. G. Mitchell (Cairo: Societe Orientale de Publicite, 1945).

10. Van Paassen, *Forgotten Ally*, p. 180.

11. *Ibid.*, p. 253.

12. The worst example is Edward Said's *The Question of Palestine* (New York: Vintage, 1980), where the mufti is never mentioned. See also Philip Mattar, *The Mufti of Jerusalem* (New York: Columbia University, 1988).

13. Schechtman, *Mufti and Fuehrer*, pp. 95–115; Sachar, *Europe Leaves the Middle East*, pp. 163–172; and Fritz Grobba, *Iraq* (Berlin: Junker and Dunnhaupt, 1984).

14. See Klaus Hildebrand, *The Foreign Policy of the Third Reich* (Berkeley: University of California Press, 1943).

15. Lukasz Hirszowicz, *The Third Reich and the Arab East* (Toronto: University of Toronto Press, 1966), p. 109.

16. On the Muftis role in Iraq, see Simon, *Iraq between the Two World Wars*, pp. 138–41, 158–59.

17. "The Arab Higher Committee: Its Origins, Personnel and Purposes" (New York: United Nations and Nations Associates, May 1947), pp. 30–32. See also Hirszowicz, *Third Reich and Arab East*, pp. 218, 262.

18. For the activities of the mufti in Berlin, see Francis Nicosia, *The Third Reich and the Palestine Question* (London: I. B. Tauris, 1985).

19. Elias Cooper, "Forgotten Palestinian: The Nazi Mufti. Roots of the Bitterness in the Arab-Israeli Conflict," special issue, *American Zionist* 69 (March/April 1978), p. 15.

20. Schechtman, *Mufti and Fuehrer*, p. 133.

21. See Hirszowicz, *Third Reich and Arab East*, pp. 250–311; John Roy Carlson, *Cairo to Damascus* (New York: Knopf, 1951).

22. "The Mufti Speaks," *Life Magazine* 33 (October 27, 1952), p. 151; Schechtman, *Mufti and Fuehrer*, p. 148; "The Arab Higher Committee," pp. 58, 68, 69.

23. Schechtman, *Mufti and Fuehrer*, pp. 152, 157, 163.

24. Hirszowicz, *Third Reich and Arab East*, p. 312; "The Arab Higher Committee," pp. 58–64.

25. Maurice Pearlman, *Mufti of Jerusalem: The Story of Haj Amin el Husseini* (London: 1947), p. 73.

26. Cooper, "Forgotten Palestinian," p. 21; Michael Bar Zohar, *The Avengers* (New York: Tower), p. 144.

27. Simon Wiesenthal, *Grossmufti— Grossagent der Achse* (Salzburg: 1947), pp. 51, 53, 54.

28. William Perl, *The Four-front War* (New York: Crown, 1978), pp. 367–71.

29. Friedman, *No Haven for the Oppressed*, pp. 155–80.

30. *Ibid.*, pp. 197–202.

31. Friedman, "The Power and/or Powerlessness of American Jews 1939–1945" in *American Jews during the Holocaust* (1984), p. 31.

32. Friedman, "The Power," p. 28.

33. Friedman, "The Power," p. 30

34. Friedman, "The Power," p. 14

35. Robert Sherwood, *Roosevelt and Hopkins* (New York: Harper, 1948), pp. 871–73.

36. Gunther, *Inside Asia* (New York: Harper, 1939); Saul Friedman, "Arab Complicity in the Holocaust," *Jewish Frontier* 42 (April 1975), pp. 9–18.

29. Postwar Palestine

1. Elizabeth Monroe, *Britain's Moment in the Middle East, 1914–1956* (Baltimore: Johns Hopkins Press, 1981); Ann Williams, *Britain and France in the Middle East and North Africa 1914–1967* (London: Macmillan, 1968).

2. *Time*, November 10, 1951, p. 35.

3. Sylvia Haim, *Arab Nationalism: An Anthology* (Berkeley: University of California Press, 1964), pp. 40ff; Richard Mitchell, *The Society of the Muslim Brothers* (London: Oxford, 1969).

4. Anne Sinai and Allen Pollack, eds., *The Syrian Arab Republic: A Handbook* (New York: American Academic Association for Peace in the Middle East, 1976), pp. 45–48, 153; A. I. Dawisha, "The Transnational Party in Regional Politics: The Arab Ba'th Party," *Asian Affairs Journal* 61 (February 1974).

5. Don Peretz, "The Palestine Arabs: A National Identity," in *People and Politics in the Middle East*, ed. Michael Curtis (New Brunswick, N.J.: Transaction Books, 1971), pp. 86–87.

6. Herbert Agar, *The Saving Remnant: An Account of Jewish Survival* (New York: Viking Press, 1960), pp. 210–13; David Holly, *Exodus 1947* (Boston: Little Brown, 1969).

7. Sachar, *Europe Leaves the Middle East*, pp. 487–93.

8. "The Arab Higher Committee."

9. Brian Saxton, ed., "The Arab-Israeli Conflict: Debates at the United Nations, 1947–1973, (Westport, Conn.: Mass Communications, Inc., 1974). See "Partition," tape 1.

10. Shlomo Moskovits, "The United States Recognition of Israel in the Context of the Cold War, 1945–1948" (doctoral dissertation, Kent State University, 1976).

11. For comments of Abdullah, Azzam, Kawukji, Ibn Saud and the grand mufti see *New York Times*, in 1947 December 1,6; 2;7; 3,6; 4,1; 22,3; May 16, 1948, p. 4; and January 10, 1954, p. 5. See also Bernard Postal and Henry Levy, *And the Hills Shouted for Joy* (New York: McKay, 1973), pp. 109–111; Harry Sacher, *Israel: The Establishment of a State* (London: Weidenfeld and Nicolson, 1952), p. 108.

12. J. Bowyer Bell, *The Long War: Israel and the Arabs Since 1946* (Englewood Cliffs: Prentice Hall, 1969), pp. 71–119; Dov Knohl, *Siege in the Hills of Hebron: The Battle for the Etzion Bloc* (New York: T. Yoseloff, 1958).

13. Samuel Katz, *Battleground: Fact and Fantasy in Palestine* (New York: Bantam, 1973), p. 133; Margaret Larkin, *The Six Days of Yad Mordechai* (Israel: Yad Mordechai Museum, 1963); Larry Collins and Dominique LaPierre, *O Jerusalem* (New York: Simon and Schuster, 1972), pp. 495–96.

14. Said, *The Question of Palestine*, pp. 44, 101; Aharon Cohen, *Israel and the Arab World* (Boston: Beacon Press, 1970), pp. 296–98.

15. Samuel Katz, *Days of Fire* (London: W. H. Allen), pp. 214–17; J. Bowyer Bell, *Terror out of Zion* (New York:

Avon, 1977), pp. 365–75; Kurzman, *Genesis 1948: The First Arab-Israeli War* (New York: World Publishing, 1970), pp. 138–49.

16. *Time* 49 (May 10, 1948), p. 28.

17. Kurzman, *Genesis 1948*, pp. 161–68.

18. Nadav Safran, *From War to War: The Arab-Israeli Confrontation 1948–1967* (New York: Pegasus, 1969), pp. 28–36.

19. Terrence Prittie and Bernard Dineen, *The Double Exodus: A Study of Arab and Jewish Refugees in the Middle East* (London: Goodhart Press, n.d.), pp. 5–6.

20. Gottheil, "Arab Immigration into Pre-State Israel," pp. 13–22. See also Joan Peters, *From Time Immemorial: The Origins of the Arab-Jewish Conflict over Palestine* (New York: Harper and Row, 1984), pp. 234–68.

21. Ziff, *Rape of Palestine*, p. 370.

22. Peters, *From Time Immemorial*, p. 23.

23. Usama Khalidi, "The UNRWA Diet," *Arab World* 16 (January 1970), pp. 13–15. See also Fred Khouri, "Arab Refugees and the Arab-Israeli Dilemma," in *People and Politics in the Middle East*, pp. 144–63.

24. *Arabic Grammar, Fourth Grade* (Cairo Ministry of Culture and Education, n.d.), p. 78.

25. Dr. Magnes Ehrenstrom, address to Canadian Jewish Congress, Ottawa, Canada, May 9, 1988.

26. Ben-Zvi, *The Exiled and the Redeemed*, passim; Schechtman, *On Wings of Eagles*.

27. Friedman, *Without Future: The Plight of Syrian Jewry*, pp. 12–13.

28. Schechtman, *On Wings of Eagles*, p. 70.

29. Friedman, "Mizug Hagaluyot: Israel's Absorption of Oriental Immigrants" (paper, Ohio State, 1963).

30. Friedman, *Without Future*, p. 14.

31. Roger Winter, "Who is a Refugee?" in *World Refugee Survey 1982* (New York: U.S. Committee for Refugees, 1982), pp. 4–5; "Evolution of the Right Asylum," *Refugees* 48 (December 1987), pp. 36–41.

32. Jon Kimche, *The Second Arab Awakening* (New York: Holt, Rinehart and Winston, 1970), p. 209. See also Peters, *From Time Immemorial*, pp. 2–32.

33. Kimche, *The Second Arab Awakening*, p. 92.

30. Egypt: Nasser

1. Kurzman, *Genesis 1948*, p. 625.

2. Robert St. John, *The Boss: The Story of Gamal Abdel Nasser* (New York: McGraw-Hill, 1960), pp. 101–04.

3. Muhammad Naguib, *Egypt's Destiny: A Personal Statement* (Garden City, N.Y.: Doubleday, 1955).

4. Kermit Roosevelt, *Countercoup: The Struggle for the Control of Iran* (New York: McGraw-Hill, 1979).

5. Gamal Abdul Nasser, *Egypt's Liberation: The Philosophy of the Revolution* (Washington: Public Affairs Press, 1955).

6. Kimche, *Second Arab Awakening*, p. 39.

7. Examples of such vitriolic rhetoric are found in Rony Gabbay's *A Political Study of the Arab-Jewish Conflict: The Arab Refugee Problem* (Geneva: Librairie Droz, 1959), pp. 504–05, 511; David Ben-Gurion, *My Talks with Arab Leaders*, trans. Aryeh Rubinstein and Misha Louvish (New York: The Third Press, 1973), pp. 270–73; and "Nasser," in *Encyclopedia Judaica*, vol. 12 (Jerusalem: Keter Publishing, 1971), pp. 841–43.

8. Kimche, *Second Arab Awakening*, pp. 104–06.

9. *Ibid.*, pp. 113–18.

10. Michael Bar-Zohar, *Suez: Ultra-Secret* (Paris: Fayard, 1965).

11. Robert Henriques, *A Hundred Hours to Suez* (New York: Viking, 1957); Hugh Thomas, *Suez* (New York:

Harper and Row, 1966); Chaim Herzog, *The Arab-Israeli Wars* (New York: Random House), pp. 109–44.

12. Tawfiq Hasou, *The Struggle for the Arab World* (London: Routledge and Kegan Paul, 1985).

13. Peter Mansfield, "The Rise of Nasserism," in *The Ottoman Empire and Its Successors* (New York: St. Martin's, 1973), pp. 114–34; Dana Schmidt, *Yemen: The Unknown War* (New York: Holt, Rinehart and Winston, 1969).

14. Walter Laqueur, *The Road to War: The Origin and Aftermath of the Arab Israelite Conflict 1967–8* (London: Pelican, 1968), pp. 67–73.

15. Theodore Draper, *Israel and World Politics: Roots of the Third Arab-Israeli War* (New York: Viking, 1967), pp. 137–234.

16. David Kimche and Dan Bawly, *The Sandstorm: The Arab-Israeli War of June, 1967* (New York: Stein and Day, 1968). See also Herzog, *The Arab-Israeli Wars*, pp. 143–92.

17. Kimche and Bawly, *The Sandstorm*.

18. Herzog, *Arab-Israeli Wars*, pp. 143–92.

19. *Oppenheim on International Law*, vol. 1, p. 508.

20. Fraser, *The Middle East 1914–1979* (New York: St. Martin's Press, 1980), pp. 115–16.

21. James Ennes, *Assault on the Liberty* (New York: Random House, 1979).

22. P. J. Vatikiotis, *Nasser and His Generation* (New York: Random House, 1978), pp. 363–64.

31. Egypt: Sadat and Mubarak

1. "The Problem of Anwar Sadat's Nazi Inclinations," *American Zionist* 68 (March/April 1978), p. 36.

2. David Hirst and Irene Beeson, *Sadat* (London: Faber and Faber, 1981), pp. 88ff.

3. "The Problem of Anwar Sadat's Nazi Inclinations," p. 37. See also Arnold Forster and Benjamin Epstein, *The New Anti-Semitism* (New York: McGraw-Hill, 1974), pp. 160–61.

4. Anwar Sadat, *In Search of Identity* (New York: Harper and Row, 1978), pp. 210–15.

5. *Ibid.*, p. 128. See also Nissim Rejwan, *Nasserist Ideology: Its Exponents and Critics* (Toronto: Wiley, 1974).

6. Sadat, *In Search of Identity*, p. 230.

7. See Mohamed Heikal, *The Road to Ramadan* (New York: Quadrangle, 1975).

8. Walter Laqueur, *Confrontation: The Middle East and World Politics* (New York: Quadrangle, 1974).

9. N. H. Aruri, "Kissinger's Legacy to Carter," *Middle East* (March 1977). See also Herzog, *The Arab-Israeli Wars*, pp. 225–324; Laqueur, *Confrontation*, pp. 88–222; Peter Kirsch, *Munich in the Middle East* (New York: Sheingold, 1978).

10. Sadat, *In Search of Identity*, pp. 297–310. See also Galil Shoukri, *Egypt: Sadat's Road to Jerusalem* (London: Zed, 1981).

11. William Quandt, *Camp David: Peacemaking and Politics* (Washington: Brookings Institute, 1986).

12. J. G. Jansen, *The Neglected Duty: The Creed of Sadat's Assassins and Islamic Resurgents in the Middle East* (New York: Macmillan, 1986).

13. Hirst and Beeson, *Sadat*, p. 13.

14. Sadat, *In Search of Identity*, p. 83.

15. *Ibid.*, p. 274.

16. George Nader, interview with Hosni Mubarak, *International Insight* 1 (July/August 1981), pp. 16–18.

17. William Brown, "Egypt's Economy: Optimism Amidst Dangers," *International Insight*, 1 (July/August 1981), pp. 10–15. See also Raymond Baker, *Sadat and After: Struggles for Egypt's Political Soul* (Cambridge, Mass.: Harvard University Press, 1990).

18. Robert Springborg, *Mubarak's Egypt: Fragmentation of the Political Order* (Boulder: Westview Press, 1989).

19. Kristen Gillespie, "Moving the Mountain," *Jerusalem Report*, vol. 16, no. 13, October 17, 2005, pp. 26–27.

32. Israel and the Palestinians

1. See statements of U.S. Defense Secretaries Frank Carlucci, Dick Cheney, and Les Aspin in *Near East Report*, November 21, 1988, p. 195; June 10, 1991, p. 97; and May 21, 1990, p. 97. See also A. F. K. Organski, *The $36 Billion Bargain: Strategy and Politics in U.S. Assistance to Israel* (New York: Columbia University Press, 1990); Saul S. Friedman, "Telling the World," *Jewish Frontier* 42 (August/September 1975), pp. 19–21.

2. *Near East Report*, June 25, 1990, p. 123.

3. Hanoch and Rafi Smith, "Judaism in the Jewish State: A 1989 Survey of Attitudes of Israeli Jews" (New York: American Jewish Committee, 1989). For results of the 1992 elections, see *Jerusalem Post*, July 4, 1992, p. 1.

4. Meron Benvenisti, *The West Bank Data Project: A Study of Israel's Policies* (Washington: American Enterprise Institute, 1984). A negative assessment may be found in David Shipler, *Arab and Jew: Wounded Spirits in a Promised Land* (New York: Penguin, 1986).

5. Foreign and Commonwealth Office, *Palestine Liberation Organization*, (London: HMSO, September 1989).

6. Thomas Kiernan, *Arafat: The Man and the Myth* (New York: Norton, 1976). For a contrasting view, see Grace Halsell, "Yasser Arafat: The Man and His People," *The Link* 15 (July/August 1982), pp. 1–6.

7. Zeev Schiff and Ehud Yaari, *Intifada* (New York: Simon and Schuster, 1989); Don Peretz, *Intifada: The Palestinian Uprising* (Boulder, Colo.: Westview, 1989); George Gruen and Karen Kramer, "The Arab States and the Palestinian Uprising: Behind Facade of Unity, Divisions Remain" (New York: American Jewish Committee, 1988).

8. Yehoshafat Harkabi, "The Palestine National Covenant: An Israeli Commentary," *Maariv*, December 12, 1969.

9. *The Middle East* (Congressional Quarterly), p. 301.

10. On Shamir's wartime record, see Gerold Frank, *The Deed* (New York: Simon and Schuster, 1963).

11. Cited in David Gordon, *The Republic of Lebanon: Nation in Jeopardy* (Boulder: Westview Press, 1983).

12. Praising violence and killing, the Hamas Charter targeted Zionists and Freemasons, along with members of B'nai B'rith, Rotary and the Lions. See *USA Today*, February 8, 1993, p. 6A.

13. Contemporary Mideast Backgrounder, "The PLO, Between the Nineteenth PNC in Algiers and the United Nations General Assembly in Geneva" (Jerusalem: Media Analysis Center, December 1988), pp. 10–12.

14. *ABC Niteline*, August 19, 1982.

15. Rustin, "To Blacks: Condemn PLO Terrorism," *New York Times*, August 30, 1979. Cf. Whitney Young, "A Black American Looks at Israel, the Arab Revolution, Racism, Palestinians and Peace," *New York Times*, October 7, 1970.

33. Lebanon

1. John Cooley, "Paradise Lost: Memoirs of a Golden Age," *Aramco Magazine* 33 (September/October 1982), p. 16.

2. *Ibid.*, p. 16.

3. Wadih Peter Tayah, *The Maronites: Roots and Iden-*

tity (Miami: Bet Maroon Publishers, 1987); Rev. Pierre Dib, *History of the Maronite Church*, trans. by Rev. Seely Beggiani (Detroit: Maronite Exilarchate, 1962); Mikhail Mishaqah, *Murder, Mayhem, Pillage and Plunder: The History of Lebanon in the 18th and 19th Centuries* (Albany: SUNY Press, 1988).

4. Sachar, *History of Israel*, pp. 203–05.

5. Norman Cousins, "Last Chances for Peace in the Middle East," *Saturday Review* 2 (March 22, 1975), p. 16.

6. Harald Vocke, *The Lebanese War: It's Origins and Political Dimensions* (New York: St. Martin's Press, 1978), pp. 35–38. See also Itamar Rabinovich, *The War for Lebanon, 1970–1985* (Ithaca, N.Y.: Cornell University Press, 1985).

7. "Accessories to Terror," Israel Ministry of Foreign Affairs (Jerusalem: October 1972), p. 24.

8. Saul S. Friedman, "The Use of Terror," *Jewish Frontier* (April 1978), pp. 17–20.

9. *Ibid.*, p. 18.

10. Lecture by George Nader (Youngstown State University, October 18, 1983). See also Jon Kimche, "Byzantine Collusion: Bloody Lebanon," *New Republic* 174 (May 1, 1976), pp. 7–10; Enver Khoury, *The Crisis in the Lebanese System: Confessionalism and Chaos* (Washington: American Enterprise Institute, 1976).

11. "There Will Be No More Forgiving," *Time* 107 (February 2, 1976), pp. 22–23.

12. David Gordon, *The Republic of Lebanon*, p. 111.

13. *Testimony of Robert Basil, Lebanon: Hearing before the Subcommittee on Near Eastern and South Asian Affairs of the House Committee on Foreign Relations*, 95th Cong., August 16, 1978, pp. 16–25.

14. Elias El-Hayek, "Raison D'Etre" (Washington, D.C.: American Lebanese League, n.d.).

15. Statement of Chamoun, American Lebanese League, 1979.

16. Sachar, *A History of Israel*, pp. 121–22.

17. *Lebanon: The Facts* (London: Britain Israel Public Affairs Committee, 1982).

18. Robert Friedman, *The Middle East after the Israeli Invasion of Lebanon* (New York: Syracuse University Press, 1986).

19. *ABC News*, July 9, 1982.

20. "Tell the World What Happened," *ABC Closeup*, January 7, 1983.

21. David Hirst, "Proud Druze Lead Tour through Corpse-Strewn Lebanese Town," *Washington Post*, September 8, 1983, p. A33.

22. Clive Aston, *A Contemporary Crisis: Political Hostage-Taking and the Experience of Western Europe* (Westport, Conn.: Greenwood, 1982); David Martin, *Best Laid Plans: The Inside Story of America's War against Terrorism* (New York: Harper & Row, 1988); *American Hostages in Lebanon: Hearings before the House Subcommittee on International Relations* (Washington: Government Printing Office, 1990).

23. "Overflight," *Aramco Magazine* 33 (September/October 1982), p. 2.

24. On Syria's overall goals in the region, see Robert Fisk, *Pity the Nation: The Abduction of Lebanon* (New York: Atheneum, 1990); Istvan Pogany, *The Arab League and Peacekeeping in the Lebanon* (New York: St. Martin's, 1987).

34. Modern Iran

1. This judgment of Shah Muhammad Reza Pahlevi was rendered by Senator Edward Kennedy, in *New York Times*, December 4, 1979, p. 1.

2. Public Affairs Forum (Youngstown State University, November 28, 1979).

3. Marvin Zonis, "Iran," *The Middle East: A Handbook* (New York: Praeger, 1971), p. 191.

4. Said Amir Arjomand, *The Turban for the Crown: The Islamic Revolution in Iran* (New York: Oxford University Press, 1988), pp. 34–58.

5. Donald Wilber, *Iran Past and Present* (New Jersey: Princeton University Press, 1976 reprint), pp. 127–29; Arjomand, *The Turban for the Crown*, pp. 59–71.

6. Donald Wilber, *Riza Shah Pahlavi: The Resurrection and Reconstruction* (Hicksville, N.Y.: Exposition Press); Amin Banani, *The Modernization of Iran 1921–1941* (Stanford University Press, 1961).

7. Bruce Kuniholm, *The Origins of the Cold War in the Near East: Great Power Conflict and Diplomacy in Iran, Turkey and Greece* (New Jersey: Princeton University Press, 1980).

8. See James Bill and W.R. Louis, eds., *Mussadiq: Iranian Nationalism and Oil* (Austin: University of Texas Press, 1988); Sepehr Zabih, *The Mossadegh Era: the Roots of the Iranian Revolution* (Chicago: Lake View Press, 1982).

9. Roosevelt, *Countercoup*, p. 4.

10. Eric Hoogland, *Land and Revolution in Iran 1860–1980* (Austin: University of Texas Press, 1982); Marvin Zonis, *Majestic Failure: The Fall of the Shah* (Illinois: University of Chicago Press, 1991), pp. 107–14.

11. Wilber, *Iran Past and Present*, pp. 332–45. See also "Iran," *Encyclopædia Britannica*, vol. 4 (15th ed.), p. 861; Rose Greaves, "The Reign of Mohammad Riza Shah" in *Twentieth Century Iran*, ed. Hossein Amirsadeghi (New York: Holmes and Meier, 1977), pp. 84–85.

12. Mohammad Reza Pahlavi, *Answer to History* (New York: Stein and Day, 1980).

13. Ann Tibbits Schultz, *Buying Security: Iran under the Monarchy* (Boulder, Colo.: Westview Press, 1989).

14. Yair Hirshfeld and Aryeh Shmuelevitz, *Mid East Contemporary Survey, 1976–77*, vol. 1, ed., Colin Legum (New York and London: Holmes and Meier, 1978), p. 379.

15. Fred Halliday, *Iran: Dictatorship and Development* (London: Penguin 1980, p. l00. See also Nikki Keddie and Eric Hooglund, eds., *Iranian Revolution and the Islamic Republic* (New York: Syracuse University Press, 1986).

16. Laffin, *Rhetoric and Reality*, pp. 110, 115.

17. Mansour Farhang and John Hossein Motavalli, "Iran: A Great Leap Backward," *The Progressive* 48 (August 1984), 19–22.

18. See Stuart Colie, "A Perspective on the Shiites and the Lebanese Tragedy," *Middle East Review*, 9 (Fall 1979), p. 17.

19. Farhang and Motavalli, "Iran: A Great Leap Backward," p. 19.

20. Oriana Fallaci, "Khomeini Unveiled," *Washington Post* interview reprinted in *Manchester Guardian*, October 28, 1979, p. 14. For a revealing view of Khomeini's dogmatic nature, see also Hamid Algar, "Imam Khomeini 1902–1962: The Pre-Revolutionary Years," in *Islam: Politics and Social Movements*, eds. Edmund Burke III and Ira Lapidus (Berkeley: University of California Press, 1988) pp. 263–88.

21. Salman Rushdie, *The Satanic Verses* (New York: Viking, 1988).

22. Farhang and Motavalli, "Iran: A Great Leap Backward," p. 20.

23. Fallaci, "Khomeini Unveiled."

24. Farhang and Motavalli, "Iran: A Great Leap Backward," p. 20.

25. *The Baha'is in Iran: A Report on the Persecution of a Religious Minority* (Baha'i International U.N. Office, 1982).

26. *Islam and Revolution: Writings and Declarations of Imam Khomeini*, trans. Hamid Algar (London: Kegan Paul, 1985); Amir Taheri, *The Spirit of Allah: Khomeini and the Islamic Revolution* (Bethesda, Md.: Adler and Adler, 1986).

27. Aryeh Yodfat, *The Soviet Union and Revolutionary Iran* (New York: St. Martin's Press, 1984).

28. *USA Today*, Jan. 4, 1994, pp. 1–2.

29. Fallaci, "Khomeini Unveiled."

35. The Radical Arab States

1. Jacques Berques, *French North Africa: The Maghrib between Two World Wars* (New York: Praeger, 1962); Elbaki Hermassi, *Leadership and National Development in North Africa* (Berkeley: University of California Press, 1972); Felix Garas, *Bouguiba et al Naissance d'une Nation* (Paris, 1961); Robin Bidwell, *Morocco Under Colonial Rule* (London: Cass, 1973).

2. David Prochaska, *Making Algeria French* (Cambridge University Press, 1990); David Gordon, *The Passing of French Algeria* (London: Oxford University Press, 1966); E. F. Gautier, *L'Evolution de l'Algerie de 1830 a 1930* (Algiers, 1931).

3. *New York Times*, May 12, p. 4 and May 13, 1945, p. 3.

4. *New York Times*, November 2, 1954, p. 1 and November 3, 1954, p. 8.

5. See Jacques Soustelle, *Vingt-huit Ans de Gaullisme* (Paris: La Table Ronde, 1968); Alf Heggoy, *Insurgency and Counter-insurgency in Algeria* (Bloomington: Indiana University Press, 1972).

6. Philip Williams and Martin Harrison, *DeGaulle's Republic* (London: Longman's 1960), pp. 189–209; Alistair Horne, *A Savage War of Peace, Algeria 1954–1962* (New York: Viking, 1977), pp. 520–23, 528–29.

7. Alexander Harrison, *Challenging DeGualle: The O.A.S. and the Counterrevolution in Algeria 1954–1962* (New York: Praeger, 1989); Yves Courriere, *L'heure des Colonels* (Paris: Fayard, 1970); Raoul Salan, *Memoires de Raoul Salan* (Paris: Presses de la Cite, 1970).

8. For varying viewpoints on the meaning of an independent Algeria, see Andre Nouschi, *La Naissance du Nationalisme algerien* (Paris, 1962); Germaine Tillion, *Algeria: The Realities* (London, 1958); Pierre Vidal-Naquet, *Torture, Cancer of Democracy: France and Algeria 1954–1962* (London, 1963).

9. Henry Jackson, *The FLN in Algeria: Party Development in a Revolutionary Society* (Westport, Conn.: Greenwood Press, 1977); David and Marina Ottaway, *Algeria: The Politics of a Socialist Revolution* (Berkeley: University of California Press, 1970), pp. 174–195; Arslan Hunbaraci, *Algeria: A Revolution that Failed* (New York: Praeger, 1966), pp. 217–45.

10. *Near East Report*, September 17, 1990, p. 175.

11. Lois Aroian and Richard Mitchell, *Modern Middle East and North Africa* (New York: Macmillan, 1984), p. 394.

12. Schechtman, *On Wings of Eagles*, p. 333.

13. *American Jewish Yearbook 1985* 85 (New York and Philadelphia: American Jewish Committee and JPSA, 1984), p. 305.

14. See Charles Gallagher, *The United States and North Africa: Morocco, Algeria and Tunisia* (Cambridge, Mass.: Harvard University Press, 1963).

15. Mirella Bianco, *Gadafi: Voice from the Desert* (London: Longman, 1975); John Cooley, *Libyan Sandstorm*

(New York: Holt, Rinehart and Winston, 1982); "Targeting Gaddafi," *Time* 127 (April 21, 1986), p. 6ff; *U.S. News and World Report*, November 10, 1986, C1, pp. 31–32.

16. Muammar al-Qadhafi, *The Green Book* (London: Martin Brian and O'Keeffe, n.d.).

17. For Qaddafi's aggressive behavior toward his neighbors, see Benyamin Neuberger, *Involvement, Invasion and Withdrawal: Qadhafi's Libya and Chad, 1969–1981* (Tel Aviv: Shiloah Center, 1982); *Libya under Qadhafi: A Pattern of Aggression* (Washington: U. S. State Department, 1986).

18. On Iraq before 1991, see Majid Khadduri, *Socialist Iraq: A Study in Iraqi Politics since 1968* (Baltimore, M.D.: Johns Hopkins Middle East Institute, 1978); Jasim Abdulghani, *Iran and Iraq* (Johns Hopkins Middle East Institute, 1984); Abbas Kelidar, ed., *The Integration of Modern Iraq* (New York: St. Martin's Press, 1979); Christine Moss Helms, *Iraq: Eastern Flank of the Arab World* (Washington: Brookings Institute, 1984).

19. Samir al-Khalil, *Republic of Fear: the Inside Story of Saddam's Iraq* (Berkeley: University of California Press, 1990); *Amnesty International Report 1983* (London: Amnesty International), pp. 308–11; *Human Rights Watch: Annual Report, 1989*, 66–67.

20. Majid Khadduri, *The Gulf War: The Origins and Implications of the Iraq-Iran Conflict* (New York: Oxford University Press, 1988); Virginia Sherry, "Kuwait before and After? What the democratic Forces Want," *Nation* 251 (January 1991), pp. 509–27; Judith Miller and Laurie Mylroie, *Saddam Hussein and the Crisis in the Gulf* (New York: Random House, 1990).

21. For events leading up to Desert Storm, see Christopher Joyner, ed., *Persian Gulf War: Lessons for Strategy, Law and Diplomacy* (Greenwood Press, 1990); Yves Debay, *Operation Desert Shield: The First 90 Days* (London: Motor Books Intl., 1990). For instant anaylsis of the war, see Martin Yant, *Desert Mirage: The True Story of the Gulf War* (Buffalo: Prometheus, 1991); James Dunnigan, *From Shield to Storm: High-Tech Weapons, Military Strategy and Coalition Warfare in the Persian Gulf* (New York: Morrow, 1992); Stephen Graubard, *Mr. Bush's War: Adventures in the Politics of Illusion* (New York: Hill and Wang, 1992); James Blackwell, *Thunder in the Desert: The Strategy and Tactics of the Persian Gulf War* (New York: Bantam, 1991); Thomas Allen, *War in the Gulf* (Atlanta: Turner Publ., 1991).

22. *USA Today*, April 28, 1992, p. 9a.

23. *Washington Post*, January 9, 1984.

24. "The Unmasking of Assad," *U.S. News and World Report*, November 10, 1986, C1, pp. 26–30.

25. Daniel Pipes, *Greater Syria: The History of an Ambition* (New York: Oxford University Press, 1990).

26. Friedman, *Without Future*; *Jews of Syria: A Chronicle* (New York: Anti-Defamation League, 1991).

27. Moshe Ma'oz and Avner Yaniv, eds., *Syria under Assad* (New York: St. Martin's Press, 1986); Patrick Seale, *Assad: The Struggle for the Middle East* (Berkeley: University of California, 1988).

28. William Spencer, ed., *The Middle East* (Guilford, Conn.: Dushkin Pub., 1988), p. 189.

36. The 21st Century

1. Alexandre Benningsen, *Islam in the Soviet Union* (New York: Praeger, 1967); *Mystics and Commissars: Sufism in the Soviet Union* (Bloomington: Indiana University Press, 1986).

2. See Adeed Dawisha, *The Arab Racicals* (New York: Council on Foreign Relations, 1986); R. Hrair Dekmejian, *Islam in Revolution: Fundamentalism in the Arab World* (New York: Syracuse University Press, 1985); John Laffin, *Holy War: Islam Fights* (London: Collins, 1988); Emmanuel Sivan and Menachem Friedman, eds., *Religious Radicalism and Politics in the Middle East* (Albany: SUNY Press, 1990); Daniel Pipes, *The Long Shadow: Culture and Politics in the Middle East* (New Brunswick, N. J.: Transaction Publishers, 1989).

3. Fouad Ajami, *The Arab Predicament: Arab Political Thought and Practice since 1967* (New York: Cambridge University Press, 1981), p. 200.

4. See Jan Schreiber, *The Ultimate Weapon: Terrorists and the World Order* (New York: Morrow, 1978); *Politics of Counter-Terrorism: The Ordeal of Democratic States* (Washington: Foreign Policy Institute, 1990).

5. *New York Times*, May 9, 1980, p. 10.

6. Salman Rushdie, *The Satanic Verses*.

7. *New York Times*, February 20, 1989, I, p.1.

8. *New York Times*, March 31, 1989, I, p. 34.

9. *Jerusalem Post*, September 25, 1993, international edition, p. 9.

Selected Bibliography

General Readings

Bill, James, and Robert Springborn. *Politics in the Middle East*. London: Foresman, Little Brown, 1990.

Cambridge Encyclopedia of Middle East and North Africa. Cambridge University Press, 1988.

Cleveland, William. *A History of Middle East and North Africa*. Boulder, Colo.: Westview Press, 1994.

Eickelman, Dale. *The Middle East: An Anthropological Approach*. Englewood Cliffs, N.J.: Prentice Hall, 1989.

Esposito, John. *The Oxford Encyclopedia of the Modern Islamic World*. New York: Oxford University Press, 1995.

Hurewitz, J. C. *The Middle East and North Africa in World Politics*. New Haven, Conn.: Yale University Press, 1975.

Kedourie, Elie. *Politics in the Middle East*. Oxford, 1992.

Laffin, John. *Rhetoric and Reality*. New York: Taplinger, 1975.

Lapidus, Ira. *A History of Islamic Societies*. Cambridge: Cambridge University Press, 1988.

Lewis, Bernard. *The Middle East: A Brief History of the Last 2000 Years*. New York: Simon and Schuster, 1997.

Peretz, Don. *The Middle East Today*. New York: Praeger, 1988.

Sachar, Howard. *The Emergence of the Middle East, 1914–24*. New York: Knopf, 1969.

_____. *Europe Leaves the Middle East, 1932–54*. New York: Knopf, 1982.

Spencer, William. *The Middle East: Global Studies*. Guilford, Conn.: Dushkin Publications, 2000.

Oil Development

Abir, Mordechai. *Saudi Arabia in the Oil Era*. Boulder, Colo.: Westview Press, 1988.

Holden, David. *The House of Saud*. New York: Holt, Rinehart and Winston, 1982.

Issawi, Charles. *The Fertile Crescent 1800–1914: A Documentary Economic History*. New York: Oxford University Press, 1988.

Nawwab, Ismail, Peter Speers and Paul Hoye. *Aramco and Its World*. Dhahran, 1891

Troeker, Gary. *The Birth of Saudi Arabia*. London: Frank Cass, 1976.

Yergin, Daniel. *The Prize: The Epic Quest for Oil, Money and Power*. New York: Simon and Schuster, 1980.

Ancient Near Eastern Civilization

Breasted, James H. *A History of Egypt*. New York: Scribners, 1951.

Contenau, Georges. *Everyday Life in Babylon and Assyria*. New York: Norton, 1966.

Erman, Adolf, ed. *The Ancient Egyptians: A Sourcebook of Their Writings*. New York: Harper Torch, 1966.

Gordon, Cyrus. *The Ancient Near East*. New York: Norton, 1965.

Gurney, O. R. *The Hittites*. Baltimore, Md.: Penguin, 1952.

Harrison, R. K. *The Archeology of the Old Testament*. New York: Harper, 1963.

Heidel, Alexander. *The Babylonian Genesis*. Illinois: University of Chicago Press, 1942.

Keller, Werner. *The Bible as History*. New York: Bantam, 1974.

Kramer, Samuel N. *The Sumerians*. Illinois: University of Chicago Press, 1963.

Moscati, Sabotino. *Ancient Semitic Civilizations*. New York: Putnam, 1957.

Oliphant, Margaret. *Atlas of the Ancient World*. New York: Simon and Schuster, 1992.

Oppenheim, A. Leo. *Ancient Mesopotamia*. Illinois: University of Chicago Press; 1964.

Parkes, Henry Bamford. *Gods and Men*. New York: Vintage, 1959.

Pritchard, James, ed. *The Ancient Near East: An Anthology of Texts and Pictures*. N.J.: Princeton University Press, 1958.

Roux, Georges. *Ancient Iraq*. Harmondsworth, UK: Penguin, 1966.

Sarna, Nahum. *Understanding Genesis*. New York: Schocken Press, 1966.

Wilson, John. *The Culture of Ancient Egypt*. Illinois: University of Chicago Press, 1951.

Woolley, C. Leonard. *The Sumerians*. New York: Norton, 1965.

Carthage, Greece and the Hebrews

Cottrell, Leonard. *The Bull of Minos*. New York: Grosset and Dunlap, 1953.

Gordon, Cyrus. *The Common Background of Greek and Hebrew Civilizations*. New York: Norton, 1962.

Harden, Donald. *The Phoenicians*. New York: Praeger, 1962.

Livy. *War with Hannibal*. Books 21–30, *History of Rome*. Translated by Aubrey de Selincourt. London: Penguin, 1972.

Meek, Theophile. *Hebrew Origins*. New York: Harper Torch, 1932.

Polybius. *The Histories*. Translated by Mortimer Chamber. New York: Washington Square Press, 1966.

Tcherikover, Victor. *Hellenistic Civilization and the Jews*. New York: Atheneum, 1959.

Jewish History

Brandon, S. G. F. *The Trial of Jesus*. New York: Stein and Day, 1968.

Cohn, Haim. *The Trial and Death of Jesus*. New York: Harper and Row, 1971.

DeVaux, Roland. *Ancient Israel*. New York and Toronto: McGraw Hill, 1965.

Fackenheim, Emil. *The Jewish Return into History*. New York: Schocken, 1978.

Flannery, Edward. *The Anguish of the Jews*. New York: Paulist Press, 1985.

Hay, Malcolm. *The Foot of Pride: The Roots of Christian Anti-Semitism*. Boston: Beacon Press, 1950.

Marcus, Jacob, ed. *The Jews in the Medieval World*. New York: Meridian, 1960.

Perry, Marvin, and Frederick Schweitzer. *Anti-semitism*. New York: Palgrave, 2002.

Sachar, Howard. *The Course of Modern Jewish History*. Cleveland, Ohio: World, 1958.

Sandmel, Samuel. *Anti-Semitism in the New Testament?* Philadelphia: Fortress Press, 1978.

Schonfeld, John. *The Passover Plot*. New York: Bantam, 1966.

Schurer, Emil. *A History of the Jewish People at the Time of Jesus*. New York: Schocken, 1961.

Stillman, Norman. *The Jews of Arab Lands*. Philadelphia: JPSA, 1979.

_____. *Jews of Arab Lands in Modern Times*. Philadelphia: JPSA, 1991.

Trachtenberg, Joshua. *The Devil and the Jews*. New York: Meridian, 1961.

Waite, Robert. *The Psychopathic God*. New York: Basic Books, 1977.

Zborowski, M, and E. Herzog. *Life Is with People: The Shtetl Book*. New York: Schocken, 1971.

Byzantium

Guerdan, Rene. *Byzantium*. Translated by D. L. B. Hartley. New York: Capricorn, 1957.

Hussey, J. M. *The Orthodox Church in the Byzantine Empire*. London: Oxford, 1990.

Kritovoulos. *History of Mehmed the Conqueror*. Translated by C. T. Riggs. N.J.: Princeton University Press, 1954.

Oxford Dictionary of Byzantium. New York: Oxford University Press, 1991.

Runciman, Steven. *The Fall of Constantinople, 1453*. Cambridge University Press, 1965.

Vasiliev, Alexander. *History of the Byzantine Empire*, vol. 1. Madison: University of Wisconsin Press, 1952.

Arabs and Islam

Beck, Lois, ed. *Women in the Muslim World*. Cambridge, Mass.: Harvard University Press, 1978.

Blair, Sheila, and Jonathan Bloom. *Art and Architecture of Islam, 1250–1800*. New Haven, Conn.: Yale University Press, 1994.

Brockelmann, Carl. *History of the Islamic Peoples*. Translated by Joel Carmichael and Moshe Pearlman. New York: Capricorn Books, 1960.

Corbin, Henry. *History of Islamic Philosophy*. Translated by L. Sherrard. London: Keegan, Paul, 1993.

Esposito, John. *Islam, The Straight Path*. New York: Oxford University Press, 1991.

Gabrielli, Francesco. *Arab Historians of the Crusades*. Berkeley: California Press, 1957.

Gibb, H. A. R. *Modern Trends in Islam*. Illinois: University of Chicago Press, 1947.

Groitein, S. D. *Jews and Arabs*. New York: Macmillan, 1968.

Hitti, Philip. *History of the Arabs*. New York: Macmillan, 1968.

_____. *Makers of Arab History*. New York: St. Martin's Press, 1968.

Hourani, Albert. *A History of the Arab People*. Cambridge, Mass.: Harvard University Press, 1991.

Jayyusi, Salma Khadra, ed. *The Legacy of Muslim Spain*. Leiden: E. J. Brill, 1992.

Jeffrey, Arthur. *Islam: Muhammad and His Religion*. New York: Library et Liberal Arts, 1958.

Lewis, Bernard. *The Jews of Islam*. New Jersey: Princeton University Press, 1981.

_____. *The Assassins: A Radical Sect in Islam*. New York: Oxford University Press, 1967.

_____. *Race and Color in Islam*. New York: Harper and Row, 1921.

Maalouf, Amin. *The Crusades through Arab Eyes*.

Translated by J. Rothschild. New York: Schoken, 1985.

Meyerhoff, Max. *Studies in Medieval Arabic Medicine.* London: Variorum Reprints, 1984.

Oxford History of Islam. New York: Oxford University Press, 1999.

Patai, Raphael. *The Arab Mind.* New York: Scribners, 1973.

Peters, F. E. *Muhammad and the Origins of Islam.* Albany: SUNY Press, 1994.

Rahman, Fazur. *Islam and Modernity.* Illinois: University of Chicago Press, 1982.

Richards, John. *The Mughal Empire.* vol. 5, *Cambridge History of India.* Cambridge University Press, 1993.

Ye'or, Bat. *Dhimmi.* New York: Associated University Presses, 1985.

Watt, W. Montgomery. *Muhammad at Mecca.* New York: Oxford University Press, 1980.

_____. *Muhammad at Medina.* New York: Oxford University Press, 1981.

Turkey: Ottomans and Ataturk

Ahmad, Feroz. *The Young Turks.* Oxford: Clarendon, 1969.

Amrstrong, H. C. *Gray Wolf: The Life of Kemal Ataturk.* New York: Capricorn, 1939.

Atil, Esin. *Turkish Art.* Washington: Smithsonian Institute, 1980.

Gokalp, Ziya. *Turkish Nationalism and Western Civilization.* Translated by Niyazi Berkes. London: Allen and Unwin, 1958.

Inalcik, Halil. *The Ottoman Empire: The Classical Age, 1300–1600.* Translated by N. Itzkowitz and C. Imber. London: 1923; reprint, New York: Praeger, 1973.

Jelavich, Barbara. *History of the Balkans.* Cambridge University Press, 1983.

Karpat, Kemal. *Social Change and Politics in Turkey.* Leiden: EJ Brill, 1973.

Kinross, Lord Patrick. *Ataturk.* London: Weidenfield and Nicolson, 1966.

Peirce, Leslie. *The Imperial Harem: Women and Sex in the Ottoman Empire.* New York: Oxford University Press, 1993.

Stavrianos, Leften. *The Balkans Since 1453.* New York: Holt, Rinehart and Winston, 1958.

Weiker, Walter. *The Modernization of Turkey.* New York: Holmes and Meier, 1981.

Middle East in World War I

Fromkin, David. *A Peace to End All Peace.* New York: Holt, 1989.

Higgins, Trumbull. *Winston Churchill and the Dardanelles.* New York: Heinemann, 1963.

Hurewitz, J. C. *Diplomacy in the Near and Middle East.* New Jersey: Princeton University Press, 1956.

Kedourie, Elie. *England and the Middle East.* London: Bowes and Owes, 1956.

Lewis, Bernard. *The Emergence of Modern Turkey.* New York: Oxford University Press, 1968.

Miller, Donald, and Larna Miller. *Survivors: An Oral History of the Armenian Genocide.* Berkley: University of California Press, 1993.

Monroe, Elizabeth. *Britain's Moment in the Middle East.* Baltimore: Johns Hopkins University Press, 1981.

Moorehead, Alan. *Gallipoli.* New York: Harper, 1956.

Werfel, Franz. *Forty Days of Musa Dagh.* New York: Carroll and Graf, 1933.

Rebirth of Arab Nationalism

Aldington, Richard. *Lawrence of Arabia.* London: Collins, 1955.

Antonius, George. *The Arab Awakening.* New York: Capricorn, 1946.

Kedourie, Elie. *Afghani and Abduh.* London: Frank Cass, 1966.

Keddie, Nikkie. *Sayyid Jamal al-Din "al-Afghani."* Berkley: California Press, 1972.

Kimche, Jon. *The Second Arab Awakening.* New York: Holt, Rinehart and Winston, 1970.

Zeine, Zeine. *The Struggle for Arab Independence.* Delmar, NY: Caravan Books, 1977.

Modern Zionism

Bein, Alex. *Theodor Herzl: A Biography.* Philadelphia: JSPA, 1941.

Esco Foundation for Palestine. *A Study of Jewish, Arab and British Policies.* New Haven, Conn.: Yale, 1947.

Herzl, Theodor. *The Jewish State.* New York: American Zionist Emergency Council, 1946.

Jabotinsky, Vladimir. *Story of the Jewish Legion.* New York: Ackerman, 1945.

Laqueur, Walter. *A History of Zionism.* New York: Schocken, 1972.

Tuchman, Barabara. *Bible and Sword: England and Palestine from the Bronze Age to Balfour.* New York: Minerva Press, 1956, 1989.

Van Paassen, Pierre. *The Forgotten Ally.* New York: Dial Press, 1943.

Vital, David. *The Origins of Zionism.* Oxford: Clarendon Press, 1975.

Weizmann, Chaim. *Trial and Error.* New York: Schocken, 1966.

Middle East Between the World Wars

Anderson, Lisa. *The State and Social Transformation in Tunisia and Libya, 1830–1980.* New Jersey: Princeton University Press, 1987.

Brown Nathan. *Peasants and Politics in Modern Egypt.* New Haven, Conn.: Yale University Press, 1990.

Deeb, Marius. *Party Politics in Egypt: The Wafd and its Rivals 1919–1939.* London: Itaca Press, 1979.

Khoury, Philip. *Syria and the French Mandate: The Politics of Arab Nationalism, 1920–1945*. New Jersey: Princeton University Press, 1976.

Safran, Nadav. *Egypt in Search of Political Community*. Cambridge, Mass.: Harvard University Press, 1961.

Stephens, Robert. *Nasser: A Political Community*. New York: Simon and Schuster, 1971.

Thomas, Hugh. *Suez*. New York: Harper and Row, 1967.

Vatikiotis, P. J. *The University of Egypt from Muhammad Ali to Mubarak*. Baltimore: Johns Hopkins University Press, 1991.

The Clash Over Palestine

Abu-Lugood, Ibrahim, ed. *The Transformation of Palestine*. Evanston, Ill.: Northwestern University Press, 1987.

Curtis, Michael, et al. *The Palestinians: People, History, Politics*. New Brunswick, NJ; Transition, 1975.

Halpern, Ben. *The Zionist Idea*. Garden City, NJ: Double Day, 1957.

Harkabi, Yehoshafat. *Israel's Fateful Hour*. Translated by Leena Schramm. New York: Harper and Row, 1989.

Hirszowics, Lukasz. *The Third Reich and the Arab East*. University of Toronto Press, 1966.

Katz, Samuel. *Battleground: Fact and Fantasy in Palestine*. New York: Bantnam, 1973.

Kurzman, Dan. *Genesis 1948*. New York: Da Capo Press, 1970.

Laqueur, Walter. *Confrontation: The Middle East and World Politics*. New York: Quadrangle, 1974.

Livingstone, Neil. *Inside the PLO*. New York: Morrow, 1990.

Peters, Joan. *From Time Immemorial: Origins of the Arab-Jewish Conflict Over Palestine*. New York: Harper and Row, 1984.

Porath, Yeoshua. *The Emergence of the Palestinian Nationalist Movement 1918–1929*. London: Frank Cass, 1973.

The Palestinian Arab Nationalist Movement from Riots to Rebellion, 1929–1939. London: Frank Cass, 1978.

Quandt, William, et al. *The Politics of Palestinian Nationalism*. Berkeley: California Press, 1973.

Reich, Bernard. *Israel: Land of Tradition and Conflict*. Boulder, Colo.: Westview, 1985.

Sadat, Anwar. *In Search of Identity*. New York: Harper and Row, 1978.

Safran, Nadav. *From War to War, The Arab-Israeli Confrontation*. Indianapolis: Pegasus, 1969.

Schechtmann, Jospeh. *The Mufti and the Fuhrer*. New York: T. Yoseloff, 1966.

Schiff, Zeev, and Ehud Yaari. *Intifada*. New York: Simon and Schuster, 1989.

Shipler, David. *Arab and Jew: Wounded Spirits in a Promised Land*. New York Times Books, 1986.

Sykes, Christopher. *Crossroads to Israel*. New York: World, 1973.

Lebanon in Turmoil

Deeb, Marius. *The Lebanese Civil War*. New York: Praeger, 1980.

Devlin, John. *The Ba'th Party: A History From Its Origins to 1966*. Stanford: Hoover Institute, 1976.

Friedman, Thomas. *From Beirut to Jerusalem*. New York: Farrar, Straus, Giroux, 1989.

Gilmour, David. *Lebanon, the Fractured Country*. New York: St. Martin's Press, 1983.

Hiro, Dilip. *Lebanon: Fire and Ember, a History of the Lebanese Civil War*. New York: St. Martin's Press, 1992.

Maoz, Moshe. *Assad: The Sphinx of Damascus*. London: Weidenfeld and Nicolson, 1988.

Modern Iran

Amjad, Mohammad. *Iran: From Royal Dictatorship to Theocracy*. New York: Greenwood, 1989.

Bkhash, Shaul. *The Reign of Ayatollahs*. New York: Basic Books, 1984.

Diba, Farhad. *Mohammed Mossadegh: A Political Biography*. Leiden: Croom, Helm, 1986.

Keddie, Nikkie, and Eric Hooglund, eds. *The Iranian Revolution and the Islamic Republic*. New York: Syracuse University Press, 1986.

Roosevelt, Kermit. *Countercoup: The Struggle for the Control of Iran*. New York: McGraw-Hill, 1979.

Sick, Gary. *All Fall Down. America's Tragic Encounter with Iran*. New York: Random House, 1985.

Wright, Robin. *In the Name of God: The Khomeini Decade*. New York: Simon and Schuster, 1989.

Zonis, Marvin. *The Iranian Political Elite*. Illinois: University of Chicago Press, 1971.

Middle East in 21st Century

Ajami, Fuad. *The Arab Predicament*. Cambridge University Press, 1981.

Dawisha, Adeed. *The Arab Radicals*. New York: Council on Foreign Relations, 1986.

Dekmejian, R. Hrair. *Islam in Revolution: Fundamentalism in the Arab World*. New York: Syracuse University Press, 1985.

Esposito, John. *Unholy War*. New York: Oxford University Press, 2002.

Al-Khalil, Samir. *Republic of Fear: Inside Story of Saddam's Regime*. Berkeley: California Press, 1990.

Mitchell, Richard. *The Society of Muslim Brothers*. New York: Oxford University Press, 1969.

Rushdie, Salman. *The Satanic Verses*. New York: Viking, 1988.

Wright, Robin. *Sacred Rage: The Wrath of Militant Islam*. New York: Simon and Schuster, 1986.

Index